The Architecture of Sir Christopher Wren

THE ARCHITECTURE OF

Viktor Fürst

SIR CHRISTOPHER WREN

published by Lund Humphries, London

By the same author: *Versailles*

ACKNOWLEDGEMENTS

The author and publishers take pleasure in recording their indebtedness to the following institutions and private collectors, without whose collaboration the production of this volume would not have been possible and to whose courtesy its illustrations are due:

The Warden and Fellows of All Souls College; Sir Edmund Craster and S. A. Webb, Esq.

The Director and Trustees of the British Museum.

Reginald W. Cooper, Esq., F.S.A., F.R.I.B.A.

The Director of the Courtauld Institute.

The Governors of the Guildhall Library and Museum.

The President and Council of the Royal Institute of British Architects, and James Palmes, Esq.

The Trustees of the National Maritime Museum.

Mr and Mrs Kirk Merrill Ruddock.

The Trustees of Sir John Soane's Museum, and John Summerson, Esq., C.B.E., F.S.A., A.R.I.B.A.

The Very Reverend the Dean of St Paul's and the Cathedral Chapter.

The Director of the Victoria and Albert Museum.

The Very Reverend the Dean of Westminster.

The Director of the Winchester City Museum.

CONTENTS

ABBREVIATIONS:
ASC   All Souls College, Oxford, Collection.
RIBA   Royal Institute of British Architects.
SM   Sir John Soane's Museum.
StPL   The Library, St Paul's Cathedral.

'I have not neglected nor transcribed those who have written before me; and if in some things I differ from them it was not out of the humour of opposing any great names, but because I intended not to deliver other men's judgments but my own.'

Edward Stillingfleet: *Origines Britannicae*, 1685.

The circumstances which conspired to effect the entry of Christopher Wren into the field of architecture have often been, and will largely remain, a subject of speculation. Whatever renown the Savilian Professor of Astronomy may have possessed at the time of the Restoration, there does not seem to have been any reason which should have prompted Charles II to confer upon him a preferment for which, superficially, Wren was hardly qualified: no reason to have made the king think that in his choice of assistant surveyor he had selected the man who would fill that office, and that of the principal surveyorship which would revert to him on the death of Sir John Denham, better than any other of his subjects. There is no reason to think that 'at the time of the death of Inigo Jones there was not one man to be found within the City seriously following the craft of Architecture',[1] for John Webb and Hugh May, without doubt, possessed far more cogent qualifications than did either Denham or Wren; Roger Pratt could have pointed to his past achievements in the field of architecture; and even Sir Balthasar Gerbier could claim a greater acquaintance with that art than either of the men of Charles's choice possessed.[2]

Thus it is obvious that reasons other than professional qualifications must have exerted an influence on Charles's appointments. Webb may have been ignored because of too facile an acquiescence with which he had worked, before the Restoration, for Lords Pembroke and St John; Hugh May, passed over in the principal appointments, was to blame the Duke of Buckingham for having brought Wren on to the architectural scene;[3] Denham, however, could claim an unstained record of Royalist loyalty and it is evident that his appointment was in the nature of a sinecure, and a reward for the not inconsiderable services which he had rendered the king's cause.[4] This fact in itself implied the necessity of an assistant surveyor, for Denham, whose poetry was of no great stature but whom Evelyn thought yet a 'better poet than architect',[5] was obviously incapable of fulfilling the duties which the appointment entailed, and while he had the benefit of Webb's assistance,[6] the king's appointment of Wren is the more surprising in view of Wren's activities and preoccupations before that date.

That Wren was a person of some renown at the time of the Restoration is evident from the numerous references which contemporaries have made to him and to his accomplishments at Oxford. After leaving Westminster School and the celebrated Dr Busby, Wren seems to have spent three years in London, probably with Sir John Scarborough,[7] before entering Wadham College as a gentleman commoner in 1649.[8] It was there that he met Wilkins, Boyle, Goddart, Ward, and Wallis; and it was there that Evelyn first met Wren and left us the first record of his impressions of that precocious intelligence.[9] It is possible, and even probable, that Wren's introduction to architecture was the result of this, and subsequent encounters; for though it has been suggested that it may have been Denham himself who proposed Wren's appointment to Charles,[10] and May has given the responsibility (if not the credit) to Buckingham, it would seem more probable that it was neither the surveyor, nor the duke, but Evelyn, the versatile and accomplished dilettante, who brought the existence of young Dr Wren to the king's notice,[11] just as it was probably Evelyn who nominated Wren for membership of what later became the Royal Society[12] and just as, ten years later, Evelyn was to be instrumental in introducing to the Court an artist of a stature equal, in his own field, to Wren's.[13]

That Wren at that period should have possessed more than a nodding acquaintance with architecture must seem doubtful[14] for his studies had been concerned with the natural sciences, his treatises had largely been devoted to mathematical problems, and the chair he held at the time of the Restoration was that of astronomy. His personal contacts with the king had been slight: he had journeyed to Windsor to return to the monarch the registers of the Order of the Garter which his father's care had preserved from the spoliation of Cromwell's men;[15] and he had dedicated, as would befit a professor of astronomy, a lunar globe to the king.[16] Thus we must seek, and suggest, more general causes which should have made Charles appoint the brilliant young scientist to an office which Wren himself does not seem to have sought, and to a career in a field which, to Wren, can then have meant no more than a minor interest. It may be that Evelyn's, or Buckingham's, promptings were responsible for the appointment; it may be that the king, with that quick apprehension and judgement which Dryden attributed to him, had recognized the potentialities of the architect in the scientist. More cogently, however, Charles showed by his appointment that, in the traditions of Renaissance humanism, he held no preconceived ideas on the separation of arts from sciences, that to him architecture was merely another department of the intellect, and that he saw nothing incongruous in the idea of making an architect of an astronomer.

On the other hand, a knowledge of architecture had already become a gentleman's prerequisite and necessary accomplishment, not least as a result of that Grand Tour which formed an essential part of his education and which entailed an acquaintance at least with archaeological antiquities. This was not the least important factor in the encouragement and connoisseurship which had already characterized the court of Charles I, and which, by the patronage of the third earl of Pembroke and the fourth earl of Arundel, had largely been responsible for that intimate knowledge of classical and Italian Renaissance architecture which Inigo Jones had been the first to bring to England. Likewise, to the polite society of the Restoration, a knowledge of architecture and antiquity was a desirable accomplishment, and thus we find the king's doctor writing tracts on the origin of Stonehenge, John Aubrey surveying Avebury, and John Evelyn translating French books on architecture and gardening.

Another consideration, however, makes it almost natural that

1. Pembroke College, Cambridge, chapel.

Charles should have looked for his assistant surveyor among that group of Oxford 'philosophers' which, however heterogeneous the background and politics of its individual members, had yet survived the strains and stresses of Commonwealth and Protectorate by the homogeneity of its widespread interests. It has, indeed, been suggested that 'nearly every member of (what later became) the Royal Society had a fair smattering of architectural knowledge, and could have filled the surveyorship without discredit';[17] but this is only the implication of a far more comprehensive truth, for philosophy, it should be recalled, signified a totally different concept to the seventeenth century than it does to our own day; and while we may regard it as an intellectual discipline distinct from science, the seventeenth century, and Wren, regarded it as the co-ordinating and superior synthesis to which the various branches of specialized knowledge (of which the assortment of Wren's 'inventions' at Wadham forms a fair cross-section) were subordinate and contributory. The speculations of philosophy and the experiments of science were yet an indivisible whole to Wren and to that group of 'diverse worthy persons, inquisitive into natural philosophy and other parts of human learning', and it is as true to say of them, as it is of Descartes, Leibniz, and Spinoza that 'their speculations about Matter, Motion, Space, Energy, Ultimate Particles, and Infinitesimal Magnitudes[18] supplied the ideas with the aid of which modern physics was gradually built'.[19]

Such an attitude was the direct heritage of Renaissance humanism and Charles, in opening up the avenue of architecture to a Savilian Professor of Astronomy, was no more inconsistent with the tenets of the times than had been the patrons of Michelangelo – who, being a sculptor, had persistently refused the commission of St Peter's; of Brunelleschi – who, though a goldsmith by training, completed the duomo of Florence; and of Perrault – who, though a physician, was preferred to Bernini when Louis XIV built the east front of the Louvre. Nor need it surprise us, in view of this attitude, that when, half a century later, an authoritative opinion was sought on whether the roof-line of St Paul's should be crowned with a balustrade or not, it was to Sir Isaac Newton that the commissioners applied.[20]

It must be a matter of regret that Wren did not accept Charles's commission to go to Tangiers to report on the state of, and suggest improvements for, the fortifications of that port which had come to the Crown as part of Catherine of Braganza's dowry.[21] Not only would the journey, if taken by way of France and Spain, have given Wren an excellent opportunity of seeing architecture in these countries, but also would it have entailed an enlargement of Wren's scope of activities which would have permitted many interesting comparisons. Had Wren accepted, he would have been following almost traditional precedent: Leonardo had spent much time and thought on the problems of fortifications; Michelangelo had actually fortified Florence; Antonio da San Gallo had built fortifications in the Papal States for Clement VII; Dürer had written a celebrated book on the subject; Sanmichele had built fortifications at Verona, at Murano, in Dalmatia, on Corfu, Cyprus, and Crete; Palladio, instructed by Trissino, has himself related his studies of military science; more recently (if tradition is to be trusted) Inigo Jones had designed the fort guarding the harbour of what later came to be known as New York; and sixty years later the Archbishop of Würzburg called on his architect for the design of the new bastions of the Festemarienburg.

It seems that Wren had actually been interested in the problems of maritime fortifications, as some of the titles among the *Catalogue of New Theories, Experiments, and Mechanick Improvements exhibited by Mr Wren at the First Assemblies at Wadham College in Oxford for the Advancement of Natural and Experimental Knowledge* indicate.[22] None the less, he refused the commission on the plea of ill health, and thus it is that his first three essays in architecture were not due to the Royal patronage to which he owed his appointment, but to the universities; thus it is to Gilbert Sheldon, successively Warden of All Souls, Chancellor of Oxford University, and Archbishop of Canterbury, that Oxford owes the theatre which bears his name; and it was in fulfilment of a vow taken during his eighteen-year-long imprisonment in the Tower that Bishop Wren called upon his nephew to furnish the plans for the new chapel to be built at Pembroke College, Cambridge.

2. Sheldonian Theatre, south front.

It has been a point of disagreement among previous authors which of the two designs is to be considered the earlier[23] as no conclusive external evidence helps to elucidate this question. The two works, however, are sufficiently close to each other, and exhibit parallels of sufficient significance, to be considered together. On purely stylistic grounds we would consider Pembroke College chapel the earlier work, for this is a very simple building, planned as a plain rectangular block, the side elevations of which were designed in a manner of sufficient regularity to allow a bay to be added during the last century without impairing the balance of the composition.[24] It is, however, the front facing Trumpington Street (Fig.1) of which it can reasonably be said that it represents Wren's first essay in the design of a classical elevation. This itself is simple and pleasing. Two pairs of Corinthian pilasters form the framework for a composition of a round-headed central window flanked by carved swags; a pair of flaming urns set off the corners against the sky-line, the whole being surmounted by an octagonal lantern. But if this whole front presents a pleasing composition, it would be difficult to claim for it either originality or great intrinsic beauty, more difficult still to find in it the 'sure command of the classical idiom' which one of Wren's critics has thought to discern.[25] For the elevation shares with those of the Sheldonian Theatre certain signs of Wren's inevitable immaturity and betrays the fact that Wren had still to learn, and to acquire the mastery of, the vocabulary of Renaissance architecture.

The Sheldonian Theatre, however, is a much more ambitious project, as the requirements, arising from Archbishop Sheldon's objections to the holding of academic functions in the university church, implied the provision of seating capacity for considerable numbers, and the desirability of a completely unobstructed floor space permitting optimum view from all parts of the hall. Wren very logically saw the solution of the problem in the form of a theatre. It is evident that technical considerations rather than classical precedent[26] were the factors uppermost in Wren's mind; given his scientific knowledge, there is little reason to assume that he should have firmly fixed on an architectural ground plan, however appositely derived from Roman examples, and then proceeded to solve the problem of how to span, without intermediate support, the given floor area of some 70 ft width. Wren solved this technical problem in an elegant fashion and the decorative treatment of the ceiling is in itself sufficiently delightful to make the spectator forget that, basically, it was not an artistic but an engineering problem which Wren here solved behind the painted figures of Streeter's cherubim and symbols of learning.[27]

The exterior elevations, however, are hardly as satisfactory. The curved front facing the Broad suffers from an unpleasant and disquiet rustication which Wren applied to the semi-circular heads of the openings which, however, in their lower portions, contain disproportionately small rectangular windows. Neither the ornate heraldic ornament nor the elaborate lucarne windows –

4

3. Emmanuel College, Cambridge, chapel.

destroyed, unhappily, at the hands of 'restorers' – can conceal the weakness of this façade with its ambiguous horizontal division and its uncertainty of grouping the masses of wall and windows. The south elevation (Fig.2) is more satisfying. It would seem that Wren first of all considered a plain façade containing two storeys of each five bays of round-headed windows, or niches, all of equal width, above a heavy, rather tall, substructure, articulated by broad keystones, while the whole ensemble was to be surmounted by a plain triangular pediment.[28] The design as executed, however, is much more complex: the lower order is enlarged to seven bays, containing the central door, two flanking windows, and niches at the extremities, while the upper order is reduced to three central bays only, and these are flanked by rectangular windows and sunk panels of diminishing size. The increasing of the lower, and the decreasing of the upper storey were obviously effected in order to build up, within a rectangular frame, a pyramidal composition, and this is finally completed by the pediment above the three centre bays and the pair of half-pediments, set slightly below, which surmount the lateral sections of the upper storey. An elaborate cornice carries a Latin inscription recording Archbishop Sheldon's munificent donation which, it is ironic to reflect, the primate was never to see.

In some respects, the south façade can be taken as a development of the Cambridge chapel: notwithstanding the totally different proportions, the centre section of the upper order of the theatre repeats, very closely, the scheme of the Trumpington Street front, even to the point of the enlargement of the centre bay – a feature which we shall meet again in later designs; likewise, the flanking niches of the chapel recur as the outer bays of the lower storey of the theatre as much as the rectangular sunk panels below are common to both; finally, the place of the heraldic emblem in the chapel's pediment is taken by the semicircular window in the theatre while Wren in both instances used

urns of very similar design to mark the terminals of both pediments.

The evidence we possess for Wren's work at Trinity College, Oxford, in 1665, is inconsiderable[29] but from the letter which he wrote to the college's president, Dr Bathurst, on 22 June,[30] we may gather that the designing of the quadrangle was a matter of rather secondary importance to him, as he seems almost completely absorbed in the anticipation of his impending visit to Paris. As with Dürer nearly two centuries earlier, the plague may have been a reason for Wren's decision to go to France, but in both cases the ultimate motive was not escape from the scourge, but the desire to see the monuments of another country and civilization. We have little doubt that Wren's chief reason was to see for himself, not only the glories of France's architectural past, but mainly the tremendous building activities which, consequent upon the end of the Fronde,[31] had begun to flourish under the young Louis XIV. Wren's well-known and often-quoted letter permits many insights into his activities while in Paris, but leaves us in tantalizing ignorance on many points of detail. Thus we have no record whether he personally met the numerous architects and artists he mentions though, well provided with introductions as he obviously was, he probably succeeded in meeting many people of importance in those fields.[32] Wren is not only explicit, but emphatic in describing his meeting with Bernini and the impression which the Italian's plan for the Louvre made on him;[33] but apart from his acquaintance with that abortive scheme, he also made himself familiar with many of the great and famous country houses of the Ile de France, not least of them Versailles which, though still largely the *petit château de cartes* which Louis XIII had left behind and not yet the stupendous edifice which Louis XIV was to complete during his long reign, was already the scene of extensive horticultural, if not architectural, activity.

Whatever may have been the tangible influence which this visit to the capital of the *roi soleil* may have exerted on Wren's development as an architect – and we shall have to give special consideration to this question in a later part of this study – there can be little doubt that he returned to England with an horizon immensely broadened by what he had seen. Considering the paucity of Renaissance architecture in the England of 1665, it is evident that his stay in France must have opened Wren's eyes to an artistic and architectural culture of which he may have known little and dreamed less. It may be too much to claim that 'the sight of a few domes brought about a climax in his artistic career'[34] for even before his visit to Paris it was clear that Wren was not going to tread the outworn paths of Jacobean and Caroline architectural traditions; but it is obvious that 'whatever he may have thought of his Uncle Mathew's amateurish efforts at Peterhouse before his visit, there can be little doubt that he felt little sympathy for it after seeing the classical achievements of Delorme, Mansart, and Le Vau'.[35]

The chapel and gallery of Emmanuel College, Cambridge, are the only works of which the designs may have been drafted before the great disaster overtook the City of London in September 1666,[36] and it recalls in many points the scheme employed by Wren in his first work at Cambridge. It displays, for instance, the same triple division, but the pilasters demarcating them embrace two storeys and thus reach the status of a giant order, the first employment of a device which was to accompany Wren throughout his life. The pediment, however, is here broken to allow the construction of a lantern more voluminous, if not necessarily more pleasing, than that which had surmounted the other Cambridge chapel; while the twin urns at the lower angles of the pediment are repeated. The interesting feature of the design, however, lies in the way the wings are linked to this central portion: the arcades, conventionally, are composed of round-headed arches though the windows above are rectangular. Each wing, moreover, is made into a self-contained unit by the break in the roof-line which permits the separate roofing of each section irrespective of the centre block. The whole arrangement, and particularly the pitch of the roofs, is reminiscent of France, and it is not impossible that Wren, in designing the arcade and gallery, may have been thinking of Fontainebleau.[37]

The Great Fire of 1666 was, unquestionably, the most decisive event in Wren's life. Whatever misery and loss it entailed for the poor inhabitants of the City, to Wren it opened up avenues of architectural activity which his mere appointment as assistant, or even his advancement to become principal surveyor, could never have offered him. Given the universality of application which was considered natural in persons such as a Savilian Professor of Astronomy and a Fellow of the Royal Society, Wren's immediate reaction to the disaster was to present the king with a draft plan for the City of London[38] which he managed to complete, and present, by 11 September, two days before Evelyn could submit

his own scheme to the king,[39] eight days before Hooke presented his version to the Royal Society.

Of the five major schemes which were proposed,[40] only Wren's has captured the attention of most later critics, an attention and evaluation which the plan may not have warranted, and which might equally have been bestowed upon the far more advanced and revolutionary schemes of Newcourt and Hooke. Yet eulogy has gone so far as to claim Wren as the true 'founder of modern town planning'[41] as 'all the modern principles of city planning'[42] are alleged to have been laid down in those 'vast and varied schemes for the reconstruction of the City'[43] which Wren is supposed to have put forward. It has been suggested that 'there was no one in France who could have taught him his plan for the rebuilding'[44] and the fact that it failed of execution is purported to be the reason for our being constrained as the years go by to spend millions in recreating small scraps of his scheme in the name of street improvements.[45] Had the plan been adopted, we are told, 'London City would have been the finest in the world'[46] because whatever legitimate criticism may have been made by modern authorities on town planning of any of its particulars, we are assured that 'Wren would probably have altered most of them'.[47]

Such views reflect the wholly uncritical esteem in which Wren's work is popularly held which denies the possibility that any of his individual designs may have failed to attain the level of unsurpassed and unsurpassable perfection. We must thus run the risk of inviting 'suspicion as a deliberate detractor of an unquestionably great figure'[48] if we are to examine the plan in a spirit of unbiased appraisal rather than partisanship. In essence, Wren's plan is based on a geometrical pattern of rectangles into which the surviving and the immovable features of the City are ingeniously fitted. That the rectangular grid scheme should have been inspired by Wren's knowledge of Roman town plans would not seem too far-fetched an assumption when his great interest in classical antiquity is recalled, and that such books on architecture as Wren knew at the time may represent a source of inspiration is a certain probability.[49] On the other hand, nothing would be more logical than to connect Wren's City plan with the visit to France from which he had returned but a few months previously and during which he had seen some of the finest of classical garden designs then in existence, not least those of that master in the art, André le Nôtre, which were based on geometrical patterns and their elaborations.[50] There, as well as in the engravings of Sylvestre and Perelle[51] which would have been known to him, Wren must have seen the horticultural, as well as the urbanistic versions of 'the vista, axial planning, through communication, and the organized relationship of street, square, and building'.[52] Finally, it can safely be assumed that Wren, at that period, was familiar with the Italian standard works on architecture and that he may have derived some theoretical precepts, if not a practical model, from

6

those sections to be found in them which are concerned with town-planning.[53]

If not Ralph, then Hawksmoor, Gwynn, and Stephen Wren may be held responsible for the creation of the legend purporting that an opportunity for the creation of a 'perfect city' was lost by turning down Wren's plan,[54] and though it is broadly speaking true that its ultimate rejection was due to the 'obstinate Averseness of a great Part of the Citizens'[55] it is legendary that the project was 'defeated by faction'[56] in spite of alleged Royal and Parliamentary approval. This assertion does not accord with historical fact. It is true that the Privy Council gave a general approval of all four plans[57] – Wren's, Evelyn's, Petty's, and Newcourt's – which it had received; but no evidence permits us to think that Wren's plan was ever adopted by the House of Lords or the City authorities; these latter, in fact, approved the plan submitted by Robert Hooke, one of their own surveyors, which had been shown to the Royal Society on 19 September. The House of Commons, indeed, actually rejected Wren's plan.[58] While finally even King Charles's statements do not permit us to think that he regarded it even as the preliminary to a final solution.

That Wren's, as well as Evelyn's, plan contributed something towards the vision which may have existed in Charles's mind is quite clear:[59] Wren ideas are echoed in Charles's recommendation that 'Fleet Street, Cheapside, Cornhill, and all other eminent and notorious streets, shall be of such a breadth[60] as may, with God's blessing, prevent the mischief that one side may suffer if the other be on fire'; both Wren's and Evelyn's ideas are clearly reflected in Charles's desire that 'we do resolve and declare that there shall be a fair key or wharf on all the river-side';[61] and a question much at Evelyn's heart[62] is expressed in the king's desire that the vicinity of the river shall not be inhabited by 'brewers, dyers, or sugar-bakers' and shall be altogether forbidden to those trades which 'by their continual smokes contribute very much to the unhealthiness of the adjacent places' and while 'they who exercise those necessary professions shall be in all respects as well provided for and encouraged as ever they have been', the Lord Mayor and aldermen of the City are to 'propose such a place as may be fit for all those trades which are carried on by smoke' so that 'other places shall receive the benefit in the distance of the neighbourhood'.[63]

But the apprehensible references to Wren's and Evelyn's schemes are hereby exhausted; in fact, Charles most probably did not envisage a City radically different from that just destroyed, as may be inferred from his reference to 'eminent and notorious streets' and the mention of Pater Noster Lane made at a later date.[64] Charles's common sense and grasp of the impracticability of Wren's project may perhaps be gleaned from his reference to 'the reducing of this great and glorious design into practice'; and lastly, bearing in mind Wren's geometrical but unhistorical

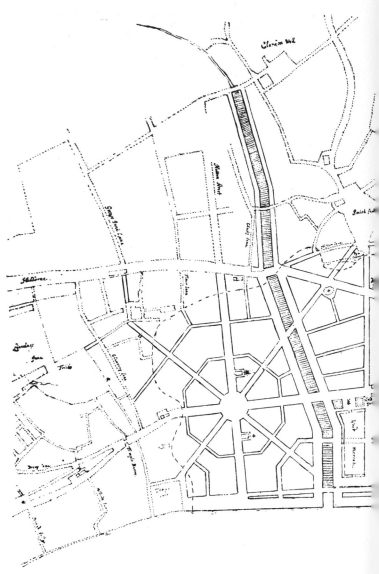

4. London City plan.

placing of the City's parish churches, Charles cannot have seriously considered the possibility of carrying Wren's plan into effect, as he urged the City authorities 'speedily to endeavour by degrees to re-edify some of the many churches, which, in this lamentable fire, have been burned down and defaced'. Charles was not blind to the artistic merits of Wren's scheme, for he was clearly aware of the desirability of unencumbered sites for these churches when he promised that 'as soon as we shall be informed of any readiness to begin such a good work, we shall not only give our assistance and direction for the model of it, and freeing it from buildings at too near a distance, but shall encourage it by our own bounty'.[65]

The reconstruction of the City churches which the king urged could not, of course, have been executed in conformity with

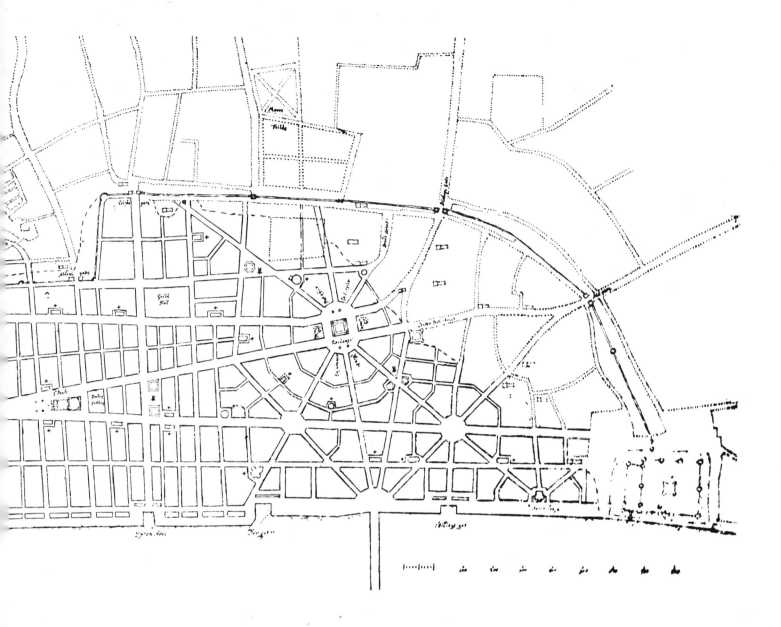

Wren's plan as the sites there projected disregarded altogether the sites of the destroyed churches, and Charles's direction that 'an exact survey be made and taken of the whole ruins' was intended 'to the end that it may appear to whom all the houses and ground did in truth belong'. The fulfilment of this command can be seen in Hollar's engraving; Pepys tells us that Hollar was actually engaged on a survey of the City before the Fire, which survey the king ordered him to complete, but, before that, Hollar executed an engraving of the City 'with a pretty representation of that part which is burnt, very fine indeed'.[66] But that Wren's plan was by no means accepted or recommended by the City authorities becomes evident from the fact that a month after the fire, as Pratt records, the committee convened and consisting of 'Mr Hugh May, Doctor Renne and myselfe' joined by the representatives of

'the citty, who sente us Mr Milles their Surveyour and Mr Hooke Professor of ye Mathematics in Gresham College, and Mr Germain an experienced man in buildings' sat down to debate the basic nature of the rebuilding scheme: 'the breadth of the streetes being already agreed upon[67] that it be next resolved whether the streets shall be laied out in the places where they formerly were, or in such other as shall be demonstrated to be more for the beauty and convenience of the citty'.[68]

Wren does not seem to have evinced much further interest once this 'committee stage' had been reached, for no further drawings are extant nor have we any record that he ever attempted an elaboration of his first project; moreover, though the City had theoretically approved Hooke's version, Hugh May told Pepys that his own design 'of building the City do go on apace' and that

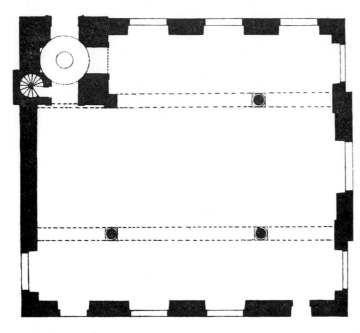

5. St George, plan.

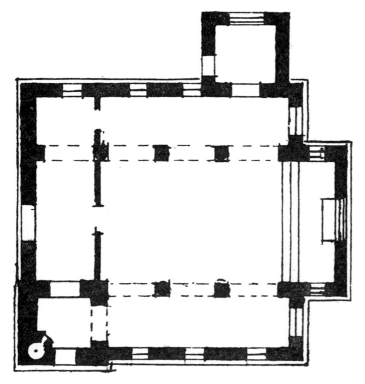

6. St Christopher, plan.

it will be 'mighty handsome, and to the satisfaction of all the people'.[69] The House of Commons debated Lord Mordaunt's Bill for rebuilding[70] in January of the following year and passed it within a fortnight.[71] Yet, Parliamentary Acts and Royal assent notwithstanding, the Lieutenant of the Tower, Sir John Robinson, encountered great difficulties in trying to carry out the provisions of the Act[72] in building a street, of 40 ft width, to run straight from St Paul's through what is now Cannon Street to the Tower,[73] in which ambition he was eventually frustrated. For even though considerable improvements on the pre-Fire street plan were made, and many of the narrow alleys of Tudor and Jacobean London disappeared, the complete provisions of the Act never materialized.

King Charles had shown much perspicacity when he exhorted the City that 'such inconveniences may and shall be prevented which may arise by the hasty and unskilful buildings many may purpose to erect for their present convenience before they can know how the same will suit and consist with the design that shall be made'.[74] But neither this warning, nor the provisions of the Act, themselves insufficiently comprehensive,[75] could prevail. In Parliament it had been proposed that the entire area of the ruins should be put in trust, to be re-sold in lots conforming to a new plan, preference to be given to the former owners.[76] But the City was too impatient to resume its normal life to listen to such projects or spend much time in discussing any schemes which would involve the relinquishing of the old leases, to receive in compensation sites the situation of which was determined by some preconceived plan.[77] The life of the City was not to be interrupted even by so 'dreadfull a conflagration' and speed in resuming its normal activities was the uppermost thought in the citizens' minds.

It is not our purpose here to decide in what degree Wren's plan would have met the conditions of the twentieth century; this the reader may decide for himself by comparing Wren's plan with that which was projected after the 1939–45 war. But, whatever its merits as an essay in urbanism, one striking fact stands out, namely that one of the considerations governing it was an illusory conception of the future population of the City. Gwynn, less than a hundred years later, realized that the City was fast losing its residential function,[78] but that fact may actually have been foreseen by the ecclesiastical authorities in 1666 when it was decided to eliminate, by merger, some thirty of the old parishes and therefore reconstruct a considerably smaller number of churches than had been destroyed.[79]

The striking thing about Wren's projected churches, however, is their siting which allocates to them positions of great prominence placed with a regularity altogether disregarding the actual boundaries of the parishes they were to serve. But while his town plan remained a dream on paper, the rebuilding of the City churches was entrusted to his hands, and the man who could

claim little more than a superficial knowledge, and slight experience of three years' standing, of architecture was thus given an
opportunity of a magnitude, importance, and scope probably
greater than had ever been offered to any single architect. Thus it
is to a consideration of some of these churches that we must now
turn.

It seems that the rebuilding of the City churches did not follow
any particular plan or sequence. Although documentary evidence
is sadly lacking which would permit a precise dating of Wren's
designs, enough circumstantial evidence exists and sufficient internal indications can be discerned to assign most of Wren's
works to periods confined within fairly narrow limits. Pepys,
indeed, complained at a very early date that 'those few churches
that are to be built are plainly not chosen with regard to the convenience of the City' for 'they stand a great many in a cluster
about Cornhill: but that all of them are in the gift of the Lord
Archbishop, or Bishop of London, or Lord Chancellor, or gift of
the City'. And though he sighed that 'thus all things, even to the
building of churches, are done in this world',[80] we can reflect that
while five[81] of the seventeen churches on which Wren was actively engaged before 1672 really lay in the vicinity of Cornhill,
the remainder are fairly sprinkled over the rest of the City.

For our purpose, the church of St Mary-at-Hill may provide a
convenient starting point for it contains not only many tokens of
Wren's immaturity at this early stage[82] but also links pointing
backwards to previous designs, and features which were to be elaborated at later dates. The plan of the church (Fig.8) can be related
to those of St Christopher's (Fig.6) and St George's (Fig.5) at
which Wren was engaged at about the same time. Yet it differs
essentially from both these examples in representing what was
clearly Wren's first essay in domed interiors. The method employed is in itself significant: Wren had a rectangular site suggestive of basilican possibilities, but he chose instead an arbitrary
division of the space so as to obtain an irregular rectangle at the
west, to contain the vestibule, tower, and vestry, leaving a somewhat irregular square for the body of the church proper. This
square is further subdivided into nine roughly equal compart-
ments, and the intersections of their dividing lines are marked by
a set of four pillars, disposed at the corners of the central square,
upon which the cupola rests, the first tentative solution of a problem which was to be Wren's chief preoccupation throughout
his life.

There is not yet any effort to give external indication of the
means by which, in a manner highly unorthodox for the England
of the time, Wren had roofed the interior. The east elevation
(Fig.7) does not provide any clue, but would rather imply the
existence of a normal double-aisled interior. The semi-circular

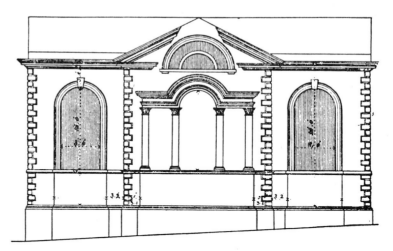

7. St Mary-at-Hill, east elevation.

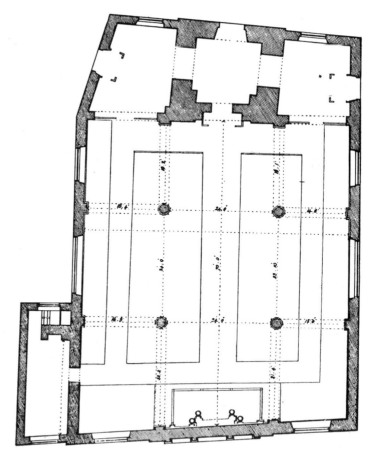

8. St Mary-at-Hill, plan.

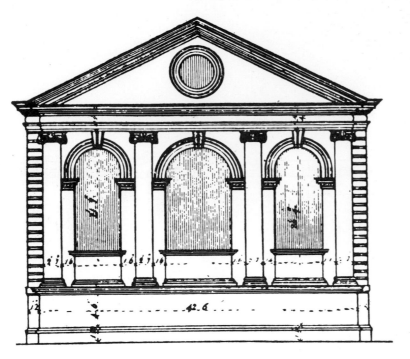

9. St Michael, Wood Street.

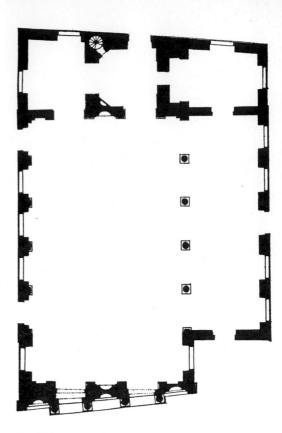

10. St Lawrence, plan.

window which, somewhat incongruously, adorns the central pediment, is a lineal descendant of that employed at the Sheldonian Theatre (Fig.2) but the four-column arcade formed beneath – the justification for breaking the cornice – shows a new invention with its flexed centre, unless we can see its predecessor in a house which Wren had designed for Henry Guy at Tring which, little known though it be, is approximately contemporaneous with St Mary-at-Hill.[83] The quadruple rustication which Wren here employed was to recur in many instances among later design. At St Michael's, Wood Street (Fig.9), Wren has confined it to the corners but the entire scheme employed points back distinctly to the Sheldonian Theatre and the chapels of Pembroke and Emmanuel Colleges. It displays the same curious enlargement of the centre bay, yet here the refusal to treat three round-headed bays as an arcade has resulted in a different method: at the Sheldonian Theatre Wren had made the side arches truly semicircular and, for compensation, had made the centre arch segmental and slightly taller, masking the difference by a clever design of keystones and a florid roundel containing the Royal cypher; at Emmanuel College Chapel the solution had been less satisfactory as Wren used a distinctly segmental arch for his centre which accords but ill with the semicircular arches of the wings. At St Michael's, Wren had not the justification which the central doors provided in the other two instances, but his solution is more subtle: treating the centre arch as a perfect semicircle, Wren here effected the compensation by raising the smaller outer arches on stilts, a feasible, if not altogether satisfactory solution of a problem created by his predilection which, particularly as it is not motivated by a nave correspondingly wider than the aisles, may be regarded as a sign of immaturity which Wren was very soon to lose.

The development of the tripartite window which we have noticed at St Mary-at-Hill, and the house in Tring, can be found

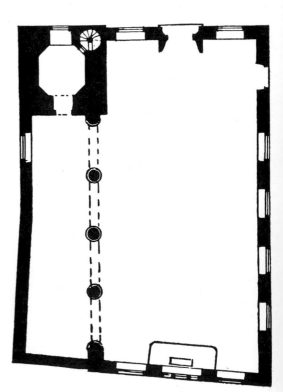

11. St Vedast, plan.

12. St Lawrence, east front.

again in the centre window of the south façade of St Mildred's, Poultry, where Wren evolved a very delightful composition characterized by triangular pediments,[84] and, more interestingly, in the east front of St Olave's, Jewry (Fig.146). The site of this church was a most unpromising narrow rectangle which left Wren but little scope for decorative treatment. In consequence, he placed his tower and porch to the extreme west, leaving the long side elevations, which could not be seen to advantage from the narrow passage leading along it, severely plain but for the windows of the three bays, and concentrated his efforts at the narrow east front which faced Old Jewry. Here Wren evolved a composition very charming in its simplicity and remarkable for the appearance of a motif unique in the whole corpus of his work, never subsequently to be repeated. The scheme of podium, rusticated angles, and plain triangular pediment is, of course, already familiar to us from previous examples; but the east window is the full development of that found at St Mary-at-Hill, and a charming version of what is frequently known as the 'motif Palladio', namely, a round-headed window flanked by rectangular ones within the framework of two pairs of pillars and a cornice flexed over the centre; a pair of small semicircular lights surmounts the rectangular sections here and thus lends to the composition a significance which will occupy our attention at a later point of this study.

Of far greater interest to our present purpose, however, is a church which Wren designed at the same period, namely St Lawrence, Jewry. It is likely that the spring and summer of 1670 should have seen the evolution of what became one of Wren's best-known churches: although a committee for the 'erecting and building of a new Parish Church' was not actually constituted until 8 April of that year, by mid-February of the following year Wren was already being pressed not only to let the parish have copies of his plan, but we have evidence that rebuilding was by then actually in progress though not, apparently, at the speed which some of the parishioners seem to have desired.[85] That Wren produced a design greatly superior to those hitherto considered, may have been due to two factors: firstly, the parish could afford to be more liberal than most in the financial provisions it made for the reconstruction of its church; secondly, Wren's friend Dr Ward had been succeeded in the living of St Lawrence by none other than Dr Wilkins who, twenty years before, had been Warden of Wadham College at the time of Wren's admission and who, though advanced to the deanery of Ripon and finally to the see of Chester in 1668,[86] had evidently retained a lively interest in his old parish church[87] in which, eventually, he was to be interred.

But Wren was not to be hurried by the impatience of the parishioners and, however much the renown of the building may have been due to the splendid, and now unhappily vanished, carving of its vestry; however much the cool reticence of the interior of the church itself may have invited criticism; it cannot be gainsaid that, in the exterior of St Lawrence, and especially in the east front, Wren produced an elevation of remarkable maturity and great beauty. In plan, the church bears much resemblance to that of St Vedast (Figs.10, 11) which must have been evolved at the same time, both examples providing a good indication of the ingenuity which Wren had already developed in solving problems inherent in irregularly shaped sites.[88] It is, however, mainly the east elevation which displays the real felicities of the design (Fig.12). Originally, this had been planned as a five-bay front the centre bay of which was to have been almost twice as tall, though only a little wider, than the side bays.[89] But Wren evidently changed his mind and reverted to the scheme of St Michael's, Wood Street, and the Sheldonian Theatre, and designed the front of five

13. St Dionis, east front.

14. St Mary Aldermanbury, east front.

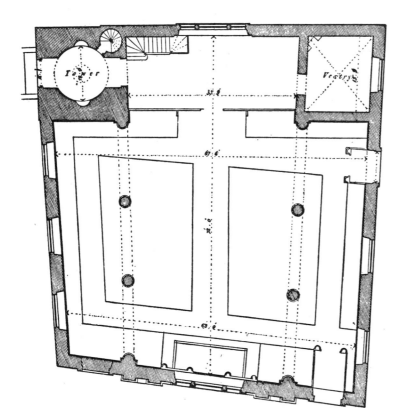

15. St Dionis, plan.

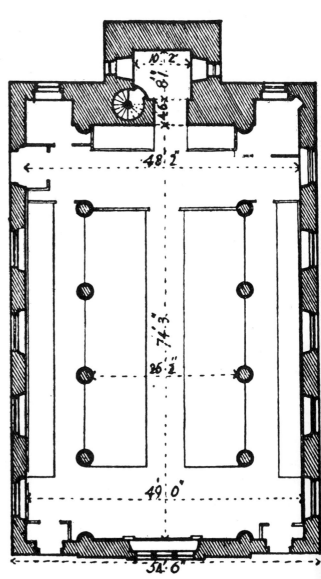

16. St Mary Aldermanbury, plan.

bays which, reminiscent of the Theatre, were partly to be niches while, reminiscent of St Michael's, the centre three were to be crowned by a pediment graced by a circular light. It is interesting to note that Wren retained the idea of enlarging the centre bay; and it is indicative of his growing accomplishment that he evolved the first truly satisfactory solution to the problem by forming the arches of all bays on equal diameters and by effecting the enlargement neither by stilts nor by deflecting them, but by a differentiated width of the pilasters of the central bay.

As can be seen, the façade introduces no feature which had not been present in the Sheldonian Theatre, the Pembroke College chapel, and St Michael's, Wood Street; St Lawrence shares the podium treatment with St Mary-at-Hill and St Olave; while the Pembroke College chapel had possessed three, and the Sheldonian Theatre seven bays, St Lawrence has five, subtly articulated by the alternation of window and niche. Only two minor features are new: there is no rustication to provide a pattern of verticals as there had been in all the preceding City church designs; and the semicircular heads of the bays are here framed by luxuriously carved swags in high relief which, barring the edges of the pediment, provide the only decoration of this very suave design which, in a manner of speaking, must represent the epitome of Wren's achievement to this early date.

The elevations which Wren designed for the east fronts of St Dionis (Fig.13) and St Mary Aldermanbury (Fig.14) are of great similarity, and this is the more remarkable for the fact that the conditions imposed by the sites, and the consequent planning, are very dissimilar. The façades represent, however, so clearly variations on the same theme to warrant being considered together even though a strict contemporaneity cannot be proved by documentary evidence.[90] In these two elevations we may see Wren's first employment of an arrangement unequivocally indicative of the interior disposition of nave and aisles. The issue had, in fact, been present at St Mary-at-Hill, but there Wren had erected a curtain wall, and superimposed a central pediment which combination gave no indication of the original and unorthodox interior planning. At St Lawrence Wren had evolved a basically similar scheme, though the front was by no means the true external expression of the interior disposition, still less of the roofing method employed. At St Dionis and St Mary Aldermanbury, however different the premiss of plan from which they spring, there can be no question of mistaking how Wren had planned his interiors and thus they represent his adaptation of the classic solution evolved by the Italian Renaissance, and as such will have to be considered again, when they will be discussed in relation to their historic prototypes.

Beyond this, the details again show unmistakable links with designs already considered and others belonging to the future. Thus both designs possess the vertical rustication which we have noticed at most preceding schemes. A substructure, or podium, such as we have already met with repeatedly, forms again the base of the central sections, but leaving free, in these two instances, the wings by reason of the twin doors, and thereby creating a rhythm which was to become a conspicuous feature of some later designs. The overall scheme is identical in both cases, even to the distinctive glazing of the large central windows, and differences are but slight, though suggestive and indicative: for example, an elaboration of the scrolls which first appeared on the pediment sections of the Sheldonian Theatre flanks the window of St Mary's; and an enlargement of the carved swags which we have noticed at St Lawrence surmounts the central window of St Dionis. The doors of the latter recall those of St Lawrence and St Nicholas as much as the triangular pediments above the round-headed doors of the former provide an echo of the windows of St Mildred's, Poultry. The rustication of the central part of St Mary's is reminiscent, moreover, of that of St Mary-at-Hill, while the pillars replacing it may be connected with those at St Olave's.

We would not, however, have stressed the similarity of these two designs but for the purpose of showing how Wren's ingenuity could derive so strikingly similar results from so widely differing premisses. Beyond this, however, both schemes are important in their relationship to that of St George's (Fig.145) and to one of Wren's best-known churches, namely St Mary le Bow. The elevation evolved at the east front of St George's represents the third variation possible in the attempt to make the exterior of the church expressive of the interior planning.[91] At St Dionis Wren had been content with a flat roof and cornice over the aisles; at St Mary Aldermanbury he had connected the central pediment with the wings by means of curved sections; at St George's he went back to the Sheldonian scheme and used a central pediment flanked by the halves of a second pediment, thus creating what must have been, before its regrettable destruction in 1904, a very charming façade.

Turning to St Mary le Bow, we have reached what is, by common consent, one of Wren's most important churches. It has been suggested that this was, indeed, the first City church to be rebuilt, reconstruction having begun in 1671,[92] but it appears that nearly two years were spent in clearing the ruins of the destroyed church and that the foundations of the new edifice were not actually laid until the middle of 1673.[93] It is clear, however, that Wren was preoccupied with the design long before that date, and while the first plan projected[94] was greatly modified when the parish acquired the site of two houses fronting Cheapside at the north-west angle,[95] it seems likely that Wren's first drafts were approved shortly after that early date, particularly as the designs, as well as parts of the executed version, bear significant relations to some of the works we have been considering.

Such relationships are evident in Wren's first design for the east end (Fig.17); the window of the attached vestry, in fact, points back to St Olave's (Fig.146), but the triple division of the central

17. St Mary-le-Bow, east front, study.

18. St Mary-le-Bow, west front, detail.

part represents, in its window arrangement, a compromise between the methods adopted at St Dionis and St Mary Aldermanbury: from the former (Fig. 13) it takes the circular lights, and from the latter (Fig.14) the triangular pediments of the flanking windows, while at the same time the intermediate position of this design is indicated by Wren's doubt whether to treat the elevation with the scrolls connecting centre and aisles as at St Mary Aldermanbury, or leave the transition plain and undisguised as at St Dionis.[96]

With the application of the whole scheme to the west front, Wren not only introduced some modifications pointing further to other designs, but also showed that a certain immaturity still attached to his design faculties at this period. That the west front was almost hidden from view at an early date[97] was thus not a matter of great regret, for it displayed an awkwardness still noticeable in Wren's handling of forms, which would suggest that the west front of Bow church actually antedates the east front of St Mary Aldermanbury, of which it is obviously the larger, but surely the less accomplished version. The quadruple lines of rustication, the triangular pediment with its oval light,[98] the curved buttresses, the slight protrusion of the central façade: all these provide unmistakable marks of a consanguinity which even the somewhat incongruously integrated door of Bow church cannot invalidate.

A cogent instance to demonstrate the rapidity with which Wren's design faculties were losing their immature uncertainties is provided, however, by that gem of a design, the porch on the north face of the tower, doubled at the west. The original of this design (Fig.76) showed a clear dependence on the original draft for the east front (Fig.17) with its oval light curiously poised on the apex of the triangular pediment below and the recurrence of this, for Wren unusual, method in a design which must be closely contemporaneous[99] goes far to show how clearly relationships and chronology can be determined by such details. However, neither the somewhat clumsy rusticated surround nor the Doric pillars with their awkwardly exaggerated entasis give an indication of how simply, yet fundamentally, so immature a conception could be transformed into one of Wren's most charming designs. The doorway as finally evolved (Fig.139) is indeed a masterpiece of great charm and one of the earliest instances where we can see Wren progress from an essentially linear to an intrinsically plas-

tic mode of design. This is achieved not solely by the profusion of charmingly carved decoration in high relief, such as the elaborate entablature and the *amorini* flanking the oval light above the door, but mainly by the simple and highly effective device of placing the entire door-frame within the striated surround making a segmental niche. While not architecturally speaking a work of truly major importance, Bow porch must yet be reckoned among those 'early works of Wren which really promised a greatness which was not to be consistently recognizable in his work'[100] of later years. It would be unjust, however, to say that the church as a whole is not impressive. Indeed, the scheme which was made possible by the purchase of additional ground, and which permitted Wren to treat the tower and steeple as a separate entity from the church proper, was one which would have added considerably to the charms of Cheapside; but the loggia which Wren had intended to extend eastwards from the tower was never to be executed, and thus, however immature the west front may be, and however open to censure the interior of the church itself,[101] the outstanding part of the edifice is that of which the charming porch provides but the first stage.

The tower and steeple raised above are justly reckoned among Wren's most remarkable achievements, and the exceptional number of drawings and engravings of it which have survived[102] testify to a contemporaneous appreciation clearly similar to our own. Even among the very varied achievements which Wren's steeples represent as a whole, that of Bow is unique, not only in form, but also in spirit and in date. While some of Wren's churches had to wait one, or even two decades after completion for the addition of their steeples, that of Bow is the first by many years to have been completed.[103] And here, in distinct contrast to most of his later compositions, Wren allowed himself what we may regard a youthful freedom in the design of this remarkable work which was not to be repeated in his later compositions. It exhibits a very remarkable degree of latitude from the 'canons' of classical architecture, which produces an imaginative whole of untramelled originality and fantasy. Critics have denigrated some of its details,[104] but in a design of this nature, immeasurable by the rules of Vitruvius and Palladio, the attribute of perfection is not to be sought in the degree of conformance to classical precedent and prescription. Thus it is only by a subjective standard of taste that Bow steeple can be judged for, however much Wren's

19. St Mary le Bow (showing
the unexecuted loggia).

plan may owe to classical inspiration,[105] it would be futile to search for similar connexions in the steeple. This is a work of art evolved from an imagination which clearly worked empirically and individualistically – we might even say, esoterically – and which owed nothing to historical precedents. It represents, *par excellence*, an aspect in Wren's conception of architecture which was to be paralleled during the latter years of his long career, and stands as a token – the most successful, we might say – of an approach to architecture which was essentially Wren's and which, in its ideological and psychological foundations, we shall yet have to examine.

The design for the church of St Edmund, King and Martyr, must have been closely contemporaneous with that of St Mary le Bow, for all the evidence, stylistic as well as documentary, suggests that the date of some two decades later, first asserted by Stephen Wren and since accepted without question by the majority of authorities,[106] must be rejected. If no other indication were available, it would suffice to know that by February 1676 the body of the church must have been roofed and completed, as early that month a deputation from the vestry of St Stephen's, Walbrook, went there 'to view the pewing',[107] obviously in search for a model which might serve for their own church, about to be completed at that time. Yet even without this piece of incidental information to supply one terminal of dates, a stylistic peculiarity comes again to our aid. There may, indeed, be some significance in the originally projected carved swags which were to have graced the curved buttresses of the tower, as these may have been inspired by a similar feature pertaining to Inigo Jones's portico of St Paul's,[108] the ruins of which, shattered but still impressive, were still standing. But the turret originally designed to cap the tower[109] is not only a simpler version of the lantern top originally intended for Bow steeple (Fig.76) but equally is of the same family as the cappings designed for the towers in an early design for St Paul's (Fig.34) which can reasonably be assigned to the same period.

That Wren signed this design with his cypher in the pediment may be yet another indication of the early date of the drawing, for with the growth of his fame, and the accumulation of work, the later years of Wren's practice are marked by a tendency to leave much of this work to draughtsmen in his office. But stylistic indications are much more cogent, as not only the windows in this drawing, but also those executed, present a treatment used by Wren only within a strictly confined, short, and early period of his career. In the same way as Wren used rectangular doorways surmounted by large circular lights only in a few, and chronologically related, instances, such as St Lawrence, St Dionis, and St Nicholas; so the type of window found at St Edmund's has been encountered at that latter church, will be found again in one of the earliest schemes for St Paul's (Fig.35) and, lastly, at St Magnus (Fig.22); as the St Paul's design must certainly ante-

date 1670, and St Nicholas can very probably, and St Magnus certainly, be assigned to the very early seventies, we have no hesitation in attributing a similar date to St Edmund's.

The design is one of considerable charm, and we are fortunate in possessing not only an original drawing for the front (Fig.20) but also a sketch for the splendid steeple (Fig.80) which we shall have to consider later. As at St Olave's, and St Mary Aldermanbury, Wren was here faced with a long, narrow site into which to fit his design. The solution in the previous instances had almost suggested itself, for the orientation indicated the placing of tower and porch at the west end. The site of St Edmund's, however, lay approximately south to north and Wren, rather than force an unsatisfactory solution so as to conform with a ruling of the Apostolic Constitution, boldly developed his south front as the principal façade, incorporating the tower and the entry. The actual features of the design are familiar by now: the four courses of rustication, the podium, the distinctive window framing, and the plain triangular pediment set against a parapet wall: all these have formed part of most of the preceding designs. The novelty, however, lies in the fact that this is the first instance in which Wren combined tower, steeple, and porch to constitute the main parts of his principal front; and the importance of this innovation will become apparent when, in anticipation, we can point to the churches of St Magnus, St Bride, and St Martin, as well as a splendid, though unexecuted project for a church which Wren was to design some ten years later.

The idea of combining porch and steeple into one artistic and homogeneous unit, and of using it as the central feature of an elevation had already been adumbrated at St Olave's and St Mary Aldermanbury. But while those two examples are of little significance here, and the instance of St Edmund's just discussed may be of great charm, if not outstanding importance, the west front of St Magnus must be reckoned among Wren's finest compositions just as the church as a whole represents one of Wren's outstanding achievements.

A number of drawings is extant which, together with such formal elements as we shall note, permit us to date the design closely to 1670,[110] which suggestion is supported by the fact that, like the parishioners of St Lawrence, the churchwardens of St Magnus resolved on 11 December 1671 to effect the 'expediting and the more vigorous carrying on the building'.[111] Wren's original plan for the church has been preserved and, as a preliminary to what was to follow, permits a most interesting insight into the evolution of this design. The plan may be regarded as a development of that of St Mary Aldermanbury (Fig.16), but the interesting difference lies in the incorporation, at St Magnus, of the tower within the façade in a manner similar to St Edmund's; equally notable is the appearance of the rectangular, eastern chancel, which feature will be found again in other plans of the same period. In principle, the scheme of St Mary Aldermanbury is

). St Edmund, elevation study.

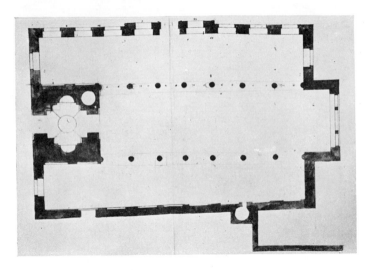

21. St Magnus, plan study.

22. St Magnus, west front study.

followed, but the plan of St Magnus betrays Wren's anxiety to achieve symmetry not only for his west front, but also for that facing north though, curiously, the south front was not meant to possess a corresponding system of fenestration.[112] The wilful imposition of a nine-bay symmetry, however, created considerable difficulties for the interior disposition of the pillars and thus, in order to preserve a north-south axis for the central door planned in the north front, Wren resorted to the expedient of eliminating two of the pillars. Even if the executed version (leaving aside later alterations such as a recession of the west front and the insertion, in 1924, of the 'missing' pillar) had necessarily deviated considerably from the original scheme in the elimination of the eastern chancel and the introduction of windows on the south side, the uneven placing of the pillars shown in Clayton's engraving is now clearly explained by the considerations which evidently had motivated the first design, which would have envisaged the north elevation of the church as the fourth side of a large 'piazza' the centre of which was to have been taken by the Monument commemorating the Fire.

A holograph drawing of the west front exists to show that Wren's final solution corresponded closely to his preliminary draft,[113] and it is here that stylistic details appear which indicate the design's chronological connexions with such as have already been discussed. For example, Wren here used again the method of rectangular door with a circular light above which we have noticed at St Nicholas, St Dionis, and St Lawrence, and which we shall meet again at Farley church, at St Anne's, Soho, and at St Michael's, Cornhill; likewise, in elaborating the original draft for the windows, he fell back (and thus provides the penultimate instance) upon the device of placing a round-headed window within a rectangular frame in the same manner as he had done at St Edmund's, at St Nicholas, and in an early draft for St Paul's.

Apart from these parallels, the façade has a beauty that is entirely new in Wren's work. Even though individual features recall previous designs – the disposition of the pillars and the pediment recalls Pembroke College chapel, the central door recalls St Dionis, the flanking niches the Sheldonian Theatre, the sunk panels of windows and doors St Olave's – this façade of St Magnus yet presents a quality of simplicity, one might even say austerity, which had not pertained to anything Wren had yet

done. There is no decoration, save for the Ionic capitals of the pillars. But apart from this simple beauty, the design possesses an importance in foreshadowing not only St Bride's and the unidentified project to be discussed later, but in pointing the way, as well, to Gibbs's St Martin in the Fields and the numerous progeny which, in England and New England, stands heir to this inspiration. One difference, however, is to be noted; in the way Wren welded porch, tower, and steeple into one architectonic unit; while Gibbs's steeple, however delightful, perches uneasily upon a porch no less dignified and thus falls short of the unity which makes St Magnus one of Wren's most impressive achievements.

It is perhaps apposite to introduce at this point the church of St Anne, Soho, which is of considerable interest for several reasons. The authenticity of the design has not always been recognized, and Wren's apologists have suggested that 'for his reputation, it is to be hoped that he had nothing to do with its erection'.[114] But evidence of a conclusive nature has come to light which renders vain that pious hope. It may be true to say of St Anne's that 'nobody ever much admired it and it was certainly not one of Wren's spectacular successes',[115] but, for all its indifferent quality, the design is no less interesting. Its dating presents some difficulty[116] for we have no circumstantial evidence to aid us. The parish of St Anne was not created until 1678, when an Act of Parliament made its constitution dependent upon the erection of the parish church which provision resulted in the consecration of a building which only by a stretch of the imagination could have been called complete.[117] However, there are cogent reasons indicative of a date considerably earlier than 1678, even though logical objections could be raised to the suggestion that Wren should have designed a church before its future parishioners had even finished building their houses.

Firstly, however, the successive lessees of the property provide circumstantial evidence in favour of an early date: the lease of the estate granted, in 1672, to the Earl of St Albans by Queen Henrietta Maria's trustees, fell in in 1677, when Charles II granted the property to the Duke of Monmouth.[118] And though Wren may have been connected with the design and building of Monmouth House, Soho Square,[119] this appears the sole, and somewhat tenuous, connexion to be established between the architect

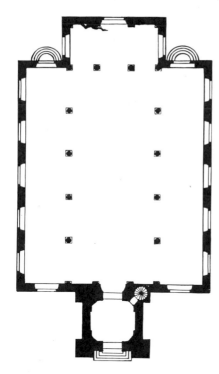

23. St Anne, plan.

24. St Anne, elevation.

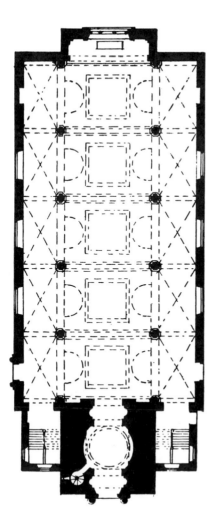

25. St Bride, plan.

and the duke. On the other hand, Wren was well known to St Albans to whom he had been introduced, as early as 1665, in Paris and, as we shall see, St Albans turned to Wren when a parish church was required for the estate which he had developed at St James's. Thus the possibility exists that Wren originally designed St Anne's church for the earl rather than the duke, in the reasonable expectation that it was only a question of time before the Soho estate which St Albans intended to develop on being first granted the lease would be made into an independent parish.

Our second reason for suggesting a date early in the seventies lies in the design itself, for not only does it bear some unmistakable signs of an immaturity which Wren had long overcome by the end of the decade, but also does it share, once more, some peculiarities with other designs clearly belonging to its earlier part. Chief among these features is the inordinately large semicircular window in the gable of the east elevation (Fig.24) which inevitably recalls those of the Sheldonian Theatre and of St Mary-at-Hill, though the difference in glazing may be of importance with regard to an ultimate derivation which will yet have to be studied; moreover, both window and glazing system are strictly identical with those found in an early design for St Paul's (Fig.34) and this fact, as well as the relationship of the central window with those of St Nicholas, St Edmund's, and St Magnus, and lastly, the connexion between the two flanking doors with those of St Lawrence, St Dionis, St Nicholas, and St Magnus: all would point to a date approximately contemporaneous with these designs, especially as some of these features were not to recur in any subsequent buildings.

Further indications may be found in the distinctive rustication which characterizes the door scheme for this, as we shall see, Wren was to use in four later designs of which none can be dated later than 1677. Equally pointing forward is a motif of the tower which, though not executed at St Anne's, was to be employed in one isolated instance many years later;[120] and lastly, the plan is clearly of great interest not only as a development of the schemes of St Mary Aldermanbury, St Michael, Cornhill, and the original plan for St Magnus, but also as serving, with its protruding tower-porch and equally protruding chancel, as the prototype of an important series of churches which includes those of St Mary,

Ingestre, St James's, Garlick Hill, Christ Church, St James's, Westminster, St Andrew, Holborn, and lastly, the celebrated church of St Bride which we must now consider.

If St Bride's must rank among Wren's major churches, its renown is not solely due to the splendid steeple which was not built until many years after the completion of the church, but also to its plan, in which Wren evolved one of his finest schemes of basilican interiors. No difficulties of siting were present to cramp the simplicity and regularity of a plan in which the foundations of the tower at the western, and the returns of the shallow chancel at the eastern end stand in line with the arcade formed of four evenly spaced pillars planned logically and consistently in symmetry of the central axis.

Of interest is also the east elevation, for here, unlike at St Dionis, the regularity of the composition is the true reflection of the interior features and reproduces the governing lines of the cross-section even though the existence of the galleries cannot be inferred from it. Not unnaturally, it is reminiscent of previous designs: the quadruple rustication is familiar from St Mary-at-Hill, and St Mary le Bow, and St Mary Aldermanbury, while the latter church and that of St Michael, Wood Street, provide the predecessors for the insertion of circular lights in triangular gables. The east window itself, however, is of some significance, for it would represent the first instance in Wren's work where he allowed the pediment to be broken at the base by the window itself; moreover, the doubling of the pillars is a characteristic of the church throughout.

It would seem that the construction of St Bride's went forward at a speed unusual for a City church, and there is nothing to invalidate the suggestion that Wren's designs should have been executed during the first half of the seventies.[121] Though the foundations of the church were not actually measured out until early in 1675,[122] the deputation from the vestry of St Stephen's, whom we have already met at St Edmund's, also came to inspect the pewing of St Bride's as early as 7 February 1676, puzzled, no doubt, by the unusual shape of their own church and still in doubt as to 'which is the best to take patterns by in order to the pewing of the Church';[123] that the church, if not the steeple, was complete before the end of the decade is thus evident even without knowing that Evelyn went there to attend the funeral of Dr Jasper Needham.[124]

While the church is clearly related to St Magnus, we must turn to consider the west front and the beginnings of the steeple for which St Bride's is chiefly celebrated; and here it is necessary to consider a drawing which, for stylistic and other reasons, must belong to the period and seems to possess at least a relationship of style to the church under discussion. The drawing (Fig.27) has been described as a preliminary study for St Benet, Gracechurch Street,[125] but the differences which it exhibits to the final version of that delightful steeple are too great to permit us to accept such an

26. St Bride, tower.

27. Steeple design; ? St Dunstan.

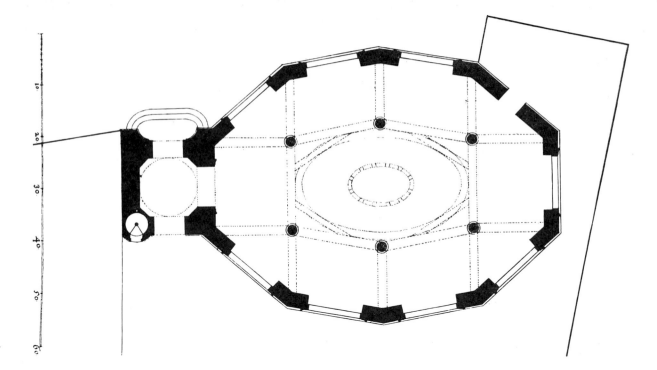

28. St Benet Fink, plan.

ascription: not only does the signature of the drawing point, as we have noticed, to an early date, while the steeple of St Benet's cannot have been designed before 1681 at the earliest; but also does that latter design show no rustication, no pillars, a very different window arrangement and – a detail of some importance – no segmental pediment.

Rejecting the above ascription, two alternatives are possible, both of which can be reconciled with our knowledge of chronology, and supported by stylistic and iconographical details: firstly, it would not be impossible to see in the design a preliminary study for St Bride's steeple, for all the stylistic features which characterize that latter design, are here present: the doorway is clearly very similar, excepting the substitution of a rectangular for a round-headed door-frame; rustication is common to both, though restricted at St Bride's to the lower stage; the inclusion, in the tower, of a triangular pedimented window, a circular light, and a round-headed belfry window are identical but for the juxtaposition which has taken place; the segmental pediment above the door, as well as that terminating the bell stage,[126] are features of striking similarity, and the doubling of the pillars, reminiscent of another design of the same period,[127] is characteristic of the church even to the pillars of the interior. Lastly, the rustication scheme of the doorways, together with the flanking pillars which appear in both draft and final design, compared with their complete absence at St Benet, Gracechurch Street, would seem to put our rejection of such an ascription beyond doubt. If the design can be related to St Bride's, it is not, however, necessarily connected with it, and there are even indications that, in fact, we may be dealing with a project for St Dunstan-in-the-East.

Such an ascription might, in view of the 'Gothic' version later executed, seem incredible at first sight. But we know that Wren was engaged on repairs, or possibly even entire reconstruction, of that church during the early seventies,[128] and we have evidence that the vestry were negotiating with workmen in June 1670 with regard to the completion of the steeple, Wren being consulted little more than a year later.[129] Furthermore, it is clear that in the nineties both church and steeple had again become defective[130] and we can be in no doubt that Wren's singular 'Gothic' design, which has called forth such varied opinions, was designed within a few years of the end of the century.[131] That Wren had been engaged on the church some thirty years earlier, seems likely.[132] But what would point quite definitely in support of our thesis is the fact that, signed holograph drawing that it is, it shows a carefully drawn weather vane in the shape of a cock – an iconographical symbol not exclusive to St Dunstan,[133] but one which forms the crowning feature of Wren's later design and thus, seeing that Wren but rarely indicated such details, may lend support to our suggestion.

Up to this point, we have considered most of the churches the design of which can be dated to the period between the Great Fire and the middle of the following decade, and have commented on the variants, as well as the similarities to be found in them. One aspect, however, has been common to all of them, excepting only the very first, namely that their ground plans are based upon rectangular patterns of greater or lesser regularity. St Olave's, St. Mildred's, Poultry, St Nicholas, and St Michael, Wood Street, St Edmund's, and the rather insignificant church of St Stephen's, Coleman Street, all followed the type of the Pembroke College chapel in being plain, rectangular halls of greater or lesser width; St Vedast and St Lawrence share the feature of a single aisle; while the St Dionis, St Mary Aldermanbury, St Mary le Bow, St Magnus, and St Bride's were designed upon basilican plans complete with double aisles, the arcades of which are disposed with regularity of spacing wherever conditions permitted it, and embracing a compromise, as at St Dionis, to achieve what illusion of symmetry could be obtained from the exigencies of an irregularly shaped site. Now, however, we must turn our attention to a number of churches where Wren chose to depart from the longitudinal plan and, sometimes because of outside circumstances,

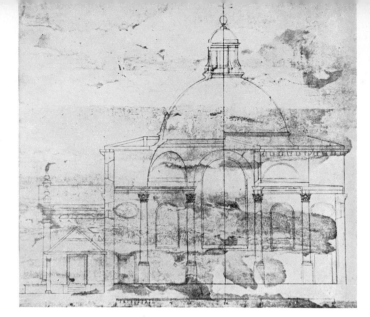

29. St Stephen, Walbrook, elevation study.

30. St Stephen, Walbrook, section.

sometimes in spite of them, designed plans based on the square, the polygon, or some other centralized figure.

We have noted, at St Mary-at-Hill, the inconsistency between the rectangular site and plan and the domical treatment; we might point to the inconsistency between the roughly square site and deliberately longitudinal plan of St Dionis. At St Benet Fink, however, no such vestiges of inconsistency can be detected: here the concept of the cupola had become sufficiently dominant to cause Wren to design, about 1670 or even a little earlier,[134] an exterior which emphasizes rather than conceals the fact. The plan cannot be compared with that of St Mary-at-Hill, as it incorporates the dome not in contradiction of the pronounced angularity of the site, but in deliberate conformity with it. It may be overstating the case to say that 'to anyone but Wren the site would have seemed almost hopeless'[135] for the exterior dimensions of 63 by 49 ft would have permitted many variations of basilican plans, variations of the aisleless, narrow rectangular plan, or, considering the narrow extremities of the site, a 'cruciform' scheme with protruding tower-porch and protruding chancel in a reduced version of what Wren was to plan for St Bride's or on the lines he was to employ, though by no means compelled by restrictions of site, at the church of St Mary, Ingestre, which he was to design within the next two or three years.[136]

Wren, however, devised a more original solution for meeting the demands of the site in the shape of an elongated decagon, surmounted by a shallow, oval dome supported upon six pillars,[137] which form an elongated hexagon within the space of the church; to this was attached a porch incorporated in the tower foundations which, though designed circular at first, was significantly changed to oval in execution. This basic motif was consistently employed throughout, and thus the basic plan is echoed in the charming design of the belfry windows which, with carved swags descending from their sides, harmonize in a delightful fashion with the domed top of the tower (Fig.75) the profile of which is equally based on an oval section.

The façade fronting the street possessed three round-headed windows disposed upon the inner faces of the decagon which, glazed in a tripartite manner recalling St Mary le Bow, with which they must be closely contemporaneous, were surmounted

by carved swags reminiscent of St Lawrence; a low balustrade crowned a delicate cornice above which the shallow dome, surmounted by a charming little lantern, remained visible. Thus, though one critic has felt little need to lament the destruction, in 1843, of this little church,[138] we feel that its interior as well as exterior must have been of an attraction only equalled by the interest which so original a work of Wren's would naturally command.

The relationship of St Stephen's, Walbrook, to the design just discussed is important, even though not at first apparent. As at St Benet's, no particular considerations of site can have inspired the employment of a centralized plan, nor is the ranging of St Stephen's five columns along the axis as against four columns placed laterally in any way comparable with the disposition of the six pillars forming an elongated hexagon at St Benet's. But, whatever criticism can be, and has been, applied to details of St Stephen's,[139] its plan is a masterpiece of design, and the originality of the arrangement has called forth the most varied and contradictory appraisals: it has been described as basilican, with a central dome carried on an octagon;[140] it has been made into a double-aisled basilica crossed by the transept and combined with the dome,[141] yet the same authority has equally regarded it as displaying 'the greatest deviation from the basilican model' which, it has been alleged, 'is tantamount to pronouncing it his masterpiece';[142] for the various combinations in which its sixteen Corinthian columns can be interpreted 'reproduce and unite almost every beauty of plan to be found in all the cathedrals of Europe'.[143] Such opinions can, at best, be taken metaphorically; but the contradictions inherent in these classifications are eloquent proof of the fact that the originality of the plan of St Stephen's defies assignation to any particular, orthodox category.[144]

The evolution of the design, however, presents problems which are not easily solved by the incomplete evidence we possess. Four drawings are extant which together with external evidence permit some insight into the initial stages of the design. That Wren had decided, from the outset, on a centralized structure crowned by a dome would seem beyond doubt, and it is likely that an elevational study represents one of the earliest surviving drawings.[145] Most of its features recall design already discussed, such as the

31. St Stephen, Walbrook.

corner keystones, the podium treatment, the flaming urns, and sunk panels; more importantly, the centre window of this, presumably eastern, front is formed in the shape of a 'motif Palladio' which, in the cross-section of the church, was to remain the basic motif of the whole design. Significantly, we meet this feature again, though enlarged into architectural importance, in the drawings which show that somewhat mysterious portion, the northern porch which was to face the Stocks Market of which the central arch cut into the triangular pediment above may conceivably represent a significant parallel, quite possibly contemporaneous, to one of the major designs for St Paul's. The three drawings

showing the projected north porch and arcade remain, however, something of a puzzle: they have been logically connected with an entry in the vestry minutes in which mention is made of the intended portico[146] and with the parishioners' petition to the Lord Mayor two years later.[147] On the other hand, it is clear that the building of a steeple had been the concern of the vestry already several years previously,[148] while the petition of 1681 already mentioned is unambiguous in recording that 'the steeple of the church was first designed to be made fronting the Stocks Market, but afterwards it was ordered that a porch should be built there instead'. This order was apparently signed by the

Lord Mayor and the Bishop of London on 10 July 1679, 'where-upon Sir Christopher Wren made a draught for the porch'.[149]

The problem created does not seem capable of resolution on such evidence as we possess; for whether this 'draught' is repre-sented by the three extant drawings[150] seems most doubtful. If they should really belong to 1679, it seems curious that no alter-native position is indicated for the tower, which, five years pre-viously, was apparently designed to stand in the place now taken by the porch. At the same time, there are considerable differences between the dome shown in the drawings and that executed, while there seems every indication that the dome had, by 1679, actually been completed: it is not likely that the deputation from the vestry whom we have met at St Edmund's and St Bride's should have set out, as early as 1676, to inspect the pewing arrangements of these churches had not their own, at that date, been nearing completion.

These inherent contradictions cannot be clearly resolved; but it is quite possible that Wren's porch as represented in these draw-ings was among such preliminary ideas as embraced the develop-ment of a symmetrical loggia along the north front of the church, embodying a central porch in the same way as we have noted in the original design for St Magnus. In view of the importance of siting which Wren, despite the failure of his City plan, attached to his churches, and considering the predilection for 'piazzas' which he continued to show in later works, it may not be unreasonable to assign the scheme to the beginning of the building history of St Stephen's rather than the end.[151] Lastly, the fact that a porch of great similarity, if greater elaboration, can with certainty be assigned to 1673 (Fig.41), may lend support to our view that we are here dealing with an attempt at retrieving a particle of the City plan rather than a remodelling belonging to the end of the decade.

The scheme, however, came to nothing. And the exterior which Wren eventually built[152] is not only cramped on almost all sides by encroaching buildings, but is not of any particular distinction. When it is remembered how, at St Benet Fink, Wren had used the basic motif of the oval even in details of the design such as the vestibule plan and the belfry windows, the exterior of St Stephen's presents no such picture of coherence and consistency: thus the introduction of oval windows above the door and in the side elevations must strike us as somewhat incongruous when recalling that the dominant motif governing the whole design is the circle which is not found in the plan only, but also in the section of the dome, the windows of the tower, the east front, and even the entry to the church beyond the front steps. Turning to the in-terior, however, it cannot be gainsaid that it must stand as Wren's most brilliant essay in an unfamiliar and wholly original form. It is unquestionably a splendid achievement for, without needing Canova's support to our opinion, it is clear that Wren here at-tained to a mastery in the handling of spatial values which finds little, if any, parallel in the rest of his work. The freedom with which he handled the components of an unusual and ambiguous plan, and the homogeneity of the whole imbue this interior with a quality of intellectual mastery and ease of accomplishment truly remarkable at this early stage of Wren's architectural career and curiously superior in facility and felicity to a good deal of his later work.

But St Stephen's possesses an importance beyond its intrinsic interest, great though it is, as it obviously served as an essay in the form which was to govern Wren's first large-scale plan for St Paul's Cathedral, for the sake of which, as well as for the sake of the approximately chronological order we have hitherto observed, we must now interrupt this examination of the City churches so as to be able to relate certain features of the various cathedral de-signs to some aspects of the field already surveyed.

It is uncertain at what time Wren's connexion with St Paul's began,[153] though it is obvious that, subsequent to his appointment as assistant surveyor, he would sooner or later be called to serve on the commission set up to decide on, and carry out, the repairs which years of neglect under Commonwealth and Protectorate had necessitated. Indeed, St Paul's had been in a sad state even during the reign of James I[154] and a Royal Commission had been set up in 1620, and renewed on Charles's accession, to deal with the problem. Laud had been able to collect some £100,000 with which to enable Inigo Jones to carry out extensive alterations and additions, by which he planned to transform, by degrees, the ancient fabric into something resembling a Renaissance edifice.[155] Jones had progressed as far as the completion of the celebrated portico,[156] the recasting of the north and south walls of the nave and transepts[157] when the political upheavals of Charles's reign put an end not only to his reconstruction, but also to his career. Cromwell's rise to power did to St Paul's what the sack of Rome by Charles V and the Connétable de Bourbon had done to St Peter's little more than a hundred years before: as horses had then stamped in St Peter's, so now they did in the canons' stalls of St Paul's: 'you know that once a stable was made a temple, but now a temple has become a stable'; and thus 'it was a bitter taunt of the Italian who, passing by Paul's Church and seeing it full of horses; "Now I perceive (said he) that in England men and beasts serve God alike".'[158]

The committee convened to deal with the repair and conserva-tion of St Paul's was thus faced with a formidable task. Wren's first proposals for dealing with the cathedral have fortunately been preserved for us: it is possible that his intention was to follow on Jones's lines in effecting a gradual transformation of the structure; significantly, however, the first step in this direction was to be the construction of a dome over the crossing to replace

32. St Paul's, pre-Fire design.

the famous spire, destroyed 100 years before. Wren must have been aware that considerable forces of conservatism would stand in the way of such drastic innovations, and it was probably with diplomacy that, to begin with, he would not 'persuade the Tower to be pull'd down at first, but the new work to be built around it, partly because the expectations of Persons are to be kept up; for, many Unbelievers would bewail the loss of old Paul's steeple, and despond if they did not see a hopeful successor rise in its stead'.[159] The second stage, however, was to be radical: perhaps actuated by the alarming state of the piers and pillars, and irrespective of 'Persons' expectations and despondency', he contemplated the total demolition of the tower.[160]

If Wren's desire for a dome was an original idea, it is highly probable that John Evelyn must have been instrumental in rendering it of such paramount importance to him that it should have dominated the entire history of the cathedral design. Evelyn was familiar with most of the domes to be seen in France and Italy.[161] Wren, on the other hand, certainly knew such domed churches and buildings as existed in Paris at the time of his visit, notably Le Mercier's Sorbonne, Mansart's three churches, as well as Le Vau's oval cupola of the Palais Mazarin;[162] and these influences, possibly combined with Wren's knowledge of the famous octagon at Ely, can be held responsible for the scheme which, enthusiastically backed by Evelyn,[163] he put before the committee on 27 August 1666. This was nothing less than startling: Wren envisaged the retention of the nave of the cathedral as it had been left by Jones; but over the crossing he projected a large, bulbous dome, raised upon a high, pillared drum, and surmounted by a giant pineapple.

The idea was not favourably received by Wren's fellow commissioners.[164] The dean, Dr Sancroft, who knew Wren from their previous encounters at Cambridge, was probably favourably inclined; the bishop might have agreed, if reluctantly, to give his blessing to the scheme. But Roger Pratt and Thomas Chicheley[165] were violently opposed to it, the former advocating the reconstruction of the steeple on its old foundations which, however much out of perpendicular Wren had proved them to be, were yet structurally sounder than he had thought.[166] But such an idea was altogether contrary to Wren's and Evelyn's intentions; and it was not solely on technical grounds that they 'totally rejected' Pratt's suggestion and persisted that 'it required a new foundation', but also, and perhaps largely, because they thought that 'the shape of what stood was very mean' and 'had in mind to build it with a noble cupola, a form of church-building not as yet known in England, but of wonderful grace'.[167]

The outcome of these differences must be conjectural. Wren's proposal, by reason of his friendship with Evelyn and Sancroft, might have been carried; Chicheley might have been persuaded into agreement, particularly as, six years later, he was doubtlessly consulted on, and evidently agreed to, the unorthodox design for St Stephen's. But the opposition of Pratt, and possibly May, could only have been overcome by being outvoted, as it seems that both resented the fact that Wren, by Royal patronage and a Privy Council appointment,[168] had been admitted into what they may not unreasonably have regarded as their own preserve.[169] But within a week, the outbreak of the Fire made an end of the dispute. Once more,

> 'Nothing could stay
> The sad decay,
> The lead was molten into drosse.'

Once more

> 'The bells fell down, and we must mourne,
> The wind it was so strong.
> It made the fier
> To blaze the higher
> And doe the church still greater wrong.'[170]

When the Fire had at last burnt itself out, the cathedral lay in ruins. The walls of choir and nave, the portico and transepts were still standing, but even so the damage was such that Wren never considered the possibility of repairing the shell. The fact emerges clearly and at an early date that, although several years were to pass before a final decision on entire reconstruction was reached, Wren never returned to his first project, but a fortnight previously proposed; and it may not be too much to conclude that, no matter how unorthodox that scheme may have appeared to the others, he himself had perhaps regarded it only half-heartedly and possibly welcomed the opportunity of redesigning the entire fabric untrammeled by any existing or surviving parts or foundations. That this opportunity was not to come for several years was due to the cathedral chapter's futile hopes to save the old cathedral and its ineffectual attempts throughout three years to patch up the ruins. But the delay thus incurred need not be regretted, for it is obvious that at that early period Wren was not possessed of sufficient knowledge and experience to have satisfactorily carried out a task of such magnitude; and in view of the fact that he did not actually finalize some of the most important details of his design until forty years later, all the difficulties, delays, and procrastinations with which he met, however galling they must have been to him, must be considered a blessing in disguise; this lapse of time permitted him to reach the full maturity of his designing faculties and attain a mastery of his technical equipment before the stones of the final version rose from the ashes of old St Paul's.

The evolution of the cathedral design must form one of the most complex and most interesting chapters in any consideration of Wren's work, and it is surprising that no detailed attempt has yet been made to interpret the sequence of concepts of major and minor importance which eventually led to the fabric as we know it today.[171] The somewhat cavalier treatment with which this problem has been dealt with has been responsible for a good

33. St Paul's, plan. Detail from the City plan of 1666.

deal of confusion further augmented by the arbitrary, and frequently inconsistent and contradictory labels of 'Rejected', 'Model', 'Favourite', and 'Great Model' design which have been attached to Wren's various schemes. On the other hand, if we are to put forward an exposition by means of which the various extant designs and available external evidence can be fitted into a logical and chronological sequence, it should be emphasized at the outset that, documentary evidence being incomplete, our reconstruction of the evolution must necessarily depend to a considerable extent on stylistic analysis and that, whatever inferences can be drawn from the application of such a method, our conclusions are not put forward as possessed of anything more than probability.

We may discredit Stephen Wren's story that soon after the Fire the architect 'was prepared with plans, elevations, and sections of every part, which he had but just finished to a large scale on vellum when the event occurred'[172] for, as we have noted, Wren never returned to the pre-Fire project once the cathedral lay in ruins. His first action was not to re-submit these plans, but to set about making a report as soon as conditions made it possible for him to survey the damage in detail.[173] Together with this report we must consider Wren's first ideas on the future cathedral – for no alternative to complete reconstruction was in his mind a week after the Fire – which we find expressed in the block plan sketched into the plan for the City. There is no reason why this should be regarded as merely diagrammatical; not only would a block plan of the ruined edifice have served such a purpose, but also this sketch contains too many indications of concepts which were to occupy Wren for the next seven years, to be thus lightly dismissed. The basic shape, consisting of a rectangular western nave leading up to a large, square, obviously domed part, clearly suggests the notions of 'quire' and 'auditory' which governed Wren's ideas not only for the temporary 'tabernacle', but also for the cathedral to come; for this, like the City plan of which it formed part, was the vision of the future.

Wren's report, however, dealt with the present: to begin with, he defined the nature and extent of the damage, largely in order to demonstrate the only reasonable position where to erect a temporary structure to serve the immediate need. He rejected the eastern parts of the ruins, where the 'New Quire' had crashed into the vaults of St Faith;[174] there, roofs and pillars had fallen so that obviously no remnant still standing could be utilized as part of a temporary structure. The 'Old Quire', however, though providing a reasonably sound foundation, was not very well suited to Wren's purpose. 'First the place is very short and little between the stone skreen and the Breach, and only capable of a little Quire, not of an Auditory';[175] nor could this latter be placed within the crossing, if for no other reason than that one would 'make such a dismall procession through Ruines to come hither that the very passage will be a Penance'. Thus, 'the properest and cheapest way of making a sufficient Quire and Auditory' was to place the structure within the body of the nave and screening it off by 'particion walls'. Beyond this, however, Wren was already looking forward to the 'time to consider of a more durable and noble Fabrick, to be made in the Tower and Eastern Parts of the Church'. The ultimate goal was not too far distant in his vision, and he was careful to hint 'in the meantime, to derive, if not a stream, yet some little drills of charity this way, or, at least, preserve that already obtained from being diverted, it may not be ill-advised to seem to begin something of the new fabric'.

The result of Wren's report can be seen in a Royal decree dated 15 January 1667/8, from which the temporary nature of Wren's suggestions, as well as the reasons for its projected location, become clear; 'it being thought necessary in the mean Time (till it shall please God to bless us with a more favourable juncture for doing something more lasting and magnificent) that some part of that venerable Pile be forthwith restored to its religious Use; and it being apparent that the whole Easte Parte of that Cathedrall is under greater Desolation than the Rest; it was this Day order'd that a Choir and Auditory for present Use be set out, repair'd and finish'd in the Course of the next summer in the Body of the Churche between the West End and the second Pillar above the little North Dores'.[176]

Of the temporary structure built in fulfilment of this command we have, unfortunately, no knowledge beyond the fact that it was short-lived.[177] What, however, becomes evident is the fact that conservative circles, and not least the cathedral chapter, were still thinking in terms of repairing the ruins, even though Wren had unambiguously expressed the impracticability of such a course. Thus, while the authorities began to waste time and money in patching up the ruins, Wren went back to Oxford, to his lectures on astronomy, and to the Sheldonian Theatre now nearing completion, his mind, however, full of ideas for a future rebuilding of the cathedral.[178] No doubt he discussed his ideas with Sancroft on his visits to London, and expressed his opinions on the irrational method of patching in which the powers that be persisted. Wren knew, though the clerics did not want to have it true, that old St Paul's was past repair; until at last the inevitable happened: piece by piece, the remnants of the shattered fabric came crashing down, bringing with them the new patchwork, so

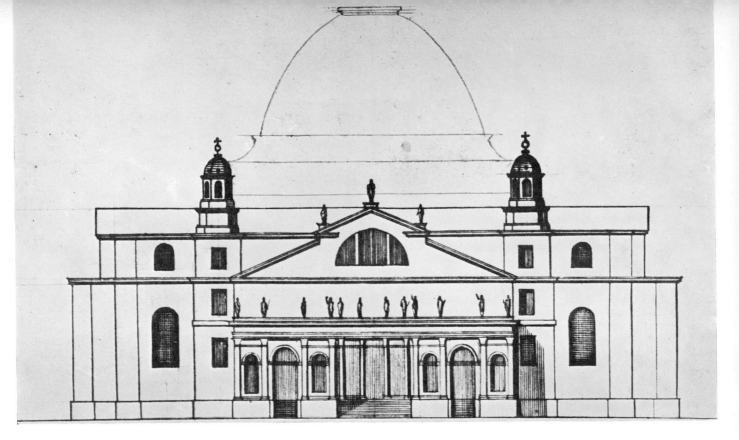

34. St Paul's, west front study.

that when fifteen futile months had passed in useless labour, Sancroft could write to Wren at Oxford that 'what you whispered into my Ear at your last coming hither, is now come to pass. Our Work at the West-end of St Paul's is fallen about our ears. 'Tis therefore, that in my Lord of Canterbury's name, and by his Order, we most earnestly desire your Presence here with all possible Speed. You will think fit, I know, to bring with you those excellent Draughts and Designs you formerly favour'd us with; and in the mean Time, till we enjoy you here, consider what to advise, that it may be for the Satisfaction of his Majesty, and the Whole Nation.'[179]

It is fortunate that some of these 'excellent Draughts and Designs' should be still in existence, and to consider what may have been the earliest of these is of the greatest interest. This crude portico, behind which looms already the faint, pencilled vision of the dome, contains the germ of the final version in spite of its amateurish awkwardness. At the same time, it reflects very clearly many design peculiarities found in work of the same period, namely the very end of the decade. Striking among these is the curiously 'broken' pediment which, in somewhat different proportion and pitch, we have met with at the Sheldonian Theatre. The balustrade crowning the portico carries a dozen statues, an arrangement reminiscent of Inigo Jones's,[180] even though the architectural features show considerable differences in Wren's curious treatment of the entries. The semi-circular window set in the upper pediment recalls, again, the Sheldonian Theatre and St Mary-at-Hill, though it provides so striking a resemblance to the east window of St Anne's, Soho (Fig.24) that we have been tempted to infer a contemporaneity of these drawings. The turrets capping the rudimentary towers equally provide points

of contact with other designs: they can pertinently be compared with the lantern of Emmanuel College, Cambridge – a feature which Dean Sancroft would have been best qualified to appreciate – and also recall, though in chronological anticipation, the turret which Wren designed for Bow steeple (Fig.76) as well as that first projected for St Edmund's (Fig.20). Most important, however, is the faint outline of a dome crowning this gauche west elevation, which gives proof – if such, indeed, were needed – that the notion 'we have in mind to build it with a noble cupola' had taken firm root in Wren's ideas.

However, Wren did not follow Sancroft's invitation immediately, but promised that he would 'wait upon his Grace and kisse your hands about the middle of next week bringing the old designes with me'.[181] The upshot of this visit was inconclusive: for Wren was explicit in telling Sancroft that 'I thinke it is silver upon wch the foundation of any worke must be first layd' and proposed deferring any further designs until 'you have found out the largeness and security of this sort of foundation' when he would 'presently resolve you what fabrick it will beare'.[182] With such a stipulation, a deadlock seems to have been created; Wren was obviously averse to spend any more time in designing cathedral plans without any knowledge of what means would be at his disposal; and it took 'my Lords of Canterbury, London and Oxford' two careful perusals of his letter to come to a decision; this however, we may imagine, would have warmed Wren's heart. Early in July arrived another letter from Sancroft who was 'commanded to give you an Invitation hither, in his Grace's name, and the rest of the Commissioners, with all Speed; that we may prepare something to be proposed to his Majesty (the Design of such a Quire, at least, as may be a congruous Part

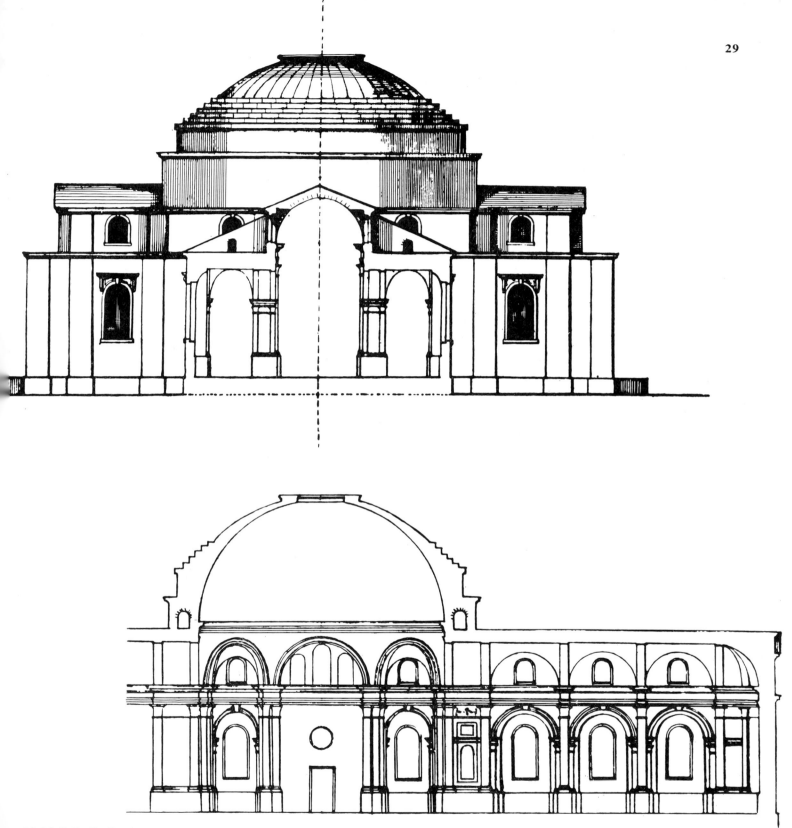

35, 36. St Paul's, 'Pantheon' design, elevation and section.

of a greater and more magnificent Work to follow) and then for the procuring Contributions to defray this'. There was to be no question of cutting St Paul's coat to fit the cloth of present means: 'for quite otherwise the Way their Lordships resolve upon it is to frame a Design, handsome and noble, and suitable to all the Ends of it, and to the Reputation of the City, and the Nation, and to take it for granted, that Money will be had to accomplish it; or however, to let it lie by, till we have before us a Prospect of so much as may reasonably encourage us to begin'.[183]

Wren's proposals must have followed the recommendations he had made some eighteen months before; for King Charles, in issuing a warrant three weeks after the date of Sancroft's letter, clearly thought the time had come 'to consider of a more durable and noble Fabrick to be made in the Tower and Eastern Parts of the Church' when he commanded 'the takeing down the walls, and cleareing the ground to the foundation at the East End, the old Choir, and the Tower, to make room for a new Choir, of a faire and decent Fabrick neare or upon the old foundations'.[184]

We may assume two extant drawings to represent what Wren then had in mind, and these are clearly the elevation and section of what had been adumbrated in a variant of the City plan (Fig.153); for the design consists of the two main components there sketched, namely a vaulted nave with a western portico leading up to a large, domed, central space, the pure expression of a 'convenient Quire and Auditory'. The nave is aisled and its three bays demarcated by pillars, and spanned by round-headed arches, with clerestory lights above the aisles. There is, significantly, a half-bay interposed between the nave and the 'crossing' and this, with short transepts and choir projecting from it, is roofed by a large dome of internally semi-circular profile, supported on eight massive piers. The surprising feature, however, is the dome itself; as we know, Wren had advocated the use of a cupola even before the Fire, and had drawn (Fig.32) a large, bulbous structure supported on a tall, pillared drum; but here, as Elmes had already noted,[185] we are confronted with a very close version of the Roman Pantheon and, clearly, the forerunner of the dome to be designed shortly afterwards for St Stephen's, Walbrook (Fig.29). Wren may have begun to disregard the 'expectations of Persons' who, mourning old St Paul's, 'would despond if they did not see a hopeful successor rise in its stead', and this disregard, explicit in his refusal to build in the style of another age, and his desire to continue the renascence of Roman architecture which Inigo Jones had initiated in England were to be responsible for many of the difficulties and disappointments which lay ahead.

Some stylistic peculiarities may help in assigning a date to this project independently of Sancroft's letters and the Royal warrant quoted above. Thus the windows shown in the elevation correspond in type to those we have noted at St Nicholas, St Edmund, St Magnus, and St Anne, and the section shows a transeptal door and window clearly of the same family as those of St Lawrence, St Nicholas, St Dionis, St Magnus, and St Anne; while lastly, the arrangement of the three round-headed windows in the upper story of the transepts provides not only a link with Jones's portico, but also foreshadows an early section for St Lawrence,[186] the west front of Bow church and the east elevation of St Bride. Thus these parallels would suggest a date towards the very end of the 'sixties, which conveniently agrees with what little external evidence we possess.

If our interpretation and dating should be correct, these drawings would constitute a preliminary step for a design, of which neither drawings nor contemporaries' references, but solely the remnant of a model remains to us by which to reconstruct Wren's design. The model fragment, which is preserved in the cathedral,[187] represents the 'nave' or 'choir', part of Wren's scheme, and we are unfortunately left in ignorance of the nature of the 'crossing', the now missing portion, to the one-time existence of which a broken hinge attached to the fragment still testifies. It may be that Wren here reversed the scheme indicated on his City plan and everything suggests that he made what we presume to have been a domed square space precede the rectangular section of the choir. This itself was demarcated by a change of floor-level at the juncture, and the aisles were, curiously, formed to provide external colonnades.[188] If we are correct in establishing a connexion between Wren's activities at that period, the Royal Warrant of 25 July 1668, and the undated design of which we only possess the model fragment, the question must arise whether Wren executed this scheme intending that it should represent a complete and final design, as some authorities suggest by pointing to parallels in Wren's later work,[189] or whether it was intended as no more than the eastern section of a 'possible new Cathedral' and thus a 'congruous part of a greater and more magnificent work'.

Our own point of departure from opinions hitherto expressed lies in our inability to assign, with them, the model remnant to 1672.[190] Whether the scale of the assumed domed section of the model was really about twice the diameter of the vestibule at Greenwich; and whether its diameter approximately equalled the width of the choir or not, is irrelevant to our ability to determine that the scheme here suggested was considerably smaller than any of the subsequent major designs, none of which measured less than some 300 ft in length – the very dimension, in fact, indicated in the City plan. Though it has never been suggested, it would seem clear to us that the model fragment represents the small-scale forerunner, the preliminary miniature version, so to speak, of what Wren was to propose as soon as financial circumstances made it possible for him seriously to consider the erection of a more 'durable noble fabric'. Such private benefactions as had been received[191] were wholly insufficient to cover the enormous cost of total reconstruction, and so Parliament, in 1670, found a feasible (and appropriate) means of raising the necessary funds. Though Sir Francis Kynaston had once ridiculed the idea,[192] Inigo Jones had held the coal smoke of London responsible for the deterioration of the stone of the cathedral: now Parliament laid a levy on coal which would provide the means of rebuilding it.[193]

Seeing that by 1670 the financial provision for entire reconstruction had been made, there is thus little reason to think that Wren should at that time have planned so relatively small a scheme as that represented by the model fragment which, therefore, could reasonably be assigned to no later date than the beginning of 1669. On the other hand, there is every reason to believe that it served, in some measure, as the prototype for the design of a similar, but much larger model, the construction of which was commenced in the autumn of that year: thus an on account payment of £50 was made, during October–November 1669, to 'Wm Clare, for Making the *New* Model of the Church in Wainscot',[194] while in January of the year following a payment of a hundred guinea pieces in gold was made 'To Dr Chr Wren His Majesty's Surveyor General and Surveyor also of these Works[195] for his directions, and towards drawing & designing a *new* draught of the whole Church for the Joyners to make a Modell in Wainscott.'[196]

That these entries cannot be related to the model fragment still extant is indicated by the phrasing specifying the 'New Model' of the church, as well as the relatively high fee paid to Wren. And further entries help to support our view when we read of a payment made, between March and April 1671, 'To Wm Clare, In full £200 . 15 . 0 for making the model of the Church in Wainscot';[197] in the autumn of that year, '2 New Rooms' were specially set aside 'for Mr Surveyor's use, and for Model of the Church';[198] and final proof is offered by an entry of June 1672[199] which records the payment of £1 to 'Wm Clare, Joyner. For mending and Removing the Model from Whitehall to St Paul's' and the disbursement of 10s 'For four Porters to carry the same and place it in C. Hse'.[200] If the size of the model is borne in mind, it will at once become clear that these entries cannot relate to it: there is no reason why the commissioners should have spent such considerable sums on a model which was to serve only a temporary purpose; there is no reason to think that a room should be specially set aside for a model which would not have been more than 6 ft long; and, whatever the size of the now missing portion of the model, it would be ludicrous to assume that four porters should have been required to carry it.

The above extracts show the difficulty of assigning the model fragment to any period subsequent to 1670, and the impossibility of identifying it with that model which in 1672 was returned from Whitehall to St Paul's. But the entries indicate that another, certainly much larger, more costly, and more elaborate model was made,[201] doubtless subsequent to that extant, which we can assume to have been put forward as a final project, not only because of the considerable sums spent on it, but also because, as we have noted, by that time such financial considerations as had cramped and restricted previous design[202] had ceased to exist. That no fragments, sketches, or drawings of this project have survived must be a matter of greatest regret, for this clearly must have been one of the major stages by which the final design of Wren's *magnum opus* was achieved. To gain an idea of the nature of that project embodied in the second model, we must turn to the accounts of those who saw it, and by whose comments we can approximately reconstruct its principal features.

Stephen Wren tells us that the 'Surveyor was directed to contrive a Fabrick of moderate Bulk but of good Proportion; a convenient Quire with a Vestibule, and Porticoes, and a Dome conspicuous above the Houses. It was to be vaulted underneath for Burials that the Pavement above might be preserved. A Model in Wood was made of this Church, which, tho' not large, would have been beautiful and very fit for our way of Worship; being also a convenient Auditory, and by the help of the Vestibule it was capable of any great Ceremonies.'[203] But Stephen Wren is not to be implicitly trusted: considering the previous resistance to a dome, we cannot guess who it was that 'directed the Surveyor' to design such a feature, and while, inaccuracies apart, this description could be applied to both the first, temporary scheme, and the second, hypothetical design,[204] it is fortunate that Hooke's references are more precise: for Hooke saw the model some months after it had returned from Whitehall to the room set aside for it,[205] and later records Wren speaking to him about 'the designe of burying vaults under Paules and the addition of a Library body and Porticoes at the west'.[206] Of greater importance, however, is the description of the model left by Sir Roger Pratt. That Pratt should not have seen it until the summer of the year following may have been due to his retirement to Ryston, and there is every reason to believe that by the time he viewed, and criticized, the model, that design had already been abandoned and Wren was busily engaged on an alternative project. What Pratt relates, however, is of great importance to complete this hypothetical picture of this stage of the evolution of the cathedral design; while the acidity of his comments may have been due to a certain amount of antagonism between the two men, existing, perhaps, ever since the day when the battle of 'Antients and Moderns' had been fought in the microcosm of the cathedral commission by Wren and Evelyn *versus* Pratt and Chicheley,[207] the concise, if incomplete picture Pratt presents suffices for us not only to envisage the outline of Wren's design, but also gather his intentions in relation to the future transformation which it was to undergo.

Pratt had very definite 'Objections against the Model of St Paul's standing in the Convocation House there as its now designed by Dr. Renne, according as it offered it selfe unto me upon the shorte and confused vewe of ¼ of an hour onely. Planta. First as to the forme of it. Its wholly different from that of all the Cathedrals of the whole Worlde besides, this being one long continued body only; all others besides in the form of a Cross more or lesse. 2ndly, That the two side aisles are wholly excluded from the Nave of the Church and turned into useless Porticos without, instead of adding a spacious Gracefullnesse to the Church within. 3rdly. In setting the Cupola at the west end of the Church instead of over the middle of the cross aisles, and then separating the whole diameter of this cupola from the Nave of the Church, as I remember, which has most causelessly and ungracefully shortened it. 4thly. Making 3 several Porticos all of the same fashion at the western ende of the Church whereas there seemeth to be no necessary use of any more than one. The upright: as to this I had scarce time to vewe it, and so can say but little to it, but see that (as I remember) there is a double portico, as it were one over the other, the lowermost looking from the Church, the uppermost looking into it, whither all the side lights of the Nave come not through that upper Portico which, if so, then how dark and ungraceful will the Nave be. 2ndly. How ungracefully and weakly do the Lucarnes stand which are over the Portico of the East end &c.[208] Ten windows[209] as I remember, make the whole Length of the Church, ye Architects in such cases usually make an odd one. That which I observed in the Cupola was that the pillars stood too thick, and consequently the Windows between too much crowded and too plain; being without all ornament: and that there were no Lucarnes in the Arch of it, and contrary to all custom, which must needs darken it.'[210]

While allowance must be made for the 'shorte and confused vewe', there can be no doubt that Pratt's description of the design is largely correct. His comments on the porticos are corroborated by Hooke; and his mention of the ten windows of the 'nave' shows to what extent the project agreed with the first model design; lastly, his description of the shape and orientation of the entire building is altogether too precise, and conform to Wren's recommendations and his grandson's description, to leave any room for doubt. The only point where Pratt's lack of comment may cause surprise is that he ignored the fact that the whole plan was designed on two levels.

The present shape, as well as the future intentions, of this project becomes clear from Pratt's remarks; the shape itself was an enlargement, and possibly an elaboration of the scheme first envisaged for a temporary structure, consisting of a fair-sized square-domed area to the east of which a ten-bay choir was attached, while provision was made for the change in floor level. But that Wren's second project, as described by Pratt, can hardly be considered final and complete is a fact which speaks plainly from Pratt's remarks as well as other circumstances; surprisingly, it has never been suggested that the model seen by Pratt might have been only the first stage, and by no means the complete design, of Wren's first major proposal for complete reconstruc-

tion. To such a view it could, of course, be objected that there was no reason for Wren's deliberate presentation of a part only, instead of the complete project, in the model, where financial considerations still present in problems of actual reconstruction did not matter. But, unless our entire thesis as presented up to now should prove false, it could be reasonably conjectured that Wren's model was to obtain an addition, at a later stage, of the part which would complete the ensemble, and by the joining of the two the two stages of construction could be graphically demonstrated.[211]

The truly cogent reasons which support our opinion, however, lie in less conjectural aspects: there is no reason to think that Wren intended his domed square, or polygon, to form the 'vestibule' of his cathedral. Not only would such an arrangement have been of great unorthodoxy and liturgical unsuitability,[212] but purely functional considerations would in that case have forced him to make the 'choir' part of the design of paramount importance, thus allocating to the domed space a subsidiary role irreconcilable with Wren's explicit and life-long predilection. These two considerations alone would offer strong reasons for the suggestion that Wren did not intend this dome-choir scheme to be final; and a close examination of Pratt's comments would make it seem evident that Wren intended the eastern part of the design to be the choir, the domed section to be the 'crossing' in which the main altar was to stand, and that he intended the addition of a nave to the west, with possibly not less than ten bays, and doubtless to be fronted towards Ludgate Hill by a majestic portico.

If this interpretation is adopted, several somewhat cryptic details of Pratt's comments attain a logical significance: thus, that Wren should have set his cupola at the 'weste ende' instead of 'over the middle of the cross aisles' becomes comprehensible the moment a future addition of a western nave is contemplated. Furthermore, 'separating the whole diameter of the cupola from the "Nave" of the Church' would be motivated by the intention of dividing the choir stalls and bishop's throne standing in the choir from the rest of the church in the same manner as it obtains today. 'That the two side aisles are wholly excluded from the "Nave" of the Church' would correspond to the intention of treating them as separate entities, either as external colonnades or internal ambulatories separated from the central part of the choir. Lastly, if Wren had intended his domed section to form the 'vestibule' only which was to precede the 'choir' as the main part of the church, he could easily, and logically, have placed his entrances to the north, west, and south. But the greatest significance attaches to the fact that he designed a 'triple portico' instead at the west end (and here Pratt is again corroborated by Hooke) for the 'Making 3 several Porticos all of the same fashion at the westerne ende' would clearly indicate that these were no more nor less than the arches of the crossing into which the central

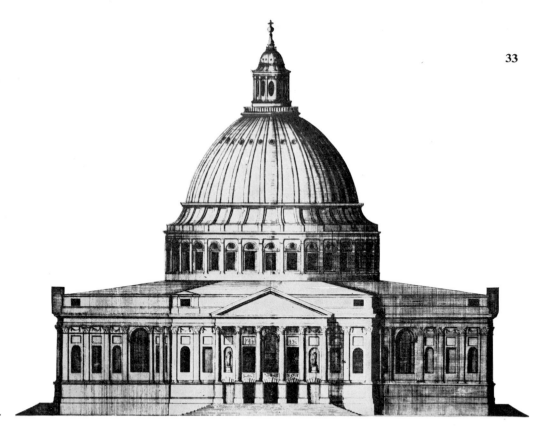

37. St Paul's, 'Greek cross design', elevation.

nave and aisles would deliver when that portion had been joined to the domed part.[213]

This would be a description, as concisely as the evidence permits us to infer, of that hypothetical project for the cathedral. Pratt's comments permit practically no conclusions to be drawn on the elevations of the design, apart from the fact that the dome, presumably supported on pillars or piers placed on an octagon plan, as well as the absence of lucarne windows, could be related to that of St Stephen's, though with the important difference that the cathedral dome was to be raised on a drum. But though we are left in comparative ignorance of the details of the elevations, the shape of the ground plan as we have construed it need not surprise us, nor appear illogical. The position of the temporary tabernacle, and the explicit specifications contained in King Charles's warrant of 1668 made it obvious and logical that the construction of the 'durable and noble fabric' should commence at the east end, thus preserving the temporary structure as long as possible to serve its function. Beyond such practical considerations, Wren's plan as here reconstructed represents an attempt to combine the domed central with the vaulted basilican plan, and though we shall have to examine this concept in greater detail in the second part of this study, we may mention here that Wren was evidently following a concept fundamental and basic to his age. Lastly, only an interpretation such as we have put forward could absolve him from the extreme unorthodoxy which the incomplete plan would have represented, an unorthodoxy for which there seems to have been neither circumstantial reasons caused by the site, nor spiritual motives responsible for so unusual a conception which, moreover, Wren must have known, would

necessarily meet with the most formidable opposition on the part of his patrons.

The design, however, was rejected, for by the time Pratt had an opportunity of criticizing this second model, namely in July 1673, Wren must already have been engaged for some time on an altogether new version. It is clear that this further project was again to be presented in the shape of a large-scale wooden model for, between April and September of that year, the sum of £42 2s 6d was paid, again to William Clare, 'For a Table and Frame for the Intended New Model of the Church to stand upon',[214] while, at the same time, workmen were apparently already engaged to 'Wheel black earth from N. side of Old Foundations in Cross Yard to the place now intended to be in the Circle of the Dome'.[215] Wren's work leading up to what is known as the Great Model design must have been accomplished in a relatively short space of time, for by 12 November 1673 a Royal Warrant was issued which stated that 'We have caused several designs to that purpose to be prepared by Dr Christopher Wren, Surveyor-General of all Our Works and buildings, which we have seen, and one of which we do more especially approve, and have commanded a model thereof to be made after so large and exact a manner, that it may remain as a perpetual and unchangeable rule and direction for the conduct of the whole work'.[216]

Two distinct stages can be discerned in the evolution of this design, and we have here entered a period where fortunately not only documentary evidence but also extant drawings permit a close insight. What must cause surprise, though, is that Wren's first approach towards the new conception was in the unusual shape of a Greek cross, where a dome of considerable dimensions

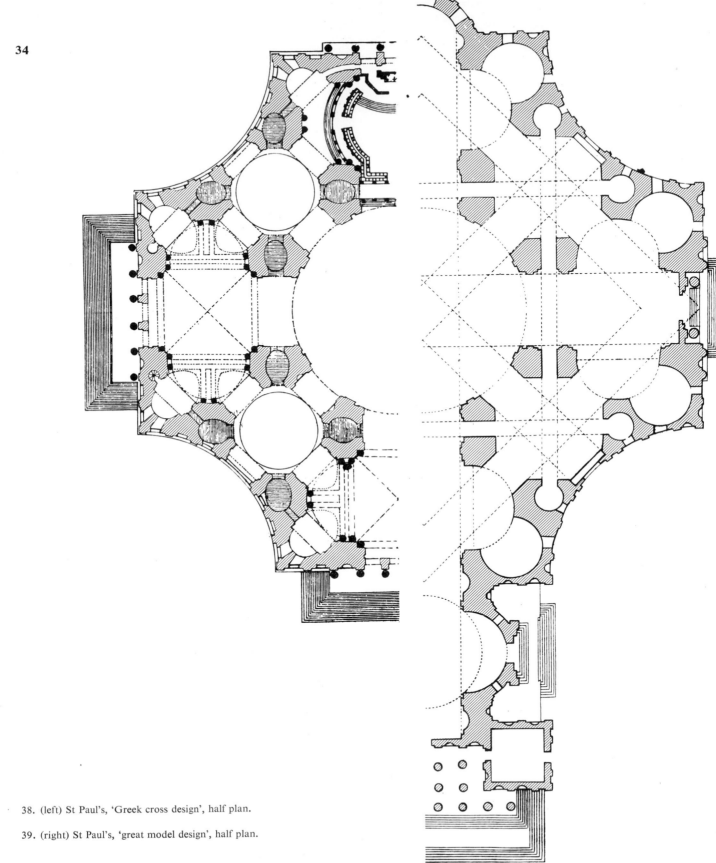

38. (left) St Paul's, 'Greek cross design', half plan.

39. (right) St Paul's, 'great model design', half plan.

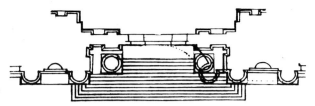

40. St Paul's, 'great model design', transept porch study.

is diagonally surrounded by four smaller, externally invisible, domes; this whole conception is fitted into a square measuring a little over 300 ft in length, the corners of which are truncated by quarter-circles (Fig.38).[217] The central dome rests on eight piers – the constructional principle to which Wren was to adhere in all future designs – while the 'transepts' as well as the western front are furnished with flights of steps leading up to hexastyle Corinthian porticos. A very elaborate setting seems to have been provided for the altar at the east end, even though the exterior elevation of that façade seems to have been identical with the others, but for the elimination of the steps.

Intriguing as the plan is in marking the entry of an entirely new conception into the sequence of cathedral designs, as well as Wren's architectural vocabulary, the elevation (Fig.37) is even more interesting, and provides far more obvious links connecting this very original work with other designs datable to the same period. Thus the windows of the drum upon which the dome rests have their exact parallels in the north door of the Sheldonian Theatre[218] while the wing elevations contain the already familiar elements of round-headed and rectangular windows and niches with their accompanying panels, such as we have first noted at Pembroke College chapel. The great portico proves to be an extension, on a monumental scale, of the five-bay east front of St Lawrence, though with significant changes: thus the podium, which was such a distinctive feature of that and other designs, is here transformed into tall plinths carrying the great order, providing the openings for the three rectangular, straight-headed doors. The pediment, however, extends across all five bays, but rises equally in front of a blocking course, the articulation of which is confined to the extreme corners only. The outer bays are niches containing statues in a manner similar to those of the Sheldonian south front, while the intermediate bays are filled with rectangular windows and their accompanying panels above.[219]

The paramount feature of the design, however, is the splendid dome which crowns this elevation, majestic on its low, polygonal drum, and subtly designed to be seen to greatest advantage from all points of view, for this consideration may actually be responsible for the curvature of the transept connexions. The dome, intrinsically as well as in relation to subsequent dome designs, is of the greatest interest. We can well believe that this conception was intended, and capable, of gratifying 'the taste of the Conoisseurs and Criticks with something coloss and beautiful', though it may be a matter of opinion whether it was really conforming 'to the best style of the Greek and Roman architecture'. But we may well believe that the design was approved of by those 'Persons of Distinction' of whom 'the generality were for grandeur'[220] though, however much the 'Conoisseurs and Criticks' may have approved, it is unlikely that the scheme would have found favour with a clergy which, whether envisaging processions or not, would see grave liturgical objections to the plan.

It is thus that came into being the scheme for a final design which, by reason of the 18 ft model[221] still preserved in the cathedral, is known as the Great Model design, or, following legend and the inscription of an engraving made half a century later, Wren's 'Favourite Design'. In a manner of speaking, Wren here returned to his very first idea as expressed in the City plan of 1666, and though the plan of the cathedral there indicated (Fig.32) is neither detailed nor to be considered more than a block plan, it is significant that in this finalization of the projects which had occupied him for five years, Wren returned to the basic idea of a dominant circular space combined with a subsidiary rectangular 'vestibule'. This arrangement of the Great Model plan (Fig.38) has not been the least cause for our refusal to believe that in previous schemes Wren should have advocated precisely the opposite concept in which, moreover, the domed sections nearest to his heart would have played a distinctly secondary part. For the Great Model seems to epitomize Wren's ideals to perfection in the clear division by which the large circular domed space, representing at once the choir, transepts, and crossing, is approached by a western vestibule of distinctly subordinate importance.

The resulting design, of which we are fortunate in having the most precise knowledge, has met with a good deal of criticism[222] for, the evidence of drawings, engravings, and the model itself notwithstanding, it has even been asserted that 'externally it would have been an architectural failure'.[223] Such esoteric judgement apart, however, we need not quote in support Wren's own opinion of this design, on which he 'always seem'd to set a higher value than any he had made before or since',[224] for the design is magnificent enough to speak for itself, splendid enough, we are tempted to think, to have caused King Charles to confer on its creator a well-deserved knighthood.[225]

It has been suggested that it was evolved by the simple addition of the western vestibule to the Greek cross design just discussed,[226] but a close study of the drawings reveals that the process was more complex than that.[227] Generally speaking, Wren retained, of course, the basic outline of the Greek cross and the placing of the eight piers is identical in both designs. But the small segmental addition at the east end is a point of significant deviation, and there are important differences in the treatment of the transept corners which the comparative half-plans here reproduced clearly demonstrate. The most important change, on plan, is the revision of the transept entrances which are now expressive of an entirely changed elevation.

The plan thus representing a development, with significant changes, from the Greek cross design, the elevations present a complete transformation which, excepting the principal dome, owe indeed but little to the preceding design. The most important difference is certainly the western portico (Fig.41): the treatment of the earlier design, where a porch some 100 ft wide was

41. St Paul's, 'great model design'.

envisaged, was by no means lacking in dignity, but the composition of the later design is of a grandeur of conception which leaves the other completely behind. The first design had possessed certain imperfections, such as the unsatisfactory placing of the order upon disproportionately tall plinths, by which means the entire horizontal division of the façade was somewhat impaired. The portico of the Great Model, however, has more than rectified this shortcoming and, utilizing a Corinthian order some 100 ft high, standing on normal bases, Wren has extended the width across the greater part of the façade. The increase from six pillars to eight and the increase of their size bring about a most impressive grandeur, by the side of which the former design looks petty and by the standard of which even Inigo Jones's celebrated portico seems almost insignificant.[228]

The transept porticoes have undergone even a greater transformation, for here we find nothing left of the static stability of the earlier composition. It seems that Wren had first envisaged a scheme in which the steps leading to the door turned at right angles;[229] but, retaining the hexastyle form, he eventually evolved an arrangement in which the spacing of the pillars is no longer even, but arranged so that those pillars flanking the entrance now appear in pairs, leaving the single member standing alone below the corners of the pediment. Originally, Wren seems to have intended to enhance the division between the pair and the single pillar by supporting them on separate plinths;[230] but the idea was abandoned when he decided to run a continuous substructure down the entire length of the elevation, to be broken only by the entrances at the transepts and the lateral entries of the vestibule. In a preliminary study[231] the horizontal division into two stories is retained and emphasized by the employment of a major, and two superimposed minor orders, but even this division was abandoned when Wren decided on a triple horizontal division, where one large order only covers the middle section which is placed on a tall substructure and surmounted by a substantial, but windowless, attic story. The change from a flat transept front into a sort of narthex is further enhanced by the placing of the pillars: not only has the even placing of the Greek cross design been abandoned, but also is the placing now varied in the third dimension (Fig.39) and thus a certain dynamism has been introduced into the composition which had been conspicuously absent in the static unity and regularity of the earlier plan. The change is completed, with great effect, by the breaking of the cornice supporting the pediment, and the sculptural treatment of the recessed semi-circular field which is carved out of it to contain what we may reasonably assume to represent the phoenix so symbolical of the cathedral.

In this transept it would be relevant to see the logical conclusion of the intention with which Wren placed semi-circular windows in the gables of St Mary-at-Hill and the Sheldonian Theatre, and the close contemporaneity suggests that Wren here planned the

monumental version of what he had projected, though not been able to execute, at the north façade of St Stephen's, Walbrook (Fig. 29). While the result achieves great force and beauty, it entails at the same time a change of character from the predominantly static conception governed by a purely linear vision to an essentially dynamic conception clearly conceived in plastic terms. This, indeed, is a point of significance which will occupy our attention at a later part of this study, so that we can now turn our attention to the two domes which are so unique and so arresting a feature of the Great Model. The main dome is closely modelled on that of the Greek cross design, but the differences bear further witness to the fact that the connexion between the two schemes is more complex than has frequently been assumed. The essential difference is shown in the drum which, most probably on account of the lengthened west front, Wren raised in height so as to make the dome really 'conspicuous above the houses'. A difference in the treatment of the windows can also be observed, and their deeper recession now achieves a more plastic impression and a more striking effect of chiaroscuro. A significant difference lies in the fact, however, that the Greek cross dome was clearly profiled to a double-flexure, thus prefiguring a most interesting bell-shaped dome which Wren was to design some fifteen years later, while in the Great Model the effect of double flexure is only indicated by the segmental buttresses which surround and support what is essentially a hemispherical dome.[232]

What must cause surprise, however, is that fact that the smaller of the two domes differs from the larger in proportion, character, and detail. Clearly planned on an octagonal base, it contrasts sharply with the smooth outline of the larger dome; and apart from the fundamental difference in volume and profile, the treatment of the lucarnes as well as the terminations themselves show significant divergences. Thus the ring of lucarne windows of the great dome are circular and fit, without elaboration, into the soft ribbing of the great structure. The lucarnes of the vestibule dome, however, are oval, embellished with ornate carved swags clearly recalling those we have noticed at St Benet Fink (Fig.75). The same divergence is found in the terminations of the domes: the lantern surmounting the larger one has been changed considerably from that planned for the Greek cross design, and it may be that the ring of pillars surrounding the central cylinder may represent the precursor of that identical feature which graces the celebrated steeple of St Mary le Bow (Fig.19). The lantern of the smaller dome, however, is an entirely different affair: planned on a square with truncated corners, the double pillars of the structure support a small stepped pyramid, conceivably inspired by the celebrated mausoleum of Halicarnassus, upon which stands the statue of what we may assume to be the cathedral's patron saint.

Although the design of this smaller dome is of considerable charm, it cannot be denied that it does not blend very well with the totally different character of the main dome, and the extreme divergence of outline, character, and treatment introduces a somewhat disturbing element into a composition which, in most other respects, is remarkably homogeneous. It certainly was a conception 'coloss and beautiful' and fit in every way to satisfy the 'conoisseurs and criticks'. On the other hand, 'the Chapter and some of the clergy thought the model was not enough of a Cathedral fashion, to instance particularly, in that the quire was designed circular and that there were no aisles or naves'.[233] Whatever the merits or demerits of the scheme, King Charles's approval was by no means sufficient to make the dean and chapter agree to its adoption. It was beginning to become clear that none but the traditional cathedral plan would prove acceptable to the clergy and though Wren would be allowed some latitude in his treatment of the elevations, the powers that be were not prepared to sanction any but the traditional plan of nave, transepts, crossing, and choir upon which England's cathedrals had been built.[234]

Wren's reaction is well known: according to one authority he actually shed tears at the rejection of what he seems to have considered his finest design[235] and, exasperated as he may well have been at the repeated rebuffs with which his projects had met, he determined that he 'would make no models or publicly expose his drawings'[236] of any further designs, and set to work on a proposal entirely different from all that had gone before; this was to 'reconcile, as near as possible, the Gothick to a better manner of Architecture, with a cupola, and above that, instead of a lantern, a lofty Spire, and large Porticos'.[237] This proved, in effect, to be an attempt to reconcile the Renaissance with the Gothic, the humanist with the medieval, the present with the past.

Wren necessarily fell back upon previous schemes. It is evident that he attempted to preserve the dome, and a study preceding the final Warrant design presents a new type of elevation, crowned by a dome of considerable likeness to Michelangelo's at St Peter's;[238] added to this, however, is a portico obviously derived from one designed some five years previously, while for the rest Wren fell back on the window-and-clerestory scheme sketched out for that early design which had been characterized by its Pantheon-like dome (Figs.34, 35). Another design[239] shows a development of a similar body, but crowned by a dome resembling that of the Great Model with most of the drum eliminated, but with a transept portico nearly identical with Inigo Jones's.

The design which obtained royal approbation by the issue of yet another warrant on 14 May 1675, and equally obtained the cathedral authorities' sanction, has met with complete condemnation on the part of modern critics.[240] It is unquestionably inferior both to the preceding Great Model design and the subsequent design to which the cathedral was eventually built, but none the less it must be regarded as one of the major steps of the evolution, thus warranting a close examination of its features

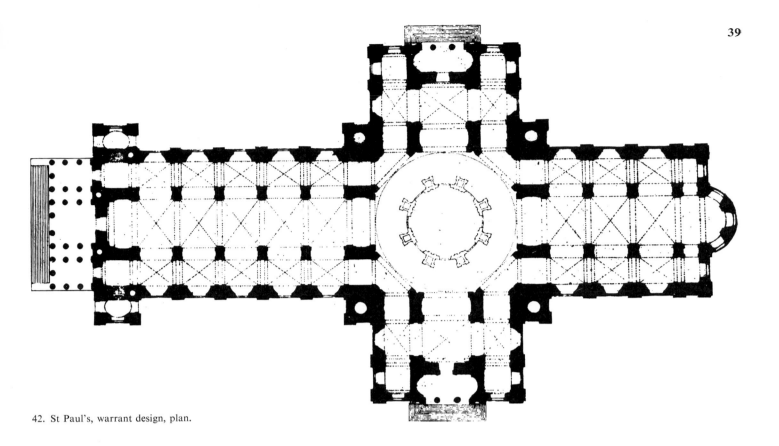

42. St Paul's, warrant design, plan.

which should serve a more useful purpose than further words of criticism.

The plan of the design represents a complete revolution from all that had gone before and its character was patently devised so as to silence such critics as had demanded a scheme in the traditional 'cathedral fashion'. Thus it is cast in the conventional Latin cross form, possessing a choir terminating in a semi-circular apse, a square crossing with short transepts, a five-bay nave with aisles fronted by a great west elevation which incorporated the western chapels allegedly forced on Wren by the Duke of York with a view to the reintroduction of the Roman Catholic faith.[241] Apart from that feature, however, Wren obtained the clergy's sanction only by presenting a plan tantamount to medieval prototypes, but if the plan shows little or no attempt to reconcile his own ideals with the wishes of his patrons, the elevation represents a truly astonishing endeavour to compromise between these different premisses.

It may almost seem that Wren had ceased to attempt the evolution of an altogether new project, disheartened by the fruitless years' labour, and was merely planning the combination of such features of Jones's building and his own designs which, individually, had met with approval. The design thus evolved is, in essence, retrogressive and clearly not of the same level of accomplishment which Wren had by that time achieved in his City churches. The heterogeneous assembly of features which had not met with previous criticism results in a rather astonishing ensemble: from the 'Pantheon' design (Figs.35, 36) Wren took the transeptal porticoes (themselves derived from Inigo Jones's) as well as the truncation of the flattened dome which supports the extraordinary steeple, while both side elevations and west front repeat the window scheme of the earlier design. The arrangement of three round-headed windows found over the transept porticoes and the western porch again recalls Jones's work, and the clerestory windows, curiously joined to the top cornice, echo the unusual method adopted in the east front of St Anne's (Fig.24). Nor are reminiscences of the Great Model entirely absent, for the domed tops of the rudimentary towers are in clear descent from the vestibule dome of that design, and the stepped pyramid of Halicarnassus lineage recurs, somewhat incongruously, crowning the buttresses[242] and the dome upon the very tall drum is no more than a reduced and simplified version of the main dome of the great model. Finally, features of some of the City churches are to be found again, such as the coupled pillars and round-headed belfry windows which the west towers of the Warrant design share with St Mary le Bow (Fig.19) and with St Bride (Fig.84) not forgetting the astonishing steeple which has, not inaptly, been described as a 'parody of St Bride's'.[243] The truly remarkable feature, however, is the combination of dome and spire over the crossing.[244] This begins upon the roof-line (where, in the Great Model, it had been hidden behind the blocking course), and rises in Pantheon-like steps to support the truncated shallow dome; this carries a lantern of considerable size, in which square-headed windows are deeply recessed between pilaster supports planned on an octagonal base which taper, in scroll

buttress fashion, towards the top of the cylinder; this in turn forms the base for a further domical structure, from the platform of which rises a spire in six stages, again designed on octagonal plans of diminishing size, with ball and cross completing this truly extraordinary composition.

Although the treatment of the west portico represents a return to earlier schemes as we have noticed, it is also possible that this return was caused by Wren's realization that the quarries upon which he could draw for materials were incapable of furnishing blocks large enough to permit the construction of a single order some 90 to 100 ft high as he had planned in the Great Model.[245] Thus the pronounced horizontal division produces a new idea for the elevation and we may point out even now that, whatever changes will be observed in the transition from the warrant design to the executed cathedral (and these were indeed momentous), the distinct horizontal division of the elevation remained to be clearly expressed in the double order portico finally built. The porch here embodies a long range of ten pillars in width and four in depth which give access to a single, square-headed door. The exterior pillars carry an entablature and balustrade upon which a range of statues, corresponding to the pillars below, stands; behind these the upper part of the front becomes visible in a pedimented centre piece containing round-headed windows, and this section is flanked, in a manner recalling St Mary Aldermanbury (Fig.14), by scroll buttresses. The transept porches are treated in a very similar fashion but for the reduction in the range of pillars, and the side elevations[246] contain clearly demarcated buttresses corresponding to the interior bays, thus balancing the predominantly horizontal rhythm introduced by the continuous cornice and roof-line.

Wren's submission of this incongruous scheme has been thought more surprising than the royal and official sanction which it received. That the design should have been the result of Wren's immaturity, as has been suggested,[247] must be ruled out in view of the contemporaneity of so accomplished a building as St Stephen's; that it should have been the result of 'the nearest thing to a bad temper of which his meek and quiet spirit was capable'[248] seems as little credible as to think that Wren 'pitched it at Charles as a joke'.[249] We can neither believe that Wren submitted it, 'thinking that the King might as well sign the silliest design he could produce as he had rejected a sound scheme'[250] nor that it was the result of 'a little experience' which 'had taught him that the King had no taste, and that the Duke of York had, if possible, even less'.[251] Least of all can we believe that 'despising the taste of the commissioners, he never seriously intended to adhere to it, anticipating that he would be his own master',[252] that he merely 'wanted the King's signature to a design',[253] which was no more than a cunning ruse by which Wren's critics 'fell into the trap thus skilfully laid'.[254] Yet few reasonable explanations can be given for this design and what seems most likely is that Wren had given

way to disappointment and produced it in a mood not likely to have been improved by the recent loss of his first wife; while Charles, at that very time, was fighting a losing battle to secure parliamentary legislation for religious toleration,[255] only to be foiled once more by the Commons' bartering his ideals for the financial support he needed. The fact, however, that Wren did not decide on some of the modifications which the warrant permitted until some twenty-five years later, makes it reasonable to break off our examination of the cathedral here to return to the City churches and other buildings of Wren.

The thirteen years which lie between the issue of Charles II's warrant for the cathedral and his brother's ignominious flight to a pensioner's life at St-Germain are patently the climax of Wren's career in ecclesiastical architecture, and within this period are to be found his maturest and most satisfying essays in that field. Indeed, one may be tempted to perceive a symbolism in the fact that Wren's churches were conceived, and largely executed, while a Stuart was yet on the throne; for the latter years of Wren's life, the years following the 'glorious revolution', represent an Indian summer of his genius largely devoted to secular architecture. It is for this reason that we would propose now to trace the development of Wren's church architecture to its end, then to consider, notwithstanding some chronological overlapping, his four great, and several small, achievements in civic architecture, to return, fittingly, to close this part of our study by an examination of the amazing changes by which the warrant design of St Paul's was transformed into the splendid fabric as we know it.

Before speaking of the major works of this period, let us consider two of Wren's smaller works: the churches of All Hallows and of St Benet, both situated in Thames Street, both executed at approximately the same time,[256] which share, in addition, a similarity of plan and conception. Wren here returned to an earlier practice, already noticed at St Lawrence, of obtaining his space for the church proper by means of pillars, piers, and screens which serve to set apart vestibules and vestries. At All Hallows, the planning is altogether arbitrary: Wren's site was a slightly irregular rectangle, of which three sides were bounded by streets, the fourth by the parish churchyard, so that his plan could have taken the form of almost any type he might have chosen. Thus the solution is somewhat surprising, for Wren chose to set his tower slightly to the east of the centre of his street front, to screen off the northern quarter of the site parallel to his south wall and in line with the tower foundations, and thus obtained an irregular rectangle no two of whose walls were of equal length, and which did not contain a right angle anywhere.

The solution arrived at, however, is practical. It may be objected that the congregation faced an altar placed against a wall

43. St Paul's, warrant design, west elevation.

44. St Benet, Thames Street, east elevation.

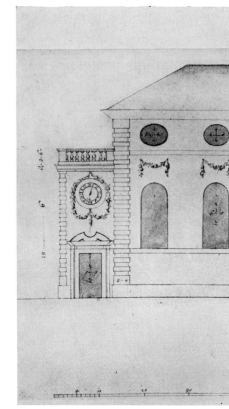

45. St Benet, Thames Street, south elevation.

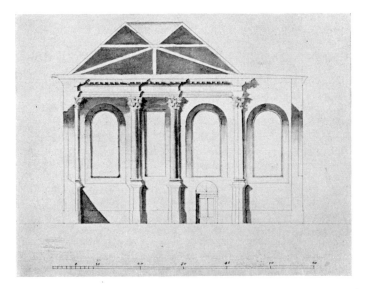

46. St Benet, Thames Street, section to west.

47. St Benet, Thames Street, north elevation.

which slanted away from it; but none the less Wren contrived a very pleasant interior south elevation which is symmetrical, though containing an even number of bays, of which the outer pair has doors leading to the churchyard. Wren being financially limited, the exterior must have been rather austere, and the tower placed asymmetrically in the street front was amoug Wren's plainest. At St Benet's, a little way up the street on the opposite side, the means at Wren's disposal were not much greater; but here he produced a building which, though small, is much more satisfactory than the one just discussed and though it cannot be ranked among Wren's outstanding works, the design possesses for us a special interest, for an unusually large number of drawings are extant[257] which permit an insight more exact and revealing than elsewhere into the way by which Wren evolved the design.

St Benet's is traditionally associated with the College of Arms, and in the pre-fire church Inigo Jones had found his last resting place. Yet, though Wren must surely have been aware of that fact, the design he produced is little reminiscent of his great predecessor. The site of St Benet's resembled that of All Hallows in being free on all sides, the southern boundary fronting Thames Street, the eastern front giving on to St Benet's Hill, the western to a narrow passage and the northern to the churchyard. Wren provided two entrances, one at the south-west angle in Thames Street, the other by a tower porch reached by the narrow passage to the west of the church. Analogous to his practice at All Hallows, he set the tower asymmetrically into the west front and used its interior foundations as the points from which to draw his screens demarcating the vestibule and a north aisle, thus reducing the irregular, trapezoid site to a fairly regular rectangle; this Wren treated as the nucleus of the design and roofed it as a separate entity, dividing his frontages on the east, south, and north into the orthodox three bays. The addition of the western vestibule, and the north aisle which he obtained by screen walls, both added an extra unit to each of the four external elevations[258] but this time Wren eschewed the symmetrical four-bay treatment evolved at All Hallows, and the solution of the problem of incorporating the fourth unit without making it appear an awkward appendage shows not a little ingenuity.

The site being small, and the desirability of galleries being apparent at an early stage, Wren first of all designed an elevational treatment which embraced an attic storey in which he proposed to place oval lights somewhat reminiscent of St Stephen's, Walbrook (Figs.43, 44). But for reasons unknown to us, the idea of the attic storey, though not of the galleries, was abandoned; Wren revised his design accordingly (Figs.45, 46) and finalized a little building which, before its destruction in 1878, must have represented, for all the criticism that had been levelled against it,[259] a picture of considerable charm. If, however, we are to turn to St Peter's, Cornhill, we shall be considering a work of far greater interest and importance. In fact, its design must have

48. St Peter, east front study.

preceded those of All Hallows and St Benet's, for we have a record of a meeting early in 1675, when it was 'Ordered that Mr Beveridge and the ch'wardens, &c. do treat with Sir Christopher Wren, and his surveyor, as to the receiving his proposals in order to the rebuilding of our parish church',[260] and though this meeting took place five weeks before Charles issued his warrant for St Paul's, the design of the parish church betrays no trace of the frustration and exasperation which have seemed to us so eloquent in that other project.

Not unnaturally, there are many parallels with preceding, as well as succeeding, works. One curious instance is provided by the carved floral scrolls originally intended for the curved buttresses of the east front which recall St Edmund's (Fig.20) but which, together with the 'flaming urns', were never executed. Of greater interest, however, is the whole design for the east front, for this, in a manner of speaking, is the mature, though simplified, development of the south front of the Sheldonian Theatre (Fig.2). The subtlety and refinement with which Wren here treated that early scheme, however, mark the great distance which Wren had covered in that decade: the lower storey is here composed of five bays of which the inner three form a slightly projecting centre, and the upper storey contains an original treatment of what, in effect, are three bays. We may note that Wren had by now abandoned his earlier practice of forming centre bays slightly larger than flanking bays, and that the subtlety with which the three centre bays are here articulated forms a motif which is found again in the belfry windows of the tower (Fig.62) which must be of slightly later date, and which will occupy our attention elsewhere. Notable is also Wren's employment of doubled pilasters[261] but more interesting still the metamorphosis of the semicircular window of the Sheldonian Theatre which here, clearly recalling the projected porch for St Stephen's (Fig.29) and the transept poticoes of the Great Model design of St Paul's (Fig.40), breaks through the upper cornice to be formed into a

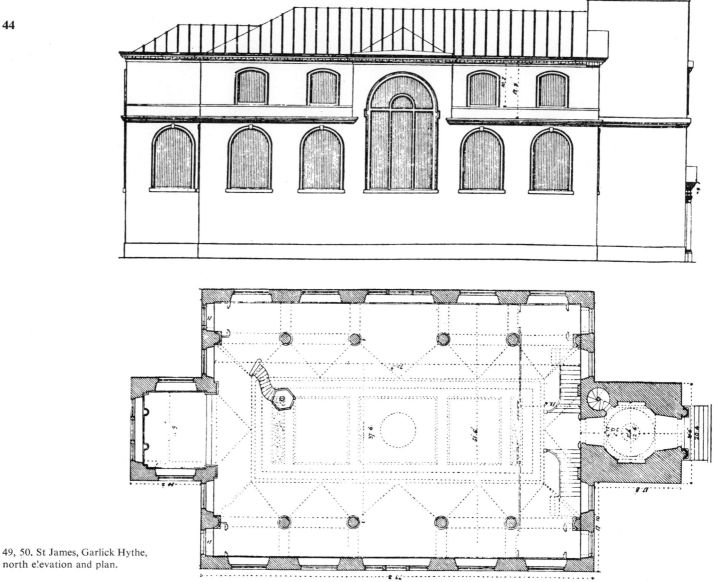

49, 50. St James, Garlick Hythe,
north elevation and plan.

large, round-headed window, forming the centre of the complete upper storey.

Of interest equally great is the plan of St Peter's, for here we find Wren following the double-aisled basilican plan even though the site precluded the incorporation of either chancel or tower-porch. From subsequent works it will become clear that, however much Wren's critics have eulogized his deviations from the basilican plan, he himself had come to regard it as an optimum solution to be employed whenever circumstances permitted. Thus not even the irregularity of the site of St Peter's; its acute north-east angle at the junction of Cornhill and Gracechurch Street; and the rather awkward means of access necessitating a porch not in line with the elevation of the church: all these draw-backs did not deter Wren from exerting much ingenuity to imbue

the plan with as much basilican regularity as conditions permitted, even going so far as to treat the placing of the nave pillars as though a regular, rectangular plan had been distorted into a parallelogram. The distortion is not great; and the illusion of regularity is complete because the accomplishment and subtlety with which the plan was drawn renders the eye practically obli-vious of the fact that there is not, indeed, a single right angle in the whole interior of the church.

The east elevation of St Michael, Bassishaw, might be regarded as a picturesque development of the east front of St Peter's, for here again a pediment, for once segmental, is broken into by a tall, round-headed window equally flanked by circular lights.[262] It is likely that the two designs are closely contemporaneous, for Wren consulted with the churchwardens on the reconstruction of

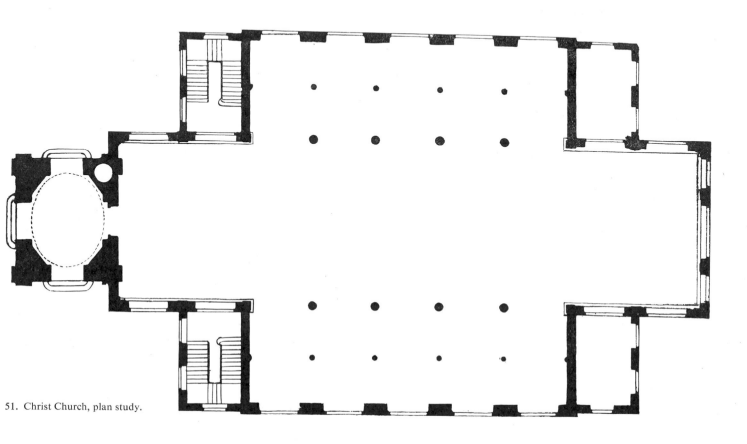

51. Christ Church, plan study.

the church early in 1676, when he was entertained to 'two dinners in Old Fish Street'.[263] But here again, Wren was foiled in an obvious attempt to plan a truly rectangular basilican scheme by the irregularity of the site; at St Peter's, as we have seen, he had treated the interior as a true rectangle distorted into a parallelogram; at St Michael's, however, the unequal lengths of the plan inspired him to a proportional spacing of the pillars, and by this means the illusion of regularity must have been contrived as successfully as at St Peter's.

It is only when we come to the church of St James's, Garlick Hill, that we find Wren once more able to develop a completely regular, symmetrical basilican plan,[264] and it is not surprising that he returned to the model of St Bride's and of St Magnus; the parallels with the latter, indeed, are more striking than would appear on first sight, for not only is an east-west symmetry created by the correspondence of chancel and tower-porch, but also a north-south axis is created through the enlarged centre of the five-bay side elevations. The reason for this treatment is not clear; at St Magnus the intention had conceivably been the insertion of a central door giving on to a piazza; but at St James's the transeptal, though doorless, treatment results in nothing but an interruption of the rhythm of the interior arcade and an enlarged centre window glazed in the manner familiar from St Dionis and St Mary Aldermanbury. The tower and steeple of St James's (Fig. 74) bears some resemblance to that of St Stephen's, Walbrook, with which it may be contemporaneous, and points forward to that of St Michael Royal, of which we shall have to speak later.

It is, however, at Christ Church that we find one of Wren's purest and most beautiful of basilican interiors. Once again, Wren was not completely free to design as he pleased, but the ruins of the Greyfriars' Gothic church, the foundations of which he had to consider, fitted admirably with what may have been his intentions irrespective of such precedent. Wren's church incorporates rather less than half the space of the old monastic edifice which had been of considerable dimensions and within

52. St Martin, elevation study.

this cadre, conforming to the dimensions of the ruined church as far as breadth of nave and aisles and disposition of pillars went, he evolved an admirable interior. His first intention, as we may gather from an early plan study (Fig.51) was to perfect the symmetry attempted at St James's by balancing the large vestibule against a spacious chancel at the east, emphasizing the north-south axis of the symmetry by a pair of (what we may presume to have been intended as) vestries at the east with two enclosed staircases at the west. This plan provided for an interior disposition of five bays marked off by a row of pillars placed in line with the vestibule and chancel returns. In execution, however, this 'ideal' basilican plan underwent considerable changes. First of all, the number of bays was increased to six; secondly, both vestries and enclosed staircases, as well as vestibule and chancel were eliminated, and what had been intended as a rhythmic, subtly articulated interior was transformed into a plain rectangular hall[265] fronted at the west by a protruding tower porch, while the plain, regular exterior elevations of no particular distinction and marred by some incongruities of design[266] border on the austere. What the exterior may lack in distinction, however, is amply made up by two things: firstly, the interior, with its quiet, regular rhythm and crystalline articulation is one of Wren's most beautiful and dignified; secondly, the steeple which was not to be erected until some two decades after the church, is rightly classed among Wren's finest and most classically beautiful as, eschewing the untrammelled fantasy of Bow steeple, it is a masterpiece of restraint and subtlety.

The three churches of St Michael's, Queenhythe, All Hallows, Watling Street, and St Mathew's, Friday Street, are not among those of Wren's works which call for much comment. Financial limitations obviously exerted an influence on design, and the sites which these three churches were to occupy contained no possibilities or promise even in the way the plot of St Benet Fink had proved the inspiration for a wholly original polygonal invention. At St Michael's, Wren made the most of a street frontage some 80 ft long in developing a south elevation similar to the north front of St Nicholas, consisting of five bays in which the round-headed windows are linked to the circular lights above in a singular and ornamental fashion. This five-bay scheme is met again at St Mathew's, where it forms a continuous arcade which, curiously, is met again in the belfry window treatment of All Hallows. This latter church presented a problem similar to St Michael's, though Wren's solution was entirely different: preserving the approximate orientation, he set the tower back from the north elevation in the same manner as at St Michael's, but instead of making a clear differentiation between the entry porch and the body of the church, he treated the front of All Hallows as one continuous façade of eight regularly spaced bays[267] which, in execution, entailed the insertion of a blind window to retain the regularity of the design. Of interest here is the way in which doors

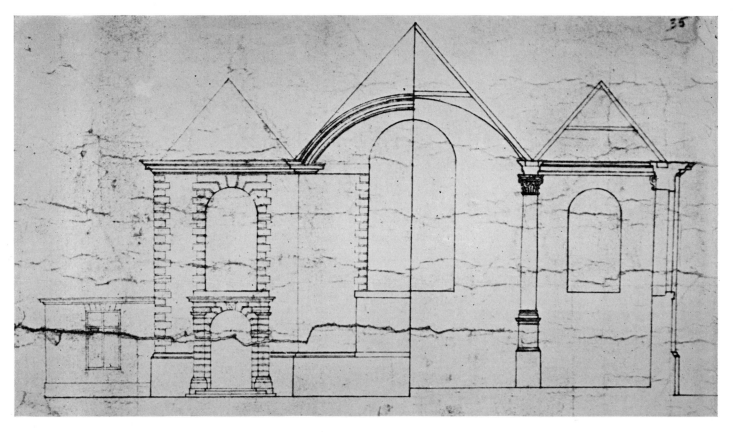

53. SS. Anne and Agnes, elevation study.

and windows are combined, as the unit formed by the segmental door head and the round-headed window above will be met again at two churches belonging, within narrow margins, to the same period.

By a singular coincidence, the two City churches which, by reason of site, could not follow traditional orientation, were treated in a remarkably similar manner by Wren; however different the plans of St Edmund's and St Martin's, their south elevations are obviously of the same cast, in a form, moreover, which finds no other strictly comparable examples among Wren's work. Much of the study here reproduced (Fig.52) was later to be altered: the steeple was to grow to a tall, slender height, additional doors were to be introduced, and the windows changed. But even at this early stage the design possessed considerable charm, though its plan, and that of the almost contemporaneous church of SS. Anne and Agnes,[268] is of greater intrinsic interest. In

both instances, Wren devised variations of a centralized plan characterized by four pillars, disposed with as much regularity as the sites permitted; that of St Martin's shows considerable affinity to that of St Mary-at-Hill, for here again the possibility of a basilican treatment was latent within the rectangularity of the site, but again rejected in favour of the centralized plan; thus, however similar the elevations of St Edmund's and St Martin's, their plans differ fundamentally. The reverse is true in relation to SS. Anne and Agnes for, however similar the plans, the elevations are essays in wholly different forms. At this latter church, Wren again portioned off a part of the site so as to obtain an approximately square body for the church; however, he set his entrances within this square portion rather than without, which decision resulted in a not altogether satisfactory south façade (Fig.53)[269] which is neither improved by the triple gables nor by the pillared porch, of which the rustication recalls the examples of St Bride's,

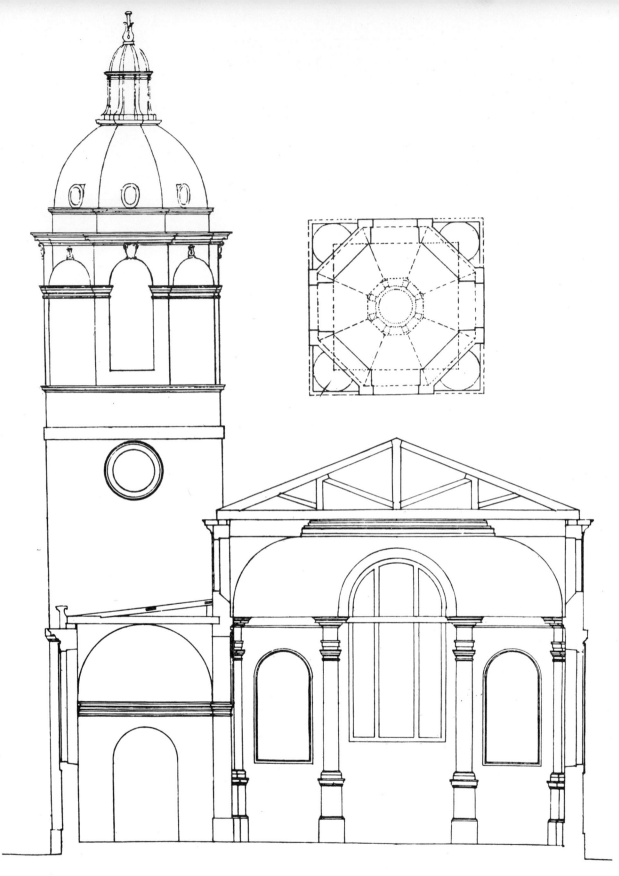

54. St Antholin, section study.

designed perhaps within a year or two of this instance, as much as that splendid design which we have tentatively described as a study for St Dunstan-in-the-East (Figs.26, 27).

Before we leave the centralized, four-pillar type of plan represented by these two churches, it must be noted that Wren projected a similar treatment for the church of St Antholin the development of which represents one of the most interesting of Wren's minor essays. Of the original project (Fig.54) the semi-cylindrical protrusions in the bell stage of the tower are the most significant feature as well as almost the only one that was to remain; practically all else was changed: the original domical top of the tower was replaced by a tapering steeple (Fig.79) not unlike that of St Edmund's (Fig.80); the plan was elongated and the outer pillars made to stand free so that they form an elongated octagon which closely corresponds to the foundations and represents, for all its originality, an interesting parallel to the solution achieved at St Benet Fink (Fig.28). The major change, however, is that from a simple gabled roof to the employment of a dome, which makes of St Antholin but the first of a whole group of domed structures belonging to this period, and, though un-lamented by others,[270] must obviously have been not only a charming, but extremely interesting design. To the same period, however, also belonged that abortive design for a mausoleum to commemorate the martyrdom of King Charles I, as Parliament apparently voted the sum of £70,000 for the purpose in 1678 and while we have no knowledge whether this amount was ever really made available,[271] it is to be regretted that Wren's design was never carried out. It is so tempting, however, to connect with this design a project, equally unexecuted, for a baptistery or chapter house for St Paul's that it will be more convenient to study these two designs together elsewhere, and turn now to three domed churches also belonging to this period.[272]

In consideration of precedent, it is surprising that the exteriors of these churches do not, explicitly, betray the existence of the dome. Once again, the centralization of plan was by no means indicated by the site of St Mildred's, Bread Street (Fig.56), where, on the contrary, a perfect opportunity for a regular basilican plan existed;[273] Wren, however, intent on experimenting with domes, rejected the opportunity as much as the possibility of using an exterior treatment as at St Stephen's, Walbrook. From the canted, pyramidal roof shapes of St Antholin, St Mary, Abchurch, and St Swithin's the existence of the dome might be suspected, but there is nothing in the west elevation of St Mildred's to give the passer by any indication of the charms of its domed interior.

The development which took place at St Mary Abchurch is also interesting, for here the evolution was the reverse of that of St Antholin. At St Martin's the parishioners could afford to buy additional ground for the enlargement of their church[274] but at St Mary Abchurch Wren had to modify his original plan (Fig.57) to meet the needs of a considerably reduced site. With this change

of plan, an important characteristic of these latter three churches is clearly brought out: in all the earlier instances, at St Benet Fink, St Stephen's, Walbrook, and even St Antholin, Wren had chosen to support his domes on sets of pillars; at St Mildred's, St Mary Abchurch, and St Swithin's, however, external conditions need not be held responsible for the fact that development tended towards the evolution of a type where the domes are supported upon pendentives which are structurally part of the wall and thus fulfil to perfection the prime function of the dome, namely, the spanning of the largest possible floor area without intermediate supports.

St Mildred's is not only the latest of these three churches, but also that in which this development found its conclusion and ultimate justification, for the relatively small scale of the building impairs neither its beauty nor the ingenuity of its conception. Viewed in such a perspective, St Swithin's may be regarded as a preliminary step. The original intention (Fig.58) seems to have been comparable to that of St Benet Fink and St Antholin in roofing the building with an oval dome, though significantly placed laterally to the axis of the church. But here again, we would hold personal preference rather than extraneous circumstances responsible for the change in disposition, by which the plan was transformed into a regular octagon (Fig.59) upon which the dome is supported on seven pillars engaged at the walls, with one remaining pillar standing free in the same manner as at St Mary Abchurch, though disguised within the partition walls.

Ingenious as was the design, and charming as was the character of these churches, Wren was not to further explore the potentialities he had here touched, for he was never to return to the pure type of the pendentive-supported dome. It would not be admissible to draw any far-reaching conclusions from this fact. But it may be relevant to point out even here, that the distinctly octagonal means of support so evident in these structures may be a cogent pointer to the system on which, almost from the first, the dome of St Paul's was to be built.

Before leaving these three interesting designs, we would draw attention to some parallels of minor features which they display. For example, the combination, at St Swithin's, of a segmental-headed door with a round-headed window above recalls the identical usage first contemplated for St Martin's (Fig.51) though there changed in execution, and also met at All Hallows, Watling Street, thus providing another significant instance of the recurrence of distinctive peculiarities of design lending support to our opinion that a correct chronology of Wren's designs can be corroborated, and even established, by such means. A further instance is also provided by the door and window combination used in the west front of St Mildred's, where both heads are formed of depressed arches, thus recalling the solution not originally intended, but eventually adopted, at St Martin's.

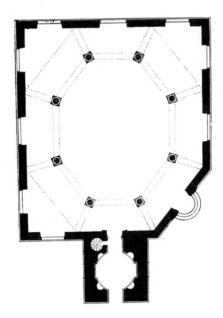

55. St Antholin, plan study.

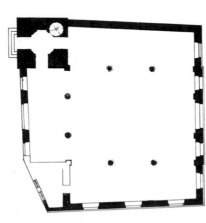

57. St Mary Abchurch, plan study.

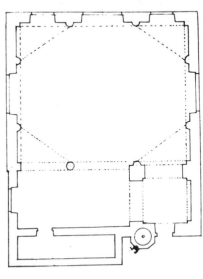

59. St Swithin, plan study.

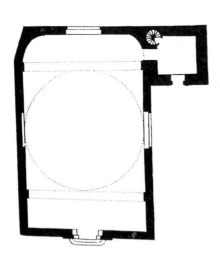

56. St Mildred, Bread Street, plan.

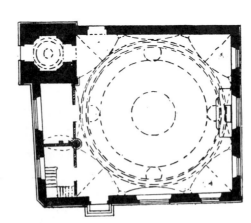

58. St Mary Abchurch, plan.

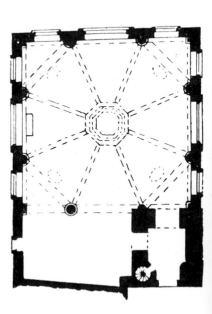

60. St Swithin, plan.

Into this period, namely the early years of the eighties, fall also three of Wren's 'Gothic' designs to form a crass, and almost incongruous, contrast to the increasing degree of suavity and accomplishment of 'classical' design which is discernible in many of the previous works. Many opinions have been voiced on Wren's attitude towards that style of the past, and many misleading inferences have been made by a selective reading of Wren's writings. But as this subject will be more appropriately examined in a later section of this study, we would here do no more than briefly notice the buildings in question.

In two of these three instances, namely at St Alban's and St Mary Aldermary, Wren was clearly not free to design in accordance with his own predilections, but had to take into consideration the wishes of others; in the third instance, however, he wisely took into consideration the cadre within which his work was to be placed: this was the gate tower which he designed for Christ Church, Oxford. The great quad there had been left incomplete when the founder of Cardinal College had fallen into disgrace, and Dean Fell felt it incumbent upon him to complete what Cardinal Wolsey had not had time to finish. We are fortunate in that Wren's letters to Fell, concerning the design and construction of Tom Tower, have come down to us, for they offer a most interesting insight not only into Wren's ideas on design, but also his methods of construction. They also make it apparent that, however much Wren may have 'disapproved' of the Gothic style, the character of Tom Tower was by no means due to Fell's insistence, as has sometimes been asserted,[275] but to Wren's sensitive awareness of the fact that the introduction of a Renaissance feature within the cadre of Tom Quad would constitute an anachronism. Wren was explicit in giving Fell his reasons: 'I resolued it ought to be Gothick to agree with the Founders worke', though 'I haue not continued soe busy as he began'.[276] When building operations were well under way, Fell suddenly suggested the possibility of using the top storey as an astronomical observatory but, however much the idea itself would have appealed to a quondam Savilian Professor of Astronomy, Wren's view on the proposed change was unambiguous, and his rejection of Fell's idea solely due to considerations of style. If such a utilitarian purpose, necessitating a wholly different approach to the design, were to be introduced at this late stage, and the half-finished structure altered accordingly, 'it will necessarily fall short of the beauty of the other way, for having begun in the Gothick manner, wee must conclude aboue with flats and such proportions as will not be well reconcilable to the Gothic manner wch spires upward & the pyramidall forms are essentiall to it'; thus 'this proposition had been much better effected had not the parts formerly built diverted us from beginning after the better formes of Architecture', but having progressed this far, Wren was decidedly against any compromise, for 'I feare wee shall make an unhandsome medly this way'.[277]

Wren's solution is not only ingenious, but also felicitous; it may be too much to claim that Wren here 'has catched the graces' of the true Gothic style;[278] but Tom Tower undeniably forms a striking centre-piece to that great quad and appears a not unworthy addition to the skyline of that city of spires. It would be invidious to criticize the detail of his composition, but it is interesting to note that features of Wren's contemporaneous design appear here in 'Gothick' disguise: thus the octagonal tower which supports the quaint domical capping recalls that of St Antholin, particularly as the four singular domical ornaments at its base seem to be a reminiscence of the domed half-cylinders which we have noted as so distinctive of that tower, and which we shall find again in one other design.

Turning to the church of St Alban, we find that, by tradition, Wren was reconstructing an original design by Inigo Jones.[279] It is not possible to adduce documentary evidence to support that tradition, just as it is impossible to suggest any reasons (beyond the probability of the parishioners' conservatism) which should have caused Jones to revert to 'the Gothick mode'.[280] We may attribute Wren's excursion into the Gothic to similar causes; at Tom Tower, the nature of the existing structure had been responsible; and it is likely that at St Alban's similar limitations were operative to those at St Mary Aldermary, for here we actually have evidence that the style of the church was a condition of a legacy which had been left for its reconstruction.[281] Whatever its ultimate aesthetic merit, the design is far from unpleasing; the tall plinths of the clustered pillars are, of course, open to criticism, but the fan vaulting of the roof is delightful, and may conceivably have been inspired by that magnificent, though late, example at Christ Church, with which Wren would have been particularly familiar at this precise period.[282]

We must now turn to six designs assignable to the first half of the eighties which, singly and as a group, show Wren at the height of his powers and give proof of a faculty of design which has lost all immaturity, and gained an accomplishment foreshadowed in previous works, yet never so consistently maintained. The first of these, to our regret, was never to attain the reality of stone in its entirety; but it is known to us from a plan and a splendid elevation (Fig.61) which does not, indeed, introduce any features not hitherto encountered, but combines them in a manner of great suavity and accomplishment. Thus we have another instance here of the tetrastyle portico treatment which so distinguishes the west front of St Magnus (Fig.22) though the pediment is here pitched at a steeper angle. This central feature is symmetrically flanked by three-bay units containing rectangular windows surmounted by circular lights, equally reminiscent of St Magnus, and the whole ensemble, articulated by pilasters in the aisles, attains a subtle unity and homogeneous quality by the fact that the outer pillars of the portico are placed so as to complete the lateral three-bay sections and to weld the whole into a nine-bay composition.

61. Tom Tower, Christ Church, Oxford.

The tower and spire which, in another reminiscence of St Magnus, rise centrally from this elevation, are splendid in the way the massive substructure, pierced by a triple belfry window, the octagonal top of the steeple, recalling some similar designs already considered, and the slender, beautiful *flèche* are combined into a truly arresting composition.

It seems that, although the design progressed to the stage of so highly finished a drawing, unknown reasons prevented its execution. Wren, however, would not willingly discard so satisfying a composition as the tower and steeple, and it is of great interest, and of great importance, as we shall have to note, that while he discarded the body of the church as far as any subsequent designs are concerned, he retained this portion of the design and incorporated both tower and steeple into the church of St Peter's, Cornhill, the rebuilding of which was sufficiently advanced in 1680 to contemplate the addition of tower and spire, thus permitting the dating of this design, which obviously must have preceded the construction of St Peter's steeple, to a period within narrow limits.[283]

The intrinsic difficulty still remains in identifying the design itself, for this is a much more complex matter than its chronological assignation. Here, indeed, we are unable to offer more than the following somewhat inconclusive observations: among the collection of drawings at All Souls College, Oxford, there are four sheets reasonably assigned to Hawksmoor's hand,[284] two of which bear an unmistakable resemblance to Wren's scheme as far as the body of the church is concerned. Wren having used the tower, as we have seen, at St Peter's, however, the design of the church is here completed by a most remarkable, huge, stepped pyramid serving as steeple, the resemblance of which to that built by Hawksmoor at St George's, Bloomsbury, is strong, if not conclusive, evidence of his authorship of these unidentified drawings. The only available clue is an inscription on the sheets, of more uncertain authorship than the drawings themselves,[285] which describes the drawings as a project for 'St Edmund the King, Bloomsbury'; and while we cannot rule out the possibility that the creation of a parish thus named may have been contemplated in Hawksmoor's later years, possibly even within the framework of Queen Anne's Act for the Building of Fifty Churches, we have met with no evidence whatever which would indicate Wren's design to have been intended for a similar dedication in a similar locality.[286]

What is certain, however, is that neither Wren's nor Hawksmoor's project was ever executed; even though Wren used the steeple at St Peter's, the body of the church of the design cannot possibly have been intended for it, as the site of that church would not have permitted such treatment.[287] On the other hand, an extant ground plan[288] is obviously related to this elevation which, with its semicircular termination at the east, suggests a connexion with St Clement Danes; there are cogent reasons, however, against

62. 'St Edmund, Bloomsbury'.

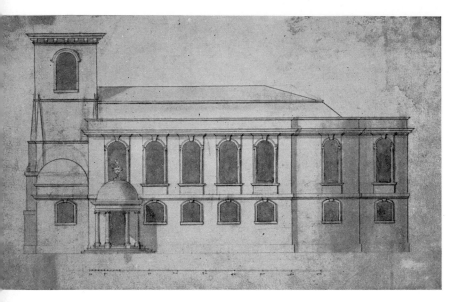

63. St Clement Danes, south elevation study.

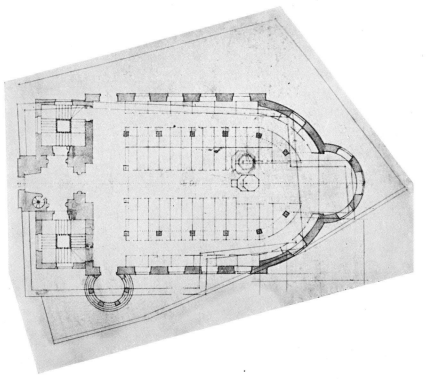

64. St Clement Danes, plan.

regarding this mysterious design as an early project for that church,[289] though it served, in some measure, as the prototype for this edifice, one of Wren's best known, to which we must now turn.

The difficulty of the site of St Clement Danes was the corollary to a splendid opportunity, for Wren had rarely before been in a position to design a church which was to occupy so striking a situation. St Clement's was not, indeed, one of the victims of the Great Fire, but it appears to have been in bad condition for many years[290] before the decision was taken to rebuild it entirely.[291] Wren's response to the challenge was splendid. Significantly he returned to a symmetrical aisled basilican scheme which by now seemed to have become his invariable preference for any church of considerable size and importance; and, obviously intent on extracting the maximum length from the irregular plot and, at the same time, retaining the old tower foundations, he devised a solution which, in its eastern treatment, recalls St Benet Fink. To fit the extreme end into the acute angle of the site, he formed the apse semicircular for, had the remainder been squared off, he could not have kept the corners within the boundary of the plot, and so resorted to the device of connecting the body of the church to the apse by curved sections, following the outline of his walls by a similar treatment of the eastern pillars of his interior arcade.[292] The west end is square, permitting the foundations of the old tower to protrude slightly from the front, but developed in a manner again reminiscent of St Magnus insofar as the square spaces to the north and south of the tower are made into vestibules; these, however, were roofed by small, hemispherical domes, a feature interesting to note as it is here met for the first, but not the last, time. These domes are echoed by the charming domed and pillared porch which was originally intended for the south front,[293] the embryonic idea of which may perhaps be seen in the original design for St Antholin (Fig.55) and the final development of which will be found in the completed cathedral of St Paul (Fig.141). Apart from this, the treatment of the side elevations is not in itself remarkable, excepting the fact that it displays a scheme of window arrangement not previously encountered, but one which set the pattern for several other churches the design of which must have followed closely that of St Clement's. The sober restraint of the exterior, however, lacking altogether in decoration but for the ornaments above the upper windows, was only a feeble preparation for the very elaborate interior of which we must record, regretfully, in the past tense, that for profusion of skilful and sumptuous stucco ornament it had no equal in London. The appreciation of this once gorgeous interior must depend on individual taste. But, although the finances of the parish were such as to cause Wren to make a gift of his design, rebuilding funds were sufficient to build the entire church in Portland stone; and while many of Wren's smaller churches, built to the exigencies of restricted budgets, are

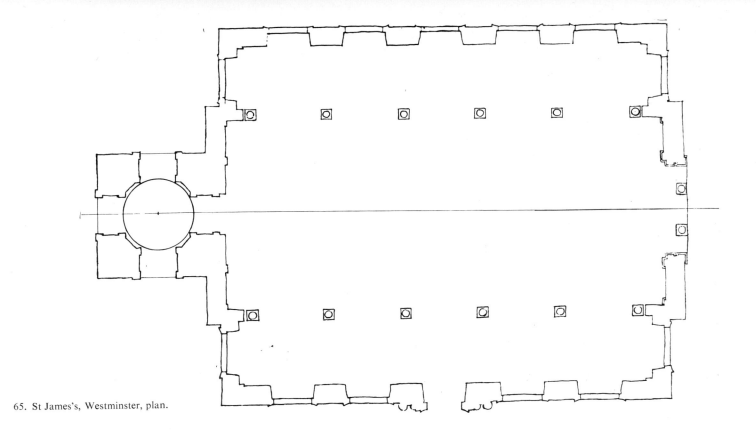

65. St James's, Westminster, plan.

simple to the point of austerity, we may perceive some significance in the vanished splendours of St Clement's decoration as
expressive of Wren's ideals realized when conditions permitted
him to indulge them to the full.

The church of St James's, Westminster, is the second in this very
important group with which we are here concerned, and possesses
an importance even beyond the rest. It is the third, and last, of
Wren's churches built outside the boundaries of the City, and
here again, Wren had the opportunity of a free and unencumbered site on which to plan his church. His patron in the enterprise was an old acquaintance: twenty years before, he had
carried his letters of introduction to Lord St Albans at Paris; ten
years before, we have ventured to think, he had planned St
Anne's, Soho, possibly for the same man; the church Wren was
now to design in Piccadilly was to become the parish church of
the estate which his patron had begun to develop twenty years
before[294] and of whose name Jermyn Street still remains a
memory.

Though we are singularly ill-informed about the building history of both St Anne's and St James's, it seems that the latter
design followed the former in some measure. The financial
premiss supplied by Wren's patron permitted the completion of
the church within a much shorter space of time than was normal
in the case of most of the City churches: while we may reasonably date Wren's design to 1682, the church was completed by
1684[295] even though a persistent tradition maintains that its
dedication was intended to be a compliment to King James II
who, however, did not accede to the throne until the following
year.[296] What Wren here achieved he himself regarded as the
finest solution of the problems set by the requirements of Anglican worship.[297] Externally, the church is far from prepossessing.

But its plan shows the dependence on, as well as development
from, that of St Anne's (Fig.23) which may be considered its
architectural and historical predecessor. The plan of St James's
is simplicity and regularity itself: a shallow recess at the east end
is all that remains of the deep chancel of St Anne's; the length is
divided into five equal bays, and the six-column arcade, of which
the extreme members are close, but not attached, to the wall,
carries the galleries which furnished as much accommodation as
Wren considered desirable for a parish church. The centrally
placed south portico does not, as at St Magnus, disturb the
rhythm of the interior arcade and contrasts, in its elaboration, a
little oddly with the general austerity of the façade chiefly remarkable, to us, for the recurrence of the window scheme previously
noted at St Clement Danes. One feature, however, is worthy of
notice: the east elevation is altogether a singular composition
interesting not only for the reappearance of the quadruple lines
of rustication so common to Wren's early designs, but also for
the remarkable feature of the nave elevation containing a 'motif
Palladio' reminiscent of St Olave's (Fig.146) but here set upon a
four-pillar arcade complete with its own cornice (Fig.66).

The church of St Andrew, Wardrobe, is not one of Wren's
more remarkable achievements; but it deserves consideration
here not only for its chronological relationship within this group
of churches,[298] but also for points of resemblance with St James's.
Indeed, were it not for the different placing of the tower and the
omission of the south porch, the plans of the two churches would
be almost identical; notwithstanding the difference in vaulting,
St Andrew, Wardrobe, is planned on the same five-bay principle,
and contains the same six-pillar arcade, though the outer members are here engaged. The window treatment furnishes the third
instance of the type first met with at St Clement's, and the east

66. St James's, Westminster, half east elevation.

67. St Andrew, Holborn, half east elevation.

68. St Andrew, Holborn, north elevation.

front, though treated here under one large pediment covering nave and aisles, shows the same keystone rustication as the church in Piccadilly.

A more interesting parallel with St James's, however, is supplied by the east front of St Andrew, Holborn, where we find again the curious composition of a 'motif Palladio' upon a four-pillar arcade; the gable contains, as that of St Andrew, Wardrobe, a circular light; the window treatment again conforms to that church, as to St James's and St Clement's, and we note with great interest the recurrence of the small hemispherical domes roofing subsidiary chambers first noted at that latter church, and here covering the registry to the south and the vestry to the north of the chancel. The east elevation being practically flat, the exclusion of these two rooms results in the creation of an eastern recess which, together with the six free-standing pillars of the arcades and the symmetrical treatment of the interior elevation, completes a striking resemblance to the first plan of St Magnus (Fig.21).

If documentary evidence were not available[299] to confirm the contemporaneity of this church and that other dedicated to Scotland's patron saint, with St James's and St Clement's, the stylistic indications we have pointed to would have made a date in the middle eighties at least very probable. For an unexecuted design of Wren's, which is indeed of the greatest interest, we can only infer a stylistic relationship, but are unfortunately unable to prove it to belong to the same period. The church dedicated to St Mary, and possibly the Twelve Apostles, which was intended to be built in the centre of Lincoln's Inn Fields, does, in fact, present some of the most puzzling problems connected with Wren's work, and the fact that it was never executed, and that our knowledge of it rests on nothing more than two engravings and a drawing, makes it altogether extremely difficult to discuss.

On the other hand, though fragmentary, our knowledge of the project is yet sufficient to make us realize that it is a design of considerable importance and seeing that it has never yet received the attention it so clearly deserves, we would propose to discuss it as fully as the evidence permits.

Two distinct and different versions of this project exist which provide the subject of some fascinating speculation. Though we cannot conclusively support the suggestion, it is likely that we are here dealing with the one essay in ecclesiastical architecture of Wren's which can be dated to the reign of William of Orange. Externally, we may note here that a perspective engraving of the whole of Lincoln's Inn Fields, complete with the church and the statues of the Twelve Apostles, is extant[300] the caption of which invites 'wealthy Persons to Subscribe' towards the realization of this project; and though it has been held that Simon Gribelin, to whom we owe the engraving, had been neither noticed[301] nor employed until he engraved some of the most beautiful views of St Paul's in 1702, there are stylistic peculiarities which tempt us to assign the project to the early years of the nineties. The inclusion of the Orange arms and motto on the engraving are proof enough that the project cannot be dated before 1689, but in a curious way the windows of the upper two storeys as shown in Sturt's engraving here reproduced remind us distinctly of the five churches just discussed, while the subsidiary domes in the angles are clearly echoes of Wren's practice at St Clement's (Fig.63) and St Andrew, Holborn (Figs.67, 68). The drawing, however, which was discovered by the editors of the Wren Society, is a much more cogent clue. Let us note first of all the introduction of the giant order embracing the upper two storeys, and the tall rusticated plinths which raise it from ground level, and note in anticipation that we shall encounter a precisely similar usage in Wren's second project for Hampton Court (Fig.94). Let us note

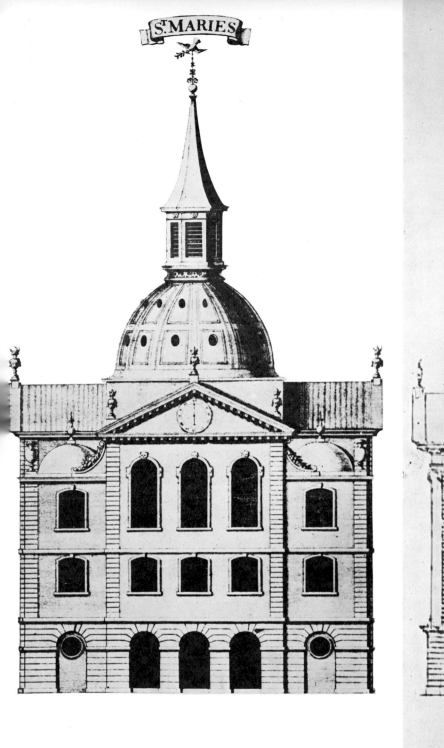

69. St Mary, Lincoln's Inn Fields, engraving.

70. St Mary, Lincoln's Inn Fields, study.

next that the change of the shape of the subsidiary domes from hemispherical to bell-shaped is a development clearly portending that splendid domical composition which graces Wren's first Hampton Court design (Fig.90). And let us remark even now that the change introduced in the major dome, and the Michelangelesque character achieved by the double row of lucarne windows and the addition of the drum is a development so closely paralleled in Wren's designs for Greenwich[302] and in the sketches for St Paul's belonging to those years of indecision before the final profile was evolved, that we would not hesitate to terminate the possible dating of this project with the turn of the century even though we have no vestige of external evidence with which to support this assertion.

It is only by reason of these very interesting connexions, as well as for the fact that 'St Mary, Lincoln's Inn Fields' has never been discussed in Wren literature, that we have devoted so much attention to it. For quite beyond its intrinsic interest, it is of considerable importance to what, ultimately, proved Wren's most lasting love, the dome. Before we can consider the evolution of that final masterpiece, however, we must discuss the remainder of Wren's work for some of it, in a manner similar to the strange church just discussed, formed the prelude and the trial for that final creation.

If St Mary's, Lincoln's Inn Fields, can be dated to William III's reign with confidence, it still remains a fact that Wren's work in ecclesiastical architecture came to an end – excepting the final touches, and some of the finest spires – with the House of Stuart and the 'glorious' revolution of 1688.[303] At the same time, this fact need not be regretted. Not only did it allow Wren the respite from church planning which he needed to embark on his great secular, as well as the greatest of ecclesiastical, schemes; but also can it be said that, within his aims and intentions, Wren had reached a final stage of development in church planning with those already built; indeed, some of his latest works in that field are insignificant when compared with such early works as St Magnus, St Stephen's, or St Bride's. But while we have traced the appearance and the supersession of small, personal predilections in the design of details running through Wren's work, it must be clear that with the clarification of his ideas on the essentials of planning, and particularly with the crystallization and the constant refinement of regular basilican schemes, Wren had reached a limit; while his range of decorative design was limited, perhaps intentionally, in elevational treatments (so as to present an endless gamut of delight in his steeples), Wren had said the last word as regards plans with the designs of St James's, Westminster, of Christ Church, and St Andrew, Holborn; these, as representative of the type, summed up all his experiments, and are the fitting and crowning achievement of a career which the calamity of the City of London had provided with an incomparable opportunity for ingenuity. Thus, the remaining City churches are not only of

secondary importance in size and scale, but do not represent any further advances beyond solutions hitherto achieved; they can therefore be dismissed with only brief discussion.

St Michael Royal[304] does not possess any particular importance beyond its truly delightful spire (Fig.73), though, in plan, it provides yet another example of Wren's tendency towards the simplicity of regular shapes. In this instance, he partitioned the site in such a way as to obtain a perfect rectangle for the church, and thus evolved a plan which is similar with its five regular bays to that of St Mary Somerset,[305] with the exception of a slight difference in the placing of the tower. Irregularity of site was overcome in a different way at St Clement's, Eastcheap, where Wren separated the irregular portion of his site by forming a wedge-shaped single aisle along the south front. The single aisle method, used some fifteen years before at St Lawrence (Fig.10) and St Vedast (Fig.11), reappears once more in the two churches dedicated to St Margaret, that in Lothbury and that in Rood Lane, which share more features than their names, as the similarity of plan produced a similarity of interior treatment which may, indeed, suggest that the constant preoccupation with a single problem which had been Wren's for nearly twenty years had resulted in a weariness giving way to repetition.[306] Thus it is equally remarkable that at St Margaret, Rood Lane, Wren returned to one of his earliest methods of forming an east elevation, for here the solution adopted by a central pediment over the nave and the two halves of a second pediment covering the aisles calls to mind what Wren had first built at the Sheldonian Theatre (Fig.2), what he had employed, albeit incongruously, at St Mary-at-Hill (Fig.7) and executed, in a more accomplished manner, at St George's (Fig.145).

What is ironic, however, is that Wren's remaining works in church architecture should largely have been in an 'alien mode', for together these form the second group of Wren's essays in the 'Gothick'. Indeed, the towers of St Dunstan-in-the-East[307] and of St Michael's, Cornhill,[308] though original works, are of a character which prevent us from regarding them as expressions of the 'essential' Wren. To the tower of St Michael's, much of what we have previously indicated, with regard to St Alban's, applies; but the structure of St Dunstan-in-the-East is a work in which Wren permitted himself considerable latitude from Gothic precedent, and it is not surprising that it should have called forth a variety of widely diverging opinions on the part of Wren's critics.[309] But whatever its merits or demerits in conforming with true Gothic style, the curved stilts which support the spire proper – possibly inspired by the scheme of Bow steeple before the Fire – are a truly ingenious piece of construction and testify to Wren's engineering skill as much as anything he ever built.

Of greater importance, however, is the project for the restoration of the north transept of Westminster Abbey, which occupied Wren's attention during the last years of his life.[310] This, in more

71. Westminster Abbey, transept. The right section shows the actual state of the building. The left shows Wren's proposed restoration.

May 20: 1719.
I doe Approve of this Design
Chr. Wren   Mich. Evans

Thos: Forot:
Jn. Barker
Wm. Morley

respects than that of scale, is a truly monumental work and quite dispels such doubts as some of Wren's critics have expressed on Wren's familiarity with the pointed style. To say, with one of them, that Wren's knowledge of Gothic forms was complete[311] is as inaccurate and as misleading as to think that 'as is clear from everything he wrote and from the work he did – he disliked and disapproved of all Gothic architecture',[312] and nothing can actually be further from the truth than to suggest that Wren 'had not the least sympathy with Gothic architecture, or taken any trouble to master its most rudimentary features'.[313]

But Wren's capacities as an architectural historian do not greatly concern us here, though we shall have to touch on that aspect of his personality elsewhere. But whatever his statements about the Goths who, according to him, were 'destroyers rather than builders',[314] there is little doubt that he was quite aware that they had not been the originators of the architecture which, incongruously, bears their name. Furthermore, however explicit Wren's dislike of the pointed styles, he was far too sensitive an artist to impose his preferences within a context where they would patently be out of place: we have already noted his respect for old St Paul's which, as 'we cannot mend this great Ruine, we will not disfigure it'; we have noted that when it fell to him to complete Tom Quad at Oxford, he designed an edifice which, however open to censure by reason of the 'impurity' of its detail, does yet form a congruous and harmonious part of the whole. And thus it is with gratification, though without surprise, that we find Wren, at Westminster, submitting a design 'of a Style with the Rest of the Structure, which I would strictly adhere to throughout the whole Intention': for 'to deviate from the whole form would be to run into a disagreeable Mixture, which no Person of a good Taste could relish'; and thus, 'for all these Additions I have prepared perfect Draughts & Models, such as I conceive may agree with the original Scheme of the old Architect, without any modern Mixtures to show my own Inventions; in like Manner as I have among the Parochial Churches of London given some few Examples (where I was oblig'd to deviate from a better Style) which appear not ungraceful but ornamental to the East part of the City'.

The project remained, apparently, under discussion for a considerable time, for even though Wren's report from which we have been quoting was dated 1713, approval was not given for a design until some six years later. Thus the drawing (Fig.71) which, by means of attached flaps, shows very graphically the changes which Wren intended to introduce, was not of Wren's own hand, for the trembling signature of the octogenarian belies the firm and precise draughtsmanship of the design. This, however, is no reason to think that the design should not have been Wren's, even if the execution was not. And we would single it out for the fact that it is indicative that Wren, even at that advanced age, should have given so much care and thought to a problem which

was obviously not very congenial to him. It is for that latter reason that we would not see any need to discuss it in detail; and rather turn to some designs, not hitherto sufficiently noted, in which the true epitome of his imagination can be most clearly discerned.

The plans and elevations of Wren's churches have suffered from a certain amount of disregard brought about by an enthusiasm for his spires and steeples which has, understandably, made his critics lavish their attention on these fascinating structures. Thus it is not merely for the purpose of restoring the balance, but also because Wren's plans and elevational treatments are of far greater architectural importance to our study, that we have hitherto concentrated on these; and if we are now going to briefly consider Wren's spires and steeples we would not see any particular purpose served by an examination and classification of each one of them, which, anyhow, has been done, or of supplying another elaborate index or catalogue in which all these structures are enumerated in their various categories; but would propose to discuss some of Wren's steeples and their details solely with a view to stylistic analyses which will offer clues not only to chronological connexions, but also permit an insight into the way these splendid creations were evolved.

We have already drawn attention to Bow steeple, perhaps the most celebrated, and if it should enter into discussion once more, it is to emphasize the fact that, splendid as it is, no other steeple can be classed with it in its general character of freedom in conception and fantasy in execution. Succeeding creations would seem to possess a character altogether different, and not least among them is the group comprised by those of St Stephen's, Walbrook, St Michael Royal, and St James's, Garlick Hill. In their essentials there is a remarkable similarity about them which is distinguished from mere repetition by the differences of decorative treatment and detail. Their towers are uniformly plain and treated with great restraint, doubtless owing to the consideration that unfavourable placing would prevent any more elaborate treatment from being seen; but above the cornices a delicate play of charming fantasy begins in the form of pillars, urns, scrolls, and drums which, carved in pearl grey Portland stone, added so much charm to the City skyline.[315]

On the other hand, the elements of which these three steeples are composed are only indicative of one aspect of Wren's inventive faculty; another, not surprisingly, makes its appearance in designs of widely differing dates and, Wren's life-long preoccupation considered, it is not strange that he should have tried on numerous occasions to incorporate the form and principle of the dome into his towers. Structurally, domical construction was, of course, an ideal solution of the problem created by progressively diminishing stages of towers.[316] Artistically, however, a visible domical termination to the tower is the distinguishing feature of several of his churches as well as, significantly, the lantern of St

72. St Stephen's, Walbrook, steeple.

73. St Michael Royal, steeple.

74. St James's, Garlick Hythe, steeple.

St Step: Walbrooke

St Mich: Royall

St Jam: Garlickhithe

75. St Benet Fink, tower.

76. St Mary le Bow, project

77. St Antholin, turret study.

78. St James's, Westminster, elevation study.

Paul's, and would have graced a number of others if radical changes had not been introduced. Lanterns with domical capping appeared, in fact, as early as Wren's work at Oxford and Cambridge in the sixties, but the fact is easily overlooked that his intentions envisage closely similar treatments for some of his City church steeples.

We have already seen that a determination of dates is not always easy in the case of Wren's churches; Stephen Wren is not to be implicitly trusted and building accounts often permit no more than approximations and the possibility of designs having been evolved long before building operations actually started. In the case of the steeples, the difficulty is even greater, and the application of methods of stylistic analysis cannot provide any precise indications simply because motifs recur in Wren's gamut of steeple design which are chronologically widely separated and which, if designed but unexecuted in an early instance, reappear in executed works many years later.

Thus it has been said with truth that 'Wren very rarely wasted his thought. If a design failed of execution, its theme or themes would surely find their way into the work of succeeding years'[317] but to how great an extent this statement is true does not generally seem to have been recognized. Yet no other department of Wren's designs than his towers and spires offers such striking evidence to show how flexibly and, indeed, interchangeably, Wren regarded these compositions. We have already pointed to an outstanding instance in the transference of a complete tower and spire from an unidentified project (Fig.62) to St Peter's, Cornhill; in general outline, this may relevantly be compared with that very

fine example eventually evolved at St Magnus, but we would consider some of those instances first where Wren seemed to intend a purely domical termination rather than a combination of dome and miniature spire.

The design of greatest charm here is perhaps that, unhappily destroyed, which graced St Benet Fink (Fig.75), for here the domical top comes truly into its own and, for all the beauty of Wren's soaring spires, it cannot be gainsaid that this provided as satisfactory a solution as any he ever devised, albeit of an entirely different character. Such treatment, in fact, may have been Wren's original intention in more than this instance. It is not easy to decide whether the domed turret first devised for St Edmund's (Fig.20) was intended to be a permanent solution or merely to serve a temporary purpose until the parish finances should permit the erection of the elegant, slim spire finally built. Yet it is the domed turret type which seems to recur with the greatest persistence, and of which the undoubtedly early example of a project for Bow (Fig.76) was almost certainly put forward as a final suggestion, even though we need not regret that it should have been replaced by the magnificent spire we still possess. It is interesting, however, to trace the connexions of this design with those of St Antholin and St James's, Westminster. The domed turret originally devised for St Antholin (Fig.77) is obviously of the same lineage, and the same period, as that of St Benet Fink, but the next step of the evolution brought with it an elongation of the bell stage of the domical top which becomes more markedly pointed, thus recalling the certainly earlier design for Bow (Fig. 76). An altogether original variation of this scheme, however,

79. St Antholin, steeple study.　　80. St Edmund's, steeple study.

occurs at St James's, Westminster; here the drum has been eliminated; the little lantern above the domical capping is identical with that of St Antholin; but the octagonal dome, pierced by circular lucarne windows, which had characterized both the St Antholin and Bow designs, is here replaced by a truly domical treatment without ribs which, curiously, was intended to be covered with metal scales, and thus inevitably points back to Wren's pre-Fire design for St Paul's (Fig.32).

Ironically, none of these designs was ever carried out. The domed turret of Bow gave way to the celebrated steeple; the little domed termination intended for St Edmund's was replaced by the tapering spire (Fig.80); and at St Antholin the precedent of St Benet Fink was ignored, though we have no means of determining whether Wren gave up the domed turret design of his own accord or whether the parishioners, possibly motivated by the same conservatism as Wren had met with during the early days at St Paul's, were responsible that this should have given way to the rather elaborate and ornamental structure which Wren finally devised and built (Fig.79).

Whatever praise may be due to Bow steeple, it cannot be gainsaid that the design finally evolved for St Magnus must rank in the very forefront of Wren's masterpieces; it is an instance in which the truly accomplished combination of a solid tower with balustrade, a tall octagonal lantern, a delightful dome, and a charming, tapering finial form a composition with which only a pedant could possibly find fault. Yet the history of this steeple in its long evolution – it was built fully three decades after the church – is even more complex, and more interesting, than that of the domed turret of Bow and its successors.

Thus it is nothing less than astonishing that what was eventually built at St Bride's was, evidently, first of all intended for St Magnus for, barring the steeple projected with the warrant design of St Paul's (Fig.43), Wren at no other occasion envisaged an arrangement of a number of identical, and successively diminishing, stages; on the other hand, the inscription of the recently discovered drawing here reproduced leaves no room to doubt that the basic idea for St Bride's steeple was originally intended for St Magnus.[318] But this is not the only parallel which the design possesses with others; for attention must be drawn to the distinctive bell-shaped top which was to crown the whole elaborate structure. Here, indeed, is a motif which, 'failed of execution' in more than one instance, was to find its way 'into the work of succeeding years'.

First of all, we may note that this was the precise form in which Wren had intended the lantern of his Greek cross design for St Paul's (Fig.37) to terminate. But more interesting still is the charming, bell-shaped turret which Wren had drawn as an 'offer for St Bride', and which thus further establishes the connexion between the St Magnus scheme and the St Bride designs. By a singular coincidence, a pencil sketch closely resembling this drawing has recently come to light,[319] which, however, lacks the distinctive, large, segmental pediment terminating the bell stage; in the former case, this feature incontrovertibly points to the veracity of the description; and the striking resemblance of the bell-shaped top, planned on a dodecagon, would make the latter sketch appear as a preliminary study to that inscribed. But when it is remembered that Wren never built such a feature, either at St Bride's or elsewhere, a different interpretation becomes equally possible.

The discrepancy between the dodecagonal capping and the octagonal plan of the stages of St Bride's steeple may not be conclusive; but this feature of the capping is clearly recalled by the twelve pillars which are no part of St Bride's, but surround the famous cylinder of Bow steeple. And while the pencil sketch lacks, as we have noted, the significant segmental pediment which Wren actually built at St Bride's, it shows a bell-stage and belfry window almost identical with those executed at St Mary le Bow. Thus it would not be too far-fetched to suggest that the pencil sketch of a bell-shaped domical capping may have been, at some

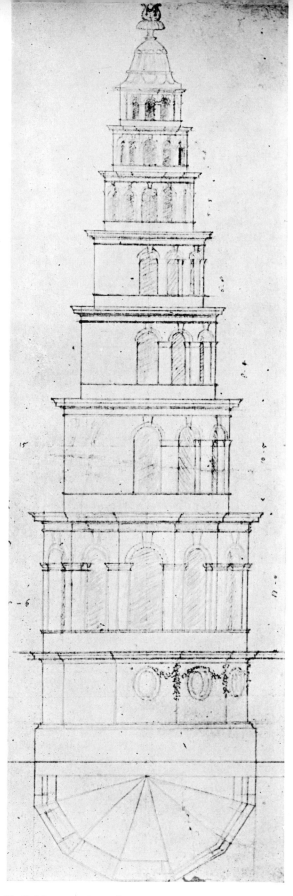

81. St Magnus, spire project.

82. St Bride's, turret study.

very early stage, intended for Bow steeple, and this suggestion seems further confirmed by the somewhat immature draughtsmanship of the design which would point to the period of Bow rather than the much later period of St Bride's; in fact, the drawing was carried out, as far as the bell stage went, with remarkable adherence to the sketch design; the apparently rejected bell-shaped top, however, found its way into the project for terminating St Bride's tower; with the significant addition of the pediment, the sketch was again carried out, again to the exclusion of the top. Wren, however, clearly had a predilection for this feature, and thus introduced it into the project for St Magnus's steeple, where it crowns a structure related to St Bride's in its stages, but related to Bow in its dodecagonal plan. Wren was foiled again, and we can trace the motif further in its reappearance, in a modified form, in the subsidiary domes of St Mary, Lincoln's Inn Fields (Fig.70) and even, on a monumental scale, in the splendid dome which characterizes his first proposals for Hampton Court (Fig.90). And thus, having been proposed no fewer than five, and possibly six, times, it was only after some forty years, at the very end of his active career, that he was able to execute it, in a purer and more beautiful form than he had previously conceived: in the western towers of St Paul's (Fig.135).

In this connexion, the final scheme for St Magnus needs to be considered. The project discussed above served, as we have seen, as the prototype for St Bride's steeple: in execution, the plan was changed to octagonal, and the number of stages was reduced from seven to four, while the warrant design steeple had possessed six. In the solution finally built at St Magnus the interdependence with other schemes becomes evident again, however original the design: we have already referred to the connexion with the domical treatment planned and later executed at St Peter's, Cornhill; it remains to point to the fact that the bell-stage of St Magnus is identical with that of Bow steeple, but for the absence of the substructure, built twenty years before; at the same time, the pairs of urns above the coupled pilasters are clearly of the same lineage as those of St Bride's; while lastly the domed lanterns which Wren had designed for Bow church and St Antholin, both of which might be open to criticism, find their refined perfection at St Peter's, Cornhill, and St Magnus.

These parallels and recurrences make chronology not only difficult but actually unnecessary, when we reflect that the reappearance of practically each of these motifs – Wren having been thwarted in his original intention – is invariably an improvement on what had gone before. The 'monstrous steeple' of the warrant design, elaborated in the hardly satisfactory project for St Magnus, is at last splendidly realized at St Bride. The somewhat awkward cupolas of Bow and St Antholin are sublimated in the beautiful compositions of St Peter's and St Magnus. It would not be reasonable to prefer the paltry little lantern of St Edmund's to the slim, graceful steeple which Wren built at last, or regret the cupola of St Antholin for the faceted steeple with its charming lucarne windows which eventually crowned the distinctive drum. Thus, with regard to the best of Wren's steeples and towers, a position similar to the cathedral obtains: the procrastinations created by financial difficulties proved a blessing in disguise; allowing Wren to attain the full maturity and accomplishment of his designing faculties. Had the City been richer, we would be the poorer for some of Wren's most splendid compositions.

We have elsewhere remarked on the fact that Wren's career in ecclesiastical architecture ended, to all intents and purposes, with the revolution of 1688; the corollary to this circumstance is the fact that Wren's essays in secular architecture, but for the overlap of a few years, are predominantly consequent upon, and not concurrent with, the years devoted to the City churches. True, he designed collegiate buildings and libraries spasmodically throughout his career; true, he was concerned with the design of some of the great houses which, in the course of London's development, were built, or intended, by great courtiers and wealthy aristocrats: but the palatial scope which only royal patronage could give was beyond the means of all but the last few years of Charles II's reign, and thus it is to that of William III that Wren's major essays in secular architecture belong. Before turning to consider these, we would briefly trace Wren's designs from the point where we left it commenting on the chapel of Emmanuel College.

Foremost among these must stand the library which Wren designed for Trinity College, Cambridge, the creation of which was due to the unsparing energy of 'that excellent, pious and most learned man, divine, mathematician, poet, traveller',[320] Dr Isaac Barrow, whom Wren had known from the time when both of them had occupied chairs of Gresham professorships. It was natural for Barrow to turn to Wren, of whom he had the highest opinion[321] even though, financial support for his library scheme having proved disappointing, he was unable to offer the architect any fee; let us note with satisfaction that Wren was happy to oblige his learned friend without any remuneration and produce what must, in some respects, be considered one of his most admirable designs.

Wren's project as first designed might logically be dated to within the very first years of Barrow's mastership of the College;[322] significantly, it took the form of a square building, the interior of which was planned circular and surmounted by a dome, while the whole was approached by a double flight of steps leading to a pedimented, hexastyle portico.[323] A remarkable feature of that design was the singular and original way in which Wren proposed to light the interior for, obviously wishing to obtain the maximum of wall space for shelving, he planned no windows at the ground level but, with considerable ingenuity, raised his dome upon a drum which was to be pierced by twelve very large semicircular windows which, together with the eight rectangular windows of the lantern, would probably have provided admirable illumination of the interior for the purpose for which it had been designed. However, like so many other of Wren's dome projects, this was rejected, and the extension of Nevile's Court planned by Barrow clearly suggested a long, rectangular shape of plan which would fittingly form the fourth side of the quadrangle. Wren finally evolved an eleven-bay scheme, flanked by a pair of domed pavilions containing the staircases, which has been variously evaluated by his critics.[324] It is true that the exterior elevations are open to criticism; yet the design is no less interesting for its obvious faults. When building a library for Dean Honywood at Lincoln,[325] Wren had conceived the idea of restoring the dilapidated fourth side of the cathedral cloisters by an appropriate colonnaded walk, and of setting his library above. In the main, he adhered to this principle at Trinity College; possibly out of common sense, possibly prompted by book knowledge, he determined to place the library on the upper floor of his structure,[326]

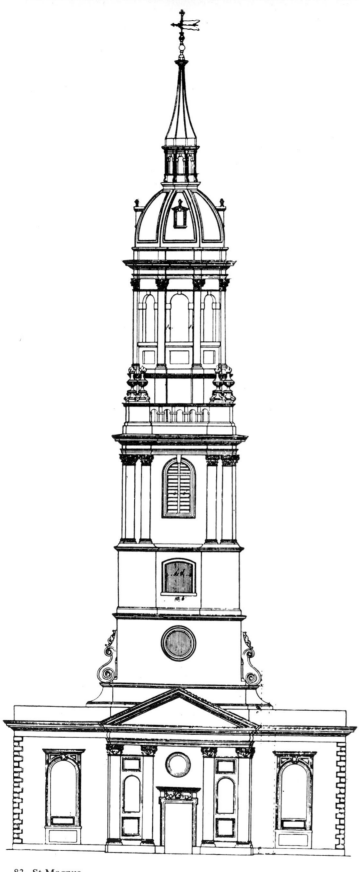

83. St Magnus.

84. St Bride's.

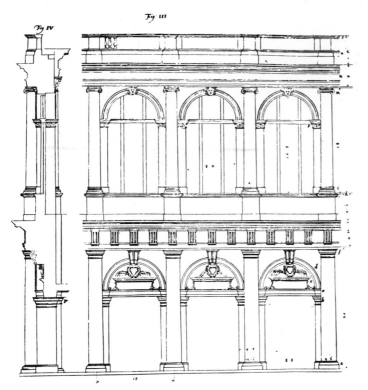

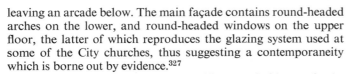

85. Trinity College, Cambridge, library, elevations, and profiles.

leaving an arcade below. The main façade contains round-headed arches on the lower, and round-headed windows on the upper floor, the latter of which reproduces the glazing system used at some of the City churches, thus suggesting a contemporaneity which is borne out by evidence.[327]

Wren's difficulty consisted in reconciling two desiderata: firstly, that of raising the library itself above ground level, yet secondly, not to raise it so high as to leave a ground floor of equal ceiling height; to make matters worse, he was clearly aware that the library windows should be placed as high as possible in the walls, not only to leave a maximum of wall space free, but also in order to obtain the superior illumination which high-placed windows would give. The solution to these problems is not, in fact, a happy one. To lend apparent height to his ground floor, Wren decided on the insertion of semicircular tympana in the arches at the level of the upper floor which, for all his fictitious claim to classical precedent, is by no means artistically satisfactory. The wall space desirable for the library again imposed a disproportionately wide separation between the tops of the colonnade arches and the bases of the windows, the awkwardness of which circumstance the design of the lower architrave and the upper mouldings does little to mitigate. Wren's desire of a floor-level at that height was the result of an endeavour to bring his cornices and mouldings in line with the buildings adjacent to the library, yet, though he has been credited with having taken 'care to harmonize the inner front with Nevile's Court'[328] his attempt was by no means successful. For all the ingenuity with which he tried to achieve an optical impression belied by actual construction, the elevation which he eventually built unfortunately fails to produce that harmony with the rest of the quadrangle which Wren had so obviously desired.

If the external elevation of Nevile's Court is not altogether satisfactory; and if the frontage to the river is disappointing in a plainness bordering on cold austerity; the interior of the building may reasonably be considered as the most admirable library of the period in existence. From a personal familiarity with all the requirements, Wren evolved a wholly felicitous disposition of the interior which permitted a great degree of privacy and seclusion to each individual bay without destroying either the architectural or functional unity of the whole. In this interior the demands of aesthetics are faultlessly married to those of functional utility, and the splendid carved decoration which adorns the woodwork contributes to create an ensemble for which no praise could be too high. There is only one library of the period which can compare with that of Trinity College, and that is that of Queen's College, Oxford.

The history of this building is unfortunately far from clear; indeed, Wren's authorship cannot be established with any certainty, for no holograph drawings seem to have survived, and such records as exist furnish no conclusive proof of either date or authorship. Thus the building has been claimed for Wren on the strength of a somewhat similar design of a ground floor formed in niches containing statuary, made in 1698 for a projected remodelling of Windsor; it has been attributed, with equal confidence, to Hawksmoor;[329] but the evidence supporting each of these claims is by no means conclusive so that it would seem

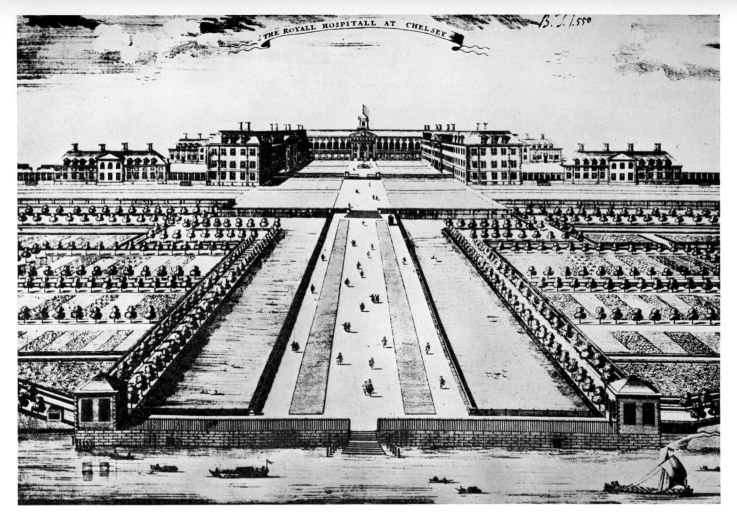

86. Chelsea Hospital.

arbitrary to proclaim in favour of one or the other with any degree of certainty. External evidence apart, however, stylistic features of the building clearly indicate that Wren either had a considerable share in the design, or else that his precepts were so closely followed that the individuality of the pupil became largely submerged in the influence of the master.

If the date of 1682 sometimes advanced for Queen's College Library could be accepted, this work would be either contemporaneous with, or the immediate successor of, a design which is not only unquestionably Wren's, but also, unquestionably, one of his most delightful. Chelsea College, though once the residence of 'my Lord Privy Seale',[330] served to house prisoners taken in the Dutch war early during Charles's reign, but it was not long after Evelyn had been there to visit 'our prisoners'[331] that the building which originally stood on the site of the Hospital was returned to the Royal Society[332] to whom Charles had given it on its foundation. The Society does not appear to have used it. It is conceivable that the Fellows found the distance inconvenient and preferred the location of Gresham College, for even when the Fire of 1666 had disorganized their meetings there, it was at Arundel House, and not at Chelsea that, in 1669, the Grand Duke Cosimo III of Tuscany was entertained and attended a meeting.[333]

This arrangement was due to Evelyn's close friendship with Henry Howard, later to be restored to the escheated dukedom of Norfolk, who had gone so far as to present the Society with a site; but even though both Wren and Hooke drew plans for a building suitable to the Society's purposes, they were never to be executed.[334] Yet even with the failure of this project, the Society does not seem to have availed itself of 'Chelsea College', though now evacuated by its Dutch prisoners, and thus, most probably owing to a suggestion of Sir Stephen Fox, the King projected to take over the buildings which he had 'sometime since given to our Society, and would now purchase it again to build an hospital; or infirmary for soldiers there'; when Sir Stephen broached the matter to John Evelyn, he knew that he would be assured of sympathetic 'assistance as one of the Council of the Royal Society',[335] which asked for, and apparently received, the sum of £1300 for the grounds.[336] The buildings then still standing being totally unsuitable for the intended purpose, it was as a matter of course that Wren, who had been elected to the Society's presidency at this very time,[337] was approached to design the hospital to be built. Charles granted £20,000 for its building together with an annual allowance of £5000 and even though the realization of the scheme still necessitated private benefactions,[338] it may be remarked that the King took on this considerable expense before contemplating the building of his palace of Winchester.

Unlike in the case of most of the City churches, the project progressed with speed; without having to suit, and modify, his designs to the tastes of churchwardens and officials of livery companies, it was no more than six months before Wren, Fox, and Evelyn called on the Archbishop of Canterbury to obtain his Grace's approbation of Wren's designs,[339] and within another month the lawns running down to the river already saw the laying of the foundations of the hospital buildings,[340] where a staff of forty was to supervise the welfare and well-being of 400 'emerited soldiers'.

Wren's design, evolved within these few months and not materially altered by his own later additions and enlargements, is simple, gracious, and betrays in its meticulous attention to detail a characteristic consideration of the function which this building was to serve. In the absence of holograph drawings, it is to our regret that he never made use of the licence obtained to publish his designs,[341] but we are fortunate in still possessing the building as he left it. To speak about it is more difficult than to speak about any of Wren's other works and the often-quoted opinion that it represents 'the work of a gentleman' does but little to convey the actual flavour and atmosphere of this, perhaps Wren's most homogeneous design. There is little that is monumental about it, in spite of the considerable scale; it is by no means impressive, as are the Invalides at Paris, or the great hospital, begun by Filarete, in Milan. But in its very reticence, in its simplicity, in the repose of its long, low-lying lines, it conveys an atmosphere of peace and calm in which, physically sheltered from the northern winds, and visually confined by an exclusion of exterior turbulence and unrest, the venerable pensioners live. Its great court, open to the south and bordered by a covered walk, is barracks, parade ground, and monastery at the same time by dint of the military maleness of its inhabitants who meditate in the cloister-like walk on their own vivid past. All this is implicit in the architecture and its function: it is neither delicate nor hard; neither ornate nor austere; it is the perfect environment for the purpose for which it was created.

Turning from Chelsea to Winchester, we turn to an almost contemporaneous work than which nothing could be more dissimilar. Both share, it is true, certain similarities: long, horizontal lines, an irrepressible preoccupation with domes, and, we might add, the fact that the one-time purpose of 'Chelsea College' was to prove identical with the last, utilitarian function of Winchester Palace, for when all the Stuart glory and Orange rule had passed, the second Hanoverian could think of no better purpose for the spoliated building than there to house some 5000 prisoners who had been captured in the war of 1756.

The earlier years of Charles's reign had not permitted him seriously to consider the building of a palace which could even in some slight degree compare with the gigantic works which were evolving at Versailles to glorify the reign of 'the King, my

Brother'. While much stress has been laid by historians of certain convictions upon the lavish expenditure which was supposedly entailed by Charles's amorous proclivities and the generosity with which he treated reigning, as well as retired, mistresses and their offspring, it is only fair to point to the fact that the privy purse equally met many of the deficiencies created by Parliamentary refusal to grant supplies as well as those deficiencies occasioned by the failure of supplies, once granted, to materialize. In consequence, Charles spent the greater part of his reign in the not altogether convenient, and, if picturesque, then hardly impressive, agglomeration of buildings known as Whitehall Palace; and it was only two years before his sudden, and possibly premature, death that he could entertain the idea of building a royal residence outside London. In choosing Winchester, Charles is not likely to have been swayed by notions of continuing an ancient tradition which once before in history had made of the city the fulcrum of English life and culture; but his choice, apart from the good hunting which the country promised, was apparently influenced also by the proximity of the sea and the possibility of seeing, from the castle hill, the masts of ships riding at anchor off the coast.

Wren's first drafts for the palace thus distinctly seem to take into consideration the desire of a king to whom the navy was, throughout his life, the first and foremost thought: he planned, not surprisingly, a large central dome, but accommodated its profile to Charles's whim by truncating its top and thus creating a flat platform aloft, above which the Royal standard was to fly. The design if of great interest and repays detailed examination. Wren here formed a lower storey of exceptional height which, we may surmise, was actually a combination of two comparatively low storeys; the front was to be largely rusticated and its twenty-seven bays were articulated by a centre-piece of five bays the upper storey of which was surmounted by a triangular pediment, flanked by a pair of two-bay sections in which the lower parts are formed into arches, which are succeeded by another pair of two-bay units, this time horizontally divided; upon these followed a duplication of the preceding section, while the terminations consisted of five-bay units reproducing the window schemes of the second pair of sections. The façades were kept exceedingly plain, there being no ornamentation save the surrounds of the drum on which the central dome rests. But even though the fenestration was almost austerely rectangular, excepting the centre window, any suggestion of monotony is banished by the organization of the whole façade, where heterogeneous units were symmetrically aligned, and the long balustraded roofline of the building charmingly enlivened by the large, central, and the pair of small subsidiary domes projected.

However, the design was to see modifications even though it is likely that the foundations were actually being laid while Wren was working towards his final solution; for this seems indicated

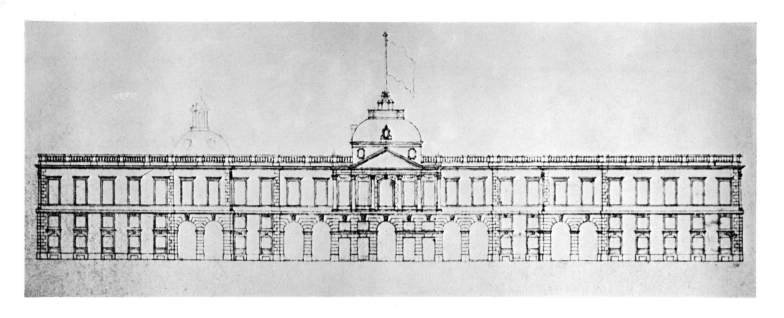

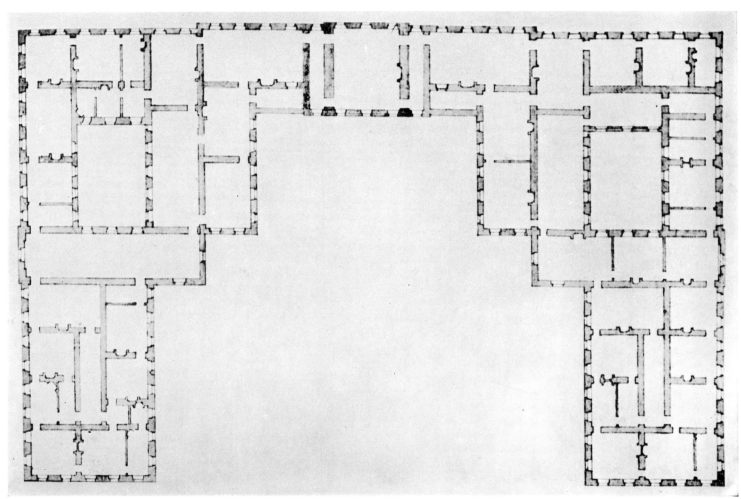

87, 88. Winchester Palace, east elevation and part plan.

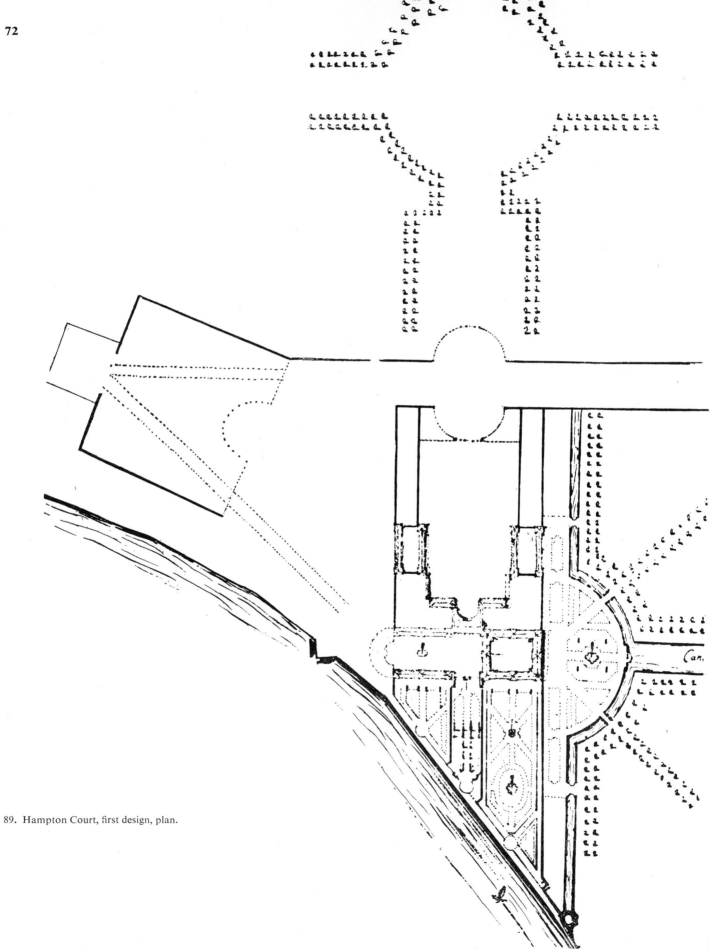

89. Hampton Court, first design, plan.

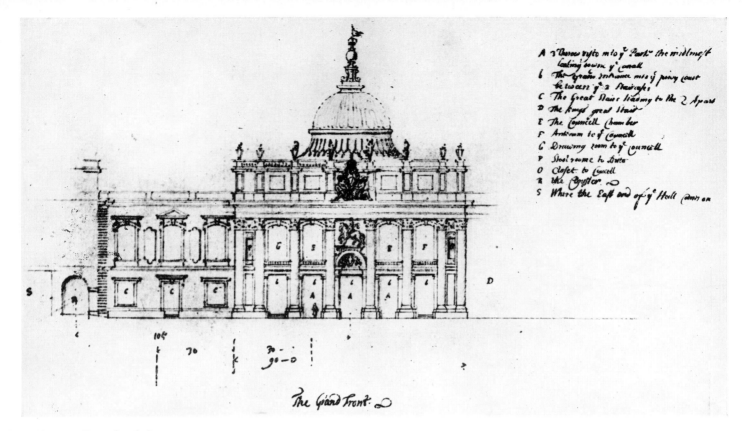

90. Hampton Court, first design.

by the fact that the scheme which presumably followed this first draft was planned on the same number of bays and clearly to the same dimensions, the differences consisting principally in changes of the elevational treatment.[342] We are reasonably well informed of the chronology of the building, for Evelyn records that the unfortunate fire at Newmarket, and the King's fortunate escape from the Rye House 'assassins, who were disappointed of their rendezvous and expectation' had been responsible for Charles's choice of Winchester, which Evelyn thought 'infinitely indeed preferable to Newmarket for prospects, air, pleasure, and provisions'. By this date, 'the surveyor has already begun the foundations for a palace, estimated to cost £35.000, and his Majesty is purchasing ground about to make a park'.[343] Unfortunately, we have not sufficient extant material to assess the exact progress and development of the design nor, indeed, any knowledge how the west front was eventually built. It is clear, however, that Wren placed the greatest importance on the east prospect, which was facing the town, and which was to include a large forecourt evidently designed for the reception of the coaches of such courtiers as Charles hoped would follow his example and build houses along the broad, straight avenue which was planned to run from the castle hill to the cathedral.

No drawings are extant of the scheme as finally built, and the evidence we possess cannot be regarded as altogether trustworthy; the most valuable are the engravings adorning the margin of Godson's map of the city[344] and that found in Milner's *History* (Fig.138); the former of these shows only the central part of the east elevation, while the latter gives a panoramic view of the whole ensemble of the east prospect, including the lawns, the horseshoe staircase, and the outbuildings. Both claim to be authentic, the former stating that it represents the palace 'as it was designed to be built', the latter purporting to have been made after a now missing original drawing of Sir Christopher's. We cannot attach too much importance to these statements, as the two representations show not inconsiderable variations in detail;[345] the main scheme, however, plainly emerges and leaves no doubt that Wren was here planning in the grand manner. Clearly his inspiration was drawn from Versailles and the great seventeenth-century houses of France even though the individual features may possess a very different character from those; but the entire project is eminently autocratic in feeling and the very symmetry enhances, as well as reflects, the conceptions of centralization which had in no small measure formed the architectural style of the age of Louis XIV. A critic of later times has considered it 'one of the ugliest piles of building in the island',[346] but we may regret that the whole magnificent project was short-lived: it is unlikely that anything more than the palace itself was completed[347] when Charles II suddenly died on 6 February 1684/5, and Charles's successor, 'his now Majesty did not seem to encourage the finishing it at least for a while'.[348] James II, in fact, seems to have taken as little interest in Winchester as did William III, and though Queen Anne settled it upon Prince George, the consort died before taking possession of it and the Queen's intention to complete it died with him. The palace, however, furnished the basis for subsequent edifices in more than one way: not only did George II allow the marble pillars of the

91. Hampton Court, first design.

portico, which Cosimo of Tuscany had presented to Charles II, to be carried off; not only did William III's parsimony make him use the palace as a quarry and timber store for his own buildings at Hampton Court and Greenwich: but also, to Wren, the design provided the remote prototype for his subsequent essays in palace architecture.

It is in many ways ironic that the first of Wren's royal palaces to be completed and inhabited should have been designed, not for Stuart glorification, but to enable William of Orange to 'give full indulgence to his unsociable inclinations'[349] and to remove his presence as far as was conveniently possible from London and its society. The reasons which motivated William's choice of Hampton Court were thus only superficially resembling those of Louis XIV in choosing a site several miles from the capital, for nothing was further from William's mind than the creation of a palace and its attendant 'courtier-town'; but while a certain quantum of the all-pervading influence of Versailles may have been active in William's mind, notwithstanding his undying enmity to the *roi soleil*, the conscious reasons for his choice were as unlike Louis XIV's as were the constitutional precepts upon which they bore their several crowns and wielded their several sceptres.

Architecturally, however, the problem which confronted Wren at Hampton Court was not unlike that which the *petit château de cartes* of Louis XIII had set his son's architects. In each case, an earlier structure was present which would either have to be incorporated in the new, or altogether removed, and the antiquity of the pre-existing edifices presented inevitable difficulties of stylistic treatment if they, or any part of them, were to be retained. The problem at Versailles was altogether easier: not only was the *château* of negligible proportions in comparison with what Louis XIV was eventually to build, but also was it an altogether easier proposition to integrate, without creating stylistic disharmonies, the brick and quoin architecture of the little *cour de marbre* within the great stone elevations of Le Vau and Mansart. Wren's problem was far more acute, for the ancient seat of Cardinal Wolsey was of a nature which, stylistically, could never form a homogeneous element within the cadre of any of Wren's architecture.

Wren's solution of this dilemma as first proposed was drastic, but simple: he planned to demolish the entire existing fabric, excepting the Great Hall, so as to be able to plan and execute a great ensemble of a palace, uniform and homogeneous, surrounded by a vast scheme of formal gardens which, however repugnant the idea would have been to William, would have formed a worthy English counterpart to those great gardens of the aristocratic seats of classic France which were so obviously its progenitors. Such was Wren's original intention: unlike later critics, he saw little to admire in the Tudor palace of Wolsey and Henry VIII, and had no scruple in advocating its destruction, retaining of it nothing but the Great Hall, which was to be incorporated, suitably masked, we may surmise, in his own gigantic layout. Wren's concept was truly grandiose: he meant to develop all four principal fronts of his palace, the northern forming the most important, and most impressive, approach: here a vast courtyard, flanked by subordinate buildings, would have been

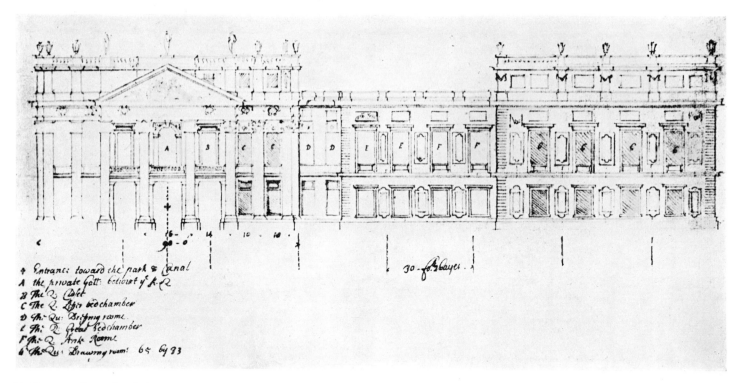

✦ Entrance: toward the park & canal
A the private Gall: below of y.ᵉ Q
B The Q. Closet
C The Q. Bed chamber
D Th.ᵉ Qu: Dressing roome.
E Th.ᵉ Q. Great Bedchamber
F Th.ᵉ Q. Ante Roome
G The Qu: Drawing room: 65 by 33

92. Hampton Court, first design.

reached by a most impressive double avenue of trees, the axis of which was to be centred on the middle of the Great Hall and the portico which Wren had planned for it. Traversing this the visitor would have found himself within a *cour d'honneur*, likewise flanked by subordinate buildings, but orientated towards the west, the centre-piece of which would have been the 'grand front' of the palace proper. Entering, the visitor would have reached a large, rectangular court, the nature of whose interior elevations we can only surmise, but traversing the court and the eastern wing of the palace, he would have found himself, just like the visitor of today, at the focal point of a horticultural design planned in a huge semicircle, from which five straight avenues radiated, the central one of which formed a canal bordered by a double row of trees. Turning to the right, the visitor would have walked along what is now known as Broad Walk and, turning the south-eastern corner of the palace, would have come into view of the Privy Garden which, accommodating its classically geometrical layout[350] to the obliqueness of the Thames's river-bank, is another feature of this great scheme to have survived, in essence, all subsequent modifications.

The elevations which Wren planned for this great project are no less interesting than is the plan. Significantly, he designed a dome as the central feature of his 'grand front', though not a dome the design of which respected utilitarian considerations such as at Winchester, but a beautiful, smooth, closely ribbed structure of double flexure the importance of which, in connexion with other domes of similar profiles, we have already noticed. This crowns an imposing façade, in which a true giant order runs

from ground level through both floors to support a tall parapet wall; the central entry is surmounted by an equestrian statue, most probably of William III, above which a large sculptured escutcheon testifies to that monarch's proud descent and glory.

The other elevations are no less interesting: that fronting the privy court has a central section very similar to the façade just discussed, though there is, of course, no dome, but which is flanked instead with a pair of towers capped by small, elongated cupolas. The central section is adorned by eight pillars of a giant order demarcating the three larger, central, and the two narrower, flanking bays, of which the latter, perhaps in a reminiscence of the scheme employed at Queen's College, Oxford, or in some ways in anticipation of the project designed for Windsor, are formed into niches containing statues. Most impressive, however, is the front towards the park. Though it may be no more than coincidence, it is worth remarking that this, like the west front of Winchester Palace, is composed of twenty-seven bays. But while Wren in the earlier example (Fig.86) had chosen a straight roofline unbroken but for the domes, and had articulated the façade by variations in the treatment of the ground floor, the solution proposed for Hampton Court was much more original, and much more daring. The design is built on a central block of seven bays which, like the other two elevations, carries a giant order of eight pillars here supporting a large triangular pediment rising from a blocking course crowned with statues. This central block is flanked by a pair of two-bay sections after which the distance between bay centres increases with the enlargement of the windows, and the ornamental panels which separate them.

93. Hampton Court, second design.

The four-bay sections following are, like the preceding, only reaching up to the cornice of the centre block, but the end sections, not only wider, are also taller by the addition of a blocking course and a top balustrade set off by urns. The entire front is certainly impressive, and neatly articulated by the three bands of keystones which demarcate the outer sections. The frames of the first-floor windows are kept simple and rectangular, excepting the round-headed centre window which again provides a link with the Winchester design. But where the latter had partly derived its articulation from the somewhat unsatisfactory partial splitting of the ground storey into two levels, the Hampton Court front dispensed with such broken rhythms and, but for the difference of width between the windows, relies on its articulation, upon its symmetrically organized roofline, and, not least, upon the decorative elements which are planned in a subtle crescendo towards the central pediment and statue-crowned balustrade.

Of the design which followed the rejection of this first project we have only partial knowledge, and what can be gleaned from extant drawings makes it clear that the successor was in most respects inferior to that first splendid scheme. The 'grand front' was enlarged by the addition of slightly projecting wings, and

Wren articulated the roofline by small degrees only which, stepping down from the solid parapet wall of the centre to the balustrades of the wings, forms an insufficient contrast to provide a dynamic or directional element to the composition. The dome was retained, but instead of crowning an ensemble which was purposefully built up towards that climax, it now sat a little incongruously upon the central block which seems too wide and too low, while the large triangular pediment in front of it provides an inharmonious contrast to the smooth curves of its profile. The tall, rusticated plinths, upon which a disjointed giant order of twin pillars stands, here brings a restless and inappropriate element into the façade, and the wings of three storeys are by no means improved by their wide centre portions, adorned with yet more pediments, and expanded by the altogether distracting niches between their windows.

The elevation towards the Privy Garden is even less satisfactory. Here, again, the five-bay centre is crowned by a disproportionately large triangular pediment,[351] but the distribution of floor levels below, and particularly the depressed arches of the ground storey give the whole elevation a low, flat character which contrasts most unfavourably with the taut and impressive

94. Hampton Court, second design.

grandeur of the preceding scheme; the squat, low centre block, a base of altogether insufficient height for the heavy pediment, is incongruously contrasted with the narrow three-bay sections adjoining the wings where not only the segmental pediments,[352] but also the completely altered proportions of the windows help to form a most disagreeable juxtaposition and give, we might almost say, an impression of amateurish immaturity. Indeed, it does not seem easy to assign to Wren so unsatisfactory a design at a period when he had reached full maturity and mastery of the medium which, some thirty years before, had almost been thrust upon him; yet though the draughtsmanship of these two drawings would point to his office rather than to his own hand,[353] it is inconceivable that he should not have been responsible for the general outlines and character of the design.

It is likely that the first and second schemes here described followed each other in fairly rapid succession; not only had William III decided on building at Hampton Court even before he had been crowned; but also is it clear that by April of the following year, 1689, work had actually been begun[354] on what proved to be Wren's final design, even though it was never to reach the complete form which he had planned and envisaged.

Though both William and Mary do not seem to have been averse to the idea of demolishing, at any rate, the larger part of the old fabric, Wren was not to have his wish fulfilled of being able to plan an entirely new palace. It is probable that, had Mary lived, not much of the Tudor palace would have been left to us to admire, instead, a greater complex of Wren's planning. But this was not to be.

Such work as Wren did at Hampton Court, however, has a character entirely of its own, for few of the churches, and none of his secular architecture before that date, had made the attempt to build on a monumental scale in the medium which is essentially that of smaller scale domestic architecture, namely brick contrasted with stone quoins and trimmings. Why Wren should have chosen this method is not altogether clear: it has been suggested that, in some measure, he wished to create not too great a contrast with the remaining Tudor portions of the building, but not only are his intentions towards these well known, but also is his own work visually sufficiently removed from them to make such a consideration negligible. On the other hand, William's nationality has been suggested as a cause, and the architect's desire to please the national taste of his patron be held responsible for his

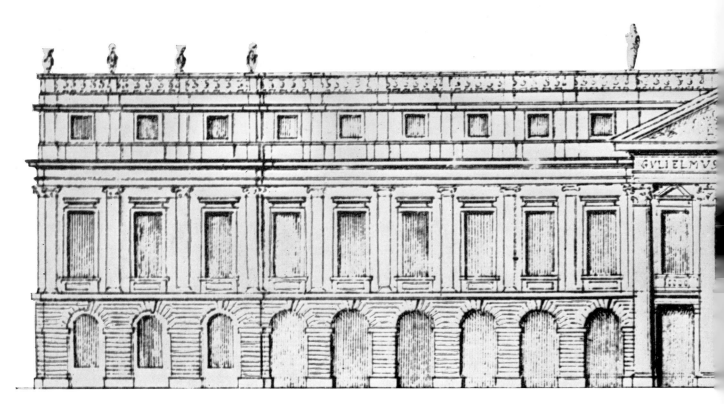

95. Hampton Court, east front study.

choice of materials. Yet while this question will have to be discussed when we come to speak of influences operative on Wren's style and development, it will suffice here to consider the edifice which, fortunately, is still left to us.

Previous generations have found but little to admire in it. Isaac Ware, not many years after Wren's death, thought, in general, that 'there is something harsh in the transition from the red brick to stone';[355] and Walpole's editor thought that the 'profusely sculptured' architraves of Wren's elevations offended 'no less than the palaces of Borromini and Mansart'.[356] And while another critic found fault with 'the great pediment not rising above the balustrade and not standing out, as it should, with only the sky as a background', this offence was 'so palpable

and gross'[357] that royal interference and the forced deference to the sovereign's ill-informed judgement needed to be suggested to explain why 'the building, as it was finally completed, should scarcely be worthy of the great architect's genius'.[358]

Such strictures notwithstanding, it is not unreasonable to say that Hampton Court represents one of Wren's happiest inventions, and one of his most delightful works; architecturally, executed as it was within a relatively short space of time, it is one of his most homogeneous and consistent designs. The method employed may be inappropriate to the scale of the edifice, and Hampton Court has been called, with justification, 'merely an English gentleman's country-house on a large scale';[359] but it cannot be gainsaid that Wren's application of methods more

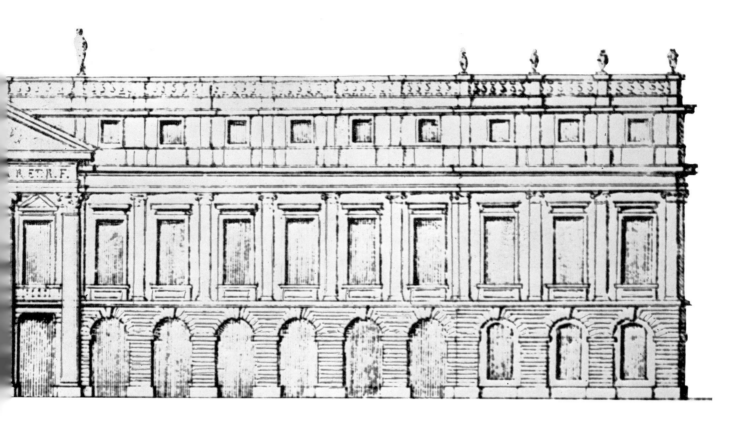

appropriate to domestic architecture to a building of which the scale recalls, though not approaches, that of Versailles,[360] has been eminently successful. And there can be today but few critics unconscious to the delight which the grand, though not over-powering, elevations yield of which the colour effect contrasts so happily, now that the brick has mellowed, with the surrounding shades of green of park and privy garden. What Hampton Court may lack in grandeur, what qualities of magnificence it does not attain, because it does not strive for them, what it must necessarily yield to the Versailles to which it is frequently, though not altogether appropriately, compared, it amply compensates for by the charm of the whole composition; and while, as we shall see, French prototypes were most certainly operative inspiration

in the evolution of the design, the attraction of Hampton Court differs as we have indicated, from that of Versailles in the same measure as the personality, the reign, and the concepts of Louis XIV differed from those of William III.

Delightful as is Hampton Court, the monumental scale of true grandeur was neither aimed at, nor attained, until Wren designed the great palace of Whitehall which, to our regret, shared the fate of so many other of his projects to an even worse degree, for of this grandiose scheme nothing, not even a multilated or dimi-nished version, was ever built.

The picturesque palace which Charles II went to inhabit on his restoration fell under Wren's care, and while Greenwich seems to have been entrusted to Denham and Windsor to Hugh May[361]

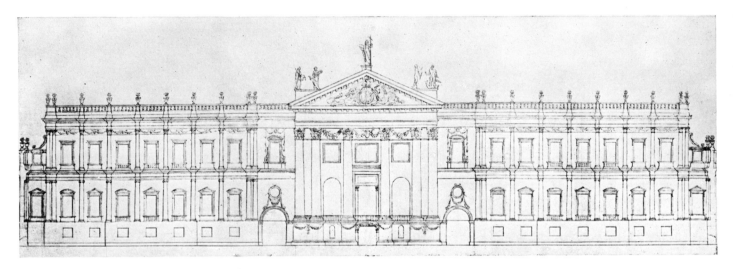

96. Whitehall Palace; for (?) James II.

it seems that Wren was consulted on the possibilities of improving Whitehall even before he succeeded Denham as principal surveyor. By reason of the decorative use of King Charles's cypher, it is clear that Wren's earliest project was designed for that monarch[362] and here we find a small reflection of Inigo Jones's ideas inasmuch as Wren intended doubling the Banqueting House – an idea which was to recur in subsequent schemes – and connecting the two buildings by a large, pedimented and statue-crowned centre-piece articulated by a double order. It is very difficult to assign this drawing to a precise date: the placing of the giant pillars is reminiscent of the distinctive rhythm and treatment of plinths which characterizes the transepts of the great model of St Paul's of 1673 (Fig.41); if, however, the design should really belong to 1669 as has been suggested, then it is clear that it did not meet with Charles's approval. Though it was Wren who 'brought us a plot for the building of our Council-chamber, to be erected at the end of the Privy-garden, in Whitehall',[363] it was, apparently, Sir Roger Pratt who was appealed to, and submitted a design for a future palace.[364] But like many another of Charles's projects, this was not to see fruition; unlike Winchester, however, it was an idea which his brother was to adopt on his accession. For it is to James's reign that we may reasonably ascribe Wren's modification of his second Whitehall design (Fig.96), for the change in the decorative sculpture from toga'ed Roman heroes to figures of some religious significance would clearly indicate a date after 1685.

Stylistically, the design possesses some interesting points.

Breaking the previous conformity with Jones's superposed orders, it introduces giant columns for its centre, at the same time equalizing the roofline. Jones's motif of carved swags is here adopted and enlarged, and forms, together with the sculpture and heraldic ornament of the pediment, a comparative richness of decoration. The carved swags which connect the pair of entries with the circular lights above are reminiscent of Wren's singular usage at St Michael's, Queenhythe, which was completed at that time; but the distinctive ornament of the windows above was a feature which was to recur in designs a decade or more hence.

None of this, however, was ever built, and Wren's work during James's reign is confined to the planning of new apartments for the Queen,[365] a terrace on the river-bank,[366] and the Roman Catholic chapel the plan of which recalls the original design for St Swithin's (Fig.59),[367] of which Evelyn thought that 'nothing could be finer than the magnificent marble work and architecture at the end, where the four statues, representing St John, St Peter, St Paul and the Church,[368] in white marble', but where the music of the Italians and the whole of the Jesuit-conducted service made him reflect that 'I could not have believed I should ever have seen such things in the King of England's Palace, after it had pleased God to enlighten this nation'.[369] But the glory of Wren's if not Gibbon's work was short-lived; not only did the chapel cease to witness the functions for which it had been designed, but also did William III, five years later, arrive back from Holland just in time to see the smoking ruins of 'all the buildings over the stone-gallery at Whitehall to the water-side' which were burned down within three years of his accession;[370] while, lastly, six years later, of what remained, all was burned in another disastrous fire, and 'nothing but walls and ruins left'.[371]

William III was not greatly concerned over this calamity, for he could write to his Dutch confidant that 'the loss is less to me than it would be to another person, for I cannot live there'.[372] Indeed, he had no need to live there: not only was Hampton Court completed, but also had he bought and enlarged the Earl of Nottingham's house at Kensington some nine years previously,[373] where he stayed when business required his presence in London. Yet it was unjust to accuse him of wilfully neglecting the re-building of Whitehall[374] for, within a fortnight of the event, we learn that 'Sir Christoper Wren has taken a survey of the ruines of Whitehall and measured the ground, in order to rebuild the same: his Majesty designs to make it a noble Palace, which by computation may be finished in 4 years'.[375]

We do not know on what information Narcissus Luttrell based his 'computation'; but we do know that Wren's design was never completed in the period estimated, for it was never begun. What Wren planned, however, was gigantic and truly magnificent and while a lack of evidence has prevented this splendid scheme from being adequately discussed before now, a detailed drawing, nearly fifteen feet long, has recently come to light which acquaints us with the elevations of the project hitherto only known in plan (Fig.98).[376]

Of all Whitehall Palace, only the Banqueting House remained after the fire, and this was again made the starting point of Wren's design. This itself is vast, and confronts us with an architectural style and pronounced mannerisms not previously encountered in Wren's work, so that hands other than his may be suspected in details of the scheme. Almost strangest is the fact that Wren proposed to alter the Banqueting House so that it is hardly recognizable: firstly, by the addition of a huge tetrastyle portico of a giant order enclosing the three inner bays of Jones's subtle and restrained façade; secondly, by a transposition of Jones's alternating triangular and segmental pediments from the ground floor to the windows above, while, not altogether con-gruously, the denuded windows receive the addition of orna-mentally carved segmental pediments; thirdly, the centre of the portico is made into an entrance, and the flanking bays are transformed into statuary-filled niches, echoing the four gesticu-lating figures upon the entablature of the portico itself. Lastly comes the addition of two circular, domed structures which flank, and tower over, the metamorphosed Banqueting House, their cylinders enclosed by a giant order, topped by a boldly projecting cornice, and capped by hexagonally shaped domes enlivened with oval lucarne windows. Symmetrically, a short connecting wing contains passage ways and links this centre feature to two identical, windowless buildings, forming a colonnade below, the upper floors of which are covered by a cross-shaped gabled roof

each of whose ends carries a large, triangular, sculpture-filled pediment. Thus far the design was known even before the dis-covery of the drawing here reproduced.[377] The remainder, how-ever, gives us the whole of Wren's intentions and shows what previously could only be surmised from the plan: the enormous gallery of communication, and the elevation of the projected new House of Lords.

It is open to question how far this stupendous design can reasonably be ascribed to Wren in its details. It is very probable that the overall planning was his but, analogous to Greenwich, we may suggest that much of the detailed planning, even of principal elevations, was left to his assistants. The treatment of Jones's Banqueting House itself suggests rather less appreciation of Wren's predecessor than his reported utterance at the time of the fire would lead us to believe though, as will presently be seen, Wren's admiration of Jones's work did not preclude him from advocating its demolition when his own plans demanded it. The circular, domed additions, however, are so clearly in line with a design concept which haunted Wren throughout his life that there seems little reason to credit another hand with their design even though the treatment is much freer, and more monumental than in other instances; they clearly recall the basic concept of the King Charles mausoleum and the St Paul's 'baptistery' (Figs.123, 124), just as the adjoining lateral wings are descended from the equally abortive project of the Cambridge Senate House.[378] But coming to the communicating gallery, we find features which raise doubts on Wren's authorship. Firstly, this would be a unique instance of Wren's designing an elevation of no less than forty-five bays with no more articulation than is provided by the centre and the extremities, particularly when recalling that at Winchester and Hampton Court, where there were no more than twenty-seven bays, he had been careful to organize the elevations by a subtle gradation which subdivided the long horizontal lines; secondly, the method of capping the extremities would be wholly novel to Wren's design repertory; lastly, though the centre porch does not contain features alien to his work and might, indeed, represent a development of the second Hampton Court design (Fig.94) with which it shares the giant Doric pillars, the heavy plinths, and the ornate centre window: these show so marked a similarity to a design for Westminster Dormitory, ascribed to Dickinson,[379] that it may be reasonable to credit his hand, if not wholly his invention, with this huge, though monotonous, design.

Turning, finally, to the projected House of Lords, we find the hand as well as the style of another draughtsman, for here are features which can decidedly be dissociated from Wren's practice; we cannot maintain, of course, that Wren's disinclination from using certain forms and motifs is indicative of his rejection of them once and for all; but their appearance in this design must throw grave doubts on any assumption that it is to be ascribed to him beyond a general outline. The first, striking peculiarity is the

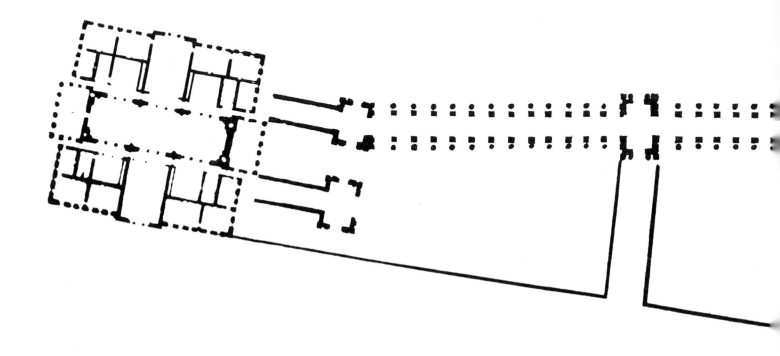

97, 98. Whitehall Palace, Communicating Gallery and House of Lords, first design, elevation, and part plan.

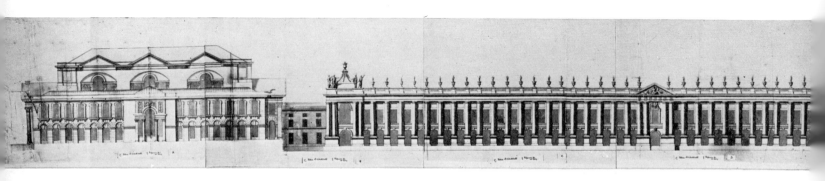

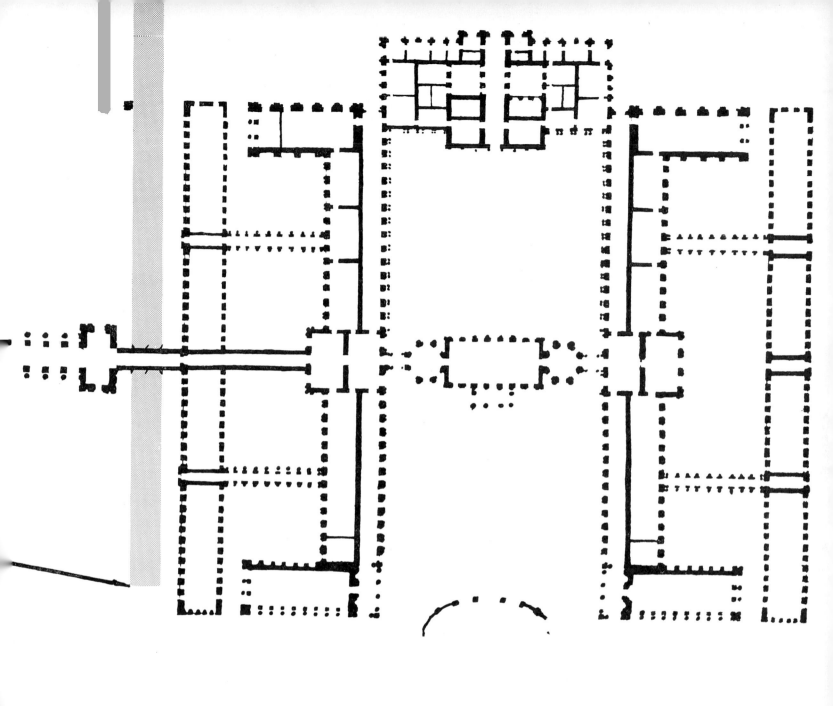
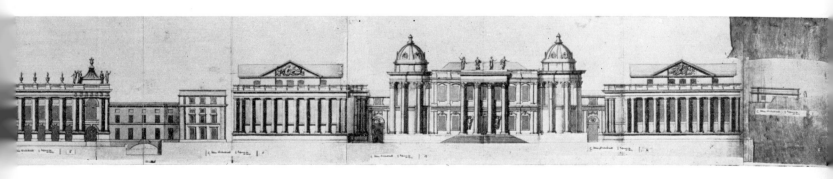

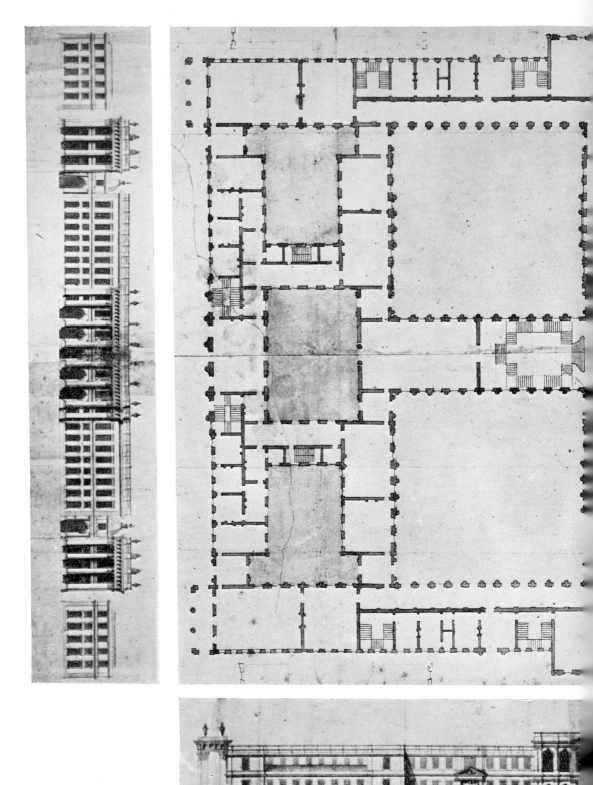

84

99, 100, 101, 102.
Whitehall Palace, second design, river front, park front,
Westminster front, and plan.

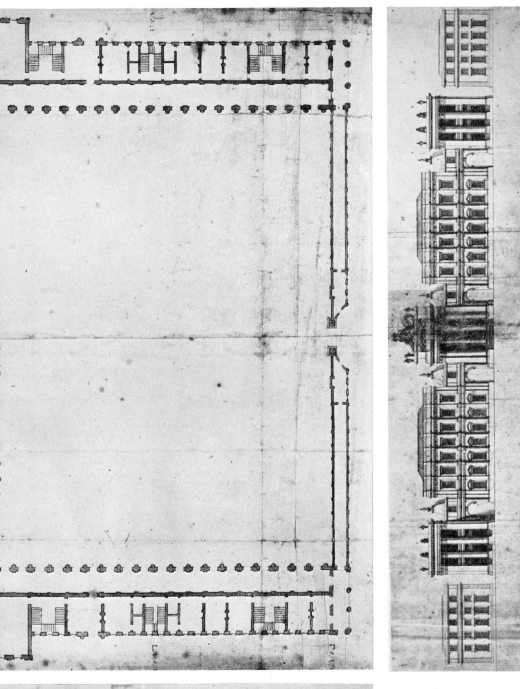

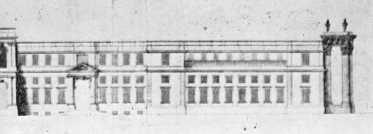

heavy rustication of the ground floor which, to be met again at Greenwich, can there, but not here, be assigned to Vanbrugh's hand. The employment of round-headed windows below such headed by flattened arches would be equally unusual for Wren: as previously noticed, the reverse arrangement was characteristic of some of his major churches of his maturity, yet the usage here displayed seems contrary to all of his design practice that has gone before. Most unusual, however, is the treatment of the porch and of what we may call the clerestorey windows, for here we find a curious employment of the 'motif Palladio' which, though its importance will have to be discussed elsewhere, we need here only point to as so rare a feature in Wren's architecture that his authorship in this particular instance may well be discounted altogether.[380]

We have no means of knowing who, and for what reason, rejected this grandiose scheme. It was not merely a question that 'his Majesty has given directions to Sir Christopher Wren to erect a range of buildings at the end of the Banqueting House, next to the Privy Garden, to contain a Council Chamber and five lodgings for his own use', while 'the rest will be omitted till Parliament provides for the same'.[381] It clearly was the case that even that 'range of buildings at the end of the Banqueting House' had not been approved, for another no less elaborate project is extant which shows Wren's second intentions for the palace itself, though it leaves us in ignorance whether the rest of the entire complex of buildings as first planned was affected.

In this project, the hand of Wren may be more clearly discernible than in the first scheme. Jones's Banqueting House is not only retained intact without additions or alterations: recalling Wren's earliest schemes, it is doubled. The centre-piece between the two parts is filled with a monumental development of the tetrastyle portico which had previously been superimposed on the Banqueting House, flanked by a pair of domed gateways,[382] which connect with the return ends of the duplicated work of Jones. These gateways are repeated at the outer parts of the Banqueting House, where they form the connexions to a simplified version of the central portico which served as the termination of the wings running down towards the river. The 'front at Westminster' is of comparable monumentality, chiefly remarkable, however, not only for the two large pedimented entrances, but for the seven-bay centre composition which, though schematically based on the elevation of Jones's Banqueting House, bears a distinct resemblance to the library of Queen's College, Oxford, the authorship of which, as we have noted, has never been conclusively established.

It is probable that King William's wars – apart from his reluctance to reside in London, least of all at Whitehall – were the ultimate cause why not even a portion of Wren's great scheme was ever executed. Yet, even if the idea of having to live in the palace may have been repugnant to William, the nation's prestige might well have called for some magnificent scheme such as Wren's. Parliament, too, might have provided a stumbling block, for this body had never – neither for James I, Charles I, Charles II or James II – been forward in financially supporting a monarch's grandiose palatial ambitions; William's Parliament no doubt considered the cost of his wars too great to envisage an expenditure such as the realization of Wren's scheme would have entailed. Nor were William's successors any more fortunate, or even interested, for three decades after the old palace had fallen a victim to the flames, Nicholas Hawksmoor could still cherish a forlorn hope, in addressing Queen Anne, that 'Whitehall is to be Raised from its ruins'.[383] By then Wren had been dead five years and though William Kent was to publish a version of Inigo Jones's original, vast project, no successor of Wren's was ever given the opportunity that was denied to him; St James's Palace was to see many modifications under both Wren and Vanbrugh; Buckingham Palace eventually became the royal residence of London. But we cannot but regretfully chronicle that, as so often in his career, circumstances of time and place should have conspired so that of Wren's great proposal for Whitehall nothing should be left to us than a dozen drawings.

As the last among Wren's great schemes of secular buildings, we must now turn to the Royal Hospital at Greenwich in which Evelyn's plan, cherished decade after decade, was finally to be materialized in tangible form. We need not speak here of the old palace where Tudor monarchs had frequently stayed, and where Queen Elizabeth was told, in 1561, of the 'burnyng of the Steeple of Churche of Poules'. Nor is it easy, or necessary, to reconstruct the history of the palace between the accession of Charles I and the foundation of the Hospital seventy years later, for while it is clear, in spite of subsequent alterations and demolitions, that Inigo Jones and John Webb had built extensively for Charles I, the further developments subsequent to the Restoration are but imperfectly documented.

The nature of the palace intended by Charles I is not easily recognizable today, but it is likely that, had the Civil War not intervened to put an end to the whole scheme, it would have been highly remarkable, though perhaps not as vast as that which Jones had planned for Whitehall. Charles II, however, did seriously think of building a palace at Greenwich, close to the sea and to the navy that was so near to his heart, very soon after his restoration; and that Wren should not, at this early stage, have been consulted may seem surprising, though evident.[384] Evelyn, however, seems to have acted in some kind of semi-official capacity as early as 1661 when, at Greenwich, he fell into disagreement with Denham on the basic question as to how the projected palace was to be planned, for Evelyn 'would have had it built between the river and the Queen's House, so as a large square cut should have let in the Thames like a bay'; a scheme which, doubtless, would have delighted the King; 'but Sir John

[was] for setting it on piles at the very brink of the water, which I did not assent to; and so came away, knowing Sir John to be a better poet than architect, though he had Mr Webb (Inigo Jones's man) to assist him'.[385] Charles's plan seems to have been to demolish Jones's work[386] as well as the remains of the old Tudor palace and, the situation and site at Greenwich offering great possibilities, it seems that, inspired by what he had seen in France, and particularly by what he heard to be going on at Versailles, he commissioned the great André Le Nôtre to design the gardens for the projected palace.[387] But for all Evelyn's eulogy of 'what your Majesty has so magnificently designed and carried on at that Your ancient Honour of Greenwich, under the Conduct of Your most Industrious and worthy Surveyor',[388] the plans were not to see fruition. The plague of 1665 and the Great Fire of 1666 may not have been as decisively instrumental in causing the failure of the scheme as the financial difficulties with which Charles was faced during, as well as after, the Dutch war. Though building probably went on,[389] it seems clear that the idea of a great royal palace must have been abandoned, for Evelyn and Pepys discussed the possibility of establishing there an institution for sick or wounded or demobilized seamen even before the Great Fire,[390] and on the same day that Pepys records the visit of Charles, the Duke of York, and Lord Brouncker to Greenwich,[391] Evelyn presented Charles with his project[392] which apparently was so well received that the King had it forwarded to the Navy Commissioners.[393] The location of the proposed infirmary was yet uncertain; Charles may not as yet have relinquished his plans for Greenwich palace altogether, and Evelyn went, not long after his audience, to Chatham, to view a site there which might be used.[394] The project, however, was not to materialize; building went on at Greenwich for some time after the Fire, but possibly came to a standstill with the death of Denham; we have Pepys's evidence that building activities had not entirely stopped by the beginning of that year,[395] but it seems likely that nothing further was done subsequent to the surveyor's death when, one would surmise, Wren would have been called in had there been either the intention or the possibility of completing the project.[396]

When Wren was first, professionally, called to Greenwich, it was not in connexion with Evelyn's project, or the King's designs, but in order to build the observatory which has since supplied the standard of longitude on the world's maps. This building, though of a strictly utilitarian function, was of considerable charm and Wren, as a one-time professor of astronomy, was alive not only to the scientific requirements of Flamsteed but also conscious of the fact that, however functional a building, the desiderata of good taste and appearance need not thereby suffer. In consequence the building for which a Royal Warrant was issued to Sir Thomas Chicheley[397] five weeks after such had been issued for Wren's design for St Paul's, is remarkable in many ways; if Wren, in the latter instance, had been thwarted in his intention of building a dome, and had passed off the 'monstrous' steeple at St Paul's to please his patrons, at Greenwich Observatory he positively revelled in domes which were not only delightful, but strictly functional. Thus the main building possessed not one dome, but two, and these were echoed in the little domed pavilions flanking the main structure. The north front was developed as the principal elevation and, while the entire structure, with its great octagon room inside, provided excellent facilities for the purpose for which it was designed, its utilitarian dedication did not prevent Wren from adorning the north front with a graceful pair of scroll buttresses, reminiscent of, and indeed almost contemporaneous with, those we have met with among the earlier City churches.[398] With the help of demolition materials from the Tudor palace given by the King, the building was completed within a year, and it was from here that Flamsteed was to dispatch his corrections and criticisms of the *Principia* which annoyed Sir Isaac Newton so much, and urge the negligent author for the return of a Greek Ptolemy, borrowed four years before; it was here that, at the turn of the century, Flamsteed was to entertain both Newton and Wren to dinner and, doubtless, astronomical discussion; and it was here that Halley, who went to St Helena to catalogue the stars of the southern hemisphere,[399] was to succeed Flamsteed, who had catalogued the northern, in spite of his faulty edition of the latter's *Historia Coelestis* and in spite of his religious non-conformity which had, once before, lost him the Savilian chair at Oxford in which he had been Wren's successor.

However, it was nearly two decades before Wren was to plan works at Greenwich again, for Evelyn's scheme, tenaciously cherished throughout three reigns, was not to see fruition until the time of William of Orange. Though he had, once more, refused the presidency of the Royal Society on account of his age and infirmities,[400] he did not decline 'the treasurership of the hospital to be built at Greenwich for worn-out seamen' which was offered to him by Lord Godolphin little more than a year later.[401] And when, three months after that, the first meeting of the commissioners took place at the Guildhall,[402] Sir Christopher was already 'nominated Surveyor of this great Undertaking; and with great Pleasure and cheerfulness engaged in it, Gratis'.[403]

Wren's design followed the pattern of previous large schemes inasmuch as a great deal of work had to be done, and many alterations adopted and incorporated, before the powers that be assented to have the final result carried out. At Hampton Court, we may regret that William III never allowed Wren the great scheme originally planned, and, for all the sentiment which rejoices in the survival of parts of Wolsey's old palace, it would have been gratifying to us if Wren had once been able to plan and complete a building according to his first intention, without interference, and without such modifications as the tastes of

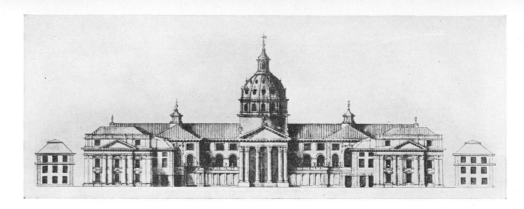

103, 104. Greenwich Hospital, 1694.

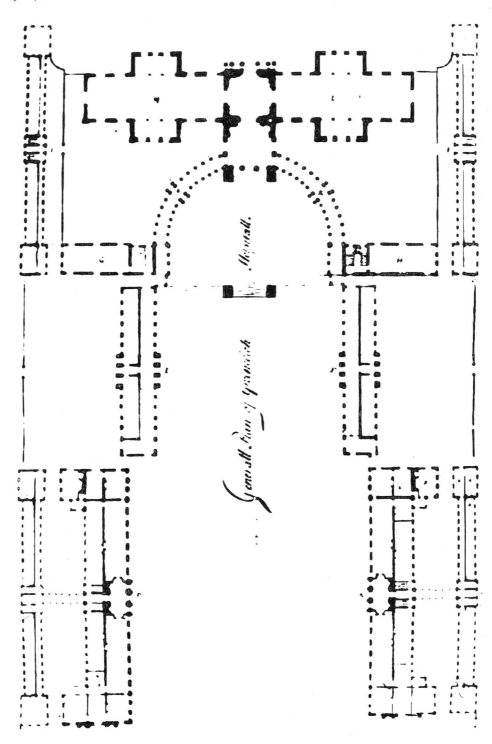

105, 106. Greenwich Hospital, warrant design, 1696.

others imposed on him. At St Paul's and at Greenwich, however, we need not so much regret that circumstances prevented Wren's designs from taking shape, even though it is now recognized that the building as finally erected owes little more than its basic idea and lay-out to Wren. Yet a reason to be glad that his first scheme was frustrated is that, with the site of Greenwich to inspire him, his first intention had involved the demolition of Inigo Jones's Queen's House to build one of these grand scenic schemes in which the Hospital would have formed the architectural nucleus of a great horticultural design on the lines of the gardens of classic France. Wolsey's palace is not so unique a gem perhaps as Jones's ravishing little palazzo for James's consort;[404] yet for all that, we might regret Wren's first project, which would have been designed some time in 1694[405] and was a truly powerful composition, for though the elevations of the long wings seem rather too simple for the complex organization of the central feature, this in itself shows a new mastery in the handling of space and masses such as can by no means be detected at Hampton Court. The central elevation facing the river is indeed splendid, its width compressed by its semicircular plan, the recession of planes of the several sections lending a powerful plasticity to the whole in which rooflines and pedimented gables echo each other's angles and sloping lines, connected by a pillared colonnade, and crowned by a proud, rather pointed, ornamental dome.[406]

The reasons for the scheme's rejection are well known: for Queen Mary, either from sentiment or from genuinely good taste, would not hear of the proposed destruction of the Queen's House and while she seems to have been the principal driving force of the scheme[407] the commencement of the new project, which respected her wish, may antedate her death, which occurred on 28 December 1694. Forced to a retention of the Queen's House, Wren devised a scheme in which the principal buildings would face each other across a wide open space and

would form two long north-to-south elevations, leaving Inigo Jones's building as the terminating point of the long vista from the river. This basic idea was adhered to even after the Queen's death, yet it is difficult to speak with less than diffidence of the design which, in 1696, obtained official sanction. The 'Principal Front of the New Building' is a composition with which it seems hardly possible to credit the mature Wren of the last decade of the seventeenth century. The low, squat building which is not improved by its three-storey return ends, is hardly graced by the clumsy pedimented portico in the centre, and the ludicrous roofline enlivened by its eight tall chimney stacks all combine into a composition which seems hardly worthy of the Wren of his earliest years of inexperience. None the less, the design was approved;[408] and Evelyn and Wren went to Greenwich where the diarist fulfilled the ambition of many years and 'laid the first stone of the intended foundation, precisely at five o'clock in the evening, after we had dined together. Mr Flamsteed, the King's Astronomical Professor, observing the punctual time by instruments'.[409]

While superficially Wren's authorship of these designs would seem indicated and alternative sources do not readily suggest themselves,[410] the warrant design of Greenwich proved as little final as did the warrant design of St Paul's; and we may thus pass to the next stage of the project's evolution, executed between 1696 and 1702, particularly as the 1696 design does not acquaint us with anything more than the nature of the two blocks nearest the river and that we are ignorant of the overall planning. Of the new project, however, we are fortunate in having complete and precise knowledge which permits a very exact evaluation of what Wren was here planning.

The entire complex of buildings was projected in two parts: the buildings fronting the river, King Charles's building to the west, and its eastern opposite, enclosed a large court between them;

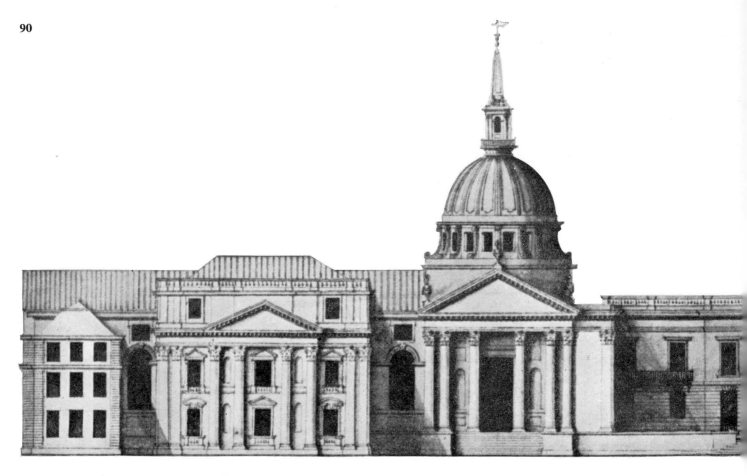

107. Greenwich Hospital, river elevation and Great Hall.

and a long range of colonnades leading up to the Queen's House, from which seven wings of 'wards' projected from each eastern and western section. The vista enclosed between them was much narrower than the court formed by the riverside buildings, and the terminations which were thus visible from the river, were formed into domed structures containing the vestibules of what eventually became the Painted Hall and the chapel. Thus the overall plan for what was eventually to be built was laid down, though the details vary very considerably from the building we still possess.

The variation causing greatest surprise, however, is caused by the fact that the two wings, though planned with exact symmetry on the axis of the vista towards the Queen's House, do not correspond and show marked differences. It is true that, embodying a most significant change from the first design (Fig.103), the dome profiles as now designed are identical. But the elevations of the buildings below are entirely different. We may notice first of all that the vestibule of the chapel shows a hexastyle portico which is clearly derived from that which characterized the first design (Fig.103), though the differences provided by the niches

with their accompanying panels and the large rectangular entry in the centre offer a remarkable parallel, in spite of the greatly different proportions, to the portico designed more than twenty years before for St Magnus (Fig.22). The western pendant, however, excepting its dome, does not answer to this elevation at all. Not only does it include a large segmental pediment resting on brackets where the other had shown a triangular pediment, but also are the floor levels arranged quite differently so that a very different horizontal subdivision results. Most striking, however, is the fact that the symmetry on the Queen's House axis is not complete, for the western block was removed by the width of one bay from the axial line in relation to the eastern block.

It is open to conjecture what reasons prompted Wren to devise a symmetry of plan which is not answered by a symmetry of elevations, but for all the obvious contradictions shown in the elevation here reproduced, we are aware of no explanation ever having been attempted for what must seem an arbitrary, needless, and altogether inconsistent and unmotivated discrepancy. Yet the only explanation which could reasonably be offered is that Wren, in submitting this drawing, was submitting two alternative

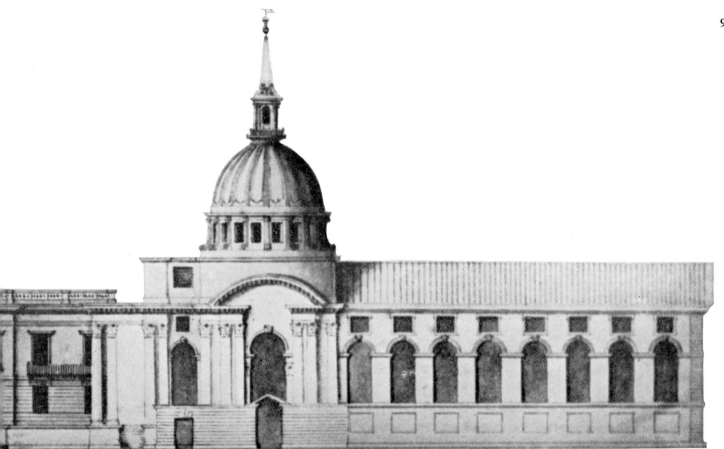

treatments for consideration, leaving it to the commissioners to adopt either of them for execution. This view seems strengthened by the plan and the two complete north-to-south elevations which belong to this scheme for, here again, two alternative versions are shown while, at the same time, we cannot possibly conceive that Wren should have ever intended building an eastern range that did not correspond exactly to the western. To take the eastern elevation (Fig.110; the drawing has been reversed for visual convenience to tally with the plan and the western elevation) first, we find a structure next to the river the design of which was evidently developed from the warrant design of 1696 (Fig.105) though the elimination of the pediment and the raising of the roof and consequent lowering of the chimney stacks constitutes an improvement on the earlier version. To this is joined the chapel, the west front of which presents an altogether different face than did the north front for, while there we found a hexastyle portico, here we find a composition of round-headed windows which clearly recalls some of Wren's early City churches. Southwards from here extends a long range of buildings, from which the six side elevations of the 'wards' stand out by being raised one storey above the connecting buildings, while the roof shapes are clearly of the same lineage as those we have noticed in the riverside tract.

That the western elevation (Fig.108) should be an alternative to the eastern, as we have suggested, seems confirmed by the complete plan (Fig.109) in which we see a completely symmetrical lay-out embodying the double colonnade which was not provided in the east elevation, but which – forerunner of the splendid composition which survives to this day – makes its first appearance in the western range as here depicted. This, however, is not the only difference to be marked: thus the riverside tract, known as King Charles's wing, is bodily taken from the 1696 design (Fig.106) without any alterations or additions. The range of buildings from the Queen's House northwards again comprises six units, which share no more than a superficial resemblance with those of the eastern wing; these display a chief difference in being treated as a symmetrical sequence which, taking the section of the Painted Hall as one extremity, organizes this whole by the alteration of two plain blocks succeeded by one identical block differentiated by the application of a giant order

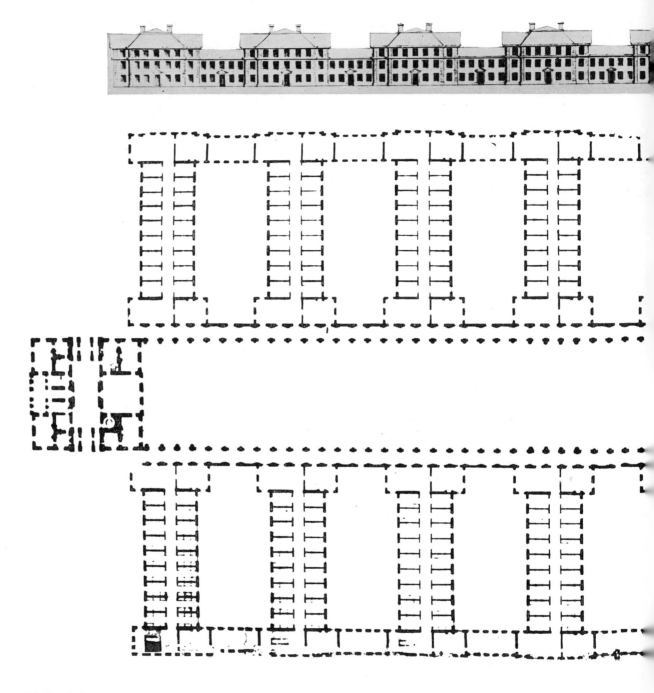

108, 109 110 Greenwich Hospital,
west elevation, plan, east elevation.

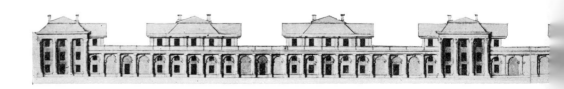

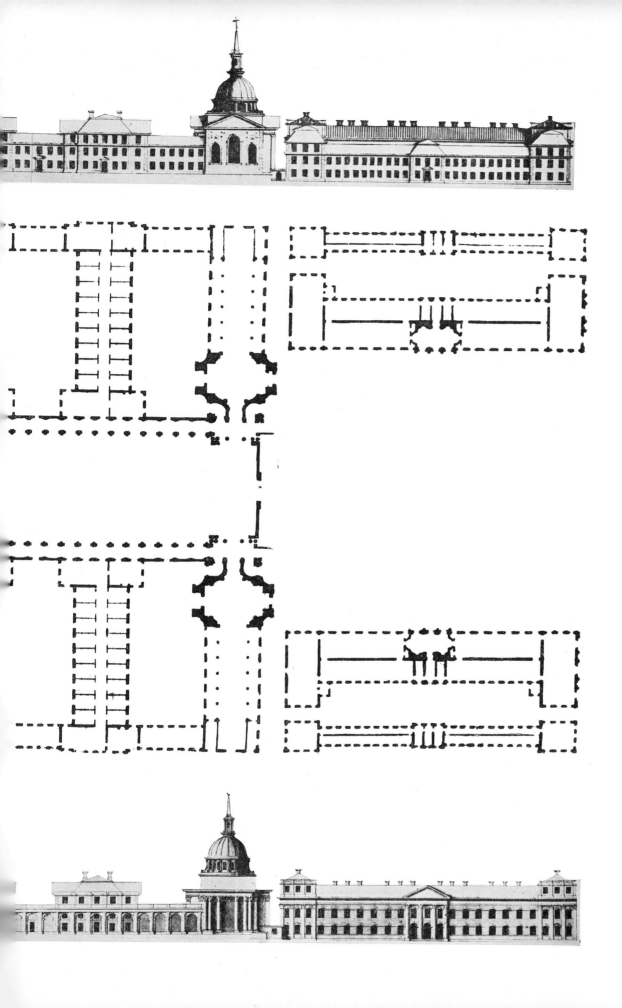

111. Greenwich Hospital, river elevation.

and thus providing a certain rhythm which, in the plain and somewhat monotonous sequence of the eastern wing, had been lacking.

The greatest difference to the latter, however, is provided by the domed vestibule to the Great Hall. If the eastern chapel had possessed a triangular pediment, and the northern front of the vestibule a segmental one, its eastern elevation has no pediment at all. Instead, it varies the interchangeability of features – and thus further supports our view that Wren was here proposing alternatives – by showing an eastern hexastyle portico similar to the northern elevation of the chapel, so that it seems that in the four distinctly different versions shown by the northern and western fronts of the chapel vestibule, and the northern and eastern elevations of that of the hall, the commissioners were being given a maximum of solutions to choose from. But, whichever version or combinations were to be adopted, the Queen's

House was to form the termination of the great vista thus provided from the river. It may be that in one design which we would consider the last to be safely assigned to Wren, the significant blank space in the centre may indicate that Wren was even now considering the demolition of that edifice, particularly if we can really credit Hawksmoor's testimony to the effect that Wren had not 'intended that his range of buildings should be brought to so poor a conclusion'.[411] But, be that as it may, Wren's ultimate ideas appear convincingly, and our suggestion that the asymmetry of previous drawings was to show only alternatives, seems finally borne out, for we may take this drawing as representing the commissioners' decision, and in the symmetry of the beautifully-shaped domes and the echoing correspondence of the various triangular pediments we may reasonably perceive a solution fully corresponding to Wren's own predilections.

With this design, the principal lines of the scheme were laid down, and even though Vanbrugh, some ten years later, was still to plan a large domed structure to close the vista from the river, his intention failed as much as Wren's had done. Wren's own design, however, formed little more than the lay-out for subsequent developments, and as we cannot share the confidence with which one writer has ascribed 'the beautiful dome, projected as early as 1702',[412] to Wren, we cannot connect his hand with any degree of certainty with any of the subsequent designs. Not only do his appearances at the committee meeting become rarer and rarer after 1702, but also was he overburdened with work in London, notably the designs for Whitehall Palace, and not least the final designs for the dome of St Paul's; moreover, it should be remembered that Wren was now a septuagenarian, and, though he was to live another two decades, it is probable that the constant strain of frequent visits to Greenwich – for we have no evidence that he had built himself a house there[413] – was beginning to prove too much for him.

Great changes were, indeed, introduced into what we have considered Wren's last design; thus the preserving of the main road running between the Queen's House and the Hospital necessitated the elimination of the southernmost three blocks of Wren's plan[414] even though Vanbrugh's ingenuity made him project a large domed building planned so that the road could pass underneath it.[415] Wren's smooth domes were to be altered beyond recognition when they were eventually built to Vanbrugh's design even though distinct traces of Wren's influence and practice, such as the coupled pillars and the treatment of the upper floor so reminiscent of the transept porches of St Paul's, are clearly discernible.[416]

When at last the foundation stone of the cathedral came to be laid, there was not, as one might have expected, any ceremony, attended by royalty, aristocracy, or civic worthies, to mark that momentous occasion; indeed, the simple act seems to have been performed by Wren with an absence of ceremonial almost amounting to furtivity. Such may actually have been intentional: if, exasperated, he had previously decided not to make any more models to be exposed to the public's view and views, it is quite obvious that no one outside the circle of his master craftsmen – Pearce, Strong, Marshall, and Wise – was in any degree familiar with his actual intentions. And these, moreover, we shall soon see to have amounted to little more than a general idea, for while, necessarily, the details of the foundations themselves had to be decided upon at an early date, the evidence we possess shows only too clearly that the entire elevational treatment was, and remained, completely fluid in Wren's mind.

It is to this fact that we may attribute the circumstance that no complete plan of the cathedral is extant which we, with any certainty, could assign to 1675 or soon after; that such actually existed, and that Wren kept its details to himself, has been suggested, yet cannot be proved. What is clear, however, is that the plan of the warrant design (Fig.42) represents substantially the shape of the cathedral as Wren was to build it during the following thirty years. For that plan, for all the vast elevational divergences, already contained the essence of the final version: it presents in a fairly final form the shape which the eastern end of the cathedral was to take; the crossing itself was carried out substantially as there indicated and, but for the alteration introduced into the transept porticos, can be regarded as the prototype; the only major change is represented in the west end where, if tradition is to be trusted, the insistence of the Duke of York brought about the addition of the chapels which, though already implicit in the earlier drawing, were to take on a greatly enhanced magnitude.

While thus the evolution of the final plan was a relatively simple matter, the physical part of laying the foundations proved of considerable difficulty. Probably in view of the unsatisfactory condition of the pre-Fire cathedral, Wren decided against following the old foundations and went out of his way to avoid a coincidence of the building lines;[417] it is clear that no liturgical considerations prevented him from deviating from the east-west axis; and, even then, he may still have harboured hope of contriving some sort of grand square and approach to the west front of the cathedral. A few extant drawings acquaint us with the elevations of the houses he planned for this 'piazza',[418] but, as we know only too well, he was to be frustrated in this ambition. The work in hand, however, was enough to occupy his mind: the laying of the foundations was no mean task. At pains to avoid the weaknesses that had caused the pillars of the old cathedral to have sunk, upon their infirm foundations, sufficiently to be visibly out

of perpendicular, the nature of the ground as disclosed by deep excavation convinced Wren that exceptional solidity of the foundations would be called for if his own edifice was to avoid the failings which he had diagnosed in the pre-Fire structure. It would be of little purpose here to detail the means by which Wren explored the nature of the ground; of less purpose still to comment on the archaeological speculations in which he indulged on the strength of the findings in different stratifications of the excavations;[419] but of greater interest to follow the course of the work, particularly as in this respect we are most fortunately placed: in the case of the City churches, circumstantial evidence had to be drawn upon extensively to establish a reasonable chronology; in the case of the cathedral, however, the books containing the contract transcripts and details of payments made to craftsmen and tradesmen provide a complete documentation which enables us to follow, step by step, the progress by which, during thirty years, the cathedral was built.

The clearing of the ruins of old St Paul's was in itself no small matter; and for months, even years, labourers were busy sorting the stones of the ruin, partly to be used for mortar, while immense quantities had to be shifted before Wren could even start the laying of foundations. In conformity with his original plan, a start was made at the east end, and thus, while demolition work was progressively clearing the ground towards the west, the new cathedral began to rise in its choir sections. Within a month of obtaining King Charles's warrant, two of Wren's master masons, Joshua Marshall and Thomas Strong, contracted for the works on the south side of the choir,[419] and two months later Marshall signed the contract for the corresponding north side;[420] the winter saw 'laborers making mortar, screening rubbish, wheeling stones &c., removing Stones from the North Cross Isle of the Old Church',[421] and while in February of the following year labourers were beginning to clear the 'ground for ye ffoundations of the great South West Peer of the Dome',[422] a month later, at a time when Marshall already received £500 in part payment 'for Masons Work done in the Choire of the Church',[423] a contract was drawn up in which it was 'agreed then with Joshua Marshall, Mason, to lay, forme, and doe the Mason rubble worke of the foundation of the S.W. Peer or Leg of the Dome'.[424]

With the import of this entry, however, the foundation of all future trouble was laid. It is a matter of speculation why Wren should have employed the very method of building his piers which he had so strongly condemned in the old cathedral. It is possible, as has been suggested, that he 'may have been unduly influenced by the old master masons, Marshall and Strong';[425] it may be that, with foundations constructed on more scientific principles, he had begun to think that the defects of the old cathedral had been due not so much to the construction of the piers themselves but to the weakness of their foundations; for by that time he must have become convinced that the structural

112. St Paul's, 'as it is now to be built', 1676.

strength of the piers was far greater than he had at first thought when he found himself forced to use, for their demolition, first gunpowder and later, when the use of such had nearly led to fatal accidents, the 'good Roman manner' of a battering ram.[426] Be that as it may, it was on that constructional basis that Wren laid his foundations,[427] and that, nine months after the labourers had finished 'to clear the ground for the ffoundations',[428] Marshall was paid 'for the Masons Rubble work of the ffoundation of the S.W. peer or leg of the Dome'.[429]

Thus, the constructional method had been decided upon; but what should also be emphasized is the fact that, however concisely the contract books and building accounts speak of the 'peers' or 'leggs' of the dome, the structure which these were eventually to support was as yet a completely unknown quantity. Seeing that Wren, a quarter of a century later, was still completely undecided as to the form and profile which the dome was finally to take, there is no reason to think that he should have had any but the most general idea at this early stage. To his contemporaries, however, it was not only the shape of the dome that was a mystery, but even the elevations themselves. John Evelyn

makes no mention of the cathedral during these early stages of construction, and the earliest intimation we possess is the folding plate representing the 'New Model of the Cathedral of St Paules as it is now to be built' appended by Richards to the new edition of his translation of Palladio's First Book.[430] However unlike the edifice, the representation so confidently offered is yet of great interest. Not only does it bear relation neither to the warrant design of 1675, nor to the elevations of which the walls were beginning to rise soon after, but also is it clearly a version of the so-called favourite, or great model design of 1673 some of whose features it undoubtedly reproduces.

This fact, that is to say, the deviation from the 'approved' scheme of 1675, warrants an examination of the woodcut which previous authorities have withheld, even though the circumstances of its production are far from clear. It is, of course, completely uncertain whether the engraver was at all familiar with Wren's intentions; in view of Wren's reluctance to make public any further designs, this does not even seem likely. At the same time, however, the picture betrays in its essentials a degree of compromise between the 1673 and 1675 designs and, seeing

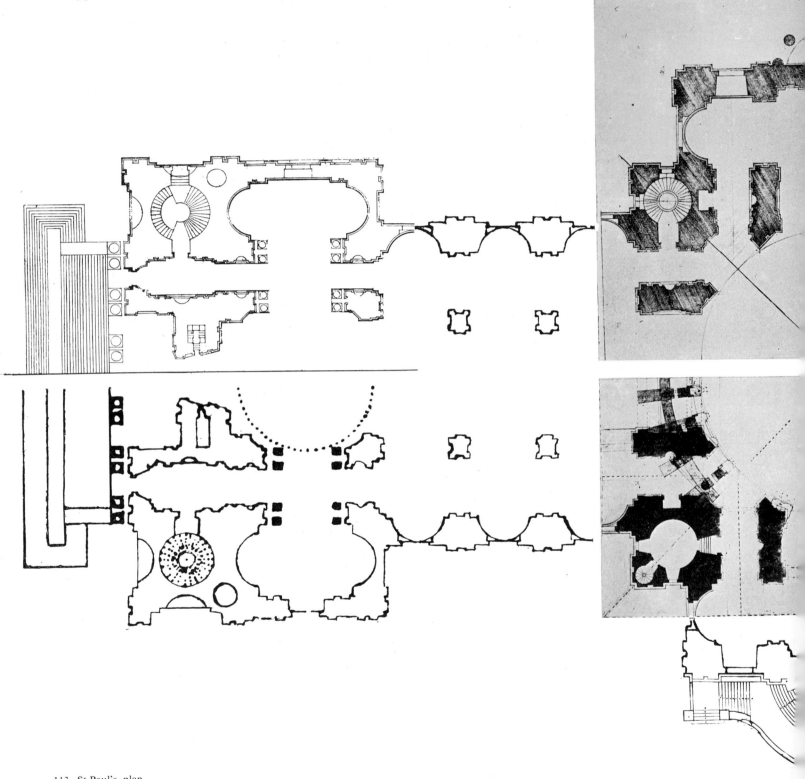

113. St Paul's, plan.

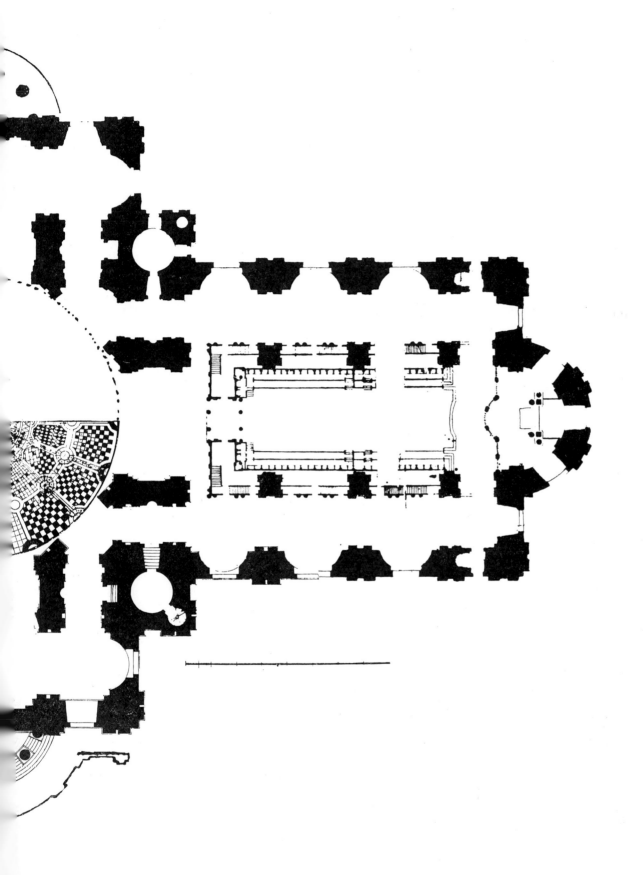

that such compromise was fundamentally the prime motif behind the evolution of the final cathedral, it would perhaps be too much to ascribe the scheme here represented entirely to the engraver's imagination. Thus the salient features of the great model reappear: albeit changed out of recognition in their shapes and outlines, the basic idea of the employment of two domes is retained; likewise, the contraction of the width in plan containing the vestibule remains, though the artist, somewhat uncertain of his perspective, has not rendered this passage unambiguous and but for our knowledge of the great model plan (Fig.39) it would be difficult for us to envisage the precise nature of this section. The transept, on the other hand, clearly reproduces the treatment devised for that scheme (Fig.41), but, with regard to the eastern parts, the uncertainty of the artist becomes painfully apparent. He probably knew that Wren would try to combine the choir of the warrant design with the east termination of the great model; but how this was to be effected was something our anonymous artist found difficult to envisage: on the one hand, his ambiguous foreshortening might be regarded as an artistically imperfect rendering of the quadrant-circles connecting transept and apse; on the other hand, the crude persrective effect produced does not even permit the inference of the semicircular apse which, as we have noted, had first appeared in the 1673 plan and was never subsequently to be altered.

The plan for which, painfully, the site was being cleared and the foundations laid during these latter years of the seventies was to exhibit none of the peculiarities which the engraver thought Wren would introduce; what Wren was to take over from the favourite design was contained in the elevations only. The plan itself is orthodox in most respects, and clearly modelled, as we have remarked, on the warrant design of 1675. This shows the degree to which Wren was forced to make concessions to clerical pressure: there is an almost complete absence of the originality and invention of previous schemes; instead, we find a conventional arrangement of choir, nave, and transepts not radically different from many a Gothic cathedral in its regularity and provision of aisles, and the way in which, without the necessity of structural alterations, the bays of the nave could conveniently be turned into chapels. It is a point difficult to decide whether this arrangement, as well as the ease with which the choir could have been screened off, may have been devised by Wren in the knowledge that the re-introduction of Roman Catholicism was a distinct possibility, should Charles II die without heir. At the time the cathedral plan was being finalized, this was not improbable; and while it is evident that many of Wren's City churches could be converted for Roman Catholic worship without structural alterations,[431] we can do no more than suggest that considerations such as the possibility of a religious re-orientation may have conditioned Wren's cathedral plan. Be that as it may, the plan itself was evolved precisely in the same fluid manner as the dome was later to be designed, and while it is clear that the complete concept was only clear to Wren in general outline, it is difficult to say precisely how many years lay between the laying of the first stone and the finalization of the western sections of the plan.

However onerous the undertaking, the laying of the foundations was progressing steadily: in July 1676, labourers were still taking up the old foundations so as 'to lay the new ffoundations of part of the S.W. Pier of the Dome', but at the same time work at the east end had progressed sufficiently for the carpenters to start 'setting up the great Centers under the W. end of the Choir to turn the Brick Arches upon'.[432] The north side was tackled before the south. The demolition of the old north transept had been contracted in March 1675/6;[433] by October of that year labourers were 'levelling ground on N. part of the W. sides of the N.W. leg of the Dome, & wheeling rubbish to fill up the ffoundation of the S.W. Angle of the S.W. leg of the same',[434] but it was not, in fact, until March of the following year that Marshall was paid 'ffor the Masons Workmanship, rubbing & setting of six Courses of plinth & Rustick Ashler with the Coines & Windowes & Rustick Arches along the N. & S. sides of the Quire' and that Strong was paid for similar work at the north and south sides of the east end.[435] In January of that year however, workmen, busy 'to bury dead bones taken up in the digging of the new ffoundations' had already begun upon the transepts by 'digging foundations of the N. & South Cross Isle',[436] and by September, Thomas Strong was paid not only for 'setting up on the South side & E. end of ye Choire 9 Courses of Rustick Ashlers & the like height in the outside Pilasters', but also 'ffor the Rubble Works of the foundations of the N. Portico'.[437]

It is at this point, at a moment when the lower parts of the eastern elevation were actually under construction, but the character of the porticos not known beyond their semicircular form, that we would introduce the successor to Richards's guess at the future shape of the cathedral: this is as unlike the final version, and as disregarded by previous authorities, as the former had been. But the engraving here reproduced possesses a greater interest than any inherent quaintness or merely the somewhat ludicrous representation of what the artist thought to have been in Wren's mind: however divergent from the actual cathedral, it yet contains sections which reproduce correctly what Wren designed and built, and the point at which divergence begins, when related to the entries of the building accounts, permits a very precise dating of the engraving.[438] Thus, the correct rendering of the windows adjoining the transept porticos makes it impossible to assign it prior to the autumn of 1678, when it was contractually 'agreed with E[dward] P[earce] to continue & build ye South Portico from ye middle of ye Window on the E. side of ye S. Cross Isle to ye middle of the Window on ye W. side of ye said S Cross Isle, taking in & including ye Whole Portico'.[439]

114. St Paul's, anonymous engraving, c.1680.

But it can almost certainly be dated between the spring of 1679, when Pearce received the first payment for the work thus contracted,[440] and the spring of 1681, when carpenters were 'makeing Bridges round the N. Portico, for the Masons to raise their Columnes upon'.[441]

If entries relating variously to the north and south porticos have here been cited, this is mainly so as to narrow down the period during which the engraving must have been made: the north portico was taken in hand before its southern counterpart; and a very precise limit is set by the fact that the engraver, assuming that the two would be identical, showed the arrangement of steps designed for the north portico in his south elevation of the cathedral, though when the south portico came to be designed and built, the difference in levels dictated an altogether different approach.

Why the engraver should have omitted any indication of the semicircular eastern apse it is difficult to imagine; what is perfectly evident, however, is that at the time of executing his work, construction at the east had not yet progressed as far as the cornice, which here appears far heavier than that actually

designed by Wren, and that work towards the west was still in its very early stages. We know in fact that Thomas Strong's masonry built up to the staybars of the windows was contemporaneous with a portion of the 'new ffoundations further Westwards' when both, having been contracted in September 1678, were paid for in March of the following year.[442] In December, it had already been 'agreed with Thomas Wise the Elder, Mason, to continue the Building of the two S.W. Leggs of the Dome with the Great Staircase',[443] but in the May following work on the nave was no further advanced than the 'digging of new ffoundations on the S. side of the Convocation house'.[444]

Within such chronological limits, it is explicable that the engraving should display a tolerably exact representation of the lower storey details, but an altogether fictitious treatment of the west end. There being three bays to the choir, the engraver guessed, if he did not know, that the nave would contain a greater number. Beyond this, however, we enter a realm of fiction and it is most unfortunate that we should have no evidence to show whether west end and the entire building above the cornice were purely a figment of the engraver's imagination or whether they

115. St Paul's, portico study.

were based on any tentative sketches of Wren's which may have existed and which he may have seen.[445] There may be some significance in the differences which the treatment of the upper sections display when compared with Richards's engraving: the vestibule dome has disappeared, and its place been taken by twin western towers unmistakably related to Borromini's of St Agnese in Rome, to the precedent of which Wren's finally completed towers have sometimes been attributed. The dome, furthermore, clearly reproduces an imaginative variation of the structure designed for the warrant design, and even though we shall point, elsewhere, to the actual limitations of Serlian influence discernible in Wren's work, the fact that such quite evidently conditioned the character of the dome as here represented[446] might raise the conjecture that some no longer extant sketch may actually have inspired the engraver. The possibility of such connexions, however, remains conjectural; and it is safer, and perhaps more instructive, to turn to the concrete evidence in following the progress of the cathedral's erection.

We have seen that the choir sections were comparatively far advanced at a time when the foundations of the nave were only beginning to be laid; and while Wren may still have been un-

decided on the entire design for the west end, financial difficulties may also have been responsible for the fact that the work did not proceed more rapidly. In 1678, Stillingfleet, having succeeded Sancroft as dean,[447] issued an appeal for funds where he contrasted the City churches, 'rising so fast of out their Ruines' with the fact that the progress of the cathedral was so slow: his appeal was cogent, and not without reproach, for 'methinks those who have already laid out so many thousands on a Monument of the dreadful Fire, should think themselves concerned to contribute freely towards a Monument of the Resurrection of the City after, and what can be more proper for that, than the Re-building of St Paul's?'[448]

The result of the appeal is difficult to estimate.[449] Yet, for all the difficulties which Wren faced, the work progressed: by 1680 practically all the work on the choir 'from the Astrogal of the small Pilasters to the height of the Stay barrs of ye Windows'[450] had been completed, and work 'from the height of the Stay-barrs of the Windows to the top of the Astragall of the inside & outside Pilasters'[451] had been begun by the end of the year. By June 1681, the joiners were 'makeing a Modell for ye Archatrave, Freeze, & Cornish',[452] but, although final work on the north portico had begun as early as 1681, and though, a year after, Sir William Dugdale thought 'the new structure of the Cathedrall Church of St Paul' so much advanced that he felt 'importuned to reprint my historicall discourse thereof',[453] it was not until 1683 that Wren had 'two Gibbets made to sett the Capitalls of the S. Portico',[454] and it was only in 1685 that Pearce, Strong, and Latham contracted 'to work sett & Carve the great Cornice of the Quire of St Paul's',[455] dividing the work between them, Pearce being assigned the south side, Latham the north, and Strong the apse.

By the autumn of 1685 work on the upper sections of the choir was begun and, by the following March, Wren's plans for the west end must have been finalized, for it was then that John Thompson contracted to 'by himselfe and Workmen lay the Foundations and carry up the walls in hight to ye floor of the Western parte of St Paul's Cathedral from the middle of ye window of the S.W. Chapel to ye middle of the great western door with the ffoundations of half ye great Portico' and promising (perhaps because he had but recently taken the place of the deceased Marshall) to 'carefully follow the designes & directions which shall be given him by ye Surveigher'.[456]

Soon after the demolition of the ruins of the west portico had begun, the carpenters were raising 'scaffolding on the S. side from the Dome Westward to bring up the Peers' and the bricklayers were 'turning the first square Vault over the S. side Isle of the Choir';[457] by the summer, the carpenters were raising the centres, and the bricklayers were turning the arches between the piers,[458] and by the late autumn the walls of the nave were sufficiently advanced for them to start 'turning over a Sphericall Arch on the W. side of the N. Portico'.[459]

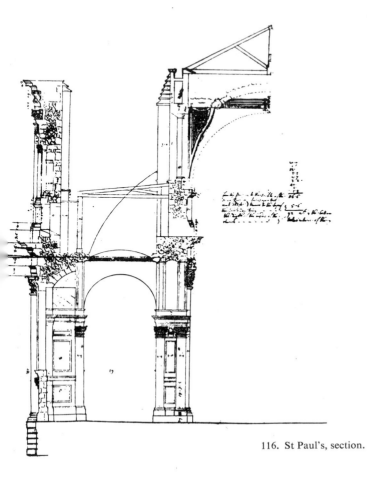

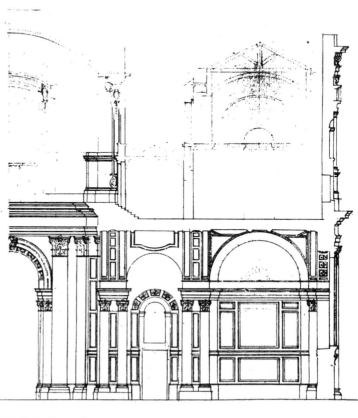

116. St Paul's, section. 117. St Paul's, section.

The last parts of the old cathedral came down in April of the following year,[460] and by May the vaulting of the whole south aisle as far as the south-west chapel was well under way.[461] By June, the corresponding northern parts had been taken in hand,[462] and in the autumn, payment was made for the 'Bricklayers Arching the Vaults in the Middle Isle of the Church towards the W. end'.[463] None the less, it was more than optimistic to think, in autumn 1687, 'that a few years will now perfect the Edifice', as a newspaper correspondent sanguinely expressed it,[464] for even a year later the vaulting of the nave was not yet complete.[465] But with the progress of the work around the crossing, the springing of the great twenty-six foot arches,[466] the first signs of trouble appeared: at the same time as the account-books tell us of a 'dinner at Tavern and at the eating of a Hunch of Venison at the passing of the Books of Accounts', at the same time as a wine bill of £5 8s 5d was incurred by 'eating Buck given by HM Queen to Officers of the Church' we read of a payment to the carpenters who had made 'Scaffolds to SE Legg of Dome for Masons to open the Joynts'.[467] We cannot be certain of the date when Wren

realized the mistake he had made in using a rubble core cased with Portland stone for the construction of piers and walls.[468] What is certain, however, is that from the time the arches were sprung to the completion of the cathedral, Wren was forced to extensive works – so delicate that he would only entrust his master masons with it – and considerable expenditure, to provide the structural stability which the piers would need to support the dome. In April 1691, the north-east pier was similarly treated,[469] and in September the masons were paid for no less than eighty-nine days' work caused by 'opening the Joynts of the Leggs of Dome'[470] and less than a year later, further payments had to be made for '56 days Sevrl Masons in sevrl Months opening the Joynts of the Leggs of the Dome & in sevrl other places'.[471]

At the same time, however, Edward Strong was paid not only for 'a little Modell for the Vaulting of the Choire' but also 'for making part of a Modell in small Stones for part of the Dome'.[472] This, indeed, may seem premature when considering that Wren was not to finalize his dome designs for another decade or more. But the building was now proceeding apace and, the details of the

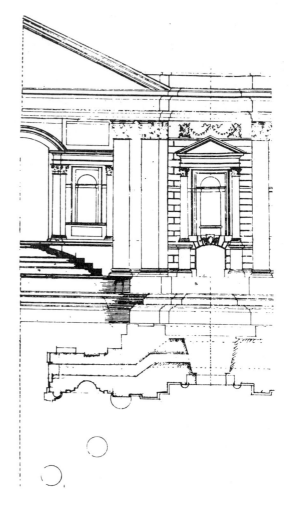

118–19. St Paul's, transept studies.

elevations being decided upon, it was but natural that Wren should have begun to turn his thoughts to the final form which the crowning feature of the edifice was to take.

The upper storeys were largely completed during the nineties; it seems that Wren was at first in two minds about the precise form of the transepts and, the masons' work being sufficiently advanced, he had Edward Strong make, and the carpenters put up, a 'Modell for the Pedament of the N. Portico'[473] which may conceivably have been the design based on a segmental pediment (Fig.118).[474] But this was not to be its final form, for it was not until 1699 that the 'Bas-relieve on ye N. Pediment' and the 'S ffrontispiece, a Great Phoenix' for which Grinling Gibbon and Gabriel Cibber were paid[475] were placed in transept pediments of an altogether different character (Fig.119), to the design of which Wren seems to have paid particularly meticulous attention.[476]

The vaulting of the nave, including the western chapels, was completed by 1695 and retains a reminiscence of the second dome of the great model design in the vestibule cupola of the executed

cathedral; but it was to be another ten years and more before the great west portico was completed and Francis Bird was paid £650 'for Carving the Great Pedament, being the history of St Paul's Conversion',[477] for, as was implicit in the constructional history from the very first, the east end was complete long before Wren devised and constructed his double-order west portico: the exterior was well advanced in 1686, when Strong was paid £420 'for Masons work and Carving done at the E. end';[478] the brick vaulting of the choir was accomplished between May 1686 and November 1689; by April 1694 the scaffolds were ready for 'Carvers & Plaisterer's use',[479] and within another two years Charles Hopson was paid not only for a 'Modell of ye Outside of E End' but also for 'a Modell for the Seats in ye Choire, a Modell for ye Altar, for the Organ Case, for the Organ Bellows, for the Dean's Seat' and 'for the Chaire-Organ Case'.[480]

The interior was nearing completion. In fact, the contract with Bernard Schmidt for the £2000 organ had been made as early as 19 December 1694,[481] and even though the last years of the century

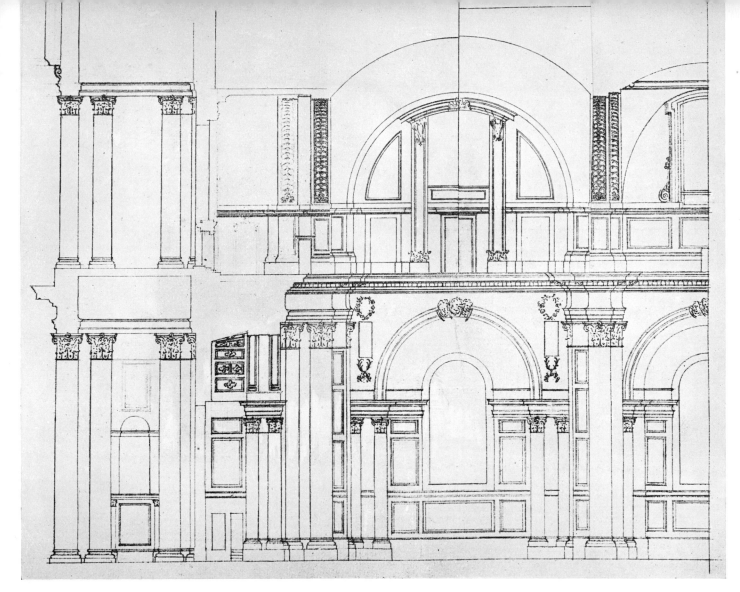

120. St Paul's, section through west end and portico.

saw vexing complications and interruptions of the work – at Portland, a landslide disrupted the supply of stones, at St Paul's itself, a fire in the organmaker's shed was fortunately brought under control before causing serious damage – it also saw the inauguration of the edifice when a Thanksgiving Service was held on the signing of the Treaty of Ryswick.

Yet St Paul's was still incomplete: the west portico was yet to be built; the western towers were not even designed; and the great piers did not, as yet, even support the drum of the dome. This, the dominant feature, must obviously have been in Wren's mind all along: we have seen that, as early as 1691, Wren had had a part model for the dome made; three years later, Edward Strong was paid for eighteen days' work spent in 'making a large Modell of $\frac{1}{8}$th of the Great Dome',[482] and three years after that, on 30 March 1697, Wren presented and read a report to the committee in which he summed up the position: 'The Work of the Choire is advanced in severall places to the Upper Cornice, and together with the Great Portico must so remain for want of large Blocks of Stone

till the peers and Cranes in the Isle of Portland be restored', he said; 'the Tambour, or Circular Walls of the Dome', he suggested, 'may be carried up with ffreestone more than 20 ft higher'; beyond this, however, 'the Cupolo, were it finished, would be so remarkable an ornament to this mighty City, that all persons natives and fforeigners will be extreamly satisfied; neither will any repine at the charge of completing the whole Work, when they see the noblest and most difficult and most expensive partes brought to a desirable effect'.[483]

However confidently Wren could forecast the artistic success of 'the Cupolo', and however decidedly the committee was to resolve 'that the Work of the Dome be set upon and carried out as fast as conveniently may be',[484] the precise shape of this dome to be built was as yet a completely fluid and undecided concept in Wren's mind. As we have remarked elsewhere, the evolution of the cathedral is only fragmentarily illustrated by drawings; but while, unlike in the case of the City churches, the majority of these reproduce the final structure very closely, and while variants are

121. St Paul's, east end and apse.

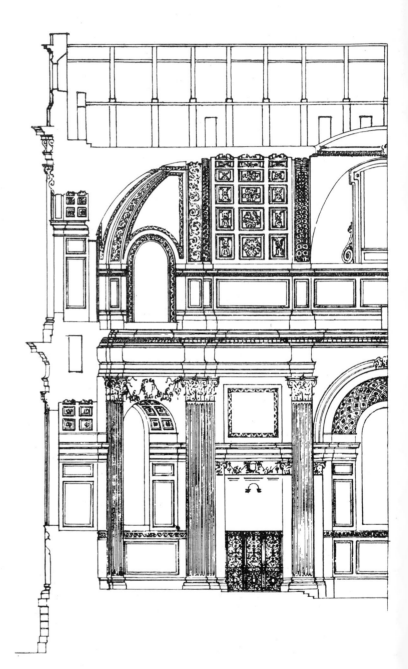

122. St Paul's, section through east end and apse.

123. King Charles mausoleum.

124. St Paul's, baptistery or chapter house.

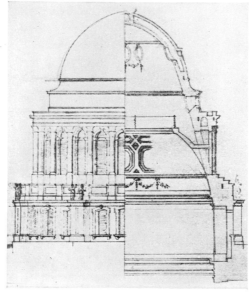

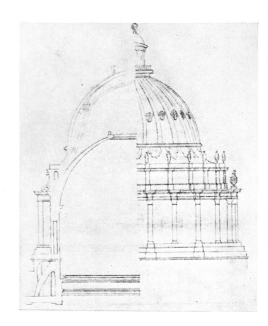

125. St Paul's, dome study.   126. St Paul's, dome study.   127. St Paul's, dome study.

rare and mostly show but minor divergences, the series of extant dome drawings represents the widest gamut of shapes and profiles which, in the absence of any evidence of holograph dating or other external testimony, can only be reduced to a conjectural sequence of development.

Chronologically retracing our steps, two dome designs need to be noticed, both of which probably belong to the latter seventies, neither of which was to progress beyond the stage of paper planning. Both are of importance to the dome of St Paul's as they display the two basic types of domes the pure employment of which, as well as their combination, proved Wren's paramount preoccupation. The first (Fig.123) represents the abortive scheme to erect a mausoleum, at Windsor, to the memory of Charles I. The scheme is dated with certainty to 1678 by Wren's surviving estimates and a Parliamentary grant of £70,000 towards its erection.[485] The design is of great interest: adopting the circular form of classical precedent, it provides for a windowless lower storey terminated by a statue-crowned balustrade above the Corinthian order; the drum rising from that level contains the windows, axially placed, and, diagonally, semi-cylindrical protrusions which clearly infer a relationship to the tower of St Antholin (Figs.54, 77, 79) as well as Tom Tower (Fig.61) already noted. Above this substructure is raised the drum proper, the sixteen sides of which contain alternately windows and protruding solid masses of masonry which latter support scroll buttresses connecting with the

dome above. This, though of reasonably smooth outline, is strongly marked by eight sets of double ribs, surmounted by a lantern with a symbolic statue, and graced by a set of lucarne lights.

Though the project remained unexecuted, its ideas were not wasted: for its basic concept was to reappear, twenty years later, at Whitehall (Fig.97). The purpose of the second design (Fig.124) is not altogether certain; a fragmentary inscription on another drawing (Fig.151) indicates it to have been intended as an ancillary building to the cathedral, but whether it was to serve as a chapter house or, less probably, as a baptistery, is impossible to determine. What is clear, however, is the relationship of this design to the King Charles mausoleum just noted; chronologically, there may not be much difference between the two, as the rapid progress of reconstruction around the future cathedral must have forced Wren to abandon his plan for the surrounding 'piazza' at the extreme western end of which he intended this edifice to stand.[476] From the point of view of design, however, the similarities are too striking to need much description, and rather should some subtle differences be noted. This principally applies to the curious dichotomies of planning: thus the mausoleum design is encircled by an array of twenty columns, while the upper portions are designed on an octagonal base; conversely, the lower part of the 'chapter house' is articulated by sixteen columns, while the upper part is designed on a dodecagonal plan. We cannot account

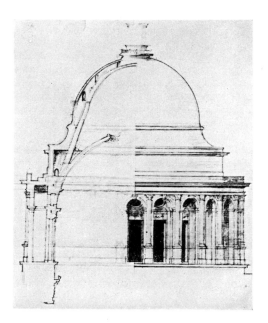

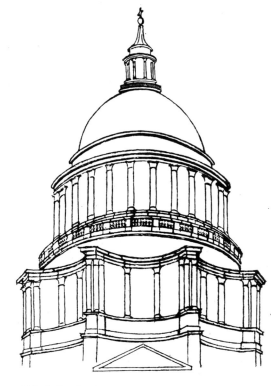

128. St Paul's, dome study.

129. St Paul's, dome study.

130. St Paul's, dome study.

for the odd syncopations created by the play of twenty against sixteen, and sixteen against twelve units; but it is possible to see here, in these first drafts, a tendency at work similar to that which, as noted elsewhere, governed the comparable changes discernible in some of the steeple designs.

More important within the present context, however, are the types of dome shown in these two designs, for both of them were to find their progeny among the many extant studies for St Paul's dome. It is probable that the hemi-spherical type of dome, exemplified in the chapter house design, proved Wren's first line of thought. Thus one early design (Fig.125) shows not only the semi-circular profile, but with its distinctive finial and its equally striking scroll buttresses provides links with designs dating from the earliest period.[487] Yet, though Wren was to return to this type in a modified form in one of the Greenwich designs (Fig.107), this did not altogether satisfy him; adhering to the idea of two distinct substructures, he eliminated the scroll buttresses in another draft (Fig.126), substituting a window-pierced lower section which was articulated by solid masonry buttresses crowned by statuary, thus recalling the method employed in the chapter house design. A variant of this scheme (Fig.127) reverses the relative height of the two portions of the dome support, curiously introducing two orders in the lower section, but this again seems to have been abandoned in favour of a more monumental treatment doing away with the previous subdivision into two series of windows and

openings and substituting one great, continuous arcade supporting a plain, solid drum (Fig.128). Apart from the intrinsic interest of these changes, however, these last three drawings are of particular importance in showing Wren's ideas on the interior treatment of these domes. It is clear that he had realized, as early as 1673, the inherent problem of a dome 'conspicuous above the houses' which would not, internally, look cavernous, for even in that early design had he projected a shallow, interior dome.[488] Yet while this expedient promised a very satisfactory solution so far as the interior view was concerned, the exterior appearance remained a problem: it was obvious that considerable height would be essential; on the other hand, the higher the dome was to be placed, the greater would be the perspective foreshortening incurred, so that a semicircular outline, seen from not too great a distance, would appear seriously distorted. Wren at first tried to solve the problem by extreme height. Falling back on the idea of a double substructure, both parts of which were considerably enlarged beyond the previous dimensions, he produced a most interesting design (Figs.129, 130): the smooth dome, with its large lantern, rests on the usual colonnaded drum; this, however, rests on a voluminous substructure which clearly recalls the device employed in the Greek cross and great model designs; but here the idea of obtaining maximum visibility is carried beyond the idea of truncating the corners of the basic square: here it is transformed into an octagon, all of whose sides are concave.[489] This treatment

131. St Paul's, dome study.

engenders a great degree of plasticity, and the interplay of curves produces so dynamic an effect of movement that it is not surprising to find that Vanbrugh should have taken up the idea when planning, as abortively as Wren had done, a central focus to the vista of Greenwich Hospital.[490]

There may be some significance in the fact that we have here the only perspective drawing to be found among Wren's dome designs, and it is likely that this was executed so as to judge the visual effect which such a dome would produce on the man in the street. But here, we would suggest, one line of development has reached its end, if we can assume a degree of consistency, for all the designs considered up to now, however divergent from each other, had in common the basic idea of a plan formed on the dodecagon and its multiples, thus emphasizing their relationship to the upper part of the chapter house design. Succeeding designs, however – and this has not been the least factor causing us to suggest this particular sequence – are characterized by plans governed by the square and the octagon.

If preceding domes were planned of comparatively modest dimensions, the first step in the new direction seems to provide for a much larger dome. Wren evidently tried to preserve the sculptural, plastic effect of the previous project, but the means now employed are altogether different and of the greatest interest: the four semi-cylindrical, domed buttress structures (Fig.131) are not only a transference of the design concept of which the transept porticos as built were the outcome; they are also the final evolutionary stage of the distinctive feature we have noted in the tower of St Antholin, in Tom Tower, and in the King Charles mausoleum which, indeed, we would not have emphasized but for this highly important final development and the interest of parallel precedents which will be discussed elsewhere.

Yet, however effective the interplay of curves and angles might have proved, the grandeur of the dome, in spite of probably increased dimensions, did not satisfy Wren, who clearly realized that the only solution lay in increasing the height. Wren's first attempt to solve the problem was by simply elongating the dome which, however, remained unpierced and smooth. Even though it possessed no indication of the nature, or even the eventual existence, of the western towers, the project was considered of sufficient importance for an elaborate perspective section of it to be engraved,[491] which shows the very interesting method which Wren proposed for a satisfactory solution of the problem of both interior view and exterior appearance. But this design was to be elaborated almost beyond recognition, for the next design belonging to the period shows an almost startling departure from the general characteristics of preceding projects: it shows, quite apart from a striking likeness to the dome of St Peter's, a distinctively pointed outline, a voluminous lantern, buttresses plastically treated in the same way as those of the chapter house design, and a degree of ornamental elaboration, manifest in the triple set of lucarne lights, the details of the lantern and the involuted scrolls capping the buttresses, which contrasts strongly with the previous designs. Of great interest, however, is the section: the lucarne lights apparently were not intended to be true windows at all, but serve a merely ornamental purpose; for the interior of the dome is only lit from a set of openings at the base of the dome which, concealed from below by a curved rim, leads us to think that Wren had in mind some elaborate pictorial treatment or scenic effect necessitating such carefully calculated lighting.

This is the first design datable within fairly close limits: in the first instance, it clearly represents an elaboration of the dome projected for the central feature of Greenwich Hospital (Fig.103) not later than 1694, but abandoned on Queen Mary's insistence on the retention of the vista to the Queen's House; in the second place, an extant complete side elevation[492] shows the dome in position of the completed cathedral largely as built, but with the western towers still in a rudimentary stage of design and the upper storey of the west end yet unbuilt.[493] Thus it is evident that the design must belong to the last years of the century; indeed, it possibly was this which the committee, in 1697, resolved to 'be set upon and carried out as fast as conveniently may be', and another probably corroborating factor will be suggested elsewhere to support the dating here advanced. Though this version was not altogether abandoned, as we shall see, once again it did not satisfy Wren completely; but even though the dome design was to undergo yet further, momentous changes, it was not long after that he began to build the drum of the dome. By the beginning of 1698, the carpenters were already erecting 'scaffolds round Inside of Dome for Masons to Set ye Intablature',[494] and as the work proceeded, the structural insufficiency of the piers necessitated again, a considerable amount of work.[495] None the less, it does not appear as though this fact influenced Wren's further designs, for the drum under construction was to carry a very different, but not smaller, dome from that last designed. At the very beginning of the new century, the committee 'ordered that Sir Chr Wren do proceed this year to carry on the Dome of the Church as high as conveniently he can, and allso the N.W.Tower',[496] but at precisely that period Wren seems to have been planning a completely different solution from that proposed three years before.

It is fortunate that we can assign the new designs to the years 1700–2 with certainty; for, following the committee's exhortation, Wren first of all began by re-designing the western towers. For these, he had a model made[497] and subsequently altered,[498] the design of which clearly betrays a debt to the chapter house project the relationship to which is indicated not only by the smooth, hemispherical domical capping, but also by the fact that the upper colonnade is based on a dodecagonal plan. Before long, however, Wren was to introduce a pattern of ribs into these little domes, possibly to harmonize them with the re-designed main dome. The change effected in the western towers is as nothing when compared with the change which this itself has undergone, for it is as different as could possibly be from the previous project. It retains, indeed, two of the latter's three sets of lucarne lights; but a notable change in shape has taken place which is discernible in all details: the dome itself is much smoother, though still retaining the pronounced double ribbing; and within this general metamorphosis of the predominantly vertical character of the previous scheme it is significant that even the shape of the lucarne lights has been altered; to make up for the height thus lost, the lantern, previously heavy and voluminous, has given way to a much more slender structure which, incidentally, also presents a very different interplay of curves. The drum supporting this dome has undergone as much change as has the dome itself. From its substructure, the upright oval lights have been eliminated altogether; the segmental-headed windows below the springing have been reduced from sixteen to eight; and the bold buttressing, fronted by double pillars, which had lent so Michelangelesque a character to the previous design, has here been replaced by a continuous colonnade which harmonizes nicely with the ring of pillars gracing the western cupolas, though the numerical

132. St Paul's, dome study.

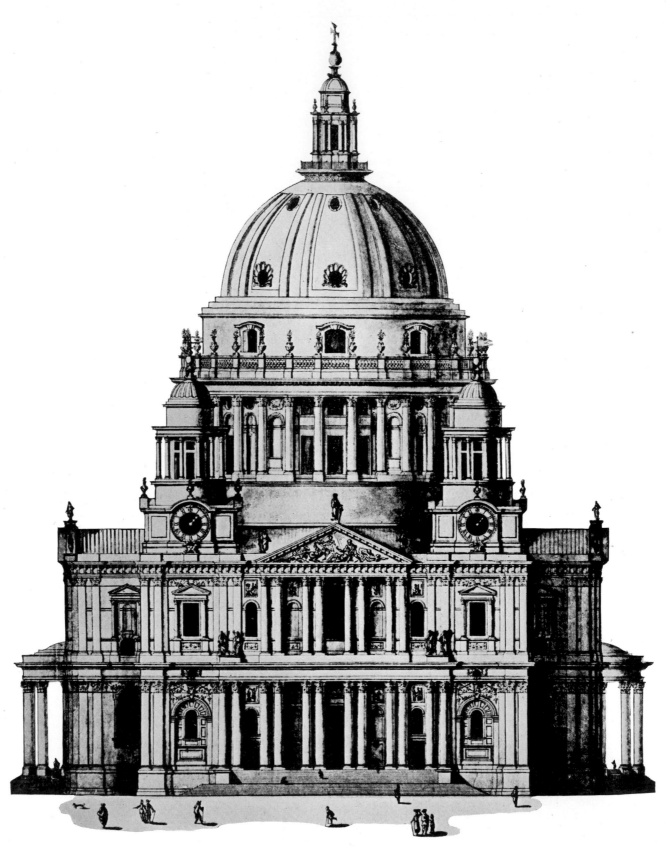

133. St Paul's, west front, 1702.

134. St Paul's, section.

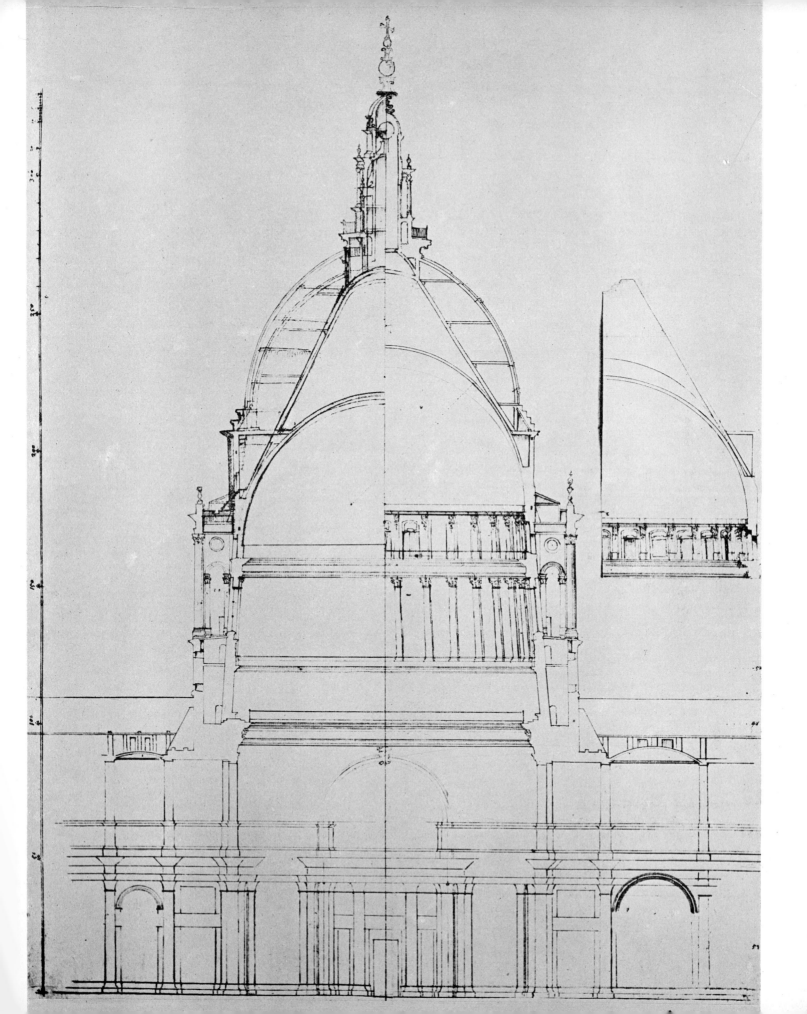

dichotomy between the dodecagonal plan of the latter and the thirty-two columns of the great drum itself still persists.

When Wren produced this novel design, the interior colonnade of the drum was already almost completed[499] and while, clearly, no further alterations up to this height were possible, Wren was still by no means certain, in 1702, of the exact shape or constructional method which the dome was to take. The proposal then put forward was obviously regarded as final, for a number of engravings were made from Wren's drawings, of which copies were officially printed and issued,[500] unlike the unauthorized representations of Greenwich, with Wren's explicit sanction. None the less, three significant things need to be noted: in the first instance, even those engravings which were issued 'ex Autographo Architecti' are not consistent and show variations of details;[501] secondly, the western towers were to be changed completely; and, lastly, the dome which was finally to crown the whole edifice was to differ considerably from this, allegedly final design. These last changes must have followed the printing and issue of the engravings fairly closely, for by 1703 another, though unauthorized, engraving was produced, and is extant in two states,[502] which shows the western towers exactly as built but for the inclusion of a clock in the north-west tower. The section is most interesting as it shows not only true lucarne lights placed differently from the 1702 project but, more surprisingly, a solid dome apparently built of masonry embodying the sloping interior colonnade already built, and ornamented with a regular pattern of coffering. In the absence of holograph drawings corroborating this method of construction it cannot be established with certainty whether this really represents one of Wren's proposed solutions of the dome problem; the delineation is accurate in all the details of the interior; but on the other hand, there is neither, as in the former case, any indication that the engraving was issued with Wren's authority, nor was the work executed by the same artist; lastly, it would hardly seem credible that Wren should, at this late stage, have suddenly envisaged such a solution when considering that already in much earlier stages of the design evolution he had been grappling with the problem of how best to avoid the unsatisfactory view which would be obtained if the true, external dome were internally visible.

One drawing (Fig.155), which is difficult to assign to any date with precision, foreshadows the method eventually adopted. It contains, significantly, a segmentally-headed window below the colonnade recalling the Michelangelesque design preceding the 1702 engravings.[503] On the other hand, it shows not only the thirty-two pillar colonnade finally built, but, more importantly, three distinct sections composing the dome. The central part already foreshadows the famous cone eventually devised and clearly forms the structural base on which the lantern rests; both the inner and outer shells, significantly different in profile from each other and from the cone, display the principle on which the dome was finally designed and built. Of this we are fortunate in having a complete section (Fig.134) which probably represents Wren's final thoughts and choice between two basically differing alternatives. The left part of the section shows the dome substantially as built, but the right section shows an attic storey above the peristyle, the inclusion of which Wren had considered once before,[504] but which, of course, was omitted in execution. This design can only be dated between 1703 and the beginning of 1705, when the actual construction of the dome began by the insertion of the first of the great chain ties at the base.[505]

From this point onwards, the rest of the history of the construction of St Paul's can quickly be told. The building of the brick cone was completed by 1707[506] but, even though it happened that ships carrying materials were 'cast away in a Storm near the Isle of Wight'[507] and 'taken & carried off by a French Privateer' to Calais where the cargo was 'condemned as Prize',[508] the final operations went forward without any serious delay. In March 1705/6, Tijou was already paid £274 16s 8d 'for the Great Iron Chain or Girdle round the Dome';[509] by June, the masons were paid for the work of letting in 'a Great chain round the S.W. Tower',[510] and in December of that year Richard Jennings was given, as a gratuity, 'for his Skill and extraordinary Pains, Care and Diligence, in the performance of the Centering of the Dome & for Modells of the same, fifty guinys'.[511] Though, with the increasing weight resting on the piers, further strengthening and repairs became inevitable,[512] the work went on without interruption: Tijou's 'Great Chain on ye Dome' was placed in position in February 1706/7[513] and the final payment for the work of letting in the 'Chain upon ye Crown of the Cone' was made in November of that year.[514]

Yet the practical completion of the work, the achievement of more than three decades of patient effort, marked equally the first of the series of disagreements which makes of the end of the story such sorry reading. It had been Wren's intention to cover the shell of the dome in copper, but the committee had other views and felt it necessary to assert them; for 'it being proposed to this Committee to cover the Cupola with Copper, and having fully considered it with all the reasons & allegations for the same. It is the unanimous Opinion of the said Committee that it is better to cover the said Cupola with Lead, and It is Ordered That it be covered with Lead accordingly'.[515] Not content with overriding Wren's wishes, when the work thus specified against his recommendations was taken in hand, he was exhorted 'to take particular care yt the same be performed in ye best and most substantial manner'.[516] The committee displayed the same attitude when it came to the decoration of the interior. On Stephen Wren's evidence, it had been the architect's intention to cover the inside of the dome with mosaics,[517] though the evidence of some drawings would lead us to think that he actually intended it to be coffered;[518] the committee, however, 'Ordered. That the inside of

The West Prospect of y. Cathedral Church of St PAUL'S London

the Dome be painted with figures', and 'that such Painters as are willing to undertake the same, do bring Designs and Proposalls (Both as to sume & time) to the Commissioners'.[519] Thornhill and Pellegrini, the latter but recently arrived in England under the patronage of the Earl of Manchester, emerged victorious from the first round of competition on the strength of their cartoons,[520] and were commissioned to paint miniature versions of their designs on model cupolas specially prepared for the purpose.[521] But, once again, Wren was to be overruled; even though 'it is understood that Wren would have preferred to employ Pellegrini'[522] it was 'almost a foregone conclusion that no foreign artist, especially one coming from a romish country, would ever receive the St Paul's commission'.[523] And thus, on 28 June 1715, after protracted deliberation, 'Sir James Thornhill was this day chosen to paint the great Dome of St Paul's, and it was Ordered to be done in Basso-Relievo, after the middlemost of the 3 Designes wch now hang in the Chapter House'.[524]

Wren seems to have offered little resistance to what he may reasonably have regarded as the commissioners' encroachment on a domain which was his sole responsibility; the divergence on the choice of material with which to cover the dome was not, inherently, a matter in which the disregard of Wren's wishes would act to the detriment of the edifice; likewise, the disagreement over the treatment of the interior dome – while few would consider the result obtained felicitous – was a matter intrinsically of decoration. But when the committee proceeded to propose alterations to Wren's design at its very architectural core, he was roused to a spirited protest which would hardly make us suspect to have come from an octogenarian. The committee, somewhat high-handedly, decided that Wren's design would be improved by the addition of a balustrade to crown the upper storey, and, perhaps characteristically, 'It was Ordered That Mr James doe inquire among the Masons for what prices a Ballastrade may be made in Stone, and also of Mr Jones & others, of the lowest price of one in Iron'.[525] Apparently the prices quoted for this aesthetic desideratum were found to be reasonable, for a year afterwards the commissioners 'resolved to set up a stone Balastrade upon the top of the Church' which resolution was subjected to the, perhaps merely theoretical, proviso, 'except Sir Chr Wren doe under his hand in writing declare that it is contrary to the principles of Architecture'.[526] This Wren did, and in no uncertain terms: he 'took leave, first to declare that I never designed a balustrade', and then proceeded to give his opinion which would have made any but the commissioners blush. 'Persons of little skill in architecture', Wren informed them, 'did expect, I believe, to see something they had been used to in Gothic architecture; and ladies think nothing well without an edging'; yet irony did not achieve its object: Wren said he would 'have gladly complied with the Vulgar taste' but the reasons he gave for not having done so are as unconvincing to us as they proved ineffective with the commissioners. Wren's explanation

that the 'statues erected on the four pediments only' were 'a most proper, noble, and sufficient ornament to the whole fabric' was reasonable enough; but when he claimed that 'such was never omitted in the best ancient Greek and Roman architecture, the principles of which, throughout all my scheme of this colossal structure, I have religiously endeavoured to follow',[527] he was proposing an archaeological justification for his design of which the commissioners may never have realized how questionable it was. Yet to them it was not a question of archaeological exactitude or classical propriety; as a matter of form, they despatched Sir Isaac Newton to formally consult Wren before proceeding, yet even before then James had been ordered to execute alternative designs for the balustrade, and, whether Newton persuaded Wren into agreement or not we do not know, it was ordered, without further ado, 'That the Balustrade be performed according to the Draught Letter-B'[528] of James's devising.

It is a matter of taste whether to rejoice in, or deplore, the balustrade thus wilfully added; yet its addition does not impair the edifice to any noticeable extent, nor, we would suggest, was its arbitrary introduction opposed, in spirit, to the edifice so fluently and empirically conceived. As to the cathedral as a whole, it must be beyond doubt or question that it represents the outstanding building of a period rich in architectural history in the same degree as the figure of Wren completely overshadows his contemporaries and makes of him, very rightly, the most celebrated architect of his time. In this sense, St Paul's has a quality of uniqueness which makes appraisal difficult and comparison impossible and, in the absence of any standard of evaluation which could cogently be applied to it, it has called forth many opinions of somewhat arbitrary judgement. Stephen Wren gleefully drew attention to the fact, which later critics have been glad to reiterate, that 'St Peter's took 176 years to build, and fourteen architects were employed upon its design and construction'[529] while St Paul's was completed by one man in less than thirty-five years; yet if some critics have rejoiced to pronounce that 'all this wonderful array of talent' epitomized by the celebrated architects of St Peter's 'did not succeed in producing a building finer than St Paul's'[530] they have confused cause and effect; for, however questionable a qualitative comparison between the two buildings must be, it is obvious that the virtues of St Paul's derive precisely from the fact that it was the product of a single mind, while the defects of St Peter's are clearly the result of the irreconcilability of the many, if brilliant, minds of different architectural ideals producing a necessarily heterogeneous edifice.

Apart from such inept comparison, St Paul's has been represented as 'the greatest church in Christendom'[531] possessed of the 'noblest dome in Christendom',[532] but such judgements are unhelpful towards an understanding of the cathedral, or of Wren's architecture in general; this, as we shall see in a later part of this study, was profoundly conditioned by the age which witnessed its

136. St Paul's, interior.

creation, and is not therefore relevantly comparable to St Peter's. It must suffice to say here, in conclusion, that St Paul's is eminently the result of the manner in which it was devised. Without applying the standards of strict Renaissance architecture, it could hardly be said that the cathedral was faultless: there are visual effects in the design of the foundations of the western towers which are open to criticism only in a lesser degree than the infelicitous solution of the crossing where the non-concentricity of arches has been generally recognized as a disturbing element. On the other hand, however much Wren has been lauded as 'scrupulously careful that the actual construction should be of the soundest',[533] and praised for his 'good, solid architecture, constructed on the finest principles of tradition',[534] we have seen that the structural insufficiency of the piers of the cathedral had become apparent even before the drum and dome were built; here we have an instance of what was, basically, unsound construction and the additional factor of Wren's building the piers at a time when he was yet far away from

any decision of the size, shape – and consequently, weight – of the dome which would rest on those piers. And if we have stressed throughout this account of the cathedral's erection the fact that, in practically every part of it, design preceded actual construction only by a short span of time; if we have emphasized that design itself was progressing in a piecemeal fashion; and if we have demonstrated that at the outset of building operations Wren's concept of the whole edifice was not only fragmentary and vague, but totally different from the edifice finally built: then we must also point to the astounding fact that such a degree of unity should have been achieved by so disjointed a method of design. And this, we think, is the highest tribute that can be paid to Wren. The faults of the building, as recognized, were the result of the manner of its contriving; its success, however, its general homogeneity, was achieved in spite of a method of design which, in other hands, might easily have produced an heterogeneous assembly of parts.

If it may be said that the selective use of precedent provides one of the most suggestive indications not only to an architect's work, but also to his mind, then an examination of such influences as may be held to have affected Wren's work will provide a clue to his sources as well as his inclinations and predilections. The question of influence on Wren has been controversial in the past. Some of our architect's eulogists have gone so far as to doubt altogether the potency of any external influences which may have contributed towards the formation of his style;[535] others, in an endeavour to credit Wren with an originality capable of supplying the inspiration which precedent and a knowledge of historical example provide, have only recognized the results of such influences in order to imply their regret at the fact;[536] others yet have reduced the architecture of the Renaissance to its dissected formal elements and, finding that Wren 'had exactly the same "properties" to work with as all others working in the same mode',[537] have ventured to see his originality in the novel combinations of such elements which he may have invented. Yet to attribute too great a share to a purely personal taste expressing itself in architectural work would be to ignore the homogeneity of a period of civilization and to reduce the sequence of styles to an arbitrary succession of individual modes of thought. If such a method is not justifiable on historical grounds, it leaves a suspicion of uncritical eulogy being at work, for 'to derive all from native power, to owe nothing to another, is the praise which men, who do not much think on what they are saying, bestow sometimes upon others, and sometimes on themselves'.[538]

In Wren's case there is neither need nor reason to deny the existence of influences. Not only is there no cause to think that a scientist, suddenly turned architect, should have evolved a style of his own in a splendid isolation of aesthetic inventiveness; but even more unreasonable would it be to claim as original a style which offers such a wealth of parallels with other architects' works and books. If we are going to trace, in detail, influences which may be clearly recognizable in Wren's work, we shall confine ourselves to such parallels which can, either by documentary evidence or by great probability, be corroborated and substantiated; but these, no less than the divergences from the work of his predecessors and contemporaries, will provide suggestive indications of the true nature of Wren's art.

The influences operative on Wren can be classed into three categories which, though interdependent and to some degree complementary, can, for convenience, be treated separately; and though we shall discuss in succession the influences stemming from national precedent, from the architecture of France as Wren saw it in 1665, and the architecture of the Italian Renaissance, these three complexes will be linked by what we would consider the most important evidence in an assessment such as this, namely the sale catalogue of Wren's library which permits a close insight not only into his theoretical knowledge, but also his predilections.[539]

It will not occupy us long to deal with such domestic architecture which may have exerted an influence on Wren's style. There having been no question at any time of Wren's career of embracing Jacobean or Tudor modes of building in a genuine spirit, the influence of English Renaissance architecture must, of necessity, have been extremely slender. Questionable claims have, indeed, been made for the 'unbroken tradition of the school of which Wren was the representative',[540] but neither such inference, nor the existence of that mythical 'school', allegedly founded by Inigo Jones, can be demonstrated. Evelyn's opinion may have been a youthful exaggeration when, arrived at Naples, he thought that there was 'little more to be seen in the rest of the civil world, after Italy, France, Flanders, and the Low Countries, but plain and prodigious barbarism';[541] but we may accept the verdict of Sir Roger Pratt who had 'no doubt that the most beautiful buildings of these times are chiefly to be seen in Italy and France' and who, in 'having nothing remarkable but the banqueting house at Whitehall and the portico of St Paul's',[542] summed up, if not the number of edifices, then at least the only personality whose work on English soil stood as the touchstone of future generations.

We can thus, ignoring Webb's and even Pratt's, confine ourselves to the work of Inigo Jones to examine its relevance to Wren's. There is no evidence to show that Wren ever met Jones,[543] but it must go without saying that he would have been familiar with most of Jones's buildings then existent. Yet two reservations impose themselves right at the outset: the influence of Jones on Wren was bound to be limited not only by reason of the small number of Jones's executed works; it was limited even more by the fact that while the bulk of Wren's *œuvre* consisted in ecclesiastical architecture, most of Jones's had been secular, be it on the princely scale of his Whitehall plans, or on the more modest scale of such houses as Shaftesbury, Ashburnham, Lindsey, and the piazza of St Paul's, Covent Garden.

Turning first to ecclesiastical architecture, Wren could, at best, have found but slender inspiration in the few examples which his predecessor had left. Not only was the early Stuart period – as, indeed, the latter would have been but for the Great Fire – occupied in only a very minor degree with the building of churches; but also must the majority of those ascribed to Jones be ruled out of consideration in this examination: we cannot here consider the church of St Alban, allegedly designed by him[544] whose scheme Wren is supposed to have followed in his own rebuilding; nor can we perceive that the church of St Catherine Cree and the chapel of Lincoln's Inn, the former ascribed to Jones with as much doubt as the latter can be with certainty, may have exercised any influence on Wren's own excursions into the 'Gothick'.

This must be considered by the way; for Jones, like Wren, 'never was designed for a Gothic architect'.[545] But likewise, the dubious ascription to Jones, as well as the nature of the famous porch of St Mary's, Oxford, must be ruled out of consideration for even if Jones's authorship could be proved, we are aware of no parallels which it might have inspired in Wren's work. We are thus left with the cathedral portico and with Jones's austere church of St Paul, Covent Garden. This latter has been severely, if unjustly, criticized[546] yet, however little we may agree with such strictures, there is nothing in Wren's own work which would remind us of Jones's little gem. True, the Doric order which graces Jones's grave portico was to be frequently employed by Wren, but the scheme of the church, and particularly of its portico, was to find no echoes in Wren's designs. For in none of his churches did Wren plan a porch permitting access from three sides – the sole instance at St Magnus being a later alteration, as we have seen – as altogether Wren never seems to have built his church porches as places of circulation and congregation, as Jones had done.[547] As to the interior planning, certain of Wren's churches may display some similarity to the plain, oblong, galleried hall which Jones had described as 'the finest barn in England'; but there is little reason to think that Jones's concept actively influenced Wren's essays in comparable types of plan beyond providing, at most, the general outline of a prototype.

The portico and exterior casing of the cathedral, however, permit more explicit comparisons and thus bear oblique testimony to the celebrity which that architectural 'piece in itself' possessed. We can point, for instance, to the windows of the side elevations which Jones had formed round-headed within a straight, rectangular frame, for this very type occurs not only in Wren's first architectural work, the chapel of Pembroke College, Cambridge, and, not unnaturally, in some of the early designs for the cathedral,[548] but is found again, as we have noted, in the elevations of St Nicholas, St Edmund, St Magnus, and St Anne, Soho. Similar parallels can be traced between Jones's employment of circular lights above such round-headed, rectangularly-framed windows, for Wren used such a scheme applied to door treatments, principally at St Lawrence, St Nicholas, St Dionis, and St Anne, Soho;[549] while lastly the resemblance of Wren's 'Dean's Door' with Jones's 'lesser doors' may perhaps be noted as a possible, but solitary link outside Wren's earliest period.

Turning to the portico itself, which 'hath contracted the Envy of all Christendom upon our Nation for a piece of Architecture not to be paralleled in these last Ages of the World',[550] it is not possible to point to any of its features and definitely attribute to their precedent such parallels as may be found in Wren's work; it is possible, as we have mentioned, that the carved scrolls originally intended for the buttresses of St Edmund's were inspired by the cathedral portico; it is equally possible that the buttresses of Jones's work were the progenitors of those at St Mary, Aldermanbury, and St Mary-le-Bow. But many diverse instances could equally be held responsible for these three examples, so that it is neither safe nor justifiable to ascribe them to Jones's influence. The most cogent case of such is found, not unnaturally, in the

warrant design of 1675, for here, dismayed by the successive rejection of his various schemes, Wren saw one way of satisfying his patrons by considerable borrowing from Jones, and it is unnecessary to point to the striking similarities of portico and transepts which exist between Jones's work and Wren's project. It is significant, however, to point to the date: for while, excepting the instance of the 'Dean's Door', none of the parallel details of windows and doors which we have mentioned can be dated much later than 1672, the striking fact appears that subsequent to that date even such minimal Jonesian influence as we have traced disappeared completely. Seen in this light, the warrant design is in the nature of an anachronism; and the fact that neither Wren's previous scheme of 1673 nor the cathedral as built bear any resemblance to any work of Jones's, would point not only to the narrow boundary, but also to the very limited period during which Wren's design can be said to have been influenced by Jones.

Turning to domestic architecture, this position appears with even greater emphasis. If Wren were really to be accepted as the creator of the 'comfortable brick-and-quoin' architecture, the divergence from Jones would be complete; but, even though such design represented by no means Wren's only concept of smaller scale domestic architecture, such other types as were possibly projected by him, on paper only, could in no way be connected with Jonesian precedent.[551]

One single parallel of significance can be found in a comparison between the scheme which Wren devised, though it failed of execution, for a piazza to surround the cathedral, and the piazza which Jones had built at Covent Garden, of which his church formed the centre-piece. Wren followed, it seems, not only the general scheme of the arcades, reminiscent of Bologna or, according to Evelyn, of Livorno,[552] but also in points of detail, such as the rustication of the arcades; and if he deviated from Jones's buildings in the treatment of the attic storeys, the giant pilasters of the intermediate floors are clearly in descent from the Covent Garden, and possibly also from the Lincoln's Inn Fields, examples.

It has been said that 'Wren inherited the secret of masculinity from Inigo Jones and tempered it with his own humanity',[553] but, whatever intangible qualities may be thus referred to, it must be evident from the above that it would be a gross exaggeration to assume that Wren's style should have been formed to any considerable extent by the one classical precedent which was before his eyes in his own country. That Wren admired Jones's work appears borne out by contemporaneous evidence which testifies to his concern for the safety of the Banqueting House at the time of the Whitehall fire.[554] But admiration for Jones's work did not entail discipleship, as can be seen in Wren's finished work; apart from this, Wren's appreciation of the classical beauties of the Banqueting House did not prevent him from projecting either the addition of a totally inappropriate tetrastyle giant order, or even the radical alteration of the whole elevation by a transposition of

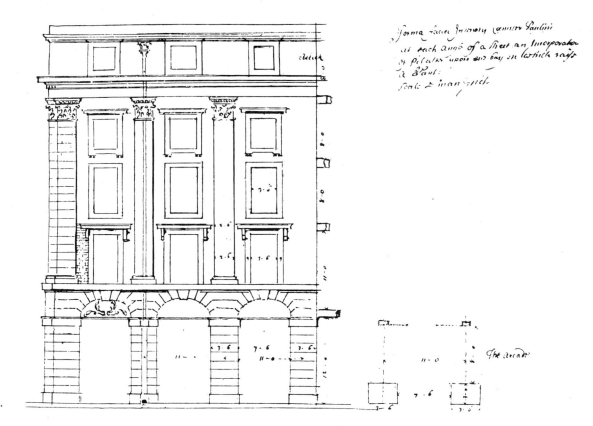

137. St Paul's, piazza design.

Jones's window pediments to the upper floors and the conversion of the inner bays flanking the entrance into niches containing statuary. In addition, Wren's attitude to the fate of the Queen's House at Greenwich provides a cogent indication of the fact that, whatever his admiration for Jones's work, it was to Queen Mary and not to Wren that we owe its preservation, for Wren, as we have seen in the preceding section, had not hesitated to project its demolition to enable the execution of one of his own schemes.[555]

Jones's influence is thus seen to have been but slight, and essentially confined to the earliest period of Wren's practice, while during his later years he seemed to have embraced concepts with which we could not presume Jones's sympathy had he known them. Thus, to have opined, as one of Wren's critics has done, that as he 'advanced in experience and mastery of his art . . . he returned to the purer and more strenuous architecture of Inigo Jones',[556] seems a perverse distortion of the facts when the advance of Wren's art into his distinct late manner[557] indicates a progressive estrangement from Jones's ideals. Beyond this stylistic comparison, however, an essential difference of character – the proper consideration of which belongs to the last part of this study – becomes apparent. For Wren's art was an intellectual synthesis composed, in an empirical fashion, of many factors; among these, however, the sensitive, poetical character associated with Inigo Jones[558] was conspicuously absent.

Before passing to a consideration of French and Italian influences on Wren's work, it is necessary to briefly discuss such as are supposed to have reached our architect from Holland. Theoreti-cally, there would be ample reason to presume that Dutch precedents should have played their part in the development of Wren's style, and that such should have been considerable has, indeed, been frequently suggested.[559] Historical precedent could reasonably have pointed to the Dutch and German pattern books which found popular acclaim in Tudor England and theory could have regarded them as the possible precursors of similar importations in later Stuart times. In fact, however, the religious ties between Protestant Holland and Anglican England have been proposed as a cogent reason and even the 'irritation at Dutch success and supremacy' in the fields of commerce and exploration has been proposed as the 'impelling force towards imitation' on the assumption that 'it was the fashion in England to adopt Dutch ideas and methods because it was seen that they invariably led to success'.[560]

Yet such conjectures transcend the bounds of the probable. If it were true that Charles II and the Royalist exiles 'came back fired with the beauty of the buildings which they had seen' in Holland, it would be difficult to explain the predominantly French orientation of the court of the penultimate Stuart in matters of dress and drama, music, or garden design. Nor was the period of commercial and naval rivalry between England and Holland after the Restoration, least of all the incursion of Dutch men of war up the River Thames, conducive to endear anything Dutch to the minds and tastes of thus humiliated Englishmen. If it were true that 'travellers like John Evelyn and Sir William Temple familiarized themselves with everything Dutch' so as to encourage and help to 'spread the already established vogue for Dutch art in many aspects',[561] Dryden would not have looked to French drama for models, nor would Wren have thought Paris the best place in which to study modern architecture. Lastly, it has been recognized that precisely at that period when Dutch influence might conceivably have been paramount, namely in the reign of William of Orange, such little as had ever existed had been superseded by the ubiquitious influence of Versailles, for the 'French Court and with it French culture, had taken the lead in Western civilization'.[562]

Thus it would seem that the importance of Dutch influence has been greatly exaggerated by previous authors. There appears little need to see any essentially Dutch sympathies in the employment of such artists as Rubens, Van Dyck, Lely, or even Godfrey Kniller, the first three of whom, we may note in parenthesis, received knighthoods from Stuart monarchs. On the other hand, the very sympathies with Holland which had characterized the Commonwealth and Protectorate would seem a potent psychological factor for causing a reversal in Restoration times, a reversal, indeed, which was not only wilful, but equally conditioned by the experiences and memories of King Charles and Royalist exiles. Finally, to stress the influence which a period of exile in Holland may have exercised on the exiles' tastes, and to minimize the impact of impressions received in France, would, in many instances, amount to an inversion of the lengths of time which Royalists spent in these several countries during the Interregnum.[563]

More concretely, the orientation of Sir Roger Pratt already hinted at, is made abundantly clear from his categorical statement that 'it is most certain, that no man deserves the name of an Architect, who has not been very well versed both in those old ones of Rome, as likewise the more modern ones of Italy and France'.[564] In analogy, even a cursory reading of Evelyn's diary reveals an incidence of superlatives pertaining to those periods of his travels in Italy and France, while Dutch architecture – and we must not forget that much of it was ultimately of Italian derivation – received but little commendatory mention. And if an undue Dutch sympathy on Evelyn's part has been inferred by the diarist's possession of an early Dutch work on the Five Orders,[565] it is not only permissible, but of greater cogency to see a more significant symptom in the fact that all the works which Evelyn translated and published were of French origin and Italian extraction.[566]

Turning, finally, to Wren, we can discuss the question of Dutch influence quite briefly. The fact that Wren had never been to Holland is well known; and if Wren's library list is examined it is found that among the numerous items concerning architecture, art, and antiquity, there is not a single Dutch book to be found.[567] Even allowing for the possibility of Wren's possessions of books which were dispersed before the compilation of the sale catalogue twenty-six years after his death, the absence of Dutch architectural books is striking and may even be interpreted as a refutation of the alleged importance of Dutch influence on the formation of his style. That Wren was not ignorant of Dutch books is quite probable, as we can assume him to have been familiar with such as possessed by Evelyn and certainly with Vingboon's work, of which Robert Hooke has recorded his possession.[568] Furthermore, it would have been strange if Wren had not been familiar with such prints and engravings of Dutch architecture as were to be bought in London, and this is the more likely for the fact that many of the engravers working for him and in connexion with his buildings had originally come from the Low Countries and northern Germany.

Dutch influence on Wren has mostly been presumed in those of his works in which brick was principally employed and elevations were enlivened by courses of stone quoins and stone surrounds to door-frames and windows.[569] Though Wren can only partially be regarded as the originator of what, in Queen Anne and Georgian times,[570] became the predominant style of domestic architecture, it is not necessarily to Dutch models that his essays in that mode are to be traced; there is no reason to minimize the influence of earlier English models[571] but, these apart, Wren's first-hand, visual experience with continental brick-and-quoin architecture provides a more logical precedent than a hypothetical knowledge of books which he may, or may not, have known or possessed. We neither can, nor need, enter here into a discussion of the connexions between the architecture of Henri IV and Louis XIII and contemporaneous work in the Low Countries; but it must be pointed out that all the prototypes for such works of Wren as have been described as 'in the Dutch manner' would have been seen by him during his visit to France in 1665.

At the time of Wren's visit, this fashion was already a style of the past to all intents and purposes, and Wren certainly had the opportunity of seeing its finest specimens. It does not seem likely that he should have been familiar with François Mansart's superb essay in this style, as the Château de Balleroy hardly lies within such a distance from Paris as we may presume to have limited Wren's excursions. But it must remain unquestionable that he had seen, and studied, the two finest examples in Paris itself, namely the Place des Vosges, then known as Place Royale, and the Place Dauphine, on the Ile de Cité, which gives on to the Pont Neuf opposite to the famous statue of Henri IV.[572] In the course of his 'prying into arts and trades' Wren is likely to have come across Pierre Le Muet's well-known book on architecture,[573] which, first published when the 'style Henri IV' was at its height, abounds in well-engraved examples. And we may well believe Wren to have been familiar with such buildings as the Château de Rosny,[574] though he has only left us a record of his impressions of 'the Mixtures of Brick and Stone, blue Tile and Gold' which he had seen at Versailles.[575]

Yet Wren's famous and often-quoted letter does not lead us to believe that much of his time was taken up with a study of examples of the 'style Henri IV', and his evident preoccupation with the essentially stone architecture of the late Valois period, as well as the more recent work of Le Mercier and Mansart, raises considerable problems in an attempt to discern what may legitimately be held to be distinct French influences on Wren's work. First and foremost, it must not be forgotten that the Renaissance in France derived its very inception and impetus from direct contact with Italy: just as Inigo Jones had gone there to 'converse with the masters', so du Cerceau, de l'Orme, and Bullant had gone to Italy some eighty years before him, on a mission exactly similar to his in its intention to study and measure the ruins and antiquities of Imperial Rome. Notwithstanding the differences between the Gallican Church and that of Rome which intermittently punctuate the entire period between the Council of Trent and Louis XIV's quarrel with the Papacy a century and a half later, the cultural connexions with Italy and the influence of Italian art on French development were inestimable: the glories of the Pléïade were of an essentially Italian begetting; and despite Leonardo's inactivity in France, despite the limitations of Serlio's, Vignola's, and Cellini's employments and the relatively unimportant nature of Il Rosso's and Primaticcio's executed work: their influence was of as great an importance as the mere presence in France of such men as Fra Jocundus, and of Tommaso Campanella a century later. It was Jean Martin who principally brought Italian architectural literature before the connoisseurs and artists of France;[576] it was due to Mazarin that the celebrated Scaramouche Fiorille collaborated with the great Molière,[577] and that, in 1640, the Sieur de Chambray was sent to Italy there to compile his well-known *Parallèle*, before long to be translated by John Evelyn.

In reality, the parallels which can be traced from Serlio's work at Fontainebleau and Ancy-le-Franc throughout a century to Mansart's[578] work in Paris and at Maisons are close enough to create a position where, in many points of detail, it becomes impossible to attribute a particular trait in Wren's design repertory alternatively to Italian derivation inspired by books, or to French derivation of the same Italian motif which he may have seen himself.[579]

But, even though Wren mentions a number of French architects and artists in his letter, it becomes quite clear from the context that the greatest impression was made on him by Bernini. The latter, at that period the most famous architect in Europe, had been invited by Louis XIV, as is well known, to submit plans for the completion of the Louvre. Bernini had been received in France with princely honours,[580] and Wren, perhaps by Lord St Alban's agency, had been able to meet the man and see the 'five little designs on paper, for which he had received as many thousand pistoles'. However brief their meeting, and however much Bernini may have been condemned by later critics,[581] it was the greatest impression Wren carried with him back to England.

Even so, it did not prove to be to the exclusion of French Renaissance architects and no more erroneous view could be held than that which would assert that 'in spite of Mansart's work' Inigo Jones's influence should have been responsible that 'Wren, on the whole, remained faithful to Palladio and the Ancients'.[582] How far Wren was 'faithful to Palladio' is a question to be discussed elsewhere. But how far Jones's supposed influence – in itself negligible, as we have seen – failed to displace French inspiration, we shall now have to consider, as there can be little doubt that 'the Kings Houses' no less than 'the incomparable Villas of Vaux and Maisons, Ruel [Rueil], Courances, Chilly, Essoane [Ecouen], St-Maur, St-Mande, Issy, Meudon, Rincy [Raincy], Chantilly, Verneul [Verneuil], Liencour [Liancour]', have left their trace in Wren's work as well as the 'many others, I have survey'd'.[583]

The most significant influence of French architecture is not, however, felt in such details as Wren's predilection for coupled pillars and pilasters which, though also to be found in Borromini's S. Agnese,[584] may point to an ubiquitious French precedent,[585] but in the planning of Wren's palatial schemes which, though none of them executed according to his first intentions, nor derivable from one particular French prototype, offer none the less the most obvious aspects of French inspiration. Such is, indeed, very noticeable in Wren's first Greenwich design in which, as we have noted, he had intended the long wings running down to the river to form a gigantic *cour d'honneur*, culminating in a paramount, dominating feature at the southern end. French inspiration is equally noticeable in the first designs for Hampton Court, where not only the prominent display of the equestrian statue of William III points to Blois and the old Hôtels de Ville of Paris and Compiègne or, perhaps with greater probability, to Bullant's treatment of the entrance court of Ecouen;[586] but where, also, the two *cours d'honneur* to the west and north are unmistakably of French lineage as the five avenues of the park converging on the centre of the east front are derived from multitudinous designs beginning with the unexecuted, but published, project for the great Porte et Place de France, and ending with the Place d'Armes at Versailles. Most cogently, French influence can be discerned in Wren's project for Winchester Palace; not only are the central dome and domed pavilions features which he had frequently seen in France,[587] but the entire layout of the scheme (Fig.138), the enormous forecourt, and organized out-buildings are eloquent echoes of the most monumental of French progenitors, such as Richelieu, the Palais Royal, and Versailles.

French influence is equally discernible in small, but significant details of design. Thus the large pediment which Wren projected for his second design for Hampton Court (Fig.93) and possibly built at the Trinity Almshouses may be an echo which the architect of Catherine de' Medici added to Philibert de l'Orme's building of St-Maur,[588] and the outline of Courances may have actually found its echo in Wren's schools at Appleby.[589] It would also be tempting

East View of the Kings House, and the adjoining Offices

Intended to have been finished by Sir Christopher Wren.

139. St Mary le Bow, porch.

140. F. Mansart, Hôtel Conti, Paris.

to look upon the elaborate entrance of Verneuil as the remote ancestor of the vaulting system which Wren employed in some of his City churches, notably at St Mary-at-Hill and SS. Anne and Agnes, for this may have been his first visual impression of a method by which a small dome is made the centre of four radiating barrel vaults forming, in plan, a Greek cross.[590] With greater confidence, we can derive the porches of St Bride and the design we have attributed to St Dunstan in the East (Figs.26, 27) to the entry which Wren had seen at the Château of Chilly.[591] But an outstanding detail of the influence of Mansart[592] can be discerned in Wren's design for the porch of Bow church: indeed, the large circular light touching the apex of the triangular pediment originally planned may not improbably have been derived from that conspicuous feature in the entry of Mansart's church of Ste-Marie de la Visitation;[593] but there can be little doubt that the final development in Cheapside had its progenitor in the monumental entry, embracing the two main storeys, of the Hôtel Conti, where not only the distinctive striated recession, but even the oval light flanked by carved figures put the derivation beyond doubt.

Many other details of French influence in Wren's work could

be mentioned: thus the centre-piece of the court of the Palais Royal[594] shows a broken cornice in a triangular pediment and an intruding round-headed window which bring to mind the east gable of St Peter's (Fig.48); the monumental treatment of this motif in the executed transepts of St Paul's, however, provides so striking a similarity to the interior east elevation of the Louvre, designed by Mansart in 1664, as to tempt us to think that Wren may actually have seen those drawings, though the addition of the porch of St Paul's points not to French, but to Italian inspiration.[595] Less strikingly, the domed pavilions and centre-piece of Le Mercier's Château Richelieu, which Wren is likely to have known from engravings,[596] are reminiscent of the original design for Winchester Palace (Fig.87); and the same architect's project for the east front of the Louvre, with its repetition of small, domed sections symmetrically articulating the façade may have provided the germinal idea for what Wren was to plan in his great project for Whitehall Palace (Fig.87). Likewise, it may not be too much to suggest the courtyard elevation of the Luxembourg Palace[597] to have been the inspiration, albeit far more elaborate, for Wren's 1696 warrant design for Greenwich (Fig.105), particularly as the

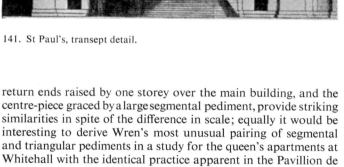

141. St Paul's, transept detail.

142. F. Mansart, design for the Louvre, east elevation of the court.

return ends raised by one storey over the main building, and the centre-piece graced by a large segmental pediment, provide striking similarities in spite of the difference in scale; equally it would be interesting to derive Wren's most unusual pairing of segmental and triangular pediments in a study for the queen's apartments at Whitehall with the identical practice apparent in the Pavillion de Flore at the Louvre.[598]

The architecture of the earlier Renaissance offers no less striking parallels with Wren's practice, but the connexions which can be established are of far greater uncertainty. The windows of the south front of the Sheldonian Theatre may, indeed, be compared with those of the old Hôtel de Ville of Paris; the *entresol* treatment first projected for Winchester Palace may actually have been derived from Bullant's usage at Ecouen[599] which is one of the few houses actually named by Wren in his letter. But though Wren had much in common with Bullant,[600] and not a little with du Cerceau and de l'Orme, we cannot validly establish any direct and indubitable influence on their part. What is more, one suggestive difference can be mentioned in that all three of them had studied in Italy, all three of them – whatever the divergences in their work

from Italian practice – had published books on the architecture of antiquity,[601] and that their achievement is national only insofar as Italian Renaissance precepts are not slavishly followed but have not, during that early period, as yet engendered what might be called a truly indigeneous tradition. Comparison with their theory and practice is, therefore, inconclusive as Italian precedent is common to both; and it is for this reason that we have here omitted any discussion of Mansart's three domed churches in relation to Wren's own dome designs; for though we would not doubt that their splendour must have made a profound impression upon him, it is feasible to discount a direct influence of Mansart in favour of Italian models; while, in anticipation, it may be said even now that Wren's solution as finally evolved was indebted neither to Mansart's nor to Italian domes, but wholly the result of his own originality.[602]

Having considered such buildings, in England, the Low Countries, and France, acquaintance with which may have influenced Wren's development as an architect, we must now turn to the inspiration, less direct but unquestionably far more potent, of Italy. Wren never saw with his own eyes the classic examples of

Renaissance architecture on Italian soil and, strange though it may seem, this deficiency, which would have been considered a serious shortcoming in the education of any gentleman of that and the subsequent century, has been suggested as beneficial to Wren's art by some of his critics.[603] What visual experience Wren may have lacked, however, was amply compensated for by his acquaintance with engravings and such Italian books on architecture as proved the keystone of European styles for 200 years and which, in countless editions, translations, and paraphrases, wielded an influence of incalculable potency on an entire period of art history throughout the length and breadth of a whole continent.

It has been suggested that 'Wren appears to have known little of what was being done in Italy and elsewhere on the Continent'[604] and that there is no 'evidence to prove him to have been intimately familiar with Italian architecture other than that reproduced by Serlio and Palladio'.[605] These assertions, however, do not accord with fact, as the sale catalogue of the combined libraries of Sir Christopher and Christopher Wren, already alluded to, proves beyond doubt that Wren must have been as acquainted with classical as with contemporaneous, with Italian as well as French architecture. Italy, past and present, is amply covered by the possession of Alberti, Serlio, Vitruvius, d'Aviler, Fontana, Bellori, de Rossi, Desgodetz, Boissard, Bosio, and no fewer than three Palladio editions; Wren's personal knowledge of French architecture was aptly complemented by a volume of du Cerceau; if, finally, the names of Scamozzi, Cataneo, and Barbaro do not appear at all in the catalogue, Wren may well have known them from copies in the Bodleian or Arundelian libraries or the libraries of friends, or, failing that, he would have found them condensed, if at third hand, in John Evelyn's translation of de Chambray which contains 'the marrow and very substance of no less than ten judiciary authors, Palladio, Scamozzi, Serlio, Vignola, Barbaro, Cataneo, L'Alberti, Viola, Bulland, and de Lorme'.[606]

Wren's familiarity with Vitruvius at a very early date can safely be presumed even though the library catalogue does not list an earlier edition than Perrault's of 1684. But it is quite likely that during his student days at Oxford[607] he had seen one of the copies possessed by the Bodleian Library and almost certain that he had seen the 'noble MS of Vitruvius' in the Arundelian Library which, by John Evelyn's agency, was given by Henry Howard to the Royal Society.[608] There are even indications that he must have been familiar with and, indeed, inspired by, the Roman author as early as his days at Wadham, for among the 'Catalogue of New Theories, Inventions'[609] which testifies to the precocious versatility of Wren, it would be tempting to connect the 'designs tending to strength, convenience and beauty in building' with the three Vitruvian stipulations[610] which, copied or paraphrased, have reappeared in the works of Alberti, Serlio, Palladio, Wotton, Pratt,

Evelyn, and Sir John Soane. Wren's study of Vitruvius during these early years was almost certainly not in connexion with architecture, but with astronomy, science, and engineering: he mentions the Roman author as an authority on eastern dialling[611] and it is highly probable that his translation of Oughtred's work on geometrical dialling led him to a study of the relevant Vitruvian passages.[612] Likewise, it would be feasible to relate to Vitruvian precedent Wren's invention of a water-clock,[613] of 'Divers Engines for raising Water',[614] for 'A Pavement, harder, fairer and cheaper than Marble',[615] for 'The best way for reckoning Time, Way and Longitude at Sea',[616] and the various items relating to fortifications and defence.[617]

But to trace Vitruvian influence in Wren's architectural work would be neither warranted nor feasible, for so completely did the Roman's precepts penetrate the architectural thought and practice of Renaissance Europe, so numerous were the editions, translations of, and commentaries on his work during the period, that it represented an all-pervasive and altogether inescapable influence.[618] On the other hand, the Ten Books of Architecture were, in many respects, of but limited use to the Renaissance, and thus we can, within the context of this study, regard its fifteenth- and sixteenth-century successors as of greater importance to Wren than the original work.

That Wren might be considered the disciple of the earliest of Renaissance architectural theorists has never, to our knowledge, been suggested. On the other hand, much, perhaps too much, emphasis has been placed upon the influence on Wren of Serlio's book and the treatise and work of Palladio. Considering, however, that much of what is contained in the Five and in the Four Books had already been adumbrated by Alberti, and considering that Wren was familiar with both the fifteenth- and the sixteenth-century theorists, it would obviously be invidious to ascribe an ascendancy of the latter two over the earlier Renaissance master solely by reason of the fact that it was Palladio whose book should attain to considerable celebrity in England.

An influence which might solely be due to Alberti is possibly represented in the podiums, or pedestals, which Wren so frequently employed as substructures to his elevations; we have met this feature at many of Wren's churches, such as St Mary at Hill, St Michael's, Wood Street, St Dionis, St Mildred's, Poultry, St Lawrence, and many others; it formed a conspicuous part of the great model design of St Paul's and would tempt us to recognize it as an instance of Wren's following Alberti's stipulation that the ideal church should stand upon a platform, in token of the fact that its function is one raised above the turmoil of everyday life.[619] The fact that Palladio does not, in fact, make any such stipulation but, on the contrary, expresses a preference for his order to stand on the ground, would lend probability to this view, even though his Church of the Redentore at Venice conforms to Alberti's demand to perfection. Furthermore, when Alberti's preferences are borne in mind, there may be some significance in the fact that Wren used piers, instead of pillars, in the interior of St Paul's and St Clement Danes;[620] for Alberti did not sanction the employment of columns supporting arches as representing a contradiction between the three-dimensional member and the two-dimensional wall,[621] and, while his stipulation links columns with straight entablatures, the arches of a vaulted building must rest on piers or pilasters – a condition which Wren would seem to have fulfilled to the letter in the interior of the cathedral.

It is true that Wren was acting quite contrary to humanist, if not Counter-Reformatory, concepts in designing the majority of his City churches on the basilican plan which Alberti, and others, had never considered proper for churches, but had relegated to juridical buildings.[622] The fact that in two churches where Wren's planning was not conditioned by tradition or cramped by site, namely at St Magnus and St James's, Westminster, he evolved a seven-bay plan recalling Alberti[623] may possess some significance, but it would not be reasonable to draw far-reaching conclusions seeing that Wren's plans were the result of circumstance more often than the expression of personal preferences which, as we shall see, show striking analogies to humanist theory and practice. It is evident that Wren's continuous preoccupation with centrally planned structures was in complete conformity with Italian humanistic conceptions:[624] Alberti had recommended nine geometrical figures to serve as basic ground plans for churches, and while three of them are developments from the square, we are left with the square itself, the circle, the hexagon, octagon, decagon, and dodecagon.[625] Serlio, explicit in recommending the centralized plan, enlarged the range by advocating the circle, the pentagon, hexagon, octagon, the square with inscribed octagon, the Greek cross plan with circular chapels, and, originally, the oval.[626] Thus, seeing that only Alberti, but neither Serlio[627] nor Palladio sanctions the decagon as a basic ground plan, his influence might be suggested in so singular a design as that of St Benet Fink (Fig.28); and if the vague attribution of the gate of the Arsenal at Venice could be substantiated, we could pertinently see its echo in the unusual design for the doorway of All Hallows, Lombard Street, unless Wren should here have been influenced by a knowledge of the several employments of this feature which Scamozzi executed in Central Europe.[628] Lastly, it would be tempting to connect Wren's semicircular breakings of the cornice of triangular pediments, such as we have seen in the great model design of St Paul's and in the projected north porch of St Stephen's with Alberti's practice at San Sebastiano in Mantua, but as Wren's knowledge of that building cannot be established, it is equally possible that he derived the motif from classical instances.[629]

If an Albertian influence has not previously been suggested, the influence of Serlio's well-known work[630] has frequently been stressed. But to regard this book as 'probably the most important single influence on Wren in early days' because Serlio was 'the first and for a long time the only great Italian writer on architecture to be published in English'[631] is not a conclusive argument in view of the predominantly Italian and French provenance of Wren's own books; on the other hand, the assertion that Peake's translation of 1611[632] should have provided a 'textbook which seems to have been used constantly by Wren'[633] is rendered of dubious veracity seeing that Wren's library did not even contain a copy of that version, but lists a Venetian edition of 1663.[634]

Wren's knowledge and possession of the work make it necessary to consider it in greater detail, but, at the outset, a reservation needs to be made: although Serlio's book contains considerable sections on historical precedent and antiquity, it is not necessary to perceive a specifically Serlian influence if such have found some reflection in Wren's work, particularly as similar, and frequently identical, material has also been treated by other writers with whom Wren was familiar: thus if among Wren drawings a large, carefully drawn plan of the Roman Pantheon has been preserved,[635] it is not necessarily from Serlio[636] that Wren derived the details, as plan, elevation, and section of the same building form not the least conspicuous part of Palladio's Fourth Book and other works in Wren's possession.[637] Equally, if the west front of St Mary-le-Bow (Fig.18) should unquestionably represent a variation on the triumphal arch motif, it is possible, but by no means unquestionable, that Wren should have derived it from the relevant illustration in Serlio.[638]

We have already indicated the alternative of a Serlian derivation for the early drafts for St Mary-le-Bow, the triangular pediments and circular lights of which Wren would have seen in the Italian book[639] as well as Mansart's actual building. Also, when Wren drew the elevation of what Elmes called an 'Ionick Temple',[640] we may regard the design as much a prototype for the west elevation of St Magnus (Fig.22) as a progeny of the classic Serlian tetrastyle Ionic portico which produced innumerable copies and paraphrases in subsequent literature and work.[641] Equally, we might establish a connexion between Wren's plan for St Swithin's with those ideal plans given by Serlio in his Fifth Book, among which we can find a square with inscribed octagon. But not only would such a connexion be tenuous; also, Serlio's own derivations are evident as his recommendation is hardly original, for in this form of centralized plan he was not only referring back to Early Christian precedent, but equally to those complex centralized structures which Leonardo had planned.

The implications of Serlian influence on Wren are further narrowed by the fact that much of his material was not original and represents an exposition of the ideas of Peruzzi,[642] and with Peruzzi we enter an intellectual territory outside Serlio's genius, the domain of Leonardo, Bramante, and the early Renaissance humanists of whom Serlio is only a relatively articulate exponent. To cite but one or two instances, the employment of small domed

143. St Paul's, west front study, detail.

subsidiary rooms we have noted at St Clement Danes and St Andrew, Holborn, may be related to Serlian illustrations,[643] just as the plan of the unexecuted church of St Mary, Lincoln's Inn Fields, could be connected with Serlian prototypes. But in both cases Serlio could only be regarded as second-hand inspiration as his versions were no more than paraphrases on Byzantine precedents and on Leonardo's ideas on centralized churches where a central dome is surrounded by subsidiary domes;[644] ideas which were to influence not only Bramante, but also Raphael and Peruzzi.

Palladio, it should be noted, had never embraced the concept of a multiplicity of domes; and when he planned domed pavilions at the extremities of one of his villas[645] a parallel may be drawn with the domed flanking staircases which Wren had originally projected for Trinity College library. Yet, reflecting that some of the more cogent comparisons we have drawn with Serlio's work either remained unexecuted or were, like the porch of Bow church, radically altered in execution, the hypothetical Palladian derivation of those unbuilt Cambridge domes is only a minor instance of Palladio's concepts as reflected in Wren's work, and we must now turn to a more detailed consideration of the influence of the architectural work which was to become the most famous in England; remarking, even at the outset, that this examination should not only serve the purpose of determining the degree of Wren's adherence to, respectively divergence from, Palladio, but

also to provide a cogent, if oblique, indication of the relationship between Wren and the Palladian movement which succeeded, and superseded, him.[646]

Before turning to architecture itself, we would point to the possibility of Italian humanist principles in general[647] and Palladian precepts in particular, making themselves felt in the City plan of 1666; there is no reason to assume that Wren should not have been familiar with Palladio's work at that date, and, while other influences can obviously be perceived in the celebrated project,[648] at least one outstanding feature seems to point to Palladio: the way in which Wren proposed to place his churches at the top of streets bears a significantly close likeness to Palladio's recommendations on street planning,[649] just as Wren's predilection for piazzas as expressed in his project clearly indicates a Palladian concept.[650] A similar derivation could be suggested for the façades of the churches envisaged by Wren, for we have little doubt that he considered the most beautiful treatment of a west front in the form of a portico based on the scheme of the Hellenic temple front[651] either of tetrastyle or hexastyle plan; the fact that in some of his finest churches, such as St Paul's, St Magnus, and the cryptic 'St Edmund, Bloomsbury', Wren used the complete scheme of a portico, and in many lesser instances used parts of it, such as a pillar-supported pediment, would point to a predilection closely paralleled by Palladio. Unlike Jones, as we have seen, but in conformity with Palladio's practice, Wren never built a portico,

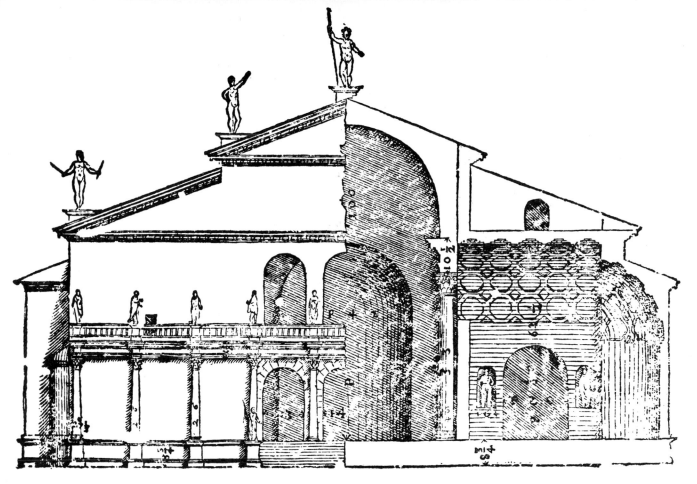

144. Temple of Peace, elevation and section (from Palladio).

excepting at the cathedral, which permits approach from three sides and affords sufficient depth for perambulation;[652] and the derivation from Italian precept seems clear, Alberti having already recommended the inclusion of porticos even in the case of circular structures, and Palladio having regarded them, on historical precedent, as indispensable.[653]

But the most interesting instance of Palladian influence is probably provided by Wren's treatment of some of his fronts, and, more particularly, the arrangement of double pediments which he sometimes, though infrequently, employed. The most primitive of these must be the early project for a west front for St Paul's which can almost certainly be traced back to Palladio's illustration of the Temple of Peace[654] and where specifically Palladian influence seems the more likely for Wren's suggestive inclusion of a semi-circular window which does not form part of the Roman temple front and to the significance of which we shall have to return again.

More concretely, Palladian influences are unmistakable in the treatment of the south front of the Sheldonian Theatre, the east fronts of St Margaret Pattens and of St George, for in these instances Wren adopted Palladio's distinctive and original treatment of the façades of his three Venetian churches by using a central pediment, supported on its own large order, which is flanked by two halves of a second pediment, also supported on its own, though smaller, order. Examining this parallel further, how-

ever, we shall find that the superficial similarity here existent masks a complete diversity of intention and purpose. Palladio's own usage may be traced back to Vitruvius[655] as well as to Lombardic Romanesque and fifteenth-century precedent;[656] within the context of his three churches, however, it represents the logical development of the premiss into the form of two inter-penetrating temple fronts,[657] each of which retains its own order of pillars and pilasters. The significance of this interpretation lies in the fact that it represents the classical solution of one of the basic problems of Christian church architecture, for this combination of two temple fronts was the logically, aesthetically, and intellectually most satisfying way of fronting a basilican church in such a manner that the design was no meaningless façade to the building, inexpressive of its interior disposition and unrelated to its plan: in the classic solutions of the Redentore and of San Francesco della Vigna, the central pediment is as clear an indication of the nave as are the sectional lower pediments of the aisles, and thus fulfil to perfection the humanist stipulation that the façade 'should correspond to the inside of the building and from it one should be able to grasp the form of the building and all its proportions'.[658]

Wren, we may note, once made use of a superposition of a double minor order over a major order of pillars[659] the latter of which carried a normal pediment; considering, though, that the lower order was not related to any imaginarily superposed front, but served merely to articulate and subdivide the front itself, this may be an instance of Wren using a motif derived from Palladio without being actuated to do so by the logical concept which had been responsible for its origination. In considering Wren's usage of double pediments, a similar position will become apparent.

It is suggestive that among the twenty-one churches on the basilican plan which Wren designed, only one displays the logical solution of the problem of external expression of internal disposition, and that this single instance should occur in a church of a very early period of Wren's career, namely St George's, Botolph Lane. While the square plan of the church (Fig.5) only permits the appellation 'basilican' by some stretch of the imagination and by the placing of the pillars and method of roofing clearly showing Wren's endeavour of making a square space appear rectangular, the exterior treatment at the east end conformed very closely to Palladio's concept, though the proportions employed (partially as a result of the steeply sloping site) did not permit an adherence to the Palladian preference for the elimination of the podium.

Palladio's device of the combination of two pediments found but two more employments in the corpus of Wren's work: at the Sheldonian Theatre, designed even before St George's, and at St Margaret Pattens some fourteen years after. In these instances, however, it is impossible to speak of a logical application of Palladian precedent: at the Sheldonian Theatre the nature of the interior did not by any means dictate such exterior treatment; and at the church of St Margaret the employment is altogether illogical as the church belongs to the group of single-aisled plans. These facts raise a doubt whether Wren was altogether aware of the significance of the Palladian device he was there using; for his rare, and mostly inappropriate employment of it might suggest that it had become, in these instances, the solution of a decorative problem and not, in three cases out of four, the solution of the design problem for which Palladio had devised it. Such usage – not to call it misuse – would mark Wren as a blind imitator of the Italian rather than a creative follower; and we would count it to his credit that it was only on so rare and isolated occasions that he borrowed from Palladio's vocabulary a motif the significance of which was evidently a matter of indifference to him.

A superficial similarity between an early elevation for Greenwich (Fig.103) and Palladio's Villa Trissino at Meledo[660] might be remarked upon, as well as the fact that a Palladian propensity might even be detected in Wren's admiration for Bernini's Louvre project which, as has been pointed out, can be regarded as a descendant of Palladio's famous cortile of the Palazzo Porto Colleoni.[661] But as external reasons must partly, though not solely, have been responsible for Wren's divergences from Palladian theory and practice, we would now turn to consider some details and peculiarities of design doubtless conditioned by personal preference rather than extraneous circumstance.

Thus it is probable that Wren derived the employment of circular and other lights within triangular pediments[662] from

145. St George's, east front.

Palladian precedent, for not only can no parallel be found with the Albertian idea of using more than one light,[663] but also is it unlikely that Wren should have been familiar with such earlier examples as Francesco di Giorgio's Sta Maria al Calcinaia at Cortona or Antonio da San Gallo's Santo Biagio at Montepulciano, from which Palladio himself may have derived the idea. The semicircular lights in the pediments of the early St Paul's draft (Fig.34), in the south front of the Sheldonian Theatre and at St Mary-at-Hill, clearly recall Palladio's façade of San Francesco della Vigna; likewise, Wren's singular employment at the latter church of a combination of the Doric and Composite orders may be related to Palladio's use of an equally unorthodox combination.[664] The semicircular window vertically divided into three is a feature which neither Wren nor Palladio would have derived from Rome or from antiquity, for this forms one of the distinct influences which the architecture of Venice exerted on the Vicentine master; if originally derived from Byzantium,[665] the type is found in such profusion at Venice[666] as to have earned it the name of 'Venetian window'. Wren, in his employments of it, could have found – or, we might even say, did find – Palladian precedent in all of Palladio's Venetian churches, that is, in the front of San Francesco, the nave and apse fenestration of San Giorgio Maggiore and of the Redentore, in the little church of le Zitelle, as well as in the triple occurrence in the façade of the now destroyed Santa Lucia;[667] likewise, he would have seen it in the woodcuts of Palladio's villas Pisani, Foscari, and Thiene, which appear in the Second Book.[668] But Wren's employment of such windows is not only rare: it is also, significantly, confined to the earliest years of his practice; on the other hand, only two of Wren's four employments[669] can definitely be traced to Palladian precedent, namely in the early St Paul's design and at St Anne's, Soho (Fig.24), where the triple division of the windows is used in preference to the concentric circles found in the Sheldonian Theatre and at St Mary-at-Hill; while, lastly, the very size of the instance of St Anne may actually also point to the precedent of several Venetian churches which, though not of Palladio's devising, may have provided a model.[670] And here an interesting similarity with seventeenth-century architecture north of the Alps is provided by the fact that there, just as in Wren's work, the type is only rarely found,[671] and we can point to an interesting divergence in that English Palladian and post-Palladian practice provides an abundance of it.

While these parallels may be of some significance, a further examination of Wren's work will reveal a degree of independence and divergence from Palladian precepts hitherto unsuspected. We have noted elsewhere that Serlian influence on Wren seems to have been exaggerated; Palladian influence, however, has been positively mis-stated,[672] though previous authorities have been altogether in disagreement as to where, or at what period of Wren's long career, such alleged influence can be said to have been evident.[673] The suggestion that English sympathies with the Palladian style should be ascribed to the fact that 'it is preeminently the style for the Protestant church'[674] must be regarded as of dubious veracity and inapplicable to Wren's theory and practice of ecclesiastical architecture. But as we need not here discuss the divergences between Palladio's theory and practice, nor draw comparisons with Wren's, we can turn to the considerable and significant deviations which Wren's work displays from true Palladian precedent.

Foremost among these must stand Wren's handling of the classic orders which has not only drawn the most severe criticism upon some of his works[675] but is also of significance to questions which we shall discuss elsewhere. Likewise, there is a surprising number of instances where Wren, whether inspired by classical, Venetian, or the Fontainebleau examples,[676] went contrary to Palladio's preference in designing the sometimes excessively high plinths on which his orders frequently rest;[677] the derivation of this practice is ambiguous, yet certainly not Palladian, for the Vicentine master had explicitly stated a preference for the elimination of plinths supporting the orders[678] which some architects, inspired by antique examples such as triumphal arches,[679] had

again brought into use but which, though 'sanctioned' by Roman antiquity, are as rare in Renaissance Rome as they are common in Venice.[680]

Equally, there is little in Wren's treatment of windows which would remind us of Palladio;[681] least of all the method adopted for the side elevations of St Michael, Queenhythe, where the combination of round-headed and circular windows, linked by carved scrolls,[682] would suggest the influence of Venetian, but not Palladian, models such as the cortile of the Ducal Palace. Palladio's custom was essentially different inasmuch as he followed earlier Renaissance models, and particularly Alberti,[683] in placing small circular windows not above, but flanking round-headed ones. In this connexion, one further significant deviation on Wren's part may be mentioned, namely that it was only on the rarest occasions that he made use of what is frequently called the 'motif Palladio'. Although his name has been given to it, it was not really of Palladio's invention as, derived from antiquity,[684] it had been reintroduced by early Renaissance practice.[685] Palladio himself employed the motif consistently[686] and the partial refutation of the allegedly Palladian character of Wren's work is found in the ubiquitious usage by most architects after Wren[687] in comparison with the very rare instances in which he made use of the device himself.[688]

The combination of the 'motif Palladio' placed on an arcade, such as Wren devised at St James's, Westminster, and St Andrew's, Holborn, may actually indicate not Palladio's influence, but that of the Roman church of Santa Maria in Via Lata, which Cortone had built in 1661.[689] As to the singular east window of St Olave, it would be feasible to establish a connexion with the arcade treatment of the Château de Liancour,[690] which Wren had seen during his Paris visit in 1665; but, if the possible derivation from Alberti's San Francesco at Rimini or an illustration in Serlio[691] may represent tenuous connexions, the greatest degree of probability attaches to Palladio's Vicentine basilica (Fig.147) as the most likely source of inspiration. But aspects of period and frequency must again be emphasized: the motif of circular openings in the spandrels of round-headed arcades, or flanking round-headed windows, is one running through the entire Italian Renaissance;[692] with Wren the occurrence at St Olave is not only a very early, but, indeed, represents his only employment of it.

In the range of such particularities, another striking divergence from Palladian theory and practice is provided by the fact that Wren considered, but never actually employed, the device of alternating segmental and triangular pediments. Here again, Serlio and Palladio could point to antiquity for precedent;[693] but even before the latter could use the motif with such effect in many of his buildings it had become a feature of widespread use in Rome, where it is met with at St Peter's, at the Palazzo Farnese, the Piccola Farnesina, and many others; at Florence, it forms a conspicuous feature of the Baptistery; but at Venice, curiously,

146. St Olave, east front.

147. Vicenza, basilica, detail (from Palladio).

there is not a single occurrence of it in any building of importance,[694] which would suggest that Palladio derived from Roman and Florentine[695] rather than from Venetian models a device which features so conspicuously in many of his designs.[696] Even if we were only to consider the precedent of Inigo Jones before Wren's eyes in his own country,[697] and the important example he had seen in Paris,[698] Wren would have had every justification in employing the device. In fact, he considered its possible use in several cases: not unnaturally, in those schemes for Whitehall Palace where the incorporation, or doubling, of the Banqueting House was envisaged; in a variant, in pairs, in a sketch study for the Queen's new apartments designed in 1687;[699] in a study for one of the City churches (Fig.52); and in one of the early designs for Greenwich.[700] But though considered, it is of some significance that the idea was never executed[701] and, once again, the frequent use which architects of the eighteenth century made of the device[702] points to a suggestive formalistic difference between them and Wren, and the necessity of considering him apart from his successors of whose school he has, however dubiously, been represented as the founder.

One further consideration will serve to elucidate the very narrow limits beyond which Wren's work cannot properly be called Palladian; a limit, indeed, which indicates that any arbitrary classification of his architecture as 'Renaissance' can at best apply to details of form, but certainly not to the principles by which these forms were conditioned. We mean to speak here of the theory of harmonic proportion which, explicit in Alberti, in

Serlio and Palladio, forms the very core not only of Renaissance architecture, but of that encyclopaedic concept of Renaissance philosophy of which architecture formed a small, but integral, part.

Alberti is explicit in his recommendations of the proportions of interior space and gives, in addition to the centralized plans already referred to, the square plus a third, the square plus one half, and the square doubled.[703] Serlio, half a century later, added the square plus a quarter, the square plus two-thirds, and introduced the root two rectangle.[704] Though Palladio accepted, in theory at least, this latter proportion, he followed Alberti and Serlio with the exception of the square plus a quarter.[705] That the proportions thus prescribed were possessed of a significance infinitely exceeding the rule of thumb character they may superficially represent will remain to be discussed in a later chapter; that Alberti, Bramante, and Palladio, however, were not only familiar with the humanistic values underlying such theories of harmonic proportions, but also consistently employed such concepts in their designs, must be beyond doubt. Even though the actual measurements of Palladio's buildings do not, sometimes, tally exactly with those so prominently displayed in the plans contained in his treatise,[706] these latter leave no room to doubt that his faculty of design was governed, beyond all else, by the overriding, paramount importance of harmonic ratio and proportion.

There is no need to further discuss this fact which, indeed, has recently been admirably analysed and demonstrated.[707] There is a need, though, to examine Wren's acceptance of, or divergence

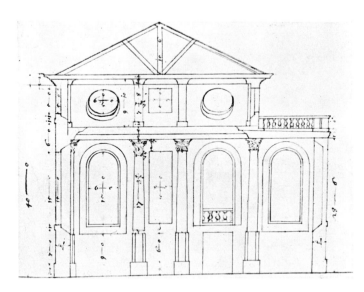

148. St Benet's, Thames Street, section.

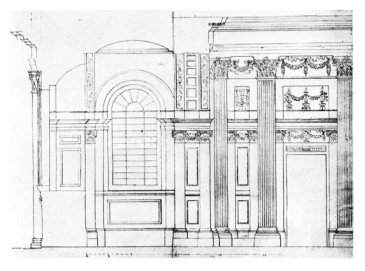

149. St Paul's, section.

from, these principles for, clearly, such an examination will permit us to draw conclusions of considerable importance. That Wren must have been familiar with these theories, just as Sir Henry Wotton, Inigo Jones, and Sir Roger Pratt can be proved to have been, must be beyond question. And it might have been assumed that the geometrical, if not the humanistic principles of Alberti's and Palladio's theories would have held a tremendous appeal to the scientist and mathematician in him; we might have thought that he would have embraced with enthusiasm so rational a mathematical concept which would have satisfied the geometrician equally as the artist in him. It has, indeed, been intimated that Wren 'deduced the beautiful by a system of logical reasoning'[708] and that 'his scientific training led him to search for true proportion in all his buildings'.[709] But we shall search in vain for the science and logic inherent in Palladio's proportions for, surprising though it may seem, an examination of Wren's work, and especially of those of his designs where considerations of site or public sentiment cannot have presented a bar to the application of preconceived concepts of proportions, does not yield any indication whatever that Wren's design was based on any system of proportional ratios such as had inspired Palladio,[710] and Wren's motto *Numero, Pondere, et Mensura*[711] does not stand for a preoccupation with number and measure in the sense which these concepts had implied for Alberti and Palladio. Wren's proportions, whatever their basis, were not built on the humanist theories of harmonic ratios, and it cannot have been with reference to these (even could we suspect him to have known them)

that William III boasted of Hampton Court that 'the new apartments for good proportions, state, and convenience jointly, were not to be paralleled by any palace in Europe'.[712] It is not necessary to cite many instances to corroborate this contention. The south front of the Sheldonian, the early date of which might argue pronounced dependence on historical models, recalls Palladio in detail but is precluded from proportional interpretation by the whim which made Wren enlarge the central bay.[713] The same peculiarity removes the east front of St Lawrence beyond the realms of Palladian harmonics. More cogent still to our contention is the fully dimensioned section of the first design of St Benet's, Thames Street, representing an intention which was to be substantially changed in execution, neither version of which can be interpreted as conforming to the principles of harmonic proportions. And lastly, when it is recalled with what precision Palladio adjusted the ratios between two orders used in combination, the actual ratio of 25:14 displayed by the two orders in the interior of St Paul's must finally dispel any illusions of Palladian inspiration.

But in conclusion, one draft must be mentioned which, among the close on a thousand extant drawings, is the only one, though never before reproduced nor even cited by those critics most anxious to clothe Wren in a Palladian mantle, to display a consistent application of Palladian concepts of harmonic proportion. It is a small, rubbed pencil sketch inserted at the end of one of the volumes of drawings in the All Souls Collection together with other fragments. It shows a square, clearly domed, building of

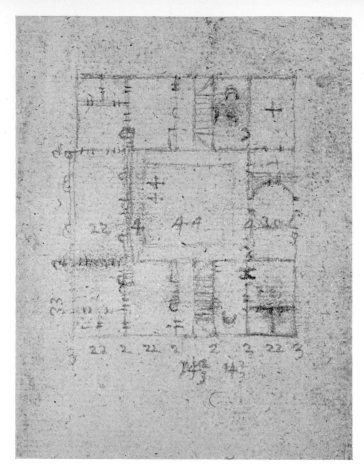

150. Wren, unidentified design.

which the sides equal twice the diameter of the dome. The module employed is a unit of 11, and the spaces surrounding the central square of four units' dimensions are designed in strict conformity with the Albertian ratios of 1:2, 2:3, and 3:4 though the first term is not, apparently, applied.

Significant as the drawing is in showing Wren not only familiar with the Renaissance theory of harmonic proportion but also inclined to experiment with it, it is equally significant that the building represented was neither executed nor can it be identified as the precursor of any later work with any degree of probability.[714] The draughtsmanship would indicate a very early date, and though Wren's familiarity with Renaissance theory, possibly even at a very early stage of his career, can safely be assumed, the nature of his executed work does not permit us to conclude that his design was ever governed by the fundamental concepts which had motivated the theory and practice of Palladio.

That Wren, throughout his long career, was preoccupied with the same problems of centralized plans as had been Alberti, Leonardo, Bramante, Michelangelo, and Palladio, must have become clear from our examination of Wren's works. We can hardly conceive the Greek cross plan proposed for St Paul's[715] to have been completely uninfluenced by a knowledge of Michelangelo's and Bramante's plans for St Peter's.[716] Wren's predilection points unmistakably to classic Renaissance inspiration for, indeed, circular churches cannot be sanctioned by recourse to Vitruvius and must therefore be regarded as a distinctive and

significant trend by which fifteenth- and sixteenth-century Italian humanists and architects turned away from the traditional basilican and cruciform plans in favour of circular structures.

Thus far the ancestry of Wren's many schemes devised on centralized lines seems clear; it is clearest, perhaps, in the chapter house, or baptistery, of St Paul's, where the striking similarity to that most classical of Bramante's designs, known to Wren from Palladio's book if from no other source, inevitably suggests it to have been modelled on, and inspired by, the celebrated Roman edifice. Yet at the same time it is necessary to point to divergences in Wren's concepts of centralized plans from those of the Italian Renaissance architects which, as will be seen, will ultimately suggest that these precedents provided no more than a formal starting point from which Wren was to evolve designs and buildings not merely divergent in form from their predecessors, but actually opposed to many of the intellectual concepts which had inspired these.

It might be mentioned, to begin with, that Wren's predilection for centralized and domed structures extended beyond the field of ecclesiastical architecture; the Italians had never conceived of circular plans for secular uses: Palladio might have planned the Villa Capra as an essentially centralized building, but there can be no comparison with such an edifice, expressive *par excellence* of his ideals, as the little church at Maser. To Wren, however, a purely centralized plan without the addition of any further design units was by no means the exclusive prerogative of such

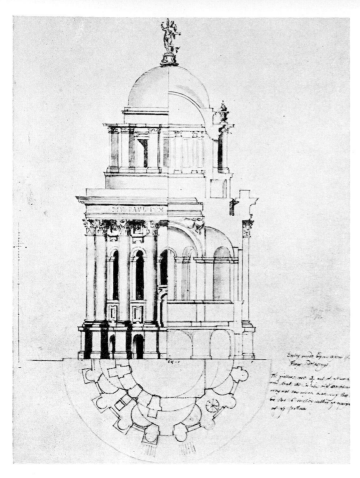

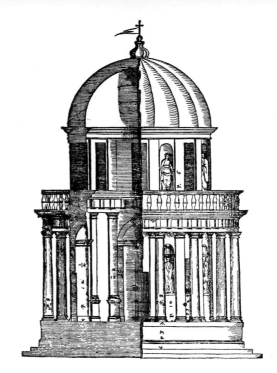

152. Bramante's Tempietto (from Palladio).

151. St Paul's, chapter house or baptistery.

ecclesiastical designs as St Stephen's, Walbrook, St Swithin's, St Mary Abchurch, and St Mary's, Lincoln's Inn Fields: he was seriously putting forward a closely related design in his first project for the library at Trinity College, Cambridge,[717] the idea of which, though rejected, still lingered on in the domed pavilions which were meant to flank the second design.

It is of some significance that Wren apparently did not hesitate to apply to purely secular uses a design concept which, to the Italian Renaissance, had been exclusively ecclesiastical. Of greater significance, however, are the manifold ways in which Wren projected, and actually roofed such domed spaces, and here we shall enter a subject which displays more cogently than others the limits within which Wren's design concurred with Renaissance practice, and the extent to which it went beyond it into realms which are clearly Baroque.

The fact that Wren never touched any of the major projects with which he was occupied throughout his long career without considering, right at the outset, the employment of domes, is, of course, inescapable even after the most cursory study of his work. This fact has been recognized by previous authorities, yet under the generic label of 'dome' have been included shapes and profiles of such divergence that it will be necessary to distinguish between the two basic types which, in their pure employment, and varying degrees of combination, must have served Wren as prototypes. The first, exemplified by the pointed examples of the Pisan Baptistery and the Florentine Duomo; the second, smooth, enclosing a perfect hemisphere or section thereof, as derived from Byzantium. Apart from the essential difference of profile, there is an equally different architectural principle discernible, for the first, the pointed, type is not in itself a truly constructional dome inasmuch as the sharp and pronounced ribs form a structural framework filled in, much in the manner of the Gothic vault; while the second, the Byzantine, type of dome is truly architectural insofar as it is its very construction that determines its curvature and profile. These two types, the Gothic and the Byzantine, are not only different, but also antagonistic in that their respective merits are opposed to each other: the first permitted the freest elaboration of external outline, while the interior, necessarily funnel-shaped, was consequently unsatisfactory; on the other hand, the low, smooth, flat dome of Byzantium permitted superb interior effects, though the inevitable restriction on height was an effective bar to the grandeur of exterior elevation.

If a broad generalization may be permitted, it might be said that once the ideological postulates of earlier Renaissance humanism had been superseded, the fundamental preoccupation of architects was to find the solution by which the exterior grandeur of Brunelleschi's dome could be combined with the advantages of interior effect as possessed by the Pantheon; the logical solution was clearly, and only, seen in a double construction which permitted the retention of the desirable, and the elimination of the undesirable, qualities of both types. The moment, however, the interior dome came to be considered as a shell attached to the true

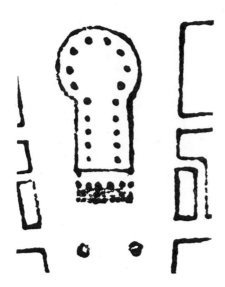

153. City of London Plan, detail.

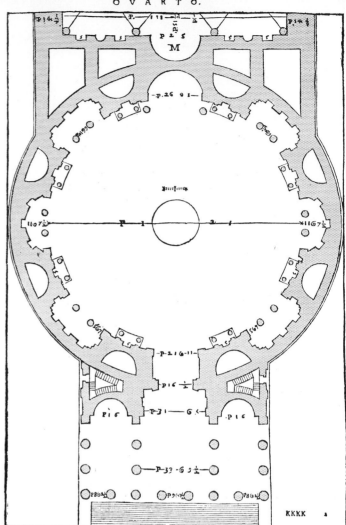

O V A R T O.

154. Pantheon, Rome, plan.

outer dome; the moment, further, that this process was reversed and the exterior dome became a shell superposed on the interior dome: a dichotomy of constructional thought was created which, while permitting the outline to be governed by taste rather than constructional necessities, was already fundamentally opposed to the true basis of Gothic, or Greek, architecture. It was the beginning of an architecture designing on the basis of principles without reference to, nor consideration of, the postulate of the indissoluble interdependence between construction and design. None the less, the diversity between the Florence dome and, let us say, that of Bramante's Tempietto were the two poles which Michelangelo tried to reconcile at St Peter's; and this very desire and process of combining the merits of these two basically different types, the endeavour to retain the tautness of the Florentine example with the smooth restfulness of the Hagia Sophia or San Marco profiles: this attempt is the keynote discernible in all the major dome designs of Wren's maturity.[718]

A chronology of Wren's designs and a classification of preponderances at certain periods proves distinctly that Wren was familiar with both the Gothic and the Byzantine-Venetian prototypes[719] but remains significantly inconclusive. The domes built by Wren up to the end of the century do not offer any conclusive evidence for any decided preference even over a relatively short period. What is clear, however, is that such 'pure' domes as Wren designed and built – St Stephen Walbrook at the one end of the scale, and Tom Tower at the other – provided no models satisfactory to him for the design of his greatest dome. And, as appears clearly from the many projected sections of the dome of St Paul's, it was the reconciliation of the two types which formed his principal preoccupation. Considering, then, that the inspiration ultimately responsible for the varying trends we can discern in these designs was of a very complex nature by no means definable by reference to one or two historic buildings, we must devote more detailed attention to this question than has hitherto been done and

examine the evolution of St Paul's dome in the light of all its historical precedents.

That the Pantheon, the most celebrated building of Roman antiquity, must be regarded as an unquestionable influence on Wren, has long been recognized. It is suggestive that among the drawings preserved at All Souls there should be found a large-scale plan of the Roman building,[720] the details of which would have been familiar to Wren from both Serlio and Palladio. More concretely, the Pantheon dome was obviously the prototype for one of the earliest of Wren's schemes for the cathedral, and if we can relate the block plan sketched into a variant of the City plan to the elevation and section (Figs.35, 36) it becomes evident that Wren was adapting the Roman plan by the addition of a western nave, by which means the simplest, and most logical solution of the 'Quire and Auditory' requirement was achieved.

However famous, though, this model did not retain its hold on Wren's imagination for long; Wren must have realized that the very fact of adding the western nave would seriously impair the frontal view of the dome itself and it must have become obvious that, for his purpose, the Pantheon curvature would have to be abandoned. In the effort, however, to achieve a satisfactory profile, so cogently exemplified in the range of dome designs we have examined elsewhere, the widest imaginable variety of influences, from classically Roman to seventeenth-century Baroque, can be discerned. It is an inadmissable and dangerous over-simplification of the facts to assert that 'Wren's masterpiece has a clear pedigree and St Peter's was before Wren as a pattern to follow and improve upon'[721] or to suggest that 'the secret of Wren is his admiration for Bernini; beyond Bernini he looked back to the dome of St Peter's which mastered his imagination'.[722] On the other hand, it is a distortion of the truth to assert that 'to quote the Baptistery at Pisa as a precedence seems to detract from the credit due to Wren for having mastered the situation without extraneous aid'[723] when 'extraneous aid' in the form of Italian and French inspiration is so patently apparent throughout the evolution of the design; while only eulogy and an imperfect acquaintance with Wren's extant drawings could have prompted the statement that whether Wren 'was acquainted with the Florentine and Pisan examples we know not;[724] but, if not, he had intuitively the knowledge they would have afforded him'.[725]

This critical digression has only been made to indicate the degree of confusion and misrepresentation which has beset an issue which, though complex, is possessed of sufficient documentary evidence to permit a fairly precise evaluation. And such indicates two points of the greatest interest: just as Wren's very extensive knowledge of historic dome types need not for a moment be doubted, so their influence, rarely pure, and frequently mixed, is discernible to such a degree that one of the major designs projected represents Wren's combination and synthesis of no less than three distinct prototypes.

Intermittently, the hemispherical form of dome seems to have been Wren's preoccupation throughout the years. It appears quite plainly in St Stephen's, Walbrook, and, rendered hemispherical externally, enters the St Paul's projects as early as in a study for the great model of 1673[726] and remains as late as the early 'nineties when its simultaneous appearance in a cathedral study (Fig.125) and a study for Greenwich (Fig.107) can be observed. Yet the restriction on height imposed by the form were irreconcilable with Wren's desire to make a dome 'conspicuous above the houses', and as soon as he realized that nothing but an elongation of the hemispherical shape would serve his purpose, the idea of double construction presented itself. This clearly underlies the dome designed for the Greek cross scheme which preceded the great model, yet this latter shows just as clearly the degree of indecision and spirit of experimentation then governing Wren's mind: we have elsewhere remarked upon the dichotomy arising between the two domes of that design, and the element of inconsistency which their divergences introduced. At the same time,

however, Wren was also experimenting with one of the first of his distinctly pointed domes,[727] which concept, as we shall see, was to reappear some twenty years later. Meanwhile, however, entirely different ideas entered into the design evolution.

When Wren planned an essentially smooth, hemispherical dome buttressed by semi-cylindrical masses (Fig.131) he was applying, on a greatly enlarged scale, the distinctive features of the tower of St Antholin's and the King Charles mausoleum, as we have noted; but in so doing, he approximated remarkably closely to the concept which had governed the dome designs of Leonardo thus suggesting that Wren, though he could not have known the originals, might have been familiar with some of their derivations. On the other hand, the distinctive ribbing which Wren introduced into many of his domes was clearly contradictory to Palladio's and earlier Renaissance precepts, and is the more surprising in designs which are related to such precedents. The mausoleum design is a case in point, for even though its semi-cylindrical buttresses may owe something to Leonardesque inspiration, the pronouncedly ribbed, taut outline of the dome points far more cogently to Florence or Rome than to Venice or Milan. When Wren introduced patterns of ribs into an essentially smooth dome, such as that projected in the engravings of 1702, it becomes clear that he was bent on combining the shape of one type with the decorative possibilities of the other. An even more remarkable adaptation occurs, however, in what clearly must be a fairly late design seeing that it foreshadows the constructional solution of St Paul's dome as finally evolved. It would seem obvious that Bramante's unexecuted design for St Peter's, known to Wren from Serlio's book if not from other sources, formed the basic inspiration of this project.[728] In fact, it is Bramante's peristyle to all intents and purposes just as the base is derived from that model; but the dome itself has been changed out of all recognition in its elongation and, however cogent the precedent, Wren clearly used it to achieve an entirely different purpose: instead of Bramante's soft, shallow dome, this was to be a soaring structure designed, moreover, on the principles which determined the final solution: the triple construction is here adumbrated, envisaging – in complete contrast to Bramante – a definite interior and exterior shell, between which lies the truly structural, though invisible, part of the dome on which the lantern rests.

However, this idea was to be contributory to, but not decisive for the final design. Before this was evolved and, indeed, before the 1702 project was engraved and published, Wren went to a dome concept the precise opposite of Palladio's, namely Michelangelo's St Peter's.[729] This model is quite clearly reflected in one of the Greenwich designs (Fig.103) where, as at St Paul's, it precedes an entirely different type. It is unfortunate that we are not acquainted with the constructional details of that Greenwich dome, but it is fortunate that a closely parallel project should have been devised for St Paul's (Fig.132) of which we have the most precise

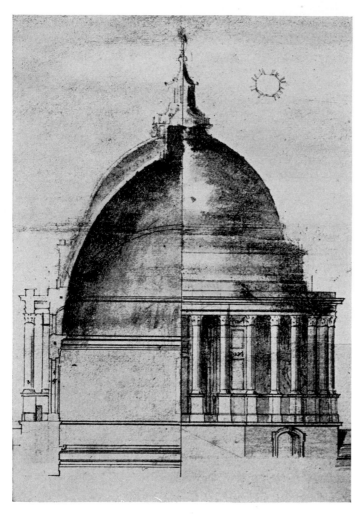

155. St Paul's, dome study.

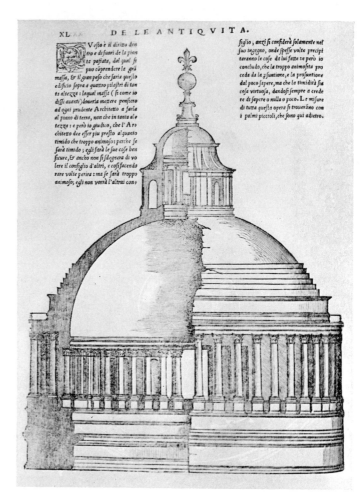

156. St Peter's, study for dome by Bramante (from Serlio).

knowledge. The resemblance of dome, curvature, and the significant triple sets of lucarne lights to St Peter's dome is, of course, inescapable. But while this is the nearest approach which Wren ever made to Michelangelo's celebrated design, the resemblance ends with these external similarities, and the differences are as profound as the superficial likeness is obvious; it is not only that this Michelangelesque dome was to be placed, not on four piers as at St Peter's, but on eight piers already constructed; it is also because completely different influences are equally discernible in the design. In the first instance, the lantern is altogether divergent from St Peter's and the connexion between it and the dome owes nothing to Rome, but everything, apparently, to Jules Hardouin-Mansart's dome of the Invalides.[730] In the second instance, whatever Wren owed to Michelangelo for his exterior effect, his treatment of the interior is completely different: in a preceding adaptation, we have seen Wren replace Bramante's solid dome construction by his triple shells. In this design, Wren modified Michelangelo's dome by the addition of a separate interior dome lit by windows invisible from below, clearly aiming at a scenic effect comparable to that which François Mansart had designed, in 1664, for the Bourbon chapel,[731] which drawings it would be tempting to think Wren to have known.

We have traced, in the first part of this study, the stages through which Wren's dome concepts went before the final solution was devised; and it remains here only to point to the fact that the method which was adopted by Wren in the final resort was one which was as much removed from Michelangelesque precedent as it was irreconcilable with Palladian notions on dome design. It represents, therefore, a unique and wholly original contribution on Wren's part which, while owing no debt to extraneous inspiration, at the same time removes Wren's masterpiece from the realms of Palladian and Renaissance architecture in which some of his critics would at all costs place his work. Yet this is not admissible: Palladian concepts of dome design were the logical development of Bramante's[732] and never attempted any compromise or reconciliation between the Byzantine and Florentine prototypes while, at the same time, his dome volumes remained, for reasons the significance of which we shall elaborate elsewhere, hemispherical.

Wren's final dome of St Paul's possesses none of these qualities. The visible domes, exterior and interior, are not hemispherical; and the concealing of what, in effect, is the true, structural component constitutes a method which Palladio would never have sanctioned; a method, in fact, not only irreconcilable with Palladian precedent but which would also have been ideologically unacceptable to the Vicentine master. This has not, indeed, been generally recognized; but to assert, as one of Wren's critics has done, that Wren's dome 'undoubtedly embodies the finest example of classical dome construction yet carried out'[733] is not only to ignore the fact that it differs in essentials from all 'classical' domes[734] but also to misinterpret the ideological fundamentals which were responsible for those designs. On the other hand, no more ludicrous suggestion is possible than that recalled in the year of the bicentenary of Wren's death, which had opined that 'St Paul's could be reduced to true architectural principles by removing the lead-covered timber dome to expose the great brick cone on which the stone lantern rests'.[735] For this is to fundamentally misapprehend Wren's purpose. What Wren wanted was the effect: this is clearly discernible in the way he had transformed historic models: the introduction of ribs into the smooth curvature of the dome projected in 1702 was essentially an anachronism; the sets of lucarne lights in the Michelangelesque design did not light up any visible part of the structure, but served a solely decorative purpose; and the elongation of Bramante's project implied the rejection of the principles on which that design had been based.

To Wren, it was of no moment that whatever the onlooker saw of his dome, internally or externally, was not a constructional piece of architecture but a piece of scenic design. We are not here concerned with an examination of whether the expedient of his dome construction can be 'justified' or not; other critics have provided answers to this question,[736] and such 'justification' or 'condemnation' as may be propounded must proceed from a given set of rules and convictions be they of a historical, aesthetic, or even ethical nature. What concerns us more directly here, however, is the fact that the conception of the dome of St Paul's presents a most suggestive instance of the 'sham' architecture of the Baroque so frequently deplored and castigated by purist critics clinging to Ruskinian traditions, that we must now, lastly, turn to an examination of Wren's work in the light of the architecture of such men as were, in Italy and elsewhere on the continent, his contemporaries and immediate predecessors. That any parallels should exist between Wren's work and the continental Baroque has, indeed, been fervently denied, and we shall need to return to this question elsewhere; here we would concern ourselves primarily with such parallels as can be demonstrated or pertinently implied. Yet even without attempting an answer to the question: is Wren's work to be called Baroque? at this stage of our enquiry, the distinct divergences from Palladian theory and prac-

tice already noted would seem to indicate that in Wren's *œuvre* 'the ideals that Palladio had sought to establish were lost' as much as they are alleged to have been in 'the unbridled licence of the Baroque';[737] the refusal to abide by Palladian rules, 'too strict and pedantick', is, if no more, an indication *per negationem* of the consanguinity of the concepts of Wren and those of the Baroque; but it will be more illuminating to examine this complex question in the light of positive similarities.

To speak expressly of sculpture in this context will not be thought inappropriate when it is recalled that to the Baroque, and the Baroque more than to any other period of Christian art, sculpture was essential to architecture to the point of becoming part of it. Considering the forces and the men to whom the style is due, this need not surprise us: in the first place, the spirit of the Counter-Reformation was essentially didactic and the abstract qualities of pure architecture offered not only but limited possibilities of expressing its ideologies but were, moreover, anathematized by the Hellenic, that is to say, pagan, derivation of their symbolism as reinterpreted by the humanists; secondly, the linear conception of the Renaissance had undergone a profound change when Michelangelo, in charging with a new dynamism the static beauties of Bramante, had become the first artist to treat an architectural composition with a plastic sense dedicated not to the organization of planes or even spatial units, but to the creation of spatial values conceived in sculptural terms. Lastly, sculpture came to be indissolubly bound up with architecture, as well as painting, when the universality of talent, first epitomized in the Renaissance ideal of man, was taken to its final and logical conclusion in a concept of art in which the separate coexistence of the arts gave place, under a fundamental Baroque impulse of integration, to a synthesis in which the independence of each is sacrificed to a complete fusion in which the boundaries between architectural sculpture and 'sculptured' architecture, as well as the dividing lines between painted architecture and painting applied to architecture, have ceased to exist.[738]

More particularly, however, the tasks to which seventeenth-century sculpture was called differed entirely from those of preceding centuries: for it had to translate, as best as stone and marble would allow, the twin ideals of the age, martyrdom and mysticism; it was called upon to show, beyond possibility of misapprehension, the ecstatic sufferings of Sant'Ignazio, St Francis Xavier, and the martyrs of Brazil and Japan on the one hand, and the ecstatic beatitudes of St Ludovico Gonzaga, St John Nepomucene, St Stanislas Kostka, and St Philip Neri on the other. And while the former category could fall back upon the earlier representations of martyrdom, epitomized perhaps most perfectly in one of the favourite saints of the Middle Ages, St Sebastian, the mysticism engendered by St Teresa and St John of the Cross called for an entirely new iconography if its representation was not to be left entirely to the artist's powers of imagination.[739] Yet even though such guidance came to the artists' aid, the difficulties inherent in painting or carving a St Diego d'Alcala lifted from earth in ecstasy, a transverberation of St Teresa or a ravishment of St Paul were incomparably greater than the problems posed by a Crucifixion, a Lamentation, or an Entombment. Just as St Teresa had emphasized the linguistic inadequacies of the vocabulary to express the mystic's experience, so art was forced to the invention of a language to give it expression. If the demands of the Apocalypse on the artist's imagination were tremendous, they were yet of an entirely different order from the problems now posed, for the essential difference lay in the fact that, however fantastic the visions of St John at Patmos, the nature of Revelation rendered permissible even the most extravagant flights of fantasy; while the problems of seventeenth-century mysticism called for a combination of the natural and the supernatural to render comprehensible the profound intrinsic nature of the mystic experience. In the plastic arts, the problem was unprecedented; for the very content to be conveyed was, in the words of one who partook of it to the sublimest degree, such that 'human nature is not sufficient to comprehend it nor human experience to describe it; because he who has passed through it will be able to feel it but not to tell it'.[740]

The solutions which Bernini, as the unquestionable creator of the style, invented are too well known to need elaborate description here:[741] suffice it to say that the astounding impact of his sculpture is the result, largely, of the extreme degree of realism with which he rendered attitudes and events of a supernatural quality, the poignancy arising from the astonishing combination of perfect naturalism in states and acts of which even the possibility was, and remains, outside and beyond the imagination and experience of the vast majority of humanity. These very attributes, implicit in the subject: the carven rhetoric, the gesticulation, the agitation, the desperate quality of quest and triumphant expression of fulfilment: these were solutions of the problem which have been the subject of much incomprehension, misinterpretation, and criticism.[742] It may, indeed, be questioned whether the felicities of the mystic's union with God, often sung, but never before painted or carved, were capable of representation in the plastic arts. It is irrelevant to debate whether such a content should, or should not, form the subject matter of a work of art. But it is as questionable to think that the 'misrepresentation of mysticism was made inevitable by the very nature of Baroque art' as it is inadmissable to arbitrarily declare the Baroque artists' 'failure to find an adequate artistic expression for the mystical experience'.[743] For, if nothing else, the contemporaneous acclaim and renown of the works of Baroque sculptors, and of Bernini in particular, do by no means lead us to believe that the people for whom their works were created considered them either inappropriate in form or inadequate in content.

These strictures have been concerned with content; but, as it

would not be relevant to pursue this enquiry further within the context of this chapter, we must now turn to the form of Baroque architecture and sculpture – no less the subject of misapprehension and criticism – for a comparison with English, and, particularly, with Wren's work, To take, first, a minor example, the frequently derided twisted pillars of Bernini's *baldachino* – a 'familiar instance of misapplied skill'[744] – are not only to be found in the celebrated porch of St Mary's, Oxford, but also in numerous other instances of seventeenth-century architectural and mortuary art,[745] and were, apparently, more highly appreciated by Wren himself than by later critics, as he was specific in his design for a *baldachino* to stand in St Paul's which was 'to consist of rich marble columns writhed, &c., in same manner like that at St Peter's at Rome'.[746] The pyramids and urns common to the tomb art of Italy and England[747] were not, as Wren thought, of Gothic, respectively French origin,[748] but graced examples of tomb architecture and sculpture in which the resemblance of many of the larger English specimens to those which, for example, Pozzo erected at Sant'Ignazio, is too striking and too general to be dismissed.[749]

More particularly, however, we must consider Wren's attitude to sculpture within the cadre of his architecture. Though he was not, like Bernini, sculptor as well as architect, it is clear that he shared the Italian's concept of the importance of the plastic art to architectural design; several explicit references found in his writings and letters[750] make it clear that he was by no means heedless of the importance of sculpture to his own work, and it is likely that, like Le Brun at Versailles, he gave ideas, directives, and, very probably, sketches suggesting his aims to the few sculptors – Bird, Cibber, and Gibbon – whom he almost habitually employed in his numerous works.

Wren's admiration for Bernini has been emphasized by several authors, as we have noted; and while nothing but conjecture can support the assumption that his admiration for the Louvre project was the result of youthful impressionability, and that 'in after years, when his enthusiasm had been tempered by a more mature judgment, this eulogium would have been materially qualified',[751] our justification for the preceding digression on Baroque sculpture is justified by a design, belonging to 1695, in which the most characteristic features of Bernini's work and of the school it engendered are to be found combined: the funeral monument for Queen Mary which Wren and Gibbon designed to stand in Westminster Abbey.[752] It would be wilful to ascribe the design to Wren's Flemish collaborator[753] in order to preserve for him that quality of simplicity and classic beauty which some critics would like to have his prime virtue. For, however dubious we ourselves may be in discerning Wren's hand in the actual drawing, it does not seem that the relationship between Wren and Gibbon was such as to allow the carver a freedom of expression which would go contrary to Wren's taste; nor was Wren the man, we would

157. Queen Mary II, monument.

suggest, to consistently associate with himself an artist whose ideas and tastes were not close to his own; while, lastly, the importance of the project would certainly indicate that the design was executed under his supervision and thus, even if we cannot establish Wren's authorship, we can pertinently suggest his approval of it.

There can be little doubt that it represents the closest approach, tantamount to identification, to that which is most exuberant in the continental Baroque: pillars, plain and twisted, festively garlanded, support an entablature which carries upon its metopes the emblems of the union of royal blood, the Star of the Garter, the Thistle of Scotland, and the fleur-de-lis of France, in allusion to the Queen's ancestry; cherubs above her support a crowned escutcheon while by her side stands one of those urns, whose profusion can be found at Versailles, at Hildebrandt's Belvedere in Vienna, and in the last book of the engraved work of Fischer von Erlach. Below, St George stands for England, while the nation's children gather around the childless Queen. In the centre of this flamboyant apparition, however, the Queen herself reclines, not altogether unlike Bernini's St Teresa, upon a couch supported by heraldic lion and unicorn, and in the joy of a beatific vision: her hand follows the attendant guardian angel's to point to a glory of clouds, broken to the passage of celestial rays, while cherubim hold crown and wreath to the departed Queen, entering a kingdom other than terrestrial.

In its very conception, as well as in all its individual features, this is the equivalent of all that is greatest, and most exuberant, in Baroque art. It is the attempt to create, in a plastic medium, a concept of beatitude not dissimilar from that of mysticism, and intention and expression, form, and content, are so close to those of Bernini and the entire school of Baroque sculpture as to be identical. For here we have, indeed, the equivalent of the Beata Ludovica Albertoni, while St Teresa's angel has lost its arrow to point instead to the glory; the clouds which hover above St Teresa are here parted, to admit the rays of a heavenly sun, and as Fischer's crowned Virgin stands upon her symbol of the crescent moon[754] so the Queen rests upon the heraldic symbols of the kingdom she has departed.

Considering, then, that even if this drawing may not be by Wren's own hand, we have reason to believe that its design and general character had met with his approval, we are naturally led to a consideration of decoration; an aspect, indeed, which has been the cause of a great deal of criticism of the Baroque. Turning from the Queen Mary monument to the City churches and other works of Wren, it becomes clear that financial considerations, as well as the frequently disadvantageous siting of buildings, often rendered the application of external ornament impossible and futile. None the less, there are sufficient indications to show that Wren shared, to a considerable degree, the Baroque taste for exuberant decoration. This taste speaks eloquently from much of the elaborate carving which can, or could, be found in his interiors; the splendid, if rather ornate screen which he designed for the chapel of All Souls is as representative as the sumptuous decoration which once graced the interior of St Clement Danes; and the admirable work of such of his collaborators as Gibbon, Maine, and Creecher; the many ornamental details of St Paul's, not least the magnificent wrought iron screens of Tijou and the lavishly carved choir stalls of Gibbon; the gates at Hampton Court no less than the numerous drawings for projected (though mostly unexecuted) carved and stucco decoration of the interior: all these bear out the suggestion that Wren was certainly the presiding spirit over all this ancillary activity, without whose sanction neither the organ case at St Paul's nor the splendid altar of King James's Chapel, so greatly admired by Evelyn, would have been executed. Such work was as foreign to the ideals of true Renaissance decoration as it was averse to the Puritan austerities of ecclesiastical architecture; and if the more exuberant details of many of Wren's early drafts were pared away in subsequent designs and executions, we need not interpret such modifications as the token of Wren's desire to render the work 'more reasonable'[755] but would prefer to regard them as the compromise which the restrictions of means dictated.

Wren was careful to explicitly pronounce on the dangers inherent in the fully developed Baroque,[756] and obviously at pains to discern that boundary of decorative treatment which, as informed criticism has recognized, is transgressed in the works of many a lesser Baroque master. But no inference can be made from his statements to the effect that he was unaware of, or even opposed to, the artistic possibilities of Baroque design and decoration. Not only would it be unreasonable to think that, had Wren disapproved of the Baroque as some critics would have us believe, he would have permitted his approbatory imprint to appear in John James's translation of the well-known book[757] of the 'lamentable'[758] Pozzo; but, more concretely, numerous instances could be cited in which Wren's first drafts were more exuberant, more ornate, and altogether of a closer affinity with continental examples than the executed work; as we have implied, it would be reasonable to think that whatever modifications these designs underwent were due to the limitations which his patrons, or the means at their disposal, imposed on him rather than to any intrinsic changes in Wren's own ideals, and a comparison of his first designs for Hampton Court (Figs.89, 90, 91, 92) with the edifice eventually built stands as the most eloquent proof of this contention.

Generally speaking, it may be said that in internal decoration Wren's work could, and did, equal that of the Baroque in such instances where conditions permitted, of which the now vanished interior of St Clement Danes, no less than the vestry, unfortunately also destroyed, of St Lawrence stood as the foremost examples. Externally, Wren's churches no less than his cathedral conformed well enough to the practice of the earlier Baroque, and it may be more than mere coincidence that two strictly contemporaneous buildings such as Fischer von Erlach's university church at Salzburg and St Paul's share the comparative restraint of their elevations equally as the exuberance of their western towers. Of greater importance, however, is a distinctive tendency inherent in some of Wren's elevations, and here chronology suggests an interesting line of development: the façade of St Mary Aldermanbury (Fig.14) may reasonably be compared with an early Renaissance edifice such as Sant'Agostino in Rome with which, incidentally, it shares the elaborate scroll motif; on the other hand, the pediment treatment of such churches as St George's points, as we have noted, to distinctly Palladian influences. The earliest of these façades, however, the south front of the Sheldonian Theatre, displays, despite its wholly different proportions, an unmistakable likeness to Vignola's first design for the Roman Gesù[759] which similarity is the more suggestive for the fact that we can hardly assume Wren to have been familiar with Vignola's design, which was considerably altered in execution, at that time.

Leaving the matter of sculpture and decoration, indicative, if not conclusive, of Wren's affinities with the Baroque, we would now turn to an element implicit in Wren's design which can be approximated very closely to its German, but not Italian, Baroque counterparts; we mean to speak here of what has been called the 're-emergence of the Gothic spirit'.[760] The suggestion that the Baroque should partake of any of the qualities of the Gothic has, indeed, been rejected with more eloquence than learning,[761] yet the subject deserves a more careful examination than either protagonists or antagonists have bestowed upon it.

An amusing, if oblique, connexion between the Gothic and the Baroque might be established by the parallels of verbiage which the detractors of both periods have used for their castigations: thus Evelyn is quoted by Stephen Wren in saying that Goths, vandals, and other barbarians were responsible for what then passed under the name of Gothic, by 'introducing a certain fantastical and *licentious* manner of building',[762] while Campbell, not many years later, spoke of 'the affected and *licentious*' works of Bernini and Fontana. Stephen Wren believed to be expressing his grandfather's opinions when he ventured to suggest that 'the moors and Arabs soon began to *debauch* this noble and useful art',[763] while the author of *Vitruvius Britannicus* charged Borromini with the attempt 'to *debauch* Mankind with his odd and chimaerical beauties',[764] On the other hand, a concrete point of similarity is touched upon when Stephen Wren speaks of the Gothic as being 'not altogether naked of gaudy sculpture, trite and busy carving' that 'gluts the eye',[765] while it is in the Baroque that a modern critic condemned 'those interminable arabesques, panels and pilasters, covered with ornament skilfully executed but destitute of meaning' which are assumed to represent 'the expression not of an artist's mind, but of a tradesman's skill paid for by the yard'.[766]

More specifically, the abundance of ornament which the Baroque, and certain aspects of Wren's work, display inevitably invites comparison with late Gothic forms. It is significant that a recent French critic should have gone so far as to call the style known as flamboyant Gothic '*le baroque médieval*',[767] and in fact, the three-dimensional curves of ogee arches cannot fail to bring to mind the intersectional curves of elliptoid vaults of the most advanced Baroque churches.[768] Yet the existence of such curves, incidental in the Gothic, but fundamental to the Baroque; the profusion of ornament; the comparable riot of pinnacles and *rocailles:* these argue a similarity, but not necessarily a connexion, between the two styles. The fact that the Gothic and the Baroque are the two epochs of European art *par excellence* which are characterized by polychrome sculpture need not be regarded as more than suggestive; but the stylistic similarities which analysis could produce, and of which the identity of conception lying behind Dürer's woodcut of the Trinity[769] and the sculptural treatment of the same subject by Egid Quirin Asam above the high altar of St John Nepomucene in Munich[770] are but two outstanding examples, points most cogently to a similarity of fundamental impulse informing the Baroque in which a 're-emergence of the Gothic spirit' may pertinently be perceived.

The mention of Dürer and Asam, however, leads us to the central point in our enquiry into the connexions between the Gothic, the Baroque, and Wren, and here we must turn to one architectural feature the presence or absence of which would seem to supply the answer to this otherwise complex question. The evidence before us is no less striking and suggestive for not having been pointed out before. But, without falling back upon criteria as intangible as Blomfield's 'virtues and serious purpose', a momentous inference can be drawn from a comparison of a view of Rome, such as obtained from Monte Pincio, a panorama of Venice as seen from the height of the Campanile, the schemata of Baroque churches of Austria, Southern Germany, and Switzerland, and a view of London such as engraved by Visscher or painted by Canaletto from the steps of Somerset House. The skyline of Rome is dominated by the dome of St Peter's which finds, like echoes, its subsidiaries scattered throughout the city; at Venice, the fact is inescapable that the domed precedent of St Mark's founded a tradition which persisted, unbroken, throughout the city's architectural history. The skyline of London, however, is dominated by the dome of St Paul's, the presence of which is rendered the more poignant for the multitude of spires which point into Canaletto's blue skies. This fact is of the greatest significance: for the re-employment, in England and Germany, of the spire in seventeenth- and eighteenth-century architecture, at a time, in fact, when the classic lands of the Renaissance were dominated by the concept of the dome, must represent a symptom of deeper meaning than the expression of a fashion.

When the Italians brought the Baroque to the lands north of the Alps, they bequeathed two prototypes to the generations of native architects which were to succeed them and transmute this heritage: the domed basilica of the Gesù type, and the centralized, circular, or elliptic plan. Both types, however, permitted the addition of a twin-tower façade and, while it is suggestive that the only two Roman churches embodying such a feature were not designed by Roman architects,[771] the fact that a twin-tower treatment was used, in Austria and Bavaria, to modify the Gesù type of façade is clearly indicative of the fact that an indigeneous concept, of manifestly Gothic derivation, was at work to transform the strict Italian heritage.[772]

We would not have stressed this point at such length if, turning to England, we were not confronted with a closely parallel situation: for just as the Baroque architects of the Catholic empire looked back, consciously or unconsciously, to the Gothic prototype of, let us say, Cologne, so Wren, in his design of towers looked back to the Gothic cathedral and parish church of England. We cannot substantiate, and therefore would not readily agree to, a view as extreme as that purporting that 'Wren, in spite of his strong classic predilections, could never free himself from the secret workings of the Gothic art of his native land within him',[773] as this seems altogether too sweeping a generalization. But if we can take, not Canterbury and York, but Norwich, Salisbury, and, not least, the old cathedral of St Paul's as typical of the English cathedral type; and if we can point to the fact that the typical English parish church is possessed of one, usually a-centrically placed tower; then it may be a token of considerable significance that Wren, when he came to design a number of churches unequalled by any of his continental contemporaries, never once even considered the possibility of a front with twin towers;[774] and, whatever he may have owed to Serlio, it is suggestive that we possess not even one single tentative sketch design which would, even remotely, remind us of the Bolognese master's unexecuted project for a twin-tower church façade.[775] Thus it may not be too much to suggest that, in the same way as we have interpreted the typically Baroque church of the continent as a 're-emergence of the Northern spirit', the church designs of Wren bear an analogous relationship to the Gothic past of his own native country.[776]

The three foregoing considerations – of sculpture, of decoration, and of elevational treatments of church fronts – have indicated such parallels as can be drawn between Wren's work and that of his Baroque contemporaries. Turning to consider the evolution of church plans, however, a question which was to Wren of as great an importance as it was to his continental colleagues, we shall be able to indicate very precisely one of the limits beyond which Wren's work cannot properly be called Baroque, for even though the premiss given was of great similarity, the solutions arrived at were entirely different.

Wren has left us a frequently-quoted statement of his ideas on church planning and the functional uses which the plan had to take into consideration. 'It would be vain', he thought, 'to make a Parish Church larger than that all who are present can both hear and see. The Romanists, indeed, may build larger churches, it is enough if they hear the murmur of the mass and see the elevation of the Host, but ours are to be fitted for auditories'.[777] The phraseology of this statement, however, has given rise to considerable misinterpretation and as Wren's views of the aims of Roman Catholic architects are themselves questionable, it is necessary to make two important reservations. Firstly, Wren could hardly have been thinking of his own times when he thought the purposes of the Roman service adequately served by the congregation's 'seeing the elevation of the Host' and 'hearing the murmur of the mass', for the Counter-Reformation had long before begun to insist on the importance of the sermon; in consequence, the Jesuit church plan was primarily designed to meet the double requirements of placing the high altar in the architectural focal point of the interior, and of providing a pulpit which, visually and acoustically, would meet the functional demands of the movement: as a Puritan apologist phrased it, Jesuit churches were planned so that 'the broad nave afforded a clear view of the altar' and 'that all could hear and see a skilfully trained preacher explode the fallacies of the heretics'.[778] From such premises, the Jesuit Order created the seventeenth-century equivalents of the friars' churches of the Middle Ages.

On the other hand, undue emphasis has been laid on Wren's stipulations concerning the 'auditory' aspect of church design; however much stress the Anglican clergy may have laid upon sermons, it would be an unwarrantable distortion of the truth to think that they regarded church architecture in terms of preaching halls; it is by no means true, as one critic would have it, that the citizens of London, when rebuilding their ruined churches, 'thought only of how they could hear and how they could see, not the elevation of the Host, but the face of the preacher'; and it is as ludicrous to think that, for St Paul's, they 'desired a vast preaching house' as to assert that, in fulfilment of such desires, 'Wren designed them such a glorified preaching house as the world has never seen' when he devised the great model.[779] This is not only to profoundly misunderstand the religious temper of the times, but also Wren's ideals and intentions. We cannot, of course, draw any general conclusions from Pepys who candidly tells us how he 'did entertain myself with my perspective glass up and down the church, by which I had the great pleasure of seeing and gazing at a great many very fine women; and what with that, and sleeping, I passed away the time till sermon was done'.[780] But it must be obvious, not only from the reaction to Puritanism and its reliance on the spoken word, but also from the pedestrian tone and content of many collections of Restoration sermons, that the sermon did by no means occupy as paramount an importance as a superficial reading of Wren's statements would lead us to believe. Yet while he, alike the Jesuits, was obviously stressing 'the importance of buildings where sermons were audible', it is quite clear that both he and they 'wished a great deal more than sermons to be heard in churches'.[781] We need only point to the elaborate setting devised for the high altar of the great model design, to the Bernini-like structure envisaged for the completed cathedral, or even the ingenuity with which he turned the converging east end of St Clement Danes into a setting for the altar which has, not unjustly, been described as theatrical,[782] to realize that, despite his own words, Wren's architectural ideas went as much beyond the requirements of the preaching house in the Lutheran, or Nonconformist, meaning of the word, as the liturgy of the Anglican Church differed from the austerities of the Puritan service.

Yet, as fundamentally similar as the intentions of Wren and of the Baroque architects are thus seen to have been, the solutions severally devised were wholly different. As outstanding a feature of the Continental Baroque as the Jesuit plan is the adoption and the development of the elliptic plan which, carried to the conclusion of an employment of combinations of elliptic plans and elliptoid vaults, was the foundation upon which the style, formalistically as well as spiritually, could be evolved to its final achievements. The ellipse was a novel introduction into the repertory of church plans when Serlio recommended it[783] and when Vignola first employed it.[784] The development of the form suffered a brief check when the Council of Trent promulgated a proscription of centralized forms and recommended a return to basilican and cruciform plans, yet with the earlier Renaissance the centralized form had obtained so powerful a hold on the architectural imagination of the times, that the primary result was the conscious combination of basilican and centralized schemes, first lucidly exemplified in Vignola's plan for the Roman Gesù.[785]

The development of centralized plans, however, was by no means permanently arrested by Tridentine anathema, and the most cogent refutation of the erroneous, though widespread, identification of the Baroque with the Jesuit Order is contained in the fact that the architects of the Baroque, particularly those north of the Alps, very soon turned to the problems and possibilities of elliptic plans, not only disregarding the Council's enactments, but distinctly dissociating themselves from the solution evolved and disseminated by the Society of Jesus. As the Gesù scheme hardened into a type, the evolution of the Baroque style passed into other hands than those of Jesuit architects, for it was the preoccupation of Borromini, Bernini, and Guarini[786] with problems of elliptic plans which constitute the real foundation of the Baroque.

In Italy, the novel form did not displace the domed basilica; beyond the Alps, however, it attained a pre-eminence which must represent a unique fact in art history. Though the ideas of the Italian originators found not inconsiderable reflections in French architecture of the seventeenth and eighteenth centuries,[787] they attained, in Austria and Southern Germany, an importance far exceeding that of any other type. Introduced to Salzburg by Caspare Zugalli,[788] Fischer von Erlach at once adopted the idea and, significantly, made the oval plan the basis for all but one of his major designs[789] culminating in the church of San Carlo Borromeo in Vienna built at the very time when St Paul's was nearing completion.

From Austria the form spread all over the Catholic empire, to be found in innumerable examples extending from Bohemia to the Rhineland,[790] yet the employment of the single ellipse was not the end of its possibilities: in the hands of one of the most brilliant of the entire school, the elliptic plan is echoed by the elliptoid vault and in the development of final refinements of a multiplicity of elliptic forms, overlapping on plan, interpenetrating in spatial elevation. What is of the greatest significance, though, is that Balthasar Neumann's masterpiece, the pilgrimage church of Vierzehnheiligen in Franconia, which unquestionably represents the late climax of the style as San Carlo Borromeo had represented its early maturity, creates an approximation to a cruciform shape composed of two circles, three major and one minor oval,[791] and thus represents, with its twin-tower façade, an outstanding instance of that fundamental Baroque impulse towards synthesis which, stylistically, renders it so unique and, ideologically, of so great a psychological interest. Speaking within the context of pure form, however, it was inevitable that such impulses, manifest in such concepts of design, had to lead to an interpretation of ecclesiastical architecture in which the long-preserved independence of the several parts had to be abandoned. With such concepts of design, the strict demarcation of spaces, as the Renaissance knew it, became obsolete, for even with ground-plans of such admirable clarity as many Baroque churches possess, the elements of nave, choir, transepts, and crossing become fluid within each other, patently and manifestly existent, yet separated by no clearly visible boundaries. Such a development would not have been possible without the employment of the ellipse, for all the basic forms upon which European architecture had been built prior to the Baroque – the square, the rectangle, and the circle – were too finite, too clearly defined to allow of a fusion of similar or dissimilar components. The suggestion lies temptingly close that the employment of the elliptic plan was not cause but effect, in that it only came to be utilized when such a fundamental impulse towards the dissolution of parts and a larger synthesis and integration had come to govern architecture. But, without attempting here to elucidate such an issue, we have here reached the most cogent point of departure to demonstrate one of Wren's fundamental, and most significant, divergences from the Baroque.

As we have seen, Wren was by no means averse to originality of form. The submission of a Greek cross plan to serve for St Paul's cathedral was as unorthodox to the clergy as his freedom and almost careless handling of the classic orders is to purists. To Wren, form was a fluid concept governed by personal predilection for, as we have seen, he perceived no incongruity or inconsistency in designing a centralized interior when the site suggested a basilican plan (as in the case of St Mary-at-Hill and St Mildred, Bread Street) or, conversely, in creating the illusion of a basilican interior when the site would have been far more congenial to a centralized treatment (as in the case of St George and St Dionis).

Wren's interest in elliptic and irregularly centralized forms, however, has an interesting history. It should be remembered that, as a youthful Savilian professor at Oxford, he had corresponded with Pascal, and written a treatise, on the subject of cycloids; the problems of conic sections apparently occupied his mind at a time when scientific preoccupations had long given place to architectural practice.[792] But the forms which so obviously fascinated the scientist did not, it would seem, particularly interest the architect.[793] It is true, he used elliptic shapes in many details of a more or less subordinate nature;[794] but, architecturally, the circle, square, and rectangle occupied his attention to the exclusion of the ellipse.

Thus there were only two among all his churches which made use of this form: St Benet Fink (Fig.28) and St Antholin (Fig.55), designed about 1670 and 1677 respectively. Both churches, unhappily, have been destroyed, but extensive as is our knowledge of their vanished charms, we are by no means convinced that Wren's intentions motivating the employment of elliptic forms were in any way comparable with those of Bernini, Fischer, and Neumann. In theory, Wren had included the oval in his recommendations of geometrical figures, though relegated to a secondary category. In practice, however, we cannot but be struck by the relative unimportance of the two buildings where it was actually employed; furthermore, were we to regard these two isolated instances as small-scale studies in the same way as the dome of St Stephen's served as the remote ancestor of the dome of St Paul's, we would find no development of the experiment, no fulfilment of the promise they contained. Lastly, if an ideological impulse towards synthesis had been the basic cause of these two designs, we could not conceive Wren forsaking that aim to return to more conservative and traditional plans, and we could never reconcile – but by an explanation of facile compliance – his return to a variety of Gothic in one of the last churches he was to build in the City of London, St Mary Somerset.

It has been suggested that 'the greatest deviation from the basilican model', allegedly represented by St Stephen's, is 'tantamount to pronouncing it his masterpiece',[795] but Wren's theory and practice show such a view to be wholly erroneous: in the first section of this study we have been able to show that Wren's increasing maturity engendered an increasing reliance on, and progressive refinement of, the basilican plan; and no further comment seems necessary upon Wren's preferences beyond pointing to the fact that when, at the end of his career, he propounded some general specifications for an ideal of church planning, he chose his own basilican church of St James's, Westminster, as the most representative prototype.

Thus in Wren's sparse and merely occasional use of the typically and symbolically Baroque form we are able to draw a distinct dividing line. Concretely, St Benet Fink and St Antholin represent experiments which Wren was not to follow up; experiments, moreover, which were not entirely unconditioned by outside circumstances for, concerning the latter, we would by no means agree that one 'can discover little of genius in it', but it is evident that its elliptic plan was no more nor less than the result of 'the adaptation of means to circumstances'.[796]

This interpretation of Wren's use of elliptic plans is germane to the contention that his design concept remained intrinsically within the limits inherent in the Renaissance without ever crossing the boundary line of the Baroque. Indeed, in a few instances conformity to Renaissance ideals goes so far that an interrelation of parts is attained which permits of neither addition nor subtraction of any of them, thus fulfilling the famous Albertian stipulation. On the other hand, there may be an occasional experiment, of which the plan of St Stephen's is the outstanding example, where the demarcation and distinction of parts is sufficiently ambiguous to resemble their dissolution in the Baroque meaning of the word. But these are exceptions to the more general impression which the corpus of Wren's work leaves on the student's mind: namely that the spatial independence of the parts is never abandoned, and that their combination is not governed by any overriding principles such as had dominated early Renaissance design; their alignment is not only arbitrary, but even interchangeable, so that design remains fluid up to the moment of actual execution, subject to no law or precept, and empirical in its selection, introduction, transference, and elimination of any parts of the original idea.

In the final analysis, it is almost possible to see a broad development of influences to which Wren was subject, inasmuch as they reflect, in his early work, an historical progression: the influence of antiquity, so clearly apparent in the earliest projects for St Paul's, is soon replaced by Renaissance models; the plan of the first definite project for the cathedral as we have construed it – the pure, domed basilica – recalls the classic Jesuit type conform to the plan of Le Mercier's Sorbonne. Yet even though Wren's late manner is more distinctly Baroque than anything that can be found in the planning of the City churches, it would be as unrealistic to regard his development as an artist as the individual progression through the history of styles, from Roman classic to early Renaissance, from High Renaissance to Baroque; as it would be ludicrous to assert the opposite, namely that with increasing maturity,

Wren 'returned to the purer and more strenuous architecture of Inigo Jones'.[797]

None the less, however cogently a progression of influences may appear, it yet remains a fact that they are never the major determinants of Wren's designs, nor do they ever dominate a period, however short, of Wren's development: the distinct Baroque qualities seen in the south front of the Sheldonian Theatre are separated by no more than half a decade from the strictly classical west front of St Magnus; the increasing refinement of the basilican plan is concurrent and contemporaneous with many of the imaginatively decorative steeples, just as the exuberant fantasy of Bow steeple is not many years removed from the pseudo-classicism of Trinity College library.

Taken as a whole, Wren's work is thus seen as a fluctuating intermingling of Renaissance and Baroque ideals, partaking of both, and yet never wholly belonging to either. Of the Renaissance ideal, it retained some of the externalities, and the conception of spatial values as distinct unities, sometimes related to, but never fused with, one another. Of the Baroque ideology, Wren possessed the disregard of classic proprieties, the disinclination to be bound by preconceived rules such as had governed the design of the orders, a tendency towards exuberance of ornamentation, and an attempt to combine, in the very concept of his towers and steeples, an essentially Northern cultural heritage with the legacy of the Italian Renaissance.

This duality was the basis for much that is fresh and original in Wren's work. But it was equally responsible for an adverse aspect there to be detected; for while Wren partially embraced Renaissance ideals, his design never attained the intellectual logic, the subtle harmony, and the complex organization which characterizes the works of Alberti and Palladio. On the other hand, his partial adherence to Baroque ideals bestows on his design the same freedom of which that style so completely availed itself; but if his design for the dome of St Paul's transcends even the maximum of Baroque subterfuge,[798] such liberties and deceptions are neither engendered by, nor do they engender the emotional intensity to which the Baroque had sacrificed the classic repose of the Renaissance. It is almost unnecessary to point out that, had Wren proceeded from such integrated and complete design concepts as Renaissance architects did, the inconsistencies and contradictions found in his work might have been avoided as much as the calamities of the piers of St Paul's, built for a dome the size, shape, and weight of which were yet undecided. But it is pertinent to emphasize that in spite of all the freedom which Wren was given and the liberties he took, he never attained to the intrinsic dynamism which is the hall-mark of the best of Baroque art.

Thus Wren's position as a European architect is far more ambiguous, and the influences to which, at various times, he was subject far more complex than has hitherto been assumed. To have been influenced, as Wren unquestionably was, by both Palladio and Bernini points to an ideological latitudinarianism which cannot easily be paralleled, and which is not easily explained; to make Wren symbolical of a 'national indifference to the rules of pure logic' and to contend that 'his was the logic of life, fluid, and adaptable as life itself, and far above the logic of schools and books'[799] proposes a qualitative judgement more cogently than an explanation. But Wren's position as we have perceived it is not to be regarded as the result of esoteric predilection availing itself capriciously of inspiration stemming from diverse, heterogeneous, and even mutually contradictory sources. Wren's position can only be interpreted and explained by the ideological diversities which differentiate the Renaissance from the Baroque, and Wren from both, and it is to such considerations that we would devote the last part of this study.

In the foregoing chapters we have discussed the corpus of Wren's work in the detail of its manifold facets, and the connexions, parallels, and divergences which it reveals when compared with such historical and contemporaneous work as can be held to have exerted an influence upon the formation of his style. But the appraisal of an architecture, be it of a period, or of an individual artist, ought not to confine itself to an application of formal analysis capable of yielding an overall impression of an architect's design faculties, his technical equipment, the inspiration operative upon him, and the stages of development which his mind undergoes during the years of his career. Architecture, as an art, necessarily contains elements which are completely extraneous to the reality of stone, brick, and mortar, elements of which these tangible materials are but the tools. Style is not merely a fashion, a vogue, or the reflection of an individual mind: it also contains spiritual qualities which find their visible expression, their token, symbol, and symptom, in the tangible reality of the edifice. Thus, if the first two parts of this study have been concerned with an examination and an analysis of form, this last chapter must be devoted to their implications; and here, necessarily, our range of reference will have to be drawn with a much wider compass, for the 'search and study of the history of the mind ought not to be confined to one art only. It is by the analogy that one art bears to another, that many things are ascertained, which either were but faintly seen, or, perhaps, would not have been discovered at all, if the inventor had not received the first hints from the practices of a sister art on a similar occasion'.[800]

There is no dearth, indeed, of indications how highly Wren was esteemed as a scientist; it may be too much to claim that 'the members of the newly formed Royal Society adored Wren' and that 'his opinion was always sought and obtained before anything definite was done',[801] but the opinions of Oughtred, Barrow, Hooke, and Evelyn cannot, even allowing for the florid verbiage of the period, be lightly dismissed.[802] On the other hand, it is strange to reflect that of Wren, the architect, not even his closest associates and friends of many years' standing should have left us more than a cursory appreciation.[803] It is not likely that Wren's career would have been so long, and his corpus of work so extensive if it had not met with contemporaneous approval and appreciation; but, like Michelangelo and Titian, he lived to see the reaction which set in against the style of his work when the fashions sponsored by Lord Burlington became the touchstone of English architectural taste. For a brief while, we can discern a dual current in architectural art, one of which drew its inspiration from Italian and French sources of the seventeenth century, and is represented by Gibbs, Archer, and White and, to a limited degree, Vanbrugh and Hawksmoor; while the other faction, headed by Burlington and including Leoni, Campbell, and Ware, advocated a strict return to the ideals and canons of Palladio. The former group, 'the scarce practitioners of the baroque',[804] managed to survive for some time after Wren's death; but it is evident that it was the latter which, even before that date, came to represent the dominant influence. Thus, inasmuch as the former represented, in some small measure, a continuation of Wren's tradition,[805] the ultimate and complete victory of the Palladians betokens the remarkable fact that Wren, the supreme architectural genius of later seventeenth-century England, neither set a fashion nor founded a school, and that the style which was the successor to his manner implied the repudiation of the concepts and ideals which had inspired him.

Much has been claimed for the school and vigorous tradition which he, allegedly as Inigo Jones's disciple, is supposed to have founded.[806] Yet not only the architecture but also the writings of the eighteenth century would lead one to think, not only that it was, at all times, at pains to emphasize its rejection of Wren's ideas, but also that it showed rather less than scant reverence for the work of the man who, without doubt, is the outstanding figure among architects since the Middle Ages. The Palladians, as we have noted, formed a reaction against, and not a continuation of, Wren's precepts and, adamant as they were in their condemnation of any architecture which could not be justified by the authority of the *Quattro Libri*, they could not but condemn the work of Wren which, as we have seen, had treated those canons with a freedom and latitude tantamount to disregard.

Yet Palladianism was not the last word; by the middle of the century, Cambridge could satirize the antiquarian researches of the Royal Society,[807] and within forty years of Burlington's and Leoni's first publication of Palladio, voices were heard to pride themselves on 'how much of late we are improved in architecture; not merely by the adoption of what we call Chinese, nor by the restoration of what we call Gothic; but by a happy mixture of both'.[808] Four years after this achievement the death blow was given to Palladianism when one of the prime instigators of the 'Attic complex', at Vicenza, 'walked out to see the different buildings of Palladio, of which I am no admirer' to find, and judge, that 'his private houses are ill-adjusted . . .'.[809]

The Grecian phase which followed was not to last long; for soon a need for picturesqueness made itself felt which expressed itself in a critical attitude of all predecessors, whether 'Attic', Palladian, Wren, or Jones.[810] And the end of the century turned the tables on all that had gone before in the previous 100 years, including Vanbrugh,[811] when it could opine that Lincoln 'is the finest of our cathedrals; and why not, when rebuilding in London, follow such a Model? How superior to lumbering Grecian [*sic*!] St Paul's!'[812]

That the critics of the nineteenth century should have found themselves unable to appreciate the art of the sixteenth and seventeenth centuries need not surprise us; for that age was not only too preoccupied with Gothic fancies, but also too self-righteous in its ideas of moral rectitude to allow any merit to an architecture which was not merely contemporaneous with but, indeed, the direct result of the patronage of a Julius II, a Cesare Borgia, a Louis XIV, or even a Charles II. It was argued, eloquently if illogically, that the corruption of those ages must needs find its reflection in the arts, and that, therefore, whatever art may have been the corollary to the Inquisition, the Counter-Reformation, the Revocation of the Edict of Nantes, or the secret Treaty of Dover must necessarily bear the stigmata of the worst moral aspects of these historic happenings. We need not here quote the rhetoric which Ruskin lavished on the 'foul torrent of the Renaissance', under which generic label he indiscriminately included the art of the sixteenth, seventeenth, and eighteenth centuries; but it is important to note the change of the criteria of appraisal which had taken place. Colen Campbell had condemned Bernini and Fontana on purely stylistic grounds;[813] the Palladians had condemned Wren for his deviations from their master, Reynolds for his lack of 'picturesqueness',[814] and the turn of the century had reproached him with the 'Grecian' character of his architecture. With the nineteenth century, however, the basis of criticism shifted from the formal, the fashionable, and the fanciful: it became moral and ethical.

We need not here consider the selective manipulation of historical evidence which permitted Ruskin to arrive at his condemnation of the Renaissance and its progeny; nor need we restate that the depravity which furnished him with a pretext was one, but neither the sole, nor even the most important, aspect of the period of his loathing; lastly, it does not seem necessary any longer to refute the notion that moral depravity must necessarily result in bad art, as neither Alberti's San Francesco nor Michelangelo's St Peter's are aesthetic achievements of lesser significance for the questionable character of Malatesta and Julius II. But in the last resort it was not only the era's preoccupation with the nobility of savages, or the romanticism of Arthurian fable, which proved the effective bar to an appreciation of the Renaissance; for equal responsibility must be assigned to the decline of ecclesiastical importance, the constitutionalism of monarchy, and the confident faith in the progressive amelioration of humanity based on strict materialism: all these were insurmountable obstacles to the appreciation of an art whose materialism was absolutist and whose spiritualism at least partly metaphysical, an art, in short, which had been the background and mirror of a social and religious climate which in itself was anathema to the English critic and social historian of Victoria's era. The consequence of this can be inferred from the dictum on Wren of a Ruskinian disciple who, in an attempt at eulogy which would not conflict with generally held taboos, was forced into saying that Wren 'was slave to no style; he took what seemed best to him from Classic, Gothic, and Moorish art, knowing that the best in art, whatever its source, must necessarily harmonize, because the best human'.[815]

What damage Ruskin inflicted on the Renaissance was not,

however, of long duration; for its masters, Brunelleschi, Alberti, Bramante, Leonardo, and Michelangelo, were eventually restored to the reverence in which their own age had held them. The Baroque, however, partly in consequence of this revaluation, came to be regarded as the decadence of the Renaissance and no less exempted from stricture, abuse, and derision for being the avowed and acknowledged successor to a great epoch.[816] It represented the worst features, both stylistically and morally, which could attach to the architecture of any period: it was the product of an age the alleged viciousness,[817] immorality,[818] and artificiality[819] of which Victorian morality could but regard with horror; it was unacceptable to contemporary taste, as it could be reconciled with neither the oriental picturesqueness of the Regency, nor with the later decades, least of all with the Hellenic and Gothic revivals which, from Pugin to Scott, dominated the popular mind. Thus it is extremely suggestive, if not surprising, that at a time when Ruskinian ideology still retained a general acceptance, an Ecclesiastical Commission of the Church of England, in remarkable ignorance of their aesthetic value, could decide upon the destruction of a number of Wren's churches and, though this may anticipate a later part of the story, let it be recalled that another commission, convened in the second decade of this century, could contemplate, with perfect equanimity, the destruction of another dozen churches, thus signifying, even at this late date, a truly astonishing depreciation of their architect's genius; while the astounding fact remains to record that the last of Wren's churches to fall a victim to utilitarian interests, before the German air force took its toll among the meagre remainder, was demolished in the year 1939.

However, Ruskinian judgements could not remain in force indefinitely; and we find that, all his strictures on St Paul's notwithstanding, a revaluation of Wren's art began to make itself felt during the latter part of the nineteenth century, significantly at a time when, on the continent, critics first began to doubt whether the Baroque was truly no more than the decadence and final decay of the Renaissance tradition, or whether virtues and qualities of a character hitherto unsuspected might not be found in it.[820] The problem of chosing a label, which arose with the revaluation of Wren's art, however, was left unsolved by avoiding it; it consisted in the fact that at the time when Wren lived and built, the true Renaissance tradition of Italy was a thing of the past, but that his life and work was contemporaneous with such continental Baroque works upon which no abuse seemed too strong to lavish. The unalterable fact remained that Wren was born in the same year as Spinoza, Bourdaloue, and Lully, and that it was not only Wren who died in 1723, but also Fischer von Erlach and Meinrad Guggenbichler. The solution of this difficulty – for it would not have done to include Wren's work with the Baroque to which it chronologically belonged, but of which the contempt was almost hallowed by English criticism – was seen in a purely dialectical differentiation: the Baroque was, and remained, an 'irregularly shaped, grotesque, whimsical style of ornamentation';[821] Wren's art was given the label of 'late Renaissance'.[822]

While the generality of writers claimed Wren's architecture as 'Renaissance' or even 'Palladian', it was in 'the literature that appeared on the occasion of the Wren bicentenary that a number of writers were at pains to present Wren in the character of a great baroque architect'.[823] Such a novelty of outlook could not, of course, go unchallenged, particularly when it is recalled that even at that late date authoritative English criticism was still castigating the Baroque in Campbellian terms; the spiritual heirs of the Palladians and of Ruskin protested vigorously[824] and gave proof to the contention, 'that there is such a phenomenon as English baroque art was often overlooked until comparatively recently; and that there is an English baroque religious art is still rarely appreciated'.[825] But, notwithstanding all protestations, the view has been gaining ground[826] and if we are to devote this part of our study to an examination of this question it is not in order to present the results of formal analysis, outlined in the previous chapter; nor for the purpose of arriving at some dialectical conclusion as to the particular category – Renaissance, Palladian, Mannerist, [827] or Baroque – Wren's work is to be classed; but in order to examine in what degree – if any – his architecture is expressive of those epochs and movements for which it has variously been claimed.

It would not be relevant here to enter into all the factors, political, social, and intellectual, which jointly were responsible for the rise of the Italian Renaissance. Suffice it to re-state that 'classic forms in Italy were indigenous and bound to reappear'[828] and to emphasize once more that the Renaissance was neither a self-conscious return to a past and defunct style, nor an artificial and sentimental revival of a mythologic age; but the recrudescence of a profound and ancient tradition which was not to be extinguished by the temporary invasion of alien forms. Despite nineteenth-century opinions to the contrary, it is not even necessary to point to such artists who, even at the height of the Gothic fashion in Italy, could remain wholly unaffected by it, to support the legitimacy of speaking of a Tuscan proto-Renaissance at a time when France, England, and Germany were wholly absorbed in the aspirations and the problems inherent in the pointed arch. The strength of the ancient, classic tradition in Italy can be judged by the ease with which it displaced the Gothic; for had the Renaissance been but a self-conscious revival it would be unreasonable to assume that it could have triumphed so easily over the Gothic, more unreasonable still to explain that a fashion allegedly so esoteric and artificial should have furnished the starting point of a tradition which was to dominate not only Italy, but also France, England, Germany, Spain, and Austria for more than three centuries.

For our present purpose, we need only point to one of the fundamental differences which exist between Gothic and Renaissance: the Gothic age has left us ample record of the religious fervour and devotion of its time, and the very quality of Gothic architecture seems expressive of the passion of faith with which 'Tyrants, Lay Potentates full of honour and riches, Nobles both men and women, bent their proud and swelling necks to the traces of waggons and drew them to the shrine of Christ like brute beasts'.[829] But if we are to search for the philosophical and ideological impulses to which the rise of the style might be attributed, we shall find the accounts of Abbot Suger as barren as the note-book of Villard de Honnecourt; thus leaving it to the historian and critic of later times to construe whatever explanations of the phenomenon he could within contexts as diverse as those of racial significance, of social structure and changes, or psychological interpretation.

On the other hand, the nineteenth century's misunderstanding of the impulses which gave rise to the architecture of the Renaissance was the result partly of ignorance, partly of a deliberate misapplication of frequently irrelevant historical material. For the Renaissance, and Renaissance architects and artists particularly, were eloquent not merely on matters of surface appearance of their arts, such as the proper dimensions and disposition of the orders, or of the limbs of the human body; but also on the philosophical and symbolical factors which were of such overwhelming importance in their selection of suitable forms from among the classic, but pagan, heritage.

Nothing can demonstrate the tendency of combining historic precedent with philosophic significance better than the Renaissance predilection for centralized plans and for the employment of the dome. Of historic precedent, there was an *embarras de richesse* from which to choose: the Pantheon at Rome no less than the early Christian remains and baptisteries, equally as the Byzantine precedent which, operative through a multitude of channels, had left the concept of the domed, centralized church as one of its prime legacies to Italian architectural thought and tradition.[830] More interesting than the structural derivation of the Renaissance dome is its symbolism: mere precedent, whether classical, Early Christian, or Byzantine, was not enough for Alberti[831] and the later theorists: they went back to antiquity and Hellenic philosophy as well as to patristic writing, and based their predilection for circle and dome on the divine symbolism which the former had possessed even for the Oprhic poets[832] and the cosmic significance which the latter had so appropriately possessed for the religious imagination of all times.

These are not relationships wilfully construed *a posteriori* to satisfy a desire of perceiving a symbolic meaning in every material form; for the writings of Renaissance architects, mathematicians, and philosophers – and, be it remembered, these were not different departments of thought – leave no room to doubt that such were actually the considerations governing the arts. When

Palladio expressed a preference for the circular, domed form as the ideal scheme for a church, he did so because he did not 'doubt that the little temple we make should resemble this very great one';[833] the choice of the circular plan was not only motivated by the consideration that the circle is 'alone among all figures, simple, uniform, equal, strong, and most capacious'[834] but also because it is 'the most proper figure to show the unity, infinite essence, uniformity, and justice of God'.[835] The corollary to this neo-Platonic sentiment was the symbolism which associated the dome with the vault of heaven, and historical writing and evidence leave no room to doubt that this significance should be made unmistakable by painting: adumbrated by Alberti,[836] the cosmic symbolism of the hemispherical vault was made incapable of misinterpretation by the painted representations of the sky which are so conspicuous a feature of many Renaissance domes.[837]

However, not only a divine, but also a humanistic significance is inherent in the basic centralized shapes, the square, and the circle, when the conscious effort is considered by which a relationship was established between these geometrical forms and the human figure, of which effort the writings and drawings of some of the greatest minds offer the most eloquent testimony.[838] Linked with such relationships is what may be considered the most important factor of Renaissance art, namely the concept of universal geometrical proportion and mathematical ratios which found its most highly developed expression in the theories of harmonic proportions by which not only the architecture, the philosophy and music, but the entire cosmology of an epoch was rationalized.[839] This in itself was not the least token of the supersession of scholastic Aristotelianism; for the classic precedent of the conception of a rational cosmos governed by harmonic ratios was to be found with Euclid, with the Pythagoreans, and, most importantly, in Plato's *Timaeus*.

It is neither possible, nor necessary within the context of this study, to discuss in detail the import of those theories which represent the intellectual achievements of Alberti, of Piero della Francesca, of Luca Pacioli, Francesco Giorgi, and Daniele Barbaro. But while it should be recalled that the predominant Aristotelianism of the Middle Ages had never dominated the world of the intellect to the complete exclusion of the Platonic system – for which fact the works of Origen and the school of Bernard of Chartres are sufficient proof – neo-Platonism was a force which not only permeated the scholastic circles of the Renaissance, such as the academy at Careggi, but represents so vital and all-pervading an element that it is difficult to overestimate its importance. Within the context of this cosmology, we can see the intellect of a century confidently striving in an aspiration towards truth, an aspiration no longer vague and emotional as had been the medieval mysticism of iconographical symbols, but an aspiration so profoundly humanistic and intellectual as to

be able to conceive of the divine purpose in the form of mathematical equations.

We would not here, as we have remarked, expound the subtleties with which the Renaissance intellect construed a cosmology from a mathematical precept; but only point to some of the ubiquitous signs by which we can measure the supreme importance of harmonic ratio to that generation. Let us point to the Renaissance endeavour of Pico della Mirandola to reconcile the Book of Genesis with Plato's *Timaeus*; to the importance which Vitruvius possessed in the eyes of Renaissance architect-philosophers, not merely for being, peradventure, the only extant classical author on architecture, but also for the constant, if vague and ambiguous, references to Hellenic proportion; we need not recall the multitudinous editions of Plato which came not only from the Aldine Press but equally from those of many other Italian printers of the sixteenth century. But let us emphasize the fact that Piero della Francesca saw his ultimate achievement not in the cool passion of his pigments, but in his treatise on the five Platonic regular solids; and that his friend Pacioli had himself portrayed, his hand resting on Euclid's Thirteenth Book by the side of a crystalline dodecahedron, very probably by the very man to whom Dürer was to appeal to learn the 'secret' theory of measurement and numbers.[840]

We can thus see Renaissance design, in theory and practice, imbued at every point with symbolic meaning. And though the ultimate derivation is unquestionably Hellenic, that is to say, pagan, the integration of Platonic and Christian thought made it possible that Alberti's stipulation should not seem incongruous in demanding that churches be placed upon a podium, just as Hellenic temples had stood upon the three sacred steps of the stylobate; and if Christian quaternities as much as Hellenic tetractyses were equally the spiritual progenitors of his choice of the simple proportions of 1:2:3:4, this was by no means considered heretical even if his derivation was not improbably the commentary on Platonic mathematics of Theon of Smyrna, in whose first progression the sum of the first four terms equals the sacred number ten,[841] the very number of books into which Alberti, following Vitruvius, had divided his famous treatise.

That the fundamental principles of harmonic proportions derive from a purely intellectual premiss need not be doubted, for in Renaissance theory and practice, in the work and writings of Alberti, of Serlio, Piero della Francesca, Trissino, and Palladio we find a reconciliation of Christian philosophy with Hellenic theory in which the system of harmonic ratios formed the keystone. Proportion in architecture was the ultimate aim, and ultimate achievement of Palladio as much as of the other architectural theorists of the Renaissance, but it was a concept of proportion in a truly cosmic sense which, though of great mathematical precision and, originally, exclusive of incommensurable ratios, was yet imbued with spiritual values and with a sense of universality which renders it one of the greatest achievements of humanism.

That the ratios productive of 'beautiful' proportions in architecture were not exclusive to that art, nor, indeed, native to it, had already been recognized by Alberti; drawing his inspiration from Plato, Pythagoras, and Vitruvius, he was fully aware that the achievement of perfect architectural proportion was the result of applying those mathematical relationships which govern the physics of musical harmonies.[842] Thus in his recommendations for plans developed from the square, the ratios given, namely the square plus one-third, the square plus one-half, and the square doubled,[843] are the architectural equivalents of the string lengths, or tensions, which produce the musical fourth, fifth, and the octave.[844] That these simple ratios, 1:2, 2:3, and 3:4, were clearly of Platonic origin, not only as representing the first four terms of one of the Timaean progressions, but also as the sum of the four numbers giving the 'perfect Pythagorean number' ten, would seem evident, particularly as the parallel development of the two series of progressions given in *Timaeus* produce, in their combination, ratios reiterating the two latter terms of Albertian theory *ad infinitum*.[845]

When Serlio amplified this range by adding the square plus a quarter, and the square plus two-thirds[846] he added, musically speaking, the major third and the major sixth; but in adding the root two rectangle[847] he introduced the first incommensurable, non-musical, ratio somewhat indicative of his academic rather than intellectually original work. Yet this incongruous addition points only to the fact that Serlio had absorbed the philosophical premisses of architectural theory but imperfectly; it does not impair the fact – lucidly demonstrated by Palladio, who accepted Serlio's innovation in theory, but does not seem to have used it in practice – that it was the concept of cosmic harmony, musically eloquent and mathematically simple, which dominated the art theory of the Renaissance. The relationships between mathematics, music, and architecture were ideas of which the Middle Ages had already been conscious;[848] but it required the neo-Platonic replacement of scholastic Aristotelianism and the full flowering of Renaissance humanism to create concepts of proportion which were to embrace all fields of human thought and endeavour in a truly cosmic comprehensiveness.

Yet neither the concepts, nor the outward forms of Renaissance design could remain unchanged; nor would we expect that a period so imbued with creative impetus could be satisfied with the achievement of a standard, however integrated and perfected, without feeling the urge for further development.[849] Thus the momentum of intellectual force resulted in a rapid further development of style from the static unity of the Renaissance to the esoteric subtlety of Mannerism, and finally, under the impact of a complete change of the intellectual climate, to the impassioned dynamism of the Baroque. 'Bramante's formula is scarcely asserted, the poise and balance of classic proportion is scarcely struck, before their fine adjustments are swept away upon the torrent that springs from Michelangelo. In the ferment of creation, of which Italy from this time forth is the scene, the greatest names count, relatively, for little. Palladio, destined to provide the canon of English classical building, and to become, for us, the prime interpreter of the antique, here makes but a momentary stand among contending creeds. His search for form, though impassioned, was too reactionary, his conclusions too academic and too set, for an age when creative vigour was still, beyond measure, turbulent. The time was past when an architecture of such calculated restraint as Sanmichele had foreshadowed could capture long attention; and the art of Peruzzi, rich though it was with never-exhausted possibilities, seems to have perished unexplored, because, so to say, its *tempo* was too slow, its interest too unobtrusive. Vignola, stronger perhaps than these, is before long forgotten in Bernini . . . .'[850]

Besides this natural development, another circumstance appeared which was to influence the further evolution of art to such a degree as it might, for with the coming of the Counter-Reformation, the entire Italian scene changed. The architecture of the Renaissance, and even more so that of Mannerism, had been esoteric art forms, no less significant for this fact, yet primarily based on purely intellectual premises, and the concern, largely, of the various academies which had sprung up in emulation of the famous progenitor at Careggi. An art form the complete appreciation of which should be confined to circles, however wide, of Renaissance *cognoscenti*, though, was not the goal which the Counter-Reformation could envisage. Its artistic weapon needed to be an art far less subtle, far less complex and less intellectualized than had been the art of the pristine Renaissance. It needed an art, for the propogation of its aims and the prosecution of its objectives, which possessed a direct and not necessarily intellectual appeal, an art which spoke more eloquently to the senses, not to reason, but to the heart. Thus, as the spirit of the age changed from the scholarly liberalism of the early part of the century to the single-mindedness of its latter end, so the change in temper was bound to produce its repercussions in the arts, a change which is significant, but which yet obeys the extraneous dictates of form to a limited degree only, to pursue again a course of logical evolution when once whatever degree of political coercion that had ever existed had ceased to operate.

The causes of which the Reformation was the eventual outcome were not only noticeable to the pastor at Wittenberg: they were equally obvious to individuals as different as St Teresa of Avila, Michelangelo, and Pierre Ronsard. In Spain, the saint strove to reform her own Carmelite Order and the laxity into which she had seen its ideals fall, in Rome the sculptor consorted with Vittoria Colonna and Cardinal Pole and the liberalism of the thought of their circle of *spirituali* is amply attested by the charge of heresy which the later Pope Paul IV brought against the cardinal; in Paris the poet lent the support of his genius to the reformatory and conciliatory spirit which informed the Cardinal de Lorraine and his circle. The serene assurance of the previous century had gone; and Catholics no less than Protestants looked critically upon the signs of decadence which characterized the papal tiara and curia of the age. This was by no means the result of an accidental succession of individuals who might have been fitter to rule with the sword than with the word; but was equally the outcome of the economic upheavals – the dislocation brought about by the spoils of the Spanish Americas, the results produced by the Portuguese voyages of discovery, the shifting balance of power in the Mediterranean as the loss of Venice's influence accrued to Islam as gain. Beyond these factors loomed large the most potent of them all: the religious division of Europe, and the challenge which Protestantism had flung at the Church of Rome. Europe had arrived at a juncture where the spiritualism of the Middle Ages must needs part from the avenues of materialism opened up by the growth and consolidation of national entities, by the discovery of unknown lands and treasures beyond the seas, and by the religious wars of the age which could not but lead to the annihilation of its one-time spiritual unity.

For the individual there were several ways which pointed to a solution of the problem; St Teresa might see it in her desire to become, by her acts of contrition, an extenuating and conciliating element in the chaos of heresy, religious strife, and growing materialism which she saw all around her. But in the wake of this noble movement came a personality of far lesser practical importance, but of far greater spiritual significance: St John of the Cross, the greatest mystic of the Renaissance, to whom the solution appeared in the utter abandonment of the material for the spiritual, to whom the Apocalypse and the Song of Songs were nearer than the Passion and in whose writing, by a remarkable historical parallel, the eroticism of Oriental carnality becomes transmuted into a system of symbolism of divine love.

Yet militant popes, alive to the challenge of Protestantism, knew that the mystic's path was not the weapon with which the new heresy could be faced. And as, in the Albigensian wars, a religious order had been made into the instrument for stamping out the heresy, so the Lutheran and Calvinist Reformation produced the historical counterpart in the Society of Jesus. If there are few institutions in history which have drawn upon themselves the condemnation of opposing contemporaries in so full a measure as the Jesuits, this fact is in itself indicative of the single-mindedness with which they pursued their objective. It is not for us to judge here whether their activities were justified or not, whether their aims were commendable or not, whether their means were justifiable or not. It remains a fact, however, that, within a definite geographical limitation, they achieved their object. It equally remains a fact that they pressed into their

service all the means which an awareness of the weapons of psychological warfare, not yet scientifically formulated, but no less subtle and penetrating for that, suggested.

To these factors, and to this movement, the character of the Baroque is due to a considerable extent. Architecture and art soon became another weapon in the Jesuits' armoury as its virile form began to be expressed in architectonic language when the negativism of witch-hunts, *autos-da-fé*, and the burning of heretics began to be balanced by the building of churches to the glory of God. The progress of the Counter-Reformation can be clearly traced in the architecture which Jesuit missions erected all over Catholic Europe: it began by the re-introduction of the basilican plan, the result of a decree of the Council of Trent which, on historical precedent, had condemned circular plans as pagan,[851] but adopted the dome and thus made the Roman Gesù the prototype of an innumerable progeny which stands witness to the cosmopolitan work of the Society not only in Italy, Spain, Belgium, Germany, and Austria, but equally in Mexico, Peru, and Brazil. Its first phase was in keeping with the austere character of the first decades of the movement, for its buildings are severe, sparsely adorned as to exteriors, and of a monumental cast akin to the monumental task of the mission. The interiors, however, became places of a splendour hitherto unknown. The psychological principle underlying this tendency was not altogether new, nor was it the discovery of the Society of Jesus: for it was the realization of Alberti's recommendation of the use of the richest materials, and of the shrewd judgement of Nicholas V who knew that 'to create fixed and unswerving convictions in the minds of the uneducated masses, there must be something that appeals to the eye. If the authority of the Holy See were visibly displayed in majestic buildings, imperishable memorials, and witnesses which appeared as though set up by God himself, belief would grow and strengthen like a tradition from one generation to another, and all the world would accept and revere it'.[852]

The Jesuits acted on this principle to the letter but, significantly, it was not their churches only, but also those of other orders which, by an outward splendour and magnificence, strove to fulfil the need of the *turbae populorum* for a visible symbol which was not only to be a reflection of the heavenly splendours, but was also to elate the soul and fortify the faith. The underlying purpose was profound: the Reformation had appealed to men by logic; it had deliberately eschewed ceremony and had insisted, as all reformatory movements must, on the condemnation of images, thus bringing about Zwingli's celebrated acts of vandalism in Zürich as much as the destruction, largely by Dowsing's fanaticism, of most of the medieval stained glass of Cambridge. The spirit of the Reformation, of necessity, had to be austere, reasoned, and iconoclast.

The Society of Jesus knew that it could not fight the Reformation with those weapons, where they had succeeded. It took precisely the opposite course: where Luther had appealed to reason, the Jesuits appealed to the senses; where Protestantism had built bare assembly halls, the Counter-Reformatory church was of undreamed-of splendour; where an iconoclast interdict lay on the artistic expression of religious sentiment, the Counter-Reformation blazed a trail of architectural, pictorial, and statuary art, and evolved a liturgy and ritual which embraced the sublimest music of the time. But the polarity was deeper than the visual, and aural, contrast: Protestantism based religion on reason; Catholicism on faith. Both had the logic of psychology on their side, as is evidenced by their respective achievements and success.

With the success of the Society's mission, and the consolidation of this success, the style of the Baroque entered into its second phase and began to unfold its true and universal character. For the phase of the militant church passed into that of the triumphant church, and all the visual delight which the earlier Jesuit architects had reserved for their interiors, and for the *theatrum sacrum* which the Society had done so much to raise to so high a level of achievement, began to adorn the exteriors. The crusade had turned into a triumph yet at the same time, this meant that whatever direct control the Society of Jesus had ever exercised upon art and architecture had come to an end.

Some critics have gone so far as to equate Jesuitry with the Baroque;[853] in the writings of others, the influence of the movement upon art and architecture has frequently been exaggerated, and some, of greater prejudice than perception, have, indeed, given certain types of ornamentation the arbitrary appellation of 'Jesuit', implying thereby in a subtle way a disapproval not only of the style, but also of the movement which is alleged to have produced it. But two aspects of this question must be considered: firstly, if close links exist between the Counter-Reformation and the Baroque, this is not tantamount to saying that it was the movement which produced the style. The manifold deviations from the classic Renaissance were already apparent at an early date and the germs of the Baroque, indeed, can be found in Michelangelo, as early as in his Medicean mausoleum, where the elements of classical architecture are first used with a complete disregard of their historic and structural function. It is thus conceivable that the Baroque would have developed towards similar solutions even without the coming of the Counter Reformation and the agency of the Society of Jesus. But, be that as it may, 'the artistic significance of the style which the Jesuits employed, remains something wholly independent of the uses to which they put it. To explain the first by the second is to misconstrue the whole matter. To condemn the first on account of the second, as has repeatedly been done, is nothing less than childish'.[854]

Our second consideration is even more important: for, whatever control the Jesuits may ever have possessed over the development of architecture was of strictly limited extent, and almost negligible importance for the future. The Roman Gesù may certainly be the prototype for the Society's churches in other towns and countries; but the names which stand out in the history of Baroque architecture are not those of the Society's official architects, but those of Bernini, Borromini, and Guarini, and of Fischer von Erlach, Hildebrandt, Neumann, and Zimmermann; these were the men who were to develop the style to its ultimate achievements, and these achievements were impossible of attainment within the limitations of true Jesuit architecture and the rigid regimentation of the Council of Trent. Suffice it to notice here that it was Archbishop Carlo Borromeo who, in 1572, first applied the Council's decree condemning round churches for the 'pagan' connotation of their form;[855] and point to the irony engendered by the fact that the crowning glory of the Vienna church dedicated to him is the splendid oval dome which Fischer von Erlach completed at the same time as Wren built the dome of St Paul's.[856]

Turning to the Catholic principalities of the empire, we find a very interesting development of architecture. The Baroque had been brought to those lands north of the Alps by Italian architects and the names which are associated with the buildings of the earlier part of the century are those of Scamozzi and Solari, followed by Zugalli, d'Allio, Carlone, Orsini, Martinelli, Gabrieli, Lurago, and Luchese. But it is significant that while Andrea del Pozzo was associated with the building of the Jesuit university church in Vienna, the Baroque churches of Salzburg eschew the type of the Roman Gesù, irrespective of whether they belong to the earlier phase, which was still the era of Solari, Dario, and Zucalli, or of the later decades, which belonged to native artists. Thus it is suggestive that neither Salzburg's cathedral, the first design for which was due to Scamozzi,[857] nor any of the city's other churches possesses the distinctive Gesù façade, and, what is even more important, that almost all of those built subsequent to the cathedral are – Tridentine decrees notwithstanding – of centralized types. Even beyond the boundaries of the principality, the territory of which was not inconsiderable, the Baroque developed on different lines from those laid down by the Jesuits and it can, indeed, be said without exaggeration that the Baroque of these countries owed its greatest debt not to the Roman Gesù, but to the concepts of Borromini and Guarini.[858] It is of no great importance that the wealth of the Fugger and Welser, added to that of the princes and prelates, created, in the sixteenth century, a cultural blossoming which was of an essentially alien begetting. For, disregarding the disruption caused by the Thirty Years' War, the foreign language became assimilated as soon as the combined forces of Emperor and John Sobieski had dispelled the last shadow of a Turkish menace; and when a new impetus of martial splendour and religious devotion began to raise new monuments to the glory of God and the princes of Church and State, the names of their creators would be Fischer, Hildebrandt, Zimmermann, and

Dientzenhofer. Before this great and last flowering, however, the empire was to be torn and all but annihilated from without and the schism of its religious strife had to draw the boundaries between Lutheran and Calvinist austerity and the Baroque splendours of Catholicism, the empire had to render the last proof of its virility in repulsing the Turks, before a triumphant Counter-Reformation could build monuments to the glory of their God and the triumph of their arms.

It was his idealized Gothic that Ruskin had in mind when he said that all art was praise; yet the dictum is no less applicable to the Baroque which he abhorred. For praise it was, indeed, in a twofold sense in the Catholic parts of the empire at the very time when James, in spite of past Exclusion Bills, ascended his brother's throne for the brevity of his futile reign, until religious convictions and a triumphant Parliamentary ascendancy put an end to the Stuarts' rule. The very reverse was the case in Austria and the empire, where a tremendous wave of renewed artistic creation celebrated the triumphs of a Church no longer militant and the glory of an emperor's victories over the infidel. It is praise which, with all the glory of Mozart's yet unwritten Credo, is writ large upon the palaces, churches, and monasteries which arose contemporaneously with St Paul's and Hampton Court. It is the high noon of a culture emerged from the dark night of the soul to move, within a century, towards its annihilation at the hands of social factors and scientific progress which brought the citadels of men's beliefs tumbling to the ground in the Century of the Common Man. Yet while it lasted, it created monuments of a beauty and spirituality which could vie with, and challenge, the greatest periods of art and the most fervent ages of faith.

Turning to France, we find a development which is as strictly conditioned by the political conceptions of the age of Louis XIV, as is that which caused the galaxy of Baroque variations which flourished within the cadre of the empire and the numerous principalities of Germany. In France, the centralization of political power, so aptly symbolized by Louis XIV's château of Marly where the ancillaries of the monarch's little palace are the attendant pavilions of the higher aristocracy, was the concomitant of a centralization in the development of art and architecture which, within the channels prescribed by Colbert's academies, produced an art of insignificant range but of great significance. It is erroneous to attach undue importance to the frequently misinterpreted character of Louis XIV in relation to the art which his reign produced;[859] nor need we try to discuss the question whether official proscription was justifiable or not[860] or examine the inference purporting the detrimental effect of such proscription on art. Here again, it is not justifiable to condemn the civilization of Versailles on whatever may be discommendable in the absolutist concepts of its creators; for even though social and political historians may disparage the arts contemporaneous with social organizations and ideological conceptions of their disapproval,

the answer to such irrelevance was given 200 years ago, and remains as cogent today, when Lord Chesterfield opined 'why the despotism of a government should cramp the genius of a mathematician, an astronomer, a poet or an orator, I confess I never could discover. It may indeed deprive the poet or the orator of the liberty of treating certain subjects in the manner they would wish; but it leaves them subjects enough to exert genius upon, if they have it'.[861]

Wren's own judgement, however immature at that early moment of his career, still stands testimony to the greatness of a national culture even at a time when Louis's reign had still half a century to run, and the finest flowers of its art had scarcely begun to unfold. It may be possible to construe the autocratic, even despotic, patronage of art into an ogre of sinister intentions, scheming the perversion of art and the enslavement of artists' talents and souls to further aims of self-glorification.[862] But it would be as unreasonable to disparage, because of their patronage, the works of Racine, Poussin, de Cotte, and Lully as it would be foolish to deny that, whatever its political conception, 'the France of Louis XIV is one of the supreme glories of European civilization'.[863]

It is important to recall the impulses and foundations on which that civilization was built; for, with the possible exception of the empire and Catholic Germany, nowhere in Europe was Italian influence so strong, so continuous and extensive. True, English patronage of Italian artists had extended from Torrigiano in the sixteenth century to Canaletto, Ricci, and Pellegrini in the eighteenth; but the first fruitful contact of French aristocracy with Italian culture must be identified with Charles VIII's Italian campaign; nor must it be forgotten that Leonardo followed the invitation of Louis XII, that Primaticcio and Serlio worked in France, and that Mazarin, who laid the foundations on which Louis XIV and Colbert were to build, was an Italian equally as Lully; it must not be forgotten that the glories of the poetry of the Pléiade were of an Italian begetting, and that a classicism derived from Rome, and antiquity, imbues the drama and the stage of France from the time when the Gesoli troupe of strolling players came to France and the celebrated Fiorille collaborated with Molière even to the time when Goldoni forsook the Venice of his triumphs to make his permanent home in Paris; lastly, let it not be forgotten that the inspiration of Poussin, no less than that of Claude, had its fountain spring in the classic grandeur of Italy.

The crystallization of absolutism, as well as the latent, if potent, influences of antiquity and its Renaissance re-interpretation were the fertile ground on which a lofty, noble, and heroic art could flourish, and it is only natural that inspiration was sought and found just in these ages which had been characterized by such conceptions. Racine went back to the drama of Hellas,[864] and the architects of this great period, beginning with François Mansart and Le Vau and ending with Jules Hardouin Mansart and

Gabriel, transmuted the classical inheritance into an architecture the grandeur, dignity, and accomplishment of which is strictly comparable to the work of Bossuet, the sermons of Bourdaloue, the writings of Fénelon, the music of Titelouze, the drama of Corneille and Racine, and the paintings of Poussin. Italian though their inspiration be, it does not entail the annihilation of the indigeneous culture; for the famous quarrel of the 'Antients and Moderns', the contending strands of Poussenists and Rubenists, were capable of reconciliation, and this proved that the tenets of the several factions were not diametrically opposed, but variations on a common theme.[865]

There can thus be little question of the annihilation of native culture by the wilful and indiscriminate importation of the outward forms of an alien civilization.[866] And this fact is very subtly borne out by the process of selection by which Italian elements were assimilated with the native tradition to produce a genuine fusion, wholly expressive of contemporaneous trends. Those who would consider the rôle of patronage paramount in the development of art, could point to the fact that what little church architecture can be found the product of the latter half of the seventeenth century is sufficiently distinctive from Italian work of the same period to stand as a token of the notions entertained by Louis XIV in seeing himself the head of the Gallican Church and in bidding defiance to the Papacy in claiming the right of episcopal presentation. But the divergences between the French and the Italian Baroque are not only explicable by the fact that the *parlement* of Paris refused to ratify the decrees of the Council of Trent; they are more subtly indicated by the fact that Martellange, an official Jesuit architect, could plan a church built on a Greek cross in Nevers; but the final explanation must rest in the fact that it was an inherent national tradition which transmuted the foreign model in the light of its own predilections, and that a Gallic sense of order, of clarity, and sobriety[867] – the very qualities, perhaps, responsible for the fact that the great mystics of the age were Spanish, Italian, Austrian, yet never French – imposed a restraint on the more flamboyant aspects of the Italian Baroque, and that a certain intellectual detachment and sophistication shrank from the final step of enthusiastic abandon.[868]

In England, however, the entire intellectual climate had been different since the days of the Tudors. Wolsey and Henry VIII, it is true, had competed with other kings and cardinals in their patronage of Italian artists and, following their call, had come Torrigiano, Rovezzano, Nunziato, Jacopo da Verona, and many others to place emperors' busts and terra-cotta medallions on Tudor façades and a tomb of cherubim and wreaths of flowers in a Gothic abbey. But the events of 1538 cut short the influx of Italian culture which, before it could have become acclimatized to the cloudy English skies, was followed by the importation of the best which Protestant civilization of the age could offer. The fact that it was an Italian Renaissance at a bad second hand which

began to exert a considerable influence on English artists and craftsmen through the medium of Dutch and German pattern books has frequently, and not unjustly, been deplored. But it must not be forgotten that this influence was but one of the aspects of a political expediency which preferred not only political, but also cultural bonds with the democratic Netherlands and Lutheran Germany than with the absolutist and Catholic powers of Italy and France. If English artists had recourse to Dutch and German representations of the orders and of Renaissance design in general, the premiss for this choice was grounded in politics. There were, indeed, many facets of ideology suggestive of Gallican sympathies with the Anglicanism of Elizabeth's time;[869] none the less, the smiling beauty of Chenonceaux was contemporaneous with the vanished vanities of Nonsuch Palace.

It is not only the violence of architectural mutation which we would emphasize, but the spiritual gulf which separates the last decades of Gothic faith from the climax of Elizabethan self-glorification. For the rejection of the political union with Spain, and with it the ideologies of St Teresa and St John of the Cross, gave England the dominion of the world at the price of the empire of the soul. In England, 'it was the world of the spirit, the "interior castle", that was left to decay, while the discoveries of scientific materialism were pursued'.[870] In the arts, the secession from Rome could not but bring a complete disruption, not, be it understood, by the termination of patronage to Italian artists, but by the change in temper, religious, and secular, which was bound to follow the schism. With Elizabeth, a new class of patrons arose, served, at best, by indifferent artists from Germany and the Low Countries, in their ostentatious tastes; parallel with the incipient beginnings of Parliamentarianism arose the architecture of Burghley and Wollaton, the work of mediocre artists for patrons of mediocre tastes, to produce a riotous, exuberant splendour for such as derived their standing from the exploration of the worlds beyond the seas and the wealth of piratical and mercantile adventures.

It is not surprising that, just as in Spain, the finer spirits revolted against the materialism of Elizabeth's England; yet they lacked the strong, dominant, unshaken, and unimpeached faith to which St Teresa had been able to turn. Nor could they, representing a young and vigorous Protestantism, take their stand on the strength of ancient tradition in the same manner as the Carmelites, however dubiously, could point to the prophet Eliah as their founder. Thus, in the hatred of the spiritual emptiness of Elizabethan splendour, but without either tradition or the spiritual rock of faith to turn to, the school arose which Dr Johnson has labelled metaphysical. Donne, the finest of them all, holds up the mirror to that torn soul of a lost religion, irreplaced and irreplaceable by other loyalties, to show a spiritual agony knowing neither hope of heaven nor fear of hell, while the ragged edges of his rugged verse are like the verbal echo of the shattered idols of persecuted Catholicism. There is a last attempt, Baroque in the profoundest meaning of the term, but pathetic in its hopelessness, to link the irreconcilables of faith and materialism. Yet the faith, for Donne, had lost its fibre and the attempt to fuse the finite with the infinite was doomed to failure from the start; for at the very core there was a void where a religious creed should have been, the same void as that of the empty niches from which, in England's reformed churches, the statues of Virgin and saints had vanished.

Not unnaturally, there were attempts to return to the Roman Church among the metaphysical poets; Donne, it is true, could never escape the shadow of that Cloud of Unknowing which had troubled another English mystic 300 years before him; but while the conversion of Jonson was of but short duration, it led Vaughan to writing his *Silex Scintillans* and Crashaw, notwithstanding his eminently anti-Papist father, to the secretaryship of Cardinal Pallotto, a canonry of Loreto, and to *The Flaming Heart upon the Book and Picture of the Seraphical Saint Teresa.*

The challenge and questioning of established religion, however, did not yet find its logical corollary in the secular field. James I was still able to anticipate no considerable opposition to the statement that 'the state of monarchy is the supremest thing upon earth, for Kings are not only God's lieutenants upon earth, but even by God himself they are called Gods',[871] thus anticipating by decades the words of Louis XIV.[872] That a quality of sanctity still attached to the crowned head in the popular mind of the reign of James I becomes eloquent, despite the failure of the Hampton Court Conference, in the writings of Beaumont and Fletcher[873] as much as in Sir John Eliot's dictum that 'The Kings prerogative' was still 'an inseperable adiunct of regalitie'.[874] On the other hand, religious and political considerations became inextricably linked with regard to Spain, and not every poet, dramatist, and pamphleteer was as fair-minded as Heywood who, in spite of his professed Protestantism, disdained to exploit the popular appeal which a tirade against Philip IV would have held. Rowley's *succés de scandale* was due not so much to brilliant writing as to the allegory with which he assigned, with sinister and evident inuendo, the black chessmen to Catholic Spain while the White Knight, standing for Prince Charles, bids check and mate.[875] Jonson, once recovered from his temporary conversion, had symbolized the Papacy by the Whore of Babylon, Beaumont had poked fun at a not long defunct chivalry. Ford's allusions to Richelieu are eloquent of his sentiments, but Fletcher's Valentinian is murdered by Maximus when the emperor – whom Amintor had not dared touch – extends the divinity of his right to the *ius primae noctis.* Lastly, against Quarles's *Divine Emblems,* the pictorial, though naïve, equivalents of Donne's oblique allegory, Webster draws an Italy of a sinister complexion, an Italy of ruthless princes and corrupt ecclesiastics, a world of utter evil, dominated by the twin arms of unscrupulous dukes and prelates.

It is thus in literature that we can find the most cogent expression of the essential dichotomy of the age, and can sense the many-sided reactions to the new tenets which disclaimed the divine right of kings as emphatically as they rejected the dogma and authority of the Roman Church. It is useless to speculate on the development of those revolutionary ideas on the premiss of a different attitude which Charles I might have taken, though, not improbably, they would have achieved a similar victory, if perhaps at a different historical moment. The fact remains that, for the first time in European history, a Parliament indicted the heads of both church and state, and, the nature of the charges rendering the verdict a foregone conclusion, did not shrink from decapitating both King Charles and Archbishop Laud. The Puritans, indeed, did not lack intellectual exponents to justify actions which political expediency had dictated, and we cannot hold Milton's *naïveté* responsible for writing a treatise on *A Ready and Easy Way to Establish a Free Commonwealth* three months before the restoration of Charles II. But there can be equally little doubt that the circumstances and preconditions of the Restoration lay not in any affection which the people of England may have held for Stuart rule, but in the fact that the intellectual – as well as the physical – demands of a Puritan régime not inconsiderably affected by its extreme Calvinist section proved too fanatic and single-minded and austere not to produce a reaction which, slowly and inevitably, turned back to tradition, not, be it noted, in the spirit of a resurrected faith, but more in the deliberate and considered choice of the lesser of two evils.

Returning to his father's palace on his thirtieth birthday, Charles found a spiritual situation which proved infinitely more difficult than the material circumstances of his return; the latter, indeed, could have been solved if Parliament had been more tractable; but the spiritual state of the country, where he and Clarendon tried to pursue a policy of conciliation, proved beyond his powers of resolution. Puritanism, it is true, had almost entirely lost the prestige it had possessed but ten years previously, but the execution of a king was not, nor ever could be, nullified by his son's restoration. What is more, if the returning Anglican dignitaries were, at first, uncertain of their position, they soon came to realize, not their own strength, but rather the weakness of their opponents and feelings of recrimination and revenge proved incapable of curbing. Clarendon, backed by the King, could eloquently champion the course of toleration: 'And shall we fold our arms toward one another', he asked, 'and contract our hearts with envy and malice to each other by any sharp memory of what hath been unneighbourly or unkindly done heretofore?'[876] But the cavaliers, whose loyalty, it is true, had entailed untold misery and deprivation, were not to be restrained from a vengeance which their unquestioned political ascendency rendered but too easy of execution.

If the situation confronting returning and triumphant cavaliers was simple and clear-cut, the choice before the returning Anglican leaders was inevitable. To them, there could be no other way open than the utter and complete repudiation of the concepts and ideals which had informed the Interregnum. It was not merely a question of rejecting the extreme Calvinist premisses on which Puritanism, in the end, had foundered; it was equally a question of reversing all the prohibitions which had been the concomitant of Puritanism. The latter, of course, had been iconoclast in its very nature: conform with Lutheran, Zwinglian and Calvinist precept, it had emulated the Lollards in rejecting as idolatrous any artistic externalization of religious sentiment; it had not only closed the theatres, but also mutilated the statues of the Laudian porch at St Mary's, Oxford, destroyed the medieval painted glass of Cambridge college chapels[877] and done untold damage to the venerable fabric of old St Paul's. These actions were, in themselves, logical from every point of view: they conformed to Protestant precedent of other countries and, what was as important, they expressed by deliberate contrast, and all the censure thereby implied, their fundamental opposition to all the sensuous beauty of the architecture and liturgy, no less than the dogma, of the Roman Church.

All these tenets, and all their outward manifestations, had to be nullified by the Anglican party and this, not unnaturally, involved an exceedingly difficult choice: any conformity with the past régime and ideology could not be tolerated; on the other hand, to imply rejection by total contradiction entailed an approximation towards the very concepts against which Protestantism had protested and Puritanism had vituperated. This was equally intolerable and impracticable to Anglicans for, whatever their fundamental divergences, psychologically Puritanism and Catholicism shared one dominant feature, inasmuch as both were creeds which no indifferent believer could embrace, both were creeds which demanded a fervent devotion and emotional intensity from their followers, both necessitated a strength of conviction demanding not only enthusiasm but, indeed, a degree of unquestioning fervour which, directed into different channels, could be transmuted into the intolerance of fanaticism.

The Anglican clergy undoubtedly recognized this problem. And a solution, indeed, in philosophical, dialectical, or logical form was possible; but a psychological solution was an impossibility, as the history of the half century following the Restoration shows. The pseudo-mysticism of the Cambridge Platonists – whose exponents occupied the pulpits of not a few of Wren's churches – gradually merged into Latitudinarianism, and the propositions of Locke and the Deists led not only to the pedestrianism of spiritual *laissez faire*, but eventually to the 'tyranny of reason' in which all problems of religious truth became mere matters of common sense.

Reaction to Puritanism, however, was not the sole conditioning factor of the development of religious and constitutional thought;

of perhaps equal importance was the development of the sciences and, in England, the foundation and activities of the Royal Society. Here again, reaction was the keynote of all enterprise. It is true, of course, that among the transactions of the Society can be found discourses and experiments only too reminiscent of medieval alchemy; but the basic attitude was a rejection of scholasticism which had ruled the universities for the past three centuries, and the conscious and persistent application of that empirical spirit which shunned all dialectic and devoted itself wholeheartedly not to the exposition of the ancient cosmology, nor the speculations of purely inductive logic, but to the attempt to reduce the visible manifestations of the tangible world to an intellectual system of irrefutable laws.

It is of the greatest interest to see how the leading Anglican clerics regarded this new endeavour, and it is of the greatest significance not only that they attempted to include within their dogma of faith the findings of the new science, nay, even used these to reinforce their teaching, but also that many of the notable ecclesiastics – as Sprat proudly pointed out – were actually members of the Society.[878] Again, this attitude is easily explicable, for history had shown only too blatantly how strong a weapon Copernican and Galilean theories had proved against orthodox Catholicism. Beyond that, however, the tenets of Anglicanism were not difficult to reconcile with the laws which the new science was beginning to establish, for by that time Anglican dogma had rejected blind faith as decisively as had the members of the Royal Society, and their methods had become truly alike in the paramount importance which both had begun to assign to reason. To the scientists, this presented no difficulty, but to the clerics it entailed a dangerous dialectic. The Cambridge Platonists, indeed, could pronounce the 'unity of faith and reason',[879] and while the Gospels proved capable of being interpreted in this new light, if more critical than devout, difficulties at once and of necessity arose over Revelation and miracles. The Latitudinarians had to hold a delicate intermediate balance to 'make the best of two worlds. Against the "fanatics" they maintained the essential congruity between reason and revelation; against the pure rationalist they insisted on the supreme importance of the truths which, because they are beyond the reach of unaided reason, God has disclosed'.[880] Wren's fellow-member of the Royal Society, the celebrated Robert Boyle, could demonstrate *The Reconcilableness of Reason and Religion*, but when Wren's fellow-student of Westminster School, Locke, published *The Reasonableness of Christianity*, the position had already changed. Boyle, as well as Bentley, had left sufficient latitude to allow the existence of miracles even if they were not explicable by reason. Newton reconciled his Christianity with his scientific mind by the proposition that miracles were the manifestations of natural laws which were not as yet understood, though not, intrinsically, beyond human comprehension. But Locke's position approaches a rationalism which finds no room for anything in Scripture which is not logically explicable; in accepting none but the bald surface meaning and in rejecting the possibility of symbolic interpretation he logically had to arrive at a point where 'revelation cannot be admitted against the clear evidence of reason'.[881] It is obvious where such a doctrine had to lead: the reconciliation of faith and reason could, in fact, point back to Port Royal; but the point of departure from Pascal was reached[882] when it was maintained that 'anything contrary to reason cannot be a miracle'.[883] Here, neither the latitude of Boyle nor even Newton's evasive reservation remains operative; for the word itself was finally robbed of its very meaning when it was postulated that a miracle 'must be something in itself intelligible and possible'.[884]

Thus, the appeal to reason on which the new science was founded, was at length found to be perfectly reconcilable with an Anglican theology which was gradually replacing faith by the human critical faculty, and the scientific and religious tendencies of the age are seen to be not contradictory, but complementary inasmuch as they represent merely different expressions of the same basic premiss. This union of science and religion is not an entirely new phenomenon when it is recalled that medieval science – whatever its shortcomings – was overwhelmingly the achievement of monastic endeavour. One basic difference, however, symbolizes the distance between the Middle Ages and beginning modernity: the science of the medieval cleric was interpreted as an enlargement of his knowledge of the divine purpose; and the same attitude still lingers in Newton. But while the Middle Ages reconciled science to dogma, Anglicanism of the seventeenth century found it necessary to accommodate religion to science,[885] and in the same measure as the latter progressed to the recognition of ever more comprehensive truths, the former inevitably lost a psychological acumen which in itself had been the very foundation of the primitive and pristine faith. Thus, if Wren's City churches have been represented as 'memorials of the faith, the fervour and the piety of the nation',[886] a more penetrating characterization is implied by the impression that 'there is no suggestion of mystery; the mood indeed is rather calm than ecstasy. Devotion here would scarcely disturb a prosperous trader's conception of the world as a pleasant place in which an honest man can await without fretful impatience the summons to another'.[887] The new philosophy, which 'called all in doubt', proved the foundation stone of modern science in shaking itself free of the preconceived notions of an earlier dogmatism; but at the same time it proved the rock on which religion finally floundered, as 'the appeal to reason lost its dignity and degenerated to the level of a pedestrian common sense',[888] and as circumspection, prudence, materialism, and non-commitment took the place of the idealism, enthusiasm, and fervour of the credulous ages of faith.[889]

The general discredit of authority which lay at the heart of the new attitude towards religion and science was bound to find its reflection also in the reinterpretation of secular authority, and it was natural that the Restoration intellect should seek to clarify an issue which both the reign of Charles I and the Interregnum had complicated. Naturally, the tenets from which the Interregnum had derived its authority had to be repudiated; more importantly still, the premises upon which the execution of Charles I had been clothed in a quasi-legal justification had to be demolished. And thus it is not surprising that the Anglican clergy fell back upon the historic concept of the sanctity and divine right of kings, as this was a philosophical foundation, hallowed by age-old tradition, which not only permitted to condemn as heretical sin the action of the Parliamentary judges and the regicides, but also was the most likely basis on which the future security of the throne might rest. Moreover, it is not inconceivable that the developments towards absolute monarchy which exiled Anglicans had witnessed in France, should have played their part in the reassertion of a principle which not only the events, but also the dialectic of the past fifteen years had invalidated.

That Charles himself was not disinclined towards absolutist concepts of kingship may seem evident; the example of Louis XIV – 'the King, my brother' – was clearly before his eyes, and he may conceivably have envied the untramelled opportunities for action which were Louis's by virtue of his absolute authority; perhaps a certain natural inclination derived from his Bourbon and Habsburg blood may also have played its part, and the tenacity with which he pursued his dominant, though secret, foreign policy aiming at the closest of possible alliances with France would point to a predisposition towards a system of international alignment in which the 'benevolent despotism' of absolute rule would present a closed front against the circumscription of royal power which was the compromise which Calvinism, at best, would offer to a crown.

The clergy did all in their power – and that was considerable – to support and propagate the claim for the divine right of kings and while Charles exhorted them that 'none are in their sermons to bound the authority of sovereigns, or determine the differences between them and the people',[890] the implications of the Act of Uniformity were further reinforced by the clause which it contained, insisting on the oath of non-resistance.[891] But the clergy which thus supported Charles's claims and of itself propagated the doctrine of passive acquiescence, was an ecclesiastical body from which all sectaries, including Presbyterians, had been excluded. This had not been Charles's intention; for there is no reason to doubt either his complete sincerity or his perspicacity, when he told Parliament that 'if the Dissenters will demean themselves peaceably and modestly under the government, I could heartily wish I had such power of indulgence, to use upon occasions, as might not needlessly force them out of the kingdom, or staying here, give them cause to conspire against the peace of it'.[892] But just as the ideals of political toleration, and a policy of non-recrimination, which had motivated the King and Clarendon, had foundered on the cavaliers' sentiments of revenge, so his ideas on spiritual indulgence were foiled by the attitude of the clergy and of Parliament. The anonymous pamphleteer could baldly propose that the commercial interests of Britain's trade would best be served by 'giving liberty of conscience to all Protestant Nonconformists, and denying it to Papists';[893] but Parliament used Charles's needs as a bargaining counter for his renunciation of any ideals of tolerance.

It would be unprofitable to speculate what course the events of subsequent years would have taken if Charles's 'divine right' had not been circumscribed by other powers at the crucial point where questions of basic policy were laid down. But it may seem that the combination of Charles and Clarendon might have been a worthy counterpart of Louis XIV and Colbert across the Channel; and, however the political consequences of such a hypothetical constellation might be viewed – and let us emphasize that this study is neither condemnation of, nor apologia for, any particular political system, but concerned with the culture and civilization which such engenders – there is little doubt that, given that absolute authority, Charles's court, its manners, arts, and graces, might have rivalled that of the *roi soleil* which was to impose its standards upon Europe from the days of its brilliance to the French Revolution.

The historical factors, however, were not to permit such a development and, ironically, it was the antithesis of Restoration rule, the arbitrariness of the Protector, which proved the stumbling block on which Charles's absolutist ambitions went to pieces. For whatever assertions of the divinity of kingship were made, its full implication signified an absolutism which, were it to be used for similar purposes, would only represent a repetition of the régime just passed; the arbitrary concentration of all power in the hands of one supreme ruler represented a centralization identical to that which the Protector had possessed, and the coronation of Charles, brought about more by weariness of Puritan rule than by loyalty to the Stuart, was solely the accomplishment of that investiture which had once been projected for Cromwell. Finally, to accept the ultimate implications of the tenets of divine right and passive obedience meant an abdication of personal choice and a surrender to blind faith and allegiance which was not merely unreasonable to expect after the events of the past two decades, but which was intrinsically irreconcilable with the temper of the age. A generation which asserted the supreme authority of reason could not acquiesce in monarchial rights the divinity of which was not logically but, at best, historically defensible. Absolutism was suspect not merely from the national historical precedent which the Interregnum had furnished, but was equally condemnable by its contemporaneous expositions: however persistently Charles might pursue his alliance with France, for the majority of Englishmen that country, as well as Spain, stood suspect and reprehensible in their twin attributes of absolutism and Catholicism; the fear of 'popery' was no less than the fear of the 'enthusiasm' of 'fanaticks',[894] and for all the sentiment that animated England in her wars against the Dutch, the ogre of the popular imagination was the absolutist rule of a despot whose pretensions were supported by Pope and Jesuits.

Thus, in a certain sense, Charles was defeated almost from the start. To return to the country which had been ruined by the preceding régime, and to return with the well-realized moral obligation to recompense those who had suffered for the Royalist cause, was a problem which would have taxed the most willing of Parliaments and administrations; but to return to England as the dependent of a Parliament was to render impossible all that Charles and Clarendon had planned to do. Parliament was not slow in perceiving its strength and realized that it was not only the arbiter of the fate of the Puritan faction, but also that it held in its hands the person and rule of the King. Almost from the first, Charles found himself in the position to have to ask Parliament for the funds with which to carry on the administration, and while the temporary rapture of his reception concealed only briefly the disunity of spirit which was, in fact, the transmutation of the conflict which had led Charles I to the scaffold, Parliament soon found that its control of finance could be used as a lever with which to make the King pliable to its wishes. And Parliament, with a consistency remarkable for so heterogeneous and discontinuous a body, contrived to foil Charles at every point. When the King advocated his policy of toleration, he echoed precisely what the cardinal of Lorraine had stated exactly 100 years before,[895] in recalling that the early Christians of the pristine faith never stooped to persecution and, in addition, subtly implied that he tended towards tolerance in explicit contrast to more recent Catholic practice;[896] when Parliament was slow to grant even adequate revenue, he very cogently pointed out that dilatoriness and lack of efficacy in granting supplies for the Dutch war would inevitably make the world 'think that I have not your full concurrence in what is done, and that you are not forward enough in the support of it';[897] but neither the appeal to religious sentiment, nor the call for at least the appearance of solidarity made any impression: Parliament was indifferent in its support, and consistent in its endeavours to circumscribe the King's power as tightly as possible. It was with bitterness that Charles, three years after the Restoration, wished for the day when he might 'call a Parliament and not ask or receive any money from them';[898] and though his critics delight in telling us that 'the King's privy purse was exhausted, no doubt, by other than pious uses',[899] he could imply a well-deserved reprimand when telling the House that 'by borrowing very liberally from myself out of my own stores, and by the kind and cheerful assistance the city of London hath given me, I have a fleet now at sea worthy of the English nation'.[900] But Parliament was not to be moved: it used finance and supplies as a lever to make Charles perjure his Declaration of Breda and withdraw his Declaration of Indulgence, without seeing that the Presbyterians thus excluded would in reaction become the nucleus of a party which would not only challenge the prerogative of the Crown, but equally of Episcopalian monopoly. At the same time, Parliament thereby provided the desired separation of Roman Catholicism, paving the way towards future Exclusion Bills, and compromising, on religious grounds, the French alliance which Charles regarded as the most desirable political aim. Finally, they brought about the discredit of Clarendon and, forcing Charles into the chancellor's dismissal, they rid themselves and the country of a man who, however increasingly difficult Charles himself might have found him, was yet the most clear-sighted and brilliant statesman of the day. With his fall, and with the stranglehold they maintained on the King by means of finance, their ascendancy became complete and by means of stigmatizing with 'popery' every factional dissent and any real or imaginary 'plot', they began to exercise an inquisitorial power which persecuted dissenters for political expediency and cloaked all its intolerance and arbitrariness under the pretence of allegiance to a King and the belief in his divine right.

The University of Cambridge could still pretend a belief in the prerogative of kingly power which 'comes to be so by a fundamental hereditary right, which no religion, no law, no fault, or forfeiture can alter or diminish'.[901] On the same day that Lord Russell was executed, Oxford University organized an *auto-da-fé* of 'certain pernicious books and damnable doctrines', and *Leviathan*, *Reformation*, and *Areopagitica* went to the flames as Convocation went on to 'decree, judge, and declare all and every of these propositions to be false, seditious and impious, and most of them to be also heretical and blasphemous, infamous to Christian religion and destructive of all government in church and state'.[902] Such demonstrations notwithstanding, the arch-enemy of kingly supremacy, and the greatest threat to the monarch's pretended rights was not seen in Puritanism, but in Rome. The days had long passed when English Catholics, trained in their colleges at Douai and Rome, where upon the walls they could daily see the terrifying representations of the torture and martyrdom which awaited them, had, like Campion, returned to their native land in a fervent, if hopeless, attempt to reconvert a materialistic England to her pristine faith. But at the same time as the Roman curia saw developments in the growing independence of Gallicanism too serious than to attempt the reconversion of a country which it had realized to be lost to its faith, cleric and pamphleteer alike began a campaign the exaggerations and distortions of which betray an hysteria which the actual, or even the potential threat of Rome would hardly seem to have warranted. The history of past misdeeds was called to mind,[903] and a sinister future was prophesied if ever the evil day were to dawn which saw Jesuits in power in England. Yet the dread was not, primarily, on purely religious grounds; it was far more conditioned by the political influence which the Roman Church, principally through its Jesuit missionaries, was supposed to wield and the extension of which to England was felt to be the greatest calamity which could befall the country.

There were, of course, pretexts to provide a bare motivation of these expressions of fear of Roman influence: Charles's queen had, not unnaturally, brought with her a number of Portuguese Capuchins, two preachers, and Antonio Fernandez, her confessor, whose presence, added to that of six English Benedictine monks, occasioned some suspicion.[904] Charles's own profession of indulgence towards the dissenters could not logically stop short of the extension of the same privilege to Catholics; and, however persistently he claimed his steadfast allegiance to the Anglican Church, those who felt the inclination did not find it difficult, and perhaps were not entirely in the wrong, to interpret his Francophile policy as a religious sympathy; the various 'plots' which were uncovered served as a further stimulus in exciting and enhancing the intolerance of the faction in furnishing a pretext on the grounds of attempted sedition; most important of all, however, was the tenacity with which the Duke of York clung to his convictions in spite of Parliament's incessant attempts to induce him to emulate his grandfather's example or to exclude him from the succession.

The culmination of all the campaign was to be found in the great work of Wren's friend and patron, Isaac Barrow, in which, in a remarkable parallel to the Gallican repudiation of Papal authority[905] he brought all his extensive learning to bear on the contention that the Pope's supremacy 'is not only indefensible but as impudent a cause as ever was undertaken by learned pens'.[906] Barrow could command considerable scholastic powers; he could copiously cite historical precedent; but his final proposition involved a dangerous dialectic: in stating that 'no power can have a higher source, or firmer ground, than that of civil government hath; for "all such power is from heaven"','[907] the way was laid open to two cogent objections: firstly, his foundation of monarchial power lay in the appeal to history and by no means in the dictates of 'reason'; secondly, in claiming that royal power was derived 'from heaven', he was doing no more than transcribe the claims of the Papacy to the Stuart dynasty. To the partisan, the divine right of kings might have appeared paramount over the pretended supremacy of the Pope; to the logical mind, however, the basis of both claims must have been equal in their pretended divinity, and no amount of dialectic could decide the superiority of either. Thus, the partisan might accept either; the historian could, at will, demonstrate the relative validity of both; but the rationalist was bound to reject both.

The doctrine of passive obedience created a dilemma when James acceded to his brother's throne. For Barrow was not alone in claiming that the loyal subject owed allegiance even to a pagan king, and the official position of the clergy still maintained that the people 'stand indispensably bound by the command of God, which exacts from them honours and obedience, even to evil kings'[908] just as 'the new very young Lord Chief-Justice Herbert declared on the bench, that the government of England was entirely in the King' and 'that the Crown was absolute'.[909] But the ineptitude of James, combined with the slow and persistent growth of the Whig party, rendered the situation incapable of solution. Anglicanism could continue to categorically deny that the relationship between king and people was to be seen in the form of a compact to which they both were parties, for this denial was, indeed, the very basis on which the Stuart dynasty had been restored. But the view, though neither widespread nor influential at first, began to assume a diffusion and importance to which the pamphlet literature of its antagonists bears eloquent witness; and it was within these very terms that the fictitious justification of the 'glorious Revolution' was invented when it was claimed that James, 'by breaking the contract between king and people has abdicated the government'.

Of necessity, 1688 proved the touchstone of the Anglican conscience, for the principles involved in the alleged 'abdication' of James and the arbitrary enthronement of William of Orange were so directly in opposition to all the tenets on which the Restoration Settlement had been built as to make a logical and justifiable transference of the oath of allegiance an impossibility. There were, of course, those to whom the taking of the new oaths proved irreconcilable with their conscience, and it would be no injustice to say that among this small minority of non-jurors were found some of the finest personalities of the age. Sancroft sacrificed the archbishopric of Canterbury to his conscience, and Granville, White, and Turner, their several episcopal thrones, but the most eloquent expression of the non-juror's sentiment, already touched by the qualities which lent so much glamour to the Jacobite protagonists of the coming half century, came from the Bishop of Chichester's death-bed, and reasserted once more the central tenets of a creed which, like the concepts of the Stuart dynasty, had begun to outlive its time; for 'whereas that religion of the Church of England has taught me the doctrine of non-resistance and passive obedience, which I have accordingly inculcated upon others, and which I took to be the distinguishing character of the Church of England, I adhere no less firmly and steadfastly to that, and in consequence of it, have incurred a suspension from the exercise of my office and expected a deprivation. I find in so doing much inward satisfaction'.[910]

But this was the minority. The rest, consistent with the 'resonableness' with which they had attempted to reconcile the irreconcilable, saw that prudence dictated the marshalling of all arguments by which the accomplished revolution could be sanctioned, and the conscientious objection to the new oaths removed. It is germane to this attitude to recall the *volte face* with which, at the Restoration, few emulated the example of Marvell, but many 'turned round with the virtuosi' to dissociate themselves from the defeated faction and ingratiate themselves with the political ascendants: we may recall that Waller, once implicated in a plot to seize London for the King, had returned to England to address laudatory verses to Cromwell and change, without much scruple, the addressee of his poems after the Restoration; similarly, Sprat's *To the Happie Memorie of the most Renowned Prince Oliver* and Dryden's *Heroic Stanzas on the Death of Oliver Cromwell*, cannot have been altogether forgotten when the latter greeted the Restoration with *Astraea Redux*. But the prudence and the very 'reason' which the majority of ecclesiastics had been advocating for so long made it possible for them to take the new oaths without undue qualms. It is true that Burnet's suggestion that the Dutchman had earned the loyalty of Englishmen by conquest and possession was an extreme of cynicism and perversion which even Parliament found impossible to sanction, and rather than admit so flagrant an assertion, and so dangerous an interpretation, ordered his Pastoral Letter to be burnt. But more 'reasonable' minds, knowing the claim of William and Mary to be tenuous, thought that the circumstances of the case commended that 'we should rather greedily catch at any appearance of proof that may justify their pretensions than dwell on such arguments as seemingly overturn them'.[911] But Burnet's compliance advanced him to the see of Sarum; Sherlock's sudden and precipitate conforming, after a stubborn allegiance to the old oaths, earned him the deanery of the yet unfinished cathedral of St Paul; and Stillingfleet, whom he there succeeded, went so far as to write that the reproaches which inevitably followed such action as Sherlock's were altogether groundless for, to him, 'the dreadful charge of perjury and apostasy, which some, of much greater heat than judgment have made use of against those who hold it lawful to take the oaths, if what I have said be true, is little less than ridiculous'.[912] Stillingfleet justified his position by the argument that political oaths were essentially different from those which bind individuals; and while much abuse had, not long before, been lavished on the papal prerogative of releasing individuals from oaths if such involved a conflict of conscience, Stillingfleet did not blush to maintain that 'if the keeping of the oath be really and truly inconsistent with the welfare of a people, in subverting the fundamental laws which support it, I do not see how such an oath continues to oblige'.[913]

Ironically, one of the first pieces of legislation enacted under the new sovereign concerned the toleration for which Charles II had so persistently fought; while he had been on the throne, Anglicanism had paid lip-service to his ideal by allowing the liberty of conscience, but what was thus given with one hand was taken away with the other, when the expression of the nonconformist spirit was proscribed, and freedom of worship was withheld. Yet the developments which this unjustifiable attitude had attempted to prevent, were not to be restrained by the factious spirit of a narrow Anglicanism; and if the credit for the legal sanction and establishment of religious toleration has undeservedly gone to William's reign, it should not be forgotten that the significance of this step was entirely different at the time when it was taken from the time when Charles had projected it. During the Stuarts' reign, toleration and indulgence meant a compromise with religious, philosophical, and political tenets which a reactionary faction would not sanction in spite of all Charles's and Clarendon's prompting and insistence. Toleration, in Charles's reign, meant the reconciliation with the upholders of religious and dynastic ideals which had led both Charles's father and Archbishop Laud to the scaffold, it meant to extend the hand of friendship to those over whom both cavaliers and clergy considered themselves the final victors. But to decree toleration and indulgence in William's reign implied neither danger, nor compromise with a warring faction: given James's ineptitude and unpopularity Queen Mary could lay a semblance of a claim to England's dynastic loyalty; while the principal Protestant parties, Presbyters and Anglicans, had found an expedient way of composing their differences by abandoning the theories of divine right and all their attendant implications; what is even more important, the factional spirit which, partly from self-righteousness, partly from sentiments of revenge, had advocated persecution where Charles had counselled moderation, this spirit had altogether lost its fibre:

the facts of Commonwealth and Protectorate lay two decades past; and 'persecution is only possible in a certain kind of intellectual environment. It presupposes an intensity of conviction so self-assured that truth is seen as the exclusive possession of one side and error as the characteristic mark of the other. In 1660 such an outlook prevailed in many quarters, but the forces at work during the period steadily corroded the confidence which maintained persecuting zeal'.[914] With the loss of this persecuting zeal, Anglicanism lost its vigour; and without the strength of conviction which is the prerequisite of that zeal, it ceased to be a religion based on faith, and became a philosophy founded on reason.

By the time of the accession of the first Hanoverian, the spiritual revolution was practically complete, which Hume attributed principally to the progress of learning and of liberty. We may question if his motivation truly touches on the fundamental causes; but we would find it difficult to improve on the cogent aptness with which he described the results of the change which brought it about that 'most people, in this island, have divested themselves of all superstitious reverence to names and authority. The clergy have entirely lost their credit: Their pretensions and doctrines have been ridiculed; and even religion can scarcely support itself in the world. The name of *king* commands little respect, and to talk of a king as God's viceregent on earth, or to give him any of those magnificent titles which formerly dazzled mankind, would but excite laughter'.[915]

It may be questioned in what degree this exposition of the ideological developments in England between the Restoration and the Revolution should be germane to the architecture of Wren; indeed, it may be argued that, briefly and superficially as the transition from the quasi-absolutism of 1660 to the constitutionalism of 1688 has been traced, the only obvious connexion existing between Wren's art and the religious and constitutional changes we have noted lies in the fact that many of the men who were instrumental in shaping these changes were Wren's friends and patrons and few, in fact, can have been entirely unknown to him. Yet the relationships between religion, politics, and Wren's architecture are deeper than Wren's mere acquaintance with the leading intellects of the period might suggest; and if the analysis of architectural forms is not an end in itself, but is to be the instrument to illuminate the ideological impulses behind the sculptured form; if we are to see in a development and change of style not merely a transmutation of form, but the expression of a changed content: then it is only within such a frame of reference as we have indicated that Wren's art can be properly interpreted and understood. To divorce it from the intellectual currents of his time would be as unrealistic as to sever it from the contemporaneous architecture of the continent, and we might reasonably suggest that it is this very disregard of the 'Zeitgeist' of Wren's England which has proved the cause of the crass and irreconcilable contradictions arising from the arbitrary application of terms to Wren's art generally accepted for continental periods of architectural history.[916]

In the task of envisaging the complexion of Wren's mind, we are not helped by an abundance of documentary material which would permit us to clearly imagine his character and personality. While Wren's 'superb dignity', his 'unfailing courtesy' and moral rectitude have frequently been pointed out, it remains a sad fact that we know next to nothing about his life and manners. A Latin epistle to his father, a letter to his first wife before their marriage, and a letter to his son many years later, are almost the only personal documents left to us, and their formal tone and reticent expression permits no insight into their writer's mind. Pepys makes but cursory mention of the architect; Aubrey, the gossip of the age, provides us with an anecdote of Wren's helpfulness to a fellow member of the Royal Society when 'Dr Wren, my deare Freinde, without my knowledge contrived an employment for me',[917] but Aubrey is not altogether to be trusted,[918] and Evelyn's references to Wren as a person are not only few, but couched in curiously distant terms, thus standing in strange contrast to the duration and alleged intimacy of their friendship.[919]

But it is necessary to examine other aspects of Wren's mind in this context to understand the true position and meaning of his architecture, and not least among these considerations must come the attitude of so singular a mind towards the political and religious issues of his times. Here, indeed, it is only with diffidence that any definite opinion can be expressed for, however confidently and enthusiastically Wren has been proclaimed a Royalist and a staunch supporter of the Church of England, we are unfortunately in no position to support such assumptions by documentary evidence: it is indicative of our poverty of knowledge that we know Wren to have sat as a Member of Parliament for various constituencies[920] at various periods of his life, but we do not even know whether he sat as a 'Whig' or 'Tory', as Stephen Wren has preserved a 'political silence which may be that of discretion or of disappointment'.[921] On the other hand, no political bias can be gleaned from the circle of his friends, or from the books on his shelves: he was on equally good terms, it would seem, with John Wilkins as with John Evelyn; in his library he had Milton's *Answer to Eikon Basilikon* by the side of his cousin Matthew's *Monarchy Asserted*.

There would have been ample reason to suppose Wren to have been the staunch Royalist as which he is normally represented: his father's position, of which Parliamentarian wrath deprived him, his upbringing at Westminster School under so noted and uncompromising a loyalist as Dr Busby, his uncle's eighteen years' imprisonment in the Tower, together with the truly royal opportunities which the favour and patronage of Charles II offered him: all these would logically point to the probability of an unflinching allegiance to the Stuart dynasty and an unwavering adherence to his father's and his uncle's Church. It is just possible 'that the small Royalist regarded the King as a kind of deity',[922] but there is no evidence at all for the adult Wren's entertaining any notions of the divinity of kings, nor could we infer with any certainty any great attachment to the Stuart; there is nothing which would lead us to believe that Wren possessed a depth of religious feeling strong enough to make him sacrifice the offers which Marvell had rejected, or fervent enough to be prepared to suffer for his convictions as his uncle had done. The fact remains that, as the Member for New Windsor in William's first Parliament,[923] Wren must have taken the oaths for the refusal of which his old friend Sancroft had sacrificed the archbishopric of Canterbury. In the work of Wren, as in that of Purcell, we are confronted with the token of a complete indifference to ideology and dynastic and religious allegiance: just as Purcell composed music at command for either Roman Catholic or Anglican services without any apparent misgivings, so Wren, too, served two religions as he served three dynasties. This fact can be held, as some critics would have it, as a sign of the greatness of Wren, the architect; but when aspects beyond the strictly technical come to be considered, this very lack of idealism strikes a curious note of indifference by his very unconcern whether his designs were intended for the worship of the Protestant or Catholic creed, and whether his palaces were to glorify the rule of Stuart, Orange, or Hanover.

However, this very indifference, again a token of a spiritual latitudinarianism beyond the confines of the religious connotation of the term, is not surprising; indeed, had Wren shown any pronounced inclinations and sentiments with regard to King or Church, such would have been difficult to explain, and impossible to reconcile with the entire intellectual climate of his age and environment. For idealism, just as imagination, was an attribute inadmissible to the mentality of the Royal Society in particular, and to latter-day seventeenth-century England in general. Idealism was regarded as the corollary of enthusiasm – and few words were in such ill favour as that during the period – and enthusiasm was indissolubly linked with the excesses of Puritan zeal which had but so recently shaken the country to its very core. Enthusiasm was seen as the dominant feature, as the inevitable adjunct of both Popery and Puritanism, and it was precisely these two points of extremes between which, as we have seen, English Latitudinarianism tried to steer a middle course. The extremes of Rome, as well as those of Geneva, were unacceptable to the Anglican clergy and the intellectual submission and surrender of individual critical faculty which both demanded of their adherents were the very antithesis of the sceptical empiricism on which the entire foundation of the Royal Society rested. It was quite certainly not 'prepared and ready to obey in all things the true Spouse of Christ our Lord, which is our holy Mother the Hierarchical Church'; it emphatically refused to believe that 'the white that I see is black, if the Hierarchical Church so determines'.[924]

From the work of Inigo Jones one might imaginatively infer a Royalist attachment even without the evidence which proclaims such; more cogently, Vanbrugh's idolatry of the Duke of Marlborough speaks plainly from the stones of Blenheim[925] and across the poles of his Protestantism and Hildebrandt's devout Catholicism an element unites the two men who were to build the palatial monuments to the glory of the two allied commanders. Jones could yet retain a dynastic loyalty rooted in the Middle Ages; Vanbrugh, with little regard to religion and notwithstanding his grandfather's attachment to Charles I, could in all sincerity exalt the Whig aristocracy and become the first Englishman to be knighted by the first Hanoverian. Wren's life, however, fell between these two poles which provided, if only in the secular sphere, an object towards which an inherent instinct of worship – and all monumental architecture, secular or clerical, has a basic purpose of glorification – could be directed. This avenue was not open to Wren. Whatever his feeling for the Stuarts – and, be it emphasized, we have no knowledge on this point – Wren could reconcile serving Charles and James no less than William, Anne, and George. Among his works there were projects which distinctly aimed at glorification: not only the palaces of Whitehall, Winchester, and Hampton Court, which were as much designed for residential as for representational purposes, but also the mausoleum for Charles I, the tomb for William III and monument to Queen Mary. In the former, Wren distinctly had recourse to a practice of earlier times; in the latter he employed,

as we have indicated in some detail, every statuary and architectural device known to Baroque tomb art. Yet whatever the similarity to such Italian and Austrian monuments as we have previously pointed to, we have no evidence to attribute to Wren an identity of sentiments with those of Bernini or Fischer von Erlach, for there is nothing known to us which would provide even the smallest clue to support a belief that Wren's attitude to his monarch and to his Church was in any way comparable to that of his continental contemporaries. This is not merely a question of knowing that Rubens attended mass every morning, that Bernini yearly withdrew into a monastery to devote himself to Loyola's Exercises, and of not knowing how often Wren went to communion; nor is it a question of ascertaining – by whatever means – whether these Catholic artists were 'really more religiously-minded than their predecessors' as has irrelevantly been suggested,[926] or of proposing an arbitrary opinion whether it was Wren's architecture or that of the Baroque which was essentially more religious.[927] But the spiritual enthusiasm implicit in the forms of the Queen Mary monument seems belied by the fact that Wren appears to have assiduously collected political pamphlets and tracts throughout his life;[928] it is irreconcilable with Sprat's apt characterization of the 'race of young men provided against the next age, whose minds were invincibly arm'd against all the inchantments of enthusiasm'.[929]

There are, as we have noted, few facts to allow us to draw any definite conclusions. But one striking instance is supplied by the friendship which we know to have existed between Wren and two of Cromwell's own family. We need not necessarily infer anything uncomplimentary from the fact that, on one famous occasion, Wren sat at the same table with the Protector – whom Stephen Wren was to call 'usurper', 'miscreant' – though it has pertinently been suggested that 'the death of Mrs Claypole checked an intimacy upon which Bishop Wren looked with little favour'.[930] But Wren was clearly indifferent to the political and religious opinions of those with whom, particularly in his earlier years, he was intimately acquainted: Wilkins, though he had been chaplain to the Prince Palatine, was actually related to Cromwell; Goddart had succeeded the celebrated Dr Harvey as Warden of Merton and become the Protector's physician; Bathurst was a staunch Royalist, while in Willis's rooms at St John's the proscribed Liturgy was daily read and Evelyn, having expressed his thoughts on *Liberty and Servitude* was 'like to be called in question by the rebels for this booke being publish'd a few days before his Majesty's decollation'.[931]

The significance of Wren's lack of discrimination is provided by its cause: the bond which united these men, and which attached Wren to them, was purely intellectual in their common desire of 'philosophical knowledge' and the degree of interest can be judged from the fact that it was sufficient to overcome even those fervent political sentiments which were so diametrically opposed to each other. This one enthusiasm – the fervent desire of scientific knowledge unimpeded by religious dogma or traditional conception – was indeed the keynote of Wren's mind and makes his final choice of architecture the more remarkable for the fact that it necessarily created a dichotomy which was incapable of resolution.

While the very absence of conclusive evidence on Wren's dynastic allegiance may argue a political latitudinarianism, it is surprising to find that, in the various fields of art, as conceived by the Renaissance mind, he seems to have moved within limits much narrower than those conceived either by Vitruvius and Alberti, or by such cultured dilletanti as Wotton or Evelyn. Wren conformed strikingly, but only partially, to the Vitruvian concept of an architect:[932] if not outstanding as Jones had been, he could not but be called a 'skilful draughtsman'; without doubt, he was 'a mathematician'; the records of the Royal Society prove that he was 'not ignorant of medicine'; as Savilian Professor of Astronomy, he could certainly claim to be 'familiar with astronomy and astronomical calculations', and the general duties of a surveyor general would make it inevitable that he should have become 'learned in the responses of the jurisconsults'.

On the other hand, we shall note that he was apparently hardly interested, and only imperfectly 'acquainted with music', and that he was by no means as 'diligent a student of philosophy' as Evelyn, who shared with Alberti a preoccupation with the evaluation of the respective merits of the active and contemplative life; furthermore, though he has been credited with the potential ability,[933] he could hardly be called a 'man of letters', and we may see in these very limitations, which we shall now examine, the measure of the distance which separates Wren from the encyclopaedic aspirations and interests which had been so conspicuous a feature of the architects of the Renaissance.

That Wren was certainly 'familiar with scientific enquiries' has been made the basis for drawing a parallel with Leonardo, yet this must remain an unwarranted exaggeration. Wren's versatility in the scientific field has frequently been stressed,[934] and though his numerous 'inventions' contrived largely during his period at Wadham may, remotely, be compared with the range of Leonardo's mechanical designs, it would be too much to claim them to be of an equal status. More important to our study, however, is an examination of Wren's strictly limited range in the fields of art, for here our architect is quite at divergence from Vitruvius, who had stipulated that 'the science of the architect depends upon many disciplines and various apprenticeships which are carried out in the other arts'.[935] Though Wren could, at the age of fifty, have claimed the ability to 'give perfect satisfaction' and be 'the equal of any other in architecture and the composition of buildings public and private', he could not have added, as Leonardo did at the age of thirty, that 'I can carry out sculpture in marble, bronze, or clay, and also can do in painting whatever may be done

as well as any other'.[936] Wren was not, like Michelangelo, architect, painter, sculptor, and poet; nor could he have rivalled the versatility with which, to Evelyn's admiration, Bernini, 'that sculptor, architect, painter, and poet gave a public opera . . . wherein he painted the scenes, cut the statues, invented the engines, composed the music, writ the comedy and built the theatre'.[937] In fact, Wren was not only incapable of work in any of the sister arts but seems to have been curiously uninterested in them.

Unlike Leonardo and Inigo Jones, Wren has rightly been said to have been 'incapable of designing a masque'[938] and here lies an indication to one of the principal differences between him and his predecessors. It remains a moot point whether Wren did not possess imagination for ephemeral tasks such as those on which Jones had spent so much love and labour, or whether the 'tyranny of the intellect' characteristic of him and his times was too oppressive to allow a flowering of a faculty so deprecated by the scientifically-minded. The fact remains not merely that Wren never designed a masque, or even the scenery for any of the elaborate presentations of the Restoration stage, but that he consistently abstained from any such architecture as was to serve only a passing purpose.[939] We would not credit Wren with an arrogance which would make him refuse any commissions which did not inherently possess that quality of the 'eternal' which he postulated for architecture, and we cannot but regret that his work did not include such theatrical designs and ephemeral works for processions as provide so much interest in the case of Inigo Jones, supply so much fascination to the celebrated Bibbiena family, and lent so much glamour to the festivities of declining Venice, for which even the best architects of the time did not disdain to design the decorations. Wren could have claimed the precedent of many illustrious names had he felt inclined to such pursuits. But the very fact that the elaborate scenic sets and effects which partly compensated for the mediocrity of the theatrical entertainments of the Restoration[940] were inevitably the work of other hands is as significant as the attitude which Wren took to art in general, and to antiquity in particular.

Jones, indeed, had been an amateur and enthusiast in the best meaning of the term in anything regarding the fine arts: when William Petty's 'Neapollitan Collection' had arrived in England, Jones was 'madde to see them'[941] and his connoisseurship of painting must be beyond question when so discriminating and knowledgeable a collector as Thomas Howard called on him for advice when buying pictures from Sir Dudley Carleton.[942] Likewise, Jones's friendship with Joachim Sandrart betokens an interest in the painter's art of which he himself was by no means an exponent to be despised, while his quarrel with Ben Jonson is certainly not indicative of any lack of interest in the art of the playwright.

Seen in these perspectives, Wren is an altogether different

figure. For beyond such painting as was to be an integral part of any of his architectural works, he seems to have evinced no interest in that art, and though he must, of necessity, have been very well acquainted with Verrio, we have no record that his appreciation of that painter's talents could even remotely be compared to Evelyn's;[943] and even the preference he appears to have shown for Pellegrini in favour of Sir James Thornhill is altogether of no account in evaluating his personal taste or, indeed, interest in the art beyond the particular context provided by the cupola of St Paul's. His attitude to sculpture does not seem to have been very different; while, as we have noted, he emphasized on several occasions the undoubted importance of sculpture to architecture, considerations of cost seem at times to have outweighed considerations of quality;[944] and though he was intimately acquainted with both John Evelyn and Sir William Fermor,[945] he does not seem to have shared the interest with which the former secured the Arundelian Marbles for Oxford University,[946] and with which the latter procured the remainder of the celebrated Howard collection.[947]

Equally, Wren does not seem to have been particularly interested in music; we have no record to show that on the day when Evelyn 'visited that miracle of a youth, Mr Christopher Wren' played any part in the entertainment 'at All Souls, where we had music, voices, and theorbos, performed by some ingenious scholars';[948] no record that, next day, he accompanied Evelyn to Magdalen to hear the celebrated Gibbons play the organ.[949] We have no record to show that Wren, like Pepys, ever stayed up till the small hours of the morning singing rounds, that he cared about, or even knew of, so illustrious a musician as Carissimi,[950] or that, like Evelyn and Pepys, he had any interest in the work of his great contemporary Purcell.[951] Wren's interest in acoustics seems to have been more concerned with the preacher's diction and enunciation[952] than with the scientific principles Vitruvius had dealt with[953] or with the dictates of the organ[954] and of the performance of music. And it is perhaps indicative of his whole attitude to music that he appears to have paid no attention whatever to the celebrated duel between the two master organ builders of the time, Renatus Harris and Bernard Schmidt,[955] reminiscent as it was of the trials immortalized in the *Meistersinger von Nürnberg*, which certainly was one of the major sensations of that year.

Wren's attitude to antiquity illustrates in a similar manner a mind dominated by intellectual concepts and of sufficient tolerance to regard, and disregard, comparatively dispassionately and with little more than a mild academic interest those phases of art which had preceded his own time. Here, indeed, we can draw a sharp dividing line between his attitude and that of his immediate predecessors. Not least in interest is their several reactions to the Gothic: Sir Henry Wotton, within the first quarter of the century, had nothing but the most explicit contempt for that style[956] and Inigo Jones, not long after, was enthusiast and partisan enough to conceive the possibility – as Alberti had done at Santa Maria Novella and Palladio at San Petronio – of transforming the body of old St Paul's into a classical edifice. Wren however, though his critics have delighted to quote his words on the 'gothic rudeness of Design' as opposed to 'the good Roman manner', was incapable of a 'bigotry of taste which, only admitting one mode of beauty, is insensible to the superior claims of order and congruity'[957] and thus unwilling to mar a Gothic ensemble by Renaissance additions: the nature of Tom Tower was due, as we have seen, to his awareness of 'the superior claims of order and congruity' just as, at Westminster, he was explicit in his intention to 'agree with the original Scheme of the old Architect, without any modern Mixtures to shew my own Inventions', for he was perfectly conscious that 'to deviate from the whole Form would be to run into a disagreeable Mixture, which no Person of a good Taste could relish'.[958]

Yet, if Wren showed tolerance and sensibility for the Gothic, his antiquarian interests were but slight: that he should have evinced but little interest for the earlier manifestations of British civilization points to a crass contrast with the attitude of Jones, Webb,[959] Sammes, Dugdale, and Norgate, or even with the archaeological preoccupations of a gifted dilletante like John Aubrey.[960] On the other hand, Wren's acquaintance with classical antiquity, and its Italian Renaissance, must have been extensive, though it is surprising that his attitude towards it was as indifferent as his conception of it was superficial. Significant is the fact that Wren has been found 'to be less careful an archaeologist than might have been anticipated',[961] for his interpretation of the mausoleum of Halicarnassus leaves the impression that in this respect not only Inigo Jones, but also John Evelyn and Fischer von Erlach were clearly Wren's superiors.[962] More important, however, is Wren's deliberate divergence from classic concept[963] and his good-humoured contempt for the 'rules' of the orders, 'too strict and pedantick', of which we shall have to speak in greater detail.

To Wotton and Jones, the appeal to antiquity and Palladian rule was manifestly unquestionable. To Wotton, Vitruvius was 'our principall Master' and 'Leon Battista Alberti the first learned architect',[964] while Jones, like John Shute before him, 'to study the arts of design . . . passed into foreign parts to converse with the great masters thereof in Italy'.[965] The attitude of Purcell, though a generation removed, is closely similar in having 'faithfully endeavour'd a just imitation of the most fam'd Italian Masters' and our sympathy is engaged by the modesty with which 'he is not asham'd to own his unskilfulness in the Italian Language'.[966] Nevertheless, by the time Cibber regarded foreign and historic inspiration with exaggerated humility,[967] an entirely different note had crept into, and become dominant of, the tenor of English artists' pronouncements on their models and inspiration: Dryden admitted that he had 'not exactly kept to the three mechanick Rules of Unity' because, in his opinion, 'the Genius of the English cannot bear too regular a play'.[968] Yet different motives and criteria were operative and came to the fore when he, notwithstanding his own indebtedness to French tragedy, could go to the length of a wholly insensitive criticism of French dramatists in asserting that 'their heroes are the most civil people breathing, but their good breeding seldom extends to a word of sense; all their wit is in their ceremony; they want the wit which animates our stage'.[969] Indeed, D'Avenant before him had thought that

'The French convey their Arguments too much
In Dialogue: their speeches are too long.
Such Length of Speeches seem not so unpleasing
As the contracted Walks of their Designs . . .'.[970]

But Shadwell, once poet laureate, could go much further than that for, having adapted *L'Avare* to the point of plagiarism, he prefaced this 'creation' by proposing that 'I may say without vanity, that Molière's part of it has not suffer'd in my hands, nor did I ever know a French comedy made use of by the worst of our Poets, that was not better'd by them', for 'it is not barrenness of wit or invention that makes us borrow from the French, but Laziness'.[971]

We would not attach too much importance to such opinions within the context of our subject were it not for the surprising fact that this kind of sentiment was closely echoed by a man of much greater mind and discernment that Shadwell, namely Wren himself. For Wren, with a surprising degree of complacency, seems to have endorsed the opinion that 'our English artists are dull enough of invention, but when once a foreigne Patterne is sett they imitate soe well that commonly they exceed the Originall'.[972]

This pronouncement is clearly of the same stamp as Wren's indifference to the precedent of architectural authority as contained in Vitruvius and in the works of the Renaissance theorists. It has been suggested that a first-hand acquaintance with Italian architecture such as Jones possessed would have rendered his art 'more informed'[973] but Wren's possession of an extensive and representative collection of works on architecture from Vitruvius and Alberti to Vignola and Blondel makes it impossible to attribute his indifference to a lack of knowledge. On the contrary, the evidence suggests that his flouting of Palladian principles was perfectly deliberate.

Wren's indifference to authority, his unwillingness to conform to any preconceived rules and abide by them merely by reason of their traditionally supposed 'inviolability' allowed him to treat the hallowed rules of the orders with a respect so scant as to have earned him the unrelenting censure of his Palladian successors and later purist critics. Indeed, Palladio himself has not escaped such criticism,[974] but Wren went beyond the position of Sir John Eliot to whom, two years after the publication of Wotton's

Elements, 'the honour of antiquitie is great, though it be not an idoll'.[975] And thus, sensing perhaps the criticism which his lack of conformity with classical canon would produce in academic minds,[976] he significantly did not invoke the Palladian provision which allowed that 'variations may well be made from the regular proportions [of columns] in order to suit them to special circumstances',[977] but boldly wrote, prophetically, we might almost say, that 'Modern Authors who have treated of Architecture seem generally to have little more in view, but to set down the Proportions of Columns, Architraves and Cornices, in the several Orders, as they are distinguished into Dorick, Ionick, Corinthian and Composite; and in these Proportions finding them in the ancient Fabricks of the Greeks and Romans, (though more arbitrarily used than they care to acknowledge) they have reduced them into Rules, too strict and pedantick, and so as not to be transgressed without the Crime of Barbarity; though, in their own Nature, they are but the Modes and Fashions of those Ages wherein they were used; but because they were found in the great Structures, (the Ruins of which we now admire) we think ourselves strictly obliged still to follow the Fashion, though we can never attain to the Grandeur of those Works'.[978]

Wren thus thought himself at liberty to modify, and disregard, the proportions of the orders as laid down by his predecessors and expounded, once more, in John Evelyn's translation of de Chambray's work. On the other hand, when Wren accepted and followed historical precedent, he was by no means motivated by the same considerations which had inspired its employment. To take but the most striking instance, we have noted that Wren's preoccupation with centralized forms and domed structures was closely parallel to that of Alberti, Leonardo, Bramante, and Palladio: there are few types of centralized plans with which Wren did not experiment, and there was hardly a project of major importance into which he did not seek to introduce the dominant feature of a dome. There are obvious parallels between Wren's various schemes for St Paul's and Bramante's, Michelangelo's, and San Gallo's endeavours at St Peter's; similarly, his projected mausoleum for Charles I followed in all essentials the concept which had governed the design of mausolea and baptisteries from Early Christian times, the tangible proof of which tradition is to be found all over Europe, from Rome to Dijon, from Ravenna to Canterbury, and from Cremona to Salzburg.[979] But the coincidence of form does not argue an identity of intention and of motivating thought: if a symbolic meaning attached to the round or polygonal baptisteries of Early Christian times, we have no reason to think that Wren was actuated by comparable considerations when he used a similar form for the projected building west of St Paul's of which, indeed, we cannot be certain whether it was intended for a baptistery or chapter house; likewise, if the circular form of church plan possessed an unmistakable significance and symbolism to the architects of the Renaissance, there was nothing in Anglican, or even Lutheran, liturgy, which could have imbued Wren's circular and centralized plans with a comparable iconographical meaning. Such an assertion is by no means conjectural: we have, elsewhere, quoted the reasons which impelled architects of the Renaissance to the employment of circular plans; but no hint of comparable sentiment can be detected in Wren's view: 'Certainly no Enclosure looks so gracefully as the circular: 'tis the Circle that equally bounds the Eye, and is every where uniform to itself;[980] but being of itself perfect, is not easily joined to any other Area, and therefore seldom can be used'.[981] This utilitarian conception of architectural forms is, indeed, infinitely removed from the ideology of the Renaissance; and it can be extended to the concomitant of the circle, the dome; for here, again, we have shown that Renaissance architects were as conscious of its symbolism as were ecclesiastics, and that their employment of the dome was principally motivated by its ability to convey a meaning which could not be expressed by any other form of vaulting. To Wren, however, the dome possessed a beauty the nature of which was akin to the mathematician's delight in a Euclidian proposition; his reasons for his employment of it are scientific and utilitarian, for as a method of vaulting, the dome is 'of all others the most geometricall; it is the lightest Manner, and requires less Butment than the Cross-vaulting, as well as that it is of an agreeable View'.[982]

The difference between Wren's arbitrary employment of forms which, to an earlier generation, had represented symbols of a mystical and religious significance, is in itself of great importance in demonstrating that although he freely used the forms of Renaissance architecture, their intellectual and symbolical implications were of no consequence to him. We have already, in a previous section, touched upon the religious significance which was inseparable from form and proportion as conceived by the Renaissance humanists; we have equally pointed to the fact that Wren's usage of Palladio's solution of the problem of fronting the double-aisled basilica was resorted to within an entirely different, even inappropriate, context; lastly, we have pointed to the fact that the designs of Alberti, of Bramante, and of Palladio were broadly based on a system of proportional ratios which was not only the *jeu d'esprit* of a superior intelligence, but had its deep roots in Hellenic and Christian philosophy.

There can be no question of Wren having been ignorant of the philosophical and religious-symbolic concepts which formed the basis of Renaissance architecture and humanist thought, for he possessed a very representative collection of books in which these theories were expounded. We can certainly expect him to have been familiar with Plato's *Timaeus* at an early date,[983] and we know him to have been familiar with the commentary on Platonic mathematics of Theon of Smyrna, of whose five original books those on arithmetic, astronomy, and music have survived;[984] from his knowledge of Kepler[985] Wren was clearly familiar with the astronomer's attempt to construct a planetary system in conformity with Platonic mathematics and particularly the five Platonic regular solids. In Vitruvius Wren would have found the adumbration of the system of harmonic ratios which formed the basis of Alberti's recommendations[986] and which had become expanded and systematized by Serlio[987] and Palladio.[988] On the other hand, he would have been familiar with the musical applications of harmonic proportions not only from the Vitruvian references[989] and the Albertian endorsement,[990] but equally from the works of Boethius[991] and those of that great musical humanist, Zarlino;[992] he would have been aware of the subtle interrelations between musical harmony and religion as expounded in Pradi's and Villalpandus's great work of interpretation,[993] while harmony and musical ratios had been the subject of the *Treatise of the Natural Grounds and Principles of Harmony*[994] of which his own former tutor and later brother-in-law was the author.

But even though Wren has been claimed to have 'soon come to realize the abstract qualities of architecture',[995] his disregard of philosophical concepts wherein mathematics, geometry, astronomy, and architecture were so closely woven into an intellectual ensemble is one of the most remarkable facts which emerges from an attempt to reconstruct the complexion of his mind. Given his predilection for mathematics and astronomy; given the fact that scientific problems occupied his mind long after one might have assumed the interests of his youthful days at Oxford to have faded into the past; given, lastly, an intelligence clearly capable of grasping the subtler intricacies of philosophical speculation: we would have expected from 'so philosophical a mind' a keen interest in Renaissance concepts of form and proportion, an interest which should have been no less intense for the fact that Albertian – and Brunelleschian – perspective had rationalized the six Aristotelian dimensions, that Copernican astronomy had superseded the Ptolemaic, and that the cosmology of Pythagoras had been replaced by that of Kepler.

If Wren's interest could be assumed, it is the very reverse that actually proves to be the case. We have no writing of his, nor reliably reported utterance from which to learn how he regarded these philosophical concepts, and in their absence, as well as on the evidence of his work, we are forced to the conclusion that he disregarded them; we may suspect that Wren had shared Dr Burnet's somewhat ironic regret at the Copernican destruction of the Platonic cosmology,[996] as the very arbitrariness with which he treated the classic canons and ideals would indicate no less than a contemptuous disregard. But no less appropriate compliment could have been paid than to 'justly admire Sir Christopher Wren's Grecian proportions',[997] and if other critics have chosen to regard his architecture as a 'translation of Palladio into English vernacular'[998] and have claimed St Paul's to be the 'perfect emblem of what England could make of humanistic ideals in art joined with robust English churchmanship'[999] then translation and joinder must have effected the annihilation of Palladio's ideals.

But we have a statement – if Stephen Wren is to be trusted – the analysis and interpretation of which permits a remarkable insight into Wren's thought and offers a profound revelation of his ideas on the final criteria of art.[1000] To Wren, 'Beauty is a Harmony of Objects, begetting Pleasure by the Eye. There are two Causes of Beauty – natural and customary. Natural is from Geometry, consisting of Uniformity (that is Equality) and Proportion. Customary Beauty is begotten by the Use of our Senses to those Objects which are usually pleasing to us for other Causes, a Familiarity or particular Inclination breeds a Love to Things not in themselves lovely . . . Geometrical Figures are naturally more beautiful than other irregular; in this all consent to a Law of Nature. Of geometrical Figures, the Square and the Circle are the most beautiful; next the Parallelogram and the Oval. Strait Lines are more beautiful than Curve . . . There are only two Positions of strait Lines, perpendicular and horizontal; this is from Nature and consequent Necessity, no other than upright being firm'.[1001]

This statement is much more than a personal canon, or esoteric preference, for the analysis of its words yields the most succinct understanding not only of his own ideas on design, but also of the influences operative upon him; it reveals a latitudinarianism capable of embracing two entirely different, contradictory and mutually exclusive canons of art in its attempt to permit the co-existence of the essentially objective with an intrinsically subjective view of aesthetics, and the somewhat dogmatic phraseology of the words belies the very range and scope of their meaning.

The classical component of Wren's theory can be traced very clearly and distinctly when he opines that natural beauty 'is from Geometry', for in this brief phrase are contained the entire dissertations of the Pythagoreans and of Plato;[1002] the postulates of Uniformity and Proportion are clearly in line with Alberti and Pacioli, and the qualifications pertaining to equality actually reflect the stipulation of symmetry and centrality of vision on which Vitruvius and Palladio had so explicitly insisted.[1003] There are, indeed, revealing parallels to be discerned between Wren's statement and the writings of classical theorists. Wren's beauty conceived as a 'Harmony of Objects' is the equivalent of Plotinus', consisting in 'the interrelation of parts towards one another and towards the whole',[1004] as much as Vitruvius', who had stated that 'proportion is a correspondence among the measures of the members of a work, and of the whole to a certain selected part as standard'.[1005] Likewise, just as Wren's 'natural Beauty' was conditioned by 'Uniformity (that is Equality) and Proportion', so Vitruvius had laid down that 'without symmetry and proportion there can be no principle in the design of any temple',[1006] Plotinus had stated 'that beauty in visible things consists of symmetry and proportion'[1007] and to Alberti, 'beauty is the result of fine proportions'.[1008]

These parallels can pertinently be extended: thus Serlio commen-

ces his discussion of forms by saying that 'I begin with the circular because it is more perfect than all the others',[1009] and Palladio, following Alberti, held that 'the most beautiful and most regular forms are the round and the quadrangular'[1010] so that Wren produced no more than a paraphrase of a universally accepted axiom in saying that 'of geometrical Figures, the Square and the Circle are the most beautiful'. In Wren's opinion that the beauty of geometrical figures derives from the fact that they 'consent to a Law of Nature' it is again possible to point to Hellenic and Roman sources of inspiration;[1011] and his third and fourth favourites, the parallelogram and the oval, are clearly indicative of their Serlian derivation, for Serlio had been the first to rank the former among his geometrical figures[1012] as he had been the first to sanction the latter as a basic ground plan.[1013]

But herewith we have indicated the limits within which Wren's ideas were clearly indebted to Renaissance theory. Wren, however, goes further than this, for to him 'there are two Causes of Beauty', and having discussed that 'natural' which 'is from Geometry', we must now turn to the 'customary'. Here, indeed, Wren was expounding the entire theory of beauty as conceived by the romantic school, and this is the more surprising for the fact not only that it was founded on wholly different premises, but also that it had been developed as the confutation of the classical theory. In this sense, Wren is equally the follower of the great Renaissance architects and theorists as he is the forerunner of the eighteenth- and nineteenth-century aestheticians; for to have said that 'customary Beauty is begotten by the Use of our Senses' betrays not only the influence of Locke, but anticipates Hume's dictum that 'Beauty is no quality in things themselves: it exists merely in the mind which contemplates them, and each mind perceives a different beauty';[1014] and when Wren permitted the possibility that 'a Familiarity of particular Inclination breeds a Love to Things not in themselves lovely', he foreshadowed Alison's theory that the 'Beauty of Forms arises altogether from the Association we connect with them',[1015] and anticipated the tenets of picturesque romanticism,[1016] for with the introduction of purely subjective criteria such as the spectator's emotional response he had, indeed, circumscribed and even discredited the very 'reason' by which the a priori principles of classic theory had been demolished, thus removing aesthetics not to the plane of Shaftesbury, but reducing it to the pedestrianism of Dubos.[1017]

While Wren was a precursor of these ideologies he was not, however, their originator. He did not, indeed, denigrate the theory of harmonic proportion as Bacon had done before him by thinking that 'a man cannot tell whether Apelles or Albert Dürer were the more trifler; whereof the one would make a personage by geometrical proportions; the other, by taking the best parts out of diverse faces to make one excellent';[1018] nor did he regard these concepts with such unconcealed irony as Donne had done.[1019] But the paradox inherent in his 'double canon' which embraced the mutually exclusive concepts of objective and subjective aesthetics is explained by Wren's work for, as we have seen, the theory of harmonic proportions had altogether ceased, in his mature work, to exert any perceptible influence and Wren's position, in practice, is thus nearer to the Baroque and to Romanticism than had been that of Jones, or even Wotton and Pratt, both of whom had, however imperfectly, still accepted the validity of the Renaissance concept.

Wren's practice is thus eminently reminiscent of Bacon's opinion that 'Houses are built to live in, and not to look at; therefore let use be preferred before uniformity, except where both may be had'.[1020] But Wren's theory contains as much of the views of François Blondel[1021] as those of Perrault inasmuch as the former, as the first director of the Académie Royale d'Architecture, still upheld the classical theory of harmonic proportions and demonstrated its validity by an analysis of classical façades and buildings; while the latter was the first French theorist to question the precepts which had governed the architecture of the Renaissance.

Wren and Perrault had, in fact, much in common: Perrault had been a physician before becoming Louis XIV's architect at the Louvre, just as Wren appeared as a doctor of medicine in the Royal Society charter; thus both entered the field of art with minds imbued with the criteria of science, and if, as we have noted, Perrault was the first exponent of a theory of beauty which, challenging Blondel's, makes aesthetic pleasure dependent on familiarity and independent of any preconceived geometrical ratios and mathematical theories, Wren's kinship with this attitude can be drawn to the closest limits and a spiritual consanguinity can be established between the two physician-architects who, to our knowledge, had never met:[1022] for a study of Perrault's book, and particularly of John James's translation which appeared in 1708,[1023] reveals beyond reasonable doubt that Wren was endorsing Perrault's thought to the point of verbal coincidence. Thus when he stipulated that 'there are two Causes of Beauty', he was reiterating the statement of Perrault's translator that 'we must suppose two Sorts of Beauties'; the first, which Wren calls 'from Geometry' was, to Perrault, that which is founded 'on solid convincing Reasons' such as were advanced by the protagonists of mathematical ratios. The second, however, 'customary' to Wren, was by Perrault found in 'Things which Custom only renders agreeable', the arbitrary beauty of which is asserted by Perrault in the full knowledge that 'they have no Beauty in themselves' just as Wren knew them to be 'not in themselves lovely'. Nor is it of little significance that such intrinsic, and subjective beauty should be the result of similar circumstances: to Perrault, such 'arbitrary' beauty was dependent 'upon the Will' and it was 'Custom, and other Reasons not positive, which induc'd this Love', while to Wren, it was 'a Familiarity or particular Inclination' which could 'breed a love to Things'.[1024]

We have not, however, gone to this length of quotation and comparison merely for the sake of establishing that probability points to Wren having endorsed a previously expressed opinion rather than produced a novel theory of aesthetics; but in order to point, once more, to the significance which attaches to this circumstance: it is immensely suggestive that Blondel, the classically trained, learned, and erudite architect, should have appointed himself one of the last great protagonists of the theory of harmonic proportions; it is equally suggestive that both Perrault and Wren, trained in a scientific discipline the orientation of which was wholly empirical, should so explicitly have rejected the tenets which Blondel, at the dawn of the Enlightenment, should still uphold. But even deeper differences and more profound divergences remain for us to indicate.

If we are to point to the fact that Alberti's architectural treatise was completed by the time he designed his first architectural work; and that Wren's writings on architecture are doubtless the fruit of a lifetime of practical experience, penned towards the end of his active career; if we are further to recall that Alberti's practice was to prepare the most detailed drawings for the masons and then depart to conduct the rest of operations by correspondence, being careful to state that the least deviation from his designs would *discorda tutta quella musica*;[1025] and compare this with Wren's method involving more or less constant supervision of his buildings under erection, and the fact that he was altering even major details when structures were well advanced, so that the vast majority of surviving drawings are no more than approximate, 'on lines as built', or 'nearly as executed':[1026] then we shall have contrasted much more than personal predilections and methods of work. For implicit in the difference of method is a fundamental difference of approach: to Alberti, and to the architects of the Renaissance, the architectural concept was worked out to the last detail before the foundations were laid; to Wren, the laying of foundations was frequently but the first stage of the final evolution of his design.

Underlying such differences, however, is an aspect of even greater significance, for they are the external tokens of how completely Renaissance architecture was evolved from preconceived designs which, once laid down on the drawing board, were of so integrated and homogeneous a nature as to permit no alteration, even of minor details, but at the risk of a 'discord' of all this 'music';[1027] Wren's faculty of design, on the other hand, was fluid and completely empirical, and while incapable of submitting to so rigid and uncompromising a discipline, it was equally unable to conceive of the possibility of any detrimental effects resulting from alterations of original designs. Unlike Alberti, Wren never considered a design as completely integral until the building was actually completed; this is amply borne out by the facts: for, no matter how confidently the City church steeples have been claimed 'as having been placed and planned with designed relation to other members around it; and in conscious and chosen connection with the whole',[1028] the transference of the steeple of 'St Edmund, Bloomsbury' to the church of St Peter, Cornhill, clearly shows the fallacy of such a view and proves no less than the remarkable transpositions of features from one context to another, traced elsewhere in detail, that Wren never considered a steeple as appropriate solely within the cadre of the first project for which it had been devised. We have met with numerous instances where certain features, unexecuted at first being projected, found their way into subsequent design: both the Cambridge Senate House and the King Charles mausoleum found their developments in Whitehall Palace; the semicircular *cour d'honneur* unexecuted at Hampton Court was revived in the first major project for Greenwich; but the most cogent illustration of how interchangeably Wren regarded the components of any structure is surely provided by the cathedral where Wren, at a time when nave, transepts, choir, and piers were complete, was still completely undecided not only what form the western towers were to take, but was still considering dome profiles of entirely different shapes. From this fact we may conclude that even though his final decision followed what he regarded as the most appropriate – and we would be the last to question the refinement of taste of which the dome profile of St Paul's was the outcome – Wren's mind, notwithstanding the advanced state of the rest of the building, was still open to the possibility of widely divergent alternatives; thus to Wren, a particular steeple is not apt and fitting only for a particular elevation of a particular church; and the elevations of the cathedral did not dictate one distinct type of dome profile to the exclusion of all others. Here Wren's approach is seen at its most fluid, at its most empiric; for his solution is never unique and inevitable, but represents only one resolution of a flexible problem. Wren's solutions are not adopted as the only possible ones; his architectural music is latitudinarian; his preferences are never exclusive to alternatives.

This is a cardinal aspect of Wren's mind; it is, indeed, the artistic attitude conform to the aura of scientific scepticism, of doubt in immutable standards and *a priori* assumptions; thus it must not be interpreted as merely personal: for it was in a very precise and symbolic manner the attitude of his time which had arrived at the denial of the concrete as well as the abstract concept of authority; the denial cogently expressed in the questioning of Aristotelianism as well as Platonism in philosophy, of the supremacy of the Pope in theology, and of the divine right of kings in constitutional theory – a denial which eventually even relinquished the very 'reason' by which these revaluations had been effected in favour of the individual, esoteric perception. Indeed, our whole digression on aspects of the religious and constitutional development of the century would have been superfluous were it not for the fact that it is only within so wide a frame of reference that a profound interpretation of Wren's art

seemed possible. In the collective attitude of the nation to the fundamental changes of the half century between the decollation of Charles I and the accession of William of Orange, just as in Wren's attitude to architecture, we can perceive the manifestations of a state of mind which did not concede any validity to tradition or precedent[1029] and which was fundamentally opposed to any notion deriving any fixed law or axiom from a purely logical precept unsupported by the evidence of concrete experiment. It was the fundamental empiricist attitude[1030] which, though it arrived at a similar mechanistic view of the universe as Descartes had done, did so by entirely different means, for the Cartesian result was achieved by logical demonstration, while the empiricist view was obtained from the observation of concrete experiment.

Thus, the profound differences existing between Wren and all his predecessors are seen to be not merely discrepancies between individual attitudes, but divergences of fundamental approach; Wren's arbitrariness, his rejection of rules, his indifference to even the greatest of his predecessors: all these are only to be interpreted as an attitude engendered by that dispassionate, dissecting spirit of a time 'which called all in doubt'.[1031] This intellectual foundation could not but create a supreme dichotomy in Wren's mind and work, the dichotomy which is so significantly expressed by the multitudinous, often seemingly contradictory and mutually exclusive, facets which constitute much of the fascination of the Restoration period. The love-poems of the age were irreconcilable with the earnest endeavour of the Royal Society, yet both were expressive of the times; the Comedy of Manners represents a sensitive indication of the spirit of the age and the mind of a patronage which did not demand, nor expect, a profundity of conviction, or the abstract treatment of ethical and moral issues; but in an inverse sense, Restoration tragedy is perhaps the most symbolically typical product of the age: Richardson was as vitally important to Baculard d'Arnaud as was Racine to Dryden. Yet the difference between *Pamela* and *L'Heureux Repentir* is small compared with that between Mademoiselle de Scudéry's and Thomas Banks's *Cyrus*; it is as nothing to the gulf which separates Corneille and Racine from Restoration tragedy: for here we have an art, modelled on a superb contemporaneous pattern, yet full of empty rant and false sentiment, an art separated by the widest of gulfs from the rhetoric of Shakespeare, the passion of Donne, and the eloquence of Webster. It rings hollow and untrue, as does much of the pomp of drums and trumpets in Purcell's *Jubilate*, and parallel to the florid counterpoint of some of his odes runs the inflated language of their words by Dryden, an empty show of the profession of a faith the lack of which not even that glamorous elaboration of word and music was able to conceal. They, indeed, to whom we owe *The Indian Queen*, could rise to greater heights, and Dryden, in the year of his death, could sound, in retrospect, a note of resigned regret of great poignancy.[1032] But the way taken out of the dilemma by Crashaw,

Dryden, Christina of Sweden, and the Cardinal of Norfolk was not that of the age: they were the exception, not the rule. To Wren, as to the majority of his time, this way was closed, for the general tendency of the time was towards the rationalization of all departments of men's knowledge and beliefs.

To Dryden, the dilemma had been one of belief; to Sancroft, the problem was not a dilemma, but an article of faith; but to Wren, the dichotomy was not as clear-cut as the choice which both the poet and the archbishop had made, for it was not merely a question of upholding and embracing one belief, and rejecting another, but a question of reconciling such elements as proved, by their very fundamental causes, to be irreconcilable; we might, indeed, see in this attempt a mentality typical, in the deepest sense, of the Baroque inasmuch as we can there discern the constant endeavour to reconcile the dictates of the heart with the demands of reason. The essential cleavage had already been recognized by Pascal, but then Pascal's faith permitted the co-existence of emotional and rational elements; but the increasingly apparent dichotomy which the Renaissance and the Reformation had created led the finer spirits to an endeavour to unify the very divergences of aspects which materialism and mysticism had created; this is implicit in Donne's allegory, in his attempt to balance the 'hemispheares'; a basic impulse towards synthesis underlies Leibniz's attempted conciliation of the creeds and his plans for the foundation of a German Academy in Vienna to re-unite what the Reformation had parted; Commenius, in London, though vainly, tried to realize his ideal of a Pansophic School under the auspices of the Long Parliament; music, freed from the constraint of an earlier homophony, develops a fugal texture of polyphony which is strictly comparable to the art language of the period where, at a certain point, the contributive branches of architecture, painting, and sculpture cease to have each its separate existence to fuse in creations – and some of Wren's works are not the least significant among these – where the boundaries have ceased to be clearly defined. Fischer von Erlach, in his church of San Carlo Borromeo, goes to the most daring conclusion in a Baroque synthesis of historical styles, where a pedimented portico of a Corinthian order is flanked by the descendants of Hadrian's Column, while the squat gate towers serve to emphasize the splendid, lantern-topped dome. In Baroque architecture north of the Alps the oval ground plan becomes in itself the most eloquent symbol of the epoch's trend towards synthesis, for no period, however preoccupied with the problems of combining the infinity of the circle with the directive of the basilica, had gone to the final logical conclusion of the fusion of the two elements; and with this fusion comes the greater synthesis of spatial creation, the dissolution of the autonomous components where the lost autonomy of each part – alike the lost independence of each art – becomes the prerequisite for a unity of a higher order.[1033] In this sense, the Baroque is the last age conscious and cognizant of the universality of all things, capable of reconciling Leibniz with Fischer von Erlach, Descartes with Guarini, Bach with Montesquieu; its scientific investigation never obscured the context of totality, its analysis was forever subservient to synthesis.

That Wren was part of this greater movement of thought need not be questioned. But for him, the possibilities of reconciliation were essentially more difficult than they were for Guarini, Fischer von Erlach, or Vanbrugh: while his faith seems to have largely conformed to the tolerant indifference of Latitudinarianism, *Parentalia's* eloquent political silence would indicate that such outlets of dynastic and political adulation as were open to Hildebrandt and Vanbrugh did not exist for him. The dichotomy arises from the fact that Wren was incapable altogether of ignoring the trends of contemporaneous architecture, just as he was incapable of following a disciple's path leading from an immutable standard to servile imitation and revivalism.[1034] Wren was, as we have shown, no Palladian; not only was he far too intelligent not to see that, for example, Palladian solutions of domestic architecture were wholly inappropriate to England, but also would we consider the attachment of the Palladian label to his name uncomplimentary when the great originality of his invention is considered, and when it is remembered that the true Palladian movement was primarily expressed in slavish imitation and as such represents but the first of all subsequent revivals which make of so much nineteenth-century architecture such a mockery. But Wren could not seek salvation in the idolization of a master dead a hundred years and more, nor could he truthfully embrace the static unity of the earlier Renaissance. The direction which his thought and design had to take, a direction of thought which he could not escape, was inevitably in the dynamic development which was the logical sequel to the Renaissance and to Mannerism; but this involved the embracing of concepts which were distinctly and decidedly monumental. It was inevitable that Wren – whom one could never accuse of being retrogressive – should have felt in sympathy with the dynamic form, if not the content, of the monumental Baroque. But true monumentality – and here we do not mean to imply mere scale – is in its very essence anti-democratic and it needs a profound conviction to raise it, and set it apart, from a mere inflated pomposity, for, as has been said with great discernment, 'to build monumentally requires faith, though not necessarily faith in the future'.[1035]

Such faith was not Wren's. Versailles, St Peter's, Vierzehnheiligen – these leave no room to doubt the convictions of their creators; but though in all his major undertakings, at St Paul's, at Winchester Palace, Hampton Court, and Greenwich, Wren was of necessity committed to working on a monumental scale and within the traditions of monumental architecture of his time, the very faith which has been postulated for its sincere expression must have been lacking.

It could not be claimed that Wren was ignorant of the spiritual implications of his art, for he was well aware that 'Architecture has its political Use'; but while, on the continent, the expression of a church triumphant and of an unquestioned secular absolutism was admirably mirrored in the monumental architecture of the Baroque, Wren's basic impulses do not seem to have gone beyond a sensible utilitarianism and a vague nationalism; for, 'Public Buildings being the Ornaments of a Country; it establishes a Nation, draws People and Commerce; makes People love their native country, which Passion is the Original of all great Actions in a Commonwealth'.[1036]

The failure, or the refusal, to see any higher purpose in architecture than the 'political Use' of attracting tourists and trade, and to engender national pride and patriotism, is not esoteric to Wren's mind but symptomatic of the age. For neither Wren nor his age could possess an adherence to a valid, unquestioned, and supreme church, or retain an unwavering allegiance to a monarchy whose 'divine rights' were so audaciously challenged, and whose very throne and crown were so patently, so pitifully, dependent upon the whims of the people's representatives. Thus the very qualities which made of English thought the pioneer of European ideology, the rationalism anticipating Rousseau by a century, and the Parliamentarianism more than 150 years ahead of 1848, these very qualities were responsible for the insoluble problem which the age set Wren. For the ideological spirit of his England proved irreconcilable with the architectural concepts of his Europe.

Here, then, lies a fundamental explanation of Wren's art, for the two components of intellect and emotion were never to be completely reconciled. Wren's first sketches for Hampton Court have pregnantly been characterized as 'the precise, modest statements of a scientific mind. And yet the raw material of the designs is quite definitely Baroque'; to have 'looked at the Baroque not with the eyes of a Baroque artist, but of an English intellectual'[1037] was an attitude which not only prevented the most perceptive English intellectuals from a sympathetic appraisal of that art, but which also proved the basic cause of 'that strain of inconsistency running through the whole of Wren's work'.[1038] Given his mind, and his time, it is clear that he was by no means in accord with the religious and dynastic implications of the Baroque; but to his progressive mind it was as impossible to retrogressively revive the styles of a former past as to imbue the Baroque forms with their profoundest meaning. The problem permitted no solution, for the architectural language of Italy, France, and the empire could not express the conceptions of Restoration and Revolution England, just as the art patrons and artists of those several countries were of a totally different background and convictions than those of Wren. The tastes of the temporal and spiritual princes of the continent do not find their counterpart in the tastes of the City companies of tradesmen and artisans; while the Baroque served in its essence an aristocratic absolutism based on a supremacy of Church and State, Wren's art was largely determined by the predilections of a bourgeois middle class. Thus Wren's Baroque form is not imbued with the pristine Baroque meaning, just as all the Baroque splendour is antipathetic to the rationalism which underlies Wren's thought and age.

This exposition should not be interpreted as a criticism on qualitative grounds; it does not intend to indicate a failure on Wren's part to attain standards which other men may have achieved. But it provides the only grounds for the assertion, so frequently made yet so rarely elucidated, of the intrinsic 'Englishness' of Wren's work. We would not claim this a qualitative criterion as other writers, anxious 'to vindicate as more excellent because more English',[1039] have done, nor can we pertinently see therein the essential greatness of Wren; for there are many indications to make us believe that, though the essentially English quality of his mind was the pre-condition of the nature of his work, his greatness may appear to lie far more pertinently in the evident desire to adapt the prevalent architectural traditions of Europe to the ideals of English intellectualism of the later seventeenth century. For, whatever allegedly English qualities are supposed to be discernible in Wren's work, it should not be forgotten that basically his architectural ideals were expressed in a foreign language, a language, moreover, of which considerable sections of contemporary authority did not altogether approve. It should be emphasized that a facile compliance with his patrons' tastes would have made life very much easier for Wren; but, excepting a conformity dictated by patron or circumstance, his artistic conscience compelled him to hold and represent his views in the face of whatever opposition it might meet; responsible English opinion would have had a steeple, *à la gothique*, where Wren would have had a dome, and in the years he spent in the frustrating struggle against the obsolete traditionalism of the chapter of St Paul's we have a token of a strength of conviction which would not lightly surrender its ideals of belonging to the common art language of Europe to the hidebound conventionalism of a timid body of clergymen. None the less, that Wren was never altogether free to design and build in accord with the dictates of his taste must seem evident, and there would seem ample indication that on other occasions than that of the famous rejection of his favourite cathedral design he was forced to accommodate his art to the tastes of his patrons; at St Stephen, Walbrook, the ultimate sanction accorded by the grocers does not seem to have impaired the final result; but it may well be suspected that elsewhere it was unfortunately true that the proposition accepted by one of Wren's most ardent admirers was the principle acted upon, that 'however eminent an architect may be, it is not the architect, but his employer, the amateur, who is entitled to make the final decision'.[1040]

That Wren, at times, had to conform to the limitations which people possessed of not a grain of his own splendid taste and originality imposed in him is no less clear than regrettable; and there is little that can rival the resigned pathos of his own words which, in dignified language and speaking in wholly impersonal terms, hint at the disappointments which his clients' whims and shortsightedness must have caused him; for, 'whatever a man's sentiments are upon mature deliberation, it will be still necessary for him in a conspicuous work to preserve his Undertaking from general Censure, and so for him to accommodate his Designs to the Gust of the Age he lives in, thô it appears to him less rational'.[1041]

Yet the influence which patronage exerted on Wren's designs should not be exaggerated. The change from the great model design of St Paul's to the warrant design was no less radical than that from the warrant design to the structure finally built, and though the first was certainly due to outside influences, we have no evidence that the second was due to any but Wren's own predilections. At the same time, the changes of which we have definite knowledge seem to generally indicate that Wren's first drafts were almost invariably of a more Baroque and Italianate character than the final structures, and it is not necessary to hold a hypothetical change in Wren's ideals responsible for the substitution of steeples and spires in the place of Italianate cupolas. It is purely a matter of taste whether to rejoice in, or lament, the changes which were thus brought about by outside influences, but, in view of the unexecuted first drafts, it seems clear in which direction his own tastes, ideals, and preferences lay. Whatever essentially English qualities are manifest in Wren's work – and these seem to be of a different nature than has hitherto been assumed – it would be invidious, as well as erroneous, to perceive in these a deliberate attempt to create a tradition of English architectural style unconnected with that of the continent; indeed, it is the very opposite that appears to have been the case for, all ideological discrepancies and contradictions notwithstanding, Wren throughout his life would seem to have done his utmost to shape a style which, though distinct and neither imitative nor retrogressive, would form a relevant and vital part of a common European tradition.

Indeed, there was little choice left to Wren. Protestantism, particularly in its Lutheran and Calvinist forms, had signally failed to establish a tradition of church architecture distinct and different from that of Rome, had, in fact, in reaction to Rome, banished the service of art from its places of worship. Wren could not, as writers of more wishful thinking than perception would have us believe, fall back on an indigeneous tradition from which to develop his own style; yet the 'translation into the English vernacular' of the art language of the Italian Renaissance and the Baroque meant far more than a naturalization of a foreign style. It equally meant the retention of a semblance of form concurrent with a rejection of the content; it meant the adoption, and the modification, of the outward appearance at the same time as the refusal to grant a validity to the very concepts of which these forms had been the expression. To Wren, it meant the employment of a monumental, dramatic,[1042] and anti-democratic form of art which was essentially irreconcilable with the religious and dynastic temper of his time; it meant a rationalism suspicious of enthusiasm and imposed a fantasy ruled by 'reason'. And it is for these reasons that Wren's work can show parallels to the Renaissance as well as to the Baroque, and that Wren could regard beauty from the contradictory points of view of classicism and romanticism. Thus, while Wren's work partakes of the forms of several epochs of art, and his canon of beauty can be identified with centuries as diverse as is the sixteenth from the eighteenth, the very irreconcilability of these premises is the ultimate cause for the fact that 'success and failure are inextricably woven'[1043] into the corpus of his work.

From such considerations, something like an appraisal of Wren's art can be attempted, not, be it emphasized again, in the nature of qualitative criticism, but in the form of an interpretation. We have no absolute standards by which to prove the contentions that Wren's 'translation' of Palladio 'surpassed the original in beauty as well as vigour',[1044] that the architects of Louis XIV were 'without a tithe of Wren's genius',[1045] nor can any but the most esoteric criteria be made to support the opinion that Wren, though he 'never possessed the perfect mastery of form of Inigo Jones or François Mansart', though 'never quite certain of his technique' was yet 'superior in skill and imagination to any architect of his time in Europe', indeed, 'the greatest architect known to history'.[1046] The importance of Wren's work is not to be sought in any arbitrary superiority over that of others, but in the ideals and concepts of which it was so sensitive an expression. As a mind, and as an artist, Wren stands on the borderline of two great epochs of Christian art; in his backward glance to the Renaissance, he was regarding values and concepts which were essentially of the past, for his own time had already discarded the foundations on which that intellectual world had rested, and it is for that reason that Wren's *œuvre*, alike the great traditions of Gibbons, Bull, and Purcell in music, and Shakespeare, Webster, and Jonson in drama, were to find no progeny in the eighteenth century. In his forward glance, however, he was anticipating a new, and even revolutionary, attitude of mind which was to abolish the rule of all authority and precedent and which was to proclaim the individual perception as the supreme arbiter above logical demonstration, which was to discard not only the validity of inductive logic, but also the authority of empiricism, to set in its place the value, however esoteric and changeable, of individual taste.

When authors have rejoiced to see in Wren's work not only the ability, but also the intention 'to redeem the Palladian style from its slavery to formulae'[1047] the argument is questionably put: for in this case, 'redemption' meant the sacrifice of very real spiritual values, irreplaced by others, in architecture, and 'slavery' signified the chains by which the humanist intellect had conceived the components of a universal cosmology linked in a complex and harmonius interdependence.[1048] And as the alleged liberation from the subservience to concepts of greater comprehensiveness here implied one of the initial stages of the fragmentation of the departments of the mind, it must remain a point open to question whether such 'redemption' was not a gift bearing within itself the seed of its own destruction. For Wren is not only the precursor of romanticism; he is also the forerunner of scientism, and our present state of knowledge does not permit us to decide whether his exaltation of the personal intellect and the supremacy of science was not a path eventually leading to a deification of values ultimately more pernicious even than the superstitions of a Counter-Reformatory past. In an age such as ours, it is impossible to view with less than diffidence one aspect of the inception of a technocratic interpretation of the universe in which the ultimate discoveries of science are to take the place of ethics and aesthetics and in which mathematics may ultimately fail to signify values which are not comprehensible by the intellect alone.

Wren's mind and work were the inevitable outcome of the time and place of his active life. In the England of 1670, none but a pedant could have built according to the precepts of a neo-Platonic treatise of 1570; none but a sentimentalist could have seen in architecture the vehicle for the expression of a secular and ecclesiastical absolutism which belonged to the past; none but a mind essentially of its own time could have built as Wren built. And this is the supremely distinguishing quality which sets him apart from all those who succeeded him, the Palladians, the Grecians, the Romantics, and the revivalists. For Wren's achievement is unique, it is wholly and completely of his soil and time. It is the epitome of an age which could confidently attempt to replace the lost ideals of the past by the newly discovered criteria of its present; an age which could glory in the belief that the advance from the 'superstitions' of religion to the 'certainties' of science was not only a progression, but progress. In this light, Wren's achievement is supreme. That his successors for long deprecated his example, and that posterity for long scorned its heritage, was due to their incomprehension, not his genius.

ABBREVIATIONS:

ASC   All Souls College, Oxford, Collection.

BM   British Museum, London.

RIBA   Royal Institute of British Architects.

SM   Sir John Soane's Museum, London.

StPL   The Library, St Paul's Cathedral.

WS   Wren Society publications.

1 Stratton, *The Life and Works of Sir Christopher Wren*, London 1897, p.48.

2 Such a claim to the surveyorship was put forward by Gerbier in the preface to *The 3 Chief Grounds of Magnificent Building*, 1662.

3 Pepys, *Diary*, 21 March 1668/9: 'Met Mr May, who tells me the story of his being put by Sir John Denham's place, of Surveyor of the King's Works, who, it seems, is lately dead, by the unkindness of the Duke of Buckingham, who hath brought in Dr. Wren: though, he tells me, he hath been his servant for twenty years together . . . and yet the Duke of Buckingham is so ungrateful as to put him by; which is an ill thing, though Dr. Wren is a worthy man.'

4 Phillimore, *Sir Christopher Wren; His Family and Times*, London 1881, p.127, states that 'Denham had been appointed by Charles I, in reversion during the lifetime of Inigo Jones'. Loftie, *Inigo Jones and Wren*, London 1893, p.152, repeats the story but does not specify which 'king had given, or sold, the reversion of [Jones's] office'. Phillimore's statement is altogether wrong; Loftie's is based, somewhat questionably, on Aubrey, *Brief Lives*, *sub* Denham (1950 ed., p.93).

5 *Diary*, 19 Oct. 1661.

6 *loc. cit.*, referring to Greenwich; *v. infra*, pp.86–7.

7 Phillimore, *op. cit.*, p.224, thinks that Wren's medical studies were undertaken at 'Oxford under Sir Charles Scarborough' but is obviously in error arising from an incorrect inference regarding Wren's entry at Wadham which she assigns to 1646; *v. infra*, note 8. Scarborough did spend some time at Oxford before going to London, but had Wren studied medicine at Oxford he would have worked under (later Sir) William Petty who held the chair of Anatomy since 1648; the Wadham group, however, was interested in medicine as well as the other sciences, one of the more remarkable experiments recorded being that of Petty reviving a woman who had been hanged, at Oxford, for felony; an account of this was published as *Newes from the Dead, or a true and exact Narration of the miraculous Deliverance of Anne Greene, who being executed at Oxford, Dec. 14, 1650, afterwards revived; and by the Care of certain physicians there, is now perfectly recovered*. Oxford, the second Impression, with Additions, 4to, 1651. The additions consist of verses in Latin, English, and French, contributed, among others, by Wren (*cf.* Bray's ed. of Evelyn's *Diary*, note to 22 March 1674/5). Wren's medical activities while at Oxford seem to have been principally concerned with matters relating to intravenous injections, experimentally tried on dogs; that the foundation of these endeavours is connected with the discoveries of Dr Harvey, the ejected Warden of Merton, seems obvious. Similar experiments were later conducted at the Royal Society.

8 The date of Wren's entry and his age resp. has frequently been misstated: Aikin, in the preface to *Elevation, Section and View of the Cathedral Church of St Paul, London*, London 1813; Phillimore, *op. cit.*, p.73; Stratton, *op. cit.*, p.2; H. H. Milman, *Annals of St Paul's*, London 1868, p.395; Cleveland, 'Sir Christopher Wren's City Churches' in *New England Magazine*, Boston 1901–2, p.481; Dimock, *The Cathedral Church of Saint Paul*, London 1901, p.56; Sturgis, in *Journal of the American Institute of Architects*, XI, No. 3, New York 1923, p.81; Gotch, *RIBA Memorial Volume*, London 1923, p.19; Hinks, *ibid.*, p.239; Middleton, *art.* Wren, in *Encyclopaedia Britannica*, 14th ed., 1932 issue; and Dutton, *The Age of Wren*, London 1951, p.21; give 1646 and fourteen years resp. Briggs, *Christopher Wren*, London 1951, p.21 is not convinced by the Wadham register which has the relevant entry *sub* 1649. Whitaker-Wilson, *Sir Christopher Wren*, London 1932, p.23, sums up the evidence and thinks it 'unthinkable that a man of Wren's stamp should have taken *five* years to obtain his B.A. degree' though Locke, we may note, took four.

9 *Diary*, 11 and 13 July 1654. Loftie, *op. cit.*, p.151 is obviously in error in giving 1644, as in that year Wren was still at Westminster and Evelyn travelling in Italy and France. Nor can any credence be given to this author's statement that Wren 'had already, at Cambridge, made a name for himself as a mathematical student'. Whitaker-Wilson, *op. cit.*, p.23, infers that Evelyn and Wren had 'seen a good deal of each other' during the two years after Evelyn's return to England early in 1652, but there is no entry in the *Diary*, nor other record, to support this assertion.

10 Dimock, *op. cit.*, p.60; Dutton, *op. cit.*, p.18.

11 Loftie, *op. cit.*, p.152; L. Milman, *Sir Christopher Wren*, New York 1908, pp.53–4; Weaver, *Wren*, London 1923, p.43; Whitaker-Wilson, *op. cit.*, p.43, all take Evelyn's agency with regard to the Tangier project as established fact. Blomfield, *The Touchstone of Architecture*, Oxford 1925, p.178, even states that 'Wren's introduction to architecture was the result of a discreditable job' as it was his 'superior patronage [compared with Webb's, which] secured for him the office of surveyor-general'. Briggs, *op. cit.*, p.33, also suggests the possibility of Wren's cousin Mathew having exerted his influence though this, as the chancellor's secretary, can at best have been slight; Clarendon's own architect, in any event, was Pratt.

12 John Evelyn, William Petty, and Sir Kenelm Digby, were already on the council when Wren, Dryden, Hooke, and Aubrey were nominated; for Evelyn's election to the council of the 'Philosophical Society' *cf.* *Diary*, 6 Jan. 1660/1; for his being sworn one of the council of the Royal Society, *ibid*, 21 Aug. 1662.

13 For Evelyn's introduction of Grinling Gibbon to Charles II, and Wren's promise to employ the carver, *cf.* *Diary*, 18 Jan. and 1 March 1671/2.

14 *Cf.* Cunningham, *Lives of the Most Eminent British Painters, Sculptors, and Architects*, 1831, IV, p.172: 'That [Wren] had silently acquired great skill in architecture, and that he had not concealed his acquirements from the king, was now [1660] to be made manifest to all.' Loftie cites no evidence for the statement, *op. cit.*, p.152, that 'Wren did not come to the office ignorant of architecture' as 'it would seem that during the Commonwealth Wren studied it'. The assertions made by Stratton, that Wren was 'well known as an amateur architect' as 'he had always had an inclination that way' clearly belong to fiction.

15 August 1660; *cf.* Phillimore, *op. cit.*, p.123; L. Milman, *op. cit.*, p.44.

16 Inscribed: 'To Charles II, King of Great Britain, France and Scotland, for the Expansion of whose Dominions since no one Globe can suffice, Christopher Wren dedicates another in this Lunar Sphere.' The globe somehow seems to have returned into Wren's possession and was sold at the auction of 1749.

17 Summerson, *Heavenly Mansions*, London 1949, p.63.

18 *Cf.* lots 237 and 515 of *A Catalogue of the Curious and Entire Libraries of . . . Sir Christopher Wren, Knt. and Christopher Wren, Esq.* of the auction sale, 24–7 April 1748 (Abstract, *v. infra*, pp.231–5): *Analyse des Infinements Petits*, Paris 1696, the publication date of which indicates Wren's continued interest in science at that late period.

19 Hampshire, *Spinoza*, London 1952, p.15.

20 *Cf.* the Minute Book of St Paul's, *sub* 1 Nov. 1717 (WS XVI, pp.130 *et seq.*): 'The Memoriall of Sir Chr. Wren was . . . now read & referred to Sir Isaac Newton, who is desired to give his opinion concerning the same.'

21 Cunningham, *op. cit.*, IV, pp.172–3, suggests that the Tangier offer was the result of an intrigue by which 'Charles proposed to rid himself of [Wren's] presence' but this interpretation will be found impossible to accept.

22 *Cf.* among the 'Catalogue of New Theories . . .', quoted by Cunningham, *op. cit.*, IV, pp.166–7, the item: 'To build in the Sea, Forts, Moles etc.' It is just possible that the now missing item 'Drawings of Fortifications' which appeared as lot 541 in the *Catalogue* may be connected with the 'invention' cited above or with some tentative drafts, particularly as these had been kept together with the printed books and not sold together with the other drawings in 1749. That Wren remained interested in the subject is indicated by his possession of Vegetius's *De Re Militari* in a 1670 edition (lot 307); we may note in passing that John Aubrey possessed a copy of Dürer's *De Urbibus* in the Paris edition, 1535; *cf.* Powell, *John Aubrey and his Friends*, London 1948, appendix.

23 Blomfield, *op. cit.*, p.181, dates both designs 1662 but gives precedence to the chapel; so do L. Milman, *op. cit.*, p.56; Sturgis, *art. cit.*, p.81; Sitwell, *British Architects and Craftsmen*, 1945, p.47; and Dutton, *op. cit.*, p.22. Whitaker-Wilson, *op. cit.*, p.265, follows, but gives 1669 for the Sheldonian Theatre. On the other hand, Taylor, *Towers and Spires of Sir Christopher Wren*, London 1881, p.5, is followed by Cleveland, *art. cit.*, p.482, who states that 'in 1663, the Sheldonian Theatre was erected; then followed the Chapel of Pembroke College'. Likewise Weaver, *op. cit.*, p.45, calls the Theatre Wren's first original work; G. Webb, *Sir Christopher Wren*, London 1937, points out that while the chapel is included in the *Parentalia* list of works, no evidence exists to prove the design to have been Wren's; *cf.* however, WS V, pp.27–9, pl.xi, where the model fragment of the chapel is illustrated and discussed. Lindsey, *Wren and his Times*, London 1951, is obviously in error in assigning the Theatre to 1670, as that building was ceremoniously inaugurated the year before; it must have been near completion late in 1667 as appears from Evelyn's *Diary*, 25 Oct. 1667; but Streeter was not completing his sketch designs for the ceiling until fifteen months later (*v. infra*, note 27) and the Theatre was not actually opened till 1669; *cf.* Evelyn's *Diary*, 9 July 1669; the reference at this date to *Sir* Christopher Wren is clearly a mistake, as Wren was not knighted till some four years later; *v. infra*, note 225. Nor is Evelyn correct in recording Sheldon's expenditure as having amounted to £25,000; according to Anthony Wood (*Life and Times*, ed. Clark, IV, p.68) Dean Fell of Christ Church kept a detailed account book of the expenditure which ran to a total of £12,239 4s 4d.

24 The opposite view has been propounded by Loftie, *op. cit.*, p.153: 'Wren . . . endeavoured to make it beautiful by proportion alone and without ornament. In this effort he succeeded completely . . . in 1881 the authorities of the College . . . allowed a modern architect to enlarge it. This he did by adding 20 feet to its length . . . what was, from its perfect proportions, one of the most satisfactory buildings in Cambridge, at once declined into an unmeaning rectangular structure, too long for its width and height, but otherwise rather insignificant.' In contrast, *cf.* Summerson, *op. cit.*, pp.63–4, who thinks the chapel 'is a strictly rational building, a plain oblong, brick box with pitched roof, ceiled internally, the whole being turned into Latin by the application of a Corinthian order'. For an examination of Wren's work in relation to Renaissance theories of proportion, *v. infra*. pp.134 *et seq*.

25 Dutton, *op. cit.*, p.23; *cf.* also Defoe, *Tour* (1726), who thought the Theatre 'infinitely superior to anything in the world of its kind'. This opinion is not general. Day, *Renaissance Architecture in England*, London 1910, p.84, thinks it 'one of the experiments in which Wren failed'; Whitaker-Wilson, *op. cit.*, p.207, called the exterior 'a trifle grim'; and Blomfield, *Touchstone*, pp.182–3, states: 'The Sheldonian Theatre . . . is about as bad as it can be. The interior is commonplace and chiefly remarkable for a well-constructed queenpost roof. On the outside the building is just a great lump. The outer walls enclose the theatre without any attempt by the designer to build up a monumental composition, and the detail is exceedingly bad. The rusticated arches are too high for their width, and Wren appears to have forgotten his own plinth in calculating the height to the springing. The upper story fails in being too high for an attic and too low for a story proper and the mouldings are coarse and ignorant. As for the south front with its slender Corinthian order below and its atrocious composite pilasters above, the misfits of its members, and the evident anxiety to make the façade imposing by swags, cartouches . . . it is, I suppose, the worst piece of architecture perpetrated at Oxford before the days of the Gothic revival . . .'

26 The derivation of the plan from Serlio's reconstruction of the Theatre of Marcellus has frequently been suggested. The connexions, however, are tenuous. The relationship with the Roman building is discussed *infra*, p.129 and note 633; the alleged Serlian provenance can be paralleled by the engraving in Du Perac, *Vestigi* . . . pl.38, with which Wren is known to have been familiar; *cf.* WS XIX, p.126.

27 Pepys, *Diary*, 1 Feb. 1668/9: 'to Mr Streeter's, the famous history painter, over the way, whom I have often heard of, but never did see him before; and there I found him, and Dr Wren, and several Virtuosos, looking upon the paintings which he is making for the new Theatre at Oxford; and, indeed, they look as if they would be very fine, and the rest think better than those of Rubens, in the Banqueting-house at Whitehall, but I do not so fully think so. But they will certainly be very noble.' For Streeter's sceneries for Dryden's *Conquest of Granada*, his murals at Sir Robert Clayton's house, his paintings for Bohun, and other work, *cf.* Evelyn, *Diary*, 9 Feb. 1670/1; 26 Sept. 1672; 31 Aug. 1679; 30 Sept. 1682; 20 June 1674/5.

28 *Cf.* the drawing StPL II, 142 (WS II, pl.xvi), which the WS editors think may have been a first draft.

29 *Cf.* ASC I, 68, 69, 71, 72 (WS V, pls.iv, v), the first of which is signed. The date of 1667, assigned to the work by L. Milman, Whitaker-Wilson, and Lindsey must be rejected on the strength of the Strong MS. quoted by Caröe, *Tom Tower Oxford*, Oxford 1923, p.109, in which the mason's completion of the work is dated 1665, having involved 'Lodgings for scholars at Trinity College, Oxford, under direction of Dr Christopher Wren of Wadham'.

30 Printed WS XIII, pp.40–1, *et al.* Whitaker-Wilson, *op. cit.*, p.208, motivates it as 'while in Paris, Wren kept in touch with Bathurst,' but the internal evidence of the letter clearly assigns it to prior to Wren's departure.

31 L. Milman, *op. cit.*, p.72, has postponed the end of the Fronde from 1652 to 1665, possibly to make the following description of the French situation applicable to the time of Wren's visit: 'Light women jerked the strings of party, ecclesiastics of unscrupulous conscience and dim religious convictions plotted in company with courtesans and adventurers . . .'

32 Phillimore, *op. cit.*, p.147, is followed by Lindsey, *op. cit.*, p.82, in ascribing the facility of Wren's contacts with French architects and artists to his alleged Deputy Mastership of English Freemasonry, but this would seem the least likely qualification in the France of Louis XIV conducive to intercourse with the artists of the court and aristocracy; it would have been a hindrance rather than a help in making the acquaintance of so devout a Roman Catholic as Bernini. However, the concrete evidence of Evelyn's and Oldenburg's agency seems far more cogent than hypothetical masonic contacts; *cf.* WS XIII, pp.40–1.

33 'Bernini's Design of the Louvre I would have given my Skin for, but the old reserv'd Italian gave me but a few minutes View.' Jackson, *Architecture*, London 1925, p.279, misconstrues this into stating that 'the crusty old Italian would barely allow him a hasty glance at his plans'. A comparable inference of Bernini's professional jealousy is made, with equally little foundation, by Killanin, quoted *infra*, note 486. This author's ludicrous assertion, in *Sir Godfrey Kneller*, London 1948, p.12, that Wren 'went to discuss the rebuilding of London' with Bernini is obviously based on ignorance of the fact that Wren was in Paris before the Great Fire.

34 Whitaker-Wilson, *op. cit.*, p.62, suggests that most previous writers (*ante* 1932) have failed to realize the importance of Wren's Paris visit and thus 'have lost the real key to Wren's greatness'. Unfortunately, this author's vague attribution of the interior of the Sheldonian Theatre to French influences does not clarify the issue, apart from the fact that we must doubt whether the 'real greatness' of Wren is to be sought in such influences; for a discussion of French motifs occurring in Wren's work, *v. infra*, pp.122–7.

35 Dutton, *op. cit.*, p.25.

36 Weaver's dating, *op. cit.*, pp.160–3, of 1668–77 is misleading. The contract was signed 17 Feb. 1668/9 (WS V, p.31), and although the building accounts end with 1673, the chapel was not consecrated until 1677. The WS editors rightly date the design to 1666 and, Wren's pre-occupations subsequent to the Fire considered, it is likely that his drawings were executed between March and August of that year. Stratton, L. Milman, and Whitaker-Wilson give 1669–77; Lindsey does not list the work at all.

37 e.g. the south wing of the Cour de la Fontaine.

38 Mackmurdo's statement, *Wren's City Churches*, London 1883, p.20, must be rejected that 'being Surveyor-General to the King at the time of the Fire, Wren was without delay summoned to the royal presence and exercised such speed in the execution of his orders, that a few days only elapsed before he had completed a plan for the rebuilding of the entire city'. This account, based on the untrustworthy evidence of *Parentalia*, is incorrect in all its details: firstly, Wren did not obtain the Surveyor-Generalship of the King's Works until 1669; secondly, no evidence exists to show that the City plan was executed in response to King Charles's command. The error of dating Wren's appointment to 1666 is repeated by Sir Aston Webb, *RIBA Mem. Vol.*, p.3, and Adshead, *ibid.*, p.165, who gives the completely fictitious date of 6 March 1666 and repeats the fable of the royal commission for the design of the plan. Wren's appointment subsequent to the Fire was as Principal Architect for the Rebuilding of the City, in which capacity, as Bell, *The Great Fire of London*, London 1920, pp.259 ff., has shown, his influence was negligible; for Wren's appointment to the principal Surveyorship, *cf.* WS XVIII, p.180.

39 13 Sept. 1666. It should be remembered that Evelyn had had greater opportunities of intimately knowing the circumstances of the City, having served, as early as 1662, on the Commission for 'reforming the buildings, ways, streets, and incumbrances' then existing; *cf. Diary*, 14 May 1662. It is to Denham's work on that commission that Evelyn refers in his dedication of the first edition of *A Parallel . . .* etc., 1664.

40 e.g. Christopher Wren, John Evelyn, Sir William Petty, Richard Newcourt, and Robert Hooke. The former four were submitted to the King, Hooke's to the Royal Society and the City authorities. Bell, *op. cit.*, p.240, also prints Valentine Knight's plan, chiefly remarkable for its great canal. Briggs, *op. cit.*, p.45, mentions seven plans in all but gives no further elucidation.

41 Blomfield, *Six Architects*, Oxford 1935, p.169.

42 Sturgis, *art. cit.*, p.82.

43 Dutton, *op. cit.*, p.29.

44 Blomfield, *Touchstone*, p.186.

45 Weaver, *op. cit.*, p.57.

46 Whitaker-Wilson, *op. cit.*, p.104.

47 *loc. cit.*

48 Summerson, *op. cit.*, p.51.

49 e.g. Vitruvius, Alberti, Palladio; *v. infra*, p.130.

50 *Cf.* the author's and L. d'Arcy's *Versailles*, London 1951, pp.50, 57, 127. Although the gardens of Versailles underwent innumerable changes between 1661 and 1715, the parterres du nord and du midi may have been seen by Wren in the same state as of today; their form, unlike that of the parterre d'eau, was determined, and never subsequently altered,

by about 1668, as is proved by Patel's painting in the Musée de Versailles. For a complete and authoritative account of the evolution of the Versailles park *cf.* Nolhac, *La Création de Versailles*, Paris 1925, with especial reference to Le Nôtre, pp.213–88.

51 Evelyn, *Diary* (Paris) 30 April 1650, records his visit to Perelle.

52 Blomfield, *Touchstone*, p.186. The layout of the town of Versailles provides an excellent example; for an instance of 'vista and axial planning' *cf.* the author's *op. cit.*, pp.12, 22.

53 Vitruvius, *De architectura*, I, v, vi; Palladio, *Quattro Libri*, III, i–vi, xvi–xviii; *v. infra*, p.130. In addition, the mutual influence between Wren and Evelyn in their town planning schemes must be mentioned: Evelyn mentions (*Londinum Redivivum*, ed. De Beer, Oxford 1938, p.46) that he 'read this discourse to the Doctor before I had seen his plot' on 11 Sept. and while at least one feature of Wren's plan (*v. infra*, note 73) contributed to the printed version of Evelyn's 'discourse', it need not be ruled out that some of Evelyn's ideas found a reflection in Wren's own plan.

54 *Cf.* Hawksmoor, *Remarks on the Founding and Carrying on the Buildings of the Royal Hospital at Greenwich*, 1728, in WS VI, pp.17–27: 'How useful had the cultivation of the Science of Architecture been, at the Rebuilding that City after the dreadful Fire in Anno 1666, if the Citizens would have been capable of Advice, and pursued the Plan laid before them by King Charles II, drawn and prepared by that incomparable Architect, Sir Chr Wren, of rendering the whole City regular, uniform, convenient, durable and beautiful, without any Man's Loss, or Infringement of Property.' Reddaway, *The Rebuilding of London after the Great Fire*, London 1951, omits any reference to this pamphlet and therefore fails to recognize the ultimate derivation of Ralph's, Gwynn's, and Stephen Wren's 'legend'; not only probability but also verbal coincidence suggest that all three authors were indebted to Hawksmoor. How closely Stephen Wren followed Hawksmoor in another instance is quoted *infra*, note 403.

55 *Parentalia*, p.269.

56 Gwynn possibly bought the original drawing of the City plan at the 1749 auction, though his engraving, published on 3 October of that year, is not an altogether accurate version. The inscription is a verbose eulogy of Wren's plan, the failure of which is ascribed to 'narrow spirited Contests about identical Property' which, quite wrongly, are stated to have triumphed over alleged Parliamentary sanction.

57 October 1666; Privy Council Registers, 2/59, ff.194–7; *cf.* Brett-James, *The Growth of Stuart London*, London 1935, p.300.

58 Bell, *op. cit.*, p.260; Reddaway, *op. cit.*, App.A.

59 Whitaker-Wilson, *op. cit.*, p.101, states that 'the King told Evelyn that, on the whole, he preferred Wren's plan, but pointed out a few details in Evelyn's that he liked better, and suggested modifying Wren's to agree with it'. This statement is entirely fictitious; were it a fact, we could hardly believe that Evelyn would have left it unrecorded in his *Diary*; the relevant entry, 13 Sept. 1666, however, reads: 'I presented his Majesty with a survey of the ruins, and a plot for a new City, with a discourse on it; whereupon, after dinner, his Majesty sent for me into the Queen's bed-chamber, her Majesty and the Duke only being present. They examined each particular, and discoursed on them for near an hour, seeming to be extremely pleased with what I had so early thought on.'

60 The dimensions proposed by Wren are not identical with those decided at a meeting of the surveyors on 11 Oct.; *cf. The Architecture of Sir Roger Pratt*, ed. Gunther, Oxford 1928, p.13: '. . . wee resolved the breadth of the severall future streetes to bee as followth. That of the Key 100 foot. That of the High Street 70 f. That of some other streetes 50f. That of some others – 42 f. That of the least – 30 or 25 f. That of the alleys, if any – 16 f.' On the other hand, the dimensions agreed upon by the surveyors recall Evelyn's recommendations (*Londinum Redivivum*, ed. cit., p.37) specifying 'none of the principal streets less than an hundred foot in breadth, nor any of the narrowest than thirty'.

61 *Cf.* the plans printed in WS XIII, pls.xxiv, xxv, and the Vertue engravings of Evelyn's three sketch plans reproduced in the *ed. cit.* of *Londinum Redivivum.*

62 *Cf.* Evelyn, *Fumifugium, or the Inconvenience of the Aer and Smoak of London dissipated, together with some Remedies humbly proposed,* London 1661; also *Diary,* 11 Jan. 1661: 'I received of Sir Peter Ball, the Queen's Attorney, a draught of an Act against the nuisance of the smoke of London, to be reformed by removing several trades which are the cause of it.' It would be tempting to connect Evelyn's recommendations with Dürer's plan of an ideal city outlined in *De Urbibus,* where section 'C' is to be allotted to the foundries 'on account of the winds [which] will drive the poisonous fumes away from the castle'. The ultimate derivation clearly must be sought in Alberti, *De Re Aedificatoria,* VII, i.

63 These quotations are extracted from King Charles's 'Proclamation to Prohibit the Rebuilding of Houses' after the Great Fire, partly quoted in Bell, *op. cit.,* pp.216 ff., from W. de Gray Birch, *Historic Charters,* and reprinted *in extenso* in *Letters, Speeches and Declarations of King Charles II,* ed. Bryant, London 1935, pp.191–4.

64 *ibid.,* 'To the Mayor and Common Council', 22 March 1666/7; *ed. cit.,* p.195.

65 'Proclamation . . .' etc. 13 Sept. 1666; *loc. cit.*

66 Pepys, *Diary,* 22 Nov. 1666. Unfortunately his note is very brief, as he quickly turns to tell us of the vests worn by Louis XIV's servants. Evelyn also refers to Hollar's 'late plan' by which either pre- or post-Fire version may be meant, in a letter to Oldenburg of 22 Dec. 1666, printed in Bray's ed. of the *Diary,* note to 13 Sept. 1666.

67 *v. supra,* note 60.

68 Pratt, *ed. cit.,* p.13; *v. infra,* note 169.

69 Pepys, *Diary,* 25 Nov. 1666.

70 *ibid.,* 28 Jan. 1666/7.

71 *ibid.,* 19 Feb. 1666/7: 'After dinner, I fell to read the Acts again about the building of the city; and indeed the laws seem to be very good, and I pray God I may live to see it built in that manner!' *Cf.* also *ibid.,* 24 Feb. 1666/7.

72 19 Car. II, c.3.

73 Pepys, *Diary,* 5 May 1667. This project, clearly a reflection of Wren's plan, was specifically noticed by Evelyn (*Londinum Redivivum, ed. cit.,* pp.45–6): 'This street from St. Pauls [eastwards] may be divaricated like a Pythagorean Y, as the most accurately ingenious Dr. Wren has designed it . . .'.

74 'Proclamation . . .' etc., 13 Sept. 1666; *ed. cit.,* p.191.

75 *Cf.* 'Address to the Mayor and Common Council', 22 March 1666/7, *ed. cit.,* p.195: '. . . shall have all assistance from His Majesty to procure the consent of all persons concerned, that such places may be enlarged, and such other things done as may contribute to the beauty, ornament and convenience of the city, although they may not seem to have full power and authority to direct and order the same by the strict letter of the Act of Parliament, as the widening of Pater Noster Row, where the same can be done . . .'

76 Pepys, *Diary,* 24 Feb. 1666/7.

77 Weaver, *op. cit.,* p.57, suggests the cause of failure to have been the fact that 'the citizens might well [have been] suspicious lest [Charles's] town-planning schemes developed into a typical piece of Caroline jobbery,' and instances, in support, 'the little affair of a vast sum of money voted for a noble monument to Charles the First'. As the monument project was not broached until 1678, it is hardly relevant to the case of the City plan failure: *v. infra,* note 271.

78 *A Plan for Rebuilding the City* . . . 3 Oct. 1749: '. . . ye Improvements made in Westminster have already drawn so many thriving Inhabitants out of ye City & the great Number of empty Houses within the Walls shows . . .'

79 The parishes of the City decreased in number even before the Fire. Richard Grafton, *A Little Treatise,* 1572 (quoted in Jenkinson, *London*

Churches before the Great Fire, London 1917, p.81) states that 'the Parishe Churches in London and adjoyning are in number CXIX besyde the Cathedrall Churches of Paules, Westminster [*sic*] and the Churche in the Rolles in Chancery Lane'. Stow, *Survey,* gives 123 churches; Brett-James, *op. cit.,* pp.38, 114; Bell, *op. cit.,* pp.334–6, lists 109. Evelyn, *Londinum Redivivum, ed. cit.,* p.38, suggests that the parish churches may 'well be reduced to a moiety, for 'tis prodigiously true, that there are some parishes no less than two hundred times larger than others'. Of the destroyed churches, thirty-five were not rebuilt; of those reconstructed, thirty-three served two parishes, one served three. We have found no evidence to substantiate Briggs's statement (*Wren the Incomparable,* London 1953, p.109), that 'Wren's first task was to recommend how many of the old churches should be restored or replaced'. Nor can we substantiate that author's assertion (*op. cit.* [1951], p.73) that Wren's alleged proposal to reduce the number of parishes to thirty-nine was approved by Parliament. An Act of Parliament passed in 1670 (Statutes of the Realm, V., 677, cited by de Beer, Evelyn, *Diary,* IV, p.243, note 7) authorized the rebuilding of fifty-one churches in the City of London.

80 *Diary,* 5 April 1667.

81 e.g. St Michael, Cornhill; St Mary, Woolnoth; St Edmund's, St Christopher's and St Bartholomew's.

82 Following *Parentalia,* the church has been dated 1672 by Phillimore, Stratton, Birch, *London Churches of the 17th and 18th Centuries,* London 1896, L. Milman, Whitaker-Wilson, Dutton and Lindsey. The building accounts (WS X, pp.48–9) commence with 1670, so that 1669 could reasonably be suggested for the design. Mackmurdo's date of 1678 lacks evidence as much as probabliity. The WS editors are precise in assigning the building period to July 1670 to Sept. 1676, and draw attention to the related plan of All Saints, Northampton, which must be dated 1675.

83 *Cf.* WS XIX, pl.lxxiii, reproducing the engraving from Chauncey's *History of Herts.,* (1700). The dedication is by John Oliver, Wren's deputy at St Paul's. The building has been dated 1673–80.

84 Clayton, *The Parochial Churches of Sir Christopher Wren,* London 1848–9, shows all pediments as triangular; in Clarke's *Architectura Ecclesiastica Londini,* London 1809, however, the window above the door is shown with a segmental pediment. In the absence of holograph drawings, the original form cannot easily be decided, but in view of the fact that Wren only rarely employed segmental pediments (*v. infra,* p.21 and note 126) and even more rarely combinations of the two varieties (*v. infra,* pp.133–4) it seems probable that Clark is inaccurate.

85 Vestry Minutes, printed WS XIX, pp.33–6.

86 L. Milman, *op. cit.,* p.236 erroneously gives 1667; *cf.* Evelyn, *Diary,* 14 Nov. 1668. The bishopric was originally intended for Sancroft who, however, declined it, 'being rather desirious to serve in the great work of "re-edifying" St Paul's church'. (Newsletter, 15 Sept. 1668, R.C. Hist. MSS., XII, app.vii, reprinted in WS XIII, p.xviii.)

87 Wilkins's possible influence on the design has been severely criticized by L. Milman, *op. cit.,* pp.236–48: '. . . it is surely permissible to trace the influence of the Doctor's notoriously Erastian leanings in what is as surely the most consistently secular as it was the most costly of Wren's City churches . . . all the more disappointing is the interior . . . it is as though Wilkins had bade his friend design an ideal lecture room for the Royal Society . . . St Laurence's is academic rather than ecclesiastical.' This view is paraphrased by Day, *op. cit.,* p.127, who would account for this 'bald and secular church', this 'preaching house of no dignity' by the irrelevant explanation that it was 'built during the rectorate of a Latitudinarian'.

88 Cunningham, *op. cit.,* IV, p.216, suggests that the plan of St Lawrence followed (Catholic) tradition in being formed in the shape of a gridiron, though this assertion is the more difficult to accept for the similarity of St Vedast, where no such iconographical concepts would be applicable.

89 *Cf.* ASC I, 61, 74, 79 (WS IX, pl.35).

90 The building accounts of both churches run from 1670 to 1686. St Dionis is dated by the WS editors 1670–86 (WS IX, p.48) and alternatively 1674–84 (WS XIX, p.146). L. Milman, Whitaker-Wilson, and Lindsey, give 1674; *Parentalia* gives 1684; Stratton gives both; Clayton assigns the tower to 1684; Dutton gives the opening of the church as 1679. The Vestry Minutes (WS XIX, p.16) record the agreement for the pewing of 23 Jan. 1672/3, specifying that it should be 'of as good stuff and materials as St Mary Hill'. The entry in Hooke's *Diary*, 19 Nov. 1672, states that 'Dr. Wren was here at St Dionis' which may indicate that Hooke was supervising operations. The dating of St Mary Aldermanbury suffers from similar confusion: the churchwarden's account of John du Bois (WS XIX, pp.38–9) covers the period Easter 1672 to Easter 1675 and states that 'during the tyme abovesayd ... the Parish Church was restored from the total ruine it received'. We have found no evidence to support the assertion made by Weaver, *op. cit.*, p.77, that the church was only repaired, but not rebuilt, by Wren. The length of time covered by the building accounts, as well as the entire character of the church, speak strongly against such a possibility. Blomfield, Stratton, Cleveland, L. Milman, and Lindsey accept the *Parentalia* date of 1677; the quotations given from the parish records by Birch, *op. cit.*, p.68, confirm our dating of 1670.

91 The fact that the east elevation of St George's (Fig.145) was placed on an exceptionally high podium and had windows, not doors, in the aisles, was the result of the steeply sloping site. Note, however, the distinctive panels below the centre window.

92 Birch, *op. cit.*, p.6; this author gives precedence to St Sepulchre and St Christopher only which, in his opinion, were repaired but not rebuilt by Wren in 1670; *cf.* however, Daniell, *London City Churches*, London 1896, p.3, who states that the repairs of St Sepulchre were probably not Wren's work at all. This opinion is supported by Phillimore, *op. cit.*, pp.182–3, who quotes Billing's *Restoration of the Church of St. Sepulchre*, according to which authority the church was not destroyed, but only damaged, and the parishioners, unwilling to wait until Wren could attend to their wants, decided on the restoration themselves.

93 *Cf.* Building Accounts, *sub* 31 July 1673 (WS X, p.60).

94 BM Sloane 5238, 58 (WS IX, pl.21; there described as a survey plan); the two houses are shown on the future site of the tower.

95 Building Accounts, 28 June and 27 Oct. 1670 (WS X, p.95).

96 The drawing reproduced (ASC I, 75) shows some very faint pencillings above the south aisle which indicate that Wren was toying with the idea of scroll buttresses.

97 As appears from one of the engravings in the Pepysian Library, Cambridge, printed in WS IX, pl.24.

98 The authenticity of this oval window cannot be established with certainty; the Clayton engravings of 1848 show identical oval windows in the gables of St Mary Aldermanbury and Bow; the latter, however, is not shown in the Hawksmoor drawing (Fig.19) or engraving of 1726 (WS XVIII, pl.xxi) executed for Christopher Wren jun. It appears, however, in two engravings from the Pepysian Library (WS IX, pl.29) which must certainly antedate the Hawksmoor drawing; for further divergences, *v. infra*, note 102. The truly accomplished version of the scheme of design illustrated in Fig.18 can be seen in the west front of St Margaret's, Rood Lane, where the central window and door combination appears beautifully balanced; the window inserted in the gable pediment is, conform with those above the lateral windows, circular.

99 i.e. the doors in the piers of the great model design for St Paul's, 1673; *cf.* the section, engraved by Hulsbergh (WS XIV, pl.iii) and the section ASC II, 23 (WS I, pl.xviii) for the significant change of this detail between the Greek cross and the great model designs.

100 G. Webb, introduction to Cobb, *The Old Churches of London*, London 1941, pp.11–12, referring to Bow Church and St Stephen's, Walbrook.

101 Summerson, *Georgian London*, 1947, p.45, suggests that other hands than Wren's may have been responsible for such 'gauche mediocrity like the

interior of St Mary le Bow' which he contrasts with a design of 'brilliant and masterly refinement like the tower of St Magnus'. This does not seem to us a cogent argument, as it is difficult, if not altogether impossible to draw a comparison between works of such different periods and functions. Moreover, it should not be overlooked that several of Wren's interiors are aesthetically unsatisfactory: even Blomfield, one of Wren's least critical admirers, in his *Short History of Renaissance Architecture in England* (1923 ed.), p.120, finds fault with those of St Andrew, Wardrobe; St Andrew, Holborn; St Peter; St Magnus; St James, Westminster; St Mary Aldermanbury; and St Mary le Bow.

102 *Cf.* ASC II, 47 (Fig.76); BM, King's Library, (WS X, pl.6); three engravings from the Pepysian Library (WS X, pl.24); the Hawksmoor drawing of the steeple only, ASC II, 76 (WS IX, pl.25) and the corresponding BM Sloane Add.5238, No.68 (WS IX, pl.26); and many prints of inferior quality. There are many divergences between different versions: *v. supra*, note 98; note also the differences in door treatment, and the partitioning of the belfry window, both shown in BM Sloane 5238, No.68, but omitted in the Hawksmoor drawing and engraving; although the latter shows oval clerestorey windows, one of the undoubtedly earlier Pepysian prints shows a roof construction following the curved buttresses. The statue on the pediment shown in the Hulsbergh engraving appears to have been fanciful.

103 The Building Accounts for Bow Steeple (WS X, pp.68–76) run from 1672 to 1682; Hooke (*Diary*, 9 March 1675/6) records an agreement with Cartwright for 'Bow Tower for £2550'. The second mason's contract is dated 15 Aug. 1678. We may take this as the latest date for the completion of Wren's design.

104 Weaver, *op. cit.*, p.145: 'in the steeple of St Mary le Bow, which is nearly perfect, the diameter of the cylinder enclosed by a ring of columns is hardly right.'

105 Hawksmoor compared the plan to that of the Temple of Peace, though the comparison does not extend very far; *cf.* Palladio, *Quattro Libri*, 1601 ed., IV, p.12.

106 *Parentalia* gives 1690, which is uncritically accepted by Birch, Cleveland, Phillimore, Mackmurdo, and Daniell; Lindsey gives 1689; L. Milman, Stratton, and Whitaker-Wilson compromise by 1689–90; Clayton correctly gives 1690 for the lantern; Weaver, who first published the building accounts in *Archaeologia*, LXVI, follows that evidence in giving 1670–9.

107 Vestry Minutes, St Stephen's, Walbrook, in WS X, pp.110–13.

108 As shown in Kent, *Some Designs of Mr. Inigo Jones and Mr. William Kent*, 1744. The carved swags do not appear, however, in the Hulsbergh engraving, BM Crace Coll., XIX, 142–3 (WS XIV, pl.liii).

109 *Cf.* also ASC IV, 112 (WS IX, pl.39) which, though unidentified by the WS editors, clearly belongs to St Edmund's.

110 The Building Accounts run from 1671–8; our dating is supported by Summerson, *RIBA Journal*, Feb. 1952, p.126; but the *Parentalia* dating of 1676 is accepted by Birch, Stratton, L. Milman, Whitaker-Wilson, and Lindsey; Cleveland assigns 'St Maglens the Martyr' to 1705.

111 Vestry Minutes, 11 Dec. 1671; WS XIX, p.26.

112 This was first noticed by Summerson, *art. cit.*, who makes the interesting suggestion that Wren may have wanted to retrieve a fragment of his City plan by building a piazza there; for a similar project in connexion with St Stephen's, Walbrook, *v. infra*, p.24.

113 ASC I, 64 (Fig.22); the WS editors failed to identify this drawing though the recession of the aisles was not effected till 1762. In WS IX, index, the drawing is captioned: '? Elevation, late style. St Lawrence?' In WS XX, p.5 (catalogue of ASC), it is described as 'Front of a Church? Four Ionic, Columns and Pediment in Centre. Shaded. See Plate XXI, Vol.V, Trinity College Library, where there are 6 Columns instead of four.' Neither of these ascriptions is correct. The obvious contradiction between 'late style' and 'St Lawrence' has been overlooked. The prototype for the design may be seen in ASC I, 58 (not in WS), described by Elmes as an 'Ionic Temple'.

114 T. F. Bumpus, *London Churches*, New York, *s.d.*, p.406. Stratton, *op. cit.*, p.50, suggests Hakewill as the probable designer.

115 Summerson, *art. cit.*, p.129.

116 Phillimore, *op. cit.*, p.300, suggests that Wren's design was made so as to 'externally resemble a Danish church . . . out of compliment to Prince George', but this notion cannot be seriously entertained; not only must the church have been completed when Evelyn heard 'Mr. Wake, at the New-built Church of St. Anns' on 20 March 1686/7, but altogether can there be no question of assigning the church to Queen Anne's reign. Summerson, *art. cit.*, suggests that as the church was 'consecrated in 1686, it will have been designed, presumably, about 1680' but the design would appear to us rather immature in comparison with others of that period.

117 Brett-James, *op. cit.*, p.396, quotes Sir John Bramston's *Autobiography* where the author records the consecration 'upon the twentie-first of the same March, 1685/6' by Bishop Compton, and gives reasons for the hasty ceremony.

118 Brett-James, *ibid.*, p.394. St Albans' development plans must have been materialized with some speed, as this author mentions the existence of a separate Soho Rate Book as early as 1675.

119 *Cf.* the cellar plan, ASC I, 20 (WS XII, pl.vii). The façade as shown in the engraving in Smith, *Antiquities of London*, pl.3, with its ludicrous broken pediments flanking a semicircular window, is, of course, not Wren's but Archer's; *cf.* WS XII, p.16.

120 The tower built for this church can be seen in Buck's panorama of 1749, printed by Phillips, *The Thames About 1750*, London 1952, Fig.108. The tower destroyed in 1940–1 had a nineteenth-century successor. The motif from Wren's original design recurs at St Benet's, Gracechurch Street, as recognized by Summerson, *art. cit.*

121 The accepted dating needs to be corrected: Stratton, Cleveland, and Whitaker-Wilson follow *Parentalia* with 1680; Birch gives 1679; the steeple is alternatively dated 1700 or 1701–2; L. Milman, *op. cit.*, p.242, assigns the plan to 1678 and states, *ibid.*, p.167, that building was begun in 1680. All these dates must be rejected as too late. Wren's visit, in the company of Woodroof and Hooke (*Diary*, 28 Nov. 1674) was probably consequent upon the completion of the demolition works, and served the purpose of inspection before finalizing the plan.

122 Ventry Minutes, 13 March 1674/5 (WS XIX, p.11).

123 St Stephen's Vestry Minutes, WS X, p.110.

124 *Diary*, 4 Nov. 1679.

125 WS editors, index and caption to WS IX, pl.37; also WS XX, p.53.

126 The significance of this feature should be emphasized, as Wren's uncommon employments of it fall into two chronologically distinct periods. The first of these concerns the years here discussed. In addition to the instance mentioned in note 127, Wren used a segmental pediment at the entrance gate of Bromley College, designed for John Warner, not later than 1672; (*cf.* the engraving, WS XIX, pl.lxxii). It is interesting to see that when, twenty-three years later, Wren designed a building of a similar kind, Morden College, he used a doorway closely resembling that of Bromley College.

127 The doorway at Arbury, dated 1674; *cf.* WS XII, pl.xlix, for draft design and photograph of the actual doorway, in which latter the pediment is triangular. For St Bride's, *cf.* ASC II, 46 (Fig.82) and Ruddock Collection, No.20. A segmental pediment also occurs on a door-frame in the Honywood Library, Lincoln, which must be dated 1674; *cf.* WS XVII, pls.lxv–lxvi.

128 *Cf.* Vestry Minutes, in WS XIX, pp.18–19; the relatively short period covered would suggest repairs only; this is supported by Weaver, *op. cit.*, p.77, though Daniell, *op. cit.*, p.165, states that Wren was called in in 1671 and 'the reconstruction of the church was carried out in accordance with his design'. No reason is given why the steeple was not completed until 1699.

129 Vestry Minutes, WS XIX, pp.18–19, *sub* 22 June 1670 and 20 Oct. 1671.

The entry in Hooke's *Diary*, 6 Sept. 1672: 'Churchwardens of St. Dunstons 5 guinnys' may refer to a gratuity. The same applies to *ibid.*, 24 April 1674.

130 *ibid.*, 18 July 1693.

131 Clayton dates the 'Gothic' steeple to 1698. Weaver, *op. cit.*, p.78, thinks it 'unique for its date and of quite extraordinary interest' though Blomfield, *Hist. Ren. Arch. Eng.*, thinks 'the details are preposterous. They are obviously insincere, and that Wren should have tolerated such work shows either that his taste must have been uncertain or his artistic conscience somewhat lax'.

132 *Parentalia* gives 1668 for St Dunstan; though obviously incorrect, as appears from notes 129–30 *supra*, the possibility exists that authors, frequently prone to follow Stephen Wren's statements quite uncritically, have here deviated from him by reason of the later steeple, and thus overlooked the possibility of an earlier structure.

133 The symbol of the cock is also associated with St Peter, in allusion to the passage in the Gospel of St John. If our interpretation of this design is correct, it would provide an instance of Wren's following the precedent of the pre-Fire structure, which was characterized by an extremely tall, tapering spire: *cf.* the Hollar engraving in Hind, *Wenceslaus Hollar* (1922), pl.xix.

134 Weaver gives the terminal dates of the building accounts, 1670–81. The *Parentalia* dating accepted by Birch, Stratton, L. Milman, Whitaker-Wilson, and Lindsey must be rejected as the design must have been executed prior to 1 Dec. 1670, when the foundation stone was laid; *cf.* Vestry Books in WS XIX, pp.8–9.

135 Blomfield, *Hist. Ren. Arch. Eng.*, I, p.156.

136 Dated by the WS editors 1673–76; *cf.* the drawings in WS XIX, pl.xxiii, also the engraving from Plot's *History of Staffordshire* (1686), *ibid.* pl.xxvi.

137 Blomfield's error, *Hist. Ren. Arch. Eng.*, I, p.156, in stating that the dome is supported by eight pillars could have been avoided by reference to the original plan reproduced.

138 Loftie, *op. cit.*, p.184: 'St Christopher, St Michael Crooked Lane and St Benet Fink were pulled down, but are not so much to be lamented.'

139 Weaver, *op. cit.*, p.78, doubtless on purely formalistic grounds, endorses Blomfield's opinion that the details of St Stephen's are 'coarse and irrelevant'. For Loftie's comparable criticism of Palladio, *v. infra.*, note 974.

140 *Cf.* Birch, *op. cit.*, p.7.

141 T. F. Bumpus, *op. cit.*, p.266.

142 *ibid.*, p.392.

143 *ibid.*, p.393.

144 *Cf.* Pevsner, *Outline of European Architecture*, 1945 ed., p.176; 1948 ed., pp.171–2.

145 ASC I, 60 (WS IX, pl.33); the crowning feature of the dome misled Elmes into cataloguing it as an 'elevation of a banquetting room, in a bad style, with a flag on the dome'.

146 Vestry Minutes, 28 Jan. 1679 (WS X, p.113): 'To attend Wren in order to have the porch built.'

147 Parish Documents at St Stephen's, box 1056, *sub* 13 Dec. 1681 (WS X, p.114).

148 Vestry Minutes, 19 Feb. 1674: 'To attend Mr Lane, the City Comptroller, to advise with him how to get a grant from the City of so much ground on the north side as will be sufficient to build our steeple thereon.' Also *ibid.*, 3 May 1675: 'To attend the Lord Mayor and Court of Aldermen to present a petition concerning building the steeple on the north side of the Church.'

149 St Stephen's Documents, WS X, p.114.

150 This was suggested by Summerson, *art. cit.*

151 The dating of St Stephen's has been controversial. The Building Accounts cover the period 1672–87, but *Parentalia* gives 1676, Chancellor, *Lives of the British Architects*, London 1909, gives 1682, Mackmurdo and

Cleveland 1681, Birch 1672; Stratton, L. Milman, and Lindsey give 1672–9. As appears from the Building Accounts (WS X, pp.77–8) construction began in Sept. 1674 and was apparently complete by Sept. 1677, though these dates may be somewhat posterior to the actual execution of the work, as they refer to payments for work completed.

152 Reference must be made to Sir Thomas Chicheley, P.C., Master of the Ordnance. The original site of the church was given by Sir Thomas's ancestor, Sir Robert Chicheley, Lord Mayor in 1421, who laid the foundation stone of the Church in 1439 (Jenkinson, *op. cit.*, p.167). Sir Thomas was present at the laying of the foundation stone of Wren's church (*cf.* Vestry Minutes *sub* 17 Dec. 1672, in WS X, p.112) for the building of which he had donated £100 (*ibid.*, 4 April 1673 and Churchwardens' Accounts, 1672–3, *ibid.*, pp.112–14); his arms are found on a doorway of the church (*ibid.*, p.42). For his connexion with St Paul's, *v. infra*, p.26 and note 165. For his connexion with Greenwich Observatory, *v. infra*, p.87.

153 According to Sprat, *History of the Royal Society*, 1663; *cf.* Dimock, *op. cit.*, p.56; L. Milman, *op. cit.*, p.56, gives 1662. Briggs, *op. cit.*, (1951) p.54 gives 1666. It should be noted, however, that neither Wren's nor Evelyn's, Pratt's, or May's names are listed in the Royal Commission for the Repair of old St Paul's, dated 18 April 1663 (WS XIII, p.13). Evelyn's first official appointment to the works at St Paul's seems to have taken place shortly before the Fire. *Cf. Diary*, 23 Aug. 1666: 'Then to my L: Chancelor, who had (with the Bish: of Lond & others in Commission) chosen me one of the three Surveyors of the repaires of Paules, & to consider of a model for the new building . . .' etc. Wren's first connexion established by documents in his report of 1 May 1666 (*ibid.*, pp.15–17), though he very probably had surveyed the cathedral before that date, as is suggested by his letter to Sancroft, 7 May 1666 (*ibid.*, p.44). The statement in Thieme-Becker, *Allgemeines Künstlerlexicon*, XXXVI, 1947, p.274, that '1662 behandelt [Wren] in einem Gutachten den baulichen Zustand' of St Paul's is not based on any evidence known to us.

154 *Cf.* Dimock, *op. cit.*, p.28.

155 Drummond, *Church Architecture of Protestantism*, Edinburgh 1934, p.26, though aware of Laud's instrumentality in making the St Paul's reconstruction possible, maintains that 'to him, the Beautiful was the Traditional, the "churchly". His aim was to build antiquarian productions of old churches. He professed admiration for the "Gothick"'. This view, based on the church of St Catherine Cree, is amply refuted by Laud's buildings at Oxford, notably the Canterbury Quadrangle at St John's and particularly the famous porch of St Mary's.

156 For details of the old west front, *cf.* Longman, *Three Cathedrals of St Paul*, London 1873, p.34; for Jones's portico, *cf.* WS XIV, pl.liii.

157 *Cf.* the pre-Fire engraving by Hollar, printed by Whitaker-Wilson, *op. cit.*, p.67, which shows the nature and extent of Jones's alterations. No conceivable reason appears why Bell, *op. cit.*, p.132, should speak of the 'bad new Gothic work at the sides'.

158 Howell, *Familiar Letters*, VIII, xxxv, quoted by Jenkinson, *op. cit.*, pp.25, 27.

159 Wren's report, quoted by L. Milman, *op. cit.*, p.90; WS XIII, p.17.

160 Whitaker-Wilson, *op. cit.*, p.82, suggests that Wren's intentions were due to the fact that 'obviously he realized that people of advanced age would not live to see the new dome. It was a kindly thought and thoroughly characteristic of him'; but this seems a tortuous interpretation of Wren's meaning which is quite clear from the passage immediately following (WS XIII, p. 17): '& chiefly because it will save a world of scaffolding poles . . .'

161 Evelyn frequently attaches the epithet 'noble' when writing of domes or 'cupolas': *cf. Diary*, Williamstadt, 22 Sept. 1641; Jesuit church, Paris, 4 Jan. 1644; Pisa Baptistery, 19 Oct. 1644; Sta Constanza, Rome, 10 Nov. 1644; Baptistery of San Giovanni in Laterano, Rome, 20 Nov. 1644; Trie Fontane, 23 Jan. 1645; the Pantheon, 21 Feb. 1645; Sant'

Andrea della Valle, 24 Feb. 1645; Sta Giustina, Padua (wrongly attributed to Palladio) June 1645; San Giorgio Maggiore, Venice, July 1645.

162 The last named is the only one mentioned in Wren's letter from Paris, though his comments are more concerned with site planning than with the dome.

163 *Diary*, 27 Aug. 1666. Evelyn mentions the offer to 'bring in a plan and estimate' which is referred to by J. S. Bumpus, *St Paul's Cathedral*, London, 1913, p.169, but this is not likely to refer to the drawings, ASC II, 2, 3, 4, 5, 6, 7 (WS I, pls.i, iv, v, vi, vii, viii), as it is not probable that Wren should have executed these in the short space of time between the meeting and the outbreak of the Fire. Cunningham, *op. cit.*, IV, p.176, assigns report and drawings to 1665 and prior to the Paris visit, which suggestion is disproved by the dates marked on the drawings themselves. Probability would indicate that they were executed before the meeting, though not submitted.

164 Stratton, *op. cit.*, p.7, states that the designs 'met with favour at once, and the order was given for its [*sic*] execution without delay', and asserts, *ibid.*, p.8, that 'the design of the cupola . . . was in the act of being carried out before the Fire'. The allegedly favourable reception on the part of the commissioners has likewise been asserted by Day, *op. cit.*, p.89, and uncritically repeated by Dutton, *op. cit.*, p.26, as recently as 1951. There is, however, no evidence whatever to substantiate this legend: on the contrary, the project was most unfavourably received, unless reason could be shown why Evelyn's passage *cit. supra* should be discredited. According to him, even the offer to bring in plans and estimates was only 'after much contest, at last assented to'. To assert that the cupola was actually under construction at that time is nothing short of ludicrous. The statement in *Parentalia* that Wren was 'ordered to provide a convenient quire, with vestibule and porticoes, and a Dome conspicuous above the houses' has been connected with the pre-Fire design by Longman, *op. cit.*, pp.96, 103, but this is obviously untenable. Stephen Wren's assertion regarding the 'order' for a dome is altogether fictitious.

165 Lindsey's statement, *op. cit.*, p.93, that 'who precisely Chichley and Prat [Evelyn's spelling] were is not clear' is unaccountable from an author writing in 1951. *DNB* deals exhaustively with the careers of both men whose names appear frequently in the documentary material published by WS. Pratt, knighted in 1668, was the best-known architect on the committee, with Clarendon House (*cf.* Evelyn, *Diary*, 22 Nov. 1666, 20 July 1670) and Coleshill (attributed by Walpole *et al.* to Inigo Jones, but shown to have been Pratt's work by Gunther) to his credit, and served on the Fire Committee as well as that of St Paul's. Sir Thomas Chicheley is frequently mentioned by Evelyn and Pepys; appointed to the St Paul's committee in 1663 (WS XIII, p.13) and also served on the 1673 Commission (*ibid.*, p.27); *v. supra*, note 152.

166 The solidity of the piers was demonstrated by the fact that Wren had to have recourse to gunpowder and battering rams when he demolished them; *v. infra*, note 426.

167 *Diary*, 27 Aug. 1666; Longman, *op. cit.*, p.84, gives 25 Aug. Dimock, *op. cit.*, p.65, unaccountably attributes the end of the passage to Wren. Pite, *RIBA Mem. Vol.*, p.51, refers to Evelyn who 'in the dedication of his "Account of Architecture" [*sic*] published in 1664, says: "You will not, I am sure, forget the struggle we had with some, who were for patching it up anyhow, (so that the steeple might stand) instead of New Building: which is altogether needed"', and suggests, *ibid.*, p.55, that 'the reference already made by Evelyn in his dedication to Wren previously shows that the possibility of substituting a cupola for the tower had been debated long before [1664]'. This perverse misrepresentation of the facts rests on its author's ignorance of the various editions of Evelyn's *Parallel*. The passage quoted comes from the dedication to 'Sir Christopher Wren, Surveyor' which neither in style nor appointment can apply to 1664; the further reference to St Paul's ('when to put an end to the contest, five days after, that dreadful conflagration happened, out of

whose ashes this phoenix, new St Paul's, is risen and was by Providence designed by you') should have made it clear that it could not have been written in 1664; just as the subsequent references to Chelsea and Greenwich would make that date an impossibility. Lastly, Evelyn's printed dedication could not have been more precisely dated than 'Wotton, 21 February 1696/7'. This was the first issue of *A Parallel*, dedicated to Wren. The 1664 edition was dedicated to Charles II, resp. Sir John Denham and does not, of course, contain the quotations cited by Prof. Pite.

168 Wren's appointment to the St Paul's Committee was not made directly by Charles II, as stated by Stratton, *op. cit.*, p.6.

169 Concerning May, *v. supra*, note 3; concerning Pratt, *cf.* the implicit criticism of Wren's City plan, in *The Architecture* . . . p.13 (continuing the quotation given *supra* p.7): '. . . being that no man can tell how to offer any acceptable designe till this be determined, nor any one to build till that design be agreed upon.' Also *v. infra*, pp.31–2.

170 (Anon.): *The Burning of Paules* (*c.*1561); printed in Simpson, *Documents Illustrating the History of St Paul's Cathedral*, London 1880, pp.126–7. Cosimo of Tuscany's statement, in *Travels* . . . etc [1669 (1821)], p.181, that the spire was struck by lightning in 1087 and never rebuilt is, of course, fiction.

171 Excepting Aikin and Godwin, Longman was the first author to dedicate a work entirely to the cathedral. He discusses at length the 'Greek cross', the 'Favourite', and the 'Warrant' designs, but confusingly calls the second of these alternately Wren's first (caption to the plate reproducing the great model) and second (p.98) design. The pre-Fire design is equally designated as 'First Design' (p.103) etc. Loftie, *op. cit.*, p.x, protests his endeavour to elucidate the sequence of the various designs, but *ibid.*, pp.191 *et seq.*, confines himself to a criticism of Phillimore and a confused discussion of the various illustrations in Longman, without discussing any but the Greek cross, the great model, and the warrant designs. Dimock, *op. cit.*, pp.62–9, gives lengthy quotations from Wren on Gothic, but commences his discussions with the great model of 1673. L. Milman, *op. cit.*, pp.90–103, 107–118, 196–216, discusses at length the building of the cathedral, but without giving any attention to the projects prior to 1673. J. S. Bumpus's inadequate account of the schemes prior to 1675 is compressed into three pages, *op. cit.*, pp.169–72. Weaver, *op. cit.*, p.63, thinks that 'the story of Wren's many designs for the new Cathedral is confusing and need not be followed here in detail'. Ward, *RIBA Mem. Vol.*, pp.216 *et seq.*, leaves out of consideration all schemes between 1666 and 1673. Pite, *ibid.*, pp.51 *et seq.*, commences his account with the 1675 design. G. Webb, *op. cit.*, can find no space, within the severely limited size of that work, to give more than brief indications, largely referring to the documentary evidence of Hooke, Pratt, Evelyn, and Royal Letters Patent. Whitaker-Wilson, *op. cit.*, pp.132–3, mentions no designs between 1668 and 1673. Dutton, *op. cit.*, pp.31 *et seq.*, commences his account with the Greek cross design which, in an ambiguous passage, is confused with the great model. Lindsey, *op. cit.*, pp.93 *et seq.*, gives no coherent account of the evolution at all. The complacent ignorance of H. H. Milman, *op. cit.*, p.402, must be dismissed on the two statements: 'Wren, it is well known, made two designs for St Paul's', and 'which of the two is that mentioned in the Royal Commission is not quite clear'. Equally, the account given by Killanin, *op. cit.*, p.11, must be altogether rejected: Wren was not 'commissioned by Charles II shortly after his restoration and before the Fire, to prepare plans for the reconstruction', nor can events be construed into asserting that he was not until 1673 appealed to to produce an alternative plan.

172 *Parentalia*, p.294: the statement is repeated by Elmes, *Memoirs of the Life and Work of Sir Christopher Wren*, London 1823, p.220.

173 The report is undated, but assigned by the WS editors to prior to 26 Feb. 1666/7. There is no reason to assign it to 1668, as Elmes and Longman have done. L. Milman, *op. cit.*, p.97, is obviously right in dating it to the period immediately after the Fire.

174 *Cf.* Evelyn, *Diary*, 7 Sept. 1666; Pepys, *Diary*, same date. The damage externally can be judged from Hollar's view of the City (reproduced in Besant, *Stuart London*, 1892) which shows the fallen roof of the cathedral, but indicates that the walls of the choir, as well as Jones's south wall of the nave, were still standing; so was the south transept front and the west portico. It is interesting to compare this engraving with Hollar's view of 1658, reproduced in Whitaker-Wilson, *op. cit.*, p.67.

175 The quotations here given are from Wren's report, printed in WS XIII, pp.20–2, from Bodl. Tanner MS.145, No.129, and reprinted by L. Milman, *op. cit.*, pp.100–2, from the *Antiquarian Repertory*, where it appeared in 1775.

176 Royal Warrant, WS XIII, pp.22–3.

177 *Cf.* H. H. Milman, *op. cit.*, pp.386–7, who quotes Dugdale in assessing the cost of this structure at £3506 5s 1½d. This temporary structure was destroyed in the accident of which Sancroft wrote to Wren, 25 April 1668; (*v. infra*, p.28) as appears from Wren's reply, WS XIII, p.47.

178 Day, *op. cit.*, p.37, maintains that Wren 'hoped to be able to retain [Jones's portico] and to incorporate it with his new work' but as the subsequent account will show, there is no evidence for such a supposition. On the contrary, Wren seems to have thought in terms of complete demolition and complete reconstruction right from the first, and certainly at the beginning of 1668; *cf.* his letter to Sancroft, 28 April 1668, WS XIII, p.47. That Wren was not actuated by any sentimental reasons to preserve Jones's work is clearly seen in the preliminary schemes for Greenwich and Whitehall.

179 Sancroft to Wren, 25 April 1668, WS XIII, p.46; L. Milman, *op. cit.*, pp.110–12; H. H. Milman dates the letter 'April or July 2nd, 1668'.

180 *Cf.* Hulsbergh's engravings from the BM Crace Coll., in WS XIV, pl.liii.

181 Wren to Sancroft, 28 April 1668; WS XIII, p.47.

182 Wren to Sancroft, 24 May 1668; *ibid.*, pp.47–8.

183 Sancroft to Wren, 2 July 1668; *ibid.*, p.49. Briggs, *op. cit.*, (1951), p.58, erroneously gives 25 April.

184 Royal Warrant, 25 July 1668; *ibid.*, p.23 *et al.* Longman, *op. cit.*, p.95, interprets the undated Wren report (*supra*, p.27) as a response to the warrant here cited, but this seems highly unlikely. Charles II would not have issued a warrant involving technicalities and constructional details without acting on Wren's advice; similarly, the warrant of 15 Jan. 1667/8, is clearly in response to the report. The 1668 warrant would hardly have mentioned the possibility of a new, permanent structure unless such had been suggested by Wren.

185 Catalogue of ASC, in WS I, pp.5–8; *sub* II, 61.

186 ASC I, 61 (WS IX, pl.33).

187 *Cf.* the illustrations, WS XIII, pp.xii–xv. It is unfortunate that the only drawing pertaining to this model only came to the writer's notice after this work was already in the press, and can therefore not be reproduced. Belonging to Sir William Worsley, it was first illustrated and discussed by Norbert Lynton in *The Burlington Magazine*, February 1955, pp. 40–4. The sheet is divided into three subjects, the first of which illustrates what we assume to be the apse, while the other two show details of the arcading. Though elucidating details of the design (such as the fact that Ionic and Corinthian orders were intended, and also correcting the floor level which Bolton proposed in his reconstruction), the drawings do not add substantially to our knowledge of the project. Stylistically, the remarkable version of the 'motif Palladio' shown in the section provides a striking parallel with Wren's usage at St Olave's (Fig.146) while the cornice broken by the round-headed window is clearly related to the intended north porch of St Stephen's, Walbrook (Fig.29) and foreshadows the transept porticos of the great model (Fig.41). The remarkable relationship between the section and the design of St Stephen's (Figs.30, 31) partly explains the accomplishment of the latter. The arcade elevation, however, is clearly the precursor of the Nevile's Court façade of Trinity College Library, Cambridge (Fig.85), and the section makes it clear that Wren was here tackling a problem similar to that which the spacing of the library floor was to present. It is unfortunate,

however, that the drawings provide no indications on the nature of the domed area or, indeed, the overall design. Our thesis that the model fragment represents the *east* end of the intended cathedral is strengthened, however, by the transverse section: this cannot possibly be interpreted either as the west end of the nave, or the nave termination towards the domed area. The orientation of the whole design has rightly been questioned by Lynton, though he has not proposed any theoretical alternative to the assumptions made by previous authors.

188 Briggs, *op. cit.*, (1951), p.60, quotes the *Parentalia* statement regarding the commission's recommendation that 'a long body with Ailes was thought impertinent, our Religion not using Processions' which passage would partly account for the external colonnades of the model fragment. Confusion arises, however, when *ibid.*, p.62, this author explains the rejection of the great model design by the alleged fact that 'the clergy disliked it . . . and said that it was most unsuitable for processions, which Wren himself considered were not part of Protestant worship'. It is not admissible to construe the successive rejection of Wren's schemes as a difference of opinion between Wren and the cathedral chapter on the proper architectural setting of Anglican worship. The point at issue is not that Wren disapproved, and the clergy approved, of processions. The *Parentalia* account is again of questionable veracity because if the clergy had really thought 'a long body with Ailes . . . impertinent' it could never have sanctioned the warrant design of 1675.

189 The connexions with Chelsea Hospital are stressed by Dean, *The Royal Hospital Chelsea,* London 1950, p.50, and WS XIII, pp.xii–xiv; G. Webb and WS XVIII, p.61, point to the connexion with Greenwich.

190 WS XIII, p.xiv; Webb, *loc. cit.* Summerson, *op. cit.*, p.73, gives 1670–2.

191 Charles II donated a yearly subsidy of £1000; *cf.* the letter of Henry Ball to Sir Joseph Williamson, of 15 Aug. 1673 (Camden Soc., CII, reprinted in WS XIII, p.xviii. J. S. Bumpus, *op. cit.*, p.174, states that 'there is no proof that one penny of it was ever paid' and thus improves on the more charitable suggestion made by Dimock, *op. cit.*, p.137, that 'these subscriptions never found their way into the fund; and forgetful how readily the Merry Monarch's money might have been intercepted *en route*, it has been assumed that he never parted with it'. *Cf.* also Denham's will (Camden Soc., LXXXIII, quoted in Jenkinson, *op. cit.*, p.37): 'And whereas I am surveyor-Generall for the rebuilding of St Paul's Church, London, I doe give and bequeath all my fees (being twenty shillings per diem) gratis towards that noble and pious worke and as a further remembrance of my affection to the same doe give the some of one hundred pounds to the said church of St Paul's to be paid when the said church shall begin to be in some forwardness to be rebuilt.' Sheldon's contribution, we may note, was £2000. Wren himself contributed £50.

192 *Cynthiades* (1642) quoted by Cunningham, *op. cit.*, IV, p.137:
'Meantime imagine that Newcastle coals
Which (as Sir Inigo saith) have perisht Paul's
And by the skill of Marquis would-be Jones,
'Tis found that smoke's scald did corrupt the stones.'

193 1 May 1670.

194 Preliminary Works, Contract Book, printed WS XVI, pp.193 *et seq.*; our italics; *cf.* also Acquittance Book (WS XIII, p.59) *sub* 27 April and 21 June 1670, where the payments are reversed: 'for making a new modell in Wainscott of ye church of St Paul in London. Wm Cleere [*sic*] £150.0.0' and 'In full for making ye Modell of S. Paul's Church, £50.15.0.' This and subsequent entries disprove J. S. Bumpus's contention, *op. cit.*, p.172, that Wren received a salary of £200 'out of which he had to pay for models and drawings'. Not only were models etc. paid for separately, but also did Wren receive additional fees for some of his designs, such as that here discussed, and £1000 for the design of Chelsea.

195 This is the first reference to Wren in his capacity as surveyor-general. The appointment was made on 15 Dec. 1669.

196 Contract Book, WS XVI, p.194; a further entry, Jan. 1669/70 – March

1670 records a payment to Edward Woodroof for further work on the model.

197 *ibid.*, p.195. The payment made was £150 15s 0*d*, for the balance *v. supra*, note 194.

198 *ibid.*, p.196.

199 *ibid.*, p.199.

200 i.e., Convocation House. A table to receive the model had been prepared earlier in the year; *cf.* the payment of £2 made to Wm. Clare, Jan.–March 1672, for a 'Table and Frame on which the New Model is to stand in C. House'. (WS XVI, p.200.)

201 Our interpretation of the evidence is further strengthened by a distinct reference to *three* models in May–Sept. 1674 (WS, XVI, pp.205–6): 'For a strong jointed Hinge for the Old Model with ten rivetts . . . for mending the little model, 5.0 . . . for plastering the inside of the Dome and Lanthorne of the Model . . .' At this stage, when the great model had been constructed, the 'little model' almost certainly refers to the extant fragment; the 'Old Model' would refer to the hypothetical design here suggested, as the reference to 'ten rivetts' cannot be related to the fragment; the last model referred to is, of course, the extant great model. It is remarkable that this evidence, taken from the records published by the WS, actually contradicts the statement made by its editors in the introduction to the Preliminary Works Accounts, WS XVI, p.185, where the June 1672 entry regarding the removal from Whitehall is quoted and suggested that the reference 'must be [to] the First Model, called elsewhere "the Old Model", paid for, in full, £200.15.' and expressly identifying this with the model fragment. It is inexplicable how the scholarly editing of the WS volumes could have failed to see the obvious contradictions between the size of the model and the price paid for it, and the number of men required to carry it.

202 *Parentalia*, pp.281–2.

203 *ibid.*, p.281. Stephen Wren's detailed knowledge of the project may be doubted. The phraseology of this passage ('our Way of Worship', 'Auditories', 'Porticos') suggests a paraphrase of Wren's 1708 memorandum. Note also the inconsistency of 'great Ceremonies' in relation to the passage quoted *supra*, note 188.

204 Longman, *op. cit.*, pp.96, 103, attempts to relate the first part of this passage to the pre-Fire design, but this is inadmissible: not only is there no evidence at all that Wren's instructions at that date specified a dome, particularly as Wren does not seem to have had any instructions at all (*v. supra*, pp.27 *et seq.*); but also can there be no question, in the pre-Fire design of the vestibule to which Stephen Wren explicitly alludes. Wren's often-quoted recommendations for 'cutting off ye inner corners of the Cross, and making a Dome in the Middle, after a good Roman manner' refer to the pre-Fire design and cannot be related to any of the subsequent schemes.

205 *Diary*, 2 Nov. 1672. Hooke says that the model was approved by the King, which statement is confirmed by the Newsletter of 10 Nov. 1672 (R.C. Hist. MSS., XII, reprinted in WS XIII, p.xviii. Summerson's erroneous dating has led him to connect this royal approbation with the first model; *v. supra*, note 190. As the Newsletter mentions this design to be 'rather bigger than the old foundation' it cannot refer to the first model which, in Stephen Wren's words, was 'not large'.

206 *Diary*, 8 Feb. 1672/3.

207 Briggs, *op. cit.*, (1951), p.60, suggests that Pratt 'wanted to rebuild St Paul's himself' though neither Pratt's writings, nor any external evidence, substantiate this view.

208 Here the memorandum is interposed: 'vide with what basement the Church raised. What ornament of the windows to the Portico', evidently with a view to a further examination of the model.

209 The model fragment is also designed with ten windows.

210 *The Architecture of Sir Roger Pratt*, pp.213–14; 12 July 1673.

211 It should be recalled that the first model was made in two sections and joined by a hinge. That the reconstruction of the cathedral was intended

to be undertaken in stages also becomes clear from the terms of the 1675 warrant (WS I, pl.ix) which specifically notes the suitability of the design because it 'could be built in parts'.

212 Mr Godfrey Allen, surveyor of the cathedral, in a personal interview, expressed the opinion that Wren could be thought quite capable of putting forward even so unorthodox a proposal. When considering the orientation of the great model, however, there seems little reason to concur with this view. Summerson, *op. cit.*, pp.73–4, accepts the possibility of the cupola forming the west termination, and suggests that 'this arbitrary reversal, implying a doubt that there could be any one inevitably right relationship of form and function in a cathedral, is characteristic of what we may call Wren's empirical method of design'. This view is, of course, supported by Wren's dictum on orientation in the 1708 memorandum: '4 . . . Nor are we, I think, too nicely to observe East and West, unless it falls out properly . . .' While largely in agreement with Summerson's very perceptive interpretation, we find it difficult to see in this instance a relevant illustration of his thesis, as the evidence, set out here, leads us to think that Wren intended the addition of a western nave to join the domed section.

213 On the basis of this interpretation, the dome would have been supported by piers placed in a regular octagon (?ASC II, 34; WS I, pl.xxiii) so that the connecting arches would be (unlike the present cathedral) of equal span and width, thus making three openings 'all of the same fashion'. It should be noted that, with the exception of the pre-Fire design, Wren adhered to the idea of eight piers, in contrast to St Peter's.

214 Contract Book, WS XVI, p.201; the entry is corroborated by John Tillison's letter to Sancroft, 22 Sept. 1673 (WS XIII, p.51): 'Dr Wren & Mr Woodroof have been the week last past in the Convocation house, drawing the Lines of ye Designe of the Church upon ye Table there, for ye Joyner's Direction for making ye new Modell.' The table built was a very elaborate construction and the entries referring to it are interesting enough to be quoted in full: 'To Wm Clare, Joiner. For a Table & Frame for the Intended New Model of the Church to stand upon. 460 ft. Braces at 5*d* per ft. £9.11.8, 212ft. Railes, 5*d*, £4.8.4. 36 Table Feet at 3*s* each, £5.8.0 & 202 ft. in cover of Table at 2*s* 3*d* per ft. £22.14.6. In all. 42.2.6 – To Wm. Clare, Joiner, contd. Two Tables & 4 Trussels to draw upon, 16*s*. A Box with lock and hinges for Designs . . .' etc. In Oct. 1763–March 1673/4 E[dward] W[oodroof] was paid £45.10.0 for 'Attendance in Works & pursuing the orders and directions of Mr Surveyor concerning the New Model of the Church'. On 21 Feb. 1673/4 Hooke was 'At Paules with Sir Chr Wren' and 'saw Module and walked through it' (*Diary*, p.87), but the setting of the model was to be elaborated even further: between 1 May and 30 Sept. 1674 (WS XVI, p.204), carpenters were paid for 'putting up two diagonal pieces of Timber with braces to them under the Floor of the Convocation House to let down the Circular Floor of the Dome within the Model', and William Clare received 14*s* 6*d* 'For 4 brass pulles for pulling the circular board of the floor of the Dome up and down', thus Wren made possible the inspection of the interior of the model itself. Close on £200 was further expended on details such as carved capitals, pillars, cherubim, festoons, gilding, plastering, etc.

215 WS XVI, p.201.

216 Royal Warrant, quoted in Longman, *op. cit.*, pp.98–9. The superficial contradiction between the date of the warrant and the fact that the commissioners had paid for a table for the model to stand upon several months before need not confuse the issue. The discrepancy further supports our view that King Charles issued his warrants after consultation with Wren; *v. supra*, note 184.

217 It is logical to call this the 'Greek cross' design by reason of its plan. The WS editors reproducing ASC II, 21, 22 (Figs.37, 38), have captioned the drawings as 'Model Design' even though no evidence exists to show that a model of this project was ever made. Blomfield, *Hist. Ren. Arch. Eng.*, I, p.167, note, calls the design both 'Model' and 'Rejected' and dates it

(*ibid.*, p.170) to 1673. Weaver, *op. cit.*, p.63, further confuses the issue by attaching the alternative labels of 'Model' or 'Second, Rejected' design to what is generally known as the great model. Longman, *op. cit.*, p.97, enumerates no designs between the temporary structure and the 1673 model and, *ibid.*, p.98, involves himself in contradictions by calling the great model the second design while captioning the Schnyvoedt perspective view and the Cole engraving of the plan as 'First Design'; confusion is completed by the statement, *ibid.*, pp.104–5, that 'patching went on for two years [i.e. 1668–70] and nearly three years more elapsed before Wren made another design'. Longman's reference to the Greek cross plan, *op. cit.*, p.110, is labelled 'Tentative Design'. Dimock, *op. cit.*, p.57, reproduces the elevation and section (ASC II, 23; WS I, pl.xviii) of the Greek Cross design, which he calls 'Rejected Design', considers to have been the first scheme and dates, *ibid.*, p.66, to 1668.

218 *Cf.* the well-known Loggan engraving in *Oxonia Illustrata*, of which a plate is inserted in ASC I, 108 (WS V, pl.ii).

219 For further parallels, the central bays of the portico should be compared with the east window of St Mary-at-Hill (Fig.7), the east window of St Olave (Fig.146), and the vestry window of the Bow church study (Fig. 17). The apsidal window shown in the transverse section (ASC II, 23; WS I, pl.xviii) is clearly related to the contemporaneous employment of this 'motif Palladio' at St Stephen's (ASC I, 60; WS IX, pl.33).

220 *Parentalia*, quoted in Longman, *op. cit.*, pp.105, 109.

221 The work on this model, and the sums paid for it, can be seen from the entries in the Acquittance Book (WS XIII, p.63) during the period 13 Dec. 1673 to 24 Sept. 1674, in addition to which the Preliminary Works Accounts (*v. supra*) contain further particulars. The entries in the Acquittance Book alone, however, make a total of £505 6*s* 0*d*, which thus supplies additional support for our theory concerning three distinct models: it is not feasible to think that the model fragment, at most 6 ft in length, should have cost £200, when the 18 ft model should have run to £500.

222 Longman, *op. cit.*, p.110: 'The whole design was given up, probably with advantage . . . there is a want of grandeur in the dome as compared with that of the present cathedral, and a poverty in the diminutive dome over the narrow nave behind the portico.'

223 Birch, *op. cit.*, p.16: 'One cannot be too thankful that the design for which Wren had a model made . . . was not carried out, for externally it would have been an architectural failure. The plan was decidedly clever and original, and almost gives the impression that it was designed as a plan only, without any thought as to how the elevation would turn out, and that the talented designer's regrets at its rejection were more on account of the plan than the elevation, which would have been unworthy of his genius.'

224 *Parentalia*. The inscription on the Schnyvoedt engraving (Fig.41) refers to this as Wren's first design ('Orthnography . . . according to the first intention of ye Architect'); *cf.* also the Hulsbergh engraving, SM and StPL II, 107 (WS XIV, pl.ii). The editors of the *RIBA Mem. Vol.* illustrate the latter engraving, repeating the mistake in calling it Wren's first design; *cf.* also Stratton, *op. cit.*, p.9.

225 Pratt was knighted 18 July 1668, possibly as a mark of recognition for his work on the Fire commission. Similarly it would be tempting to connect Wren's knighthood with the great model design. The WS editors (XVIII, p. 193, note) give 12 and 20 Nov. as alternative dates, and (XIII, p.5) refer to Hooke's *Diary* in giving 14 Nov. But neither these dates, nor even the year, has been conclusively proved as correct. The Vestry Minutes of St Swithin (WS XIX, pp.53–6) refer to 'Dr' Wren as late as 10 Aug. 1675. The accounts of St Clement Danes (*v. infra*, note 291) refer to 'Dr' Wren as late as 1680. The Preliminary Works Book of St Paul's, however, refers to 'Sir' C. Wren as early as 1671/2 (WS XVI, p.197). The confusion in Wren literature is comparable. Taylor, *op. cit.*, p.6, refers to Sir Christopher in a context *temp.* 1668; Cunningham, *op. cit.*, IV, p.204, quotes a MS list of knighthoods in the BM which gives

12 Nov. 1673, but omits to supply the reference. Lastly, *cf.* the following, if contradictory passage in L. Milman, *op. cit.*, p.154: 'Wren was knighted in 1672; [note] according to most authorities; but in a letter in the Sloane Collection, British Museum, addressed by the younger Christopher Wren to Mr Ward (author of Lives of Gresham Professors) dated Hampton Court, 24 Jan. 1740, an inquiry of Mr Ward's . . . is answered as follows: "I have no account of the exact time when he was knighted. In the Royal Commission for building St Paul's, dated Nov. 12 1673, he is still Doctor of Laws. A Warrant signed by Lord Arlington signifying his Majesty's pleasure, dated 18 Feb. 1674/5 is directed to Sir Chr. Wren Kt., so there can be little or no mistake to assign the time to the year 1674"'.'

226 This is implied by Longman, *op. cit.*, p.109. *Cf.* also Weaver, *op. cit.*, p.64, and Dimock, *op. cit.*, p.67, and caption to plate, p.66. This author's suggestion, wrongly supported by the passage in *Parentalia*, pp.281–2, that Wren's first considerations on the great model were influenced by financial difficulties would seem a perverse thesis in view of the size and magnificence of the scheme evolved. That the design should fall prior to 1670 (in which year the coal dues were granted) as Dimock implies, *ibid,*. p.67, is a suggestion not to be seriously entertained. Whitaker-Wilson goes so far as to date the great model to 1678, apparently in complete ignorance of the unimpeachable evidence.

227 The drawing ASC II, 60 (WS I, pl.xxviii) indicates the possibility that Wren once envisaged a totally different development whereby the transept connexions of the Greek cross design were to be changed from concave to convex, the transepts and choir to be formed by semi-circles joined to the circular dome area, an addition for a 'vestibule' being provided by a short western arm with a portico clearly based on a triumphal arch motif and possibly flanked by towers. It is unfortunate that no further evidence exists for elucidation.

228 Loftie's description, *op. cit.*, p.193, of the west portico as 'very like that of Inigo Jones' is, of course, completely unwarranted and suggests this author's confusion between the great model and the warrant designs.

229 StPL [Sotheby 1(2)]; a faint pencil sketch by the side of the inked drawing gives a variation in which the stairs curve.

230 The change in the pillar spacing is first adumbrated in StPL II, 168 (WS XIII, pl.iii) upper subject, where, however, the pair is formed by the outer two pillars. This arrangement is reversed in the drawing StPL I, 50 (WS II, pl.xviii) though the shading here seems to indicate that pilasters were intended for the outer two members.

231 StPL I, 50 (WS II, pl.xviii). The WS editors interpret this as a proposal for the west end, but the spacing of the pillars and the significant break in the cornice clearly relate it to the transepts of the great model; indications of the semi-circular recession in the pediment appear already in StPL II, 168, referred to above.

232 An interesting comparison is afforded by the sections of the Greek cross design, ASC II, 23, and the Hulsbergh engraving of the great model, WS XIV, pl.iii: both domes are double structures; the exterior dome of the great model is considerably taller, though the interior curvatures are practically identical. A very interesting point hitherto unnoticed is the fact that Wren envisaged, as early as 1672/3 the structural desirability, and the optical illusion thereby created, of sloping the interior order of the drum.

233 Elmes, *op. cit.*, p.319.

234 The date of the actual rejection is not recorded in any extant evidence. Payments for details of the great model continue up to Sept. 1674 (WS XVI, p.204) when Wren received £83 6*s* 8*d* 'For his direction in the Work and finishing the Model' and £2 was expended on 'Calico . . . for Curtains in the Conv. House to keep the heat of the sun from the Model'.

235 Spence, *Anecdotes*, quoted by Longman, *op. cit.*, pp.114–15.

236 *Parentalia*, p.283.

237 *ibid.*, p.282. Longman, *op. cit.*, pp.105, 114, rightly quotes the passage in connexion with the warrant design, but also relates the same quotation to the pre-Fire design (*ibid.*, p.97). Attention should be drawn to the wholly erroneous account of the evolution of the cathedral given by Middleton in *Encyclopaedia Britannica*, 14th ed., 1932 issue: 'Dean Sancroft was anxious to have [the cathedral] wholly rebuilt and in 1668 asked Wren to prepare a design for a wholly new church. This first design, the model of which is preserved . . . is very inferior to what Wren afterwards devised. In plan it is an immense rotunda surrounded by a wide aisle, and approached by a double portico; the rotunda is covered with a dome taken from that of the Pantheon in Rome; on this a second dome stands, set on a lofty drum, and this second dome is crowned by a tall spire. But the dean and chapter objected to the absence of a structural choir, nave and aisles, and wished to follow the mediaeval cathedral arrangement. Thus, in spite of its having been approved by the king, the design was happily abandoned, much to Wren's disgust; and he prepared another scheme with a similar treatment of a dome crowned by a spire, which in 1675 was ordered to be carried out. Wren apparently did not himself approve of this second design . . .' This account is incorrect in every respect. Sancroft, as dean, was not in a position to commission Wren to do any design, nor was the financial position in 1668 such as to permit contemplating complete reconstruction. What Middleton here calls Wren's 'first design' and assigns to 1668 is a confused medley between the Greek cross design of 1672–3, the great model of 1673, and the warrant design of 1675. The former two did not, of course, possess any steeples, so that the latter could never have presented a 'similar treatment'. Had the two schemes been alike, there is no reason why Wren should have received the rejection of the first with disgust while disapproving of the second. In fact Middleton has invented an imaginary model at a wholly unacceptable date, compounded of the features of the two later major designs. It is surprising that so completely unauthoritative an account should come from a one-time director of the South Kensington Museum, where the great model had been kept for many years before returning to the cathedral trophy room.

238 ASC II, 32 (WS I, pl.xxi).

239 ASC II, 31 (WS I, pl.xxi).

240 Weaver, *op. cit.*, p.69: 'So unworthy is it of Wren's genius that his apologists have been ingenious in explaining it away.' *Cf.* also Longman, *op. cit.*, p.115, Dimock, *op. cit.*, p.69; Birch, *op. cit.*, p.16; J. S. Bumpus, *op. cit.*, p.173; and Loftie, *op. cit.*, p.195.

241 Elmes, *op. cit.*, p.319: 'The side oratories were added by the influence of the Duke of York and his party who wished to have them ready for his intended revival of the Papist service.' Spence, *Anecdotes* (quoted by Longman, *op. cit.*, p.115) adds that the addition 'narrowed the building and broke in very much upon the beauty of the design. Sir Christopher insisted so strongly on the prejudice they would create, that he actually shed tears in speaking of it; but it was all in vain. The Duke absolutely insisted on their being inserted, and he was obliged to comply'. Birch, *op. cit.*, p.17, is almost the only author to discount this legendary tradition.

242 *Cf.* the south elevation, ASC II, 13 (WS I, pl.xii).

243 Weaver, *op. cit.*, p.61.

244 The combination of dome and steeple is not as unique as some critics have represented it to be; the same underlying intention governs Borromini's chapel of St Ivo in Rome (*c*.1640) which Wren would have known, though at a later date, from de Rossi's *Insignium Romae Templorum*, 1684, pls. 40–1. The same idea recurs, in a charming version, in Franze's little church at Hirschberg, (*cf.* Hager, *Die Bauten des deutschen Barock*, Jena 1942, pl.48).

245 Despite the reasons suggested by *Parentalia*, Birch, *op. cit.*, p.17, held that Wren decided on the double-order portico for purely artistic reasons and thinks 'it would be a waste of time to notice further the remarks of critics on such points as the employment of the two orders, the coupled columns, etc. etc; we accept them, and are, on the whole, glad that Wren

employed them, for we know how poor in effect St Peter's looks with its one order, and Wren realized that his building would not long enjoy the advantage of standing in the midst of a wide piazza, but that the streets and houses would encroach upon it on every side; therefore he was wise to do as he did. One has but to look at the Cathedral from one of the bridges . . . to see how immensely it has gained by the adoption of these two orders'.

246 *Cf.* ASC II, 13 (WS I, pl.xii).

247 *Cf.* Blomfield, *Touchstone*, p.189: 'I have never understood how Wren could have seriously put forward this design, except on the assumption that when he first attacked this immense problem he was technically unequal to it and had only a glimmering of its ultimate solution.' It is noteworthy, however, that the universally criticized arch supports of the executed version are clearly inferior to the solution planned in the Greek cross design: *cf.* ASC II, 23 (WS I, pl.xviii) and the modification in the great model, WS XIV, pl.iii.

248 Loftie, *op. cit.*, p.195.

249 Weaver, *op. cit.*, p.69.

250 *loc. cit.* This criticism of Charles II is evidently based on this author's ignorance of the Royal Warrant of 12 Nov. 1673; the rejection of the great model was obviously due to the clergy and commission, not the King.

251 Loftie, *op. cit.*, p.195.

252 Dimock, *op. cit.*, p.60.

253 Loftie, *op. cit.*, *loc. cit.*

254 Stratton, *op. cit.*, p.10.

255 *Cf.* Charles's speech to Parliament, 13 April 1675, in *Letters . . . ed. cit.*, p.261.

256 The *Parentalia* date of 1683 for both churches is accepted by Phillimore, Stratton, L. Milman, Birch, Whitaker-Wilson, and Lindsey; Caröe gives 1680 for All Hallows, which is equally unacceptable, as the building accounts run from 1677–87. A credit of £500 was granted to the parish for the reconstruction of the church on 17 March 1676, so that it would be reasonable to date Wren's design to that year or shortly after. For St Benet's the date 1683 is at least six years too late; the building accounts run from 1677–85. Moreover, Caröe prints an abstract of a MS. concerning the Strong family (*op. cit.*, p.109) which states that Thomas Strong began the building in 1677.

257 Apart from the drawings illustrated on p.42 there remain: 1st scheme: Ruddock Collection No.17 (erroneously described in the Sotheby Catalogue as a duplicate of Ruddock Collection No.14); Ruddock Collection No.15 (plan and section looking west; the section illustrated *infra*, Fig.46); 2nd scheme: ASC I, 94 (WS IX, pl.33, part sections looking south); a plan assignable to either scheme, Ruddock Collection No.14. A survey plan in the Cooper Collection [Sotheby No.15(54)]; and a further plan in the RIBA Collection.

258 The west and north elevations were changed when the vestry at the north-west angle was added; *cf.* the ground plan as given by Clayton, reprinted in WS IX.

259 Mackmurdo, *op. cit.*, p.76, draws attention to the 'wretchedly bad and exceedingly poor' sculpture, adding that 'it is one unfortunate circumstance connected with this beautiful architecture, that the architect had no sculptor. All, therefore, Wren could do was to design position and effect of the carving. For the rest leaving it to take its chance. Here it is sufficient to say that Wren was not responsible for the character of the carving that enriches his architecture'. It is curious to note that, in the case of Gibbon's splendid carvings, some critics have credited Wren at least with partial responsibility, but *v. infra*, pp.142 *et seq.*

260 Niven, *Churches of the City of London destroyed since 1800*, London 1887, p.28, quotes Whittington, *Trans. Lond. Midx. Arch. Soc.*, IV, and Vestry Minutes, 8 April 1675. The *Parentalia* date of 1681, followed by most authorities, is again inadmissible, as the building accounts run from 1677–87; the design must certainly have preceded 1680, as the tower of the church (assigned by Clayton to 1681) was bodily taken

from a totally different design: *v. infra*, p.52. There is no evidence to support Whitaker-Wilson's statement, *op. cit.*, p.173, that, attempts to repair the old fabric having failed, Wren pulled it down in 1679 and rebuilt it. The church must have been finished by 1681, as in that year Bernard Schmidt was paid £210 for his organ (Jenkinson, *op. cit.*, p.122).

261 For another example of such placing of pillars, *cf.* the early Bow steeple design, Fig.76.

262 *Cf.* ASC I, 87 (WS IX, pl.34).

263 Churchwardens' Accounts, 1675–6, in WS XIX, p.41. In spite of this evidence, the church is usually dated later: Lindsey 1678; Stratton, L. Milman, and Whitaker-Wilson 1678–9; *Parentalia* 1679. According to Birch, construction preceded design, as this author, *op. cit.*, p.71, dates the former 1676–9 and *ibid.*, p.8, the latter, 1678. The building accounts cover the years 1676–82.

264 The design should be dated, with Birch, to 1676; but Lindsey gives 1677, L. Milman is followed by Whitaker-Wilson with 1677–83, and Cleveland gives 1683. The ruins of the old church were demolished from 1674–6 (Churchwardens' Accounts, WS XIX, p.21) and a meeting with Wren is recorded in 1676/7 (*loc. cit.*) while the Vestry Minutes record the appointment of a committee, on 27 Jan. 1681/2, 'for finishing the church'. (*ibid.*, p.20.)

265 Two part interior elevations in the RIBA Collection may refer to the first and the revised scheme resp. The first shows a flat ceiling, with rectangular panels for clerestorey lighting; the second shows the vaulted ceiling, with clerestorey windows inserted by 'Welsh vaulting', a method severely criticized by Blomfield, *Short Hist.*, p.120. The two drawings are discussed at length by Summerson, *art. cit.*

266 The east elevation, containing a large round-headed window flanked by two smaller ones, with a circular light in the pediment, clearly recalls St Mary le Bow (Figs.18, 19) and Inigo Jones's portico, re-employed by Wren in the warrant design (Fig.43). An incongruity is introduced by the diversity of the size of the aisle windows. The breadth of the church, imposed by the foundations, results in a somewhat awkward proportion of the east front.

267 *Cf.* ASC IV, 70 (WS IX, pl.32).

268 The building accounts of both churches run from 1677–87. Stratton and L. Milman give 1679–80 for SS. Anne and Agnes; Birch and Blomfield follow *Parentalia* with 1680; Clayton, possibly by a misprint, dates the lantern 1673. The *Parentalia* dating of 1684 for St Martin's is accepted by Birch, Cleveland, and Lindsey; L. Milman, Stratton, and Whitaker-Wilson give 1684–5.

269 Fig.53 was described in the Sotheby sale catalogue as 'probably a preliminary study for St Mary-at-Hill' but as it shows so singular a scheme of rustication, we would prefer to assign it to SS. Anne and Agnes. A similar roofing scheme was employed by Wren at St Augustin, some four years later.

270 Whitaker-Wilson, *op. cit.*, p.232: 'St Bartholomew . . . would not have engrossed our attention any more than St Antholin.' But this author, *ibid.*, p.185, thinks 'St Stephen, Coleman Str. well worth a visit' even though Wren's most ardent admirers have found difficulty in speaking of this church with any degree of enthusiasm.

271 Weaver, *op. cit.*, p.57, states that 'the money was forthcoming' for the monument but the design 'remained on paper, to the benefit of Charles the Second's pocket'. There is, however, no proof for this partisan assertion. It seems altogether remarkable that Parliament, with such unaccustomed generosity, should have voted £70,000 for the state funeral and the monument, the latter of which was to have cost £43,663 (*cf.* Wren's holograph estimate, ASC II, 90; WS V, pp.52–4). It is unfortunate, as appears also elsewhere, that Weaver's interpretations should occasionally be distorted by his anti-Jacobite sentiments.

272 St Antholin must have been designed prior to 1677, for even though the Vestry Minutes (WS XIX, p.6) record a meeting with the 'Parish of St John Baptist to treat about church' as early as 28 April 1671 and

Hooke records details of demolitions on (*Diary*) 22 Dec. 1673 and 14 Jan. 1673/4, the building was not under way until 1678 when, by 26 March, the Parish seemed dissatisfied with the progress of the work and wanted to 'expedite the building'. The steeple was the subject of discussion as late as 1694/5. According to the Strong MS. printed by Caröe, *op. cit.*, pp.109–10, Edward Strong sen. began St Mildred's, Bread Street, in 1681. This accords with the building accounts which run from 1681–7. The church, according to Daniell, was opened for worship on 23 March 1683; according to Seymour, on 20 March. Most authors have accepted the *Parentalia* date of 1683, except Caröe. St Swithin's must have been designed before 1678. The Vestry Minutes (WS XIX, p.54) record negotiations with Dr [*sic*] Wren regarding the demolition on 10 Aug. 1675, but the committee for Rebuilding the Church did not 'treat with Sir Chr Wren about building' until 29 March 1677. Wren was first engaged on St Mary Abchurch in 1672 in connexion with a temporary tabernacle. The Vestry Books (WS XIX, p.30), record, on 10 March 1680/1 that 'the Rt. Hon. Sir Patience Ward, Lord Mayor, desired to know of this Parish what they would require his Lordship to do towards Rebuilding of the Parish Church' and on 21 June 1681 it was decided that 20 guineas were 'to be given as a present to Sr Christopher Wren, or others, for encouraging the forwarding of the building of the Church'. The *Parentalia* date of 1686 must therefore be rejected, as the design must certainly have been made prior to 1680; the building accounts cover 1681–7.

273 Attention should be drawn, however, to the drawings, ASC IV, 110, 111 (WS XII, pl.xxxi); catalogued (*ibid.*, p.20), as 'Plan for a Domed Room. Possibly an idea for Trinity College, Cambridge. On the other hand, the plan might have some relation to the orangery at Kensington Palace. The Section on the same plate may be a square garden pavilion (?). 37 ft. with pendentives and dome; 48 ft. high to crown. It might be another idea for the Library smaller in scale'. These suggestions must be altogether rejected: the section almost certainly relates to St Mildred's, Bread Street with which it agrees very closely in dimensions. Considering the proximity of these two drawings to ASC IV, 113 (Fig.56) and the tendency in architects' offices for sets of plans to remain together, it would be very tempting to regard the plan ASC IV, 111 as a first proposal for the same church; the idea of a garden pavilion seems untenable as there would have been no reason for the different treatment of the four elevations. On the other hand, the intended blank north wall would conform with the conditions of the site of St Mildred's. Our only reason for not describing the plan with certainty as a preliminary idea for that church lies in the fact that the dimensions as marked, 60 ft square, could not have been accommodated within the site (*cf.* Clayton's site plan, reprinted in WS IX) without purchase of additional ground. In fact the irregularity of the site does suggest such a possibility; and we might conjecture that Wren devised the plan pending negotiations for the acquisition of additional ground, which did not, in the end, materialize.

274 *Cf.* Birch, *op. cit.*, p.103, quoting the parish books: 'Dr Wren had staked off 127 feet of ground part of the Stationers gardens which the parish purchased for £25.'

275 Day, *op. cit.*, p.72: 'At Oxford [Wren] consented to carry out Dr Fell's wishes.' Briggs, three decades after Caröe's publication of the documents, still maintains, *op. cit.* (1951), p.112 and *op. cit.* (1953), p.156, that Wren was 'instructed' to design the tower 'in the Gothick manner'. For a discussion of Wren's attitude towards the Gothic, *v. infra*, pp.169–70.

276 Wren to Fell, 26 May 1681; Caröe, *op. cit.*, p.23. Briggs's reference, *op. cit.* (1953), p.249, to Wren's correspondence with Sprat on the subject of Tom Tower is obviously erroneous.

277 Wren to Fell, 3 Dec. 1681; Caröe, *op. cit.*, p.31. For Wren's parallel opinion, thirty years later, *v. infra*, p.60.

278 Walpole to Bentley, Sept. 1753; quoted by Carritt, *A Calendar of British Taste, 1600–1800*, London 1948, p.264.

279 Day, *op. cit.*, p.33, ascribes St Alban's to Jones with certainty, though without giving his evidence. Birch, *op. cit.*, p.3, dates Jones's rebuilding to 1632 but is careful to point to the lack of evidence. The dating, however, is questionable as Monday's *Continuation* of Stow (1633) still records the dangerous state of the building, and parishioners' anxieties.

280 Birch, *op. cit.*, pp.4, 187, and Drummond, *op. cit.*, p.26 (quoted *supra*, note 155), have held Archbishop Laud's influence responsible for Jones's Gothic design by pointing to St Catherine Cree. Stratton's view, *op cit.*, p.5, that 'at Oxford, Gothic traditions, owing to Laud's influence, had lingered longer than anywhere else in England' is in no way supported by this author's mention of the Christ Church staircase, with the erection of which Laud cannot be associated. Whiffen, *Stuart and Georgian Churches*, London 1948, cogently points to that 'school of thought which likes to see William Laud as the first Gothic revivalist' but his statement that the terms 'Laudian Gothic' and 'Laudian Baroque' are 'about equally inexact' does not supply the answer to whether Laud is to be regarded as a belated straggler of the past tradition, or forerunner of a future style. G. Webb, intro. to Cobb, *op. cit.*, p.7, explicitly links Jones's Gothic Lincoln's Inn Chapel with the Canterbury Quad of St John's, Oxford, in spite of the pronounced Italianate character of the arches which, with their busts in the spandrels, even recall Brunelleschi's Florentine Foundling Hospital, while there is nothing Gothic about the two gateways containing Le Sueur's statues of Charles I and Henrietta Maria. Laud's predilection, notwithstanding St Catherine Cree, would seem most pertinently epitomized by the famous porch built to St Mary's, Oxford, and dubiously ascribed to Jones; its iconographical significance formed part of the Parliamentary indictment of Laud; it is significant that he never defended himself by a denial of his responsibility for the porch's erection.

281 *Cf.* Daniell, *op. cit.*, p.233: 'A legacy of £5000 had been left by a Mr Henry Rogers for the rebuilding of a church, and his widow and executrix consented to apply it for the reconstruction of St Mary Aldermary; she stipulated, however, that the new church should be an exact imitation of Keble's church and the architect was thus compelled to follow a system widely different from his ordinary methods.'

282 *Parentalia*, for once accurate, gives June 1681 to Nov. 1682 for the construction of Tom Tower; St Mary Aldermary is assigned to 1682 by the WS editors X, p.13.

283 The striking similarity between the steeple of this design, Ruddock Collection, No.22, and that of St Peter's was overlooked by the compiler of the Sotheby sale catalogue; these are the only two instances, though, in which Wren made use of a triple belfry window.

284 ASC IV, 61, 62, 63, 64 (not in WS; the catalogue of ASC in WS XX, follows the inscription of the drawings); the portico in 61 and 62 is tetrastyle, though the pediment extends over five bays; apart from that it is identical, even in dimensions, to Wren's design.

285 The authorship of the inscriptions is unknown, as neither Sir Edmund Craster, librarian of All Souls, nor Mr Webb, the sub-librarian, can suggest any probabilities. Though the hand may be early nineteenth century, it is not Elmes's who never catalogued ASC IV, it is certainly not the hand of one of the WS editors or contemporary scholars, who have mostly initialled the slips bearing comments inserted in the volumes.

286 An eighteenth-century project concerning this hypothetical parish does not fall within the limits of this study; there is no mention, however, of it in Besant's volumes dealing with the seventeenth and eighteenth centuries.

287 Iconography supports the improbability of regarding the design as a preliminary for St Peter's; analogous to our suggested identity of another steeple (Fig.27) we might have expected the keys, or even the cock, of St Peter to have been drawn on this finished elevation, if that dedication had been intended. The vane shown unfortunately provides no clue.

288 Ruddock Collection No.21. The plan tallies very closely with the six outer bays and the portico of Fig.62, though it indicates a greater protrusion of the tower from the body of the church than one would infer from the depth of shadow drawn on the elevation.

289 This was suggested by the compiler of the Sotheby catalogue; the following reasons, however, speak against it: (a) the width of the project seems too great for the restricted site of St Clement's which presented considerable problems (*v. infra*, pp.52–4); (b) faint pencil markings on the plan indicate that Wren considered squaring off the east end instead of the curved treatment inked in, which alternative would have been impossible on the site of St Clement's; (c) the two extant plans of St Clement's (Fig.64 and ASC II, 57) show that Wren was incorporating the tower foundations of the old church in his design (*cf.* WS IX, index, *sub* pl.12) but no such intention is indicated in the plan Ruddock Collection No.21 as there an entirely new structure was clearly envisaged, Wren placing the stairs in the north-east angle, while the old tower had its stairs in the south-west angle.

290 Daniell, *London Riverside Churches*, London 1897, p.199, quotes Stow's Continuator who gives previous 'repairs and adornments' in 1608, 1616, 1632–1633, the total cost of which was £1586. From parish records (WS X, pp.108–10) it appears that the churchwardens paid for repairs to the church as late as 1669–70.

291 The design must be dated 1680, in which year subscriptions were first received (WS X, p.110); the entries in Hooke's *Diary*, 15 April 1680, 'By water to Sir Ch. Wren, advised him about St. Clements Church' and 23 July 1680, 'At Sir Ch. Wrens . . . to St. Clements church by water' clearly refer to St Clement Danes, and not St Clement's, Eastcheap. Tradesmen's contracts are preserved (BM Add. MS. Chart. 1605, in WS X, pp.108–9) and cover 1680–82, the dates given in *Parentalia*. In the churchwardens' accounts Wren is still referred to as 'Dr'. The church (excepting the tower, added by Gibbs thirty years later) was completed by 1684 (*cf.* Evelyn, *Diary*, 28 Oct.).

292 Wren's ingenious solution was criticized by L. Milman, *op. cit.*, p.243: 'This converging, however, is unpleasantly theatrical and St Clement's has more of grace than of dignity and little of devotional feeling.' The building, however, must have impressed contemporaries considerably, as Whiffen, *op. cit.*, p.27, in discussing Price's St George's at Yarmouth, mentions that 'the committee of trustees appointed to oversee the work stipulated that St Clement Danes should be taken as model. Sir Reginald Blomfield pronounced in his airy way that the building erected "bears not the slightest resemblance" to Wren's church; in point of fact the plan of the interior and the arrangement of the galleries . . . do follow St Clement's very closely'.

293 Mackmurdo's reference, *op. cit.*, p.78, to the 'circular columniated porticos . . . roofed with cupolas, that stood on either side of the main building' is entirely fictitious. That Wren planned an entry opposite the south porch is indicated in the two extant plans. But neither shows any trace of a corresponding porch on the north side which could not possibly have been accommodated on the site.

294 *Cf.* Pepys, *Diary*, 2 Sept. 1662; Brett-James, *op. cit.*, pp.296, 370 *et seq.* St Albans' house in 'Jarman' Street was rated as early as 1667. Grand Duke Cosimo of Tuscany was lodged there during his visit, Easter 1669; *cf. Travels*, pp.163 *et seq.*

295 The church must have been completed in 1684, as it was consecrated that year. *Cf.* Evelyn, *Diary*, 7 Dec. 1684, who 'went to see the new church at St James's, elegantly built . . .' and *ibid.*, 17 April 1684/5 (Good Friday) when he heard Dr Tenison preach at St James's; this was a week before James II's coronation.

296 Hatton's statement, *New View of London* (1708), I, p.298, that the church was 'founded by Authority of Parliament, an Act having passed 1 Jacobi II, constituting this Church parochial' has probably been the origin of the story of the church being dedicated to the King's patron saint; this is perpetuated by Birch, *op. cit.*, p.94; L. Milman, *op. cit.*, p.243; and Whitaker-Wilson, *op. cit.*, p.189, though these authors are aware that the church was consecrated before James's accession.

297 *Cf.* the reference to St James's in Wren's 1708 memorandum.

298 The records of this church are somewhat contradictory; the churchwarden's accounts (WS XIX, pp.5–6) record, in 1684/5, that the churchwardens were 'waiting on Sir Chr. Wren in order to the building of the church, several times', and contain a memorandum concerning 'the new erected Parish Church . . . finished in 1693, being near 7 years in hand'. 1686 would seem the latest date to which to assign Wren's plans, and there is no reason to accept the *Parentalia* date of 1692, which has been followed by Stratton, L. Milman, Cleveland, Whitaker-Wilson, and Lindsey.

299 The church was not destroyed in the Great Fire; *cf.* Pepys, *Diary*, 24 Jan. 1667/8, 9 May 1669; Evelyn, *Diary*, 21 Feb. 1679/80 records his son's marriage to Mrs Martha Spencer at St Andrew's. Rebuilding was clearly contemplated in 1683/4 when a report was drawn up on 26 March (WS X, p.95) that the 'Rev. Eden [*sic*] Stillingfleet Rector, John Philpott & Thomas Harris Churchwardens & others were appointed to treat with workmen'. The first mason's contract is dated 7 Aug. 1684; Other tradesmen's accounts extend to Jan. 1692.

300 *Cf.* WS IX, pl.31, reproducing Gribelin's engraving from a print in the Pepysian Library. The domes shown in this engraving, similar to those reproduced in Fig.69, should be compared with the drawing ASC IV, pp.114–15 (WS XIII, pl.xxvi), a design for the library and triforium of St Paul's, which display the same type of dome, thus furnishing the last example of this chronologically related group.

301 *Cf.* the biographical details of Gribelin's career in WS XIV, p.15. The WS editors' suggestion that the engraver was not noticed before 1700–2 is invalidated by the inclusion of his name in a list of 'Gravers at that Time' [e.g. 1697] drawn up by Vertue; being listed second, we may surmise that he had even then attained to some renown. This is further corroborated by his (signed) engraving of Greenwich, 1699 (WS VIII, pl.xxiv); that he should not have been employed at St Paul's before 1702 is solely due to the fact that no engravings of the cathedral were made before that date, *v. infra*, pp.111 *et seq.* Wren's choice of Gribelin, in preference to well-known engravers such as Emmet, to produce the autograph set of engravings in 1702 may indicate that the artist was then by no means as obscure as is alleged.

302 *Cf.* SM II, 7, 24 (WS VI, pl.xxi and VIII, pl.xix). The connexion between the church and Greenwich is further indicated by (a) the four subsidiary domes shown in the Gribelin engraving of 1699 (WS VIII, pl.xxiv) and the drawing ASC V, 34 (*ibid.*, pl.xxv); (b) by the second drawing from the Westminster P.L. Pennant (WS XVIII, pl.viii) which, though ascribed to the church by the WS editors, is clearly related to the domed chapel, and hall of Greenwich.

303 *Parentalia* dates six churches subsequent to 1688: St Michael's, Crooked Lane, 1688; St Edmund's, 1690; St Andrew, Wardrobe, 1692; St Michael Royal, 1694; St Mary Somerset, 1695; St Vedast, 1697; but *v. supra, infra, passim*, for datings derived from documentary evidence.

304 The *Parentalia* date of 1694, accepted by Chancellor, Birch, Blomfield, Stratton, L. Milman, Cleveland, Whitaker-Wilson, and Lindsey represents the termination of the building accounts, which begin in 1686.

305 *Parentalia* is again followed by most authorities with 1695. This is altogether unacceptable as the building accounts close with 1694, having commenced with 1686.

306 Birch, *op. cit.*, p.130, suggests that 'it may be that at this period Wren's extensive works at Hampton Court tempted him to repeat himself in these churches', but this is not even tenable on the basis of this author's inaccurate datings. Work at Hampton Court did not begin until 1689; but St Margaret Pattens must be dated 1682, or very soon after, as on 11 May of that year the churchwardens were 'waiting on Sir Chr. Wren with an Order from my Lord Mayor concerning the building of the Church'. The building accounts begin with 1684, thus giving no reason

to accept the date of 1690 put forward by Stratton, L. Milman, Whitaker-Wilson, and Lindsey; or accept the contemporaneity with Hampton Court suggested by Birch.

307 *Cf.* the preliminary study, Ruddock Collection No. 27, and the drawing from the King's Library, BM, in WS X, pl.3.

308 *Cf.* the drawings by (?) Dickinson and (?) Wren, dated May and July 1716, from the King's Library, BM, in WS X, pl.9.

309 *v. supra*, note 131.

310 Stratton's cryptic remark, *op. cit.*, p.19, that 'from [Wren's] designs and models, the Western Towers were, for the most part, brought to their present state, but he was not altogether responsible for them' is unacceptable. Wren's proposals for Westminster included a central tower and spire (*cf.* WS XI, pl.v) but it is now established that the west towers are Hawksmoor's.

311 Stratton, *ibid.*, p.41.

312 Lindsey, *op. cit.*, p.115.

313 Blomfield, *Hist. Ren. Arch. Eng.*, I, p.164.

314 Memorandum, 1713; *Parentalia*, pp.296 *et seq.*

315 The similarity of draughtsmanship displayed in the three drawings printed, p.61, may perhaps be connected with the fact that all three steeples were built by Edward Strong jun.; *cf.* Caröe, *op. cit.*, p.110.

316 *Cf.* Clayton's careful analysis of the constructional details of the spires of Bow, St Bride's, St Vedast, St Stephen's, Walbrook, St Michael Royal, and St James's, Garlick Hill, in a paper read to the RIBA, 5 and 26 April 1852, reprinted in WS IX, pp.27–8, and quoted, without acknowledgement, by T. F. Bumpus, *op. cit.*, pp.291, 292, 350.

317 Summerson, *art. cit.*, p.128. This author points to the very interesting instance provided by the 'trefoil' motif in the pediment idea proposed, but not built, at St Anne's, and later incorporated in the tower of St Benet's, Gracechurch Street.

318 The idea of towers in the form of successively diminishing stages is clearly expressed in a crude, and evidently very early sheet in the Cooper Collection (No.59) inscribed 'scitches of Towers', the main drawing of which shows a very tall, thin tower, in which solid sections of varying proportions alternate with arcaded sections the arches of which increase from one to nine. In a most rudimentary fashion, this is the progenitor of the steeple of Christ Church, in which the same augmentation occurs in the inter-columnar spaces of the three main stages. The similarity is rendered even more striking by the fact that the solid stages of Christ church are not equal, but change in proportion, getting taller with the height of the steeple.

319 Ruddock Collection No.20. The drawing unfortunately offers no conclusive evidence substantiating the suggested relationship to Bow Church. It has, *verso*, an ink plan which Summerson has related to that of the tower of St Anne's, in which case our dating for that church (*v. supra*, pp.18–19, note 116) may offer some corroboration for our theory, for Bow steeple was finished by 1680 as far as the mason's work was concerned, and St Bride's steeple cannot be dated before 1700, though the bell stage of the tower may have been completed by 1682.

320 Evelyn, *Diary*, 25 April 1675.

321 *Cf.* the inaugural lecture of Barrow at Gresham College, 1662 (printed in *Works*, 1895, IX, and quoted by Caröe, *op. cit.*, pp.115–16) but *v. infra*, note 802.

322 Barrow was a close friend of Wilkins, Seth Ward, and John Pearson; Pearson succeeded Wilkins both as Master of Trinity and Bishop of Chester; Barrow succeeded Pearson in the mastership by King's Patent dated 13 Feb. 1672, though he had been Lucasian Professor of Mathematics at Cambridge since 1664. There is no reason to assume his special interest in the college before his appointment to the mastership, though Phillimore, *op. cit.*, p.146, Loftie, *op. cit.*, pp.155–6, and Stratton, *op. cit.*, p.5, date the origin of the design to 1665. Adshead, *RIBA Mem. Vol.*, p.163, equally questionably, dates it to *c.*1669.

323 ASC I, 39, 40, 42, 43, 44 (WS V, pls.xvi, xvii, xix, xx, xxi).

324 *Cf.* L. Milman, *op. cit.*, pp.145–7:, the meanness of the plain ashlar strips which frame the windows' and 'nor can the solid upper half of the tall doorways . . . be esteemed a happy contrivance; the disproportion between the architrave of the doorways and the top mouldings of the low windows is, moreover, very unpleasing', and Richardson, *RIBA Mem. Vol.*, p.157, who thinks that in the river front 'the architect has risen to inspired heights'. *Cp.* also Weaver, *op. cit.*, p.109, and Summerson, *Heavenly Mansions*, p.85.

325 1674; *cf.* WS XVII, pls.lxv–lxvi.

326 *Cf.* Evelyn's translation of Naudé, *Instructions concerning erecting of a Library*, 1661, where it is specified that 'it will always be fit to place it in the middle stages to avoid the dampness of the ground which engenders mouldiness'. Although Evelyn thought the book 'miserably false printed' (*Diary*, 16 Nov. 1661) the Royal Society was pleased at its publication (*ibid.*, 3 Dec.).

327 *Cf.* for example the drawing for Christ Church, RIBA Collection; and Wren's letter to Barrow, WS V, p.32.

328 Briggs, *op. cit.*, (1951), p.111.

329 Pro Wren: Stratton, *op. cit.*, p.23, dated 1683; WS editors date the design 1682, and print the building accounts, 1693–6; *cf.* also WS VIII, index to plates *sub* xiv: The remodelling project for Windsor shows '13 bays of which three form a centre. Ten Statues of Kings and Queens in the arcades of the wings of the ground storey, which is rusticated. In view of the composition of this centre feature, the authorship of the Library at Queen's College, Oxford, which has been claimed to Hawksmoor, must be regarded as no longer in doubt'. This evidence does not seem conclusive to us, particularly as the very same feature occurs also in a design for Hampton Court (Fig.91) though the possibility remains that Hawksmoor may have copied it. Pro Hawksmoor: Day, *op. cit.*, p.157; Dutton, *op. cit.*, p.113, writing some twenty years after the publication of WS VIII, confidently gives the building to Hawksmoor and dates it 1695, stating, *ibid.*, p.123, that 'the invitation to Hawksmoor to design a new library . . . was probably a tentative trial of his competence to undertake the whole scheme' of rebuilding the college. The 'invitation' is stated to have been made in 1692, though unfortunately this author does not give his sources, and we are told that 'under the critical eyes of the great provost, Dr Lancaster, and of Wren, Hawksmoor produced a building of great beauty'. This assertion should not be readily accepted. Firstly, it should be noted that Dr Lancaster was not provost of the college at this time, but only succeeded on Halton's death in 1704. Secondly, if the date and the ascription to Hawksmoor are accepted, the implication would be that Hawksmoor's design of statue-filled niches provided the prototype for Wren's Windsor design of 1698, which is hardly probable. S. Sitwell, *op. cit.*, p.99, seems nearest the truth in crediting Wren with the design, and Hawksmoor with the execution. The statement in Thieme-Becker, *Allgemeines Künstler-lexicon*, ed. cit., XXXVI, p.275, referring to 'vom Louvre beeinflusste Entwürfe von Wrens Hand, undatiert' refers to no drawings known to us.

330 Pepys, *Diary*, 30 Sept. and 21 Oct. 1661.

331 Evelyn, *Diary*, 8 March 1664/5.

332 *ibid.*, 24 Sept. 1667 and 19 May 1669.

333 *Cf.* Cosimo of Tuscany, *Travels*, pp.186 *et seq.*, where he recounts in some detail a meeting of the Society; for the Grand Duke's visit, *cf.* also Evelyn, *Diary*, 19 May 1669. Wren apparently was not on the council at that time. It is also unfortunate that Cosimo did not meet Wren when at Oxford, where he went to hear the 'lecturer in geometry, John Wallis, who has the reputation of being the greatest arithmetician in Europe; the lecturer in Anatomy [Dr] Paris; and the lecturer in experimental philosophy, Thomas Willis, the most distinguished of all the learned men in the university'. (*Travels*, p.260.) The description of the Sheldonian Theatre (*ibid.*, p.266) as 'being painted almost all over in fresco' must be regarded as fanciful.

334 Pepys, *Diary*, 17 Jan. 1667/8. The evidence for the scheme is contained in a letter from Wren, at Oxford, 7 June 1668, to the Royal Society; printed by L. Milman, *op. cit.*, p.105; *cf.* also *infra*, note 551.

335 Evelyn, *Diary*, 14 Sept. 1681.

336 The legend of Charles's gift of the grounds to Nell Gwynn, and the actress's return of the present, recounted most recently by Briggs, *op. cit.* (1951), p.102, seems amply discounted by the fact that Charles actually bought, and eventually paid for, the property from the Royal Society, to whom he had given it in 1669; *cf.* Pepys, *Diary*, 18 Nov. 1667.

337 Evelyn, *Diary*, 30 Dec. 1681.

338 *ibid.*, 27 Jan. 1681/2; Evelyn does not mention the extent of Fox's munificence.

339 *ibid.*, 25 May 1682.

340 *ibid.*, 4 Aug. 1682.

341 *Cf.* Dean, *op. cit.*, p.122.

342 The drawing, Fig.87, should be compared with the drawings from the BM King's Library, printed in WS VII, pl.v; it is impossible to assign these to Wren, and the ludicrous dome suggests inferior draughtsmanship. Nevertheless, we may suppose the general character of the elevation to have been approximately resembling Wren's intentions, at least in the revision of the floor scheme.

343 *Diary*, 19 Sept. 1683; according to Bray (note to 16 Sept. 1685), Charles laid the foundation stone on 23 March 1683.

344 WS VII, p.231.

345 The divergences are as follows: the central dome in Milner (Fig.138) is circular, in Godson hexagonal or probably octagonal; the windows of the drum are round-headed in Milner, rectangular in Godson; the central dome has a lantern in Milner, a statue in Godson; the domed turrets over the chapels are square in Milner, hexagonal or octagonal in Godson; the cupolas of the chapels are crowned by a ball in Milner, by miniature spires in Godson; Milner shows three distinct storeys to the chapels, and the base of the pediment slightly below the balustrade of the wings, Godson shows only two storeys to the chapel and draws the base of the pediment in line with the top floor windows of the wings; the number of chimney stacks to each wing differs between eighteen in Milner and seven in Godson; Godson shows basement windows in the south wing and two, resp. three in the east returns, while Milner only shows five in each of the east returns, none in the wings; the proportions vary considerably between the two engravings, the giant order portico shown in Milner being relatively wider, and the pediment pitched at a more acute angle than those shown by Godson; etc.

346 Walpole, quoted by Cunningham, *op. cit.*, IV, p.226.

347 *Cf.* the engraved views of the east front printed in WS VII, pl.iii; that by Peake shows that the large forecourt and outbuildings were never built, and indicates a certain amount of spoliation, such as the missing dome and partial demolition of the centre portico; the engraving by S. and H. Buck of 1733 shows the building in a ruinous condition, nothing but the pillars left standing of the central portico, and the domed entrances of the chapels completely demolished. Luttrell, *Diary of Events*, 10 March 1694, records William III's visit to Winchester, whence he procured quantities of timber etc. for his own buildings at Hampton Court and Greenwich; *cf.* WS IV, p.23, note.

348 Evelyn, *Diary*, 16 Sept. 1685.

349 Law, *History of Hampton Court*, III (1891), p.2.

350 In parenthesis, the question of garden design should be briefly discussed. It is by no means certain to what extent the garden layouts drawn in Wren designs, such as those for Hampton Court, can be associated with Wren's own hand. Dean, *op. cit.*, p.83, ascribed both the Chelsea and Hampton Court gardens to Wren, though pointing to the undoubted influence of Le Nôtre. The evidence for Le Nôtre's supposed designs for Greenwich is discussed elsewhere. For the gardens of Hampton Court, Dutton, *op. cit.*, p.62, makes the unsubstantiated statement that 'it is far

more probable that the ingenious and incredibly versatile Monsieur Marot, who was conveniently on the spot, furnished the design'. There are considerable difficulties preventing us from accepting this suggestion: firstly, the character of the Hampton Court gardens as shown in the drawings is altogether different from Marot's work, and it is only necessary to glance through his engraved books to realize that this designer furnished neither the inspiration nor the design. The evidence points far more cogently to Le Nôtre himself, whose designs were of an entirely different character from Marot's (*cf.* the author's *op. cit.*, pp.37, 48, 50, 57, 88, 127), and whose influence seems particularly noticeable in the Windsor designs. The documentary evidence confirms that the inference of Marot's influence is erroneous: the pipe rolls containing the payments for the Hampton Court gardens show £12,750 paid to George London (WS IV, p.29) and while Dutch gardeners only appear in subordinate positions (*cf.* the references to William Wahup, Henrick Quellinburgh, Samuell van Stadan, Caspar Comperle, and Tille Bobart, *ibid.*, p.35 and *passim*), the name of Marot does not appear at all. Evelyn specifically mentions London as Wren's gardener (*Diary*, 9 June 1698). *Cf.* however, Switzer's statement, *Ichnographia Rustica*, I, p.75, that in William III's gardens 'the only fault was being stuffed too thick with box, a fashion brought out of Holland by the Dutch gardeners'.

351 An excessively large triangular pediment of similar pitch appears on the entry of the Trinity Almshouses, Mile End Road, which, according to Papworth, date from 1695 and are sometimes attributed to Wren; *cf.* Godfrey, *History of Architecture in London*, London 1911, pl.168. The prototype for this practice may be seen in Wren's Custom House (1668).

352 A similar scheme was devised by Wren some years previously, *c.*1682, for Christ's Hospital; *cf.* WS XI, pl.xliv, showing the large segmental pediment over the centre and the triangular pediments over the narrow sections; the idea, in reverse, is also apparent in ASC II, 100 (WS V, pl.xxxi) representing stables, probably for Winchester, designed for Charles II. It is not improbable that Wren was here modifying Hooke's treatment of Bedlam Hospital, which was completed by 1676; *cf.* the engraving, *Diary*, opp. p.130.

353 It is difficult to determine holograph drawings with certainty; in consequence we would hesitate to draw any far-reaching conclusions from such inferences. The drawing in question would hardly be by Wren's hand, particularly as the numerals differ from what we know as Wren's handwriting. Whoever the draughtsmen, he would not have been responsible for the nature of the design.

354 *Cf.* the 1st Pipe Roll for the building, dated 1 April 1689 to 31 March 1691, in WS IV, pp.20–3; the 1st Pipe Roll for the gardens, dated 1 May 1689 to 25 March 1696, *ibid.*, pp.29–36.

355 *Complete Body of Architecture* (1756).

356 Dallaway's edition of the *Anecdotes*, quoted by Law, *op. cit.*, III, pp.43–4.

357 *ibid.*, p.44.

358 *ibid.*, p.5.

359 L. Milman, *op. cit.*, p.263; *cf.* the similar opinion in Weaver, *op. cit.*, p.100: 'Hampton Court, for all its size, is a gentleman's house rather than a palace.'

360 *Cf.* however, Loftie, *op. cit.*, p.171, stating that if Wren's entire scheme had been carried out, William III would have had 'a palace superior to any other in Europe'. Equally Blomfield, *Touchstone*, p.188: 'Jules Hardouin Mansart's vast palace is architecturally inferior to Hampton Court.'

361 For Denham at Greenwich, *v. infra*, pp.86–7. May seems to have been in charge of Windsor until his death in 1684. Wren's work for Windsor consisted in some unexecuted projects for turning parts of the old castle into a classical disguise, and a garden layout; *cf.* ASC V, 15, 16, 17, 18, 19, 20 in WS (WS VIII, pls.xi–xvi).

362 The drawing ASC II, 73 (WS VII, pl.x) bears Charles's cypher of linked C's comparable to those at the Sheldonian Theatre (and recurs in the

design for stables, possibly at Winchester, ASC II, 100); the WS editors have tentatively dated the design to 1669.

363 *Diary*, 24 July 1671.

364 *The Architecture* . . ., pp.194–5, gives a brief specification for 'the house of the prince'.

365 Evelyn, *Diary*, 18 Oct. 1685: 'The King was now building all that range from east to west by the court and garden to the street, and making a new chapel for the queen, whose lodgings were to be in this new building, as also a new Council-chamber and offices next the south end of the Banqueting-house.' *Cf.* ASC I, 85 (WS VII, pl.xv), though the WS editors suggest the possibility that these were designed not for Mary of Modena, but for Mary II. Evelyn, *ibid.*, 24 Jan. 1686/7, however, comments on the 'Queen's new apartment at Whitehall'.

366 *Cf.* ASC IV, 59 (WS VII, pl.xvi).

367 *Cf.* ASC II, vii and II, 69 (WS VII, pl.xiv) for plan and altar-piece of the chapel.

368 *Cf.* WS XI, pl.xxix. The statues of the altar now appear to be in the garden of Westminster School. The identification of the figures is not clear; Evelyn's description has been rejected both by C. F. Bell and Professors Saxl and Wittkower of the Warburg Institute, the former describing them as SS. Peter and Paul, and two allegorical figures, the latter two authorities as SS. Peter and Paul, and Fides and Spes.

369 *Diary*, 29 Dec. 1686.

370 *ibid.*, 10 April 1691.

371 *ibid.*, 5 Jan. 1697/8. The fire actually took place on 2 Jan.

372 William III to Heinsius; Grimbolt's ed. of the *Letters*, I, p.144, quoted by Law, *op. cit.*, III, p.62.

373 Luttrell, *Diary*, 18 June 1689, gives the price paid as 18,000 guineas; *cf.* also Evelyn, *Diary*, 25 Feb. 1689/90 and 23 April 1696: 'I went to see the King's house at Kensington. It is very noble, though not great. The gallery furnished with the best pictures [from] all the houses . . . and a pretty private library. The gardens about it very delicious.'

374 Macaulay, *History*, ch.xxiii, quoted by Law, *op. cit.*, III, p.63.

375 Luttrell, *Diary*, 20 Jan. 1697/8.

376 Fig.98 [Sotheby, 16(1)] now ASC II, i, is unquestionably lot 45, 'A long ditto [large high-finished drawing] of an intended New Palace at Westminster' which fetched £2 4s 0d at the auction sale 4 April 1749 when Wren's drawings were dispersed. For a discussion of the provenance of the collections as now existing, *v. infra*, p.229. The plan printed together with the elevation as Fig.97 is ASC V, 1 (WS VIII, pl.i) which volume of ASC was discovered in 1930 by the WS editors.

377 *Cf.* ASC V, 4, 5, 6 (WS VIII, pl.iv) which show the river and street fronts with variants. The principal differences are the retention of Jones's pediments, the domes are octagonal instead of hexagonal, the statues are replaced by ornamental cartouches, and there is a much greater profusion of ornament.

378 *Cf.* ASC I, 55 (WS V, pl.xiv); the principal differences are only the divergence in the number of clerestorey lights and the elimination of the corner turrets designed for the Cambridge project.

379 *Cf.* the drawings, Bodleian Library, Gough Maps 23, fol.42 *verso* (printed in *Architectural Drawings in the Bodleian Library*, Oxford 1952, pl.11) and the part elevation of the same building, dated 24 Jan. 1718/9 in WS XI, pl.xxi. These should suffice to dispel the WS editors' somewhat derogatory notion of Dickinson as 'the Gothic man in the Office' (X, p.127). Two lines of interpretation are possible in view of the chronological distance between the Whitehall and Westminster Dormitory designs: (a) that the communication gallery at Whitehall was designed by Wren and, not being carried out, was developed by Dickinson years later when Wren's own designs for the dormitory (which were essentially different: *cf.* WS XI, pl.xv, dated 15, 17 March 1710/11, and ASC III, 28, WS XI, pl.xviii, examined 14 Jan. 1718/19) had apparently been rejected; this would be analogous to Hawksmoor's using Wren's discarded and unexecuted ideas in the cryptic 'St Edmund's, Bloomsbury'

discussed *supra*, pp.51–4.(b) It is equally possible that the Whitehall design was Dickinson's, though, of course, influenced by the rejected Hampton Court design and, failing of execution, its author revived it more than twenty years later to be utilized for the other project; analogous to Wren's incorporating features from previous unexecuted designs in later structures. The similarities between the Whitehall and Westminster designs are very striking: the coupled Doric pilasters are identical, though the centre of the dormitory possesses three storeys; it is also noteworthy that in both designs the plinths are carried up to the springing of the centre arches: similar characteristics are also found in the street front ASC V, 5 (WS VIII, pl.iv) both in the central portico, where the Doric pillars are doubled, and in the two lateral wings, where they stand singly. If the College of Physicians could be assigned to Wren with any degree of certainty, it would provide the ultimate prototype for the coupled pillars on tall, heavy plinths; *cf.* Soane, *Lectures on Architecture*, ed. Bolton, 1929, pl.86.

380 Unlike in the case of the gallery, the House of Lords design provides no clue to any architect who could be reasonably connected with the scheme. Hawksmoor might be suggested, particularly on account of the 'motif Palladio' windows which he used so successfully in the Codrington Library, All Souls; on the other hand, Hawksmoor's draughtsmanship was far more accomplished than is suggested by the hand which drew the House of Lords. (*Cf.* Bodl. Libr. Top. Oxon., a 37 fol. 134 in *Arch. Drawings*, pl.16.)

381 Luttrell, *Diary*, 5 March 1697/8.

382 A pencil study for these domed gateways is in the Hampton Court Vol. of SM (WS VI, pl.li); its presence there has probably been responsible for the WS editors' failure to identify it.

383 Hawksmoor, *Remarks* . . . (1728), WS VI, p.17.

384 Cunningham, *op. cit.*, IV, p.204, counts Charles II's palace 'among the earliest finished works of Wren' but more recent scholarship has discredited the attribution. Loftie, *op. cit.*, p.152, thinks that 'when Charles decided to complete the building of the palace at Greenwich, it is probable that Evelyn recommended Wren to the King', but this assumption is doubly erroneous, as the *Diary* shows; Charles neither intended to complete his father's building, nor is there any evidence that Evelyn recommended Wren; *v. infra*, note 386.

385 *Diary*, 19 Oct. 1661.

386 *ibid.*, 24 Jan. 1661/2: 'His Majesty entertained me with his intention of building his Palace at Greenwich, and quite demolishing the old one; on which I declared my thoughts.'

387 Le Nôtre's connexion with the design for the park has been more confidently asserted than the evidence would seem to warrant. L'Estrange, *The Palace and the Hospital; or Chronicles of Greenwich*, II, London 1886, p.63, dates the supposed Le Nôtre designs to the reign of Charles I, when 'the park was re-formed. It had been walled in by James I, and was now laid out by Sir William Boreman in accordance with the designs of Le Nôtre, who planned Louis XIV's ornamental gardens at Versailles.' Hawksmoor in his *Remarks* of 1728 also speaks of Le Nôtre as the designer of the park, and this tradition has been perpetuated by subsequent writers. None of these, however, cites the only direct reference to Le Nôtre's employment, which is found in *Letters* . . . etc. *of Charles II ed. cit.*, p.167, in a letter to his sister, the duchesse d'Orléans, 17 Oct. 1664, P.S.: 'Pray let Le Nôtre go on with the model and only tell him this addition, that I can bring water to the top of the hill, so that he may add much to the beauty of the descent by a cascade of water.' It is improbable that this should refer to any location but Greenwich.

388 *A Parallel* . . . etc. 1664, dedication to Charles II. The reference to the 'worthy surveyor' is, of course, to Denham. For the various editions of the work, *v. infra*, note 606.

389 *Cf.* L'Estrange, *op. cit.*, II, p.68: 'In April, 1667, Sir John Denham reports that the charge of building Greenwich Palace from Feb. 1664 to Feb. 1667 was £26.433, whereof £17.606 has been paid, and he requests

£10.000 for this year.' As this author does not state his sources, and his assertions are frequently at variance with the facts, this statement should not be accepted without reserve; the citation of actual figures, however, lends some degree of veracity to it.

390 Pepys, *Diary*, 29 Jan. 1665/6: 'Mr Evelyn ... entertained me with discourse of an Infirmary, which he hath projected for the sick and wounded seamen ...'

391 *ibid.*, 8 Feb. 1665/6.

392 Evelyn, *Diary*, 8 Feb. 1665/6.

393 *ibid.*, 20 Feb., 1665/6.

394 *ibid.*, 13 March 1665/6.

395 Pepys, *Diary*, 16 March 1668/9: '... the King's house, which goes on slow, but is very pretty.' Braybrooke, Pepys's editor, mentions in a note that the wing then completed had cost £36,000 and had been built by Webb, making no mention of Denham. Loftie's guess, *op. cit.*, p.152, that Webb 'seems to have died before Denham' is, of course, erroneous, as Webb only died in 1672.

396 That Wren was not called in at Greenwich by Charles II cannot be satisfactorily explained; particularly in view of the connexions between Wren and Evelyn, Evelyn and Pepys, and the frequent occasions when Pepys was in contact with Mathew Wren, Clarendon's secretary. In consideration of Denham's virtual supersession by Wren in many of the King's Works, as well as the offices created subsequent to the Fire, the King's ignoring the architect in the case of Greenwich is surprising, unless he wished to leave Denham the semblance of the authority of his appointment. L'Estrange, *op. cit.*, II, pp.64, 68, makes mention of *Sir Hugh May* in connexion with the works at Greenwich, but we have found no confirmation of either knighthood or employment. Stratton, *op. cit.*, p.25, assigns the 'alterations for Charles II' to Wren and to 1663, neither of which can be supported by evidence. Webb was acting as Denham's deputy as late as 1668; *cf.* Brett-James, *op. cit.*, p.384; May acted as paymaster at St Paul's until 1669; *cf.* WS XVI, p.192. Jackson's statement, *op. cit.*, p.283, that Wren built the river front in 1678 must be regarded as fictitious.

397 22 June 1675; Milman, *op. cit.*, p.158; Caröe, *op. cit.*, p.58.

398 *Cf.* the engraving reproduced by Caröe, *op. cit.*, pl.xxi; and *v. supra* Figs.14, 18, 20.

399 Halley's enterprise was backed by Charles II (*cf. Letters ... ed. cit.*, p.286), possibly on the instigation of Sir Jonas Moore. Moore was also instrumental in the building of the observatory, and was the benefactor to whose generosity Wren's design and building of the Mathematical School at Christ's Hospital and the school at Appleby were due. *Cf.* also Charles's letter to the East India Co., the Muscovy Co., the East Land Co., the Royal African Co., and the Levant Co. (*ibid.*, p.285), with reference to his patronage of Christ's Hospital. In view of the many interests common to Wren and Moore, it is unfortunate that practically nothing is known of their personal relations.

400 *Diary*, 30 Nov. 1693.

401 *ibid.*, 17 Feb. 1694/5.

402 *ibid.*, 5 May 1695.

403 Hawksmoor, *Remarks ...*, WS VI, p.19. Stephen Wren's indebtedness to Hawksmoor, referred to *supra*, note 54, is further indicated by a comparison with the relevant passage in *Parentalia*: '... and the Surveyor [being] nominated a Director, and chief Architect of this great Undertaking, he Chearfully engag'd in the Work, gratis.'

404 Phillimore, *op. cit.*, p.269; Loftie, *op. cit.*, p.168; L.Milman, *op. cit.*, p.274; Blomfield, *op. cit.*, p.134; and Richardson, *RIBA Mem. Vol.*, p.144: are in error in stating that the house had been designed for Henrietta Maria.

405 The earliest project was the completion of Webb's palace for Charles II; *cf.* ASC V, 21, 25, 26 (WS VIII, pls.xvii, xx); this is clearly derived from the Winchester plan, and prefigures the development at Whitehall.

406 *Cf.* for an interesting comparison the parallel plan and elevation,

ASC V, 23, 24 (WS VIII, pls.xvii, xix); the most interesting difference is the semi-circular encroachment into the pediments of the central building which, though changed in the SM drawings here reproduced, will be found again in the domed vestibules. *Cf.* SM I, 28, 43 (WS VI, pls.xlii, xxvii).

407 For early projects by James II and Queen Mary, *cf.* Evelyn, *Diary*, V, p.203, note 1.

408 The warrant most probably followed the 'meeting at Guildhall of the Grand Committee about settling the draughts of Greenwich Hospital' recorded by Evelyn, *Diary*, 21 April 1696.

409 *ibid.*, 30 June 1696.

410 The drawing of King Charles's wing (Fig.106) is not original, of course, but part of Jones's building; *cf.* SM II, 9 (WS VI, pl.xx) which is tentatively ascribed to Webb by the WS editors. For the 'New Building' it is difficult to suggest an alternative designer: Hawksmoor cannot be held responsible, though it is probable that he executed the drawing (*cf.* Minute Book, *sub* 8 Oct. 1697, WS VI, p.36). Vanbrugh, at this early period, cannot be seriously considered as Bray's note to Evelyn's *Diary*, 31 May 1695, is erroneous, the secretary to the commission being William and not John Vanbrugh. *Cf.* Wren's letter to 'Mr Vanbruck' printed in facsimile in *RIBA Mem. Vol.*, p.138; William Vanbrugh died Jan. 1716/7 (WS VI, p.74, note); John (later Sir John) Vanbrugh's association with the hospital was by no means due, as Phillimore, *op. cit.*, p.286, asserts, to his 'first start in life was his being engaged by Wren to act as clerk of works at Greenwich' which position was held by Hawksmoor. John Vanbrugh's name first appears in the Minute Book on 14 Oct. 1703 (WS VI, p.44), by which time, of course, he was well known both as a dramatist and architect.

411 Quoted by L. Milman, *op. cit.*, p.276; this report written, according to Milman, for Parliament, is not verbally identical with the *Remarks ...* previously quoted; on the other hand, Milman's dating of 1778, uncritically copied by Whitaker-Wilson, *op. cit.*, p.218, cannot be correct as Hawksmoor died in 1736. *V. infra*, note 555.

412 Briggs, *op. cit.* (1951), p.107. The opinion of the WS editors, VI, pp.11 ff., published twenty-three years earlier, must be considered authoritative: 'The truth of the matter is that in the buildings at Greenwich, as now existing, the share of Sir Chr. Wren, apart from his general control as Surveyor-General ... can almost be limited to the idea of the grand layout ... on the accession of Queen Anne in 1702 ... it must be recognized that the initiative passed over to Vanbrugh. It is further probable that this new impulse goes back to 1699 and that the notable raising of the two Cupolas ... was due to the indirect influence of the younger man, whose design for Castle Howard produced an immediate impression.' The last designs with which Wren's name can be confidently associated are very likely those which were engraved, though later repudiated by the Greenwich Commissioners (*cf.* WS VI, where the prints are reproduced and the evidence set out); this becomes apparent from Evelyn, *Diary*, 3 April 1700: 'I went with Sir Chr. Wren, Surveyor of his Majesties Workes & Buildings, to Kensington, to present the King with the Model & several drafts ingraved, of the Hospital now erecting at Greenwich for Sea-Men, the A:Bish: of Cant: introducing us; His Majestie receiving us with greate satisfaction, & incouraging the prosecution of the Work ...'

413 L'Estrange, *op. cit.*, II, p.85.

414 *Cf.* the plan, WS VI, pl.xxvi.

415 *Cf. ibid.*, p.92, and pl.xli.

416 The doubling of the pillars, but not the semi-circular protrusion into the pediment, is already apparent in the drawing SM, I, 44 (WS VI, pl.xxvi) which the WS editors ascribe to Wren's hand; the significant pediment treatment, as well as the coupled pillars, appear in SM I, 43 (*loc. cit.*) also ascribed to Wren, but which lacks any indication of the dome, while the former possessed a small sketch of a cupola pasted on to the main drawing. The second drawing must be considered rather early, as it

shows a different treatment of the entresol from that built; the first cannot be later than 1702 as by that time the peristyle of the drum was 4 ft high above the bases of the columns, which are not even shown in that drawing, but appear in the two elevations, National Maritime Museum, Vol. III, 12 and SM I, 28 (WS VI, pls.xxix, xlii), both of which show the break in the pediment and niches flanking the central window where Wren's drawing had shown flat panels. It should, lastly, be noted, that Wren's elevation of the Great Hall (SM I, 43) shows two small doors at the western end closely resembling the 'Dean's Door' of St Paul's.

417 For the comparative plan, *cf.* ASC III, 45 (WS XIII, pl.i).
418 StPL II, 174, 175 (WS III, pl.xxxii), 176 (WS XIII, pl.xxxiii).
419 Contract Book, 18 June 1675; WS XVI, pp.7–8.
420 Contract Book, 2 Aug. 1675; *ibid.*, p.8.
421 Account Book, Nov. 1675–Feb. 1675/6; WS XIII, p.75.
422 *loc. cit.*
423 Building Accounts, March 1675/6, *ibid.*, p.76.
424 Contract Book, 9 March 1675/6; WS XVI, p.13. There is no foundation for the assertion made by Clinch, *St Paul's Cathedral*, London 1906, p.126, that the excavations were completed by 1674.
425 WS editors XVI, p.ix: 'Had Sir Chr Wren's travels extended to Italy he might have been influenced [by] the Roman practice of through bonding with brick at five-foot levels.' The opposite view had previously been expressed by Clarke, quoted by Clinch, *op. cit.*, p.130, who opined that Wren 'fortunately was not acquainted with the Roman systems of construction' and, notwithstanding actual fact, states that in St Paul's 'we have a building which not only seems to be, but really is built of stone, within and without. The arches, cornices, vaulting arches, and all wall surfaces and carvings are of stone'. This is, of course, untrue; for the vaulting arches, *cf.* the numerous payments made to bricklayers in the Building Accounts; for the actual method of construction, *v.* Fig.116.
426 *Cf.* Building Accounts, April 1676; WS XIII, p.76, recording payments to 'Carpenters . . . making a Triangle for the Ram and helping at that work'. The method seems to have been continued throughout the work of demolition: *cf. sub* June 1682; *ibid.*, p.162: 'Labourers clearing and wheeling away Stones from the Piller which was ramd down the last Month.'
427 *Cf.* Building Accounts, Sept. 1677; *ibid.*, p.96; payment to Marshall 'ffor Rubble Work of the ffoundation of the South Portico from the first bed of loam'.
428 Building Accounts, June 1676; *ibid.*, p.78.
429 Building Accounts, March 1676/7; *ibid.*, p.86.
430 *The First Book of Architecture by Andrea Palladio . . . Translated by* G[odfrey] R[ichards]; *v. infra*, Abstract of the Wren Library catalogue, lot 214. The author has not been able to see a copy of the 1676 edition, the first to contain the plate here reproduced: the copy listed in the BM catalogue was apparently destroyed; neither the Victoria & Albert Museum, nor the RIBA Library possess a copy of the 1676 edition. The plate, however, was included in later editions of the work, and it is amusing to note that it still appeared as late as 1708, at a time when the cathedral was actually complete. It is unfortunately impossible to establish whether Richards's representation is in any way connected with the plaster model made by Grove which Hooke records to have seen on 5 Jan. 1675/6.
431 This was already recognized by Loftie, *op. cit.*, p.202.
432 Building Accounts; WS XIII, p.79.
433 Contract Book, 9 March 1675/6; WS XVI, p.13. (John Simpson, John Hoy, John Parker.)
434 Building Accounts; WS XIII, p.82.
435 Building Accounts, March 1676/7; *ibid.*, pp.86–9.
436 *ibid.*, p.84. The work was already begun in the previous November (*ibid.*, p.83); continued in February (*ibid.*, p.85) when the foundations for the crypt below the dome area were also cleared; and possibly completed by May (*ibid.*, p.90).

437 Building Accounts, Sept. 1677; *ibid.*, p.95. Payment to Marshall for work to the same height on the north sides of the choir, under same date; contracts dated 11 Jan. 1676/7.
438 The date and provenance of this undated and unsigned engraving from the Guildhall Library is not easily established. The fact that the details of the lower storey are rendered substantially correctly, while the features above the cornice are imaginary, points to a period specified in the text below. What is noteworthy, however, is the very striking resemblance of this representation of the cathedral to that which appears in sheet 3 of Hollar's *Prospect of London and Westminster, Taken from Lambeth* (Hind, *op. cit.*, pl.xxiv). In the latter, the body of the building agrees perfectly with the anonymous engraving here reproduced; the drum and dome are very similar, though not identical; and of the two western towers, Hollar shows the southern one already built. The exact date and authorship of this Hollar engraving, however, is unfortunately not clear: Hind, *op. cit.*, p.49, rightly rejects the 1674 date proposed in the Crace Collection Catalogue, and notes that sheets 3 and 4 have apparently been reworked on some impressions by an inferior hand. This may account for the fact that steeples later than this stage of the cathedral (such as St Augustin and St Benet, Gracechurch Street) are shown. The close similarities between Hollar's and the anonymous engraving here reproduced need not, however, imply the possibility of Hollar's authorship of the latter, in spite of an obvious technical accomplishment. In any event, as Hollar died in 1677, he can, at best, have been responsible for the representation of those architectural features completed or projected by that time.
439 Contract Book, 7 Sept. 1678; WS XVI, p.16.
440 Building Accounts, up to Dec. 1680; WS XIII, pp.117–44: £350; April 1679, £200; July 1679, £350; Sept. 1679, £300; Dec. 1679, £500; June 1680, £464 10s 0d.; Dec. 1680, £730; leaving a balance of £215 13s 5¾d.
441 Building Accounts, May 1681; *ibid.*, p.149.
442 Building Accounts, March 1678/9; WS XIII, p.116.
443 Contract Book, 12 Dec. 1678; WS XVI, p.17.
444 Building Accounts, May 1679; WS XIII, p.119.
445 Wren eventually broke his resolution not to have any more models made; though certainly not for public exhibition, Pearce executed, and was paid in Jan.-March 1684/5 (WS XIII, p.198), 'for making Divers Modells, & other extraordinary Works, by Order of Mr Surveyor (viz.) in the two Yeares past: For ye Modells of ye great Tribune of ye Dome, and for ye Model of ye small Arches & part of ye S.Isle, & for ye Tribune of ye S. Windows of ye Quire. For ye Model of ye Portico, & a second Model of ye great Tribune with ye Cornish continued round. For ye Model of ye great Modelion Cornish, & for several Modells for ye Head of ye great S. Door,' a total of £47 1s 3d.
446 *Cf. Regole* (1537 ed.) V, fol.11 *verso*.
447 Sancroft was elevated to the archbishopric in 1677; *cf.* Wren's letter of congratulation, 30 Dec., in WS XIII, p.51. Lindsey, *op. cit.*, is altogether in error in stating that 'Edward Stillingfleet, in 1677, succeeded Sancroft as archbishop of Canterbury,' as Stillingfleet succeeded Sancroft as Dean of St Paul's, and never rose to the primacy at all, ending his life as Bishop of Worcester.
448 Pamphlet, no title, dated 30 May 1678; BM pressmark 1897 c. 19(49). Clinch, *op. cit.*, p.133, mentions a 'very earnest and urgent address' published by the Bishop of London in 1678, which we have not been able to trace. It is possible that the authorship stated is erroneous, and should refer to the Dean of St Paul's.
449 The yearly totals do not offer any indication. Expenditure remained fairly stable up to 1682 (Oct. 1675–Oct. 1676, £9446; 1676–77, £12, 419; 1677–8, £13,121; 1678–9, £14,019; 1679–80, £10,373; 1680–1, £12,784; 1681–2, £10,710); the year 1682–3 showed a marked falling off to £6651; in 1683–4 it rose again to £13,153, to fall again to £7164 in 1684–5.
450 The contracts, dated 5 Sept. 1678, are printed in WS XVI, pp.15 *et seq.*

451 Building Accounts (Pearce) Jan. 1680/1; *ibid.*, p.143.
452 *ibid.*, p.149.
453 Letter to Sir R– F– [?Sir Richard Ford;? Sir Ralph Freeman] R. C. Hist. MSS., XII, reprinted in WS XIII, p.xviii.
454 Building Accounts, April–June 1683; *ibid.*, p.175.
455 Contract Book, 18 April 1685; WS XVI, pp.20 *et seq.*
456 Contract Book, 18 March 1685/6; *ibid.*, p.22.
457 Building Accounts, May 1686; WS XIV, p.6.
458 Building Accounts, June 1686; *ibid.*, p.7: 'fframeing of six 16 foot Centers to turn over a Brick Arch at the S.E. Leg of the Dome. In making a Scaffold to turn over the Arch at the N.E. leg of the Dome . . .' and July 1686, *ibid.*, p.8: 'Bricklayers turning over two Sphericall Arches one on the S. side and the other on the N. side Isles of the Choir & bringing up the Spandrells of three other Sphericall Arches . . .' and Aug. 1686, *ibid.*, p.9: 'Bricklayers turning over a Sphericall Brick-Arch on the N.E. Legg of the Dome . . . turning over the Shell on the N.W. Legg of the Dome . . .' etc.
459 Building Accounts, Nov. 1686; *ibid.*, p.19.
460 *ibid.*, p.22.
461 Building Accounts, May 1687; *ibid.*, p.23: 'Bricklayers turning over the Brick Vaulting on the S. side of the Dome as farr as the S.W. chapel westward.'
462 Building Accounts, May, August; *ibid.*, pp.27, 31.
463 Building Accounts, Oct. 1687; *ibid.*, p.31.
464 Newsletter, 1 Sept. 1687; in WS XIII, p.xviii.
465 Building Accounts, Feb. 1687/8; WS XIV, pp.40–64.
466 Building Accounts, Feb. 1689/90, *ibid.*, p.70: 'To E. Strong. Work on the 3 Peeres on N. Side within Church and W. of N.W. Vestry . . . together with ye Springer Stones in 2 Cources of ye 26 ft Arches, & also severall faces of ye Corinthian Capitalls.' *et al.*
467 Building Accounts, Jan.–Feb. 1690/1, WS XIV, p.80.
468 The WS editors, XVI, p.ix, think as early as 1680, referring to Wren's letter to Fell regarding Tom Tower, 11 June 1681.
469 Building Accounts, WS XIV, p.85.
470 *ibid.*, p.89.
471 Building Accounts, July 1692; *ibid.*, p.98.
472 Building Accounts, April 1691; *ibid.*, p.86. Strong had already been paid for a 'modell of 1/4 part Dome' in Jan.–Feb. 1690/1; *ibid.*, p.80.
473 Building Accounts, Dec. 1695; WS XV, p.5; *cf.* also WS XIV, p.148.
474 *V. supra*, notes 126–7 for an earlier chronology of the incidence of segmental pediments. The design here referred to is related to the contemporaneous instance occurring in Morden College and to the Windsor Castle project ASC V, 17 (WS VIII, pls.xiii, xiv) dated 1698.
475 Building Accounts, WS XV, pp.45, 50
476 Apart from the drawing here illustrated, *cf.* StPL II, 131, 132, 133.
477 Building Accounts, Jan. 1706/7; WS XV, p.146.
478 Building Accounts, Sept. 1686; WS XIV, p.10.
479 *ibid.*, p.131.
480 Building Accounts, Aug. 1696; WS XV, p.11.
481 Contract Book, WS XVI, pp.23–4. The final payment was made in Aug. 1703; WS XV, p.98.
482 Building Accounts, June 1649; WS XIV, p.134.
483 Wren's memorandum, in Minute Book; WS XVI, p.85.
484 Minute Book, 30 March 1697; *ibid.*, p.84.
485 *V. supra*, note 271.
486 *Cf.* the two plans of the 'piazza' around St Paul's, SM and StPL II, 173 (WS III, pl.xxxi) but note that the plans of the 'chapter house' are not identical. The oblique approach from Ludgate Hill indicated shows that that section was already largely reconstructed. Killanin's statement, *op. cit.*, p.12, that 'Wren was very anxious to copy Bernini's colonnaded arcade of St Peter's,' is as ludicrous as the assertion that 'the Italian would not let him have the plans to copy'. For Wren's piazza, *v. infra*, pp.120–1; the St Peter's colonnade would have been known to Wren,
without seeing Bernini's drawings, from engravings; for example, de Rossi, *Insignium* . . . (Abstract, *infra*, p.231), pl.10.
487 The finial is reminiscent of the pre-Fire design (Fig.32); the idea of the scroll buttresses is probably derived from ASC II, 32 (WS I, pl.xxi).
488 *Cf.* the section ASC II, 23 (*ibid.*, pl.xviii). The drawings here discussed demonstrate the fallacy of Dimock's statement, *op. cit.*, p.89, that 'to the end, Wren's wish seems to have been to have made the external height [of the dome] no greater than was required by the formation of the interior cupola'. In view of the double construction of the dome of the Greek cross design as early as 1672–3, this statement seems incomprehensible. The passage from *Parentalia* quoted in support unquestionably refers to the 1675 design. A double dome, obviously intending optimum interior effect and maximum height, was already projected for the pre-Fire design; *cf.* the section, ASC II, 7 (WS I, pl.viii).
489 It is possible that such a treatment for the substructure was already envisaged in connexion with the dome design StPL II, 164 (Fig.128), on the basis of the related drawing StPL II, 166 (WS III, pl.xxviii); the dome section there sketched is practically identical with 164, and the portion of the substructure clearly shows the quadrant truncations.
490 *Cf.* Vanbrugh's scheme, in WS VI, pp.91–2.
491 *Cf.* WS XIV, pl.ix.
492 ASC II, 29 (WS I, pl.xix). In our interpretation of the evolution of St Paul's, it is impossible to accept the date of 1675 for this drawing as suggested by Summerson, *Arch. in Brit.*, *1530–1830*, London 1954, caption to pl.81.
493 Only a close scrutiny of the work as completed reveals the fact that the west end was still incomplete; the best clue is given by the oval feature in the cornice above the round-headed window of the extreme western bay; the fact that the sunk panels above and below the flanking windows of the morning prayer chapel are not shown indicate that this part was not yet built. Both these features are shown in the Emmet engraving of 1702 (WS XIV, pl.xv) which is clearly posterior to the drawing here discussed.
494 Building Accounts, Jan.–March 1697/8; WS XV, p.37.
495 *ibid.*, p.35: 'Picking Mortar out of the Beds of the Stones in ye N.W. Legg of ye Dome'; *ibid.*, p.38: 'Splitting Mortar out of the joynts of part of the N.W. Legg of the Dome'; *ibid.*, p.51: '6 days Masons opening Joynts inside ye Church', etc.
496 Minute Book, 8 March 1699/1700; WS XVI, p.98.
497 Building Accounts, July–Sept. 1700; WS XV, p.62: 'To John Smallwell. For the Modell of one of the Towers at the W End, £13.'
498 Building Accounts, Sept. 1701; *ibid.*, p.74: 'To John Smallwell, Joyner. For 52 days 1 man Altering the Modell of one of the Towers at the W End to show the Winding Stairs & Raising it higher & making ye corners square which were hollow before . . . £7.16.0'. *Cf.* the drawings StPL II, 145, 146, 152, 155 (WS III, pls.xviii, xix), the first of which clearly shows the 'hollow corners'; the shape of these domed west towers is clearly derived from the 'chapter house' design (Fig.124); if Kneller's portrait (*cf.* Killanin, *op. cit.*, pl.57) is correctly dated, Wren had envisaged this form as early as 1687.
499 Building Accounts, July–Sept. 1700; WS XV, p.64, recording a payment to Edward Strong 'for 834 ft 3 in sup. Inside Circular Freestone, inclining to ye Centre of the Dome 1 inch in a foot at 14d per ft.' The colonnade was completed before 1703.
500 Building Accounts, WS XV, pp.70 (Kip), 84 (Gribelin), 89, 94, 96 (Gribelin).
501 Two drawings of the west front are extant, ASC II, 39 (Fig.133) and StPL I, 49 (WS II, pl.xvii); the differences are principally in the western towers: the latter drawing shows a segmental pediment on brackets above the clock, while the former has only a curved flexure in the cornice. Also the drum of the domical cappings is shown plain in the ASC drawing, but with sunk panels in the StPL version. Both the Emmet and Gribelin (autograph set) engravings of the west front show the segmental pediments and panels of the StPL drawing; the latter of the two engravings

shows recumbent figures on all sides of the pediment; in the Emmet engraving of the south elevation and the Gribelin (autograph set) engraving of the north elevation, however, the bases are shown truncated, and the pediment replaced by the centrally flexed cornice; there are flaming urns instead of sculpture; in both engravings, the sunk panels of the drums are omitted.

502 SM (WS XIV, pls.xxxvi, xxxvii).

503 StPL II, 162 (WS III, pl.xxvi); the windows appear in ASC I, 29 (WS I, pl.xix), this being the principal difference between this complete south elevation and the dome study StPL II, 171 (Fig.132).

504 StPL II, 170 (WS III, pl.xxix).

505 *Cf.* WS editors, XIII, p.15, pointing to the fact that in Fig.134 'the lower part of the drawing is taken from an earlier drawing dating back to the accession of James II' as 'a 12-ft. arch, smaller than that finally adopted, is shown at the start of the nave'.

506 Building Accounts, WS XV, p.159. Construction begun Nov. 1706 (*ibid.*, p.144).

507 *ibid.*, p.128.

508 *ibid.*, pp.130, 144.

509 *ibid.*, p.133.

510 *ibid.*, p.137.

511 *ibid.*, p.145.

512 *ibid.*, p.146 (Jan. 1706/7): 'K & B [Kempster and Beauchamp] 17 days ea Piece & Mend of ye Corinthian Capitals & Pilasters at ye S.E. Legg of ye Dome.' From Dec. 1709 repair entries become frequent; *cf.* WS editors, XVI, p.10: 'From Dec. 1709 to Dec. 1710, say £5,016.7.3 was spent in repairs of "flaws and fractures". With some earlier repairs from Oct. to Dec. 1697, and some later from Dec. 1710 to June 1711, a total of, say £7,471.19.3 was reached.'

513 Building Accounts, WS XV, p.148.

514 *ibid.*, p.158.

515 Minute Book, 25 Aug. 1707; WS XVI, p.105.

516 *ibid.*, p.106; *cf.* also Simpson, *op. cit.*, pp.173–4.

517 *Parentalia*, p.292, note; the statement is accepted by Longman, *op. cit.*, p.141, Weaver, *op. cit.*, p.70, Dutton, *op. cit.*, p.28, and discussed by Dimock, *op. cit.*, pp.107–8. The whole idea of mosaics, however, is regarded as 'of very doubtful authority' by the WS editors, XIV, index, *sub* pl.xlv.

518 *Cf.* the section of the great model of 1673, engraved by Hulsbergh (WS, XIV, pl.iii) and the Emmet engraving, though of doubtful authenticity, mentioned *supra*, note 502.

519 Minute Book, 3 March 1708/9; WS XVI, p.107.

520 One of Pellegrini's cartoons was acquired by the Victoria and Albert Museum in 1953; Thornhills designs are printed in WS XV, pl.lv, and XVII, pls.xvii–xviii.

521 *Cf.* Minute Book, 5 April 1709 and 28 Jan. 1709/10; WS XVI, pp.108, 109.

522 WS editors, XIV, index *sub* pl.xlv.

523 F. J. B. Watson, *Eighteenth Century Venice*, Whitechapel Art Gallery, exhibition catalogue, p.6.

524 Minute Book, WS XVI, p.116.

525 Minute Book, 9 July 1716; *ibid.*, p.126.

526 Minute Book, 15 Oct. 1717; *ibid.*, p.127.

527 'The Memoriall of Sir Chr Wren', dated 28 Oct. 1717, transcribed in Minute Book, 1 Nov. 1717; *ibid.*, pp.130–1.

528 Minute Book, 17 March 1717/8; *ibid.*, p.133.

529 Birch, *op. cit.*, p.15; J. S. Bumpus, *op. cit.*, p.177, gives the alternative of 145; Dimock, *op. cit.*, p.73, of 153 years and twelve architects 'from Bramante to Berninus' [*sic*] but rightly comments on the difference in scale in relation to the cost of the two buildings. The ineptness of the comparison is recognized by Weaver, *op. cit.*, p.76; but *cf.* Birch, *supra*, note 245.

530 Birch, *op. cit.*, p.15

531 Blomfield, *Touchstone*, p.189; *cf.* also J. S. Bumpus, *op. cit.*, p.172.

532 Loftie, *op. cit.*, p.196; *cf.* also Dutton, *op. cit.*, p.35: 'It would be bold to claim the dome of St Paul's as the finest in Europe, but which can be said to exceed it in beauty of proportion or detail?' and Drummond, quoted *infra*, note 536.

533 Day, *op. cit.*, p.91.

534 Dutton, *op. cit.*, p.12. Dimock's contention, *op. cit.*, p.95, that 'Wren's regard for stability caused him to make his vast square supports of a solidity exceeding those of Mainz and Speier' is not corroborated by the structural soundness of these Romanesque edifices when compared with the insufficiency of the piers of St Paul's.

535 Loftie, *op. cit.*, p.158, found it 'impossible to believe . . . that [Wren] learned much, if anything, from Mansart or Perrault' and suggests that St Paul's and Greenwich 'must have proceeded from a mind uninfluenced by what he had seen in Paris, but working on lines parallel with those of the great foreign architects'.

536 *Cf.* Weaver, *op. cit.*, p.51: 'It would have been better if Wren had relied more on English decorative motives', and Blomfield, *Short Hist.*, p.121: 'As Wren advanced in experience and mastery of his art, he gradually shook off the artificial manner which he learnt in France' and *ibid.*, p.302: 'he went to see Bernini in France and talked with Mansart and Perrault, yet their influence on him was merely superficial. It spoilt his ornament, but left his faculty of design untouched'. Lastly, *ibid.*, p.111: 'In all the earlier work of Wren's middle period, the influence of the French architects is very marked; but it gradually disappeared towards the end of the seventeenth century, and in his later work he shook off the exuberant ornament which disfigures some of his earlier designs.' Day, *op. cit.*, p.85, thought that 'the French visit influenced deeply and not altogether favourably his work in succeeding years'. It should be noted that these anathemata are strictly couched in general terms, without pointing to any specific features as illustration of these judgements. The only qualitative criticism on specific grounds is to be found in Drummond, *op. cit.*, p.35: 'Wren's brief but intensive study in France is revealed in the chastity of the vast dome [St Paul] majestic with a kind of humility, untroubled and smiling; the clumsy and proud pomposity of the southern dome is exchanged for one that expresses a genuine religious spirit without any loss of dignity.' For Wren's attitude to religion, *v. infra*, pp.167 ff.; for the dome as an expression of religious spirit, pp.153–4.

537 Eberlein, 'Sir Christopher Wren, 1632–1723', in *Architectural Forum*, New York, Feb. 1923, p.50.

538 Reynolds, *Sixth Discourse*.

539 *Cf.* the annotated abstract of *A Catalogue of the Curious and Entire Libraries Of that ingenious Architect Sir Christopher Wren, Knt. and Christopher Wren, Esq*; auction sale, 24–27 October 1748 (hereafter cited as Abstract), pp.231–5. Most of the references found in subsequent pages are taken from the specific editions listed in the catalogue. It should be pointed out that the account given of Wren's Library by Briggs, *op. cit.*, (1953) p.262, is entirely erroneous. The books did not, as there stated, form part of the 1749 sale of Christopher Wren's medals and Sir Christopher's drawings; as the Abstract printed *infra* shows, there can be no question of a 'dearth of treatises on scientific, mathematical and mechanical subjects', as Briggs alleges, as there are not 'only three or four in all' but their total number is nearer one hundred. The same correction must apply to this author's figures given for works on antiquity, archaeology, and travel. Briggs suggests the absence of scientific works to be due to dispersals prior to the sale; his account, however, is due to an acquaintance only with the abridged list of books given in WS XX, pp.74–7, and obvious ignorance of the sale catalogue itself.

540 Longman, *op. cit.*, p.22.

541 *Diary*, 8 Feb. 1645.

542 *The Architecture of Sir Roger Pratt*, pp.289, 23. The statement is neatly corroborated by 'A Character of England in a Letter to a Nobleman of

France' in *Harleian Misc.*, X, p.191, quoted by Jenkinson, *op. cit.*, p.5: 'Among the pieces of modern Architecture I have never observed above two which were remarkable in this vast City; the portico of St Paul, and the Banqueting-house at Whitehall.'

543 Their meeting, however improbable, has been suggested by Phillimore, *op. cit.*, p.93.

544 *v. supra*, note 279.

545 Pennant, quoted by Jenkinson, *op. cit.*, p.286.

546 Birch, *op. cit.*, p.5, finds that 'Horace Walpole's strictures upon this church were singularly correct; he could find nothing to admire in it ... If architecturally it was a failure it is interesting as being the first church on the new model in which galleries were to form an important part.'

547 The depth of Jones's portico was intended to provide a place for much of the commercial negotiation which customarily went on in the nave of the cathedral.

548 *Cf.* ASC II, 61 (Fig.35); the 1675 design, ASC II, 11 (Fig.43), 12, 13, 15 (WS I, pls.xii, xi).

549 The instance of Farley church could be added.

550 Webb, *Vindication of Stone-Henge restor'd* ... (1664), p.27.

551 *Cf.* for example the drawings BM Sloane 5238, Nos.57, 60, 66 (WS V, pls.xxxiii, xxviii, xxvii). The second of these agrees roughly with the specifications given by Wren in a letter to Oldenburg for the Royal Society premises projected in 1668, in possessing four distinct storeys, and a central feature very likely intended to serve as an observatory; the dimensions, however, do not tally, and the WS editors (XIII, pp.48–9) suggest No.66 to represent Wren's proposals for this abortive scheme on the strength of the scale specified. Although Briggs, *op. cit.* (1953), p.60, agrees with the WS editors in regarding this elaborately ornamented façade as a 'characteristic Wren design' we cannot ascribe the drawing to him on purely stylistic grounds, and certainly not to the immature period of 1668; Mr John Summerson, in a private communication, has rejected the possibility of regarding the drawing as by Wren's hand. Details of style point to a relationship to the centre feature of Hooke's Bedlam Hospital (*cf. Diary*, pl. opp. p.130).

552 *Diary*, 21 Oct. 1644; for the Covent Garden piazza, *cf.* Summerson, *Georgian London*, pl.1; for Wren's design, *cf.* StPL II, 174, 175 (WS III, pl.xxxii) and 176 (WS XIII, pl.xxxiii).

553 Richardson, *RIBA Mem. Vol.*, p.159.

554 *Cf.* the deposition of John Evans. 1698. in WS XVIII, p.166, which illuminates Wren's desire to save the Banqueting House at the time of the Whitehall fire.

555 *V. supra*, p.151. L. Milman, *op. cit.*, p.276, quotes a report by Hawksmoor, allegedly written by order of Parliament in 1778 [*v. supra*, note 411] containing the statement, referring to the Queen's House as the terminal point of the vista, that Wren 'had not intended that his range of buildings should be brought to so poor a conclusion'. The passage is not contained, however, in the *Remarks on the Founding* ... etc. of 1728 referred to elsewhere. For the relationship between the Banqueting House and the final cathedral design, *v. infra*, note 585.

556 Blomfield, *Short Hist.*, p.121.

557 *Cf.* Summerson, *Heavenly Mansions*, pp.84 *et seq.* and *v. infra*, pp.175–6.

558 Summerson, *Georgian London*, p.20.

559 For instance, Richardson, *RIBA Mem. Vol.*, pp.120–5, referring to the Custom House and the Grand Storehouse of the Tower. A general Dutch influence is also discussed by Pevsner, *Outline* (1948 ed.), pp.165 *et seq.*, with especial reference to Vingboon's book and van Campen's *Mauritshuis*. The inherent contradiction invalidates Blomfield's thesis, *Short Hist.*, p.267, that 'the use of fine rubbed brickwork, with very thin joints seems to have been introduced by Wren early in the reign of Charles II and was probably suggested by the Dutch noblemen who came over with William'.

560 Stratton, 'Dutch Influence on the Architecture of Sir Chr Wren', in *RIBA Mem. Vol.*, pp.180–1. This author reproduces, with doubtful

relevance, plates from Vingboon, Danckert, and Dahlberg's *Suecia antiqua et hodierna*, Stockholm 1691; the second plate drawn from the latter work, a view of St Mary Magdalen at Stockholm, though showing a vague resemblance in its steeple to some of Wren's work, betrays far more strongly Italian influence shown in the great transept porch, obviously a paraphrase on the Roman Gesù, with the somewhat inappropriate addition of Venetian-looking windows.

561 *loc. cit.* These generalizations are altogether contrary to fact: apart from architecture, Restoration literature shows very clearly the negligible extent of Dutch influence. Dryden, though unduly critical of French authors in spite of his indebtedness to them, is positively contemptuous of Dutch commentators; *cf. Essays, passim*, esp. Preface to *Sylva*. As a matter of small but significant detail, the King's twenty-four violins noted by Evelyn, *Diary*, 21 Dec. 1662 were in obvious emulation of the *vingt-quatre violons du roi* of Louis XIV.

562 *art. cit.*, p.192.

563 H. H. Milman, *op. cit.*, p.393, states that 'Charles II had invited ... Claude Perrault' which is clearly fictitious. The implication that the 'invitation' was extended prior to 1660 is contradicted by Perrault's description as having 'built the new front of the Louvre'.

564 *The Architecture of Sir Roger Pratt*, p.23; the continuation of the passage *supra*, p.119.

565 Stratton, *art. cit.*, p.184; the reference is to H. Bloem, *Een Constich Boeck van de Vijf Columnen*, Amsterdam 1598, which Stratton states was found in the attic of Wotton House. The intrinsically Dutch character of the work is, however, questionable, as it is one of the many paraphrases on Serlio and Palladio which were published all over Europe in the seventeenth century, not infrequently in a somewhat unlearned way misinterpreting Italian authors and frequently representing 'Rules' as principles.

566 *Cf.* (a) *The French Gardener, transplanted into English by Philocepos* [i.e., J.E.]1658; (b) *Instructions concerning ... Libraries*, 1661, translated from Naudé; (c) *A Parallel of the ancient Architecture with the modern*, 1664 ff. translated from de Chambray (*v. infra*, note 606 for list of editions and issues); (d) *Treatise of Statues*, printed with *A Parallel*, from Bartoli's edition of Alberti; (e) *Kalendarium Hortenses, or the Gardener's Almanac*, 1666; (f) *Idea of the Perfection of Painting*, 1668, also translated from de Chambray; (g) *Rapin of Gardens* [*Rapinus Hortorum*] 1673; (h) *The Compleat Gard'ner*, 1693, and (i) *Directions concerning Melons* [?] 1693, were both translations from J. de la Quintinye. Briggs's mention, *op. cit.* (1953), p.29, of a book on sculpture is misleading, as the work deals with engraving (*Sculpture, or the History and Art of Chalcography and Engraving on Copper; to which is annexed A New Manner of Engraving on Mezzotint*, 1662, 1755). In view of this formidable list, as well as the fact that Evelyn never translated a Dutch work into English, Stratton's opinion, *art. cit.*, seems perverse that 'cultivated amateurs ... convinced of the adaptability of Dutch models to English use ... by disseminating knowledge of what they had seen, helped to spread the already established vogue for Dutch art', as there was neither an 'established vogue for Dutch art' worth talking about, nor did cultured dilletanti do anything to encourage it. Evelyn's orientation is made abundantly clear from his *Account of Architects and Architecture* (printed with *A Parallel*) in which not a single Dutch book or artist is mentioned, but where constant reference is made to Vitruvius, Palladio, Alberti, Barbaro, Bramante, Raphael, Michelangelo, and Bernini of the Italians, Wotton of English architectural writers, and Desgodes (Desgodetz), d'Aviler, Perrault, and Blondel among the French. Finally, we may quote Dryden, *Musical Drama*: 'Italy, the mother of learning and of arts ...; and the other parts of [Europe], in relation to those delightful arts, are still as much provincial to Italy as they were in the time of the Roman Empire.'

567 *Cf.* Abstract, pp.231–5. Marolois's *Perspective* does not deal with architectural style. The Amsterdam edition of d'Aviler cannot, of course, be

regarded as a Dutch work, particularly as it deals with Vignola and Michelangelo. For the paucity of Dutch works in Sir Roger Pratt's library, *v. infra*, note 605.

568 Eberlein, *art. cit.*, p.49, repeats other authors with the mention of Vingboon's book, but declines an opinion how far Wren may have been influenced by that work.

569 Briggs, *op. cit.*, (1951) p.122, calls the Winchester Schoolroom 'very Dutch looking'.

570 No evidence seems to exist to prove Wren's authorship of such houses as those at Chichester, Groombridge, and most of the others attributed to him.

571 L. Milman, *op. cit.*, p.186: 'the fact that there was a long tradition of brick building in England before Wren's time, and that Wren himself constantly made use of the material in his Caroline period, justifies a denial of this debt to Dutch architecture.'

572 The Place des Vosges still retains its pristine character; of the original Place Dauphine, only a pair of houses remains intact which, fronting the bridge, give a good impression of what it must originally have been like, though the arcades have been turned into shops.

573 *Manière de bien bastir*, 1623.

574 *Cf.* de Ganay, *Châteaux de France, environs de Paris*, Paris 1948, pl.75.

575 This was the remnant of the 'château de cartes' of Louis XIII, portions of which are preserved in the cour de marbre of Louis XIV's building; *cf.* the author's *op. cit.*, p.17.

576 Jean Martin's editions of Italian works form an impressive list: *Hypnerotomachia Poliphili*, [Francesco Colonna, Venice 1499] Paris (Kerver) 1554. *Des antiquités, le troièsme livre* [of Serlio] Anvers, 1545, 1550. *Livre extraordinaire d'architecture* [Serlio, bk VI] Lyon, 1551. *Regole* [Serlio] Paris, 1545. *De architectura* [Vitruvius] Paris, 1547, 1572.

577 *Cf.* Mellers, *François Couperin and the French Classical Tradition*, London 1950, p.55.

578 The careers of the two architects have been amusingly, if not very correctly, compared by Blomfield, *Six Architects*, pp.20, 125: 'Serlio's career ended among the adventurers at the court of François I' and 'François Mansart was lost among the adventurers who crowded the Court of Louis XIV.'

579 No more than two examples need be cited here: the design for Trinity College, Cambridge, may be compared with either the south side of the cour ovale at Fontainebleau, or with Serlio, *Regole* (1537 ed.), III, xlviii. Secondly, the large round-headed windows poised on the apex of a triangular pediment in the early studies for Bow Church (Figs.17, 76) may be derived from either Mansart's Ste-Marie or from Serlio, *Regole*, IV, xxxiii; (1663 ed., p.278).

580 *Cf.* Fréart de Chantelou (ed.) *Journal du voyage en France du cavalier Bernin*, Paris 1930, *passim*.

581 Blomfield, *Six Architects*, p.43, calls Bernini's work 'the most grotesque travesty of Christianity'; for a contrasting view, *cf.* Sencourt, *The Consecration of Genius*, London 1947, p.235.

582 Weaver, *op. cit.*, p.51.

583 Wren, letter from Paris, 1665.

584 *Cf.* Fokker, *Roman Baroque Art*, Oxford 1938, II, pl.130.

585 The origin of this usage may be sought in Michelangelo, as early as the Medici chapel; it is comparatively rare in earlier French Renaissance architecture, though found at Ecouen, the Valois mausoleum, the 'Fontaine des Innocents', the chappelle Montmorency, at Chantilly, and in du Cerceau's Louvre elevations. In seventeenth-century French architecture it is only in isolated instances that the doubling of pillars and pilasters is *not* found. Summerson, *Arch. in Brit. 1530–1830*, p.141, suggests that the St Paul's elevations may be due to Jones's Banqueting House, Wren taking over the rusticated wall-face, the general two-storey design, and doubling the pillars and pilasters. This last, and most prominent feature, however, would seem to point quite clearly to French influence, many examples of which Wren would have seen himself in 1665.

586 Blunt, *François Mansart*, London, 1941 pl.28b.

587 e.g. Vaux-le-Vicomte, Montceaux, Richelieu, Berni, in the church of the Minimes, the corner pavilions of the Palais Mazarin and the Hôtel d'Aumont.

588 *Cf.* the du Cerceau drawings printed by Blomfield, *History of French Architecture 1494–1774*, London 1911, I, pl.xliii, and the engraving from the Bibliothéque Nationale, printed by Brissac, *Châteaux de France disparus*, Paris 1947, p.47.

589 *Cf.* ASC IV, 48, 49 (WS XI, pl.liv).

590 *Cf.* the engraving printed by Brissac, *op. cit.*, p.66; a remarkable parallel is to be found in a drawing of the *Procession de Louise de Lorraine . . . en 1584* printed by Yates, *French Academies of the Sixteenth Century*, London 1947, pl.13b; here, however, unlike at Verneuil, the vaults intersect without a central dome just as in SS. Anne and Agnes; the 'chapel' shown has a semi-circular eastern apse roofed by a conch, the vaults being supported by double pillars standing on a balustrade.

591 *Cf.* Brissac, *op. cit.*, p.78.

592 Wren's personal acquaintance with Mansart as well as Perrault has been presumed by Blomfield, *Short Hist.*, p.302. Though out of favour at court, Mansart was certainly still alive in 1665, as the date given by Pevsner, *op. cit.*, p.169, 1664, for his death, is erroneous; *Biographie Universelle* gives 1666. The portal of the Hôtel Conti is normally taken to be the precedent for Bow porch; it should be pointed out, however, that a very similar doorway existed at the Hôtel Carnavalet which, if Marot is to be trusted, was incorporated by Mansart in his new building.

593 Blunt, *op. cit.*, pl.5a.

594 *Cf.* the Perelle engraving printed by Blomfield, *Hist. Fr. Ren. Arch.*, II, pl.clxii.

595 e.g. S. M. della Pace, Rome, by Cortona; this suggestion was first made by Saxl and Wittkower, *British Art and the Mediterranean*, London 1948, p.47; Wren's derivation may be traced either through Falda's *Nuovo Teatro*, 1665, as these authors suggest; through Hooke's possession of an engraving of the 'chiesu di St. Maria della pace, 1s. 3d.' (*Diary*, 10 June 1677), or through de Rossi's *Insignium Romae Templorum* (Abstract, 551), pl.72.

596 *Cf.* the Perelle engraving printed by Blomfield, *Hist. Fr. Ren. Arch.*, II, pl.cxxxviii.

597 *Cf.* the Marot engraving, *ibid.*, II, pl.cxi.

598 *Cp.* the Marot engraving, *ibid.*, II, pl.ci and ASC I, 85, left subject (WS VII, pl.xv).

599 *Cf.* the du Cerceau drawing, *ibid.*, I, pl.liii.

600 Among Wren's early inventions was a sundial for All Souls; *cf.* Bullant, *Recueil d'Horlogiographie contenant la description, fabrication et usage des horloges solaires*, 1561 and *Petit Traicté de géometrie et d'Horlogiographie*, 1562.

601 Bullant, *Reigle Générale*, 1564, 1568; de l'Orme, *Premier Livre d'Architecture*, 1568; du Cerceau published books on Triumphal Arches, Grotesques, and Fragments from the Antique in 1549 and 1550, and *Edifices Antiques Romains* in 1594.

602 Briggs's statement, *op. cit.*, (1951) p.39, that in Paris Wren 'made a particular study of the fine domed churches recently erected or actually under construction' is conjectural, as there is no mention whatever of such in Wren's letter; in fact, none of Mansart's churches is mentioned by name; the only dome remarked on is that of the Institut.

603 Day, *op. cit.*, p.85: 'A longer period of travel and observation might not improbably have weakened rather than strengthened his work . . . and by leading him to rely overmuch upon precedent and to seek inspiration from the work of others, would have checked the natural development of his own powers, and fettered the free expression of his ideas.' This view is endorsed by T. F. Bumpus, *op. cit.*, p.262: 'One is inclined to think that it is as well, on the whole, that Wren did not go to Italy. His work would, in all likelihood, have been far more delicate and refined in detail had he done so, but he would have inevitably lost much of the

originality and freedom of treatment, which is undoubtedly the great charm of his work.' The theory purporting ignorance of historical precedent to be beneficial, and knowledge of such to be detrimental, to the development of originality seems largely novel in art historical literature.

604 Blomfield, *Six Architects*, p.165.

605 L. Milman, *op. cit*., pp.145–6. The ludicrous suggestion made by Ward, *RIBA Mem. Vol*., that 'it is hardly open to question that, at a period when technical works were still relatively scarce, engraved and manuscript copies of notable designs and even sketches of modern buildings passed from hand to hand in architectural circles' cannot be seriously considered. Pepys's mention, *Diary*, 6 Nov. 1667, of Allestry 'who is bookseller to the Royal Society' where one could find a 'great variety of French and foreign books' should suffice to dispel such a wholly erroneus notion of seventeenth-century book trade. That Wren's library was by no means exceptional is indicated by the book list of Ryston Hall, representing the remainder of works formerly belonging to Sir Roger Pratt, printed by Gunther as appendix II to *The Architecture of Sir Roger Pratt*, pp.302–4, which includes Italian and Dutch editions of Vitruvius, Alberti 1550, Serlio 1551, Le Muet's *Traicté*, 1647, as well as Boissard, François du Jon, Villalpandus's *Apparatus Urbis*, 1604, etc. A reference to books no longer extant at Ryston indicates Pratt's possession of Cataneo, Dom. Fontana, du Cerceau, Scamozzi, Rubens's *Palazzi di Genova*, Palladio, Perier, Meibomius, Labacco, and du Choul; the only Dutch work, we may note, is van Campen's *Stadt Huys van Amsterdam*, 1661.

606 *A Parallel* . . . etc., pref. ded. This statement is a transcription of the full title of the original French work, *Parallèle de l' Architecture Antique et de la moderne avec un recueil des dix principaux autheurs qui ont écrit des cinq ordres: Sçavoir Palladio et Scamozzi, Serlio et Vignola, D. Barbaro et Cataneo, L. B. Alberti et Viola, Bullant et de Lorme, comparez entre eux* . . . [Edme Martin] Paris, 1650. Evelyn's translation, entitled *A Parallel of the ancient Architecture with the modern . . . to which is added an account of Architects and Architecture . . . with L. B. Alberti's Treatise of Statues; made English for the benefit of builders* . . . was first published in 1664, and reissued in 1669, both of which editions are dedicated to Sir John Denham; *cf. Diary*, 15, 27 Oct. 1664. The title of the 1680 edition, printed for J[ohn] P[lace], was changed to *The Whole Body of Antient and Modern Architecture, With L. B. Alberti's Treatise of Statues . . . adorned with fifty-one copper plates*. The 1697 issue was dedicated to Wren; although the Wren library catalogue only lists a copy of the 1707 issue, Wren's knowledge of the 1664 edition is established by his reference to it in a PS to his letter from Paris, and Evelyn's letter to Wren, 4 April 1665 (printed WS XIII, p.40), which mentions a presentation copy. A third edition of *A Parallel* was printed posthumously, in 1723, including the addition of Wotton's *Elements*; a reissue, called the 4th edition, was published in 1733. The value of de Chambray's book has been variously assessed. Briggs, *op. cit.* (1953), misdates it to 1651 and describes it misleadingly as 'based upon the rules of Palladio'; Blomfield, quoted by Hiorns, *Symposium*, p.17, calls it 'one of the most valuable treatises on the details of Renaissance architecture ever written' but in *Touchstone*, p.179, condemns both Serlio's 'very inaccurate *Architettura*' and Fréart's 'still more inaccurate *Parallel*'.

607 *Cf.* Thomas Hyde's *Catalogus impressorum librorum Bibliothecae Bodlejane*, 1674 which lists no fewer than seven Vitruvius editions: Venice 1523; (Barbaro) Venice 1567; (Philander) 1552, (*id*.) Lyon 1586 and 1550; (Cesariano) Como 1521; (de Laet) Amsterdam 1649. The catalogue also lists the Paris 1512 and Florence 1550 editions of Alberti; Serlio, 1545–7, 1544, and 1569; and the (3rd) edition of Palladio, Venice 1601 (*cf.* Abstract, lot 529, and *v. infra*, note 646).

608 *Diary*, 29 Aug. 1678.

609 Cunningham, *op. cit*., IV, pp.166–7.

610 *De Architectura*, I, iii, 2.

611 Cunningham, *op. cit*., IV, p.171.

612 *De Architectura*, IX, vii–viii.

613 *ibid*., IX, viii, 8, describing the water clock of Ctesibius.

614 *ibid*., X, iv.

615 *ibid*., VII, i.

616 *ibid*., X, ix.

617 *ibid*., X, *passim*.

618 The strictly Vitruvian precedent discernible in the plan study for St Magnus (Fig.21) and the plan of St Anne (Fig.23) has been pointed out by Summerson, *art. cit*., pp.127, 129. In the latter instance, this would support our early dating as Wren is more likely to have been influenced by classical models during his formative years than later.

619 *Cf.* Wittkower, *Architectural Principles in the Age of Humanism*, London 1949, p.7.

620 Wren changed the pillars to piers in the lower order; *cf.* ASC II, 54, 56 (WS IX, pl.13).

621 *Cf.* Wittkower, *op. cit*., p.30.

622 *De Re Aedificatoria* (1550 ed.) pp.251 *et seq. Cf.* also Palladio, *Quattro Libri* (1661 ed.) III, cap.xix 'Delle Basiliche Antiche,' referring to SS. Cosmo and Damian, 'nellaquale rendeuano giustitia'. Alberti is following Vitruvian precedent; *cf. De Architectura*, V, *passim*.

623 *De Re Aedificatoria* (1550 ed.) p.251.

624 Drummond, *op. cit*., p.29, thinks, however, that 'to 17th and 18th century Germany we owe a debt, not so much for architectural style, as for experimentation in the plan and arrangement of Protestant churches' and cites Furttembach's treatise of 1649 and Sturm's *Anweisung* of 1718 in support, in the latter of which recommendations for centrally planned churches are to be found. The connexion is as difficult to accept as this author's conception of the centralized plan as a Protestant expression of religious feeling on the premises, *ibid*., p.31, that 'as Religion is "Purity" rather than "Pomp", the beauty of a church should be derived from Form rather than Ornament', the thesis that 'the reformed service called for compression and simplicity, and the natural tendency was to approximate to the square of circular "Zentralbau" type that became so popular in Germany', and lastly, the contention that 'the Catholic finds a natural delight in Colour, which the Puritan cannot find theologically acceptable and temperamentally congenial; thus the Puritan is thrown back on Form, expressive of clearness, sobriety, and dignity'. It is difficult to decide whether this monochrome/polychrome concept of religion and all its implications is the result of ignorance or a partisan distortion of the facts. The centrally planned church was derived in both Wren's and Sturm's case from early Renaissance models, and not a novel and inherently Protestant conception of church architecture. Wren's indebtedness to Furttembach appears to us as non-existent as the Palladians' debt to Sturm. Also *v. infra*, note 858.

625 *De Re Aedificatoria*, ed. *cit*., pp.207, 208. Alberti is explicit in his derivation of centralized plans from early Christian precedent; for Palladio's recommendations of circular plans, *v. infra*, p.154. Circumstances prevented Palladio from carrying out the precept in his two major Venetian churches, but the church at Maser, as well as his pupil Francesco Zamberlano's octagonal church of B.V. del Soccorso at Rovigo can be pointed to as practical realizations.

626 Serlio, *Regole generale di Architettura* . . . (hereafter cited as *Regole*) 1663 ed., V, pp.369, 377, 379, 382, 386, 389, 375.

627 The decagon appears only *ibid*., I, p.26, among geometrical figures, but not in V, Temples.

628 First at the Hradčany Palace in Prague; for derivations from that prototype, *cf.* Donin, *Vincenzo Scamozzi und sein Einfluss auf die Salzburger Architektur*, Innsbruck, 1948 pl.72.

629 e.g. the triumphal arch at Orange and the so-called Isis temple at Pompei. Alberti's most easily accessible precedent, which he doubtless knew, would have been the Roman Tempio Clituno at Campello near Perugia, the fifth-century porch of which is thus formed. Wren certainly

would have known the instance of the temple at Trevi, *Quattro Libri*, (1601 ed.), IV, p.101.

630 Serlio's book was first published in Venice, 1537–40; L. Milman, *op. cit.*, p.134, erroneously gives 1560, Blomfield, *Six Architects*, p.19, 1532, as publication dates.

631 G. Webb in Cobb, *op. cit.*, p.11.

632 *The First booke of Architecture, made by S. Serly* . . . translated out of Italian into Dutch, and out of Dutch into English, five parts [E. Stafford] London 1611. This version was based on the Dutch edition of P. Coeck, *Den eersten boeck van Architecturen S. Serlii* . . . Antwerpen 1553, which is itself a version of the German edition of Coeck and Rechtlinger, *Die gemaynen Regeln von der Architectur* . . . Antorf 1542 (*cf.* Vasari, *Lives*, Divers Flemish Artists) so that Peake derived his version at third hand.

633 L. Milman, *op. cit.*, p.134; the suggestion is repeated by Whitaker-Wilson, *op. cit.*, p.210, and Sitwell, *op. cit.*, p.47. The passage in question, *Regole* (1663), III, p.125, furnishes no corroboration of Briggs's statement, *op. cit.* (1951), p.36, that for the Sheldonian Theatre 'Wren deliberately adopted the design of the ancient Theatre of Marcellus' from Serlio.

634 *Cf.* Abstract, lot 540. The fact that Peake's edition does not appear in the 1674 Bodleian Library Catalogue (*v. supra*, note 607) is significant; as the work was never reprinted, it is likely to have been out of print and unobtainable long before Wren took up architecture.

635 ASC IV, 58 (not reproduced in WS).

636 *Regole* (1663), III, p.89

637 *Quattro Libri* (1601 ed.), IV, pp.73–83. Other duplications between Serlio III and Palladio, IV, are: the temple of Bacchus (Serlio, p.100, Palladio, pp.85–7); Temple of Peace (Serlio, p.103, Palladio, pp.11–14); Temple of Vesta (Serlio, p.107, Palladio, pp.90–4); Bramante's Tempietto (Serlio, pp.122–3, Palladio, pp.64–6); *cf.* also Desgodetz (Abstract, lot 547), pls.5, 64, 82, 105 for engravings of the Pantheon, the Temples of Bacchus, Vesta, Tivoli, and Temple of Peace.

638 *Regole* (1663), III, p.143.

639 *ibid.*, p.394.

640 ASC I, 58 (not reproduced in WS).

641 *Cf.* for example, the numerous variations of such tetrastyle porticos given in the German paraphrase of Scamozzi, *Grund-Regeln der Baukunst oder klärliche Beschreibung der Fünff Säülen Ordnungē und der gantzen Architectur des berühmten Baumeisters Vincent Scamozzi aus dem Italienischen ins Hochdeutsch übersetzt*, Nürnberg 1678, caps.xxii–xxiv, pp.79–89, esp. fols.81, 86, 87 referring to Ionic porticos only; sections of comparable length are given to the Doric, Corinthian, and composite variants.

642 *Cf.* the explicit reference in *Regole* (1537 ed.) II, fol.1 *recto*, to 'consummatissimo Baldassar Peruzzi'. The possibility even exists that Leonardesque material found its way into Serlio's treatise: Cellini possessed a MS. copy of Leonardo's treatise on architecture, sculpture, and painting, of which he gave the former two sections to Serlio whom he had met while working in France; these parts of the treatise must now be presumed lost; the Treatise on Painting survived in several copies. *Cf.* Leonardo da Vinci, *Traité de la Peinture*, ed. Péladan, Paris 1940, p.3.

643 *Regole* (1663), p.395.

644 The Paris (Institut de France) MS. B (*c.*1488–9) esp. fols.18 *verso* and 57 *verso*; also the Paris (Bibliothèque Nationale) MS. 2037, *passim*.

645 *Quattro Libri* (1601), II, p.67.

646 As appears from the Catalogue (*cf.* Abstract), Wren possessed Leoni's edition of 1715, Richard's translation of the First Book, and a Venetian edition of 1601. This is actually a reissue of the (2nd) 1581 edition, also printed by Carampello. There are no textual differences between these and the *editio princeps* of 1570.

647 Wren may have had knowledge of the town-planning essay of the town of Richelieu, to which both Evelyn and Pratt refer in their writings; that

the cardinal's enterprise was very probably influenced by Italian philosophical conceptions seems indicated by his appointment of Tommaso Campanella, the author of *Città del Sole* (1623) to head the theological academy of St Victor; for Campanella's significant dedication of the 1637 edition of his work to Richelieu, *cf.* Yates, *op. cit.*, p.292, note 1, and *Journ. Warb. Court. Inst.*, III, 3–4, p.250, note 6. Yates, however, makes no mention of the academy of which Evelyn speaks in his *Diary*, 14 Aug. 1644, but the reference to the 'houses . . . built exactly uniform, after a modern handsome design' as well as Pratt's references to the town make it appear as if Campanella's town-planning ideas had found some reflection in the building of Richelieu, though the designs are due to Le Mercier.

648 *v. supra*, notes 52, 53.

649 *Quattro Libri* (1601), III, cap.xvi: '. . . rendono ancho molto ornamento, ritrouandosi à capo di vna luogo bello, e specioso, dalque si veda l'aspetto di qualche bella fabrica, e massimamente di qualche Tempio.'

650 *ibid.*, *loc. cit.*

651 It is amusing to recall the opinion of Birch, *op. cit.*, p.10, holding that Wren 'never attempted huge columns, porticos, and pediments borrowed from heathen temples.'

652 Wren was aware of such functions even though he did not provide for them; this is clear from his advice that churches should be 'adorned with *useful* porticos.'

653 *Quattro Libri*, *ed. cit.*, IV, cap.ii, p.7: 'Deuono hauere i Tempij i portici ampij, & con maggior colonne di quello, che ricerchino le altre fabriche, & stà bene che essi siano grandi, e Magnifici . . . & con grandi, e belle proportioni fabricati.'

654 Possibly also the Tempio del Sole, *ibid.*, cap.x, p.37.

655 Wittkower, *op. cit.*, p.83, points to the somewhat vague description in Virtuvius, V, i, 10, of the basilica at Fano, with its 'double arrangement of gables', but whether this represented a similar solution to Palladio's is not clear. While the reconstruction of the building in Philander's Virtuvius edition of 1544 (*ibid.*, pl.32b) may be largely fanciful, the possibility exists that the extant twelfth-century duomo of Fano reflects at least some features of Vitruvius's original building; but *v. infra*, note 656.

656 A large number of Lombard churches show similar systems of roofing double-aisled basilican structures; the outstanding examples are S. Celso and S. Vincenzo in Milan, S. Michele in Cremona, S. Fedele in Como, and that most interesting example in the same town, S. Abondio, where the angles and breaks of three pediments are used to articulate the four aisles. The classic examples are, of course, S. Zeno and S. Fermo in Verona; none of these, however, possesses orders or pediments in the classical sense (*cf.* Porter, *Lombard Architecture*, Yale 1917, IV, *passim*); these were probably first used by Bramante at S. Maria di S. Satiro, Milan, and the cathedral at Carpi, attributed to Peruzzi (*cf.* Wittkower, *op. cit.*, p.81, pls.32a, c).

657 In addition to the examples quoted above, old St Peter's must be mentioned as well as the very interesting church of Sant'Agostino in Rome, both of whose façades retained the horizontal division of the central section and thus foreshadowed the design of the Gesú.

658 Memorandum on San Francesco della Vigna by Francesco Giorgi, quoted by Wittkower, *op. cit.*, p.137. The same stipulation is implied by Evelyn's remarks on Montague House, *Diary*, 10 Oct. 1683, where 'the fronts of the house are not answerable to the inside'.

659 St Paul's, west front study, StPL II, 140 (WS III, pl.xiv).

660 *Quattro Libri*, *ed. cit.*, II, p.60.

661 Wittkower, *op. cit.*, p.71.

662 St Mary Aldermanbury; St Michael Wood Street; St Lawrence; St Mary le Bow; St Bride; Christ Church; St Margaret Pattens; St Andrew Wardrobe; St Andrew Holborn; the Custom House; Tring House; Fawley Court; Middle Temple Gateway; Winchester Palace; Winslow Hall; St Paul's transepts; and [?] design for a house, BM Sloane 5238, 60 (WS V, pl.xxviii).

663 For instance, at San Francesco, Rimini, and Sant'Andrea, Mantua.

664 T. F. Bumpus, *op. cit.*, p.362, has noted the unusual combination, but failed to draw attention to the side elevation of the Loggia del Capitaniato (also known as the Palazzo del Consiglio) at Vicenza, where Palladio employed a Tuscan over a Composite order, a combination probably derived from the Porta de' Borsari at Verona (*cf.* Wittkower, *op. cit.*, p.78). Anderson, *The Architecture of the Renaissance in Italy* (1927 ed.), p.210, quotes Palladio's rules for the disposition of the orders, citing the Basilica and the Palazzo Porto Barbarano as examples of conformity, but fails to draw attention to this instance where the superposition of Tuscan over composite is not sanctioned by Palladio's writings.

665 e.g. the Hagia Sophia. Fletcher, *Andrea Palladio*, London 1902, calls the type Roman for no apparent reason known to us.

666 To cite only the most outstanding instances: S. Fantino, S.M. della Carmine, S. Fosca, S. Giacomo di Rialto, S. Geremia, S. Giovanni decollato, S. Gallo, S. Guiseppe, S. Lorenzo, S. Margherita, S.M. Mater Domini, S.M. della Salute, S. Moisè, S. Pantaleone, S. Rocco, S. Silvestro, S. Vitale, Scamozzi's S. Lazzaro dei Mendicanti and S. Niccolò dei Tolentini, and the chiesa della Pietà.

667 Francesco Guardi's painting at Vienna (Akademie der bildenden Künste) shows the front extremely well; *cf.* Goering, *Francesco Guardi*, Vienna, 1944, pl.vii.

668 *Cf. Quattro Libri, ed. cit.*, II, pp.47, 49.

669 In addition, the occurrence, though bipartite, in the unidentified drawing ASC IV, 66 (not reproduced in WS).

670 Particularly in S. Francesco di Paolo, S. Trovaso and S, Pietro in Castello. Whether this last instance is due to Palladio is impossible to decide. Palladio's original design for this church of *c.*1588 is now lost. Wren's treatment of the central window of St Mildred, Bread Street, recalls the present S. Pietro in Castello, built by Francesco Smeraldi, 1594–6.

671 The earlier instances found are significantly due to Italian architects, such as S. Maria at Alt-Bunzlau in Bohemia, built 1617–23 by Jacopo Evaccini, and the small church of S.M. della Vittoria in Prague, built 1636–40 by an unknown architect clearly influenced by Scamozzi. Similar windows are also found in Scamozzi's design and Solari's execution in Salzburg cathedral (*cf.* Donin, *op. cit.*, p.57), which provided very probably the model for Fischer von Erlach's similar windows in the church of the Hospital of St John in the same city, though he does not seem to have used the type in any later designs.

672 Loftie, *op. cit.*, pp.vii–viii, motivates his application of the term 'Palladian' to Wren by the allegedly undefined meaning, and the 'foreign sound' of the word 'Renaissance'; and opines, *ibid.*, p.180, that though the design of St Mary Aldermary is 'Gothic in its general form, it was strictly Palladian in details' of the spire; lastly states, *ibid.*, p.279, that Inigo Jones and Burlington, as well as Wren, 'were and acknowledged themselves to be, under the influence of Palladio rather than Bramante or Vignola, or Sansovino, or San Gallo, or any other great Italian of that time'. There is nothing, though, in Wren's writings to confirm this assertion. Palladian influence, through Jones's agency, is also stressed by Stratton, *op. cit.*, p.5; and Weaver, *op. cit.*, p.57, thinks that Wren's allegedly French orientation might have led him to become a follower of Vignola rather than Palladio.

673 According to Adshead, *RIBA Mem. Vol.*, p.164, Wren's work at Trinity, Pembroke, and Emmanuel Colleges, when 'compared with his later works shows that he was directly influenced by the work of his predecessor Inigo Jones, and by such Palladian architecture to the illustration of which he would, at the time, have access'. In contrast, Blomfield, *Short Hist.*, p.121, thinks that 'as Wren advanced in experience and mastery of his art . . . he returned to the purer and more strenuous architecture of Inigo Jones'.

674 Loftie, *op. cit.*, p.98.

675 *V. supra*, note 25, *infra*, note 975.

676 The arcade of the Cour Ovale.

677 To cite but the principal examples: St Paul's: ASC II, 22; StPL I, 50, and interior, WS XIV, pl.iii; drum, StPL II, 161; studies, ASC II, 31, 32, 59, 61, StPL II, 145, 163; east end, ASC II, 36; south elevation (WS XIV, pl.xv); north elevation (WS XIV, pl.x); dome study, StPL II, 171; chapel screen [Sotheby 3(28)]; also St Mary Aldermanbury, St Lawrence, St Dionis, Bow, St Antholin, St Nicholas, St Stephen Walbrook, St Mary Ingestre, St James Garlick Hill, St Michael Bassishaw, SS. Anne and Agnes, St Peter, St Michael Cornhill, St Martin, Christ Church, St Benet, Thames Street, All Hallow, Thames Street, St Swithin, St Augustine, St Clement Eastcheap, St Margaret Pattens, St Magnus, St Bartholomew, Abingdon Town Hall, Christ's Hospital, Westminster Dormitory, St Paul's Chapter House, Winchester Palace, etc.

678 *Quattro Libri, ed. cit.*, IV, cap.v: 'Ma però ne' Tempij Antichi non si veggono piedestili, ma le colonne cominciano dal piano del Tempio; ilche molto più mi piace . . . si anco perche le colonne, le quali da terra cominciano; rendono maggior grandezza, e magnificenza.' High plinths occur, of course, on the front of S. Giorgio Maggiore, and were praised by Fletcher, *op. cit.*, p.86, for achieving a better proportion [*sic*] than that of the Redentore; equally, *ibid.*, p.89, he thinks S. Francesco has 'another fault' in 'the management of the orders, for too great a contrast is obtained by starting both the principal and subsidiary order from the same base, the treatment of S. Giorgio being preferable'. This criticism must rest on disregard or ignorance of the passage from *Quattro Libri* quoted above, as well as ignorance of the fact that the west front of S. Giorgio was executed, after Palladio's death, to a revised design by Scamozzi, who introduced the plinths in deviation from the original design (ill. Wittkower, *op. cit.*, pl.33b). Fletcher's preference of 'better proportions' is as arbitrary as his condemnation of the 'too great a contrast', as both façades were designed strictly on a system of geometrical proportional ratios; *v. infra*, pp.134 *et seq.*

679 Notably those of Septimus Severus, of Titus, of Constantine and of Drusa. The Roman practice was, of course, also carried over the empire: *cf.* the triumphal arch at Orange, the Porta Nigra at Trèves, *et al. Cf.* also Alberti, *De Re Aedificatoria, ed. cit.*, p.294, and Serlio, *Regole*, III, cxi, cxix, cxxiii.

680 The Roman examples are rare and confined to: Raphael's and San Gallo's Villa Madama, Bramante's S.M. della Pace, Maderno's S. Susanna and S. Andrea della Valle, Vignola's Gesù and Porto del Popolo, Fontana's S. Marcello, the so-called Palazzina di Pio IV, and the Palazzo Venezia. The examples in Venice are too numerous to cite, but *cf.* Donin, *op. cit.*, p.25. The Venetian predilection can already be seen in the illustrations of Colonna's *Hypnerotomachia Poliphili*, 1499.

681 Palladian influence may have been responsible for the three-bay terminations of the transepts of the Greek cross design (Fig.37). The sequence of round-headed units flanking a central rectangular one can be traced to *Quattro Libri, ed. cit.*, II, p.42, and III, p.34; the internal usage in the apse of the Maser church is clearly related to *ibid.*, II, pp.39, 40.

682 A similar scheme occurs in the Abingdon Town Hall; *cf.* WS XIX, pls.lvii–lviii; as well as in a design for Whitehall, ASC II, 106 (WS VII, pl.ix).

683 San Francesco, Rimini.

684 For instance, the peristyle of Diocletian's palace at Spalato; *cf.* Adam, *Ruins of the Palace* . . . etc. (1764), pl.viii.

685 For example, Peruzzi's Palazzo Linotto and the house in Via Julia, Rome.

686 Basilica, Casa di Palladio and Loggia del Capitaniato, Vicenza; Villa Poiana Maggiore; designs for S. Petronio, Bologna.

687 *Cf.* Vanbrugh: garden pavilions, King's Weston; 1st floor windows of corner turrets, Grimsthorpe Castle; top storey of corner turrets, Eastbury House. Inigo Jones: central window of 1st and 2nd floors of

Whitehall Palace. Isaac Ware: Wrotham, Middlesex. Wm. Kent: five occurrences in the north front of Holkham (Loftie, *op. cit.*, p.234, mistakenly gives seven). Adam: three in each side pavilion, Kedleston. Burlington: at Burlington House, Chiswick, Gen. Wade's house. Gibbs: St Martin's in the Fields, All Saints, Derby. Paine: entry of Middlesex Hospital. Flitcroft, St Giles. Stuart, Montagu House, Portman Square. James and Vanbrugh: St Alphege, Greenwich; Hawksmoor: porch of Christ Church, Spitalfields; etc. as well as Gibbsian and other derivatives in New England, such as Christ Church, Cambridge, Mass., the Baptist Meeting House, Providence, R.I., *et al.*

688 As we have seen, Wren considered the employment of the motif on several occasions, principally in the vestry window of Bow Church (Fig.17)**,** the study for St Stephen's Walbrook, ASC I, 60 (WS IX, pl.33) and the chronologically related Greek cross design (*cf.* esp. the section, ASC II, 23; WS I, pl.xviii).

689 Wren's familiarity with this building is proved by his possession of de Rossi's *Insignium* (Abstract, lot 551), which contains an engraving of the façade, pl.51, although St James's was completed in 1684, when the book was published.

690 *cf.* Brissac, *op. cit.*, p.82.

691 *Quattro Libri*, IV, xxxii.

692 This applies to painting as well as architecture; the spandrels of the arcade of Brunelleschi's Foundling Hospital in Florence are perhaps the earliest instance; see also Masaccio's Trinity at S.M. Novella, Florence; Gentile Bellini's St Mark preaching, at the Brera, Milan; Cima da Conegliano's Presentation at Dresden; Filippo Lippi's Madonna at the Palazzo Riccardi, Florence; and particularly Vecchietta's San Bernardino in the Walker Art Gallery, Liverpool, where the entire scheme of the 'motif Palladio' with flanking circular lights is developed into a most elaborate architectural background.

693 For instance, Temple of Jupiter, *Quattro Libri*, IV, 43 and 47; as well as the Temple of Diana at Nîmes, Serlio, *Regole*, III, cxlviii and Palladio, *Quattro Libri*, IV, cap.xix [*sic.* a misprint in the 1601 ed. for xxix].

694 The sole instance, the bell tower of S. Giacomo a Rialto, is too whimsical and insignificant an example to warrant inclusion. Scamozzi's Palazzo Cornaro of 1602 is, of course, of Palladian derivation.

695 Apart from the Baptistery, Raphael's Palazzo Pandolfini and Vasari's Uffizi.

696 Palazzi Chiericati, Thiene, Porto Barbarano, Teatro Olimpico, the so-called Casa del Diavolo (Antica Posta); *cf. Quattro Libri*, II, 7, 8, 14, 15, 23, 74.

697 The Banqueting House, Whitehall; also Brympton, and the river front of Somerset House, sometimes attributed to Jones.

698 1st floor windows of the Galérie du bord de l'eau, Louvre, by Louis Métezeau, 1595–1610. Also the additions of du Cerceau and du Pérac, *cf.* Blomfield, *Hist. Fr. Ren. Arch.*, II, pl.c.

699 ASC I, 85 (WS VII, pl.xv); *cf.* also ASC V, 5 (WS VIII, pl.iv); and the version, in pairs, in the Abingdon Town House, *c.*1677 (Caröe, *op. cit.*, pl.xxvii).

700 ?1694; SM II, 7 (WS VI, pl.xxi) and ASC V, 24 (WS VIII, pl.xix); *cf.* also the design retaining the same features, before 1702, SM II, 16 (WS VI, pl.xxi) where the bases of the triangular pediments are complete, but the segmental pediments rest on brackets only.

701 The employment of the device at the Ashmolean Museum, Oxford, may be taken as proof *per negationem* against Wren's alleged authorship proposed by Bray (ed. *Diary*, note to 23 July 1678); Milman, *op. cit.*, p.306; Stratton, *op. cit.*, p.23. The same reason could be advanced for discrediting Wren's authorship of Fishmongers' Hall alleged by Phillimore, *op. cit.*, p.340 (*cf.* the engraving printed by Phillips, *op. cit.*, p.47), where ground floor, first floor, and attic windows all have alternating pediments; in this instance, documentary evidence (*ibid.*, p.60) conclusively supports Jerman's authorship.

702 For example, Gibbs: Senate House, Cambridge; St Mary le Strand.

Vardy: Spencer House. Burlington: Burlington and Westminster House Dormitory (WS XI, pl.xxvii). Wood: Priory Park, Bath. Flitcroft: Wentworth Woodhouse, *et al.*

703 *De Re Aedificatoria* (1550 ed.), VII, cap. iiii, p.206: 'Ne Tempi quadri usarono gli Antichi che la pianta fusse una meza volta piu lungo che largo. Altri usarono il terzio piu lungo che larga. E altri volzano che la fusse lunga due largezza.' For the Vitruvian connexion of these proportions, *v. infra*, note 844.

704 *Regole* (1663 ed.), p.27. The latter was probably not entirely novel but derived from *De Re Aedificatoria, ed. cit.*, p.31, where the root two rectangle is adumbrated in a diagram, though not, of course, recommended as a preferred proportion for plans. The ultimate derivation may be in *De Architectura*, VI, iii, 3.

705 *Quattro Libri, ed. cit.*, I, p.52: 'Le più belle e proportionate maniere di stanze, e che riescono meglio sono sette: percioche ò si faranno ritonde, e questa di rado; ò quadrate; ò la longhezza loro sarà per la linea diagonale del quadrato della larghezza, ò d'vn quadro & vn terzo; ò d'vn quadro e mezo, ò d'vn quadro e due terzi, ò di due quadri.'

706 Loftie, *op. cit.*, p.viii, interprets Palladio's occasional disregard of the 'rules' as a 'freedom' which 'as much as anything recommended his views on the Italian style . . . to the admiring notice of posterity' and to its eventual adoption in England. This view is superficial and distorted in so far as it not only ignores the fact that Palladio's design is only very rarely contrary to theory, but also takes no account of the fact that the *Quattro Libri* contain explicit sanction for specific divergence from the 'rules'. For Palladio's express sanction of variations in the proportions of the orders, *v. infra*, note 977; for his sanction of other than the three classical proportional means applied to the height of rooms, *cf. Quattro Libri, ed. cit.*, I, p.54.

707 Wittkower, *op. cit.*, pp.51–88, 110–24. This author, however, in his final chapter on 'The Break-away from the Laws of Harmonic Proportions' mentions only Wotton and the eighteenth- and nineteenth-century English theorists and aestheticians, without mentioning Jones, Pratt, and Wren. The works of the former two cannot be adequately discussed within the scope of this study; for the important references found in Sir Francis Bacon and John Donne, *v. infra*, p.173 and note 1019.

708 Stratton, *op. cit.*, p.29.

709 Sir Aston Webb, *RIBA Mem. Vol.*, p.4. In contrast, T. F. Bumpus, *op. cit.*, p.285, thinks that Wren's proportions were not the outcome of logical deduction or scientific search, but of instinct, and gives, *ibid.*, p.320, St James, Westminster, as 'an example of Wren's love of harmony in proportions' whose 'breadth is half the sum of its height and length, its height half its length, and its breadth the sesquilateral of its height, the numbers being 86, 63 and 42 feet,' and *ibid.*, p.382, points to St Peter's, Cornhill, of which 'the length within the walls is 80 feet, the breadth 47 feet and the height 40 feet, being nearly a double cube'; these mathematical relationships do not seem to indicate 'instinctive' proportions, unless such, ideally, would amount to arithmetically correct ratios. Concretely, Wren's drawings do not offer any evidence for the application of geometrical ratios; *v. infra*, p.136, for the only drawing which can thus be interpreted.

710 *Cf.* the highly significant passage in Dryden, *Nature and Dramatic Art* (1681): 'But as in a room contrived for State, the height of the roof should bear a proportion to the area . . .'

711 Cunningham, *op. cit.*, IV, p.147.

712 *Parentalia*, p.326; *cf.* however the measurements given by Law, *op. cit.*, III, pp.88, 92, of the Guard Chamber, 60 ft 6 in × 37 ft 3 in × 28 ft, and the Great State Bedchamber, 33 ft 9 in × 23 ft 7 in. × 30 ft.

713 It is, of course, possible to construe the façade into conformity with Palladio; the centre part of the upper storey, including the pediment, approximately forms a square, as do the sections covered by the half pediments; the dimension of the latter practically equals the height of the ground storey minus the podium, but inclusive of the architrave. But

the two units thus established do not harmonize, as they are related in the ratio of (approximately) 11:7.

714 The drawing recalls the four corner pavilions of the plan for Norfolk House, ASC II, 102 (WS XII, pl.xv), but the dimensions differ; the latter design is broadly based on a 30 ft module, with a total site of 630 ft by 600 ft, but the application of the module, if intentional, is inconsistent: measurements of 10 ft, 20 ft, 40 ft, and 50 ft, occur as well as 170 ft, 230 ft, and 320 ft.

715 Loftie's opinion, *op. cit.*, p.192, that Wren's Greek cross design 'made no provision whatever for Roman Catholic worship' must be based on ignorance of the classical R.C. Greek cross plans, such as Michelangelo's S. Giovanni dei Fiorentini, Bramante's St Peter's plan, and all of Leonardo's designs.

716 The parallel with Bramante becomes particularly clear in the study plan for St Paul's ASC II, 64 (WS I, pl.xxvi, lower subject). In the same way as Bramante's plan represents an agglomeration of Greek cross units, so Wren in this one plan designed both nave and choir as identical units in the shape of a Greek cross; the parallel falls short of completeness in the transepts which represent fairly closely the final solution, but a part section included in the drawing shows that the choir, and doubtless the nave also, were to be (externally invisibly) domed. The fact that the choir shows a semi-circular apsidal termination makes the basic concept more similar still to Bramante's.

717 *Cf.* ASC I, 39–44 (WS V, pls.xvi–xxii).

718 Mackmurdo's judgement, *op. cit.*, p.23: 'In Brunelleschi's dome how much individuality, in St Peter's, how little!' does credit neither to the author, nor to Wren in view of Wren's project illustrated p.111.

719 The question of Wren's knowledge of historic prototypes has aroused some controversy. *Cf.* Blomfield, *Short Hist.*, pp.116–17: 'Mr Fergusson has sought for the origin of this masterly conception [i.e. St Stephen's] in certain eastern domes. But Wren had certainly never seen such domes, even if he knew of their existence, and it is more probable that he arrived at his result by pure ingenuity and constructive skill.' Loftie, *op. cit.*, p.280, goes even further when, referring to Fergusson's remark of the dome being 'long a favourite mode of roofing in the East' he opines that 'what Fergusson meant by "the East" I do not know. There was nothing to compare with St Stephen's in India, Syria, or Egypt before the time of Wren, whose design, in any case, must be accounted wholly original'. That domes of this type existed in Armenia and Byzantium centuries before Wren has been shown by Strzygowski, Diehl, and other Byzantine scholars. However, that Wren was interested in such eastern domes, as well as familiar with them from descriptions, becomes clear from evidence. *Cf. The Lives of Francis North* ... etc. (1826), III, p.42, quoted in WS XIX, pp.116–18: 'Our merchant [Sir Dudley North, 1641–91, who lived for many years in the Near East, returning to England in 1680] was a great builder himself, and no foreigner ever looked more strictly into the manner of the Turkish buildings than he had done. But he could not give Sir Christopher Wren satisfaction about their covering their vaults with lead. For, when he had the covering of the great dome of St Paul's in deliberation, he was pleased to enquire of that matter ...' etc. We might further cite John Evelyn's acquaintance with Paduan and Venetian domes to have contributed towards Wren's knowledge, or quote from works in his library from which he could have derived information. But the definite, if chronologically indeterminate refutation of Blomfield's and Loftie's assertions is contained in Wren's 'Tract' II (WS XIX, pp.131–2): 'Another Way [of Vaulting] (which I cannot find by the Ancients, but in the later eastern Empire, as appears at St. Sophia, and by the Example, in all the Mosques and Cloysters of the Dervises, and every where at present in the East), and of all others the most geometrical is composed of Hemispheres, and their Sections only; and whereas a Sphere may be cut all manner of Ways, and that still into Circles, it may be accomodated to lie upon all Positions of the Pillars. I question not but those at Constantinople had it from the Greeks before them; it is so

natural, and is yet found in the present Seraglio, which was the episcopal Palace of old. Now, because I have for just Reasons followed this way in the vaulting of St Paul's. I think it proper to shew, that it is the lightest Manner . . .' etc.

720 ASC IV, 58 (not in WS).

721 Ward, *RIBA Mem, Vol.*, pp.213–14.

722 Sencourt, *op. cit.*, p.xxi. Mackmurdo's statement, *op. cit.*, p.20, that Bernini had 'fired [Wren's] enthusiasm for the architecture of the "New Birth" by showing him his drawings of St Peter's just completed, and of the Louvre, then building' is questionable in inference and wholly erroneous in fact.

723 Stratton, *op. cit.*, p.32.

724 For the Florence duomo, *cf.* ASC II, 43 (WS I, pl.xxvii) which is a comparative section of St Peter's and Brunelleschi's dome.

725 Wightwick, quoted by Longman, *op. cit.*, pp.210–11.

726 StPL II, 168, upper subject (WS XIII, pl.iii).

727 ASCII, 32 (WS I, pl.xxi).

728 The connexion is touched on somewhat contemptuously, though without reference to any specific Wren drawing, by Anderson, *op. cit.*, p.146: 'It is possible that [Bramante's] design, pulled out, so to speak, and with solid masses at intervals in the colonnade, gave Sir Chr Wren a suggestion for his most beautiful dome of St Paul's, in which case Bramante's design had its uses.' The inference, however, is erroneous as far as the completed dome is concerned as the 'pulling out' was clearly inspired by Brunelleschi and Michelangelo, to which latter the 'solid masses at intervals' found in several of Wren's designs are clearly due.

729 In parenthesis, it should be noted that Michelangelo's unexecuted design for S. Giovanni dei Fiorentini does not appear to have influenced any stage of the St Paul's evolution, though Wren would have been familiar with it in or after 1684, when it was published in de Rossi's *Insignium Romae Templorum* (Abstract, 551) pl.48. As regards St Peter's, we cannot establish Wren's knowledge of Michelangelo's design prior to della Porta's and Fontana's alterations. It is suggestive, however, that Wren's identical treatment of the windows conforms to Michelangelo's intention and deviates from the dome as built, as can be seen from the model in the Museo Petriano, where the windows of the drum have triangular pediments throughout, just as the introduction of alternating pediments to the lowest row of lucarnes was a deviation from Michelangelo's original. As an interesting detail, it would be tempting to relate the reclining figures on the pediments of the western towers as shown in some of the 1702 engravings to Michelangelo's Medici chapel, or derivations therefrom, such as, for instance, Palladio's Palazzo Porto Colleoni, Vicenza (*Quattro Libri, ed. cit.*, II, p.9) *et al.*

730 The author is indebted to Prof. Wittkower for drawing his attention to this fact; *cf.* Saxl and Wittkower, *op. cit.*, 46, pl.d, for the Invalides dome reproduced from *Description Générale*, 1683. Loftie's question, *op. cit.*, p.157, 'did Mansart show him any sketches for his future dome of the Invalides' was recognized as patently absurd by Ward, *RIBA Mem. Vol.*, p.206, though this author [followed by Briggs, *op. cit.*, (1953) p.260] makes the equally ludicrous suggestion that it is 'highly probable that the younger Mansart was fired with the ambition of emulating the success of St Paul's the designs for which must have been perfectly well known in Paris by 1690'.

731 Blunt, *op. cit.*, pl.7c.

732 It is only necessary to point to the essential similarity, in spite of differences of scale, between the Bramante design illustrated in Fig.156 and the section of the Maser church printed by Wittkower, *op. cit.*, pl.9b.

733 Hiorns, *art. cit.*, p.20.

734 Wren must, of course, have been aware that his dome construction had no precedent among Renaissance structures; apart from his familiarity with the Pantheon, St Peter's, Florence, and probably Pisa, he knew all details of seventeenth-century dome construction as exemplified in the Gesù, S. Agnese, S. Andrea al Quirinale, S. Carlo alle Quattro Fontane,

S. Ignazio, S. Andrea della Valle, and others from de Rossi's *Insignium*, 1684 (abstract 551).

735 *Cf.* Clark, *RIBA Mem. Vol.*, p.73.

736 *Cf.* Jackson, *op. cit.*, p.281.

737 Blomfield, *Six Architects*, p.16.

738 Newton's illuminating remarks, *European Painting and Sculpture*, London 1945, p.100, are worth quoting: '. . . baroque sculpture . . . tends to fade from the memory, not because it is not memorable but because it is, in the fundamental sense, baroque. It is almost always part of a whole, a detail in a larger conception, and it therefore loses its meaning when it is detached from its context.' The misrepresentation of this tendency, on the other hand, is most clearly stated by Blomfield, *Modernismus*, London 1934, pp.37–8, who holds that Baroque artists 'never recognized the limitations of the arts. Complete inability to realize that each art has its own peculiar province appears in the works of the illusionists, men such as Pozzo, Fumiani, and the Bibbiena family'.

739 The reader must be referred to Mâle, *L'Art religieux du XVIIe siècle*, Paris 1951, as the only large-scale scholarly work on seventeenth-century iconography, in which the question of clerical supervision of iconographical details in works of art is corroborated by a wealth of documentary evidence.

740 St John of the Cross, prologue to *Súbida del Monte Carmelo*, quoted by Brenan, *Horizon*, 89, p.331.

741 We can refer the reader to the admirable plates found in Fokker, *op. cit.*, II, *passim*. It is to be regretted that the illustrations accompanying S. Sitwell's *Southern Baroque Art* (1924) and *German Baroque Sculpture* (1927) are qualitatively not comparable with the sensitive interpretation presented by the texts which, though lacking the documentation of Fokker's study, offer a very penetrating and evocative insight into the concepts of the style. The caustic strictures passed by Blomfield on these works, to be found in *Modernismus*, ch.i, and elsewhere must be taken with the reserve dictated by this author's prejudices and proneness to dogmatic judgements.

742 Numerous quotations could be given from both Ruskin and Blomfield; it is significant, however, that even so perspicacious a critic as Rolland should interpret (*Musiciens d'autrefois*, 1908, p.151) 'une façade de Bernini' as 'surchargée de statues épileptiques, dont les draperies s'envolent, qui agitent les jambes, et tordent leur échine, qui ont la danse de Saint-Guy et tombent dans des colvulsions . . .'

743 A. Huxley, 'Death and the Baroque', *Horizon*, 112, pp.290 *et seq*. In this essay an attempt at a purely psychoanalytical interpretation of Baroque sculpture is made which culminates in the pronouncement that 'in Baroque art, the mystic is represented either as a psychic with supernormal powers, or as an ecstatic, who passes out of history in order to be alone, not with God, but with his or her physiology in a state hardly distinguishable from that of sexual enjoyment'.

744 Blomfield, *Touchstone*, p.206. It should be noted that these were not, as is frequently assumed, of Bernini's invention. The concept of spiral motives decorating pillars has an extremely long history, the first great period of which was the Romanesque (among innumerable examples, *cf.* the cloisters of S. Giovanni in Laterano), while the earliest English instance is most probably found in the Saxon crypt of Repton church. For Vignola's precedents knows to Wren, *cf.* Abstract, 376, pls.41, 42, pp.107, 111.

745 For example, the doorway in King's Lynn, illustrated by Dutton, *op. cit.*, pl.85, and the wall tablets reproduced in WS XII, pl.lii.

746 Quoted by Longman, *op. cit.*, p.112; *cf.* WS XIII, pls.xxvii, xxxi (ASC IV, 74), and xxxii.

747 The reader must be referred to the excellent introduction to that little known subject: Esdaile, *English Church Monuments, 1510–1840*, London 1946.

748 'Tract' I, WS XIX, p.127. Sir Thomas Browne, though not an architect, could see deeper causes than such hypothetical provenances: 'Pyramids, Arches, Obelisks, were but the irregularities of vain-glory and wilde enormities of ancient magnanimity.' (quoted by Whistler, *Sir John Vanbrugh*, London 1938, p.1.)

749 The connexions, particularly during the later seventeenth century, are suggestive: Bushnell, for example, was working in Venice when Lord Tyrconnel persuaded him to return to England. Francis Bird was a pupil of Le Gros, and it may be noted that the skeletons which Huxley, *art. cit.*, considered so significant a feature of the Roman Baroque, recur in a wall monument (the Benson tablet, St Leonard's, Shoreditch), by the very man whom Wren chose to execute the tomb of his daughter Jane.

750 *Cf.* 'Tract I (WS XIX, p.127): 'No pinnacle is worthy enough to appear in the Air but Statute.' Also Wren to Bathurst, 1675 (WS V, p.33): 'The Statues will be a noble Ornament,' and 1692 (*ibid.*, p.15); lastly, Wren's memorandum to the commissioners of St Paul's, 1 Nov. 1717 (Minute Book, WS XVI, pp.130–1): 'My opinion, therefore, is to have statues erected on the four pediments only, which will be a most proper, noble and sufficient ornament.'

751 Dimock, *op. cit.*, pp.59–60.

752 Weaver, *op. cit.*, p.108, expressed a somewhat inappropriate preference, for the monument over the King Charles mausoleum, but fails to identify the drawing in spite of the very obvious symbolism of the decorative details.

753 As done by Blomfield, caption to his plate reproducing the drawing in *Hist. Ren. Arch. Eng.*, I.

754 The criticism of this monument ventured by Blomfield, *Modernismus*, p.39, is indicative of the surprising degree of ignorance masked by dogmatic judgements: 'In the Collegien Kirche, at Salzburg, Fischer von Erlach filled up the lower part of his windows with fat clouds modelled in stucco which go wandering up the walls until they lose themselves in the vault. The impression this sort of thing leaves on the spectator is that of a confused sort of nightmare, in which reason totters, because the evidence of the senses is no longer to be trusted.' Had Blomfield described the complete monument instead of confining himself to one portion of it, it would have become evident to the reader that what is here represented is a literal translation into plastic terms of the passage from Revelation 12: 'And there appeared a great wonder in heaven: a woman clothed with the sun, and the moon under her feet, and upon her head a crown of twelve stars.' Whether 'nightmare' is an appropriate description, and 'the evidence of the senses' a relevant criterion in such a context, need not be discussed. It should be noted though, that the monument is not the work of Fischer himself, as Blomfield assumes, but of Diego Francesco Carlone and Paolo de Allio; analogous to the Queen Mary monument are discussed, however, we feel confident that it reflects Fischer's intentions.

755 WS editors, IX, p.13: 'the apparent extravagance of some of [Wren's] designs can be explained as compromises . . . and nothing is more remarkable than the transition by which the actual work is rendered more reasonable.' The design illustrated in Fig.27, ascribed by the WS editors as for St Benet's, Gracechurch Street, and the Clayton engraving of that structure as built are suggested as supporting this statement. For our rejection of the ascription, *v. supra*, p.21. Nor can we agree that Wren's 'extravagance' should have been due to such motives as pandering to people's attachment to the old fabrics, as implied by the editors; this would certainly not have been the case in such instances as the carved swags of flowers originally designed for the curved buttresses of St Edmund (Fig.20) the omission of which in execution could hardly be said to have rendered the work 'more reasonable'.

756 *Cf.* 'Tract' I (WS XIX, p.127): 'In Buildings where the View is sideways, as in Streets, it is absolutely required that the Composition be square, Intercolumnations equal, Projections not great, the Cornices unbroken, and everything strait, equal and uniform. Breaks in the Cornice, Projectures of the upright Members, Variety, Inequality in the Parts, various Heights of the Roof, serve only to confound the Perspective, and make it deformed, while the Breaches and Projectures are cast one upon another,

and obscure all symmetry.' The WS editors suggest that these strictures be interpreted as observations on the 'Jesuit' façade of de Brosse's St-Gervais in Paris, but this is not likely in view of Wren's explicit reservation of 'where the view is sideways'. Such was never possible at St-Gervais as even at the time of Wren's visit an open space strictly comparable to that of today extended between the Hôtel de Ville and the façade which de Brosse built to the Gothic church. An oblique view of it was as impossible when as it is now, as neither the rue de Brosse, nor the rue Beaudoyer permit a view of the façade. The principal approach to the church is admirably seen in the engraving in Merian's *Topographica Galliae*, I, Paris 1655.

757 *Cf.* Abstract, 542.

758 Blomfield, *Modernismus*, p.35.

759 *Cf.* the Cartaro engraving printed by Fokker, *op. cit.*, II, pl.16.

760 *Cf.* Read, *The Meaning of Art* (1931 ed.), p.95: 'between Northern art and Baroque art there is a bond of natural sympathy which does not exist between Northern and Classical art.' And *ibid.*, p.100: 'it has been suggested by Professor Worringer – and it is a brilliant suggestion – that Rococo is really the re-emergence of the northern spirit in art . . . first fully typified in Gothic.'

761 *Cf.* Blomfield, *Modernismus*, p.42: 'Mr Read ingeniously finds in the Baroque a "re-emergence of the Northern spirit in art, first fully typified in Gothic". But this is exactly what it is not. It had none of the virtues and serious purposes of northern Gothic architecture.' Against this magisterial pronouncement, however, *cf.* Hager, *op. cit.*, pp.45, 127, 131, 142, 149, and the statement, though somewhat over-simplifying the issue, made by Watkin, *Catholic Art and Culture*, London 1947, p.98: 'Baroque is the employment of classical forms by Gothic feeling.'

762 *A Parallel*, quoted in *Parentalia*.

763 *Parentalia*, quoted by Longman, *op. cit.*, pp.85–6.

764 *Vitruvius Britannicus* I, introduction.

765 *Parentalia*, quoted by Longman, *loc. cit.*

766 Blomfield, *Touchstone*, pp.203–4; it is apposite to quote, in this connexion, from the building accounts of the City churches; for example, St Stephen's Walbrook (WS X, p.119), William Newman's account for carving: 'ffor 36 ffoot of huske at 6d per fft. 0.18.0. ffor 6 Boys an ffestoones at 30s each 9.0.0. ffor 30 ffoot of Lace at 2d per fft. 0.5.0; ffor 30 ffoot of large Rafel Leaves at 1s per fft. 1.10.0. ffor 44 ffoot of Small Leaves 5d per ft. 0.18.6' etc. That this account was by no means unusual, and that not only Wren's churches, but others as well, are covered by 'ornament skilfully executed' but clearly representing 'a tradesman's skill paid for by the yard' is borne out by all other contracts for City churches and St Paul's; *cf.* also Whiffen, *op. cit.*, p.24, for the carving work specified in May 1711 for St Philipp's, Birmingham, where the carver was to execute 'architrave and cornish round the said ailes for half-a-crown the foot running measure'.

767 Réau, *L'Art religieux du Moyen-Age*, Paris 1946, p.36. *Cf.* also the comparable use of the term by Focillon, *Peintures Romanes*, Paris 1950, p.37, and by Kendrick, *Anglo-Saxon Art*, London 1938, pp.171, 184, 185, and 193: 'the Ethelwulfian "Baroque"'.

768 *Cf.* on this subject Pevsner, *op. cit.*, p.147; Hager, *op. cit.*, pp.124–8; and *v. infra*, p.157.

769 Dodgson, *Catalogue of Woodcuts in the British Museum*, No.116, dated 1511.

770 Completed 1743; illustrated by Hager, *op. cit.*, pl.128.

771 e.g. S. Agnese by Borromini and the Trinità dei Monte by de Sanctis, possibly based on Gueffier's plan; S. Anastasio was, of course, a Greek church.

772 Modifications of the Gesù type significantly occur already in the earliest Austrian Baroque churches, such as the (Jesuit) university church, 1627, the 'Scots' church, 1638–48, in Vienna; St Charles Borromé in Antwerp, 1621, with a compromise solution of domed towers, attests to the diffusion of the modification. The geographical distribution of types is also

significant: the twin-tower façade became practically the standard type in Austria, Bavaria, and Switzerland, as exemplified by Fischer von Erlach's Holy Trinity and university church in Salzburg, Hildebrandt's St Peter's in Vienna, Salzburg Cathedral, the Innsbruck churches of St James and Wilten, Prandtauer's church of Melk Abbey, Dientzenhofers' Banz, Neumann's Würzberg 'Käppele' and Vierzehnheiligen, Einsiedeln, St Gall *et al.* In the east, the twin-tower scheme is only rarely found which fact may corroborate our thesis (the monastic church of Grüssau in Silesia, by an unknown architect, is altogether exceptional in such a location; while the churches of St John Nepomucene, St Nicholas in, and the church at Kladno, near Prague as well as St Magdalene at Karlsbad are not by native, but by a Franconian architect). The instances of façades employing a single tower, such as Neubirnau, Dürnstein, die Wies *et al.* are numerically too few to invalidate our theory.

773 *Cf.* in this context, the statement in 'Tract' I (WS XIX, p.127): 'Fronts ought to be elevated in the middle, not the Corners; because the Middle is the place of greatest Dignity, and first attracts the eye.'

774 The west front of St Paul's does not, of course, invalidate this generalization, as its twin towers are the only logical corollary to the dome.

775 *Regole*, 1663 ed., V, pp.390, 420, where twin towers with domical cappings are shown, and p.398, where the towers are capped with obelisks; the former type would have been known to Wren from the concrete example of S. Atanasius in Rome, illustrated by de Rossi, *Insignium Romae Templorum* (Abstract, lot 551), pl.62.

776 That Gothic elements should have contributed towards the formation of Wren's style was vaguely suggested by Mackmurdo, *op. cit.*, pp.10–12, in describing Wren's style as Renaissance 'slightly seasoned with the salt of Gothic character'; Wightwick's critical interpretation of the St Paul's west front, quoted by Longman, *op. cit.*, p.206, as a 'Gothic idea Romanised' seems largely beyond the limit of formalistic analysis.

777 WS IX, p.17.

778 Drummond, *op. cit.*, p.28.

779 Loftie, *op. cit.*, pp.188, 191.

780 *Diary*, Sunday 26 May 1667.

781 Addleshaw and Etchells, *The Architectural Setting of Anglican Worship*, London 1948, p.54. *Cf.* also L. Milman, *op. cit.*, p.117.

782 L. Milman, *ibid.*, p.243.

783 *Regole* (1540), V, fol.4 *recto*; (1663), p.375.

784 Sta Anna dei Palefrenieri, *c.*1570.

785 It should be noted that the idea was not wholly original; it had been theoretically expounded by Francesco di Giorgio, *c.*1470 (*cf.* Wittkower, *op. cit.*, pl.1a) and concretely carried out at Siena, Pisa, Florence, Pavia, and Loreto.

786 *Cf.* Borromini's San Carlo alle Quattro Fontane, Rome, begun 1633, the plan of which is clearly derived from Serlio as quoted *supra*, note 783. For Bernini, *cf.* the oval Piazza San Pietro in Rome, enclosed within the famous colonnade, and S. Andrea al Quirinale as well as the Capella Cornaro in S.M. della Vittoria. For Guarini, *cf.* the (posthumous) *Architettura Civile*, Torino 1737, *passim*. Wren's knowledge of all but the last is documentarily established by his possession of de Rossi's *Insignium Romae Templorum* (Abstract, lot 551) which illustrates the St Peter's colonnade, pls.8, 10, the San Carlo alle Quattro Fontane plan, pl.16, the plan of S. Andrea al Quirinale, pl.25, and the Cornaro chapel in the appendix.

787 For example, Le Vau's oval hall of Vaux-le-Vicomte and the Collège des Quatre Nations, 1657 and 1661.

788 St Cajetan, 1685–1700.

789 Holy Trinity, Salzburg, National (former Imperial) Library, Vienna; the exception being the university church, Salzburg.

790 The plan seemed to be popular in Bohemia even before the Dientzenhofers' influence; *cf.* Hegemann, *Die Deutsche Barockbaukunst Böhmens*, Munich 1943, pp.24, 25, 27, 32, 36, 38, 41, 42. For Austria and Southern

Germany, *cf.* Hager, *op. cit.*, Figs.121, 162, 175, 176, 186, 187, 196, 200, 201, 202.

791 *Cf.* the holograph plan, dated 1734, printed by Hager, *ibid.*, pl.94.

792 *Cf.* Abstract, lot 234.

793 *Cf.* 'Tract' I (WS XIX, p.126): 'Of geometrical Figures, the Square and the Circle are the most beautiful; next the Parallelogram and the Oval.'

794 To instance: St Mary Aldermanbury, Fig.14; St Mary-le-Bow, Figs.18, 139; St Benet Fink, Fig.75; St Stephen's, Walbrook, Figs.29, 30; St Benet, Thames Street, Figs.44, 45; the original plan of St Swithin, Fig.59; St Mary Abchurch, lucarne windows of dome and upper windows of east wall St James's, Westminster, Fig.66; the oval ceiling of St Clement's, Eastcheap; the oval windows in the steeple design, Fig.27; Cambridge Senate House, ASC I, 55 (WS V, pl.xiv); Christ's Hospital schoolroom, BM Sloane 5238, 51 (*ibid.*, pl.xxx); the stable design, BM Sloane 5238, 89 (*ibid.*, pl.xxxii); and the interesting hesitation between circle and ellipse discernible in the elevation study for St Michael's, Crooked Lane, ASC II, 110 (WS IX, pl.27).

795 T. F. Bumpus, *op. cit.*, p.392.

796 Godwin and Britton, *Churches of London*, London 1838–9.

797 Blomfield, *Short Hist.*, p.121.

798 *Cf.* for example Fischer von Erlach, *Civil and Historical Architecture* (translated by Thos. Lediard) London 1730, IV, pls.x and xiii, for sections of the Salzburg university church and Vienna San Carlo Borromeo domes which are both double constructions. The same applies to the instances of Roman domes cited *supra, note* 734.

799 Ramsey, in *Symposium*, p.13.

800 Reynolds, *Seventh Discourse*.

801 Whitaker-Wilson, *op. cit.*, p.42.

802 Oughtred, quoted in Ward, *Lives of Gresham Professors*, p.96: 'Mr Christopher Wren . . . a youth generally admired for his talents, who, when not yet sixteen years old, enriched astronomy, gnomonics, statics and mechanics, by brilliant inventions, and from that time has continued to enrich them, and in truth is one from whom I can, not vainly, look for great things.' Barrow's view, however (*Works*, IX, pp.176–7, quoted by Caröe, *op. cit.*, pp.115–16) leaves a suspicion of polite lip-service, particularly in view of his erroneous reference to Wren as professor of geometry, a post which Wren never held. For Evelyn's often-quoted opinion, *cf. Diary*, 11, 13 July 1654 and 25 Oct. 1664. For Hooke, *cf.* preface to *Micrographia* (1665): 'Since the time of Archimedes, there scarce met in one man, in so great perfection, such a Mechanical Hand and so Philosophical a Mind.' This passage should suffice to dispel the misrepresentation of the relationship between Hooke and Wren first expounded by Elmes, perpetuated by Phillimore, *op. cit.*, p.247: 'Wren whom one can never imagine but with all the courtesy and refinement of a finished gentleman, and Hooke half a miser, utterly slovenly, and jealous of any rising fame . . .' apparently still accepted by Weaver, *op. cit.*, p.119. We may note in passing that when Dr Busby decided on building his church at Willen, he chose, from among two of his old pupils at Westminster School, Hooke to design it.

803 Though Evelyn is one of the chief sources for a study of Wren, the fact that he offers practically no qualitative comments on Wren's architecture has never been remarked upon. It is surprising that there are no references to Wren's work comparable to those to Pratt's Clarendon House (letter to Lord Cornbury, 20 Jan. 1665/6, printed by Bray as a note to 18 Sept. 1683) and to 'Bedlam Hospital, magnificently built' (*Diary*, 18 April 1678). Evelyn's only appreciative comments on Wren's architecture are on 'St Laurences . . . cheerfull pile' (*Diary*, 28 May 1682), on St Clement Danes, 'that pretty built and contrived church' (*ibid.*, 28 Oct. 1684), on St James's, Westminster, 'elegantly indeede built' (*ibid.*, 7 Dec. 1684) and Christ Church, 'which is a modern noble & ample fabric' (*ibid.*, 13 March 1687); while the only reference to St Paul's, *ibid.*, 5 Oct. 1695, does not seem to betray much enthusiasm: 'I went to St Paul's to see the choir, now finished as to the stone work, and the

scaffold struck both without and within, in that part. Some exceptions might perhaps be taken as to the placing columns on pilasters at the East tribunal. As to the rest it is a piece of architecture without reproach.' This opinion compares unfavourably with Evelyn's outspoken and repeated praise of Verrio and Gibbon. It seems suggestive that there is no comment on the quality of the City churches (*ibid.*, 5 May 1681), on the Chelsea designs (*ibid.*, 25 May 1682 and 12 May 1691), the Tenison Library (*ibid.*, 15, 23 Feb. 1683/4), or Greenwich Hospital (1695 *et seq.*), though in the latter three instances he was intimately concerned and doubtless familiar with every stage of their development. The entry referring to Greenwich (*ibid.*, June 1705) of which 'the buildings now going on are very magnificent' must clearly apply to Vanbrugh's, and not Wren's work. The eulogistic passage in the dedication to Wren of his *Account of Architects and Architecture*, 21 Feb. 1696/7, is rendered of dubious significance in view of the comparable dedication, to Sir John Denham, of the 1664 edition of *A Parallel*.

804 Dutton, *op. cit.*, p.15, with reference to Vanbrugh, Hawksmoor, and Gibbs.

805 *ibid.*, pp.127, 108, where White's 'flamboyant' Worcester Guildhall is suggested to have been inspired by Wren. Sitwell, *op. cit.*, p.105, likewise classes White as a Wren pupil, but Whiffen, *op. cit.*, p.35, has pertinently pointed out the entirely fictitious nature of the statement in Nash's *Worcestershire* that White accompanied Wren to Rome. In fact, there is no evidence that White, forty-one years Wren's junior, ever met Wren. It is interesting to note that, for all evident Italian influences, White in 1734 presented a model of a Gothic church to be built in Worcester (*cf.* Carritt, *op. cit.*, p.210). Gibbs certainly, and Archer very probably, studied in Rome, as Whiffen pointed out in a letter to the *Times Literary Supplement*, 8 Feb. 1952. There is little evidence which would permit Gibbs being called Wren's pupil, as Phillimore, *op. cit.*, p.286, and Whitaker-Wilson, *op. cit.*, p.241, suggest, nor any reason to think that Wren was responsible for Gibbs's employment in adding the steeple to St Clement Danes. Hawksmoor is the only one who can truly be called Wren's pupil, though in his later work he was to be equally influenced by Vanbrugh. The confusion which besets the subject of Wren's successors is well illustrated by Fletcher, *Palladio*, pp.116 *et seq.*, who includes Hawksmoor, Vanbrugh, Gibbs, and Archer among the Palladians. *V. infra*, note 809.

806 *Cf.* Loftie, *op. cit.*, pp.99, 180, 279, where the names of Jones, Wren, Gibbs, Burlington, and Chambers are indiscriminately linked, and p.215, where it is stated that Wren 'both founded a school and lived to see it flourish' which school is supposed to have consisted of 'several architects well able to take up and carry on his tradition', among which Burlington, Hawksmoor, Campbell, and James are named as well as Kent, 'whose work singularly resembles Wren's'. Stratton, *op. cit.*, p.28, opined that though 'Wren did not willingly acknowledge his obligations . . . he must be considered the direct successor of Inigo Jones, not only in the school of design founded by him, but also in the methods in which that school worked', while we learn, *ibid.*, p.48, that the 'natural outcome' of Wren's works was 'a school of vigorous and consistent design, unequalled in the pages of history alike for its productions and for the period of its duration'. Blomfield is involved in contradictions by stating, *Hist. Ren. Arch. Eng.*, I, p.162, that in his later works, Wren 'returned to the purer models of Palladianism' but, according to *Short Hist.* (1921 ed.), p.143, he 'cannot be said to have had an immediate following either among his contemporaries or successors'. Weaver, *op. cit.*, p.51, explains Wren's allegedly Palladian inclinations by Jones's supposed influence. Drummond, *op. cit.*, p.39, considers that Hawksmoor, Gibbs, and Archer 'continued his tradition vigorously'.

807 *Cf. The Scribleriad*, esp. V, ii, 88–108.

808 *The World*, 1754; quoted by Carrit, *op. cit.*, p.267.

809 J. Adam, *Diary*, 1760, quoted *ibid.*, p.412. This passage should suffice to discredit Fletcher's assertion, *op. cit.*, pp.116 *et seq.*, that the English

school of Palladianism included not only Jones, Webb, and Hawksmoor, but also Campbell, Vanbrugh, Gibbs, Archer, Talman, Kent, *Adam*, and Chambers.

810 *Cf.* Miller, *The Man of Taste*, quoted by Whistler, *Vanbrugh*, p.292:
'Sure wretched Wren was taught by bungling Jones,
To murder mortar and disfigure stones.
Who in Whitehall can symmetry discern?
I reckon Covent Garden Church a Barn.
Nor hate I less thy vile Cathedral, Paul!
The Choir's too big, the Cupola's too small;
Substantial walls and heavy roof I like,
'Tis Vanbrugh's structures that my fancy strikes.
Such noble ruins every pile would make,
I wish they'd tumble for the prospect's sake.'

811 *Cf.* Memoirs of the Earl of Ailesbury, quoted by Carritt, *op, cit.*, p.143, to whom Blenheim was 'like one mass of stone, without taste or relish'. *Cf.* also Chesterfield to Stanhope, 9 Dec. 1766 (*ibid.*, p.311) who, at Nîmes, thought Serlio's 'bellissimo Amphitheatro' (*Regole*, III, iii) 'the clumsiest and ugliest; if it were in England, everybody would swear it had been built by Sir John Vanbrugh'.

812 Torrington *Diaries*, 28 June 1791, quoted by Carritt, *op. cit.*, p.412. In view of the evidence of which only a small part is here quoted, it is difficult to see how the WS editors, XIX, p.125, could speak of Wren's 'great and lasting influence'.

813 *Vitruvius Britannicus* I, introduction: '. . . for the Italians . . . are entirely employ'd in capricious Ornaments, which must at last end in the Gothic. For proof of this assertion, I appeal to the Productions of the last Century. How affected and licentious are the works of Bernini and Fontana? How wildly extravagant are the Designs of Borromini, who has endeavour'd to debauch Mankind with his odd and chimaerical Beauties, where the Parts are without Proportion, Solids without their true Bearing, Heaps of Materials without Strength, excessive Ornaments without Grace, and the Whole without Symmetry? And what can be a stronger Argument, that this excellent Art is near lost in a Country, where such Absurdities meet with Applause?'

814 This quality has become a controversial point among Wren's critics; Cleveland, *art. cit.*, p.483, calls St Martin's one of Wren's 'less picturesque' designs, Eberlein, *art. cit.*, p.49, contends that 'the "picturesque" in architecture made no appeal to' Wren. *Cf.*, however, Reynolds's criticism of the City plan in the *Thirteenth Discourse*.

815 Mackmurdo, *op. cit.*, p.59.

816 For an indication of the change in taste, *cf.* the Earl of Arundel's advice to Evelyn (quoted by Hervey, *The Life . . . of Thomas Howard . . .*, Cambridge 1921' p.453) not to miss 'ye famous monastery of the Certosini called la Certosa de Pavia' which is 'well worth ye seeing for ye fairnesse of ye monastery & church' as contrasted with Blomfield's opinion on the same edifice, *Touchstone*, pp.203–4, quoted *supra*, note 766. The most recent champion of the somewhat worn views of the Campbell-Blomfield school is Scarfe, who conceives of the Baroque as 'some grand nightmare, where the victims are trying to resolve the struggles of their childhood' and who considers Bernini 'just a bragging caricature of all the most superficial aspects of Michelangelo, a pompous effulgence of the baroque'. (*Rome*, London 1950, pp.47, 52.)

817 Not that such concepts were confined to the nineteenth century: *cf.* Whitaker-Wilson, *op. cit.* (1932), p.59: 'The later Stuart period was as vicious as any that succeeded it, with the possible exception of that of George IV.' This statement is made to enable its author to 'draw a pleasant comparison by pointing to the superb dignity and clean living of Wren and Evelyn, who stood above the moral filth of the times. No two finer characters or more perfect Englishmen lived in *any* period of our history, from the Stone Age to this included'.

818 Drummond, *op. cit.*, p.28, defines the Baroque as 'the ecclesiological expression of an artificial and pleasure-loving age, which delighted in

stilted dramas, pompous palaces, powder and paint', and considers Versailles adequately characterized by 'opera, mistresses, and obsequious chaplains'.

819 Blomfield, *Modernismus*, chapters i–iii.

820 The credit must go to Burckhardt. Read's judgement, *op. cit.*,p.95, reiterated by Hauser, *Social History of Art*, London 1951, pp.424–5, that 'not only the attitude of Winckelmann, Lessing and Goethe, but also that of Burckhardt is guided fundamentally by the point of view of classicist theory; they all reject the baroque on account of its "irregularity" and "capriciousness" . . . Burckhardt and the later purists, such as Croce, for example, who were incapable of liberating themselves from the often narrow-minded rationalism of the eighteenth century, perceive in the baroque merely the tokens of illogicality and lack of structure . . .' is only true of Burckhardt's earliest writings. Thus in his *Cicerone* (1854) he still accepted the generally held view that the Baroque was 'der verwilderte Dialekt der Renaissance'; but in 1870 he wrote to von Preen (quoted by Waetzholdt, postscript to the Phaidon, Vienna ed. of *Die Kultur der Renaissance . . .*, p.402): 'Die vorgebliche Ausartung bestand meist in genialen letzen Konsequenzen und Fortschritten, und die Stile starben in der Regel, wenn sie in der Höhe waren . . .' Burckhardt's final opinion is diametrically opposed to his earlier views, as expressed in his letter to Alioth, Rome, 5 April 1875 (quoted by Hager, *op. cit.*, p.2): 'Mein Respekt vor dem Barocco nimmt stündlich zu und ich bin bald geneigt, ihn für das eigentliche Ende und Hauptresultat der lebendigen Architektur zu halten.' It is significant that Burckhardt reached this opinion thirteen years before the publication of Wölfflin's *Renaissance und Barock*, and thirty-two years before Riegl's *Die Entstehung der Barockkunst in Rom*, the two works in which Read and Hauser have perceived the recommencing appreciation of the style. For another interesting example of Burckhardt's development, *v. infra*, note 830.

821 *Concise Oxford Dictionary*, 1921.

822 Fletcher, *Hist. Arch.* (1950), p.781; Blomfield, *Hist. Ren. Arch. Eng.*, *et al.*; *cf.* also Dimock, *op. cit.*, p.78: 'St Paul's is often called "classical", or "Roman", or "Italian"; it is not one of these three: it is English Renaissance.'

823 Scott, *The Architecture of Humanism* (1947 ed.), p.262.

824 *Cf.* Blomfield, *Touchstone*, *passim*; *Modernismus*, pp.1–82; *Short Hist.*, p.303: 'We alone of European peoples steered clear of rococo art, the decadence of the Renaissance.' For this author's confusion between Baroque and Rococo, *cf.* his reference to Read, *op. cit.*, in *Modernismus*, p.41. The lack of precision with which the two terms are used is also apparent in the reference in Caröe, *op. cit.*, p.50, to the work of Cibber 'which is apt to incline to the Rococo of Bernini and his school'.

825 Webb, introduction to Cobb, *op. cit.*, p.8.

826 Among recent publications, *cf.* Weaver, Webb, Whistler, Pevsner, and Newton.

827 The term is not used here in the connotation given by Whiffen, *op. cit.*, p.10, with reference to St Catherine Cree and Bishop Wren's Peterhouse chapel, or the definition given by Webb, introduction to Cobb, *op. cit.*, p.7, as 'the curious mixture of Gothic and Renaissance', but in the meaning defined by Pevsner, *op. cit.*, pp.77 *et seq.*, and *Gegenreformation und Manierismus*, *passim*.

828 Scott, *op. cit.*, p.20.

829 Haymon, a thirteenth-century abbot of St-Pierre-sur-Dives, quoted by Jackson, *Gothic Architecture*.

830 Wittkower, *op. cit.*, p.2, draws attention to an interesting development of Burckhardt's thought: 'Burckhardt changed his ideas about the meaning of centrally built churches. At first he thought them due to aesthetic considerations (*Cicerone*), later concluded that "die Renaissance hat den Zentralbau einer künftigen Religiosität zum Vermächtnis hinterlassen".' (*Geschichte der Renaissance in Italien*, 1920 ed., p.114.)

831 It is significant that Alberti mentions the Early Christian circular buildings, but not the Pantheon.

832 Wittkower, *op. cit.*, p.26, mentions the definition of God as a circle to be found in Plato, Plotinus, Dionysius the Areopagite, Dio Cassius, Nicolas of Cusa, and John Donne; for Du Perron's Cusanian 'spherical' interpretation of divinity, *cf.* Yates, *op. cit.*, p.168, note 7.

833 *Quattro Libri, ed. cit.*, IV, sig. AAAA 2 *recto*: '. . . & come i Cieli co'l continuo lor girare vadino in lei stagioni secondo il natural bisogno cangiando . . . che douendo esser simili i piccioli Tempij, che noi facciamo'.

834 *ibid.*, IV, cap.ii: '. . . elleggeromo la più perfetta, più excellente [forma] e consciosia che la Ritonda sia tale, perche tra tutte le figure è semplice, vniforma, eguale, forte e capace, faremo i Tempii ritondi.'

835 *loc. cit.*, '. . . [perche] finalmente ritrouandosi in ogni sua parte l'estremo egualmente lontano dal mezo, è attissima a dimonstrare la Vnità, la infinita Essenza, la Vniformità, & la Giustitia di DIO.'

836 *De Re Aedificatoria*, III, cap.14.

837 *ibid.*, VII, cap.11. *Cf.* Wittkower, *op. cit.*, p.28, for Campanella's recommendation for a dome painted with stars in *Città del Sole* (1623). *Cf.* Mâle, *op. cit.*, p.151, for typical examples, e.g. Correggio at Parma, Lanfranc at Sant' Andrea della Valle, Rome, the Val-de-Grâce, Paris, *et al.*

838 The derivation is from Vitruvius, *De Architectura*, III, i, 3. For Francesco di Giorgio, Francesco Giorgi, Fra Jocundus, and Cesariano, *cf.* Wittkower, *op. cit.*, pls.1a, 2a, 2c, 3, 4; for Leonardo, *cf.* the drawing Venice, Accademia, 228, and *Codex Huyghens* (ed. Panofsky), London 1940, esp. fol.7, as well as the drawings Royal Library, Windsor, 19,130–3. For Michelangelo, the drawing Windsor, 12,765. For Bernini, Brauer-Wittkower, *Die Zeichnungen des G. L. Bernini*, II, 54.

839 Pacioli, *De Divina Proportione*, Venice 1509, and Francesco Giorgi, *De Harmonia Mundi Totius*, Venice 1525, and Paris 1545, 1579, are the most important works, the former derived from Piero della Francesca's unpublished MS. preserved at Urbino.

840 e.g. Jacopo de' Barbari; the portrait, dated 1491, is in the Museo Nazionale at Naples, and the accessories shown are full of neo-Platonic symbolism, such as the slate inscribed EVCLIDES on the rim, on which a circle inscribed with an axially halved equilateral triangle is drawn; giving two scalene triangles as mentioned in *Timaeus*. This is related to the complex crystalline body suspended on the left and the dodecahedron on the right.

841 If our exposition may be thought too far removed from our subject, *cf.* Abstract, 498.

842 *De Re Aedificatoria*, IX, cap.6 (1550 ed., p.340): '. . . Caueremo adumque tutta la regola del finimento da Musici, a chi sono perfettissimamente note tali numeri ma non andrò dietro a questo cose sinon quanto farà bisogno al proposite dello Architettore . . .' Having discussed the mathematics of musical harmonies, Alberti concludes (*ibid.*, p.344): 'Di questi numeri que noi habbiamo racconti si seruono gli architettori nō confusamente, ne alle mescolata; ma in modo che corrispondono & consento da ogni bāda alla Armonia.' Without further quotations, Blunt's opinion, *Artistic Theory in Italy, 1450-1600*, Oxford 1940, pp.18 *et seq.*, must be rejected, who, discussing the treatise *Of Statues*, thinks that 'the very matter-of-fact averaging technique' of finding measurements 'characteristic of Alberti and illustrates how far he was removed from any sort of idealistic Neoplatonic conceptions'. This is not borne out by a study of Alberti's other writings. That the inspiration of his art theory was not exclusively Platonic is proved by his explicit reference to Aristotle in connexion with the 'sacred number 10', *De Re Aedif.*, p.340. The analogy between visual and musical harmony, however, is a purely Platonic, or rather, Pythagorean concept which, largely derived from *Timaeus*, furnished the basis for the neo-Platonic cosmology of harmonics. Blunt's misapprehension arises from a wholly erroneous identification of humanism with rationalism, and neo-Platonism with the Counter Reformation; *v. infra*, note 855.

843 *De Re Aedificatoria*, 1550 ed., VII, p.206; quoted *supra*, note 703.

844 *Cf.* Vitruvius's 'concords', *De Architectura*, V, iv, 7: 'concentus quos natura hominis modulari potest, graece qua symphoniae dicintur, sunt sex: diatesseron, diapente, diapason', the fourth, fifth, and octave; 'et disdiatesseron, et disdiapente, et disdiapason'; the octave plus a fourth, octave plus a fifth, and double octave. *Cf.* also *ibid.*, I, i, 9, I, i, 16. That Renaissance musical theorists were aware that these intervals were not only produced by strings of equal tension and proportional length is borne out by the lower left picture in Gafurio's *Theorica musice*, 1492 (but used already in 1480; *cf.* Wittkower, *op. cit.*, p.109, note 1; the woodcut reproduced pl.37b) where 'Pitagoras' stands before an apparatus on which strings of equal length are kept at various tensions by weights marked 4, 6, 8, 9, 12, 16.

845 Plato, *Timaeus*, in *Plato Selections*, ed. Demos, New York 1927, pp.398–9; after interpolation of new terms corresponding to arithmetic and harmonic means into the two principal series, two new progressions are generated, the latter of which represents a progression of ratios of 3:2, 4:3, 3:2, 3:2, 4:3, 3:2 . . . *ad. inf. Cf.* also Alberti, *De Re Aedificatoria*, p.347, and Palladio, *Quattro Libri*, I, p.54, regarding the relationship of height to the length and width of rooms.

846 *Regole* (1537) I, 15 *recto*.

847 *V. supra*, p.134.

848 We must point to the fairly common occurrence of illuminations representing Pythagoras and music, frequently as parts of the Trivium and Quadrivium of the mediaeval syllabus. The subject of Vitruvian and, more generally, Platonic influence during the Middle Ages has not yet been extensively studied. References to Vitruvius occur in Vincent of Beauvais, William of Malmesbury, and certain mediaeval French works (*cf.* Langlois, *La connaissance de la nature et du monde au moyen âge*, Paris 1911). The most recent work, however, is the scholarly study of Klibansky, *The Continuity of the Platonic Tradition during the Middle Ages*, London 1950.

849 Drummond, *op. cit.*, p.27, represents the development of latter sixteenth-century Italian architecture as a split between 'conservative' and 'radical' elements: 'On the radical side, the opposition broke away from precedent and convention, refusing to accept the "verbal inspiration" of Vitruvius. The conservative tendency became known as Palladian: the radical as Baroque.' This wholly erroneous interpretation serves to support this author's favourite theory that 'the first or formal [Palladian] style was generally followed by Protestants, the second or romantic version of the Renaissance [*sic*] was the style of the Counter Reformation.' This naïve partitioning results in a confusion between cause and effect. For outstanding proof of the fallacy of this distortion, *cf.* our exposition of the non-Palladian character of Wren's work in the preceding chapter; the wholly Baroque character of Schlüter's work in Berlin (*cf.* Hager, *op. cit.*, pp.155 *et seq.*), and the fact that the door of the Ostkerk at Middleburg (*cf.* Sitwell, *The Netherlands*, pl.114) is a replica of Maderno's at Sta Susanna, Rome, must suffice to dispel this partisan notion.

850 Scott, *op. cit.*, pp.15–16.

851 The supposedly 'pagan' character of Alberti's S. Sebastiano in Mantua had been criticized even during its construction by clerical opinion which did not 'see if this is meant to turn out a church, or a mosque or a synagogue' (quoted by Pevsner, *op. cit.*, p.92).

852 Quoted by Pastor, *History of the Popes*, II, p.166. Nicholas V was undoubtedly influenced in matters of architecture by Alberti, who was in Rome during his pontificate; *cf.* Vasari, *Lives*, L. B. Alberti.

853 The extreme of distorted presentation is found in Drummond, *op. cit.*, p.27: 'The Jesuits were wise in their understanding of men and of the Zeitgeist. Baroque was "up to date". Its showiness and magnificence of scale impressed the masses, and did not make it less "eine Hofkunst und Priesterkunst". Speedy building was possible for the craftsmanship and honesty of the Middle Ages was long past . . . The Jesuits found Baroque architecture an effective and relatively inexpensive architecture, for the

appeal could be varied according to the country and degree of culture. In France, moderation, refinement, and sound workmanship would be necessary; in Italy, more colour; in Spain, a version in accordance with the sombre religiosity of the country; in Spanish America, plenty of cheap glitter to bewitch the natives.' Apart from the inherent contradictions of this characterization, this author evidently thinks that 'national' versions of the Baroque were designed, presumably by the executive officers of the Order in Rome, upon considerations of racial psychology. He seems apparently ignorant of the fact that native Mexican and Indian labour and talent was to a considerable extent responsible for the 'cheap glitter' and that the Baroque version known to art historians as Churigueresque takes its name from the most outstanding of native Spanish American artists. L. Milman, *op. cit.*, p.74, speaks of 'the Church of St Paul and St Louis, whose façade, an extreme example of the onerous type of decoration known as "Jesuit" ' which she ventures to guess 'must have filled the austere Englishman rather with amazement than admiration'. This, however, is to attribute Victorian and Edwardian sentiments to Caroline England and proves wholly erroneous if we can apply the standard of Evelyn's taste: *cf. Diary*, 8 Nov. 1644, with reference to the 'fair church', the Chiesa Nova at Rome, with its 'most precious oratory of Philippus Nerius'; *ibid.*, 12 Nov. 1644, the 'noble *facciata*' of Maderna's Sta Susanna and 'Santa Maria della Vittoria ... with the most ravishing front'. *Cf.* also the reference to Borromeo's San Carlo alle Quattro Fontane which 'is a singular fabric for neatness', and what in Naples (*ibid.*, 31 Jan. 1645) is 'above all to be admired, is the yet unfinished church of the Jesuits, certainly, if accomplished, not to be equalled in Europe'. References to the 'gloriuos front' of Sta Maria in Navicula in Rome (*ibid.*, 14 Feb. 1645) are as eloquent as the opinion of the 4th Earl of Arundel quoted *supta*, note 816; for the countess's impressions *cf.* Vercellini's letter to the earl printed by Hervey, *op. cit.*, pp.175–6, from Antwerp: 'Piaccia v[ot]ra ecc[elen]tia far saper al sr. Server [i.e. Inigo Jones] che Madam ha veduta la Chiesa delli Gesuitti, et la trova cosa maravigliosa.'

854 Scott, *op. cit.*, p.25.
855 *Cf.* Wittkower, *op. cit.*, pp.27–8, referring to Borromeo's *Instructionum Fabricae Ecclesiasticae* ... and pointing to the parallel in Cataneo's *I Quattro Primi Libri*, 1554. It is surprising that Blunt, who discusses Borromeo's *Instructions* at some length, *op. cit.*, pp.129 *et seq.*, persists in the broad identification of the Counter Reformation and neo-Platonism, on the argument that the cosmological mysticism of the latter was the logical adjunct of the 'sacrifice of the intellect' demanded by the former. He points to the fact that 'there is considerable play in Lomazzo with the symbolism of numbers, with the seven circles of heaven, and with all the apparatus of medieval astrology. Even Zuccaro, who is in general clear of this particular lumber, [*sic*] ... cannot resist dragging in Mercury, Jupiter, and the rest...' But the thesis that 'the Neoplatonist Christianity' of Zuccaro is a sign of 'the tendency in the Mannerist period for theorists as well as artists to give up rational ideals which had dominated the Renaissance ... and to return to non-humanist theological values of medieval Catholicism' and that 'in the system of the later Mannerists the individual reason, which was the foundation of all Renaissance progress, was replaced by the acceptance of authority, exactly as the individual conscience had been crushed by the Counter Reformation' represents a perverse distortion of historical fact. We have commented elsewhere on the Platonic inspiration which governs Alberti's system of proportions; and the fact that not only Francesco Giorgi's neo-Platonic treatise of 1525 was put on the *Index*, but also that the Tridentine decree condemned circular plans because of their Platonic symbolism points to the distinct effort of the Counter Reformation to dissociate itself from every expression of neo-Platonic, humanist thought. Blunt's allegedly rational basis of humanist aesthetics is wholly fictitious; Lomazzo and Zuccaro are independent survivals from the neo-Platonism of the early Renaissance.

856 In Salzburg, an attitude comparable to that of the Sorbonne towards the Jesuits obtained. The university, objecting to Jesuit influence, had the matter settled by law; *cf.* Etienne Pasquier, *Exhortation aux Princes et Seigneurs ... pour obvier aux séditions qui semblent nous menacier le faict de la Religion*, Paris 1561; Pasquier was counsel for the Sorbonne in its action against the Society in 1564; significantly, his *Catéchisme des Jesuits* was translated into English by Edward Aggas, 1594. Parallel to this action, Marcus Sitticus, Prince Archbishop of Salzburg (1612–19) refused to entrust the administration of his 'gymnasium' (later university) which he founded in 1617 to the Jesuits, but charged the Dominicans with the task. This action achieves its true significance when it is remembered that Sitticus's decision went contrary to the wishes of his own cathedral chapter as well as those of his powerful neighbour, the Duke of Bavaria, and lastly, that he carried out his intention despite the fact that he was himself a nephew of San Carlo Borromeo. *Cf.* Martin, *Salzburgs Fürsten in der Barockzeit*, Salzburg 1948, pp.98 *et seq.*
857 Scamozzi's connexion with the building dates from 1599, although the extant plans are to be dated *c.*1606; it is probable that he was invited by Archbishop Wolf Dietrich, who had possibly met Scamozzi in Italy, as he would hardly have gone to Salzburg uninvited: not only was he expected in Prague by Rudolf II, but also did the journey from Venice to Prague via Salzburg entail a considerable and troublesome detour, which Scamozzi would not have undertaken without good cause; *cf.* Donin, *op. cit.*, p.30.
858 *V supra*, note 624, where attention is drawn to Drummond's thesis, *op. cit.*, pp.31 *et seq.*, that circular plans were an essentially Protestant concept. The examples cited only serve to prove the untenability of this theory. Thus, St Aegidius in Nürnberg is as neither due to the fact that 'many of [Sturm's] ideas were carried out' nor was it 'the first oval church': the publication of Sturm's book and the building of St Aegidius were strictly contemporaneous, so that it is not feasible to see in the latter the result of the former; oval churches had been built north of the Alps many decades before this instance. Nor is there any reason to think that 'from the Catholic point of view, such a church as the oval Paulus-kirche in Frankfurt would be frigid and repellent' for the oval plan had been considered eminently suitable by Catholic architects from Vignola and Borromini to Fischer and Zimmermann. Finally, Sturmian influence in Bähr's church of Our Lady at Dresden (1722) seems far less cogent than early Renaissance influence, as (however clumsy the domes) the idea of four subsidiary domes surrounding a large central one points back to Bramante, Leonardo, and San Gallo. It is clear, of course, that the neo-Platonic concepts originally responsible for these forms had been forgotten, and the forms had survived merely as types; this is recognized by Drummond: 'if there is little symbolism, there are finely carved organ cases, pulpits, and magistrates' stalls ...'.
859 *Cf.* L. Milman, *op. cit.*, pp.262–3: 'Louis XIV, morally unstable, a bigot, a voluptuary, delighting in flattery and display of every kind, regarding Versailles and the reckless expenditure it entailed as the symbol of his glory ...' Hauser, *op. cit.*, p.445, expresses the questionable view, as though it were a statement of fact, that 'neither the King, nor Colbert had a real understanding or a genuine love of art'.
860 The two extreme protagonist views on this subject are expressed by Scott, *op. cit.*, p.21: 'The influence of patronage on art is easily misstated ... most that rulers can do towards determining the *essence* of an art is to impose upon it a distinctly courtly character, and the coherence which comes from a strongly centralized organization.' And Hauser, *op. cit.*, p.444: 'the suppression of all individual effort, the supreme glorification of the idea of the state as personified in the king, these are the tasks which the academies are called upon to deal with ...'
861 Chesterfield to Stanhope, 7 Feb. 1749; quoted by Carritt, *op. cit.*, p.248.
862 *Cf.* Hauser, *op. cit.*, pp.444–5: 'The government wishes to dissolve the personal relationship between the artist and the public and make them directly dependent on the state. It wants to bring to an end both private

patronage and the promotion of private interests and aspirations by artists and writers. From now on they are to serve only the state and the academies are to educate them and hold them to this subservient position . . . [for Colbert] art is nothing but an instrument of state government with the special function of raising the prestige of the monarch' and subsequent to the foundation of the Académie de Rome in 1666, 'artists are purely the creatures of the state educational system'.

863 Mellers, *op. cit.*, p.28.

864 Hauser, *op. cit.*, p.441, holds the 'cosmopolitan outlook' allegedly prevalent in seventeenth-century France responsible for the fact that 'in all the tragedies of Racine . . . not a single Frenchman appears', but this would seem a far-fetched argument to prove the contention that 'it is absolutely wrong to see in the classicism of this court the French "national style"'. The titles of Racine's dramatic works are sufficiently indicative in themselves of Hellenic inspiration; *cf.* the author's *op. cit.*, p.69.

865 *Cf.* Meller's admirable exposition of this question, supported by apt quotations from de Nyert (*op. cit.*, p.132) who sought to 'ajuster la méthode italienne avec la française', to J. J. Fux (*ibid.*, p.125) and his *Concentus Musico-instrumentalis* of 1701, and finally to Couperin (*ibid.*, p.234), *Les Goûts Réünis*, 1724: 'Le goût Italian et le goût François ont partagé depuis longtemps (en France) la République de la Musique . . .' These instances, however, are the latter end of a tendency of many years' standing, the beginning of which may be sought in Jean le Maire de Belges, *Concorde des Deux Langues*, 1513.

866 The suggestion is made by Hauser, *op. cit.*, p.441, that 'the French court attains the international recognition of its manners, fashion and art at the expense of the national character of French culture.'

867 *Cf.* Poussin, quoted in Mellers, *op. cit.*, p.75: 'Mon naturel me constraint de chercher les choses bien ordonnées, fuyant la confusion qui m'est aussi contraire et ennemi comme est la lumière des obscures ténèbres.'

868 In the literary field, the position has been pertinently described by Marcel Raymond, 'Propositions sur le Baroque et la littérature française' in *La Revue des Sciences Humaines*, juillet-décembre 1949: 'Il est entendu que la France a manqué le temps du grand art baroque. Alors qu'il triomphait ailleurs, il n'a pu s'y réaliser pleinement. Il en résulte que dans les textes littéraires que nous séduisent aujourd'hui (dans lesquels nous croyons discerner la stylistique du baroque ou la présence diffuse de son esprit) nous poursuivons presque toujours à notre insu l'image de ce qui aurait pu être.'

869 *Cf.* Yates, *op. cit.*, pp.224 *et seq.*

870 Kathleen Raine, 'John Donne and the Baroque Doubt', in *Horizon*, XI, 66, p.373.

871 *Basilikon Doron*, quoted by Cragg, *From Puritanism to the Age of Reason*, Cambridge 1950, p.158. Drummond, *op. cit.*, p.26, is inconsistent in taking exception to the fact that Inigo Jones's portico at St Paul's 'characteristically contained statues of King James and King Charles – not even genuine saints' as he raises no objection to 'the whitewashed walls and wooden galleries' of German Lutheran churches 'often naïvely decorated with representations of Luther, Melanchton, and the Apostles'. (*ibid.*, p.30.)

872 Quoted in Mellers, *op. cit.*, p.43: 'Celui qui a donné des rois aux hommes a voulu qu'on les respectât comme ses lieutenants.'

873 *Cf. The Maid's Tragedy* (1610–11), especially: *Amintor*:
'Y' are a tyrant; and not so much to wrong
An honest man thus, as to take pride
In talking with him of it . . .
. . . As you are mere man,
I dare as easily kill you for this deed,
As you dare do it, but there is
Divinity about you that strikes dead
My rising passions; as you are my King,
I fall before you.'

874 (Grosart) *Negotium Posterorum*, I, p.139.

875 *A Game at Chesse* (with Middleton), 6 Aug. 1624. The entire cast is allegorical: Black Knight stands for Count Gondomar, Spanish ambassador to James's court; the Fat Bishop, Marco Antonio de Dominis, sometime Archbishop of Spalato who, however, joined the Church of England and became Dean Wren's predecessor at Windsor and Master of the Savoy; the Black King stands for Philip IV; the White King for James I; the White Knight symbolizes Prince Charles, and the White Duke stands for Buckingham.

876 Clarendon, speech to both Houses, quoted by Cragg, *op. cit.*, p.193.

877 Dowsing went beyond the Zwinglian practice in this respect, as the Swiss reformer had differentiated between statues and pictures on the one, and stained glass on the other hand.

878 *Cf.* Sprat, *History of the Royal Society* (1702 ed.), p.132: 'Of our churchmen, the greatest and most reverend, by their care and passion and endeavours in advancing this institution, have taken off the unjust scandal from natural knowledge, that it is an enemy of divinity. By the perpetual patronage and assistance they have afforded the Royal Society, they have confuted the false opinions of those men who believe that philosophers must needs be irreligious.'

879 *Cf.* the lucid exposition by Cragg, *op. cit.*, pp.37–60. Exception might, however, be taken to this author's somewhat exaggerated presentation of the mystic tendencies of the Cambridge Platonists, *ibid.*, p.51. The degree to which they could be called mystics is not necessarily indicated by the 'loving care' with which 'they brooded over the obscure passages of the neo-Platonists' but rather by the fact, *ibid.*, p.53, that 'their writings are never reminiscent of bizarre regions wholly beyond normal human experience'. It is a question of opinion whether to rejoice, with this author, over the fact that 'there is a complete absence of that atmosphere of oppressive extravagance which is unfortunately so common to mystics', a question which can only be decided by a comparison, let us say, between the works of Wichcote and of St John of the Cross.

880 Cragg, *ibid.*, p.70.

881 This position is not invalidated by the loophole which, somewhat charily, he suggests by designating such phenomena as cannot be reasonably explained as 'the proper matter of faith', as the contradiction is obvious between the statement that Revelation must be true even 'against the probable conjectures of reason' and the counter-claim that 'it still belongs to reason to judge the truth of its being revelation'. (*Essay on Human Understanding*, IV, 18, 5–8); *cf.* also O'Connor, *John Locke*, London 1952, pp.198–202.

882 *Cf. 18e Provinciale*, VII, 49–50: 'D'où apprendrons-nous donc la verité des faits? Ce sera les yeux, qui en sont les légitimes juges, comme la raison l'est des choses naturelles et intelligibles, et la foi des choses surnaturelles et révélées . . . Et comme Dieu a voulu se servir de l'entremise des sens pour donner entrée à la Foi, *Fides ex auditu*, tant s'en faut que la foi détruise la certitude des sens, que ce serait au contraire détruire la foi que de vouloir révoquer en doute le rapport fidèle des sens . . . la parole de Dieu étant infaillible dans les faits mêmes.' And further, *ibid.*, 273: 'Si l'on soumet tout à la raison, notre religion n'aura rien de mystérieux et de surnatural. Si l'on choque les principes de la raison, notre religion sera absurde et ridicule.'

883 [John Toland] *Christianity not Mysterious* (1696), p.150, quoted by Cragg, *op. cit.*, p.151.

884 *ibid.*, p.152; quoted in *ibid.*, p.152.

885 *Cf.* Burnet, *A rational Method for proving the Truth of the Christian Religion as it is professed in the Church of England*, London 1675.

886 T. F. Bumpus, *op. cit.*, p.258.

887 L. Milman, *op. cit.*, p.220.

888 Cragg, *op. cit.*, p.11.

889 *Cf.* the significant passage from Patrick's *Autobiography*, quoted by Cragg, *op. cit.*, p.85, recording his sentiments on his elevation to the See of Chichester: 'I fell into a meditation of the goodness of God, who had

brought me into the world, and let me live sixty-three years in such wealth, ease, and pleasure . . . and made me a minister of the Gospel, and placed me in an advantageous position . . .'

890 Letters to the archbishops, 14 Oct. 1662; *Cal. S. P. Dom.*, Car.II, 1661–2, p.517; quoted by Cragg, *op. cit.*, p.33.

891 *Cf.* Harris, *Life of Charles II*, II, p.94.

892 Speech to Parliament, 18 Feb. 1662/3, in *Letters . . .* etc., *ed. cit.*, p.140.

893 *The Present State of England, stated by a Lover of his King and, Country* 1671, quoted by Tawney, *Religion and the Rise of Capitalism*, London, 1948 p.311, note.

894 Anti-Catholic sentiments were not confined to the mob which, as Evelyn describes, plundered the Spanish ambassador's house, but also extended to the educated classes; a remarkable indication is provided by the proviso contained in Sir William Petty's plan for London, 1666, that no Papist should live within its confines; *cf.* Brett-James, *op. cit.*, p.319.

895 *Cf.* Yates, *op. cit.*, p.204.

896 'I am in my nature an enemy to all severity for Religion and Conscience, how mistaken soever it be, when it extends to capital and sanguinary punishments, which I am told were begun in Popish times . . .' Speech to Parliament, in *Letters . . . ed. cit.*, p.140.

897 Speech to Parliament, 24 Nov. 1664; *ibid.*, p.171.

898 Speech to Parliament, 12 June 1663; *ibid.*, p.143.

899 H. H. Milman, quoted by J. S. Bumpus, *op. cit.*, p.174.

900 Speech to Parliament, 24 Nov. 1664, in *Letters . . . ed. cit.*, p.171.

901 Address to Charles II, quoted from *History of Passive Obedience*, by Cragg, *op. cit.*, p.164.

902 *The Judgment and Decree of the University of Oxford*, 21 July 1683 (mistakenly dated 31 July by Cragg, *op. cit.*, pp.164–5), quoted in Miller, *Philosophical History*, III, p.385; *cf.* also Brodrick, *History of the University of Oxford*, 1886, p.158.

903 *Cf.* Peter de Moulin, *The Papal Tyranny as it was Exercized over England for Some Ages*, 1674.

904 *Cf.* Cosimo of Tuscany, *Travels*, pp.168–71, for a description of Catherine's religious establishment, including the Italian musicians of her chapel under Matteo Battaglia.

905 *Cf. Cleri Gallicani Ecclesiastica Potestate Declarato*, 1682: '. . . Reges ergo et principes in temporalibis nulli ecclesiastice potestati Dei ordinacio subjici, neque autoritate clavium Ecclesiae directe nel indirecte deponi, aut illorum subditos eximi e fide atque obedientia, ac praestito fidelitatis sacramento solve posse, eamque sententiam publicae tranquillitati necessariam, nec minus Ecclesiae quan Imperio utilem a verbo Dei, Patrum historici et sanctorum exemplis censenam omnino retuendam.'

906 *Treatise of the Pope's Supremacy*, preface; quoted by Cragg, *op. cit.*, p.167.

907 *Treatise* . . . quoted *ibid.*, p.168.

908 *The True Protestant Subject*, quoted *ibid.*, p.169.

909 Evelyn, *Diary*, 27 June 1686.

910 *A Defence of the Profession which the Right Reverend Father in God, John* [Lake], *late Lord Bishop of Chichester, made upon his death-bed; Concerning Passive Obedience and the new Oaths*, 1690, quoted by Cragg, *op. cit.*, p.182.

911 William Nicolson, *Epistolary Correspondence*, 15 May 1689; quoted *ibid.*, p.178.

912 *A Discourse Concerning the Unreasonableness of a New Separation, on Account of the Oaths, with an Answer to the History of Passive Obedience, so far as relates to them*, quoted *ibid.*, p.179.

913 *A Discourse* . . ., quoted *ibid.*, p.180. *Cf.* also Locke, *A Letter Concerning Toleration*, passim.

914 Cragg, *op. cit.*, p.223.

915 Hume, *Essays* (1741), I, vii.

916 The difficulty has been summarized by Whiffen, *op. cit.*, p.14; but no answer to the problem is given by the proposition that 'his style is best called, simply, Wren'.

917 Bodl. Libr. Aubrey MS Wood, quoted in Powell, *op. cit.*, p.145.

918 Aubrey is not to be altogether trusted; the anecdote recounted in the *Miscellanies* of Wren's being ill in Paris, dreaming of palm trees and recovering on eating dates is of highly questionable authenticity, particularly as Aubrey's date cannot be reconciled with Wren's only visit to Paris known to us, although the apocryphal story is accepted by Briggs, *op. cit.* (1951), and transferred to the only date at which Wren was in Paris, 1665.

919 Whitaker-Wilson's opinion, *op. cit.*, p.247, that 'looking back on the early part of Wren's career, it is almost impossible to gauge the depth of John Evelyn's friendship. Surely no man ever had such a friend!' is typical of the extravagant exaggerations and distortions to which this author is prone. Evelyn's respect for the prowess of the young Oxford scholar has been frequently quoted (*Diary*, 11, 13 July 1654). But the only other references to Wren in the *Diary*, apart from records of meetings attended by both at the Royal Society, in connexion with Greenwich, Chelsea, and St Paul's, occur under 12 Feb. 1670/1: 'This day dined with me Mr Surveyor Dr. Chr: Wren, Mr. Pepys, Cleark of the Acts, two extraordinary ingenious and knowing persons, and other friends . . .', and 26 April 1681, when Evelyn entertained Wren and Sir William Fermor to dinner and commented on the former: 'A wonderful genius had this incomparable person.' These entries do not convey, by their somewhat distant phraseology, any degree of intimacy between Evelyn and Wren; nor can such be inferred from Evelyn's dedication of the 1696 edition of *A Parallel* to Wren as he had dedicated, with comparable fluorish, the 1664 edition to Denham with whom we have no evidence of Evelyn to have been more than acquainted. The possibility exists that events caused a certain amount of estrangement between the two subsequent to 1688; the statement made by Phillimore, *op. cit.*, p.263, that 'it is evident that [Wren] took the new oaths of allegiance, probably holding with Evelyn and other honourable men that King James had abdicated and that therefore the throne was vacant' must be rejected. Evelyn's sympathies, as is clearly revealed from the *Diary*, were with Sancroft and the non-jurors.

920 Wren's Parliamentary career extended over many years, though its total active duration was short. According to Briggs, *op. cit.* (1951), pp.135–6, Wren stood unsuccessfully as candidate for Oxford in 1674; sat as Member for Plympton St Maurice in 1685; was involved in the contested election for Windsor in 1688 (*v. infra*, note 923); and held his last seat, for Weymouth, 1701–2.

921 Phillimore, *op. cit.*, p.x.

922 Whitaker-Wilson, *op. cit.*, p.6.

923 The election was contested on the grounds of a faulty poll count; *cf.* Adderley, *The Case of William Adderley Esq. duly elected a burgess to serve in Parliament for the Borough of New Windsor . . .* etc., 1688.

924 Ignatius of Loyola, *Spiritual Exercises*, quoted by Peers, *Studies of the Spanish Mystics*, I (1927), p.25.

925 It must have surprised many contemporaries that Marlborough did not choose Wren to design the palace which was to have been the nation's gift to the victor of Blenheim. 'But could he have made it a symbol, a monument to the triumph of British arms? The Duke was right. Only Vanbrugh could evoke such arrogance from masonry – the glance of Tamburlaine from a capital – and turn a Roman triumph into gesturing stone.' Whistler, *op. cit.*, pp.111–12.

926 Hauser, *op. cit.*, p.435.

927 Drummond's view, *op. cit.*, p.29, that 'the Baroque temple was infinitely further from the spirit of Christianity than the Gothic shrine of the Middle Ages' can be accepted by a Puritan partisan, but not by the architectural or ecclesiological historian. Psychologically as well as stylistically the comparison is not valid, though much of the splendour of (particularly later) Gothic architecture is nearer to the Baroque spirit in

Catholicism than to the Lutheran preaching halls; *v. supra*, pp.144–5.

928 *Cf.* the Sale Catalogue, lots 51, 173, 203, 290, 480, 481, and 505, the total of which gives no less than forty-three volumes of collected tracts and pamphlets.

929 Sprat, *History of the Royal Society* (1702 ed.), p.53.

930 Phillimore, *op. cit.*, p.100.

931 *Cf. Of Liberty and Servitude*, 1649, and *Diary*, 21 Jan. 1648/9; also *An Apology for the Royal Party*, 1659, and *Diary*, 7 Nov. 1659.

932 *De Architectura*, I, i, 3: 'Et ut litteratus sit, peritus graphidos, eruditos geometria, historias complures noverit, philosophos diligenter audierit, musicam scierit, medicinae non sit ignarus, responsa iurisconsultorum noverit, astrologiam caelique rationes cognitas habeat.'

933 Gotch, *RIBA Mem. Vol.*, p.10, suggests that 'we can well believe that in [music and literature] also he would have excelled had leisure permitted him to turn his versatile mind to them'. Loftie, *op. cit.*, p.151, believes that Wren 'dabbled successfully in poetry'.

934 There is nothing to substantiate the full implications of H. H. Milman's opinion, *op. cit.*, p.395, that 'there was no branch of scientific inquiry of which he was not master, in which he had not advanced as far as any man, and surpassed most'. Nor have we any evidence for the 'very valuable astronomical instruments' which Wren, according to Cleveland, *art. cit.*, p.481, is alleged to have designed before going up to Oxford. Nor does historical evidence support Mackmurdo's statement, *op. cit.*, pp.18–19, that 'by victories over the first mathematicians of the age by his profound mathematical tracts, and astronomical dissertations, by his ingenious inventions, and by his newly applied methods of scientific investigation, Wren was celebrated throughout Europe'. Lastly, not only would it be too much to claim Wren as 'one of the best geometricians in Europe' (Phillimore, *op. cit.*, p.132), and 'a scientist of European fame, a compeer of Newton and Harvey' (Gotch, *RIBA Mem. Vol.*, p.10); but evidence actually disproves the allegation first made by Stephen Wren, and perpetuated by L. Milman *et al.* that Wren not only solved the problem set by Pascal, but also that the promised reward of twenty pistoles was 'withheld by some trickery'. The most reasoned and balanced opinion is that of Weaver, *op. cit.*, p.35: 'It appears clear that in withholding the prize Pascal wronged neither Wren nor the other contestants. The suggestion that Wren was the master mathematician of Europe will not do. It is enough to affirm of him that he was an ingenious geometrician who made several minor advances in that science.' For a facsimile reproduction and discussion of Pascal's problem and Wren's solution, *cf. RIBA Mem. Vol.*, pp.244–5, and the article by Hinks.

935 *De Architectura*, I, i, 1: 'Architecti est scientia pluribus disciplinis et variis eruditionibus ornata ab ceteris artibus perficiuntur.'

936 Letter to Ludovico Sforza, *c.*1482, in Codex Atlanticus (Bibl. Ambros.) 391; in J. P. Richter, *Literary Works of Leonardo da Vinci*, No.1340.

937 *Diary*, 19 Nov. 1694.

938 Clark, *RIBA Mem. Vol.*, p.158.

939 We are here excepting the temporary 'tabernacles' built in a number of parishes after the Fire. References to these occur in parish records, and Wren's name is mentioned on several occasions. No drawings, however, of any of these structures survive.

940 *Cf.*, for example, the stage directions for Purcell's *Dioclesian*, printed by Westrup, *Purcell*, London 1937, p.126.

941 Lord Maltravers to William Petty, 13 Jan. 1636; quoted by Hervey, *op. cit.*, p.355.

942 *ibid.*, p.101 (ref.1616).

943 Evelyn's repeatedly expressed admiration need not be cited here in detail; but *cf. Diary*, 23 July 1679; 18 April 1680; 16 June 1683; 10 Oct. 1683; 10 May 1684; 29 Dec. 1686. His interest in painting extended to the translation of de Chambray's *Idée de la perfection de la Peinture* (Au Mans, 1662) which appeared in 1668 as the successor to the better-known *Parallel* (*cf. Diary*, 28 Aug. 1668) and was dedicated to Henry Howard.

944 *Cf.* Wren's letter regarding Trinity College library, quoted by Caröe, *op. cit.*, p.51: 'The Statues are supposed of plaister, there are Flemish artists that doe them cheape.' *Cf.* also Robert Bridges's amusing reference to Wren's apparent disinclination to spend much money on statuary, quoted *ibid.*, p.111:

'. . . one of those column-heads which Wren
compounded for at two-pound-ten . . .
But jealous Time, who was unwilling
to suffer those poor fifty-shilling
presentments of the brows of Hellas
snubb'd them as readily & as well as
his frost and rain make scald & sorry
the ashlar of our suburban quarry . . .' etc.

945 Sir William was godfather, with Evelyn, to Wren's son; *cf. Diary*, 17 June 1679 and 5 May 1681.

946 *ibid.*, 19 Sept., 8 Oct., 17 Oct., 25 Oct. 1667.

947 *ibid.*, 21 March 1691: 'Sir William [Fermor] had now bought all the remaining statues collected with so much expense by the famous Thomas, Earl of Arundel, and sent them to his seat at Easton, near Towcester.'

948 *ibid.*, 11 July 1654,

949 *loc. cit.*

950 Pepys, *Diary*, 22 July 1664, when, returning home, he found 'Mr. Hill, and Andrews, and one slovenly and ugly fellow, Signor Pedro, who sings Italian songs to the theorbo most neatly; and they spent the whole evening in singing the best piece of musique counted of all hands in the world, made by Signor Charissimi [*sic*] the famous Master in Rome'. *Cf.* also *ibid.*, 12 Feb. 1666/7.

951 *Cf.* Evelyn, *Diary*, 30 May 1698: 'I dined at Mr Pepys, where I heard the rare voice of Mr Pule, who was lately come from Italy . . . he sung several compositions of the late Dr Purcell.'

952 *Cf.* Wren's Memorandum, para (7), in WS IX, p.17. It is surprising that Gibbs should appear to have been far more considerate of acoustics than Wren; *cf.* his reasons for the design of the ceiling of St Martin's, quoted by Daniell, *London Riverside Churches*, p.185: 'The ceiling is elliptical, which I find by experience to be much better for the voice than the semicircular, though not so beautiful.'

953 *De Architectura*, V, viii.

954 *Cf.* Wren's contemptuous reference to Schmidt's organ as a 'box of whistles'.

955 Hopkins and Rimbault, *History of the Organ* (1870), quoted by Jenkinson, *op. cit.*, p.244.

956 *Elements of Architecture*, 1624, p.51: 'Both for the naturall imbecility of the sharp Angle itselfe, and likewise for their very Uncomeliness, pointed Arches ought to be exiled from Judicious Eyes, and left to their first inventors, the Gothes or Lombards, amongst other Reliques of that barbarous Age . . .'

957 Aikin, *op. cit.*, p.2.

958 Report on Westminster Abbey restorations, 1713, *Parentalia*, pp.269 *et seq.* The only instance of Wren's ignoring the unsuitability of Gothic-Renaissance combinations occurs at St Michael's, Cornhill, the incongruity of which has been remarked on by Jenkinson, *op. cit.*, p.118. It is interesting to compare Wren's and Evelyn's opinions, popularly assumed to be identical. In his *Account of Architecture and Architects*, a lengthy tirade similar in content to Wotton's opinion can be found, together with a eulogy of Jones and Wren, in which the juxtaposition of the Oxford Schools and the Sheldonian Theatre is the most questionable. Against this, however, must be set a considerable number of appreciative remarks occurring in the *Diary*; e.g. 17 Aug. 1641 (Haarlem); 4 Oct. 1641 (Vrou Kirk, Antwerp); 12 Nov. 1643 (Abbeville); 18 March 1644 (St-Ouen); 28 March 1644 (Evreux); 30 Sept. 1644 (Avignon, Ste-Madelaine and St-Martial); 4 Nov. 1644 (St-Sauveur, Aix-en-Provence); 21 May 1645 (Siena); July 1645 (SS Giovanni e Paolo, Venice, Milan

Cathedral); 31 July 1654 (Gloucester); 2 Aug. 1654 (Worcester); 15 Aug. 1654 (Newstead Abbey); 17 Aug. 1654 (York Minster); 19 Aug. 1654 (Lincoln); 30 Aug. 1654 (Peterborough); 16 Oct. 1671 (Norwich) etc.

959 *Cf. Stone-Heng restor'd ... the most Notable Antiquity of Great Britain ...* etc., 1655, where Jones describes the remains as circular in plan, and interprets them as the ruins of a Roman temple dedicated to Coelus. The refutation of his theory was attempted by Dr Walter Charleton, in *Chorea Gigantum, or Stonehenge restor'd to the Danes*, 1663, which was followed by John Webb's retort entitled *A Vindication of Stone-henge restor'd, in Answer to Dr Charleton's Reflections*, 1665. The three tracts were re-published together in 1725; *cf.* also Powell, *op. cit.*, p.108.

960 For works on the subject in Wren's library, *cf.* Abstract, pp.231–5. The only reference to his interest in Anglo-Saxon antiquities is confined to a note (pr. Aubrey, *Monumenta Britannica*, I): 'on Lurgeshall Hill (or neere there) in Wiltshire, is a Campe ...' written by Wren to 'Mr Darsyth, Almanack-maker there'. We may also note that in 1673 a new edition of Camden's *Britannia* was being planned, and questions of editing were discussed by several members of the Royal Society, notably Wren, Hoskyns, Hooke, Ogilby, Aubrey, and Gregory King, and possibly Evelyn (*cf.* Powell, *op. cit.*, pp.151–2). Significantly, however, Wren made no contribution to the edition eventually published by Gibson in 1695, though Evelyn was responsible for the additions pertaining to Surrey; *cf. Diary*, 8 March 1695.

961 Weaver, *op. cit.*, p.132.

962 *Cf. A Plan of Civil and Historical Architecture ...* etc. (translated by Thos. Lediard) London 1730 (original edition, French and German, published posthumously, Leipzig 1725), which contains the antiquities of Halicarnassus, Niniveh, Knossos, Spalato, Palmyra, Stonehenge.

963 Wren's explanation of the origin of the proportions of the orders is wholly different from Vitruvius: *cf.* 'Tract' II (WS XIX, p.129): 'at first the Columns were six Diameters in Height; when the Imitation of Groves was forgot, the Diameters were advanced to seven; then to eight; then to nine, as in the Ionick Order; then, at last, to ten, as in the Corinthian and Italick Orders.' Vitruvius's account is altogether different: firstly, he derives the 1:6 proportion of the pristine Doric order from the relationship between the length of a man's foot to his height; *De Architectura*, IV, i, 6: 'in ea aede cum voluissent columnas conlocare, non habentes symmetrias earum et quaerentes quibus rationibus efficere possent, uti et ad onus ferendum essent idonea et in aspectu probatam haberent venustatem, dimensi sunt virilis pedis vestigium et id retulerunt in altitudinem. Cum invenissent pedem sextam partem esse altitudinis in homine, item in columnam transtulerunt et, qua crassitudine fecerunt basim scapi, tanta sex cum capitulo in altitudinem extulerunt. Ita dorica columna virilis corporis proportionem et firmatetem et venustatem in aedificiis praestare coepit.' For Vitruvius's account of the extension of the proportions, *ibid.*, III, v, *passim*; IV, i–ii.

964 *Elements*, preface. Pratt's opinion on Alberti, *The Architecture of ...*, p.285, is identical.

965 Cunningham, *op. cit.*, IV, p.77.

966 Preface to *Sonatas of III Parts, for two Violins and bass with organ or harpsichord*, dedicated to King Charles II, 1683; *cf.* also Dryden, *Musical Drama*.

967 Quoted in Whistler, *op. cit.*, pp.111–12: 'Not long before this time [i.e. beginning of the eighteenth century] the Italian opera begun first to steal into England, but in as rude a disguise, and unlike itself, as possible; in a lame hobbling translation into our own language, with false accents, and metre out of measure to its original notes, sung by our own unskillful voices, with graces misapply'd to almost every sentiment, and with action lifeless and unmeaning through every character'

968 1689; *cf.* Nicoll, *A History of Restoration Drama*, Cambridge 1923; Dryden's *Essay of Dramatic Poesy*: 'The drift of the ensuing discourse was chiefly to vindicate the honour of our English writers, from the censure of those who unjustly prefer the French before them ...' and

Preface to *All for Love*: 'I have endeavoured ... to follow the practice of the Ancients ... Yet, though their models are regular, they are too little for English tragedy; which requires to be built in a larger compass.'

969 *Ibid.* The words 'all their wit is in their ceremony' ironically suggest a French source for this criticism of French drama: *cf.* Montaigne, *De La Praesumptio*. In contrast, however, *cf.* Nicoll, *op. cit.*, p.119: 'Not one of the heroes, heroines, or villains of the exalted tragedy acts rightly. Their psychology is hopelessly wrong. Whether it is love or war or death, their actions and their words are the actions and words of unreality.

970 *The Play-House to be Lett.*

971 Preface to *The Miser*, 1672.

972 Wren to Nathaniel Hawes, 24 Nov. 1692, quoting a conversation at a previous meeting; *cit.* L. Milman, *op. cit.*, p.337.

973 Weaver, *op. cit.*, p.51: 'It is useless to speculate how Wren would have developed on a fuller Italian basis. His art would have been more informed: he would almost certainly have avoided the technical uncertainties that mar some of his finest achievements ...' but *v. supra*, note 603.

974 *Cf.* Loftie, *op. cit.*, p.viii: 'the faults of Palladio, as set forth, not so much in his drawings as in his actual buildings, are easily discovered, though they hardly concern us here. He was careless of details, his ornaments are often coarsely cut, and though he had laid down such exact rules for proportions he was always ready to break them himself when occasion arose.' This author's opinion on Palladio's ornament should be compared with that of Blomfield and Weaver, *supra*, note 139. For his criticism of Palladio's proportions, *v. infra*, note 977.

975 Grosart, *op. cit.*, II, p.91.

976 *Cf.* Blomfield, *Touchstone*, p.183, with reference to Pembroke College chapel: 'The Corinthian pilasters of the front are some 12 diameters high. If Wren had consulted his Serlio, he would have found out his mistake'. And *Six Architects*, p.163: 'Wren made his order 12 diameters high because he thought it looked nice and did not know any better.' Stratton, *op. cit.*, p.43, explains Wren's 'lapses' from classical precedent by suggesting that 'he never allowed himself to be fettered by changeless rules of proportions in the use of the Orders, but evolved his own with a nicety which never fails to please'. It is significant of Loftie's uncritical attitude that he severely criticizes Vanbrugh for a 'fault' with which Wren could be, and has been, reproached; *cf. op. cit.*, p.215: 'If [Vanbrugh] had any knowledge or any artistic perception, he carefully concealed them ... his style consisted in the negation of style. If a composite column should be no more than ten diameters high, Vanbrugh made it twelve or fourteen.'

977 *Quattro Libri*, quoted by Fletcher, *op. cit.*, p.49; the reference there given as I, ch.ii, is incorrect; the passage occurs at the end of ch.xiii (1601 ed., p.16, sig.B 2 *verso*): 'onde potrà ciascuno facendo il Modulo maggiore, et minore, seconda la qualità della fabrica seruirsi della proportioni, & della sacome disegnate a ciascun'ordine conuenienti.'

978 'Tract' II, WS XIX, p.128.

979 Apart from classical precedents, *cf.*, for example, the Merovingian and Carolingian baptisteries of Riez, Fréjus, and Savona; the Romanesque baptisteries of Parma, Pisa, and Florence; the Renaissance counterparts in St Gabriel's chapel at St Sebastian, Salzburg (by Elia Castello, 1595–1600); Mansart's Valois mausoleum; or the basic plan in Jacques Androuet du Cerceau's volume of drawings, Pierpont Morgan Library, fo.86 *recto*. The ultimate derivation for Renaissance usage is found in Serlio, *Regole*, V, 2 *recto* (1663 ed., p.369).

980 This characterization is clearly derived from Palladio; *v. supra*, notes 834, 835.

981 'Tract' IV, WS XIX, p.137; the reference is to the temple of Mars Ultor, Rome.

982 'Tract' II, WS XIX, pp.131–2.

983 *Cf.* Abstract, lot 310; it is clear, however, that Wren was familiar with Plato's works before the publication of that edition: *cf.* the suggestive reference to the Platonic concept of the soul-stuff in relation to the

universe (*Timaeus*, 35–6, 41–2) in his address to Gresham College (pr. Cunningham, *op. cit.*, IV, p.161): 'It were pedantic to tell you of the affinity of our souls to Heaven – of our erected countenances given us on purpose for astronomical speculations; or to acquaint you that Plato commended it in his commonwealths.'

984 *Cf*. Abstract, lot 498.

985 *Cf*. Abstract, lot 416, Kepler's edition of Tycho Brahe's *Astronomia*, 1609; in Wren's address to Gresham College occurs only a reference to Kepler's 'Dioptricks', but a knowledge of *Mysterium Cosmographicum* (1597) and possibly *Harmonia Mundi* (1619) is suggested by the passage (pr. Cunningham, *loc. cit.*): '. . . glorious in their starry ornaments, of which every one affords various cause of admiration, most rapid yet most regular – most harmonious in their motions . . .'

986 *De Architectura*, III, i, 1, 3; also *v. supra*, note 844. *De Re Aedificatoria*, VII, iiii, quoted *supra*, note 703.

987 *Regole*, V, *supra*, p.155.

988 *Quattro Libri*, I, xxi, quoted *supra*, note 705.

989 *De Architectura*, V, iv, 7.

990 *De Re Aedificatoria*, IX, vi, quoted *supra*, note 842.

991 *Cf*. Abstract, lot 286; this, the Bâle 1570, edition contains the *De Musica* originally published Venice 1491.

992 *Cf*. Abstract, lots 282, 283.

993 *In Ezechielem Explanationis*, Rome 1596–1604 does not appear in the Wren library list; his knowledge of the work, however, is indicated by his reference in 'Tract' V (WS XIX, pp.141–2); and corroborated by the entry in Hooke's *Diary*, 6 Sept. 1675, 'Long Discourse with [Wren] about the Module of the Temple at Jerusalem'. Significantly, Hooke records the purchase of 'Villalpandus, 30sh.' exactly four months later.

994 *Cf*. Abstract, lot 323.

995 Richardson, *RIBA Mem. Vol.*, p.160. Wren's only recorded opinion on proportion is inconclusive: *cf*. 'Tract' I (WS XIX, p.127): '. . . a Portico [here meaning colonnade] the longer the more beautiful, in infinitum; on the contrary, Fronts require a Proportion of the Breadth to the Heighth [*sic*] higher than three times the Breadth is indecent, and as ill to be above three times as broad as high.'

996 *Cf*. Abstract, lot *32: [Thomas] Burnet's [*Sacred*] *History of the Earth*, 1719 [1689], 'If the sea had been drawn round the earth in regular figures and borders, it might have been a great beauty to our globe . . . What a beautiful Hemisphere [the stars] would have made if they had been placed in Rank and Order; if they had been disposed into regular Figures . . . according to the Rules of Art and Symmetry . . .' (quoted by Carritt, *op. cit.*, p.119).

997 Warton, *Milton's Minor Poems*, quoted by Carritt, *op. cit.*, p.388.

998 Drummond, *op. cit.*, p.35.

999 Weaver, *op. cit.*, p.74.

1000 Before analysing Wren's canon, the following reservation should be made: the first four 'Tracts' here quoted were published in *Parentalia* in 1750; the fifth has been transcribed from the original MS. in the 'Heirloom' copy of the work. now at the RIBA. The exact provenance of the material cannot be established with certainty; the drawings of the temple of Diana at Ephesus, the city of Babylon, Noah's Ark, etc. have been suggested to be Flitcroft's work, based on sketches by Wren. The reliability of *Parentalia*, as noted, has been proved doubtful in many respects. The thirty pages of printed matter included in the 'Heirloom' copy are most probably proofs of the text matter to be included in a book for which Christopher Wren had a number of engravings made. On the other hand, the WS editors have noted the inclusion of a passage drawn from a book published in 1730, so that it seems that Wren's opinions, as presented in *Parentalia* were edited either by his son or grandson. The basic authenticity, however, is attested by Wren's references to the tomb of Lars Porsenna, which are corroborated by the discussions on the subject recorded by Hooke (*Diary*, Oct. 1677); internal evidence may suggest the frequently dogmatic phraseology to be due to Christopher or Stephen Wren, but questions of expression apart, there seems no reason to doubt the authenticity of the views expressed.

1001 'Tract' I, WS XIX, p.126.

1002 For Wren's familiarity with Plato's *Timaeus v. supra*, note 983; he would also have been familiar with the quotations occurring in Junius's [François du Jon] *De Pictura Veterum* (*cf*. Abstract, lot 82).

1003 *De Architectura*, I, ii, 1, 4; III, i, 1; *cf*. also Bassi, *Dispareri in Materia d'Architettura et Prospettiva* . . . etc., Brescia 1572 (quoted by Panofsky, 'Die Perspektive als "Symbolische Form"' in *Vorträge der Bibliothek Warburg*, 1924–5, Leipzig-Berlin 1927, pp.324–7, note 68), in which Palladio's stipulation occurs that 'after all the rules of perspective the viewpoint must lie central in order to lend the view "maestà e grandezza"'.

1004 *Amnead*, I, 6, 1, quoted by Richter, *Rhythmic Form in Art*, London 1932, p.3.

1005 *De Architectura*, III, i, 1, and VI, ii, 1. *Cf*. the parallels in *De Re Aedificarotia*, VI, ii, and IX, v, and *Quattro Libri*, I, i: 'La bellezza risulterà dalla bella forma, e dalla corrispondenza del tutto alle parti, delle parti fra loro, e di quelle al tutto; conciosache gli edificij habbiano da parere vno interio, e ben finito corpo: nelquale l'vn membro all'altro conuenga, & tutte le membra siano necessarie à quello, che si vuol fare.'

1006 *De Architectura*, III, i, 1: 'Namque non potest aedis alla sine symmetria atque proportione rationem habere compositionis.'

1007 *Amnead*, *loc. cit.*,

1008 *De Re Aedificatoria*, IX, 5.

1009 *Regole* (1663 ed.), p.368: 'Et perche la forma rotonda è la più perfetta di tutte l'altre, io da quella cominciarò.'

1010 *Quattro Libri*, IV, ii,: 'Ma la più belle, e più regolare forme, e dalle quali le altre riveuono le misure, sono la Ritonda, & la quadrangulare.'

1011 *De Architectura*, I, ii, 4; III, i, 3, and III, i, 4: 'Ergo si ita natura composuit corpus hominis, uti proportionibus membra ad summam figurationem eius respondeant, cum causae constuisse videntur antiqui, ut etiam in operum perfectionibus singulorum membrorum ad universam figurae speciem habeant commensus exactionem.'

1012 *Regole*, I, 2 *verso*.

1013 *Ibid*., I, 13 *recto* & *verso*, V, 4 *recto*; *v. supra*, p.129.

1014 'Of the Standard of Taste', in *Essays Moral, Political and Literary*, quoted by Cassirer, *The Philosophy of the Enlightenment*, Princeton 1951, p.307.

1015 *Essays on the Nature and Principles of Taste*, quoted by Wittkower, *op. cit.*, p.133.

1016 Summerson, *Heavenly Mansions*, p.81, analyses Wren's 'Two Kinds of Beauty' as a differentiation between geometrical design and applied ornament. This, however, would amount to no more than the Albertian distinction (*De Re Aedificatoria*, VI, 2) between beauty conceived in purely geometrical terms, and ornament. Wren's 'Customary Beauty', however, seems to us of an entirely different significance. Summerson's restricted interpretation is the more surprising for his penetrating exposition of empiricist ideologies in relation to Wren's work.

1017 For an admirable exposition of the development of eighteenth-century aesthetics, *cf*. Cassirer, *op. cit.*, esp. ch.vii.

1018 *Essays*, 'Of Beauty' (1612); it is surprising that Wittkower, in his lucid work here frequently quoted, omits all reference to this most important passage, just as he makes no mention of Pratt or Wren in their relationship to harmonic theory. Bacon's passage is quoted in the *Third Discourse* where Reynolds approvingly cites Proclus' retort that 'he that takes for his models such forms as nature produces, and confines himself to an exact imitation of them, will never attain to what is perfectly beautiful. For the works of nature are full of disproportion and fall very short of the true standard of beauty'. Bacon's position in this context was already recognized by Goethe: *cf*. *Farbenlehre*, in Jubiläums-Ausgabe, XL, p.202: '. . . the disinclination to acknowledge authority becomes more and more marked, and as one has protested in religion, so one will protest in science, and at last Bacon of Verulam dares to wipe out . . . everything that had been inscribed upon the tables of mankind.'

1019 Satire, *On the Court*:

'And then by *Durers* rules survay the state
Of his each limbe, and with strings the odds trye
Of his necke to his legge, and waste to thighe.
So in immaculate clothes, and Symetrie
Perfect as circles, with such nicetie
As a young Preacher at his first time goes
To preach, he enters . . .' etc.

The reference, plainly sarcastic, is to Dürer's *Vier Bücher von menschlicher Proportion*, Nürnberg 1528, which Donne may have known in the original, the Latin translation by Camerarius of 1532, or the French translation by Louis Meigret, which appeared in 1557.

1020 *Essay on Building.* For Wren's knowledge of Bacon's works, *cf.* Abstract, lots 17, 118, 523.

1021 *Cf.* Abstract, lot 549. A lengthy exposition of the theory of harmonic proportions, with quotation of numerous examples is found in II, pp.727 *et seq.*

1022 The WS editors, XIII, p.42, note, and XIX, p.124, suggest that Wren 'would certainly have come in contact with both Claude and Charles Perrault' but we cannot share the confidence with which this assertion is made. It would, of course, be of the utmost interest to have documentary evidence that at least portions of Wren's 'Tracts' were 'ideas gained in converse rather than from books' but there is neither evidence nor even probability to support this view. Claude Perrault's Louvre front was built 1668–70; at the time of Wren's visit he was not even officially appointed to the works; there is no mention of either of the Perraults in Wren's letter; lastly, at the time of Wren's visit, Claude was new to architecture in a similar way to Wren. We have no evidence to show that at that period he had formulated his 'canon' of beauty: his Vitruvius edition, and his work on the Five Orders, as well as his brother's *Parallèle des Anciens et des Modernes*, which the WS editors quote as the derivation of some of Wren's ideas, were not published until some twenty years after Wren's visit.

1023 *Cf.* Abstract, lot 561. This book provides some clue to the hitherto controversial question of dating the Wren 'Tracts' (*cf.* WS editors, XIX, pp.123–5). Internal evidence suggests 'Tract' I to belong to widely differing dates: the first section, completely conservative, states that 'Architecture aims at Eternity; and therefore the only Thing incapable of Modes and Fashions in its Principles, the Orders'. Up to the clearly Vitruvian-derived paragraph on 'Beauty, Firmness and Convenience' the 'Tract' may really belong to the period of the middle 1660's, as the WS editors suggest. The passage following, however, is clearly in line with James's translation of Perrault (quoted *in extenso* in our text) that the dating of this part to post-1708 seems almost a certainty, and indicates the comparative insignificance of the passage from Charles Perrault's *Parallèle* cited by the WS editors in support, which book, for that matter, does not even appear in Wren's library list. (The entry, Perrault's *Characters* clearly refers to [Charles's] *Les Hommes Illustres* . . . 1698.) The divergence of dates of the 'Tracts' is clearly demonstrated by the dictum on the orders quoted above, and the completely contradictory opinion with which 'Tract' II commences: 'Modern Authors . . .' (quoted *in extenso*, p.171).

1024 The quotations here given are taken from James's translation, preface, pp.v–vii.

1025 Letter to Matteo de'Pasti, quoted by Clark, *Piero della Francesca*, London 1951, p.18. *Cf.* also *De Re Aedificatoria* (1550), pp.162–3: '. . . che la Bellezza è vn consento . . . di maniera che e non ui si possa aggiungnere o diminuire, o mutare cosa alcuna, che non stesse peggio . . .'

1026 The best instance is provided by the two extant plans for St Clement Danes, Ruddock Collection 23 (Fig.64) and ASC II, 47 (WS IX, pl.12).

Both are advanced in date, one having been used during erection, but vary from the actual church.

1027 Such a quality of organic conception of design has actually been claimed for the steeple of St Vedast: *cf.* Mackmurdo, *op. cit.*, p.46: 'Alter one finger's breadth you cannot, without destroying the beauty of the proportions.' *Cf.* also Keen, *RIBA Mem. Vol.*, p.34: 'The divisions of the tower [of Bow Church] are faultless in proportion.' Unfortunately these authors do not elucidate their conception of the 'beauty' and 'faultlessness' of the proportions there found.

1028 Mackmurdo, *op. cit.*, p.25.

1029 This appears clearly from Wren's address to Gresham College, printed by Cunningham, *op. cit.*, IV, p.161: 'I might be too verbose should I instance this particularly in showing how much the mathematical wits of this age have excelled the ancients (who pierced but to the bark and outside of things) in handling particular disquisitions of nature, in clearing up history, and fixing chronology.'

1030 *Cf. loc. cit.*: 'For mathematical demonstrations, being built upon the impregnable foundations of geometry and arithmetic, are the only truths that can sink into the mind of man void of all uncertainties.'

1031 Credit must be given to L. Milman, who in her work published in 1908 was the first author on Wren to recognize, however parenthetically, the influence of philosophy on the conceptual basis of Wren's architecture; *cf.* her *op. cit.*, pp.39, 220, 221. And it is surprising that this aspect has been completely disregarded by all subsequent critics until the publication of Summerson's essay, first in the *RIBA Journal* and later incorporated in *Heavenly Mansions*.

1032 *Cf.* Dryden's *Secular Masque*, inserted for the revival of Fletcher's *Pilgrim*, 1700, quoted by Whistler, *op. cit.*, p.92, where Chronos replies to Diana, standing for James I, to Mars, standing for the Civil War, and to Venus, standing for the Restoration:

'All, all of a piece throughout;
Thy Chase had a Beast in View;
Thy Wars brought nothing about;
Thy Loves were all untrue.
'Tis well an Old Age is out,
And Time to begin a New.'

1033 This subordination of the autonomy of each art to a greater synthesis has been stipulated as the prerequisite of true canonical (as opposed to religious) art by Ouspensky, *L'Icone; Vision du Monde Spiritual*, Paris 1948, p.11.

1034 The differences between the European implications of the Renaissance and the Baroque have been aptly summarized by Hager, *op. cit.*, p.13: 'Die Renaissance war eine Geistesströmung die, in Florenz und Rom geboren, Italien ergriff und seinen Geist und seine Sitten umbildete. Von dieser Hochburg aus gewann die Renaissance Einfluss auf das spätmittelalterliche Europa, der sich je nach Entfernung und Empfänglichkeit der Länder unterschiedlich auswirkte, und dabei keineswegs feste Zustände schuf, sondern treibende Gärung auf lange hin vorbereitete. Der Barock dagegen war ein allgemeiner Kulturzustand Europas. Er hatte zwei hundert Jahre Zeit und erzeugte im ganzen Abendlande eine einheitliche politische, soziale, geistige, künstlerische Grundlage, in der, wie gesagt, wesentliche Erungenschaften der Renaissance und Reformation zur Ausgestaltung und allgemeinen Wirksamkeit gekommen sind.'

1035 Henry-Russell Hitchcock, in 'Symposium on Monumentality', *Architectural Review*, 621, p.124.

1036 'Tract' I, WS XIX, p.126. The derivation of this passage may be sought in Alberti, *De Re Aedificatoria*, VIII, i.

1037 Summerson, *Heavenly Mansions*, p.84.

1038 *ibid.*, p.79.

1039 Sencourt, *op. cit.*, p.270.

1040 Loftie, *op. cit.*, p.x.

1041 'Tract' V, WS XIX, p.140.

1042 Wren's critics are at variance on the question of dramatic qualities in his work. The extremes of opinion are to be found in Mackmurdo, *op. cit.*, p.22, holding that St Paul's is 'the completely developed example of the dramatic form of architecture', and Dutton, *op. cit.*, p.12, maintaining that Wren's work was 'free from all attempt at undue dramatic effect'.

1043 Summerson, *Heavenly Mansions*, pp.85–6.
1044 Drummond, *op. cit.*, p.35.
1045 Blomfield, *Touchstone*, p.178.
1046 *Ibid.*, pp.184–5, and *Hist. Ren. Arch. Eng.*, p.140.
1047 Drummond, *op. cit.*, p.35.
1048 *Cp.* Gilpin, *Three Essays on Picturesque Beauty* (1792), quoted by Wittkower, *op. cit.*, p.127: 'The secret is lost. The ancients had it . . . If only we could discover their principles of proportion!' and Gide, *Notes on Chopin*, New York 1949 (*Journal*, 28 Feb. 1928): 'There is a certain relationship between the third and the fifth which is found from one octave to the next, giving by inversion the sixth, the whole forming the perfect chord. Yes, from octave to octave the number of vibrations (a number I do not know) [*v. supra*, note 844] must be in a constant relationship. And this in all keys. And I would doubtless find them, with infinitely higher vibrations, in the visual domain, in the perception of colours. [The relationship between colours and musical harmonies was expounded in several Renaissance treatises; *cf.* Louis de Montjosieu, *Gallus Romae Hospes*, Rome 1585, pt.III; Mersenne, *Harmonie Universelle*, Paris 1636, and especially Zarlino, *Instituzioni harmoniche*, Venice 1558, III, cap.8.] The ear and eye allow an immediate intuition of these relationships. And it surprises one that both our senses, as a result of gradual familiarity, a kind of domesticating, reach a point of enjoying other relationships, whose effect, at first, they consider as disagreeable to the ear and eye, as *dissonant* . . . I cannot think that our senses have grown sharper; but perhaps they are more capable of enjoying any musical relationship whatever.' This view is highly questionable; for visual capacities of appreciating certain proportions, *cf.* Doni, quoted by Wittkower, *op. cit.*, p.12, note 2.

The dating of Wren's works has been a matter fraught with error in the past, as many of the notes referring to the building of the City churches show. The question is complicated by the fact that previous authorities, in assigning dates to Wren's buildings, have very frequently failed to indicate the meaning of such dates, and thus the lists of works which have variously appeared, beginning with that compiled by Stephen Wren, are of only questionable value.

   The catalogue here printed has been devised on a chronology of dates determined by the period during which we know, or can surmise, Wren to have executed his designs. The dates given must not, however, be taken to imply complete precision in the majority of cases: as has been seen, Wren was not in the habit of carrying his designs to completion before building began, and it is therefore wholly probable that certain features and details were actually not finalized until long after building accounts indicate construction to have begun. In this sense, our dates are to be taken as the earliest to which designs can be assigned; the completion of the work, usually indicated by the building accounts, supplies the other terminal. The aim of this catalogue is further to give a picture as complete as possible of Wren's verified and authentic works. Previous authorities have assigned numerous buildings to his hand which cannot be proved, by documentary evidence, to have been designed by him. The prime instance of such wholesale attribution is the case of the City companies, all of whose halls have, at various times, been credited to Wren alone, or in collaboration with Jerman, Hooke, and others. It has now been recognized that Wren cannot be associated with any of them, nor with the Royal Exchange, and therefore no further reference is made to these. A number of buildings doubtfully attributed to Wren has been included in this catalogue, but placed at the foot of the page, relevant material being indicated. Unidentified drawings, however, even if likely to be authentic, have been omitted.

1662–1663 PEMBROKE COLLEGE, Cambridge, chapel. *Cf.* pp.2–3, note 24; Loggan, *Cantabrigia Illustrata*, 1690, where the chapel is shown before the nineteenth-century additions. There are no extant drawings, but a fragment of a wooden model is preserved: *cf.* WS V, 27–9, pl.xi.

1663 SHELDONIAN THEATRE, Oxford. *Cf.* pp.3–4, Loggan, *Oxonia Illustrata*, 1675, has two plates of the building, one of which is given as Fig.2. StPL II, 142, may be an early study. There are no other drawings extant.

1664 TOWER OF LONDON, Storehouse. This is one of Wren's earliest works, though its authenticity cannot be established by documentary evidence; *cf.* Pepys, 8 Nov. 1664.

1665 TRINITY COLLEGE, Oxford, 'quadrangle'. *Cf.* p.4, note 29. Material: ASC I, 68, 69, 71, 72.

1665–1666 EMMANUEL COLLEGE, Cambridge, chapel and library. *Cf.* p.5. Material: ASC I, 100 (Fig.3).

1666, May–August, ST PAUL'S, pre-Fire design. *Cf.* pp.24–6. Material: ASC II, 2, 3, 4, 5, 6 (Fig.32), 7.

1666, 6–11 Sept. CITY OF LONDON, plan. *Cf.* pp.5–9, notes 38–76. Material: ASC I, 7 (Fig.4), 8, 101.

1668 CUSTOM HOUSE. *Cf.* Evelyn, 22 Sept. 1671. There is no extant material, but *cf.* the representation of the building on a Custom House certificate printed by Phillips, *op. cit.*, Fig.31.

1668 SALISBURY CATHEDRAL, report and repairs to spire. *Cf.* Wren's report, printed WS XI, pp.21–6.

1668 ROYAL SOCIETY, project for London premises subsequent to evacuation of Gresham College. *Cf.* Evelyn, *Diary*, 24 Jan. 1668, and editor's note, III, p.505; and Wren's letter, Oxford, 7 June 1668, partly printed by L. Milman, *op. cit.*, p.105. For our rejection of the WS editors' and Briggs's association of the drawing BM Sloane 5238, 66, with this project, *cf.* note 551. It seems that Wren's proposals were rejected: although the Royal Society eventually returned to Gresham College (*cf.* Hooke,

Diary, 14 March 1672/3, 1 Dec. 1673), and Hooke, on 20 June 1674, went to Hoskins, 'with whom much discourse about R.S. module', it was Sir William Petty who was eventually 'desired to draw up a new module for Royal Society' (*ibid.*, 29 Sept. 1674). The project came to nothing: six years later Hooke was still discussing designs with Henshaw (*ibid.*, 6 July 1680).

1668–1669 ST PAUL'S, 'Pantheon design'. *Cf.* pp.29–30. Material: ASC II, 59, 61, 62 (Figs.35, 36).

1669 ST MICHAEL, Cornhill. This early Wren design is not discussed in the text. The Vestry Minutes (WS XIX, pp.45–7) record the agreement with Nicholas Young, on 24 Nov. 1669, 'that he perform the mason's work . . . according to the model shown at the Vestry . . .' The Building Accounts (WS X, p.50) cover the years 1670–7. There are no extant drawings. For the tower, *v. infra, sub* 1715.

1669 ST MARY-AT-HILL. *Cf.* pp.9–10, Figs.7, 8; for dating, *cf.* note 82. A report by Jerman on the ruins of the church was called for on 7 Aug. 1668 (Vestry Minutes, WS XIX, p.31); Wren's name only appears by 6 July 1674, though owing to Jerman's death, he was doubtlessly engaged on the church at least four years earlier. The Building Accounts run from 1670–6. There are no extant drawings.

before 1670 ST PAUL'S, 'dome-nave' design. The project is discussed pp.30–1; the only extant drawing in note 187. The model fragment is preserved in the cathedral Trophy Room.

1670 or before, ST BENET FINK. *Cf.* pp.22, 63. For dating, *cf.* note 134. Material: Building Accounts, in WS X, p.46, Vestry Book and Churchwardens' Accounts, WS XIX, pp.8–9. ASC II, 58 (Fig.28). The church was demolished in 1843.

1670 TEMPLE BAR, London. Now removed to Theobald's Park, Herts. There are no extant drawings or accounts.

1670 ST DIONIS. *Cf.* p.13, Figs.13, 15. For dating, *cf.* note 90. Material: Building Accounts, in WS X, p.48, Vestry Minutes and Churchwardens'

1662–1684 WOLVESEY, Winchester. Wren is credited by Papworth with the bishop's palace, but the suggested dating makes the attribution highly improbable.

?1663 ELY CATHEDRAL, doorway. The resemblance of this work to the porch of Bow Church (Fig.139) has been responsible for the ascription to Wren. The WS editors, XIX index, *sub* pl.xiv, give the alternative dates of 1663 and 1699–1702, and derive the design from 'a famous example by François Mansart which Wren saw in Paris 1665–1666'. The reference is to the Hôtel Conti (Fig.140), but is inapplicable to the first of the dates given. L. Milman, *op. cit.*, p.56, considers it Wren's very first work, but Caröe, *op. cit.*, pp.18–19, denies the work to Wren on impressive,

though not completely convincing evidence.

?1669 TRING, house for Henry Guy; *v. infra, sub* Easton Neston.

c.1668–1669 ST SEPULCHRE. Wren's association with this church cannot be established. Repairs to the apparently not wholly destroyed church are recorded as early as 7 May 1667 (Vestry Minutes, WS XIX, pp.50–2); Wren is not mentioned by name in any subsequent entry. The reference, on 19 April 1670, to 'The Doctor to discharge Mr Hodgkins Bill' is likely to refer to Dr Bell, who was previously recorded as dealing with Marshall's accounts. The Building Accounts (WS X, p.52) cover 1670–7. No drawings survive.

Accounts, WS XIX, pp.16–17. The drawing ASC IV, 89, is perhaps for the east window. The church was demolished in 1878.

1670 *et seq.* ST MARY-LE-BOW. *Cf.* pp.13–16, 63–4; Figs.17, 18, 19, 76. The Building Accounts are printed in WS X, pp.57–76. Material: ASC I, 75 (Fig. 17); ASC II, 47 (Fig.76), 76; BM Sloane 5238, 68; RIBA, D 6/30 (Hawksmoor) (Fig.19); ? ASC I, 66. The church was badly damaged in 1940–1, but is to be reconstructed (1955).

1670 *et seq.* ST LAWRENCE. *Cf.* pp.11–13, Figs.10, 12. The Building Accounts (WS X, p.48) run from 1670–86, so that the date of 1677 advanced by *Parentalia* and accepted by most authorities seems to possess no significance. Daniell's statement, *London Riverside Churches*, p.191, that the foundation stone was laid 12 April 1671 is erroneous, as appears from the entry in the Vestry Minutes quoted *supra*, p.11. Similar complaints occur until 1677. Material: Cooper Collection, 30 (Fig.10); ?ASC I, 61, 73, 74, 103; IV, 78, 79. The church was burnt in 1940, but is being reconstructed (1955).

*c.*1670 ST DUNSTAN IN THE EAST. *Cf.* pp.20–1. The rebuilding was made possible by the gift of £4000 by Lady Dyonis Williamson. Wren's name first occurs in the Vestry Minutes (WS XIX, pp.18–19) in Oct. 1671. The extent of work done at that date cannot easily be established. There are no extant drawings apart from the hypothetical connexion of Fig.27; for the Gothic steeple, *v. infra, sub* 1697.

*c.*1670 ST EDMUND, Lombard Street. *Cf.* pp.16, 64. For our rejection of the universally accepted date of 1689–90, *cf.* note 106. Material: Building Accounts, WS X, p.48, Vestry Minutes and Churchwardens' Accounts, WS XIX, p.19. ASC II, 44 (Fig.20); ASC IV, 112; Rudock Collection 25 (Fig.80) with variant.

*c.*1670 ST CHRISTOPHER. *Cf.* p.9, Fig.6. Phillimore, *op. cit.*, p.185, calls this 'the first church which came under Wren's hand' but the claim is as ill-founded as those made for St Nicholas and St Mary-le-Bow. Birch, *op. cit.*, p.145, suggests works in 1696 in addition to repairs assigned to 1671, without quoting his evidence. The Building Accounts (WS X, p.46) cover 1670–5; the Vestry Minutes (WS XIX, p.15) provide little indication of the extent of the work, and no mention of Wren before 1684/5. No drawings survive. The church was demolished as early as 1781 to make room for the Bank of England.

*c.*1670 ST MICHAEL, Wood Street. *Cf.* p.10, Fig.9. The *Parentalia* date of 1675 universally accepted is erroneous. The Building Accounts (WS X, p.50), cover 1670–87. There are no extant drawings. The church was demolished in 1894.

*c.*1670 ST MILDRED, Poultry. This church is not discussed in the text. In plan it was a slightly irregular rectangular hall, with a tower at the south-west corner. Externally the south front was a pleasing composition of windows topped by triangular pediments (but *cf.* note 84) of varying sizes. The tower was very plain. The Building Accounts run from 1670–9, but the church was in use before 1678, when a deputation from St Bartholomew's (*q.v.*) came to inspect the pewing. There are no extant drawings. The church was demolished in 1872.

*c.*1670 ST OLAVE. *Cf.* p.11, Fig.146. This church has been variously dated: *Parentalia* and Birch give 1673; Phillimore, L. Milman, and Whitaker-Wilson, 1673–6; Caröe, 1672–5; Dutton gives the completion as 1679, but the church must have been in use by April 1678, when its pewing was inspected by members of St Bartholomew's vestry (*q.v.*). There are no extant drawings. St Olave's was destroyed in 1888.

*c.*1670 ST VEDAST. Plan, Fig.11. This church is only mentioned in passing in the text. *Parentalia* has misled most authorities into accepting its date of 1697 for the church, though this is varied by Stratton, L. Milman, Whitaker-Wilson, and Lindsey to 1695, and 1698 is given by Birch for

the completion of the church, by Dutton for the steeple. The Building Accounts (WS X, p.52) cover the years 1670–3; the steeple, and possibly alterations to the west end, can be assigned to 1695 on the strength of the Strong MS. printed by Caröe, *op. cit.*, p.110. One drawing of the steeple is in the King's Library, BM., the only other extant drawing, ASC IV, 99, relates to details of a window and a cornice. St Vedast was badly damaged in 1940 but is being restored (1955).

1670–1671 THE MONUMENT. Designed by Wren possibly with Hooke's collaboration, to commemorate the Great Fire; erection authorized by Parliament 1667. For Wren's various proposals, *cf.* ASC II, 71 and BM Sloane 5238, 69, 70, 71, 72, 73, 77, and Hawksmoor's drawing (V&A) for the Hulsbergh engraving of 1724. *Cf.* Hooke, *Diary*, 19 Oct. 1673, 1 June 1674, 7 Aug. 1674, 23 March 1675.

1670 or later, but before 1672, ST PAUL'S, 2nd model design. This hypothetical scheme is discussed, pp.30–2. There are no extant drawings or other evidence.

1670–1671 ST NICHOLAS. This church is noticed only in passing in the text. Though dated 1677 by *Parentalia*, Birch, Stratton, Daniell, Cleveland, L. Milman, Caröe, Whitaker-Wilson, and Lindsey, the design is clearly much earlier. The Building Accounts (WS IX, p.50) run from 1671 to 1681. There is no evidence for T. F. Bumpus's statement, *op. cit.*, p.376, that this was 'the first church built and finished after the Fire'. Stylistic details support the early date indicated by the Building Accounts and the Churchwardens' Accounts (WS XIX, p.48): the increased width of the centre bay is analogous to Wren's early practice at the Sheldonian Theatre, Emmanuel College chapel, St Michael's, Wood Street, *et. al.* The type of window used corresponds to those of St Edmund, St Anne, St Magnus, and other early designs; the same applies to the rectangular door with a circular window above. Material: ASC I, 105, may be a study for the west end; a plan is in the RIBA Collection.

1671 ST MAGNUS. *Cf.* pp.16–18, 64; Fig. 83. For dating, *cf.* notes 110–11. The history of this church has been clarified by the discovery of early, important drawings in the late Bute Collection. Building was begun early in 1671 and completed by about 1677, when the Vestry Minutes of St Lawrence (WS XIX, p.24) record: 'Peirce to view the Pulpit of St Magnus Church and give his price for doing the like carved work.' The entry, 1677, in the Committee Book (*ibid.*, p.27) for the execution of the north portal may be connected with Wren's original plan. Material: Cooper Collection, 31, 32 (Fig.81). Five drawings in the RIBA Collection, of which one is reproduced as Fig.21; ASC I, 64 (Fig. 22).

*c.*1671 ST GEORGE. *Cf.* p.9, Fig.145. Material: Building Accounts, WS IX, p.48; Churchwardens' Accounts, WS XIX, pp.19–20. The first mention of 'the Doctor' occurs 8 July 1672. The *Parentalia* date of 1674, accepted by Stratton, Birch, L. Milman, Whitaker-Wilson, Dutton, and Lindsey, must be rejected. St George was begun 1671. The only extant drawings are Ruddock Collection, 26 (Fig.5), 27. The church was demolished in 1904.

*c.*1671 ST MARY ALDERMANBURY. *Cf.* p.13, Figs.14, 16. For dating, *cf.* note 90. Building Accounts, WS X, p.50, Vestry Minutes and Churchwardens' Accounts, WS XIX, pp.36–9. No extant drawings. The church was burnt in 1940, only the walls and tower remaining.

1671–1673 ST PAUL'S, Deanery. Erroneously assigned to 1684 by Birch. No extant material.

?1671 DUKE OF NORFOLK, house for. *Cf.* Evelyn, 24 Feb. 1667/8, 17 Oct. 1672. ASC II, 102, ? IV, 118.

? before 1672 WHITEHALL PALACE, first design, for Charles II. *Cf.* pp.79–80. ASC II, 73.

1672 ST STEPHEN, Walbrook. *Cf.* pp.22–4, note 151. Material: Building

---

1670–1677 ST MARY, Woolnoth. Wren's authorship cannot be established. The much later entry in the Churchwardens' Accounts (WS XIX, pp.35–6), 10 Jan. 1707, 'Spent with Mr Cozens waiting on Sir C. Wren', is inconclusive. The rebuilding of the church was decreed by Act of Parliament, 1712. It was eventually rebuilt by Hawksmoor, 1716–27.

Accounts, WS X, pp.77–87, 1674–82. ASC I, 60, is a preliminary study. A drawing of the steeple is in the King's Library, BM (Fig.72); three drawings in the RIBA Collection, of which two are reproduced (Figs. 29, 30). The church was badly damaged 1940, but has been entirely reconstructed.

1672 BROMLEY COLLEGE. Not discussed in the text. Godfrey assigns the building to 1666 which, however, is the date of its foundation. The design is generally accepted as Wren's. There are no extant drawings, but *cf.* the prints in WS XIX, pl.lxxii.

c.1672 ST PAUL'S, 'Greek cross design'. *Cf.* pp.33–5. Material: ASC II, 21, 22 (Figs.38, 37), 23, 80; StPL II, 168 may be a study sheet.

1673 or earlier, ST ANNE, Soho. *Cf.* pp.18–19, note 116. Material: three drawings in the RIBA Collection, of which two are reproduced as Figs.23, 24; ? ASC III, 46.

1673, spring, ST PAUL'S, 'great model design'. *Cf.* pp.33–8. Material: the model preserved in the cathedral; the accessions to StPL from the late Bute Collection, four drawings of which No.3 is reproduced as Fig.40. Possibly StPL I, 50 and II, 141; ASC II, 24–8, 79.

1673–1674 ST BRIDE. *Cf.* pp.20, 64–5; Fig. 84. Material: Building Accounts, WS X, p.46, Vestry Minutes and Churchwardens' Accounts, WS XIX, pp.11–14, ASC II, 46 (Fig.82); ASC IV, 85–6; King's Library, BM; ?Ruddock Collection, 20. The church was burnt in 1940, but the steeple survived.

1673–1676 ST MARY, Ingestre. The attribution is cogent; the only surviving drawing (V&A) relates to the lantern of the tower.

c.1674 ST STEPHEN, Coleman Street. This minor Wren church is not discussed in the text. It was one of the plainest of the City churches, in plan resembling St Olave, without any particularly remarkable features. As appears from the Vestry Minute Book (WS XIX, pp.52–3) the means of the parish were limited. Wren's name does not appear, though the design was certainly his. The building was begun about 1674 and completed by April 1678 when the vestry deputation of St Bartholomew (*q.v.*), already noticed elsewhere, came to inspect the pewing for which Creecher had contracted in March 1676. There are no extant drawings. The church was destroyed in 1940.

c.1674 ST BARTHOLOMEW. This minor church is not discussed in the text. The 'Churche Acoumptes' and Vestry Minutes are in WS X, p.46, and XIX, pp.10–11. A survey of the steeple, by Hooke, is recorded in Jan. 1673/4 as well as an inspection by Dr Woodroffe, churchwardens, etc., to St Mildred, Poultry, St Stephen, Coleman Street, St Olave, St Edmund, and St Magnus, on 3 April 1678 'to view severall churches in order to a Patterne for the workemen to make Pewes by'. There are no extant drawings. The church was demolished in 1841.

1674 ARBURY, Warwickshire, stables and (?) house for Sir Richard Newdigate; *cf.* note 127; WS XII, pl.xlix.

1674 BASE TO KING CHARLES'S STATUE, Charing Cross. Assigned to 1678 by Stratton, L. Milman, Whitaker-Wilson, and Lindsey; the statue was erected in 1674. Material: ASC IV, 54, 55, 56.

1674 LINCOLN CATHEDRAL, Honywood Library, for Dean Michael Honywood. There are no extant drawings. *Cf.* WS XVII, pls.lxv–lxvi; L. Milman, *op. cit.*, pl.12a.

?1674 SENATE HOUSE, Cambridge. Assigned to Wren and to 1674 by Stephen Wren. There seems no reason to doubt the attribution. The thirteen-bay arcade of the lower floor shows the enlargement of the centre bay characteristic of Wren's early practice. Material: ASC I, 52, 53, 54, 55.

1675 ST PETER, Cornhill. *Cf.* pp.43–4; for dating, *cf.* note 260. Wren was not at once appointed to the task of rebuilding this church. The Vestry Minutes (WS XIX, pp.49–50), record the appointment of Jerman on 9 April 1668 'to view, survey and direct the building erecting and setting up the walls of the Parish Church as [he] . . . shall judge most fit and convenient'. On Jerman's death, John Oliver was appointed surveyor on 2 Feb. 1668/9. In 1672 Wren was presented with a gratuity of five guineas 'for his pains and furtherance of a Tabernacle', but plans for rebuilding were not mooted until April 1675. The Building Accounts (WS X, p.52) run from 1677 to 1687. Material: a survey plan is in the Cooper Collection (56); a plan and an ink drawing of the south door are in the RIBA Collection; the steeple, incorporated in 'St Edmund, Bloomsbury', appears in the drawing from the Ruddock Collection, Fig.62; the drawing of the east end, ASC I, 77, is illustrated in Fig.48.

1675 GREENWICH OBSERVATORY. *Cf.* p.87. The building is exhaustively discussed by Caröe; relevant documents are printed in WS XIX, pp.113–15. There are no extant drawings.

before 14 May 1675, ST PAUL'S, 'warrant design'. *Cf.* pp.35–40. Material: the warrant itself, preserved as ASC II, 9; and the drawings ASC II, 10 (Fig.42), 11 (Fig.43), 12, 13, 14, 15, 16; ASC II, 7, 31, 32 may be studies.

1675–1708 ST PAUL'S, the cathedral as built. The evolution is discussed pp.96–106, 108–17. The extant material is extensive and comprises the StPL collection exclusive of those few drawings concerned with preliminary schemes, the 'chapter house' and the piazza designs; in addition, the 1951 accessions to StPL from the late Bute Collection; lastly, the study drawings ASC I, 16, 92, 98, 107; II, 17–20, 29, 30, 33–42, 64, 72, 74; III, 44–5; IV, 71–4, 95, 98, 102, 106–9, 114–15, 152; and one drawing in the RIBA Collection.

before 1676 TRINITY COLLEGE, Cambridge, library, first design. Material: ASC I, 39, 40, 41, 42, 43, and the description, 44; ASC IV, 53.

1676 or earlier, ST MICHAEL, Queenhythe. *Cf.* p.46. It is difficult to date this design with precision. Stylistic indications point to the middle of the decade, but Wren was consulted as early as Oct. 1672 (Churchwardens' Accounts, WS XIX, p.42) though building was not commenced until 1676. The Building Accounts, WS X, p.50, cover 1676–87. Two drawings are preserved in the RIBA Collection. St Michael was demolished 1876.

1676 SS. ANNE AND AGNES. *Cf.* p.47. The church is usually dated 1679–80, though it was neither begun nor finished at that time. *Cf.* note 268. The Building Accounts (WS X, p.46) cover 1676–87; *cf.* also Vestry Minutes, WS XIX, pp.4–5. The elevation, Fig.53, and a plan in the RIBA Collection are the only extant drawings. The church was damaged in 1940.

1676 ALL HALLOWS, Thames Street. *Cf.* pp.40–3; for dating, note 256. Material: Building Accounts (WS X, p.46) and Vestry Minutes and Churchwardens' Accounts (WS XIX, p.2). A survey plan is in the Cooper Collection: an original plan in the RIBA Collection. The church was demolished in 1894.

1676 ST JAMES, Garlick Hythe. *Cf.* p.45, Figs.49, 50. The ruins of the old church were taken down 1675–6 (Churchwardens' Accounts, WS XIX, p.21), and in the following year Wren was consulted on reconstruction (*loc. cit.*). This progressed relatively quickly, as the church was opened for service on 10 Dec. 1682 (Vestry Minutes, *ibid.*, p.21), so that the *Parentalia* dating is, for once, correct, though ironically not followed by subsequent authorities. *Cf.* note 264. There are no extant drawings except that of the steeple in the King's Library, BM (Fig.74). The church was damaged 1940–1, but is being restored.

1672–1674 DRURY LANE THEATRE. Wren's authorship cannot be established. *Cf.* ASC II, 81.

1673–1676 SESSIONS HOUSE, Northampton. Attributed to Wren, with Henry Jones's collaboration, by the WS editors.

1673 EXETER HOUSE. Attributed to Wren by the WS editors; material: ASC IV, 67, dated Jan. 1672/3.

1675–1680 ALL SAINTS, Northampton. *Cf.* Evelyn, 23 Aug. 1688. The church was rebuilt after a fire on 20 Sept. 1675. Attributed to Wren by the WS editors on the similarity of plan with St Mary-at-Hill. Whiffen and Summerson consider Wren's authorship doubtful. *Cf.* WS XIX, pp.58–60.

1676 ST MICHAEL, Bassishaw. *Cf.* pp.44–5. Wren's designs were probably discussed early in 1676 at the 'Two dinners in Old Fish Street' (Churchwardens' Accounts, WS XIX, p.41) which cost the parish £9 19*s* 0*d*. Hooke records building agreements with Fitch and Scarborough on 2 May 1676. The Building Accounts (WS X, p.50) cover the years 1676 to 1682. The drawing, ASC I, 87, may be a study. The church was demolished in 1900.

1676 TRINITY COLLEGE, Cambridge, library. Second, executed design. *Cf.* pp.66–8. Material: ASC I, 45, 46, 47, 48, 50 (Fig.85), 51 (Fig.85), IV, 50–2; and one drawing at Trinity College.

1677 ALL HALLOWS, Watling Street, *Cf.* p.46. The Building Accounts (WS X, p.46) cover 1677–87, though the church is normally dated 1681 or 1684. Material: ?ASC IV, 70. The church was demolished in 1878.

1677, or slightly earlier, ST ANTHOLIN. *Cf.* pp.49, 64. Dated by all authorities, except Caröe, 1682; *cf.* note 272. Material: Building Accounts, WS X, p.46, Vestry Minutes and Churchwardens' Accounts, WS XIX, pp.6–7. ASC II, 51 (Fig.54); ASC II, 52 (Fig.77). The church was demolished in 1875.

?.1677 CHRIST CHURCH. *Cf.* pp.45–6, notes 265–6. The dates generally proposed for this church must be rejected. According to Birch, construction preceded design, as the latter is given (*op. cit.*, p.8) as 1687, the former (*ibid.*, p.120) as 1686–7. Likewise, the *Parentalia* date of 1687, accepted by Daniell, Macmurdo, Stratton, L. Milman, Lindsey, and Whitaker-Wilson appears to be a decade too late. The Building Accounts run from 1677–91. Material: five drawings in the RIBA Collection, of which one is reproduced as Fig.51; ASC II, 53 is a study for the west front. The steeple was not added until 1704. The church was badly damaged in 1940–1, though the steeple has survived.

.1677 ST BENET, Thames Street. *Cf.* pp.40–3; for dating, note 256. Though one of Wren's lesser works, it is amply documented by extant drawings: *cf.* Figs.44, 45, 46, 47, and note 257.

.1677 ST MARTIN. *Cf.* pp.46–7; for dating, note 268. Material: Building Accounts, 1677–87, WS X, p.48, Vestry Book and Churchwardens' Accounts, WS XIX, pp.29–30. ASC II, 50 (Fig.52).

1677–1678 ST SWITHIN. *Cf.* p.47, Fig.60. Wren was consulted about the demolition of the ruins and repairs to the steeple as early as Dec. 1670 (Vestry Minutes, WS XIX, p.54); the rebuilding committee, however, was not formed till 1677 (Committee Book, *ibid.*, p.55); by 1679 the church was sufficiently advanced for the agreement for pewing to be made, and the pulpit was placed in position in 1680 even though the Building Accounts (WS X, p.52) were not closed until 1687. Material: one early plan, RIBA Collection (Fig.59); the church was practically destroyed in 1941.

1678 ABINGDON, Market House. This building has been ascribed to Wren with a great degree of probability. The WS editors have drawn attention to the possible influence of the side wings of the Collège des Quatre Nations at Paris, but the design is more cogently compared with Wren's own Trinity College library, with which it shares the arcade and round-headed windows, though not the unsatisfactory filling of the tympana of the lower arches. The building is exhaustively discussed by Caröe; *cf.* also WS XIX, pp.100–2.

1678 KING CHARLES MAUSOLEUM. *Cf.* pp.107–8. The following material relating to this unexecuted project is extant: Wren's holograph estimate,

ASC II, 90; plan, elevation, and section, ASC II, 91, 92 (Fig.123), 93; and two drawings for the sculptured group of the interior, ASC II 94, 95. [*Cf.* also Hooke, *Diary*, 2, 9 Feb. 1677/8.]

?1677 or later. ST PAUL'S, ? chapter house, ? baptistery. *Cf.* pp.107–8. Stratton gives no evidence for dating this unexecuted project to 1684. Material: StPL II, 158 (Fig.151), 159 (Fig.124), 160.

?1679 ST PAUL'S, piazza. Unexecuted project; our approximate dating is not supported by any evidence. Material: StPL II, 174, 175 (Fig.137), 176.

before 1680 'ST EDMUND THE KING, Bloomsbury'. This cryptic scheme is discussed pp.51–4, and notes 284–6. Material: Ruddock Collection, 21, 22 (Fig.62); and (?Hawksmoor), ASC IV, 61, 62, 63, 64.

1680 ST AUGUSTIN. This relatively minor church is not discussed in the text. It was chiefly remarkable for its unusual method of roofing nave and aisles with three separate gables which seems to be related to SS. Anne and Agnes (Fig.53). In plan a four-bay basilican scheme, with a gallery on the north side. A study drawing (RIBA Collection) shows a pointed domical top to the tower and a flexure of the cornice over the centre window of the west elevation reminiscent of the treatment at St Swithin. Two drawings for an alternative termination of the tower (ASC IV, 88 and RIBA Collection) show a charming slim finial; in execution a straight tapering spire was substituted. The church has been variously dated, as early as 1680–3 (Caröe) and as late as 1695 (Cleveland). The Building Accounts (WS X, p.46) run from 1680 to 1687. *Cf.* also Vestry Minutes, WS XIX, p.7; and the corroborating entry in Hooke's *Diary*, 17 Aug. 1680: 'Made Contract at Paules with Strong for St. Austins.' Apart from the drawings mentioned above, a section is preserved in the RIBA Collection. The church was burnt in 1940.

1680 ST CLEMENT DANES. *Cf.* pp.54–5; for dating, note 291. The Vestry Accounts are preserved and printed in WS X, pp.108–17. The church has been correctly dated by all authorities, following *Parentalia*. Material: Ruddock Collection, 23 (Fig.64); ASC II, 54, 55 (Fig.63), 56, 57. The church was burnt in 1941.

1680–1690 FARLEY CHURCH. For Sir Stephen Fox. The WS editors draw attention to the fact that the transept entrance agrees with the original plan of St James, Westminster, in which case it would have provided the prototype for the latter. For Almshouses, see below.

c.1680 ST MARY ABCHURCH. *Cf.* p.49; for dating, note 272. The rebuilding of this church was slow. The Vestry Books (WS XIX, p.30) record a meeting of the 'Committee to advise with the City Surveyor about the form of building the Church' as early as 24 June 1670, but it was only in 1680 that definite steps were taken. The Building Accounts (WS X, p.48) run from 1681–7, in which latter year the church was roofed. Material: the only extant drawing is in the RIBA Collection, printed as Fig.57.

1680–1681 ST MILDRED, Bread Street. *Cf.* p.49; for dating, note 272. Material: Building Accounts (WS X, p.50), Vestry Minutes (WS XIX, p.47); ASC IV, 113 (Fig.56); ASC IV, 110 is almost certainly a section, and ASC IV, 111 probably a preliminary plan. The church was destroyed in 1941.

c.1681 ST BENET, Gracechurch Street. Generally dated 1685. The Building Accounts (WS X, p.46) cover 1681–7. The church was inaugurated 1686 when the Churchwardens' Accounts (WS XIX, p.8) record expenditure of £1 14*s* 0*d*. 'To wine and sweetmeates for treating the Lord Mayor

---

1677 LAMB'S CONDUIT, Snow Hill. Attributed to Wren by Papworth, but Hooke's authorship seems indicated by the entry in the *Diary*, 2 Aug. 1677.

'1677 NEW COURT, Temple. Assigned to Wren by Papworth and WS editors. No extant material.

.1680 KILMAINHAM HOSPITAL, Dublin. Wren's authorship of this building has not been established. Stylistic details speak against assigning the work to him. Lindsey, however, credits Wren with it and Richardson, *RIBA*

Mem. Vol., p.137, thought that 'the design could not have been produced by any other hand or devised with such certainty of purpose. The building is one of Wren's most consistent designs'. On the other hand, Dutton, *op. cit.*, p.72, states categorically that 'it has now been conclusively proved that it was the work of Sir William Robinson'.

1680–1690 ALMSHOUSES, Farley, Wilts. For Sir Stephen Fox. *Cf.* WS XIX, p.88. Dutton, *op. cit.*, p.54, however, thinks it 'impossible to suppose that Wren can have had any hand' in the design of the warden's house.

at opening of the Church'. There are no extant drawings; for our rejection of the drawing from SM, Fig.27, *v. supra*, p.20. The church was demolished in 1867.

1681 ST MATTHEW. This insignificant church is noticed p.46. The Building Accounts (WS X, p.50) cover the years 1681–6. Clayton assigns the tower to 1685. There are no extant drawings; the church was demolished in 1881.

1681 TOM TOWER, Christ Church, Oxford. *Cf.* p.51. Fig.61. There are no extant drawings. Wren's letters to Fell were first printed by Caröe.

1681 *et seq.* CHELSEA HOSPITAL. *Cf.* pp.68–70. A range of documentary evidence is printed in WS XIX, pp.61–86, including sections of building accounts. There are no extant drawings, but *cf.* ASC I, 6.

before 1682 ST MARY ALDERMARY. *Cf.* p.51. Hooke records the employment of a man 'for pulling down Alderman [*sic*] church' on 15 Nov. 1675; on 8 Jan. 1675/6 he went 'To Aldermary church' to find that 'Clark had taken down the greatest part of the parapet'. Apart from this, documentary evidence regarding the church is lacking, the accounts being missing and no drawings being extant. The record of Henry Rogers' donation of £5000 (*v. supra*, note 281) occurred in a Latin inscription above the west door. The upper part of the steeple, of which the cost was defrayed out of the coal dues fund, was not completed until 1701. The church was damaged in 1940–1, but has been restored.

1682 ST MARGARET PATTENS. *Cf.* pp.131–2. The decision to rebuild the church was evidently taken in the spring of 1682: *cf.* Churchwardens' Accounts (WS XIX, p.28) *sub* 11 May. Wren must have been very busy elsewhere, as on 11 Aug. the churchwardens were 'Going with several of the Parishioners to Sir Christopher Wren to put him in mind of building the Church' which errand entailed the expenditure of 4*s*, and on 25 of the same month, Wren had to be put 'in mind of the Order of my Lord Mayor', this time at the cost of 5*s*. The design was probably executed in the autumn, following these summonses. There are no extant drawings.

1682 ST JAMES, Westminster. *Cf.* pp.55, 63–4; for dating, note 295. Material: two site plans are in the Cooper Collection, 28, 29 (Fig.65); ASC II, 45 (Fig.78); ASC II, 68 (Fig.66). The church was badly damaged in 1940–1, but has been restored.

1682 CHRIST'S HOSPITAL, Mathematical School. *Cf.* the documents printed in WS XI, pp.60–80. There seems no evidence to support Dutton's assertion that the structure was designed as early as 1672, though not carried

out until ten years later. Material: BM Sloane 5238, 50, 51. The building has long been demolished.

1682 ST ALBAN. *Cf.* p.51. Material: Building Accounts, 1682–7, WS X, p.46. There are no extant drawings. The church was burnt in 1940.

1683 ST MARY MAGDALENE. This minor church is not discussed in the text. Wren's design was probably executed subsequent to the churchwardens' visit in 19 July 1683, recorded in the accounts (WS XIX, p.33). The date of 1685 advanced by *Parentalia* and uncritically accepted by later authorities must be rejected. According to the Strong MS. printed by Caröe, Edward Strong, Sen., began the building in 1684. ASC I, 67, is a sketch for the turret. The church was burnt and demolished in 1886.

1683 ST CLEMENT, Eastcheap. *Cf.* p.58. The evidence concerning this church is contradictory. The Vestry Minutes, WS XIX, p.15, record, on 26 Aug. 1684, 'Persons appointed to meet and consult with the Parish of St Martin's Orgar about the Building of the Parish Church', but the Building Accounts (WS X, p.48) commence with 1683, and the Strong MS. printed by Caröe states that Edward Strong, Sen., began building in 1683. There are no extant drawings.

1683 WINCHESTER PALACE. *Cf.* pp.70–4. Material ?ASC I, 76; II, 96–8 (part illustrated as Fig.88); ASC IV, 77; one elevation in Winchester City Museum (Fig.87); two drawings in the King's Library, BM; ?Stables, ASC II, 100.

1683–1684 ST MICHAEL, Crooked Lane. Not discussed in the text. The design was evolved between 1682/3 – 1683/4, at which latter date (not further specified) the Churchwardens' Accounts (WS XIX, p.44) record a present of 10*s* 'given the Draughtsman'. Material: two drawings in the RIBA Collection; ASC II, 110; and one drawing of the steeple in the King's Library, BM. The church was destroyed in 1831.

1684 ARCHBISHOP TENISON'S LIBRARY. Assigned to 1688 by Stratton, L. Milman, and Lindsey in spite of the explicit entries in Evelyn's *Diary*, 13, 23 Feb. 1683/4, 15 July 1685. Demolished in 1861.

1684–1685 ST ANDREW, Holborn. *Cf.* p.56, Figs.67, 68. For dating, *cf.* note 299. The Building Accounts (WS X, pp.95–106) cover 1683–92. There are no extant drawings. The church was burnt in 1941.

1684–1685 ST ANDREW, Wardrobe. *Cf.* pp.55–6. The church is usually dated 1692, but *cf.* note 298. The Building Accounts (WS X, p.46) cover 1685–95. The Churchwardens' Accounts are printed WS XIX, pp.5–6. There are no extant drawings. The church was burnt in 1941.

1681–1683 ASHMOLEAN MUSEUM, Oxford. The building is given to Wren by Bray, Stratton, and Whitaker-Wilson; Phillimore and Caröe date it to 1677; for our rejection of the ascription, *cf.* note 701.

1681 MATRON'S COLLEGE, Salisbury. Assigned to Wren, by the WS editors, though without documentary evidence.

?1682 QUEEN'S COLLEGE, Oxford, library. Discussed pp.68–9.

?1682 EASTON NESTON. Wren is sometimes stated to have been consulted on additions to Sir William Fermor's house prior to Hawksmoor's rebuilding. This suggestion is now substantiated by the following MS. letter (sold by auction at Sotheby's, 6 July 1953) to Sir William, which, though undated as to the year, also corroborates Wren's concern in the house at Tring (*v. supra*, p.221): '14 May. Sr, I had hoped to have had an easy opportunity to have waited on you by goeing first to Tring this Whitson-weeke, but Mr Guy is not certain of his Journy, & thinges soe fall out with me that I can goe nor whither till the King be settled at Windsor, & other-thinges now incumbent upon me be at least put in such a method as I may safely leave them. You are happy who can enjoy your Quiet in a Garden undisturbed, with wealth & plenty about you, wee are bound to our good behaviour uncertain wch way the next wind may tosse us, wee are afrayd of being absent from our charge, & therefore watch as those who travell in suspected places. if Mr Guy had been assured, I had wrote to you as wee had agreed when I last had the honour to see you, but businesse detaines him till the end of next weeke & the beginning of the

following I must be engaged, soe that I must begge your excuse this time, being desirous to hear how your affaires prosper as well as your health. if you ask me any questions wee can resolue by letter, I shall readily serve you till I can find opportunity to wait on you I remaine Your most affectionate & most humble servant Chr. Wren'. The dating of the letter presents great difficulties: it is unlikely that Wren's reference to his patrons should refer to 'Sir C. Wrens disfavour with King' recorded by Hooke on 3 Oct. 1674; on the other hand, the following dates given by *DNB* are relevant: Fermor succeeded as 2nd baronet in 1671; Henry Guy was granted Tring Manor on the death of Henrietta Maria in 1669, but acquired Hemel Hempstead Manor in 1680.

1683–1687 WINCHESTER COLLEGE, Schoolroom. Attributed to Wren by Stratton, L. Milman, and Dutton (all dating the building 1684), and the WS editors. Eberlein rejects the attribution. There is neither extant material, nor accounts.

1684 MIDDLE TEMPLE GATEHOUSE. Generally accepted as Wren's, but there is no extant material.

1684–1688 FAWLEY COURT, near Henley. Assigned to Wren by the WS editors; *cf.* XVII, pls.lii–lvii.

*c.*1685 BELTON HOUSE, Lincs. Accepted as Wren's by Papworth and L. Milman. The WS editors suggest the possibility of Hooke's authorship.

1685–1692 GRAND STOREHOUSE, Tower of London. No extant evidence, but *cf.* WS XVIII, pl.v.

1685 CHAPEL ROYAL, Whitehall, for James II. A plan is in the RIBA Collection; drawings relating to the altar-piece are ASC II, 69, IV, 97.

c.1685 ALL HALLOWS, Lombard Street. The Vestry Minutes of this church (WS XIX, pp.3–4) are unfortunately fragmentary. Entries between 15 Feb. 1669/70 and 24 Feb. 1671/2 relate to demolition work and to the proposed raising of £500 towards reconstruction. No further particulars are given until 1693. The Building Accounts (WS X, p.46), cover the years 1686–94; there are no extant drawings. The church was demolished before the war.

1685–1688 WHITEHALL PALACE, for James II. The project remained unexecuted; material: ASC II, 106 (Fig.96), ASC II, iv; IV, 142, 143. Fragmentary works of the period are discussed, pp.79–86. Material: ASC I, 85.

?1685, or ? after 1688, ST MARY, Lincoln's Inn Fields. This unexecuted project is fully discussed and illustrated, pp.56–8. The one surviving drawing from the Westminster P.L. Pennant is reproduced as Fig.70.

1686 ST MARGARET, Lothbury. Cf. p.58. The Building Accounts (WS X, p.48) cover 1686–93. The gallery was an addition to the original design dating from the resolution of 25 March 1690 recorded in the Parish records, WS XIX, p.28. There are no extant drawings.

1686 ST MICHAEL ROYAL. Cf. p.58. The Building Accounts, WS X, p.50, run 1686–94, though the Strong MS. printed by Caröe, op. cit., p.110, gives 1687 as the commencing date. But cf. note 307. No Vestry Minutes earlier than 1706 are extant. The only surviving drawing is of the steeple, King's Library, BM (Fig.73).

1686 ST MARY SOMERSET. Cf. p.58. The Building Accounts (WS X, p.48) are extant, and cover 1686–94. The only extant drawing is ASC I, 106, a plan and elevation. The church, excepting the tower, was demolished in 1867.

1687 CHARING CROSS ROYAL MEWS. A project, left unexecuted probably by reason of the change of dynasty in 1688. Material: ASC II, 105.

1688 ETON COLLEGE, New School. Dated 1670 by Papworth, but cf. WS XIX, pp.108–10.

1688–1690 KENSINGTON PALACE, remodelling. For William and Mary; Material: ASC I, 4, 9, 11, 12, 14; III, 2, 4.

1691–1692 CHRIST'S HOSPITAL, Sir John Moore's Writing School. The submission of Wren's designs is recorded in the Court Minutes, 2 March 1691/2 (WS XI, p.72); one drawing is in the Gough Collection, Bodl. Libr.; further material: ASC IV, 28–34.

1689 et seq. HAMPTON COURT. The evolution of this design is discussed in detail pp.74–8. Material: practically all extant drawings are preserved in SM, with additional material in ASC I, 10, 27, 34–6, 79, 80, 104; II, 66; IV, 1–18, ?104–5, 144.

1694 or earlier. GREENWICH HOSPITAL, first scheme, completing the existing palace. Material: ASC IV, 20, 26; V, 21, 23, 25, 26, 28.

1694 GREENWICH HOSPITAL, second design. Cf. pp.87–9; material: SM 6, 7 (Figs.104, 103); ASC IV, 19, 25, ?83; V, 24, 27.

1694 MORDEN COLLEGE. Usually dated 1695; but the Strong MS. printed by Caröe, op. cit., p.110, states that the building was begun in 1694. There are no extant drawings; but cf. the engravings reproduced in WS XIX, pls.lxx–lxxi.

1695 QUEEN MARY MONUMENT, for Westminster Abbey. Cf. pp.142–4. Material: ASC I, 5 (Fig.157).

1696 GREENWICH HOSPITAL, warrant design. Cf. p.89. Material: National Maritime Museum (Figs.105, 106).

1697 ST DUNSTAN IN THE EAST, steeple. Cf. pp.21, 58. The steeple, normally dated 1698, must have been designed some time before. The Vestry Minutes (WS XIX, p.19) record on 21 June 1697: 'Upon the promise of Mr. Bechamp [Beauchamp] to hasten the fitting up the Church and finishing the Steeple, he is to have £30.' The nave of the church was rebuilt in 1817, the tower remaining. The drawing, Ruddock Collection 24, is probably a preliminary sketch. A further drawing, though hardly by Wren, is in the King's Library, BM.

1698 WINDSOR CASTLE, projected, unexecuted remodelling. Material: one drawing at SM; ASC V, 15–20.

c.1698 GREENWICH HOSPITAL, fourth design, with wings extending to the Queen's House. Cf. pp.89–95. Material: ASC V, 29 (Fig.109); SM II, 12 (Fig.108); 13–14 (Fig.110).

1698 WHITEHALL PALACE, with new House of Lords, for William III. First design; cf. pp.81–6. Material: ASC V, 1 (Fig.98), 3, 4, 5, 6, 7; ASC II, i (Fig.97).

after 1698, before 1703 WHITEHALL PALACE, second design. Cf. p.146.

1687 ROCHESTER, Town Hall. Ascribed to Wren by Eberlein, L. Milman, and Whitaker-Wilson; no evidence.

?1687–?1724 ST JAMES'S PALACE, alterations, etc. The bulk of this work was done in collaboration with Vanbrugh, or even by Vanbrugh alone. There seems no positive means of separating Wren's work, if any, from Vanbrugh's in the existing drawings (ASC I, 2, 29–33, 83, 86; III, 1, 5).

c.1688 COLLEGE OF PHYSICIANS. The authorship of this building is not established. Evelyn, Aubrey, and Pepys refer to it, though without giving a clue as to its architect. Papworth, Phillimore, Stratton, L. Milman, Birch, and Whitaker-Wilson accept it as Wren's; Whiffen gives it to Hooke; Sitwell credits Inigo Jones with the old lecture theatre. Material: ?ASC IV, 80–2.

1688 WINDSOR, Town Hall. Ascribed to Wren by Stratton, L. Milman, Weaver, Whitaker-Wilson, and Lindsey.

1689–1692 RANELAGH HOUSE, Chelsea. Assigned to Wren by Dean. Material: ?ASC II, 84, 86, 87.

1691 TRINITY COLLEGE, Oxford, chapel. The authorship of the building is a matter of controversy. The drawing ASC II, 103 (reproduced in WS V, pl.vi, but erroneously described as ASC I, 82), if by Wren, would establish his authorship with certainty, in spite of the differences from the completed building. Dutton, op. cit., p.103, assigns the building to Aldrich, but the interpretation of Wren's letter to Bathurst leaves open the possibility of Wren's original design having been altered, though not necessarily by Aldrich. If the WS editors' dating of 1682 were accepted, the doors of the drawing here mentioned would furnish the prototype of that of St James, Westminster.

1691 THE MINT, Tower of London. Variously assigned to Wren, though without documentary evidence.

1692 ST MARY, Warwick, restoration. Cf. the drawings ASC IV, 35–46. According to Stratton, L. Milman, and Whitaker-Wilson, only the tower of Wren's design was executed. According to Whiffen, the whole of Sir William Wilson's scheme was carried out, in preference to Wren's.

1693 SCHOOLS, Appleby, Leics. This building is given to Wren by the WS editors and dated 1693–7; Dutton assigns it to Sir William Wilson, with the possibility of Wren's collaboration. Whiffen, op. cit., p.19, states that Wilson's design was preferred to Wren's. Cf., however, WS XI, pp.84–107, for relevant documents. Material: ASC IV, 47, 48, 49.

1694–1697 WILLIAM AND MARY COLLEGE, Williamsburg, Va., U.S.A. Briggs, op. cit., pp.97, 123, thinks the building was executed 'to plans made in the office of Sir Christopher Wren' of which 'it does seem probable that Wren may have supplied the design'. There is no evidence, however, to support this 'probability', as the assertion that the college 'closely resembles Wren's work in England' must be treated with reserve due to the lack of specification which of Wren's works the college is supposed to resemble.

1695 TRINITY ALMSHOUSES, Mile End Road. Assigned to Wren by Papworth, though without evidence.

?1698; ?1709–1712 ST JOHN'S COLLEGE, Cambridge. The WS editors suggest Hawksmoor's collaboration. Cf. WS XIX, pp.103–7; ASC IV, 76.

1698 MARLBOROUGH HOUSE. No concrete evidence for Wren's work exists. The possibility of Christopher Wren, Jun., having been concerned has been suggested. Material: ASC II, 82, 85.

Material: ASC V, 10 (Fig.102), 11 (Fig.99), 12 (Fig.100), 13 (Fig.101), 14.

1700 DIVINITY SCHOOL and DUKE HUMPHREY'S LIBRARY, Oxford, repairs. *Cf.* Warren, in *RIBA Mem. Vol.*, pp.233–8. The nature of Wren's work is entirely technical.

before 1702 GREENWICH HOSPITAL, modifications to fourth design. Material: SM II, 16, ASC IV, 21–4. Two plans of the Queen's House are preserved as ASC IV, 136–7.

1702 MAUSOLEUM FOR WILLIAM III. This unexecuted project was unknown until the appearance of four relevant sketches at the Bute sale in 1951. The drawings are now preserved at the Victoria and Albert Museum.

1710/11–1718/19 WESTMINSTER SCHOOL, dormitory. Referred to, note 379. The somewhat confusing sequence of the five successively rejected designs preceding that of Lord Burlington is illustrated in WS XI, pls.xi–xxviii. The authorship of some of the drawings, preserved in the Gough Collection, Bodl. Libr., and in ASC cannot be easily established. Even much earlier, Wren had his designs drawn by others in his office; one at least of these, Dickinson, submitted a design of his own, but his style is not sufficiently distinctive to enable us to pronounce on the set of drawings with any degree of certainty which are to be assigned to Wren and which are the result, not only of Dickinson's hand, but also imagination.

1713, 1715, 1719 REPORT ON, and PROJECTS FOR WESTMINSTER ABBEY. *Cf.* pp.58–60; WS XI, pp.15–20, for Wren's report. The proposed transept alterations are illustrated as Fig.71. Further material: a site plan, dated 8 June 1716, ASC III, 42; two plans, for the tower and the 'light shell' in the Gough Collection, Bodl. Libr.; and two drawings (by Dickinson) dated 1722 for the central tower and spire in the Abbey library.

c.1715 ST MICHAEL, Cornhill, tower. *Cf.* p.58. The date of 1721–2 universally accepted for this work appears to be erroneous. According to the Vestry Minutes (WS XIX, p.47) the project of rebuilding the structure originated as early as Oct. 1713. The authorization for taking down the old, and erecting the new tower is recorded on 24 Aug. 1715. On 13 Aug. 1719, however, the Minutes record the receipt of a letter 'from Mr Strong, Mason, employed in Rebuilding the Tower, intimating that for want of money he could not proceed further in the building thereof'. This is borne out by the Strong MS. printed by Caröe, *op. cit.*, p.110, which states that the old tower was demolished, and the new begun, in 1715. Two drawings by Dickinson are preserved in the King's Library, BM.

1700 WINSLOW HALL, Bucks. Ascribed to Wren by the WS editors and Dutton. *Cf.* WS XVII, pls.lviii–lxiv.

1702–1724 KENSINGTON PALACE, remodelling for George I, very probably largely by Vanbrugh.

1704 KENSINGTON PALACE, orangery. Attributed to Wren by Weaver, L. Milman, and Lindsey.

?1705 ALL SAINTS, Isleworth. Phillimore *et al.* have attributed this church, much altered since, to Wren, but there is no substantiating evidence.

1705 NEWBY HALL, Yorks. Attributed to Wren by Papworth. According to the WS editors the authorship cannot be established.

1713 COURT HOUSE, Windsor. Ascribed to Wren by Papworth. According to the WS editors the design was due to Sir Thomas Fitz, but the building was completed by Wren.

1713 HYDE PARK BARRACKS. *Cf.* ASC II, 99, 101; *cf. Parentalia*, p.334.

UNDATED:

BLICKLING HALL, Norfolk, alterations. No evidence exists to establish Wren's authorship; but *cf.* the drawings ASC IV, 131, 132, 133.

LORD NEWCASTLE, house for. *Cf.* ASC I, 26, 28.

LONDON BRIDGE, projected repairs; *cf.* ASC IV, 69; also 1748 Sale List, lot 214.

BUCKINGHAM HOUSE, Gardens. *Cf.* ASC II, 6 and SM II, 42.

ALL SOULS COLLEGE, Oxford, screen to ante-chapel. The attribution to Wren seems cogent. *Cf.* ASC II, 65, 67.

SIR EDWARD ALSTON, house for. *Cf.* ASC I, 24.

ASPLEY HOUSE, Aspley Guise, Beds.; assigned to Wren, 1695, by Eberlein, without evidence.

Owing to the fact that an extensive and important collection of Wren drawings, deriving from the collection of the Marquess of Bute, was rediscovered and sold by auction in 1951, subsequent to the index of Wren drawings published by the Wren Society in Vols.III and XX, a revision of the material seems called for.

Our basic knowledge of the extent of surviving Wren drawings derives from the particulars of the auction catalogue of April 1749, at which time Christopher Wren's numismatic collection and his father's drawings were dispersed. This listed:

LOT 30. 82 designs, & 2 large prints of St Paul's, in portfolio.
LOT 31. 114 large & finished drawings of St. Paul's, Bow and other churches in London; also the Monument, Whitehall, Winchester Castle, Trinity College, Cambridge, etc. & 3 prints, pasted into a large book.
LOT 32. 32 very large drawings of Whitehall, Windsor and Greenwich.
LOT 33. A Book of Astronomical Schemes.
LOT 34. 100 drawings & sketches of London churches in a portfolio.
LOT 35. 66 drawings of Hampton Court.
LOT 36. 102 drawings & sketches of Kensington Palace, & miscellaneous Architecture.
LOT 37. 101 ditto, in a cover.
LOT 38. 113 ditto, in a Portfolio.
LOT 39. 69 do of Hampton Court, Warwick church & other buildings, in cover.
LOT 40. 7 large finished drawings of St Paul's, 1 of Monument, & plan of London after the Fire.
LOT 41. large Port Folio of finished drawings of Hôtel des Invalides.
LOT 42. 150 drawings and sketches of Winchester Palace, & Miscellaneous Architecture, with a parcel of papers relating to the subjects.
LOT 43. A large high-finished Drawing of St Paul's.
LOT 44. ditto of the inside of St. Paul's.
LOT 45. A long ditto of an intended New Palace at Westminster.

The majority of these lots have not survived intact into their present collections; however, it is possible to trace most of them from the 1749 dispersal to their present ownerships, though the intermediate hands through which they passed are largely obscure. To establish the present distribution of the sixteen lots catalogued in 1749 it is necessary to reject the suggestion made by the compiler of the 1951 sale catalogue, who sought the provenance of the Bute Collection in LOT 31 of the 1749 sale. Superficially, the '114 large & finished drawings of St. Paul's, Bow and other churches in London; also the Monument, Whitehall, Winchester Castle, Trinity College, Cambridge, etc.' correspond to the 122 drawings of the Bute Collection. On examination, however, two objections prevent us from accepting the suggested identity. Firstly, the Bute drawings show no sign whatever of ever having been 'pasted into a large book' (which passage was mis-transcribed in the 1951 sale catalogue as 'packed into a large book') and the condition of the drawings barely suggests the presence of a protective cover; secondly, numerical objections arise: the St Paul's Collection numbered, before the 1951 accessions, 185 items, of which 162 were drawings and 23 prints. Vol.I may correspond exactly, as to drawings, to the 82 items of LOT 30 of the 1749 sale; for the remainder, however, it is only to the questionable LOT 31 that we can turn, for no other lots (excepting the 8 drawings of 40 and 43) contain any mention of St Paul's. It seems inconceivable that the 80 remaining drawings of the St Paul's Collection should not have been individually mentioned, but included under the generic label of 'miscellaneous architecture'.

In rejecting the hypothetical provenance of the Bute Collection as LOT 31, we are accepting the WS editors' suggestion that the St Paul's Collection should consist almost precisely of LOTS 30 and 31; and with this distribution established, the rest of the material can feasibly be assigned to the present collections.

Three lots have been preserved intact: LOT 32 is unquestionably ASC V, which was rediscovered by the WS editors in 1930 and subsequently published as WS VIII, in 1931. LOT 35 undoubtedly represents the Hampton Court Volume preserved at SM, which bears an inscription 'from G. Dance to John Soane, 1817'. LOT 45 is without doubt the drawing which formerly belonged to the Bute Collection and which has now acceded to ASC (Fig.98).

LOTS 30 and 31 make a total of 196 items, of which we have suggested 162 to be found in StPL I and II, the remaining 34 items of which must have, at least partly, accrued to the Bute Collection. LOT 36 must form part of ASC, as no drawings of Kensington are found elsewhere. LOT 42 is very likely to be now found in ASC IV, and as that volume contains 11 more drawings than catalogued, it would be tempting to see the remainder of (actually 12) drawings of Warwick church in having come from LOT 39, of which the rest would largely account for the remainder of the SM Collection. LOT 40 is clearly part of ASC I, as this contains the only City of London plans. LOTS 43 and 44 may be presumed missing.

The remainder, LOTS 34, 37, and 38 make a total of 314 drawings, which are to be divided between the c.160 unaccounted drawings of ASC, the remaining c.115 drawings of the Bute Collection, losses, and isolated drawings and small sets still extant. It is unfortunate that the lack of precision in cataloguing does not permit an elucidation of the position in greater detail; the ultimate derivation of the Bute Collection, however, is thus circumscribed.

Though the precise identification of the 1749 items with present collections is not completely verifiable, it is now possible to account for practically all the drawings dispersed in 1749, which could not be done before the rediscovery of the Bute Collection. The position now apparent is as follows:

The total of drawings listed in 1749 was	939.
The five volumes of ASC comprise	463,
the two volumes of StPL comprise	162,
the late Bute Collection (now dispersed in accessions to ASC, StPL, the Cooper and Ruddock Collections, RIBA, Trinity College, Cambridge, Winchester Museum, and Victoria and Albert Museum) had	122,
the Hampton Court volume of the SM	66
and the remainder of the SM Collection	68 drawings
which gives a total of	881

extant drawings in the major collections. The remainder of 58 items is clearly made up of losses, and small sets and isolated drawings in the British Museum (King's Library, and Sloane Collection, 5238), the Bodleian Library (Gough Collection), and the Royal Institute of British Architects. (The series of Greenwich drawings preserved at the National Maritime Museum has here been excluded, as this evidently did not form part of the 1749 sale.)

Thus it is gratifying to know that no important or considerable part of the material has been lost, as had been feared, in the fire at Luton Hoo in 1771, or elsewhere. And while it is possible that actual losses may mount to no more than perhaps three dozen items out of the 939 originally catalogued, we may reflect with satisfaction on the constellation of circumstances which has preserved this unique corpus of drawings practically intact. At the same time, this fact indicates that no further major discoveries of hitherto unknown material are probable, and that it is highly unlikely that any documentary evidence, in the form of drawings, should yet come to light which would call for a revision and revaluation of the work of Sir Christopher Wren.

A CLASSIFIED AND ANNOTATED ABSTRACT OF
SIR CHRISTOPHER WREN'S LIBRARY

compiled from

A CATALOGUE OF THE CURIOUS AND ENTIRE LIBRARIES OF
THAT INGENIOUS ARCHITECT, SIR CHRISTOPHER WREN, Knt.
AND CHRISTOPHER WREN, Esq:

Which will be sold by Auction on Monday the 24th of this Instant, October, 1748, and the three following Evenings.

A short abstract of this catalogue was printed by the editors of the Wren Society in Vol.XX, pp.74–7. The present, more comprehensive, abstract has been prepared to illustrate more explicitly the range and extent of Wren's interests; works of which the subject matter and publication date point to Christopher Wren's possession and acquisition have been omitted. For the reader's convenience, the abbreviated entries of the catalogue have been expanded to permit reference to full title, date, and place of publication, and have been annotated for elucidation; such editing having been placed within square brackets.

Lot

545 [*Les dix livres d'*]*Architecture de Vitruve* [*corrigez et traduits . . . en François, avec des notes et des figures. Seconde édition; corrigée et augmentée*] par [M.C.] Perrault. Paris, 1684.

443 [Leon Battista] Alberti *De Re Aedificatoria*, Florent. 1512. [No Florentine edition of this date is recorded; the only edition is that printed in Paris by B. Remboldt and L. Hornken, a copy of which must have been the work in question.]

540 *Architettura di Sebastiano Serlio* [*nuovamente impressi in beneficio universale in lingua latina & volgare con alcune aggiunte*] Ven[eto] 1663.

529 *Il Quattro Libri dell'Architettura di Andrea Palladio*, [in] Ven[etia, Appresso Bartolomeo Carampello.] 1601.

214 *Palladio's First Book of Architecture* [translated by G. R(ichards) from the French of P. Le Muet.]. [Several editions of Richards's translation were published, notably the 1st, London 1663, 2nd 1668, 3rd 1676; this entry probably refers to the latter or any subsequent edition which contain an appendix on 'the new Model of the Cathedral of St. Paul's, as it is to be built'. *v.* pl.112.]

548 [Giacomo] Leoni's [*The Architecture of A.*] *Palladio* [*in four books . . . to which are added several notes and observations made by Inigo Jones, revis'd, design'd, and publish'd by G. Leoni*] 3 vol. [London] 1715.

376 *Cours d'Architecture* [*qui comprend les ordres*] *de Vignole* [*avec des commentaires, les figures, et descriptions de ses plus beaux bâtiments, et de ceux de Michel Ange*] par [le sieur] Daviler [i.e. Augustin Charles d'Aviler] avec fig., Amst[erdam] 1700.

562 [*Les plus excellents*] *Bastiments de* [*la*] *France* par [Jacques Androuet du] Cerceau, vol.2d. 1708.

563 *Œuvres d'Architecture* [*Desseins de plusieurs palais, plans et elevations en perspective geometrique*] d'Anthoine le Pautre, Paris [1652].

439 Hospital of the Invalids. [*s.d.* This cryptic entry may be compared with Lot 41 of the sale, in April 1749, of Wren's drawings: 'Large Portfolio of finished drawings of the Hôtel des Invalides', then bought for £1 11*s* 0*d* and now at the Soane Museum.]

549 *Cours d'Architecture* [*enseigné dans l'Académie Royale d'Architecture*] par [François] Blondel, [seconde édition] 2 vol. Paris 1698.

561 [Claude] Perrault's [*A Treatise of the five orders of columns in*] *Architecture . . .* by [John] James, [London] 1708 [with engravings by J. Sturt]. [Translated from *Ordonnance des cinq espèces de colonnes . . .* Paris, 1683.]

567 [John] Evelyn's [*A*] *Parallel of* [*the ancient*] *Architecture* [*with the modern . . . In a Collection of Ten Principal Authors who have written upon the Five Orders . . . to which is added an Account of Architects and Architecture, with Leon Battista Alberti's Treatise of Statues; made English for the benefit of builders . . .* London] 1707. [Translated from

Roland Fréart de Chambray, *Parallèle de l'Architecture Antique et de la moderne . . .* Paris, 1650; *v. supra*, note 606.]

542 [Andrea] Pozzo's [*Rules and Examples of*] *Perspective* [*proper for Painters and Architects . . . done into English from the original printed at Rome, 1693, in Latin and Italian*, by John James, London] 1707.

531 *Perspective* by Marolois, Amst. 1625. [The date may be erroneous; the entry refers either to *Perspettiva . . . obersehn und verbessert durch Samuel Marolois*, 1628, which is a version of the work of Jan Vredeman de Vries; or *Perspectiva . . . in haltende Theorie und Practicke*, 1628.]

541 Drawings of Fortifications. [*s.l., s.d.*]

300 [S. le Prestre de] Vauban's [*New Method of*] *Fortifications* [London, 1693].

307 Vegetius *De Re Militari*, 2 vol., cum fig., Vesalii 1670.

522 *Il Templo Vaticano descritto dal Cav. Carlo Fontana*, Rome 1694.

125 [P.] Bonnani *Historia Templi Vaticani*, cum fig., Rome 1696.

528 [Johannes Jacobus] Boissardus [*I. pars*] *Romanae Urbis Topographiae* [*ex antiquitatum J.J.B.*] 2 part [of 6] cum fig., [Francofordii] 1597 [–1602].

532 [O. Panvini, B. Marliani, P. Victoris, J(ohannes) J(acobus)] Boissardi *Antiquitat*[*es*] *Roman*[*ae*] [*Topographia Romae . . .*] 8 part 2 vol. [Francofurti] 1627 [1597–1602].

80 [Hildebrandus F.] Rosini *Antiquitates* [*Potissimum*] *Romanae* [*e Rosino Allisque . . . contractae*] notis Dempsteri, Amst[erdam] 1685.

543 Antique Statues. [? Perrier, *q.v.*; ? de Rubeis, *q.v.*]

136 [François] Per[r]ier's Statues of Rome by [N.] Vis[s]cher [i.e. *Eigentlyke Afbeelingde van Hondert der aldervormaersdte Statuen . . . binnen Romen*] Amst[erdam] 1702.

210 *Figures, Antiques, Designes a Rome*, par François Per[r]ier, Par[is. *s.d.*].

533 *Icones & Segmenta illustrium e Marmore Tab*[*ularum*] *quae Romae adhuc extant* a F[rancisco] Perrier [delineate] Romae, 1645. [*cf.* Evelyn's critical comments, *Diary*, 21 June 1650.]

537 [Giovanni Giacomo] Rossi's Roman Statues [i.e. *Admiranda Romanorum Antiquitatum ac veteris Sculpturae Vestigae*, notis J. P(ietro) Bellori, editit J(ohannes) J(acobus) de Rubeis, 1693] stained, the first twenty wanting.

551 *Insignium Romae Templorum Prospectus* [*exteriores, interiores . . . cum plantis ac mensuris* a J(ohannes)] per J[acobus de] Rubeis [i.e. Giovanni Giacomo de Rossi] Rome 1684.

568 *Romae Vetus, Capitolii, Templorum, Amphitheatrorum, Theatrorum, Circi, &c.* ex Officine D[omenico] de Rubeis.

569 *Heroicae Virtutis Imagines* [*quas Petrus Berrettinus pinxit . . .*] cura & sumptibus [J.] J. de Rubeis [i.e. Giovanni Giacomo de Rossi, ?1693].

553 *Columna Antoniana* [*M. Avrelii Antonini . . . edita cum notis*] par [J.] P[ietro] Bellori, Romae [?1672].

554 *Columna Trajano [con l'espositione latina d'A. Ciaccone* (i.e. A. Chacon)] par [Giovanni] P[ietro] Bellori, Rome [1673].

508 [J.] Vignolius[i] *de Columna Imperatoris Antonini Pii [dissertatio]* Rome, 1705.

544 *Arcus L. Septimii Severi.* Rome, 1676.

564 *Thermae Diocletianae.*

78 [Raffaello] Fabretti *Bellum [et excidium] Trojanum ex Antiquarum [Antiquitatum] Reliquis,* cum fig., Berolini, Lipsiae, 1699.

369 Fabrettus *de Aquis & Aquiducti[bu]s Veteris Romae [dissertationes tres]* Romae, 1688.

429 Salengre *Thesaurus Antiqu. Roman.* 2 vol., Hague, 1716.

557 *Reliquiae Antiquae Urbus Romae [opus postumum]* per [M.] Overbeke, 3 vol., Amst[erdam] 1708.

77 *Religio Veterum Romanorum Auct. G[uillaume] du Choul,* cum fig., Amst[erdam] 1686.

560 *Sacelli Crucis ab Hilaro Papa,* apud Baptist. Constan. Exaedificati & Marmorea Incrustatione Emblemat. Ornato Deformatio. Rome, 1658.

503 *Ager Puteolanus sive Prospectus ejusdem Insignores,* Romae 1652.

137 Bartoli *Lucernae Veterum Sepulchrales Ionica [ex cavernis Romae subterraneis collectae . . . cum observat. J. P(ietro) Bellori]* Col[oniae Marchicae] 1702.

555 *Roma Sotterranea [opera postuma]* di Ant[onio] Bosio, Rome 1632. [*Cf.* Evelyn, *Diary,* 11 April 1645.]

534 *Signorum Veterum Icones,* par Ger. Reynst, Amst. [*s.d.*].

82 Junius [i.e. François du Jon] *De Pictura Veterum,* Amst. 1637.

139 Hugenio *Sygnorum Veterum Icones.*

422 [Joachim] Sandrart *Sculpturae Veteris admiranda* [sive delineatio . . .] Nor[imbergae] 1680.

547 [*Les] édifices antiques de Rome [dessinée et mesurés très exactement]* par [Antoine Babuty] Desgodetz, Par. 1697. [?1695]

409 [?Tezio, G.] *Aedes Barberini [anae ad. Quirinalem descriptae]* cum fig. Roma 1647 [?1642].

205 Fleetwood, *Inscriptiones Ravennatis Geographia,* Par. 1688.

19 (prints) Eleven historical prints, after Raphael, P. Testa, Baroccio, etc.

28 (prints) Antient and Modern Rome.

566 Collection of Prints and Drawings, relating to antient Architecture, 79 in number.

135 The Effigies of the most famous Painters and Artists of Europe. 1694.

246 [Jacob] Sponii *Miscellanae Eruditae Antiquitatis,* Lugd[uni] 1685.

476 [John] Battely *Antiquitates Rutupinae,* chart. mag., Oxon. 1711.

96 [John] Evelyn's *Discourse on Medals,* 1697. [*Cf. Diary,* note to 7 Feb. 1696/7, Christmas 1697/8.]

37 *Antiquities of Salisbury and Bath,* 1719.

287 [Aylett] Sammes's *Antiqu[ities] of antient Britain* [London, 1676].

389 [J.] Seldeni *Eadmerii [Historiae nouorum . . . libri VI.* In lucem ex Bibliotheca Cottonia emisit Iohannes Seldenus . . . Londoni . . . 1623].

251 [Sir William] Dugdale's *History of St. Paul's Cathedral,* best cuts, [London] 1658.

252 [Sir William] Dugdale's *[The] Antiquities of Warwickshire,* best cuts, [London] 1656.

253 [Sir William] Dugdale's *Monasticon Anglicanum,* with Stevens's Cont[inuation] 3 vol., 1718.

254 [Sir William] Dugdale's *Monasticon [Anglicanum] abridged [epitomised in English . . .* London] 1693.

530 [John] Webb's *Vindication of Stoneheng Restored [in Answer to Dr. Charleton's Reflections,* London] 1665.

102 [Humphrey] Prideaux *Marmora Oxoniensa [ex Arundellianis]* 1676.

100 & 276 [Edward] Stillingfleet's *Origines Britannicae [or the Antiquities of the British Churches,* London] 1685.

377 Guidot [i.e. T. Guidotti] *de Thermis [Britannicis tractatus . . .* Londini 1691].

160 Sprat's *Sorbier* [i.e. Samuel Sorbière, *A Voyage to England in 1667*] 1709. [*Cf.* however, Voltaire's comment on the original work, quoted by

Cunningham: 'He stayed three months in England and, equally ignorant of its manners and language, thought fit to publish a relation, which proved but a dull and scurrilous satire upon a nation of which he understood nothing.']

484 [*A New]View of London* [by Edward Hatton] 1708.

105 [Robert] Plot's *Natural History of Oxfordshire* [Oxford] 1677.

106 [Robert] Plot's *Natural History of Staffordshire* [The Theatre, Oxford] 1686.

277 [Charles] Leigh's *[The] Natural History of Lancashire [Cheshire and the Peak . . .* Oxford] 1700.

457 *Account of Livonia.*

457 *Travels thro' Denmark,* 1707.

457 *Account of Switzerland.*

86 [J. J.] Scheuchzeri *Itinera[ris]e Alpin[i]ae,* cum fig., [3 pt.] London, 1708.

157 [Charles] Patin's *Travels [thro' Germany, Bohemia, Swisserland, Holland . . .* London 1696].

160 [Martin] Lister's *[A] Journey to Paris [in the year 1698.* London 1699].

69 [Bernard de] Montfaucon *Diarium Italicum [sive Monumentorum veterum, Bibliothecarum, Musaeorum . . . notitiae . . .]* Par[isiis] 1702.

472 [Bernard de] Montfaucon's *[The] Travels [of Father Montfaucon from Paris] thro' Italy* [made English from the Paris edition . . . with cuts . . . London] 1712.

556 Ross's *Silius Italicus.* 1661.

439 [Richard] Lassell[s]'s *[The] Voyage (to) [of] Italy* [Paris, London 1670. *Cf.* Bray's notes to Evelyn's *Diary,* 17 Oct. 1644 ff.].

303 *Journey to Naples.* 1704.

177 *Delices d'Italie,* 3 vol., avec fig., Leide 1706.

319 *Voyage d'Italie [? dans la Grèce, L'Asie Mineure, la Macédonie . . .]* du sieur [Paul] Lucas, Par[is] 1712.

25 [François Maximilien] Misson's *[A New] Voyage to Italy* [fourth edition] 4[2] vol. with Cuts [London] 1714.

221 *Silius Italicus* [Arnold] Drakenbor[ch]shi, 1717.

318 *Voyage d'Italie, [de Dalmatie] de Grece & de Levant* [fait] par [J.] Spon [et G. Wheeler] 2 vol., Amst[erdam] 1679.

114 [Sir George] Wheeler's *Travels [i.e. A Journey into Greece . . . in the company of Dr. Spon of Lyons]* with Cuts, 1682. [*Cf.* Evelyn, *Diary,* 24 Oct. 1686.]

140 [C.] Le Brun's *Voyage to the Levant,* with fine Cuts, 1702.

143 Thevenot's *[The] Travels [of Monsieur de Thevenot] into the Levant,* [3 pt. London] 1687.

366 [J. Pitton de] Tournefort's *[Relation d'un] Voyage (to the) [du] Levant,* [Amsterdam] 2 vol., with Cuts, 1718.

207 *Voyage to Constantinople.*

367 *Relation d'un Voyage de Constantinople,* Par[is] 1689.

109 Sandy[s]'s *Travels [containing a history of the originall and present state of the Turkish Empire.]* 1670.

559 *Explication des Cent Estampes qui Representent differentes Nations du Levant.* Par[is] 1715.

471 [Henry] Maundrel[l]'s *[A] Journey from Aleppo to Jerusalem [at Easter],* Oxon. 1703.

145 *Journal du Voyage du Chevalier* [J.] *Chardin en Prose [sic. scil: Perse] & Aux Indes Orientales,* avec fig., [London] 1686. [Possibly a presentation copy: *cf.* Evelyn, *Diary,* 27 Aug. 1680.]

439 [Charles Jacques] Poncet's *[A] Voyage to Ethiopia [made in the years 1689, 1699 and 1700 . . .* translated from the French original . . . London 1709].

539 [John] Ogilby's *Description of Africa,* vol. 1st, with Cuts, 1679 [1670?].

238 Frazier's *Voyage to the South Seas.* 1717.

305 *Voyage to Borneo.* 1718.

452 [François] Leguat's *Voyage to the East Indies* [London 1708].

458 *British Empire in America,* 2 vol. 1708.

157 *Relation of a Voyage to Buenos Ayres,* 1716.

439 [William] Dampier's *Voyage to* [? *Observations of Capt. W. D. on the Coast of New*] *Holland*, [? 1677–88; ? 1699].

209 [Willem] Bosman's (*Account*) [*A New Description of the Coast*] of *Guinea* [London] 1705.

452 [Edward] Cook[e]'s [*A*] *Voyage* [*to the South Sea and*] *round the World*, [2 vols. London] 1712.

207 [William] Hacke's [*A Collection of original*] *Voyages* [*... Round the Globe ... over the Isthmus of Darien ... through the Streights of Magellan ... the Levant ...* with maps, draughts ... 3 pt. London 1699].

309 Wood's Rogers's *Voyage round the World*. 1712.

320 *De l' Utilitate des Voyages*, 2 vol. Par[is] 1696.

371 [Jacobus] Tollii *Epistolae Itineraria*[*e*], cum fig. Amst. 1700.

161 [A. G.] Busbequii [i.e. Augerius Gislenius de Bousbecq] *Epistolae* [*omnia quae extant*. Ludg. Bat. ex officina] Elz[everiana] 1633.

273 Corvini Commentaria Geograph. [i.e. *Geographiae Commentariorum libri XI*] *Dom*[*inicus*] *Marii Nigri* [editi ... L. Corvini ... Basilieae] 1557.

131 Strabonis *Geographia*, Gr. & Lat. [ed. Morelli] L[utetia] Par[isiorum] 1620.

15 [Periegetes] Dionysii *Orbis Descriptio*, Oxon. 1710.

132 Pausanias *de Tota Gr*[*a*]*e*[*cia libri decem*] Inter. A. Loeschero, Bas[iliae] 1551 [?1550].

98 [*A*] *Commentary on Antoninus* [*his*] *Itinerary* [by W. Burton, London [1658.

122 Herodoti [Halicarnassei] *Historia*[*rum*]*e* [*libri IX*] Gr. & Lat. [ed. sec.] H. Steph[anus, Paris] 1592.

15 Herodiani *Historiarium* [*Libri 8*] Oxon., 1678.

15 Xenophontis *de Cyri Institutione* [*libro octo*] London, 1720.

123 Xenophontis *Historia* [transl.] Leunclavii, Gr. & Lat., Franc[ofurti] 1596.

15 [Flavius] Eutropii [*Brevarium*] *Historiae Romanae*, Oxon. 1702 [1703].

83 [Isaac] Vossii *Observationes ad Pomponium Melam*, [Hagae] Com[itis] 1658.

59 Pliny's *Panegyrick*[*e, Translated out of the original Latin ... by Sir Robert Stapylton, Oxford, 1644.*]

66 Plinii [Caecilii Secundi] *Epistola*[*rum*]*e* [*Libri X*] *cum Comment*[*ariis*] *J.* [*M.*] *Catan*[*a*]*ei*, P. Steph[anus, Geneva] 1600 [?1601].

188 [C.] Plinii *Historia Naturalis* [*Libri xxxvii*] 3 vol. [ed. J. de Laet] Elz[evir, Ludg. Bat.] 1635.

292 [Caii] Plinii [secondi] *Hist*[*oriae*] *Naturalis* [*libri xxxvii*, ill. J.] Harduin-[us]i, 3 vol., Par[isiis] 1723. [The work is included in this abstract, as Wren knew the previous (1685) edition of it, as appears from a reference in 'Tract' IV, WS XIX, p.138.]

330 Valerii Maximus [cum selectio variorum observat.] L[ugd.] Bat. 1670.

191 [T.] Livii *Historia*[*rum Libri, ex recensione Heinsiana*] 3 vol. Elz[evir, Lugd. Bat.] 1635 [?1634].

171 [Rev. William] Wotton's *History of Rome* [*from the death of Antoninus Pius ...* London] 1701.

28 & 180 [Humphrey] Prideaux [*The true Nature of Imposture ... displayed in the*] *Life of Mahomet.* [One copy apparently Hooke's gift: *cf. Diary*, 13 Jan. 1678/9.]

265 Froysart's *Chronicle*, black letter [R. Pynson, London] 1525.

400 [Anthony à] Wood's *Athenae Oxoniensis*, 2 vol. in 1, 1691.

259 & 412 [Elias] Ashmole's [*The institution, laws & ceremonies of the most noble*] *Order of the Garter*, with fine Cuts, 1672.

478 *History of the Order of the Garter*, 1715.

20 *Critical History of England.*

20 *History of Parliament*, 1700.

20 *Art of governing by Parties.*

20 *History of Faction.*

101 [Enrico Caterino] Davila's [*Historie of the*] *Civil*[*l*] *War*[*re*]*s of France* [London] 1647. [*Cf.* Pepys, *Diary*, 14 July 1666.]

39 [Charles] D'Avenant's *Essays on Peace* [*at Home*] *and War* [*Abroad*. London 1704].

37 Life of Sir Thomas More.

129 [William] Prynne's *History of King John*, [*King Henri III and ... King Edward the I. Wherein the ancient sovereign dominion of the Kings ... over all persons ... and causes ... is indicated.* London] 1670.

395 [Francis] Sandford's *Genealogical History of the Kings of England* [with additions and annotations] by Stebbing, best Edit., 1707.

196 & 314 Dryden's [L. Maimbourg, *The*] *History of the League* [translated by Mr. Dryden, 1684.]

154 Milton's Defensio Populi Anglicani [i.e. *pro Populo Anglicano defensio ...* ?London, 1650].

59 [Mathew] Wren's *Monarchy Asserted*; [*or, the State of Monarchicall and Popular Government ...* Oxford] 1659.

90 Collection of Treaties from 1630 to 1687.

93 [Sir William] Dugdale's [*A Short*] *View of the late Troubles* [*in England*] 1681.

104 [Bulstrode] Whit[e]lock's *Memorials of* [*the*] *English Affairs*, 1682.

59 [Gilbert] Burnet's [*History of the*] *Rights of Princes* [*in the disposing of ecclesiastical benefits and Church lands ... relating chiefly to the pretensions of the Crown of France ... and the late Contest with the court of Rome*. London, 1682].

141 [Gilbert] Burnet's *History of the Reformation*, 3 vol. 1679 [–1715].

128 Sleidan's [i.e. J. Philippson, *The General*] *History of the Reformation* [*of the Church from the errors and corruptions of the Church of Rome ...* London] 1689.

196 [?George] Dawson of Loyalty and Obedience. [? *Origo Legum*, 1694.]

514 *Cabala*. [? Moor; *cf.* Hooke, *Diary*, 26 May 1677.]

113 *Sacheverel's Tryal.* [Jac. Tonson, London 1710.]

158 [Edward] Chamberlain's [*The present*] *State* [*of Great Britain ... ed.* John Chamberlain] 1708.

482 Political States, 3 vol. 1715. [?Boyer.]

303 [Charles] Perrault's [*historical*] *Characters* [*of the greatest men that have appeared in France ...*] 2 vol., [London] 1704. [Translated from *Les Hommes Illustres ...* Paris, 1697–1700.]

21 [John] Wilkins [*A Discourse showing the gift*] *of Prayer and* [*whereunto may be added ... a discourse showing the gift of*]*Preaching.* [London 1690.]

32 [Samuel] Clarke's [*The*] *Scripture Doctrine of the Trinity*, [London] 1712.

56 [W.] Nichol[l]s's [*A*] *Conference with a Theist*, 5 parts in 3 vol., 1703.

61 [Simon] Patrick [*A Commentary upon the First Book of Moses, called*] *Genesis*, [*A Commentary upon ...*] *Exodus* (*and*) [*A Commentary upon ...*] *Leviticus*, 3 vol., 1695 [–1697–1698].

63 [Nicholas] Fulleri *Miscellane*[*orum*]*a Theologic*[*orum*]*a*, [? 1612 ff.]

67 [Edward] Stillingfleet's *Origines Sacrae* [*or a rational account of the grounds of Christian faith*] bound in Turkey. [?1663 ff.]

390 [Edward] Stillingfleet's [*A*] *rational Account* [*of the grounds of Protestant Religion*] bound in Morocco [London] 1665.

208 [Edward] Stillingfleet's Pieces, 4 vol., bound in Turkey.

95 [John] Pearson on [*An exposition of*] the Creed. 1715.

208 [John] Tillotson's [*The*] *Rule of Faith*, bound in Morocco [London] 1666.

391 [Henry] Hammond [*A Paraphrase and Annotations up*]*on the New Testament*, 2nd ed., 1659.

445 [Robert] South *Opera posthuma* [London 1717].

470 [Edward] Young's *Sermons* [*on several occasions*], 2 vol. 1702 [–1703].

199 [John] Milton's [*Eikonoklastes, in*] *Answer to* [*a book call'd*] *Eikon Basilikon* [Amsterdam] 1690.

199 [John] Toland's [*Amyntor, or a*] *Defence* [*of Milton's Life ...*] 1699.

491 [William] Coward's [*Second*] *Thoughts on the human Soul*, 2 vol. 1702.

194 [Richard] Bentley against Boyle, 1699. [i.e. *A Dissertation upon the Epistles of Phalaris with an answer to the objections of the Hon. C. Boyle*.]

280 [Nehemiah] Grew's *Cosmologia Sacra* [London] 1701.

*32 [Thomas] Burnet's [*Sacred*] *Theory of the Earth*, 2 vol. [4th ed., London] 1719.

18 [William] Whiston's *Theory of the Earth* [*wherein the Creation ... Deluge*

and Conflagration . . . are shewn to be perfectly agreeable to reason and philosophy. London] 1696.

6 [William] Wotton's Reflections of antient and modern Learning, 1697. [Cf. Evelyn, Diary, 6 July 1679.]

286 Boethii Opera [omnia, 2 pt.] Bas[iliensis] 1570.

193 Republicae, 7 vol.

310 Plato's Works by [A.] Dacier, 1701.

498 Theonis Smyrnae[orum]i [quae in] Mathematic[is]a [ad Platonis lectionem utilia sunt, expositio] Gr. & Lat. Notis illustr. J[smaele] Bullialdi [i.e. I. Boulliau, Lut. Par. 1644].

31 [Desiderio] Erasmus's Praise of [Morea Encomium or A Panegyric upon] Folly, with Holbein's Cuts, 1709.

355 [Desiderii] Erasmi Stultitia Laus, Latin and English, with fine Cuts, 1717.

434 [Desiderii] Erasmi Opera, 5 vol.

273 [Desiderii] Erasmi Adagio. [Probably the Editio Novissima . . . repurgata . . .printed by W. Hall, Oxford 1666.]

326 [Desiderii] Erasmi Colloquia [cum notis selectis . . . C. Schreivelio] L[ugduni] Bat[avorum] 1664.

186 [Desiderii] Erasmi Colloquia. [? Flesher, London 1676; ? 1697.]

275 [Pierre] Gassendi [De] Vita [moribus, pacitisque] Epicuri, 2 vol. Lugd[uni] 1649.

374 [Pierre] Gassendi Claudii Fabricii de Peiresc Vita. [?Paris 1641; ?Hague 1651, 1655.]

496 [Pierre] Gassendi Tychonis Brahe Vita [Parisiis, 1654].

387 [Robert] Burton's Anatomy of Melancholly. [Oxford, 1621.]

385 [René] Descartes Traite de l'Esprit de l'Home [sic] Paris 1666.

352 Clarke's and Leibnitz's Letters. [i.e. A Collection of Papers which passed between the late Mr. Leibnitz and Dr. Clarke . . . relating to the principles of Natural Philosophy and Religion.] 1717.

18 [John] Keil[l]'s [An] Introduction to [Natural] Philosophy, 1720.

312 [? John Keill] Introduction to Natural Philosophy, 1720.

362 [Isaac] Newton's Principia, Cant[abrigia] 1713.

386 [Isaac] Newton, Idem Liber. [?Philosophiae Naturalis Principia Mathematica] London 1687.

506 Philosophical Transactions [of the Royal Society], vols.1, 2, 3, 4, 11, 12, 13, 14, 15, 16, 17, 18. 1665 [vol.1, 1665 & 1666, John Martyn, 1667].

365 [Thomas] Sprat's History of the Royal Society, London 1667.

118 [Francis] Bacon's Opera Omnia [quae extant: philosophica, moralia, politica, historica . . .] Franc[ofurti] 1665.

17 [F.] Bacon's [The] Remains [of . . . Francis Lord Verulam . . . being Essays and severall Letters and other pieces of various and high concernment not heretofore published. London 1648].

380 Claudii Ptolemaei Harmonicorum [libri tres] Gr. & Lat., interpr. [John Wallis] Oxon. 1682.

282 Dimonstrationi Harmoniche del[la Musica] del [Gioseffo] Zarlino, Ven. 1571.

283 [Le] Institutioni Harmoniche del [di M. G(ioseffo)] Zarlino, Ven. 1573.

216 [M.] Meibomius [de] Antiqua[e] Musica[e Auctores septem] Amst[erdam] 1652.

323 [William] Holder [A Treatise on the Natural Grounds and Principles] of Harmony [London] 1694.

18 [William] Whiston's Astronomical Principles of Religion [natural and reveal'd [London] 1717.

242 Baptistae Astronomiae Vetus & ac Nova duae part. Bon. 1651.

241 [David] Gregorii Astronomiae [phisicae et geometriae] Elementa, Oxon[iae] 1702.

416 Tychonis Brahe Astronomia [nova . . . seu physica coelestis . . .] per Keplerum, 1609.

215 Galilaeus Systema Mundi. [? London 1663.]

522 Opere di Galileo, 3 vol. Firenze 1718.

501 Ulugh Beig(hi) [Ibn Sharukh] Tabula Stellarum, per [Thomas] Hyde, Oxon. 1665.

212 [C. Huygens] Cosmotheoros [sive de Terris coelestibus aerumque ornatu, conjecturae. Hagae Comitum, 1698].

212 [C. Hugenii] Systema Saturnium, Hagae [Comitis] 1659.

248 Helvelii Dissertatio de native Saturni Facie Gedani, 1656.

527 [Ismael] Bullialdi [i.e. I. Boulliau] Astronomia [philolaica . . . Parisiis, 1645].

502 Astronomica Danica. [T. Brahe?]

378 [Thomas] Street's Astronomia Carolina, [a new theorie of the celestial motion. The first edition, London 1661, or the Latin edition, Norimbergae 1705].

499 [Thomas] Street's Astronomia Carolina, 2nd edit. [2 pt.] 1710.

312 [John] Keil[l]'s [An] Introduction to [the] true Astronomy, [London] 1721.

244 [Athanasius] Kircheri Ars Magna Lucis & Umbriae [in decem Libros digesta] Amst[erdam] 1671. [Cf. Evelyn, Diary, 8, 20, 23 Nov. 1644.]

247 [Athanasius] Kircheri Phonurgia Nova, Campi 1673.

424 [C.] Hugenii [i.e. Huygens] Horologium Oscillatorium . . . [Parisiis] 1673.

212 [C.] Hugenio[i] Opuscula [postuma, quae continent Dioptricam . . . Lugd. Bat., 1703].

235 Essay de Dioptrique, par N. Hartfoeker. Paris 1694.

526 Aquilonii Optic.

361 [Sir Isaac] Newton Opticks; [or, a Treatise of the Reflexions, Refractions, Inflexions and Colours of Light. Also two Treatises of the Species and Magnitude of Curvilinear Figures.] 1704.

284 Ubaldi Mechanica, Ven. 1615.

374 [John] Wallis's Mechanica sive de Motu, 3 vol. 1670.

81 P[aolo] Casati Mechanic[orum]a [libri octo] Lugd[uni] 1684.

386 Recueil de Plusieurs Machines [de nouvelle invention] par [Claude] Perrault, Paris 1700.

1 Euclidis Elementa. [Probably Gregory's edition, Oxford 1703; Barrow's edition, Cambridge 1655-7 or London 1659-60, 1678; alternatively Elementa Decimi Euclidis in Oughtred, 1652.]

88 Opere di Euclidi tradotta N. T. Brisciana, Ven[ice] 1565.

418 [Henry] Brigg[s]e Arithmetica Logarithmica, London 1624.

89 [J.] Wallisii Oper[um]a Mathematic[orum]a, [i.e. Arithmetica Infinitorum sive nova Methodus inquirendi curvilineorum quadratum . . .&c.] Oxon. 1656.

266 [J.] Wallis's [A] Treatise of Algebra, [Oxford] 1685.

517 [Thomas] Hobbes's Examinatio [et emendatio mathematici . . . in libris 3] Wallisii Mathemat. 1660.

184 [Joannes] Alexandri Synopsis Algebraica [opus posthumum, Londini 1693].

248 Les Oeuvres Mathematiques de Simon Steven, reveu Corrige & Augmentee par Gerard, Leide 1634.

425 Forstler's Mathematical Lucubrations, 1659.

250 Salisbury's Mathematics, vol. 1st, 1661.

182 [J.] Wilkins's Mathematical Works, 1708.

236 La Science du Calcul, Par[is] 1714.

517 Analysis Geometrica.

234 Traite Analytique des Sections Coniques [et de leur usage pour la résolution des equations . . .] par le Marquis [Guillaume François Antoine] d[e] '[l]Ho(s)pital, Par[is] 1707.

237 & 515 [Guillaume François Antoine de l'Hôpital] Analyse des Infiniment Petits, Par[is] 1696.

285 [Vincenzo] Vivian[i]us de Maximis & Minimis [geometrica divinatio . . .] Florent[iae] 1649.

108 [Robert] Hooke's Micrographia [or some Physiological Descriptions of Minute Bodies made by Magnifying Glasses, with Observations and Inquiries Thereupon] with Cuts, 1665.

245 [John] Evelyn's Physiologia Expermentalis.

107 [Robert] Hooke's [The] posthumous Works [of R. H.] with Cuts, [London] 1705.

299 [Robert] Boyle's Pieces, 5 vol.

358 [Robert] Boyle's Essays [? of the strange subtlety of efflusions, 1673].

281 [Nehemia] Grew's *Rarities of Gresham College* [*Museum Regalis Societatis*] 1681.

16 [Thomas] Gibson's *Anatomy* [*of Humane Bodies epitomized*. ? 1697].

357 [Thomas] Willis's [*De*] *Anima Brutorum* [1672] *Cerebr*[*i*] *Anatome* [*cui accessit nervorum Descriptio et Usus*. Londini] 1664.

16 [Thomas] Willis's *Practice of Physick*, 1685.

357 [Thomas] Willis's *Pharmaceuticae Rationalis* [Englished by S. Pordage, *The remaining medical works of T. W. . . .*, London, 1681, 1683, 1684].

523 [Francis] Bacon's [*Sylva Sylvarum, or a*] *Natural*[*l*] *Histor*[*ie*]*y*, with large MSS. Notes.

62 Godartius [i.e. Joannes Goedaert, *of*] *On Insects*, [York] 1682.

528 *Theorique de la Conduite des Eaux.*

437 Nerus *de Arte Vitraria*, Amst[erdam] 1686.

250 Parker's *Treatise on japanning and varnishing*, 1688.

249 [John] Minshe[u]w's Dictionary [i.e. *Minshaei emendatio . . . the guide into the tongues*] with Notes by Dr. Wren, colour'd, 1625 [London, 1626].

272 Minshew's Dictionary.

127 Hofmanni Lexicon Universale, 4 vol. Bas[el] 1677.

473 Rapin of Gardins, 1714. [i.e. a reissue of Evelyn's translation of *Rapinus Hortorum*, 1673; cf. *Diary*, 3 Jan. 1672/3.]

120 [John] Parkinson's *Flower Garden* [i.e. *Paradisi in Sole Paradisus Terrestris*] 1656.

121 Johnson of Gerard's Herball [i.e. J. Gerarde, *The Herball or Generall Historie of Plantes . . . very much Enlarged and Amended by T. Johnson*, third edition] 1636.

Note: Works listed in the preceding Abstract of the Library of Sir Christopher Wren are not enumerated below, unless consulted in editions different from those given above.

ADDERLEY, William: *The Case of William Adderley Esq. duly elected a burgess to serve in Parliament for the Borough of New Windsor . . . etc.* 1688.

ADDLESHAW, G. W. O., and ETCHELLS, Frederick: *The Architectural Setting of Anglican Worship*, London 1948.

ADSHEAD, S. D., 'Sir Christopher Wren and his Plan for London', in Royal Institute of British Architects, *Memorial Volume*, London 1923.

AIKEN, Edmund: *Elevation, Section and View of the Cathedral Church of St Paul, London, engraved by J. Le Keux after drawings by James Elmes.* London 1813.

ALBERTI, Leon Battista: *De Re Aedificatoria.* Florence 1485; [tr. Cosimo Bartoli] Florence 1550; Venice 1565.

ANDERSON, William J. [ed. Stratton]: *The Architecture of the Renaissance in Italy.* London 1927.

AUBREY, John: *Miscellanies.* London 1696.

AUBREY, John: *Brief Lives.* London 1949; London 1950.

BARTHEL, A., and HEGE, W.: *Barockkirchen in Altbayern und Schwaben.* Berlin 1941.

BELCHER, J., and MACARTNEY, M. E.: *Later Renaissance Architecture in England.* London 1901.

BELL, W. G.: *The Great Fire of London.* London 1920.

BESANT, Sir W.: *Stuart London.* London 1892.

BIRCH, George: *London Churches of the 17th and 18th Centuries.* London 1896.

BLOMFIELD, Sir Reginald: *History of French Architecture 1494–1774.* 4 vols. London 1911.

BLOMFIELD, Sir Reginald: *History of Renaissance Architecture in England.* London, 1897.

BLOMFIELD, Sir Reginald: *A Short History of Renaissance Architecture in England.* 6th ed. London 1923.

BLOMFIELD, Sir Reginald: *Six Architects.* (esp. ch.vi) Oxford 1935.

BLUNT, Anthony: *Artistic Theory in Italy, 1450–1600.* Oxford 1940.

BLUNT, Anthony: *François Mansart.* London 1941.

BOAS, F. S.: *Stuart Drama.* Oxford 1946.

BORROMINI, Francesco [ed. S. Giannini]: *Opera della Chiesa e Fabbrica della Sapienza di Roma . . .* Rome 1720.

BOYCEAU, Jacques: *Traité de Jardinage.* 1638.

BRETT-JAMES, Norman G.: *The Growth of Stuart London.* London 1935.

BRETTON, J., and PUGIN, A.: *Illustrations of Public Buildings in London.* 2 vols., suppl. London 1825, 1838.

BRIGGS, Martin S.: *Baroque Architecture.* London 1913.

BRIGGS, Martin S.: *Christopher Wren.* London 1951.

BRIGGS, Martin S.: *Wren the Incomparable.* London 1953.

BRINCKMANN, A. E., *Die Baukunst des 17. und 18. Jahrunderts in den romanischen Ländern.* Neubabelsberg 1919.

BRISSAC, Philippe de Cossé: *Châteaux de France disparus.* Paris 1947.

BRITTON, John: *Cathedral Antiquities.* London 1836.

BROCK, Henry D.: *Colonial Churches in Virginia.* Richmond, Va. 1930.

BRYANT, Arthur: *King Charles II.* London 1946.

BUKOFZER, Manfred: *Music of the Baroque Era.* London 1948.

BULLANT: *Règle Générale des Cinque Manières.* 1564.

BULLOCK, A. E. [ed.]: *Grinling Gibbon and his Compeers.* London 1919.

BUMPUS, J. S.: *St. Paul's Cathedral.* London 1913.

BUMPUS, T. F.: *London Churches.* New York, *s.d.*

BURCKHARDT, Jakob: *Die Kultur der Renaissance in Italian.* Vienna, *s.d.*

BUSS, S.: *Sir Christopher's Church of St Anne and St Agnes.* 1909.

BUTLER, C.: *Western Mysticism.* London 1927.

CAMPBELL, Colen: *Vitruvius Britannicus.* London 1715 ff.

CAMPBELL, W. S.: *The Passer by in London.* London 1908.

CAMPEN, Jacob van: *Afbeelding van't Stadt Huys van Amsterdam.* Amsterdam 1661.

CARÖE, W. D.: *Tom Tower, Oxford.* Oxford 1923.

CARRITT, E. F.: *A Calendar of British Taste from 1600 to 1800.* London 1948.

CASSIRER, E.: *The Philosophy of the Enlightenment.* Princeton 1951.

CASTELLS, Francis de P.: *Was Sir Christopher Wren a Mason?* 1917.

CERCEAU, Jacques Androuet du: *De Architectura Opus.* Paris 1559.

CERCEAU, Jacques Androuet du: *Les Plus excellents bastiments de la France.* Paris 1576–9.

CHAMBRAY, Roland Fréart de: *Parallèle de l'Architecture Antique et de la moderne, avec un recueil des dix principaux autheurs qui ont écrit des cinq ordres.* Paris 1650.

CHANCELLOR, E. Beresford: *Lives of the British Architects.* London 1909.

CHANCELLOR, E. Beresford: 'Wren's Restoration of Westminster Abbey; the Drawings', *Connoisseur*, 1927; vol.LXXVII.

CHARLES II [ed. Bryant]: *The Letters, Speeches and Declarations of.* London 1935.

CHARLETON, Walter: *Chorea Gigantum, or Stoneheng restor'd to the Danes.* London 1663.

CLARKE, C.: *Architecture Ecclesiastica Londini.* London 1811–21.

CLARK, S.: 'Observations on Wren's System of Buttresses . . .' etc. in *RIBA Mem. Vol.*, 1923.

CLAYTON, John: *The Parochial Churches of Sir Christopher Wren.* London 1848.

CLAYTON, John: 'On the Towers and Spires of the City Churches – the Works of Sir Christopher Wren', paper read to the RIBA, 5, 26 April 1852; reprinted WS IX.

CLEVELAND, Ralph D.: 'Sir Christopher Wren's City Churches', in *New England Magazine*, Boston Sept. 1901–Feb. 1902; vol.XXV, pp.478–96.

CLINCH, George: *St Paul's Cathedral.* London 1906.

COBB, Gerald: *The Old Churches of London.* London 1941.

COLONNA, Francesco: *Hypnerotomachia Poliphili.* Venice 1499; Paris 1554.

COSIMO III, Grand Duke of Tuscany: *Travels of,* [1669] London 1821.

CRAGG, G. R.: *From Puritanism to the Age of Reason.* Cambridge 1950.

CUNNINGHAM, Alan: *Lives of the Most Eminent British Painters, Sculptors and Architects* (esp. vol.IV) London 1831.

DANIELL, A. E.: *London City Churches.* London 1896.

DANIELL, A. E.: *London Riverside Churches.* London 1897.

DAVISON, T. R.: *Wren's City Churches.* London, 1923.

DAY, Ernest Hermitage: *Renaissance Architecture in England.* London 1910.

DEAN, C. G. T.: *The Royal Hospital Chelsea.* London 1950.

DE L'ORME, Philibert: *Le Premier Livre de l'Architecture (avec Nouvelles Inventions)* Paris 1576.

Dictionary of National Biography.

DIMOCK, A.: *The Cathedral Church of Saint Paul.* London 1901.

DONIN, Richard: *Vicenzo Scamozzi und sein Einfluss auf die Salzburger Architektur.* Innsbruck 1948.

DRUMMOND, Andrew Landale: *The Church Architecture of Protestantism.* Edinburgh 1934.

DU BREUIL, Jacques: *Théâtre des Antiquitez de Paris* [édition augmentée] Paris 1639.

DUTTON, Ralph: *The Age of Wren.* London 1951.

DVORAK, Max: *Die Entstehung der Barockkunst in Rom.* 1908.

EBERLEIN, Harold Donaldson: 'Sir Christopher Wren, 1632–1723', in *Architectural Forum*, New York, Feb. 1923; vol.XXXVIII, No.2.

ELMES, James: *Memoirs of the Life and Works of Sir Christopher Wren.* London 1823.

EMBURY, Aymer: *Early American Churches.* New York 1914.

Encyclopaedia Britannica. Fourteenth edition, 1932 issue.

ENTICK, J.: *A New and Accurate History and Survey of London.* 1766.

l'ESTRANGE, A. G.: *Greenwich Palace and Hospital.* 2 vols. London 1886.

EVELYN, John [tr.]: *A Parallel of the ancient Architecture with the modern . . . to which is added an Account of Architects and Architecture . . . with*

L. B. Alberti's Treatise of Statues . . . etc. London 1664; 1669. *The Whole Body of Antient and Modern Architecture* . . . etc. London 1680 London 1697; *A Parallel* . . . *The Third Edition, with the addition of the Elements of Architecture; collected by Sir Henry Wotton Knt* . . . etc. London 1723; *A Parallel* . . . etc. *The Fourth Edition* . . . [with] *other large additions* [*sic*] London 1733.

EVELYN, John: *Londinum Redivivum, or London Restored not to its pristine, but to far greater Beauty Commodiousness and Magnificence* . . . ed. E. S. de Beer, Oxford 1938.

EVELYN, John: *Diary*, ed. E. S. de Beer, 6 vols. Oxford 1955.

FERGUSSON, J.: *History of Modern Styles of Architecture*. London 1862.

FISCHER von Erlach, Johann Bernhard, [tr. Thos. Lediard]: *A Plan of Civil and Historical Architecture* . . . etc. London 1730.

FLETCHER, Bannister F.: *Andrea Palladio* . . . etc. London 1902.

FOKKER, T. H.: *Roman Baroque Art*. Oxford 1938.

FORCE, Piganiol de la: *Le Châteaux de Versailles*. Paris 1730 ff.

FRASCHETTI, S.: *Bernini*. Milan 1900.

FREY, D.: *Architettura della Rinascenza*. Rome 1924.

FUERST, V., and D'ARCY, L.: *Versailles*. London 1951.

GANAY, Ernest de: *Châteaux de France; environs de Paris*. Paris 1948.

GAXOTTE, Pierre: *La France de Louis XIV*. Paris 1946.

GEYMÜLLER, H. von: *Les Projets primitifs pour la Basilique de St-Pierre*. Florence–Paris–Vienna, 1875–80.

GODFREY, W. H.: *A History of Architecture in London*. London 1911.

GODWIN, G.: *A History and Description of St Paul's Cathedral*. London 1837.

GOTCH, J. A.: *The English Country House; Charles I–George IV*. London 1918.

GOTCH, J. A.: 'Sir Christopher Wren from the Personal Side', in *RIBA Mem. Vol.*, 1923.

GRASSHOFF, E. W.: *Raumprobleme des protestantischen Kirchenbaus im 17. und 18. Jahrhundert*. Berlin 1938.

GRIMSCHITZ, Bruno: *Wiener Barockpaläste*. Vienna 1944.

GUARINI, Guarino: *Architettura Civile*. Turin 1737.

GUNTHER, R. T. [ed.]: *The Architecture of Sir Roger Pratt*. Oxford 1928.

GURLITT, Cornelius: *Geschichte des Barockstils in Italien*. Esslingen 1887.

GURLITT, Cornelius: *Geschichte des Barockstils in Deutschland*. Stuttgart 1887.

GWYNN, John: *London and Westminster Improv'd*. London 1766.

HAGER, Werner: *Die Bauten des deutschen Barock*. Jena 1942.

HANSON, R. J. E.: *A Brief Tribute to Sir Christopher Wren*. 1931.

HARRISON, Sydney S.: *The Wren Screen from the Temple Church*. 1935.

HAUPT, A.: *Renaissance Palaces of Northern Italy and Tuscany*. London s.d.

HAUSER, Arnold: *The Social History of Art*. London 1951.

HAUTECOEUR, L.: *L'Histoire du Châteaux du Louvre et des Tuileries*. Paris–Bruxelles 1927.

HAWKSMOOR, Nicholas: *Remarks on the Founding and Carrying on the Buildings of the Royal Hospital at Greenwich*. London 1728; reprinted WS VI.

HIND, A. M.: *Wenceslas Hollar and Views of London and Windsor in the Seventeenth Century*. London 1922.

HIORNS, Fred. R.: in *Sir Christopher Wren Symposium*. London 1923.

HOOKE, Robert: *Diary*, ed. Robinson and Adams, London 1935.

HOWELL, J.: *Londinopolis*. 1657.

ILG, Albert: *Die Fischer von Erlach*. 1895.

JACKSON, Sir T. G.: *Architecture*. London 1925.

JENKINSON, W.: *London Churches before the Great Fire*. London 1917.

JONES, Inigo: *Stone-heng Restor'd* . . . etc. London 1655.

KEEN, Arthur: 'Sir Christopher Wren's Parish Churches', in *RIBA Mem. Vol.*, 1923.

KENT, William: *Some Designs of Mr. Inigo Jones and Mr. William Kent*. London 1744.

KENT, W. Winthrop: *The Life and Works of Baldassare Peruzzi*. 1925.

KER, C. H. B.: *Sir Christopher Wren*. London 1828.

KYP: *La Grande Bretagne*. 1724.

LANCASTER, Robert Alexander: *Historic Virginia Houses and Churches*. Philadelphia 1915.

LAURUS, J.: *Antiquae urbis* [Romae] *splendor*. 1612.

LAW, E. P. A.: *History of Hampton Court*. 3 vols. London 1888, 1891.

LETHABY, W. R.: *Architecture*. 1912.

LINDSEY, John: *Wren and His Time*. London 1951.

LOFTIE, W. J.: *Inigo Jones and Wren*. London 1893.

LOFTIE, W. J.: *History of London*. 1884.

LOGGAN, David: *Oxonia Illustrata*. Oxford 1675.

LOGGAN, David: *Cantabrigia Illustrata*. 1690.

LONGMAN, William: *Three Cathedrals of St. Paul*. London 1873.

LOUKOMSKI, G. K.: *Andrea Palladio*. Paris 1927.

LÜBKE and SEMRAU: *Die Kunst der Barockzeit*. 1905.

MACARTNEY, M. E.: 'Some Recent Investigations at St. Paul's', in *RIBA Mem. Vol.*, 1923.

MACKMURDO, A. H.: *Wren's City Churches*. London 1883.

MAGNI: *Il Barocco a Roma*. Turin 1911.

MÂLE, Emile: *L'Art religieux du XVII siècle*. Paris 1951.

MARIE, A.: *Jardins Français Classiques des 17–18 siècles*. 1949.

MAROT, Jean: *Le magnifique Châteaux de Richelieu*. Paris 1660.

MAROT, Jean: *Recueil des Plans, Profils, etc. des plusiers Palais, Châteaux, Eglises, Sépultures, Grotes et Hôtels*. Paris [*c*.1676].

MAROT, Jean: *Architecture Française. Plans, Elévations, Coupes, et Détails des Principaux Palais, Châteaux, Hôtels particuliers, etc., existant à Paris ou aux Environs sous le Règne de Louis XIV*. Paris [*c*.1680].

MARTIN, C.: *La Renaissance en France*. Paris *s.d.*

MARTIN, Franz: *Erzbischof Wolf Dietrich von Salzburg*. Vienna 1924.

MAURICHEAU–BEAUPRÉ, Charles: *Versailles*. Monaco 1950.

MELLERS, Wilfrid: *François Couperin and the French Classical Tradition*. London 1950.

MILMAN, H. H.: *Annals of St Paul's*. London 1868.

MILMAN, Lena: *Sir Christopher Wren*. New York 1908.

MERIAN, M.: *Topographia Galliae*. Paris (vol.I.) 1655.

MINNS, Ellis H., and WEBB, Maurice: 'Pembroke College Chapel, Sir Christopher Wren's First Building', in *RIBA Mem. Vol.*, 1923.

MUET, Pierre le: *Manière de bien bastir pour toutes sortes de personnes*. Paris 1623.

NEW, E. H.: *Twenty Drawings of Sir Christopher Wren's Churches* [together with an edition of *Parentalia*] London 1908.

NEWBOLT, W. C. E.: *St Paul's Cathedral*. 1897.

NEWCOURT, Richard: *Repertorium*. London 1708.

NICOLL, Allardyce: *A History of Restoration Drama*. Cambridge 1923.

NIVEN, W.: *Churches of the City of London destroyed since 1800*. London 1887.

NOLHAC, Pierre de: *La création de Versailles*. Paris 1899.

NOLHAC, Pierre de: *Histoire du Château de Versailles*. Paris 1911.

PALLADIO, Andrea: *Le antichità di Roma*. Venice 1554.

PALLADIO, Andrea: *Il Quattro Libri dell' Architettura*. Venice 1570, 1581 London [Leoni] 1715; London [Ware] 1738.

PEPYS, Samuel: *Diary*.

PERELLE: Estampes de Versailles.

PERRAULT, Claude: *Ordonnance des cinq espèces de colonnes*. Paris 1683.

PETTY, Sir William: *Growth of the City of London*. 1683.

PEVSNER, Nikolaus: *An Outline of European Architecture*. London 1948.

PHELPS, Albert C.: 'Sir Christopher Wren and the Wren Ideal in Modern Architecture', in *Architecture*, New York, May 1924; vol.XLIX, No.5.

PHILLIMORE, Lucy: *Sir Christopher Wren; His Family and Times*. London 1881.

PHILLIPS, Hugh: *The Thames about 1750*. London 1952.

PINDER, Wilhelm: *Deutscher Barock*. Leipzig 1929.

PITE, A. Beresford: 'The design of St. Paul's Cathedral', in *RIBA Mem. Vol.*, 1923.

POST, Pierre: *Les Œuvres d'Architecture*. Leyden 1715.

POULAIN, A.: *The Mysticism of St. John of the Cross*. 1893.

POWELL, Anthony: *John Aubrey and His Friends*. London 1948.

POZZO, Andrea: *Prospectiva Pingendi*. Rome 1693.

PRATT, Mario: *Studies in 17th century imagery*. 2 vols. London 1947.

RALPH, J.: *A critical Survey of the Public Buildings in London*. London 1734, 1771.

RAMSEY, Stanley C., in *Sir Christopher Wren Symposium*, London 1923.

READ, Herbert: *The Meaning of Art*. London 1931.

REDDAWAY, T. F.: *The Rebuilding of London after the Great Fire*. London 1951.

REYNOLDS, Sir Joshua: *Fifteen Discourses*.

RICHARDSON, A. E.: 'Sir Christopher Wren's Public Buildings', in *RIBA Mem. Vol.*, 1923.

RIEGL, Alois: *Die Enstehung der Barockkunst in Rom*. Vienna 1908.

ROYAL COMMISSION ON HISTORICAL MONUMENTS: vol.II (1925); vol.IV (1929); vol.V (1930).

SAXL, F., and WITTKOWER, R.: *British Art and the Mediterranean*. London 1948.

SCAMOZZI, Ottavio Bertotti: *Le Fabbriche e i Disegni di Andrea Palladio*. 4 vols. 1776.

SCAMOZZI, Vincenzo: *L'Idea dell'Architettura Universale di V. S.* Venice 1615.

SCOTT, Geoffrey: *The Architecture of Humanism*. London 1914, 1947.

SEDLMAYR, Hans: *Österreichische Barockarchitektur, 1690–1740*. Vienna 1930.

SEDLMAYR, Hans: 'Die politische Bedeutung des Barock', in *Festschrift für Heinrich von Sbrk*. Munich 1938.

SENCOURT, Robert: *The Consecration of Genius*. (esp. ch.xviii). London 1947.

SERLIO, Sebastiano: *Regole Generali di Architettura . . . etc.* Venice 1537 and 1540.

SIMPSON, W. S.: *Documents Illustrating the History of St Paul's Cathedral*. [Camden Society] London 1880.

SITWELL, Sacheverell: *British Architects and Craftsmen*. London 1945.

SMALL, T., and WOODBRIDGE, C.: *Houses of the Wren and Early Georgian Period*. 1928.

SOANE, Sir John: *Lectures on Architecture* [ed. Bolton]. London 1929.

SOTHEBY & Co.: *Catalogue of Important Architectural Drawings . . . etc.* London, May 1951.

SPRAT, T.: *History of the Royal Society*. 1702.

STILLINGFLEET, E.: *Pamphlet, no title*. 30 May 1678.

STRACK, H.: *Central- und Kuppelkirchen in Italien*. 1882.

STRATTON, Arthur: *The Life and Works of Sir Christopher Wren*. Liverpool 1897.

STRATTON, Arthur: 'Dutch Influences on the Architecture of Sir Christopher Wren,' in *RIBA Mem. Vol.*, 1923.

STURGIS, R. Clipston: 'Sir Christopher Wren', in *Journal of the American Institute of Architects*, New York 1923, vol.XI, No.3.

SUMMERSON, John: *Georgian London*. London 1947.

SUMMERSON, John: *Heavenly Mansions*. London 1949.

SUMMERSON, John: 'Drawings for the London City Churches', in *Journal of the Royal Institute of British Architects*, London, Feb. 1952, 3rd ser. vol.59, No.4.

SUMMERSON, John: *Architecture in Britain, 1530–1830*. London 1954.

TANNER, Lawrence E.: 'Wren's Restoration of Westminster Abbey; the Signatures', in *Connoisseur*, 1927, vol.LXXVII.

TAYLOR, A.: *Towers and Steeples of Sir Christopher Wren*. London 1881.

THIEME & BECKER: *Allgemeines Künstlerlexicon* (esp. vol.XXXVI). Leipzig 1947.

TILLEY, A. L.: *Studies in the French Renaissance*. Cambridge 1922.

TIPPING, H., and HUSSEY, C.: *English Homes. Late Stuart, 1649–1714*. London 1920.

VENTURI, A.: *Storia dell'arte Italiana*. vol.XI, 1, 2, 3. Milan 1938–40.

VIGNOLA [Giacomo Barozzi]: *Regole dei cinque ordini d'architettura*. Rome 1563.

VINGBOON, Philip: *Gronden on Afbeeldsels det Vornaamste Gebowen;* Amsterdam 1648.

VITRUVIUS: *De Architectura Libri Decem*. Venice 1511; Rome 1544; Venice 1556; New York 1932.

WACKERNAGEL, Martin: *Die Baukunst des 17. und 18. Jahrhunderts in den germanischen Ländern*. 1915.

WATKIN, E. I.: *Catholic Art and Culture*. London 1948.

WARD, W. Henry: 'French and Italian Influences on Sir Christopher Wren's Work', in *RIBA Mem. Vol.*, 1923.

WARNER, S. A.: *St. Paul's Cathedral*. London 1926.

WARREN, Edward Prioleau: 'Sir Christopher Wren's Repair of the Divinity School and Duke Humphrey's Library, Oxford', in *RIBA Mem. Vol.*, 1923.

WEAVER, Sir Lawrence: 'Building Accounts of the City Churches', in *Archaeologia*, LXVI.

WEAVER, Sir Lawrence: *Sir Christopher Wren*. London 1923.

WEBB, Sir Aston: Introduction to *RIBA Mem. Vol.*, 1923.

WEBB, Geoffrey Fairbanks: *Sir Christopher Wren*. London 1937.

WEINGARTNER, Josef: *Römische Barockkirchen*. Munich *s.d.*

WEISBACH, Werner: *Die Kunst des Barock in Italien, Frankreich, Deutschland und Spanien*. London 1937, Berlin 1924.

WESTRUP, J. A.: *Purcell*. London 1937.

WHIFFEN, Marcus: *Stuart and Georgian Churches*. London 1948.

WHISTLER, Laurence: *Sir John Vanbrugh*. London 1938.

WILSON, C. Whitaker-: *Sir Christopher Wren*. London 1932.

WIESENHÜTTER, A.: *Protestantischer Kirchenbau des deutschen Ostens*. Leipzig 1936.

WITTKOWER, R.: *Architectural Principles in the Age of Humanism*. London 1949.

WÖLFFLIN, H.: *Renaissance und Barock*. Munich 1908.

WOTTON, Sir Henry: *Elements of Architecture*. 1624 and *v. sub* Evelyn, John.

WREN, Dr Christopher: 'Account of the State of S. Paul's Cathedral after the Fire of London, 1666', in *Antiquarian Repertory*, London 1775 (reprinted by L. Milman).

WREN, Sir Christopher and WREN, Christopher: *A Catalogue of the . . . Libraries . . .* London 1748.

WREN, Sir Christopher and WREN, Christopher: *A Catalogue of . . . Greek and Roman Medals . . . etc.* London 1749.

WREN SOCIETY: *Publications*. 20 vols. London 1924 ff.

WREN, Stephen: *Parentalia . . . etc.* London 1750.

YATES, Frances A.: *The French Academies of the Sixteenth Century*. London 1947.